Beginning
Components for ASP

Richard Anderson
Alex Homer
Dr Simon Robinson

Wrox Press Ltd. ®

Beginning
Components for ASP

wrox

Published by Wrox Press Ltd, Arden House, 1102 Warwick Road, Acock's Green,
Birmingham, B27 6BH, UK
Printed in the United States
ISBN 1-861002-88-2

Trademark Acknowledgements

Wrox has endeavored to provide trademark information about all the companies and products mentioned in this book by the appropriate use of capitals. However, Wrox cannot guarantee the accuracy of this information.

Credits

Authors
Richard Anderson
Alex Homer
Dr Simon Robinson

Additional Material
Brian Francis
Stephen Mohr
David Sussman

Technical Reviewers
Michael Corning
Richard Harrison
Ivor Horton
Rockford Lhotka
Davide Marcato
Sophie McQueen
Todd Mondor
Boyd Nolan
Jim Pierre
Kenn Scribner
Marc Simkin
Thearon Willis

Cover
Chris Morris

Technical Editors
Jon Duckett
Jon Hill
Ian Nutt
Karli Watson

Managing Editor
Chris Hindley

Project Manager
Tony Berry

Index
Andrew Criddle
Robin Smith

Design/Layout
Tom Bartlett
Mark Burdett
Jonathan Jones
John McNulty
William Fallon
David Boyce

Figures
David Boyce
William Fallon

About the Authors

Richard Anderson is an established software developer who has worked with Microsoft technologies for nearly 10 years. He works for a small yet globally known software house in Peterborough (England), where he currently holds the position of "Research and Development Manager". What that means is that he plays with lots of great new technologies, and then tells people how they work, ensuring they are correctly understood and adopted correctly and successfully in new applications. He also writes applications too, and is responsible for mentoring and managing C++ and VB developers.

Richard can be contacted via his private email account rja@arpsolutions.demon.co.uk (and will work for anybody provided they supply him with free blueberry muffins, pizza and pepsi max). On a more serious note, he'd love to hear from anybody regarding his or her thoughts on this book—constructive criticism or praise is very welcome.

Simon Robinson lives in Lancaster, UK, where he shares a house with some students. He first encountered serious programming when doing his PhD in physics. He would program in FORTRAN when his supervisor was watching (physics lecturers like FORTRAN) and C when he wasn't. The experience of programming was enough to put him off computers for life, and he tried to pursue a career as a sports massage therapist instead until he realized how much money was in programming and wasn't in sports massage.

He then spent a year writing some very good cardiac risk assessment software but he and his business partner never got round to selling it to anyone. Finally, driven by a strange lack of money, he looked for a—whisper the word quietly—job. Which somehow ended up—after a year of his working for Lucent Technologies in Welwyn Garden City—leading to him writing books about computers.

You can visit Simon's web site at http://www.simonrobinson.com/

Author Acknowledgements

Richard Anderson

OK, first I'd like to say thanks to a few people, actually, quite a lot of people.

Firstly, a special thanks to the other two authors, especially Simon who put a bucket load of effort and value into this book. Also thanks for the additional material guys (Stephen, Dave and Brian) who helped out with the MSMQ and Data Access chapters when we were short on time. Finally, a big thank you to the editors, who apart from losing the odd change (sorry Ian, couldn't resist that) did a great job of ensuring the book flowed well, rewording and adding text when clarification was needed. All of which you did whilst putting up with my terrible email humor, sorry.

Thanks must also go to John 'COM' Franklin, Richard 'It worked in the hotel room' Grimes, Lindsey 'Save the Village' Annison, Simon Thomas, Craig Berry and Alex Stockton, all of whom have helped me progress my writing career in some way shape or form.

Now for the more personal thanks which anybody other than my family will probably want to skip over!

I'd like to say a huge lifetime Thank You and send a big family hug to my Mum, Dad and Sister—three very special people in my life. I owe you for bringing me up with the beliefs and values I have. Thanks for letting me sit up late into the night playing on my computer when I was very young, and thanks for all the advice, direction, guidelines and DIY assistance you give me on a fairly regular basis.

Another big family hug and thank you goes to Bob and Thelma, my wife's parents. You're also very special to me, and I can't really thank you enough for everything you've done for us. I think you'll agree you daughter is very unique and special.

Finally, I'd like to dedicate my contributions to this book to Sam, my loving wife—you're my sunshine babes. You know how much you mean to me, so I shan't prolong this acknowledgment anymore, I'll just say those three you probably here too much anyway—I Love You.

Simon Robinson

This has been an experience!

But everyone's been great. The editors—Karli, Jon, Jon and Ian—who carefully worked through all the code samples, making sure they worked correctly, and who in the last weeks were still at work at midnight reworking everything we'd written until it actually said what we wanted it to say—I couldn't have asked for a better editorial team. The reviewers, as well as Richard Anderson who picked up all sorts of potential problems and made the book a lot better in the process.

Would I repeat the experience? Well, put it like this. I'll never forget sending an email to Richard with some comments about chapter 10, wondering why I was up at 3.30 in the morning doing this - only to get a reply half an hour later.

Thank you everyone. Now when's this party?

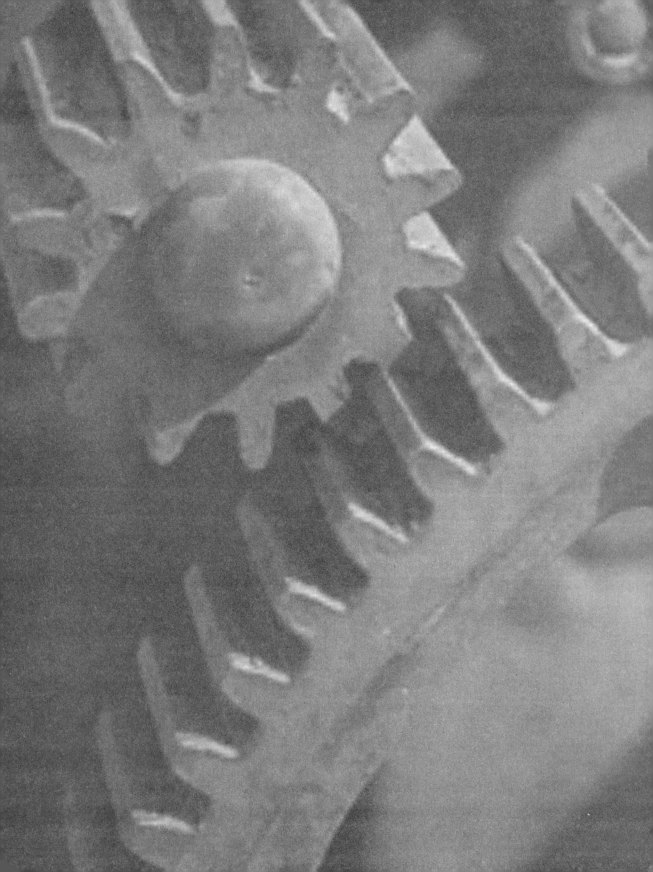

Table of Contents

Chapter 3: Interfacing With Hosting Environments   **85**

Chapter 4: Universal Data Access Through ADO and COM   121

Chapter 5: Application Architecture and ASP Component Design   165

Chapter 6: Introducing MTS   197

Chapter 7: Transactions, Scalability, and Resource Management

247

Chapter 10: Writing C++ Components Using the Active Template Library   401

Chapter 11: Developing An ASP Component Using C++   431

Chapter 12: Threading, Scope and Performance 467

Chapter 13: Accessing Databases with ATL: The OLE DB Consumer Templates 507

Chapter 14: MTS—Transactional Data Access and the ASP Intrinsic Objects in C++ 533

Chapter 15: Document Management Case Study—Part 1 573

Chapter 16: Document Management Case Study —Part 2   623

Appendix C: Microsoft Transaction Server Type Library Reference 743

Appendix D: Microsoft Message Queue Object Library Reference 747

Introduction

Component building is as relevant to web application development as it is to any other kind of application development. Moreover, most ASP developers know that components can bring considerable benefits in terms of overall performance, maintainability, scalability of applications, reusability and transportability of code, and so on. However, in order to program components effectively, there are hurdles to be faced:

❑ The biggest problem that most ASP developers face lies in the transition from writing script-based applications to understanding the apparent complexities of COM—the Component Object Model—and how to use it in the context of web solutions

❑ In many cases, the ASP developer is further intimidated by the need to learn a new programming language (and perhaps development environment) in which to build their components

❑ Arguably, the most popular component programming language among web developers is Visual Basic—but Visual Basic hides a lot of the workings of COM, and can hinder the developer from gaining a genuine understanding of their components

The move from pure ASP development to component development may therefore appear to involve a huge investment in learning. This book aims to counter these difficulties by introducing the necessary concepts step-by-step, in a logical order, with demonstrations and commentary along the way.

This book is all about creating components. In particular, it's about creating COM components for *web-based* applications—that is, components that can run on your web server and can be used within your ASP pages. We'll build a foundation of knowledge that firmly establishes the motivation for using components, and the techniques and considerations involved. We illustrate each chapter with complete, working examples that are designed to demonstrate the points of the discussion.

The components that we develop in this book are all used within ASP pages. Some of the components in this book make very specific use of the fact that they'll exist as part of an ASP application; others are more generic. All the components in this book are COM components—that is, they adhere to the COM specification, which allows COM-compliant components to work together.

There are many languages that we can use to create COM components. In the first chapter, we'll create a COM component in no time at all by using the Windows Script Components (WSC). In Chapters 2–9, we'll be using Visual Basic. And in the later chapters of the book, we'll see how C++, in conjunction with the Active Template Library (ATL), can give us that extra bit of control in terms of things like scalability and resource usage. Along the way, you'll develop an appreciation of COM and an understanding of good component design. We'll also show you the associated design and structure of the applications that employ the components we build.

We should be clear: while this book is about ASP components, it isn't *only* about components that make use of the ASP object model. When we develop ASP applications using script alone, we're quite able to interact with component-based technologies such as Microsoft Transaction Server, Microsoft Message Queue Server, directories, mail servers, and text-based files (including HTML and XML files). In this respect, there's no reason why component-based ASP applications should be any different! Therefore, we'll also be looking at how our components can interact with technologies such as those listed above. The components that you see will help you to harness and employ the power of COM components within all areas of your ASP application development.

Who Is This Book For?

This is *not* an entry-level ASP book—it won't teach you about the ASP object model or how to start programming ASP. Newcomers to ASP might like to try our *Beginning ASP 2.0* or *Beginning ASP 3.0* titles (ISBN 1-861001-34-7 or 1-861003-38-2) instead.

This book is for all other ASP developers. The word *Beginning...* in the title of this book is intended to reflect the fact that the book gives ASP developers an entry point into componentization. So, we'll assume that you have a basic understanding of web development, and—in particular—that you've spent some time creating your own ASP pages and building up a good understanding of ASP and VBScript. We're also going to assume that you've seen at least a smattering of Visual Basic—a leaf through the first couple of chapters should tell you whether you know enough; if you're happy with what's there, you'll have no problems anywhere else in the book.

Because ASP applications often benefit from the use of supporting Microsoft technologies—such as Microsoft Transaction Server (MTS), Microsoft Message Queue Server (MSMQ) and Active Directory Service Interfaces (ADSI)—we'll be devoting at least one chapter to each of these topics. These chapters do not assume an in-depth knowledge of these technologies—we'll briefly cover installation and set-up requirements for them when it's appropriate to do so—but they are approached from the perspective of component use in ASP, and should not be treated as a general tutorial. All of these technologies are free for download from the Microsoft web site at http://www.microsoft.com.

The examples in the C++ chapters—in the latter part of the book—build on the COM foundation laid down earlier on. They are written predominantly for those with prior experience of the C++ programming language. However, the purpose of these chapters is also to demonstrate situations in which C++-based components can give us greater control than their Visual Basic-based counterparts. The samples in these chapters all use ATL, but you won't need any prior experience of *that* topic, since we cover ATL from the basics. Even if you don't understand all of the code that's used in the examples, they'll explain some of the benefits of C++-based ASP components, and perhaps sow the seeds of motivation for exploring Visual C++ and ATL further.

What's Covered in this Book?

The first part of this book (Chapters 1–9) takes you from your first COM component (using the free Windows Script Components download) through to the development of components that perform a variety of complex tasks. We'll cover key concepts of component design, and how these components interact with ASP applications. In this part of the book, we'll be using Visual Basic to write the components.

We will see sample components that interact with the ASP object model; we'll also discover how our components can interact with some important technologies that are associated with ASP applications. So we'll focus in on data access, MTS, MSMQ, directories accessed using Active Directory Services Interfaces (ADSI), and text based files (such as HTML and XML files). If you are new to these technologies, these chapters will give you an opportunity to learn about the functionality offered by each one.

Having laid down a firm foundation in COM, component design, and technologies in the first part of the book, the second part (Chapters 10–14) takes a different angle—coming at ASP component design from the point of view of a C++ developer. We'll see how ATL plays its part in building components, and we'll look more closely at how control over issues like threading can give us better components.

Finally, we've included two case studies. First, Chapters 15 and 16 explain a system that automates the storage, retrieval and indexing of text-based information using XML and HTML—it's a component-based solution with a browser-based user interface. Second, Chapter 17 contains a straightforward cinema booking system that uses C++ components and OLE DB to manage the bookings and the necessary data access functionality.

What You Need To Use This Book

The requirements for this book are flexible. While it is possible to test many of the examples on a single machine with Windows 9x and Personal Web Server, some of the chapters use features that are only available on Windows NT 4 running IIS 4 as the web server. (We have also tested much of the code on a pre-release version of Windows 2000 with IIS 5, and while there are some differences, we expect the code to port smoothly to such a platform.) In addition, while it's not a prerequisite, some of the examples are designed to run across several machines.

Here's a list of other software that's used at various points in this book. Each of the examples will have its different software dependencies:

❑ **Windows NT 4 Option Pack.** The Windows NT 4 Option Pack is an oddly named collection of additional functionality for use with Windows NT 4.0 *or* Windows 9x. Among other things, it includes Internet Information Server 4.0, Microsoft Transaction Server and Microsoft Message Queue Server. It is freely available for download from Microsoft's web site.

❑ **Windows NT 4.0 Service Pack 5.** Since the initial release of Windows NT 4.0, Microsoft has made a number of service packs available—they feature bug fixes and enhancements to the operating system. However you're using Windows NT, it makes sense to take advantage of these updates, which can be downloaded freely from Microsoft's web site. The Windows NT service packs are of particular interest to COM developers—we certainly recommend that you install Service Pack 5, which is the latest release at the time of writing and fixes a number of known problems with IIS.

- **Microsoft Visual Basic 5.0 or later.** Most of the examples written in the first section of the book require Visual Basic. The latest version is 6.0, but version 5.0 will suffice for most of these examples. Again, we recommend downloading the relevant service packs for Visual Studio from Microsoft's web site. For version 6.0, the most recent one at the time of writing is Visual Studio 6.0 Service Pack 3; for version 5.0, you need Visual Studio 97 Service Pack 3.

- **Microsoft Access 97** and **SQL Server 6.5 or later.** Some of the data access examples make use of Microsoft Access databases or SQL Server databases. Where appropriate, we've made these databases available as part of the source code that supports this book. The latest service pack for SQL Server 6.5 is Service Pack 5.

- **Microsoft Data Access Components (MDAC) 2.0 or later.** Contains components used in the data access examples—ActiveX Data Objects (ADO) and OLE DB. MDAC 2.1 Service Pack 2 is the current version at the time of writing. MDAC 2.1 is supplied with Internet Explorer 5 and Microsoft Office 2000, and with a number of other products. It is also available for free download from Microsoft.

- **Microsoft Visual C++ 6.0.** Necessary if you decide to compile the components in Chapters 10–14 and 17—they are written using ATL 3.0, which ships with this version. Again, don't forget the latest service pack; this was Service Pack 3 at the time of writing.

Conventions

We use a number of different styles of text and layout in the book to help differentiate between the different kinds of information. Here are examples of the styles we use and an explanation of what they mean.

Bullets appear indented, with each new bullet marked as follows:

- **Important Words** are in a bold type font.

- Words that appear on the screen, such as menu options, are in a similar font to the one used on screen, for example the File | New... menu. The levels of a cascading menu are separated by a pipe character (|).

- Keys that you press on the keyboard, like *Ctrl* and *Enter*, are in italics.

Code has several styles. If it's a word that we're talking about in the text, such as a `For...Next` loop or a file name like `Videos.mdb`, we'll use `this font`. If it's a block of code that is new, important or relevant to the current discussion, it will be presented like this:

```
<%
    Response.Write "Beginning Components for ASP"
%>
```

Sometimes, you'll see code in a mixture of styles, like this:

```
<%
    Response.Write "Beginning Components for ASP"
    Response.Write "...enjoy the book"
%>
```

The code with a white background is code we've already looked at, or that has little to do with the matter at hand.

Advice, hints, background information, references and extra details appear in an italicized, indented font like this.

> **These boxes hold important, not-to-be forgotten, mission-critical details that are directly relevant to the surrounding text.**

Customer Support

We've tried to make this book as accurate and enjoyable as possible, but what really matters is what the book actually does for you. Please let us know your views, either by returning the reply card in the back of the book, or by contacting us via e-mail at feedback@wrox.com.

All the source code for all the examples in this book is available for download at the Wrox Press web site at http://www.wrox.com or at http://webdev.wrox.co.uk. You'll find more information about COM at a related web site, http://www.comdeveloper.com.

We've made every effort to make sure that there are no errors in the text or the code. However, to err is human and as such we recognize the need to keep you informed of any mistakes as they're spotted and corrected. Errata sheets are available for all our books at http://www.wrox.com. If you find an error that hasn't already been reported, please let us know. We've included an appendix that gives more information about support and errata.

Our web site acts as a focus for other information and support, including the code from all our books, sample chapters, previews of forthcoming titles, and articles and opinion on related topics.

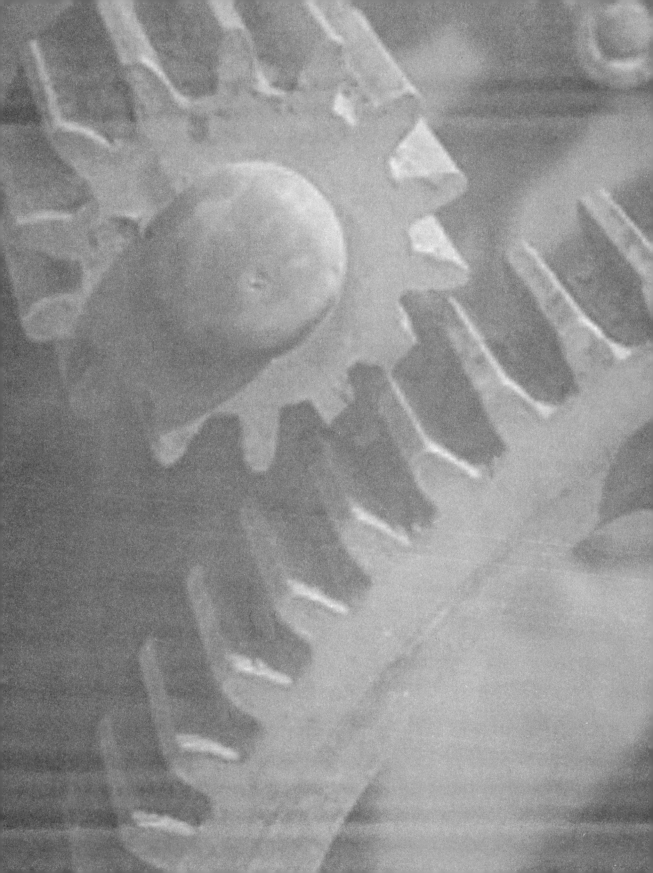

Starting Out With Components

As our customers, our managers and the sales team ask for increasingly complex applications, the demands made of software developers are growing at an ever-increasing rate. Lately, the vogue for companies, quite rightly, has been to automate their business processes. Now the drive is to integrate all of these disparate systems together, often with the addition of a web interface so that access to these products and services is more widely available.

The continual growth in the adoption and expansion of computer-based systems leads to more sophisticated (or complicated) applications—some of which take years to develop, or evolve without direction into unmanageable systems that no single developer fully understands. When the system requires maintenance or an upgrade, where's the developer who built the thing in the first place? They're either 'too busy', or they've moved on to richer pastures (not uncommon in today's market). That means that some other poor developer has to bear the pain and hardship of working out where changes need to be made—and the ramifications that these changes will have on other parts of the system.

Concerns over scalability, structure and maintenance of these increasingly complex systems, coupled with the demands that are the very nature of software development, mean that something is needed to ease the burden. **Components** have got a lot to offer us. If you think of a component as a small, self-contained nugget of code that we write to sit at a well-defined point in a system's architecture and perform certain (related) tasks, we can begin a list of the benefits of components right here:

- ❑ Because by itself it is a lot simpler than the entire application, we can maintain it easily.

- ❑ Because it's self-contained, we can upgrade simply by taking out the old component and putting the new one in its place. The same applies to components that we discover to contain bugs.

- ❑ If it's useful elsewhere, we can reuse it—we may borrow it for our own purposes, or put it on the market.

We could go on, but we'll save that for later. The point is this: everything we've said so far is just as applicable to ASP and web development as it is to any other kind of development. Web sites are becoming more complicated: our ASP applications are being asked to incorporate the functionality of traditional applications; to centralize the point of access for end users who need to get at different applications; to handle increasing numbers of users. The fact is, we need to give components some serious consideration.

Components are already an important part of programming and software development, and the ability to build and use components is a valuable tool in any programmer's arsenal. In fact, these days, component building is arguably an essential skill.

In this chapter, we're going to convince you that you already know quite a bit about programming with components; we'll look at some typical scenarios in which components are used; and we'll begin to investigate the impact that component programming has on application design. By the end of the chapter, you should understand that componentization isn't *just* about code reuse—it implies a new way of creating applications, opening the door to techniques and technologies that aren't available in 'traditional' programming. Specifically we will see:

❑ The advantages of using components

❑ The basics of COM—Microsoft's Component Object Model

❑ An introduction to 3-tier and *n*-tier application development

❑ Examples of situations where you're probably using components already

❑ How to build and use our first component

The Advantages of Componentization

Consider the question, "What's the best approach to the solution of a complex problem?" Perhaps the most obvious answer is this:

❑ Break it up into a number of smaller parts, each of which is self-contained and can be easily understood

❑ Solve each of the smaller parts (or use a ready-written solution—you might have a solution lying round from a previous project, or you might buy in a third-party solution)

❑ Bring each of the smaller parts together to create the overall solution

This approach generally works very well—and programming is no exception. The reason is probably its simplicity—but this simplicity is the key to good software engineering and development.

COM—the Component Object Model

The good news is that there is an established technology available to us today that allows us to build our applications this way. It is called **COM**—the **Component Object Model**. COM is the software industry's favored solution for solving the complex problems relating to large applications and code reuse on the Windows platform. Using **componentization**, large applications can be assembled from smaller, self-contained packages of software, each of which performs a particular task.

By using components, we only need to write a small amount of application code to act as 'glue', sticking the pieces together. The 'glue' then simply calls the components into being, provides them with the information they need to do their work, and then either lets them get on with it or waits for them to produce a result. In this sense, they can be like little "black boxes" of functionality: you don't need to know how each component achieves its task; you just need to know what it's capable of doing and what values you can provide it so that it will accomplish the task it is built for.

A Couple of Analogies

If that sounds a bit esoteric, consider what happens when you need to ask the operator for your uncle's telephone number. You call the operator, and you give the name and address of your uncle. Then, they go away and do their thing... and eventually they come back with a number (or not, if your uncle has no telephone). In this sense, the operator is acting like a component—maybe the request would be programmed like this:

```
Dim objOperator
Set objOperator = Server.CreateObject("Operator")
Response.Write "The phone number you require is " & _
               objOperator.GetNumberFor("Uncle Brian", "Chicago")
```

The point here is that we're not particularly worried about how the operator finds the number—we just give them the information and expect them to do the job.

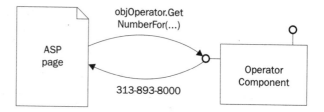

As another example, think about hi-fi 'separates'. You buy an amplifier, a pair of speakers, a CD player, and you wire them all together with some leads. Then, a month later, you decide that you wanted a turntable so that you can play all your old vinyl. But you don't go out and buy a whole new system—after all, you already have an amplifier and speakers. You just expand the existing system by purchasing the turntable and plugging it into your amplifier.

In your average software house, this is how customers and the sales/marketing department think that application development works. Wouldn't it be nice if it really did?

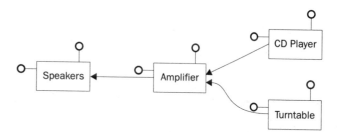

Well, there can be a strong similarity. You may not have realized it, but you're already using COM components. For example, in your software development, you've probably already come across ActiveX Data Objects (ADO)—a set of components for data access. Or perhaps you've used the Ad Rotator component, the Content Rotator component, or some of the other components that are provided as standard with ASP?

Better still, look at the software you use every day—things like Microsoft Word and Internet Explorer. Many of these kinds of application are written using components. The Internet Explorer executable (Iexplore.exe) is only 77Kb in size; all of its sophisticated functionality is handled by numerous other components, which the executable only calls into action when necessary.

What Do Components Do for Us?

Hopefully, we've given you an incentive for wanting to learn about components. The *advantages* of packaging up our code into components rather than using script are numerous, and we'll outline the main ones here.

Code Reuse and Distribution

Possibly the two most common reasons for using components are:

❑ Breaking up a complex application into manageable chunks, as we've already discussed

❑ Packaging up code that you are likely to need more than once so that it can be re-used

Having written a piece of code that performs a specific function, cutting and pasting the appropriate pieces into another program can often be difficult. If you've ever done this with your own code, you'll know how tricky it is to remember how you originally intended the code to work—you may have to work out what each line is doing in order to select precisely the correct lines. And if you've ever done it with someone else's code, you'll know that it's even harder!

When you package code into a COM component, you are automatically providing a clear definition of precisely how to use the functionality of that component. You'll still need to document it, but you won't need to do any cutting and pasting of code.

Easy Distribution

Of course, this also makes for a convenient code distribution technique. When passing your neatly packaged component to your colleagues and customers, they don't need to understand the code behind it to get it to work—you just tell them what tasks it can achieve and what information they'll need to pass to it.

For example, we don't need to know how the ADO components work in order to use them. We can just retrieve them from the Microsoft web site, install them, and let Microsoft's documentation tell us the rest.

Binary Distribution and Reuse

As we'll discuss in more detail later on, COM components are **language neutral**—they can be written in one language and used in another. If you ask a Visual Basic compiler to compile some C++ code, you'll see some interesting errors and it won't work. Ask a Visual Basic application to use a COM component that was written in C++, and it will work fine.

Maintenance and Replacability

Here's a case in point: if you have to do a lot of form field validation, you can write a component that performs the task for you—that way, you centralize the code in a component, and you can simply reuse it time and time again.

If you ever find a problem with your validation code, you can just correct the component and reinstall it in place of the faulty one. Drawing an analogy with our telephone operator example, this is comparable to the operator being off work. The telephone company just installs another operator as a stand-in. We, as clients, don't care *which* operator is on the other end of the 'phone—so long as they can do the job.

Commercially Available Components

There are an ever-growing number of components that are available commercially. If you have a programming task to achieve, it's quite possible that there's already a component out there in the marketplace that will help you to achieve you goal, or even provide a complete solution. Buying a suitable third-party component means that we don't need to research, write and test the component ourselves—this brings three immediate advantages:

- ❑ We can acquire the component immediately, and therefore we should be able to deliver our final solution faster

- ❑ We've effectively replaced the cost of development and testing (for that part of the project) with the cost of a fixed-price lump of pre-written code—which is usually cheaper

- ❑ Highly specialized components are usually written in consultation with specialists in the field. In that case, we also avoid the cost of employing a specialist

In addition, commercial components should be tried and tested in their market situations, so you can be fairly confident that it will perform well at the task it is intended to achieve (although it's worth restricting yourself to buying components only from trusted suppliers, as you generally don't get to see the source code). One very popular example of such a component would be a credit card verification component for use in e-commerce sites.

> *To get an idea of the number of components on the market, check out some sites that specialize in selling components over the Web. For starters, try* http://www.componentsource.com, http://www.greymatter.co.uk, *and* http://www.serverobjects.com.

Performance Advantages

When you're executing complicated code, you're always looking to reduce the time it takes to process. However, if your code is in the form of ASP or some other script, you can reasonably expect it to take a while. That's because scripting languages are **interpreted**. That is to say, each line of code needs to be converted into more elementary instructions (binary code) that the processor can understand, before that line can be executed. That happens *every time* a script is run.

By contrast, components are usually already **compiled**, which means that they have already been converted into the binary format. This means that the component's **methods**—the functions that it makes available—can be executed straight away. The result is that components often execute much more quickly than plain scripts do.

Hiding Sensitive Code

If you're distributing code, then you need to think about whether you want other people to see it. If they can see it, they can figure out how it works, and they can probably also tamper with it. If you're distributing script files, your code is open to these kinds of threat.

Writing components in languages such as Visual Basic and C++ requires you to compile them. By compiling the component, you produce the binary representation that we mentioned in the previous section—not only does this execute efficiently, but also it protects your code from snoopers and code-changers. Your component's business logic is safe from anyone who may wish to meddle with it.

Splitting Tasks Into Distinct Areas

If you have several developers or teams working on an application that is split up into discrete chunks, componentization makes it possible for each of the different groups to work on a different part of the application. Each task can be clearly defined, and you can specify the values that the different parts of the application need to share in order for the application to come together as a whole afterwards.

Ease of Debugging

While the Script Debugger is a very useful tool, it isn't nearly as sophisticated as the debuggers in Visual Basic and (in particular) Visual C++ . The debugging tool in the Visual C++ development environment, for example, allows you to look right down into the computer's memory to see what is being stored where.

This kind of capability means that, if you're using Visual C++ or Visual Basic to write components that are intended to perform complex tasks, you gain the edge in terms of finding out exactly why your code isn't working properly.

That covers some of the major advantages of componentization, although we will see others as we go through the book—in fact, we'll see some more in this very chapter. If you take all of these advantages into account as you write your ASP applications, you may soon find yourself writing less of your programming logic in script, and placing more of it into components. The ASP script becomes the 'glue' that binds the component pieces of your application together.

How It All Comes Together

So, to recap: **COM** stands for the **Component Object Model**, which is a framework for creating and using components.

Microsoft introduced the COM framework back in 1993, as a model for describing and implementing components in such a way that they could interact with each other and with all COM-enabled platforms and applications. COM is the specification to which components are written and used on the Windows platform—and there are now implementations of COM on many non-Microsoft platforms. Every component that we develop in this book will be a COM component, and will therefore conform to this specification.

Let's backtrack a little. We've just made a rather lofty claim. All COM components will be able to interact with all other COM-enabled platforms and components? How do they do that?

The foundation of COM is a **binary specification** that defines how the code using a component—usually called a **client**—can use the functionality that a component makes available. On the flip side, it also defines how a component exposes that functionality to a client.

Because COM is a binary specification, it allows **language neutrality**. As long as a given language can produce compiled code that complies with the binary specification, it can be used to write COM components—and it can also interact with COM components written in any other COM-enabled programming language.

There are a number of languages in which you can write COM components. In this book, we will mainly see how to write COM components in Visual Basic and C++, although there are many more languages you could use, including Visual J++, SmallTalk and Delphi.

So, while this book is about components for ASP, the components that we'll develop are all COM components—and that means that (with some exceptions) they can be used in other COM-aware programs, such as standalone applications written in Visual Basic or Visual C++. As we will see in Chapter 3, the ability to do this is dependent upon whether our components are designed to interact with the environment that calls them. If we develop a component that relies on some functionality of the ASP object model, for example, we will only be able to use it within ASP applications. There are, however, very many occasions when our components will be reusable in different environments.

COM is not the only specification for components—CORBA and JavaBeans are two others. However, as this book is about components for ASP, we will be focusing on COM components.

ActiveX and COM

A term that you may have come across in the context of component-based development is **ActiveX**, and we should make clear that in most situations, ActiveX means pretty much the same thing as COM. An ActiveX component is the same as a COM component. In addition, an ActiveX control is the same as a COM control, and an ActiveX server is the same as a COM server. But don't let all that confuse you—we'll come back to these terms shortly.

Today, ActiveX is little more than an outdated brand name that was introduced by Microsoft a few years ago when they redirected folks towards the Internet and revamped and optimized some of their technologies to meet the low-bandwidth requirements of the Net. There was ActiveX Scripting, ActiveX Components, ActiveX Data Objects, ActiveX Controls, and ActiveX Documents.

ActiveX achieved its original goals and got lots of media attention, but since then people have been confused about the differences between COM and ActiveX. Essentially, however, in modern-day parlance and as far as ASP component development is concerned, ActiveX implies COM.

Components and Objects

We've established that a COM component describes a set of related functionality and the code required to achieve that functionality. When we want to use a component's functionality, however, we don't make constant references to the component itself. Rather, we use the component as a blueprint, and we use it to create an entity that we refer to as an **object**.

The process of creating an object from a component is called **instantiation**. An object is a single instance of a component. The object is created in the image of the component, and is the vehicle by which we make use of the component's functionality.

> **In code, we use** objects. **An object represents a single entity within our code; we use a component as the blueprint for creating an object.**

We may want to use several instances of a single component at any one time, within different applications. Or we may have a single application that uses several instances of the same component—just like having many variables (or 'instances of variables') to hold different strings.

You should be aware that the term 'component' is often used to refer both to the COM component and to the instance—relying on the context to imply the exact meaning.

Interfaces and Implementation

So far, we've talked only in general terms about how we can pass some relevant values to a component and ask it to perform a task for us. We haven't yet talked about how we *tell* the component what we want it do, or how we pass in the required values. That's what this section is about.

One of the key characteristics of all COM components is that they are able to perform tasks for us without telling us *how* the task is going to be performed. To achieve this, the component must give us clearly defined information saying what the component can do, what type of information it expects us to pass, and what it will return when the task is complete. In other words, we need to know what methods the component exposes, the parameters that each method expects, and the return value from each method. In order to facilitate this, COM distinguishes the description of a component's functionality from its internal workings.

❑ This description of the component's functionality is defined by the component's **interface**. A component can have many interfaces, but related methods are generally grouped together within the same interface. A lot of people in the COM world (including the authors of this book!) agree that **interface-based programming** is the single most important and powerful aspect of COM.

❑ The 'internal workings' of the methods and properties—that is, the code that allows them to perform their tasks—is generally referred to as the component's **implementation**.

An interface is really nothing more than a list of **methods**, **properties** and **events** (you'll meet the second and third of these terms in a moment). When we want to use the component, the interface tells us how to do it. The interface doesn't give any details of the component's implementation, but its existence implies a promise that the functionality it describes will always be available.

The distinction between interface and implementation is an important one. It's the interface that provides the link between our applications and the component itself. We can replace an old component with a new one that has a different implementation, provided that the new component provides the same interface as the old one. Otherwise, applications designed to use the original interface may break.

Understanding Interfaces

To help us understand interfaces, let's think about cars. We're going to model a car in terms of a component. If you want to be really imaginative, you can pretend that you're an ASP page (rather than a human being) driving the car. The car component provides functionality that can be defined by a number of interfaces. For example, the component has an interface that defines how you drive the car—we'll call it `IDrive` (by convention, interface names often begin with `I`).

Methods

The `IDrive` interface has these methods:

Method	Description
Accelerate()	Push the accelerator down by the specified amount
Brake()	Stop the car
BrakeHard()	Stop the car fast!
SteerLeft()	Turn the steering wheel left by the specified amount
SteerRight()	Turn the steering wheel right by the specified amount

The methods are the object's way of allowing us to use it to perform a task. The methods above allow us to accelerate, brake, and steer the car. By using the object's methods to perform the tasks, we don't need to worry about what is going on inside the object. If we want to turn the car to the left, we don't need to get under the car to find out how the steering mechanism works—we just sit in the driver's seat and call its `SteerLeft()` method (equivalent to turning the steering wheel).

Some methods need additional information, and will adjust their behavior accordingly. For example, the `SteerLeft` method would need to be told just how far to turn the steering wheel to the left. To this end, such methods are capable of receiving **parameters**—values required to execute the method.

Properties

Properties are the settings or stored values that are contained within an object, some of which are exposed to the user. These values tell us about the appearance or behavior of the object—and we can change some properties too. The `IDrive` interface might include properties that tell us the temperature of the engine, and the amount of gas in the tank.

There are three types of properties: read-only properties, write-only properties, and read–write properties. For example, the car probably has a read-only property that tells us what mileage it has done. You can affect the values of some read-only properties indirectly—driving the car will increase the mileage—but you're not permitted to set the mileage directly. The tripometer (which tells you how far you have gone) would be a read-write property—you can write to it by pressing the button that resets it to 0, and you can read it by looking at the display that tells you how far you traveled since you last pressed the button.

Events

We should also briefly mention **events**. If methods are our way of telling an object what to do, events are the object's way of telling us that something has happened. For example, many modern cars have a device that is capable of monitoring the amount of gas in the tank. If the gas level falls below a certain level, the device fires an event, which informs the object that the gas level is low. This allows the object to react to the event—in this case by displaying a bright-red warning sign on the dashboard. Reacting to an event in this way is called **event handling**.

Using the Interface

The nice thing about cars is that generally, once you know how to drive one, you know how to drive them all. All cars use a steering wheel to steer; you make them go faster by pressing the accelerator pedal, and slower by pressing the brake pedal. The same is true for trucks and juggernauts. How does this relate to components? Well, we can have lots of different types of component that all expose the same interface. The car component exposes the `IDrive` interface, but so do the truck component and the juggernaut component. Once we know the methods and properties exposed by the `IDrive` interface, we know roughly how to use that interface on *any* component that exposes it.

You will often see methods written with parentheses after them, like this:

```
BrakeHard()
```

Within the parentheses, you might need to include one or more other items—these are the parameters we mentioned earlier. The `BrakeHard()` method doesn't have any parameters (when we ask the car to brake hard, it will stop quickly—the car doesn't need any more information than that). By contrast, when we accelerate we'll need to tell the car by how much we want to accelerate—and to do that we use a parameter like this:

```
Accelerate(3)
```

This will work provided that the object knows what we mean by an acceleration unit of 3. This should be defined in the documentation for the component: "Insert an integer as the first parameter and I'll convert that into *miles per hour* and increase the speed by that amount". Again, as a driver we don't mind *how* the car component achieves this acceleration—we just have the promise that it will.

Lollipop Diagrams

To represent the interfaces that a COM component supports, we use a simple, pictorial technique called **lollipop diagrams**. A lollipop diagram represents the component in the form of a box; the interfaces extrude from the left side of the component. A name that appears within the box is the name of the component. The single line sprouting from the top of box represents an interface called `IUnknown`—this is a rather special interface in COM, so it gets special attention in lollipop diagrams.

> Every *component implements* `IUnknown`, *but programming languages like Visual Basic shield us from* `IUnknown` *and other COM-specific workings on the supposition that they're difficult to understand. We could explain* `IUnknown` *here, but there's no gain, because we'll be using Visual Basic until Chapter 10. We'll come back to talk about* `IUnknown` *in some detail in Chapter 10, when we start using C++.*

The following figure shows the lollipop diagrams for the car and the truck in our example. Both components provide all the basic functionality needed to drive such a vehicle.

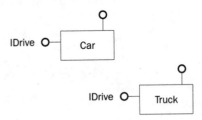

It's not a great diagram, but it clearly shows what we can do with our vehicles. Let's look at a more realistic lollipop diagram for our car example. Interfaces generally group together related functionality, so in the following we have three interfaces (or four, if you include IUnknown extruding from the top):

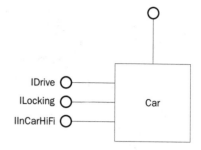

One interface provides methods for driving the car, another for controlling the locks and the alarm, and yet another for controlling the in-car music system.

Identifying the Component

IDrive is quite a nice name for our driving interface. The trouble is, it's such an obvious name that it wouldn't be at all surprising if someone else designed an interface of their own that did something similar, and they might call it IDrive as well. That's going to cause severe problems if a component that exposes my IDrive gets installed on the same machine as a component that exposes this other developer's IDrive interface. An application could easily end up talking to the 'wrong' interface—which will almost inevitably cause it to crash.

COM resolves such problems by ensuring that each COM interface (and, for that matter, each component) has a 'real' name that is guaranteed to be unique. An interface's unique name is called an interface identifier (IID), and a component's unique name is called a class identifier (CLSID). IIDs and CLSID are both types of **globally unique identifier (GUID)**; a GUID is a 128-bit number that can be generated with special a utility supplied by Microsoft.

For example, the IID for my IDrive might be 67741683-547D-11D0-8236-00A0C908DB96. Inspection alone should tell you that it's more than a little unlikely anyone else will come up with that name by chance.

The utility that generates GUIDs does so partly at random, and partly by scrambling information like the address of the Ethernet card in the machine on which it's running and the current time (to 100 nanosecond intervals). The algorithm used has been carefully designed to guarantee that identical GUIDs will not be accidentally generated for at least several thousand years. This should guarantee that there won't be any confusion between interfaces!

Where Are Components Stored

Normally, when you run a program, you're actually running an executable file. The executable file might call up some other files called **dynamic-link libraries** (or **DLLs**) to perform some tasks. A DLL is like an executable file, in that it contains instructions that the computer can run directly. But a DLL differs from an executable file because a DLL *cannot* be run independently. A DLL really is like a library that can be called up by any executable that's already running.

*Executables can also call upon the functionality contained in other files, such as **OLE control extensions** (or **OCXs**). An OCX is essentially a DLL that implements a visual interface. We won't deal with OCXs in this book.*

COM is designed to allow any application or component to call up any other component, no matter where the other component is. This means that COM components can be stored within executable files or as DLLs. When you create a component in Visual Basic or by using the Visual C++ ATL Wizards, you get to choose what type of file you'd like to host the component—a .dll or a .exe file.

There are several factors to consider when choosing which type you want, but broadly speaking an executable offers greater security, while a DLL can give greater performance. This is because an executable will run in a separate process, which means that in order to use the component within the calling application, COM has to spend time passing data back and forth between the application's process and the component's process. A DLL-hosted component doesn't run in a separate process, so for components hosted in DLLs, this overhead is not normally an issue. Because of this, components hosted in DLLs are referred to as **in-process components**, while those located in executables are referred to as **out-of-process components**.

COM Servers

One of the slightly confusing aspects of COM is that there are several different names for some of the concepts involved. For example, what we have been referring to as a component, a Visual Basic programmer might call an "externally creatable class module". To confuse matters even further, C++ programmers may refer to the same thing as a "COM server", or a "COM object". We'll generally stick to the term *component* here.

Strictly speaking, a **COM server** is a file (such as a DLL or an EXE) that contains all the executable code for one or more COM components, like this. One corollary of this is that related components can be hosted within the same COM server if necessary.

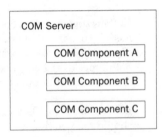

Using Components from ASP

The majority of this book is about creating your own components for use in your ASP applications, and in this section we'll use a custom-built component in an ASP page.

We'll begin by looking at how to call components from ASP. It's likely that you'll have done something like this before during your time as an ASP developer, but you may not have completely understood the detail of what your code was up to. Let's put that right with a quick example.

Did You Know You Were Using COM Components?

Whether you realized it or not, the Server, Request, Response, Application, and Session objects are in fact COM components. They are known as ASP's **intrinsic** or **built-in** objects—they are hosted in a COM server called asp.dll, which you'll find on your machine if you have IIS or PWS installed. There are also a number of other COM components that come with ASP, such as the Ad Rotator and the Content Rotator. The components available to you will depend upon which version of ASP you are running.

In ASP pages, the ASP intrinsic objects are treated a bit differently from other COM components. The ASP intrinsic objects are there and ready-to-use in the page—the ASP environment takes care of this for us.

When we want to use other components on our ASP pages, we have to create them explicitly using the `Server` object's `CreateObject()` method. We also have to pass the CLSID or the ProgID of the object to the `CreateObject()` method, so that it creates an object of the appropriate type for us to use in our script (we will meet ProgIDs later in this chapter).

Using Our First Component

Later in the chapter, we will build a component called `BrickCalc.wsc`. Its job is to calculate how many bricks we would need in order to build a wall. At this point, we'll talk about how that component is used in a simple user interface called `wroxblox.asp`. This page asks the end user to specify the size of the wall they want to build. It also allows users to specify the type of brick (breeze block or house brick), using a drop-down list box. This information is held in an HTML form:

```
<HTML>
   <HEAD>
      <TITLE>Wrox Blox Building Supplies</TITLE>
   </HEAD>

   <BODY>
   <P><FONT FACE="Arial" SIZE="6">Wrox Blox Building Supplies BrickCalc.</FONT></P>

   <FORM ACTION="WroxBloxResult.asp" METHOD="post">
   <P>Length of wall in feet: <INPUT ID="WallLength" NAME="WallLength" ></P>
   <P>Height of wall in feet: <INPUT ID="WallHeight" NAME="WallHeight" ></P>

   <P>Select Type of Brick:
      <SELECT ID="BrickType" NAME="BrickType" STYLE="HEIGHT: 22px; WIDTH: 131px">
         <OPTION SELECTED VALUE="BreezeBlock">Breeze Block</OPTION>
         <OPTION VALUE="HouseBrick">House Brick</OPTION>
      </SELECT>
   </P>
   <P>Click here to calculate the number of bricks you will need: 
      <INPUT TYPE="submit" VALUE="Calculate">
   </P>
   </FORM>

   </BODY>
</HTML>
```

The code for this example and the component it uses is available from our web site at http://webdev.wrox.co.uk/books/2882. *You'll also find a compiled version of the component there. Before you use this component, however, you need to install the Windows Script Component download that's available from* http://www.microsoft.com/scripting; *this will be discussed in more depth when we see how to create the component later in the chapter.*

Here is what the `WroxBloxForm.asp` page looks like:

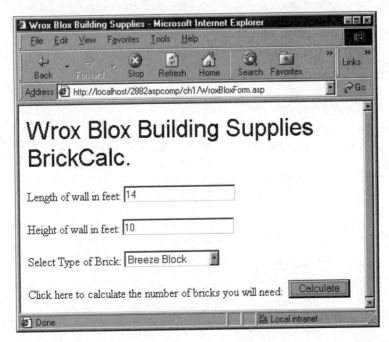

When the user clicks on the **Calculate** button, the values are sent to our `WroxBloxResult.asp` page. Before we take a look at that page, let's just see what the component allows us to do.

The Brick Calculator Component

The Brick Calculator component `BrickCalc.wsc` is a **Windows Script Component** (hence the `.wsc` file extension). Windows Script Components (WSC) is a Microsoft technology that allows us to create COM components using VBScript or JScript. They are excellent for speedy prototyping of components, because—as we will see later in the chapter—the interface is generated by a Wizard, and the methods are implemented using script.

The Brick Calculator has one property, `BrickType`, which specifies the type of brick. It also has one method, `HowManyBricks()`, which requires the `WallHeight` and `WallLength` as parameters in order to perform its calculation. Given the type of brick and the size of the wall, it will work out the number of bricks we need to build the wall.

Using the Brick Calculator Component

When the user clicks on the **Calculate** button of the HTML form, the values are sent to our `WroxBloxResult.asp` page. This is the page that uses the Brick Calculator component and returns the result of its `HowManyBricks()` method to the browser. The page starts by creating an instance of the component so that we can use it from the page:

```
<%
    Dim objBrickCalc
    Set objBrickCalc = Server.CreateObject("BrickCalc.wsc")
    ...
```

Here, we create an object variable in the first line, then set this variable to an instance of the component we want to create. In this case, the ProgID is BrickCalc.wsc. Recall that the instance of the component created is called an **object**.

People often use the terms component and object interchangeably, but in strict terms an object is an instance of a component.

Now we collect the wall dimensions from the form to submit to the object's HowManyBricks() method. We set the BrickType property of the object to the value of the select box, and write the dimensions of the wall back to the browser:

```
. . .
WallLength = Request.Form("WallLength")
WallHeight = Request.Form("WallHeight")

objBrickCalc.BrickType = Request.Form("BrickType")

Response.Write "<FONT FACE=arial SIZE=6>" & _
               "Wrox Blox Building Supplies BrickCalc Result</FONT><BR><BR>"

Response.Write "Calculation for a wall " & WallHeight & _
               " foot high and " & WallLength & " foot long."
. . .
```

Having created an instance of the component in the ASP page, we can treat the object just as we would any other object in ASP. So we can reference the methods our component implements using dot notation:

```
objectname.methodname(parameter1, parameter2, ..., parameterN)
```

You should be familiar with this notation already, because it's exactly the same as the one we use when using the ASP intrinsic objects, and all other COM components in ASP. For example, when we want to write something back to the browser in ASP, we are using the Write() method of the Response object.

In our case, however, we have the objBrickCalc variable holding the reference to our component, so we can access the methods of the component using:

```
objBrickCalc.methodname(parameter1, parameter2, ..., parametern)
```

On this occasion, the component only has one method, so we'll be using:

```
objBrickCalc.HowManyBricks(WallHeight, WallLength)
```

We want to save the return value of the method in a variable strResult so that we can use it in the ASP page. To do this, we just make sure that the variable we want to use in the ASP page is set to the above line, simply by using:

```
. . .
strResult = objBrickCalc.HowManyBricks(WallHeight, WallLength)
. . .
```

Finally, we write the value of the variable `strResult`, which holds the return value of the component's `HowManyBricks()` method, to the browser:

```
      ...
      Response.Write "<BR><BR> You will need " & strResult & " bricks."
   %>
```

And that's it. Here is the result:

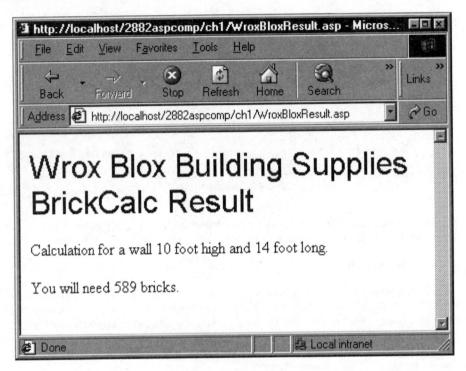

So, we have created an instance of our Brick Calculator component, and used it from script in our page. Obviously it's a very simple example, and it's a task that could have been achieved using script within the form. But it does show you how to use components from your ASP script, and how we talk to objects via their methods and properties.

Having seen how to use components from our ASP pages, let's take a look at some of the common types of component, and how they might fit into our applications.

Different Kinds of Components

Components come in all manner of different types. To try to get an idea of the range of tasks that could be performed using custom-designed components, it can be useful to categorize components according to their nature. In this section we'll describe a few of the commonly used categories.

Note that we've only categorized in this way for guidance. We've intended this as a useful way of understanding what can be done with components, but nothing more—there are no hard and fast rules about categories, and they are not mutually exclusive. A given component may fit into more than one of the categories we describe. If you've used many components in your ASP development, you'll probably recognize some of these varieties, and may even be able to name some examples of each. If not, don't worry—you'll have seen plenty before long!

Generalized or Universal Components

Some components are of a generalized nature, and designed to be used in many different environments. Typical examples that display this behavior are the members of another group that you may well have met before: the set of **ActiveX Data Objects** (**ADO**) components that provide programmatic access to data stores.

The ADO components ship with all current Microsoft operating systems and data-aware applications, and they can be used from programming languages such as Visual Basic, Visual C++ and Visual InterDev. However, they are equally at home within applications that contain programming or scripting features, such as Microsoft Office, Windows Script Host (WSH), Internet Information Server (IIS), and so on. And, of course, we can use them from ASP—we'll be focusing more closely on ADO and ASP in Chapter 4.

The Brick Calculator component we just saw (and which we'll be building later in the chapter) is an example of a generalized or universal component.

Environment-Specific Components

Other components are designed specifically for use in a particular environment, and rely on some of the facilities of that environment in order to operate. The standard Browser Capabilities component that ships with ASP, for example, is designed specifically for use within IIS and ASP, and useless in any other environment. On the other hand, the Progress Bar component (which is supplied with Windows programming languages like Visual Basic and Visual C++) is totally unsuitable for use in IIS, as it provides a visual interface that is designed to provide feedback on a standalone workstation, as opposed to a web page served across a network or the Internet to a client.

> We will come back to a discussion of client–server and n-tier architecture when we've completed our 'categorization'. But for the moment, if you think about the **client** as being the machine that makes a request for the pages, and the **server** as a different machine where your ASP pages reside and get processed, with some kind of network in between, you will be able to follow the descriptions of components.

Visual Interface Components

The Progress Bar component we just mentioned also hints at a second way of classifying component types: by their support for a visual interface. Some components are more often described as **controls**, and the term is generally used to indicate that a component has some sort of visible representation that forms a significant part of its operation. The ActiveX Calendar control that ships with MS Office, the Structured Graphics control that ships with Internet Explorer 4+, and the FlexGrid control (shown here) that ships with Visual Basic 6.0 are also examples of components with visual interfaces.

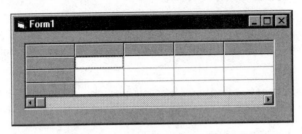

Because controls are usually implemented on client machines, as opposed to being run on the server as part of an ASP script, we will not be covering them in this book.

Business Rules Components

Business rules are the rules to which the operation of your component, application or system (or even your business) must adhere. These rules might involve checking that customers remain within agreed credit limits, that discounts are applied in a uniform manner, or that a manufacturing cycle is correctly scheduled. Business rules components are components that implement this kind of programming logic.

Because business rules components are chiefly concerned with the internal logic of the application, they often have no visual interface. However, there are many exceptions to this very general rule.

Transactional Components

Some applications require multiple, separate actions to take place in order to achieve the desired result. For example, if we're updating a local database and then sending an order to a remote server, we want *both* actions to succeed: if the order request succeeds but the data update fails, our database won't contain an accurate reflection of our orders. It is usual to implement a system that *guarantees* either that all of the required actions are successfully completed, or that none of them takes place. This is called a **transaction**, and we can create components that work with a **transaction monitor** to ensure the completion or complete undoing of each transaction. We'll cover transactional components in Chapters 6 and 7.

Active Server Components

If you're reading this now then you probably don't need to be told about the increasing popularity of Active Server Pages as a server-side programming language. This has produced an explosion in **Active Server** (sometimes called **ActiveX Server**) component usage. These components are specifically designed to run on the server under IIS, and to interface with ASP directly. They can provide better performance than pure script code, and encapsulate complex tasks. We'll be looking at what programming features characterize Active Server components and how to write them in Chapter 3. Active Server components can be considered to form a sub-category of environment-specific components.

Utility/Commercial Components

This is the catchall that covers all the 'leftovers' from the other categories—for example, components designed to perform specific tasks within other components, and highly generic components that can be used in a variety of ways. You can make almost any block of code into a component, and so there is really no limit to the components you might create. Common examples are the commercial components that you can purchase off-the-shelf, such as registry access components, HTTP transfer components, and XML data parsing components.

How Components Are Made Available

OK, we've had an example of using a component from ASP, and we've talked about some of the ways we can think about categorizing the components we're going to build. Despite that, what we've yet to do is establish exactly how components are made available to our client code. You know that components are stored in DLL and EXE files, but there have been no references to those in the code you've seen so far. There must be another mechanism in operation.

The first questions to ask are: How do we know how to reference the component that we want? Where do applications get the information about components? The answer to both these questions lies in the **system registry** (often known simply as "the registry"). The registry currently plays a lead role in the world of COM. It's a hierarchical data store that's used to hold COM-related information and lots more.

> *The role of the registry with COM+ in Windows 2000 has changed slightly; the general concept of having a 'central repository' for component information is the same, but the registry is no longer that repository, except for legacy components.*

Generally, applications don't access the registry directly for the COM information they need. Instead, they use some Application Programming Interface (API) functions provided by COM that encapsulate its usage. To take a closer look at the registry, run the registry editor program Regedit.exe (just choose Run... from the Start menu and type Regedit). When it starts, you'll see a number of **keys**:

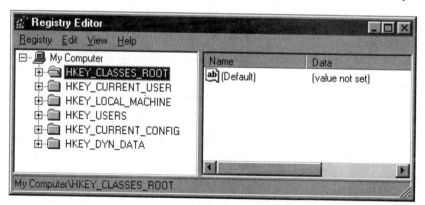

COM information is stored under the HKEY_CLASSES_ROOT key. We won't discuss the registry editor or the various keys in detail here, but feel free to have a look around it when you have a spare moment.

> Looking around is fine, but never *change* anything in the registry unless you know exactly what you're doing. The registry holds a lot of information that's used by the Windows operating system. If you accidentally change something important, it's possible to render your computer unusable.

If you expand the HKEY_CLASSES_ROOT key, you'll find a number of interesting sub-keys. Those of interest are shown here:

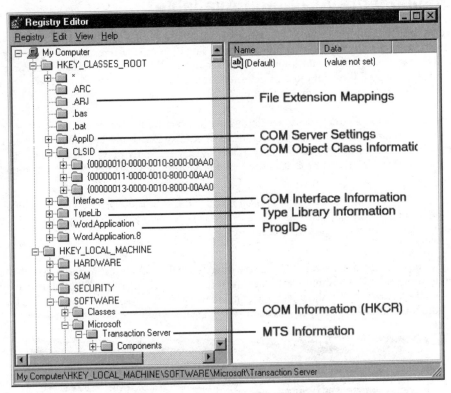

Most of the COM components installed on your machine will be listed under the key HKEY_CLASSES_ROOT\CLSID, where you'll find a large number of sub-keys whose names are all CLSIDs of the form you saw earlier. There will a sub-key for every component registered on your machine. As we've explained, these identifiers are the *actual* names of your components, and each sub-key stores information about the component whose name it bears. One of these pieces of information is the location of the server that contains the component, and it's by this means that components are found and subsequently instantiated on request.

When your client is compiled (if, for example, it's a Visual Basic or a Visual C++ application), the CLSIDs of the components it uses are generally "hard-wired" into the code. This means that if the CLSID of the component it uses should change, the client will no longer work.

However, in our Brick Calculator example, when we created the component instance within the ASP page, we did not use the CLSID to reference the component. Instead, we used the **programmatic identifier**, or **ProgID**.

Programmatic Identifiers

In our first example of using a component in an ASP page, we created an instance of the component like this:

```
Dim objBrickCalc
Set objBrickCalc = Server.CreateObject ("BrickCalc.wsc")
```

When you create a class module in Visual Basic, it generates a ProgID for you, in the form:

```
[ProjectName].[ClassModuleName]
```

At the end of this chapter, we'll build the Windows Script Component using the Wizard provided by Microsoft. There, you'll see that WSCs store the ProgID in the same file as the rest of the component's implementation:

```
<registration
    description="BrickCalc"
    progid="BrickCalc.WSC"
    version="1.00"
    classid="{f954a720-67c1-11d3-99b1-00104b4c84a4}"
>
</registration>
```

As the next screenshot shows, ProgIDs are also sub-keys under HKEY_CLASSES_ROOT. They provide a way of looking up a CLSID at runtime from a "friendly" string identifier. Using the Brick Calculator component as an example, we can see that the ProgID key has a sub-key called CLSID. This has a Default string value that contains the GUID in string format:

Whether you use ProgIDs or CLSIDs to call your component from ASP is up to you. While CLSIDs are less easy to write and less logical to read than ProgIDs, they do ensure that (in the unlikely event that there is a component with the same name and method as the one you are calling) you get the correct method of the correct component.

The COM Runtime

An important part of the COM is the **COM runtime**, which provides the API functions that enable applications use to create and manipulate COM objects. As ASP programmers, we don't really *see* the COM runtime, but functions like the `Server` object's `CreateObject()` method are layers upon it. If you asked ten C++ programmers to name a COM runtime API, you'd probably find 99% of them would say `CoCreateInstance()` or `CoCreateInstanceEx()`. These APIs are responsible for the creation of COM objects—they are the equivalent of `CreateObject()` in ASP. The COM runtime is a large topic, and we will not be covering it in depth here.

There is a lot more to learn about COM in general, but both ASP and Visual Basic make COM very easy to work with. While we could introduce all manner of topics to help you understand what is going on under the hood, the ASP and Visual Basic environments are designed to hide much of the complexity from you until you're at a stage when you really need to dig into the inner workings. We will be looking into COM more deeply in the section on C++, starting in Chapter 10, but what you have seen so far is enough to get you used to building components and using them in your ASP pages.

Will Microsoft Replace COM?

Unlike a lot of Microsoft technologies, COM has a fairly stable history that can be tracked back long before the official release in 1993. Since its release, COM has slowly evolved, but this has largely involved additional features such as security and the ability to call up components on different computers. There have been no major architecture changes.

COM has a solid future. These days, almost every new technology that Microsoft introduces is based to some extent—and in some cases entirely—on COM. This is true for all the technologies we will be examining in this book—ADO, MTS, MSMQ ADSI, and OLE DB. All the Microsoft Office components expose COM interfaces, as does Internet Explorer. The next version of COM, known as COM+, already has a pivotal role in Windows 2000, so you can rest assured it is here to stay. There are some big changes between COM and COM+, but nothing that invalidates or outdates the code that we will be writing in this book.

Network Application Architectures

ASP is a relatively new technology, but people have been building network-based applications for many years. To help us see where our components fit, it's worth taking a look at the options available for network development as whole, since the same considerations will be relevant when it comes to designing our component-based solutions.

Two-Tier (or Client–Server) Systems

Older types of network application were invariably made up of a **server** (which did the real grunt-work of running the application) and multiple **clients** (which connected to that server). The clients provided instructions to the server and accessed the results it produced. The clients in this situation are referred to as **thin clients**, because they do not have to do much work—most of the functionality is hosted on the server.

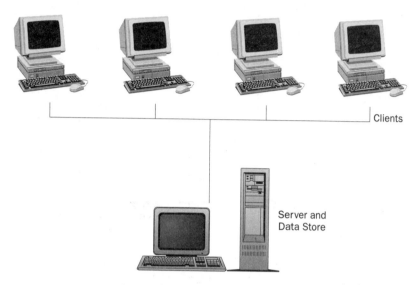

Clients

Server and
Data Store

As time went by and computing power got cheaper, the temptation was for the clients to perform more of the processing work, easing the strain on big expensive servers. When more of this processing work is passed to a client, the typical client application needs to contain all the code needed to process the required tasks. If such a client were accessing a database, for example, the client application would need to be capable of accessing the database and manipulating that data—while the data alone still resides on the server. This is known as a **fat client** because some of the processing has been passed onto it.

While this relieved the load on the main server, any changes either to the client or to the database then have rippling effects across all client installations. Any changes that need to be made are not just made to the central server; each individual client has to be updated for each change, and potentially several *different* applications have to be recompiled and updated if data manipulation and access code is shared between them.

> To help reduce the maintenance of 2-tier systems, *database views* and *stored procedures* can be used. Both provide an elementary level of indirection that can sometimes help reduce the impact of database changes on client code. However, neither works very well in the case of distributed, heterogeneous databases; unless the same provider (SQL Server, for example) is used for each database engine, and inter-database interoperation is non-existent. This means that stored procedures have to be duplicated, which can be a potential concern for enterprise applications.

As computers spread into more areas of the workplace, the demands on computer-based applications rose rapidly. These applications are often referred to as **enterprise applications**, and incorporate many servers and data stores. They tend to be organic in that they are always growing, and tend to be difficult to design and to maintain.

To help programmers work with programs and data spanning increasing areas, it made sense to divide up the application into layers or **tiers**. The important thing to remember when talking about tiers in an application is that they can be **logical** or **physical**.

A physical tier is one that actually resides in a distinct physical place, while logical tiers are a more conceptual way of thinking. Logical tiers help us plan and view the different parts of an application, removed from concerns about where they reside physically.

Thinking about architecture changed, along with the expansion of networked applications, to **three-tier models**. We shall take a quick look at this next so that you can understand where we are using our components (you may also have heard of *n*-tier applications, which are an extension of the three-tier model, and which we will come back to in Chapter 5).

Three-Tier Applications

You can view the client–server model as being a 2-tier application structure. This is extended in the three-tier model by the addition of a middle layer that sits between the client and the data sources. The three physical tiers break down as follows:

❑ The **client tier** is the front-end tool with which the end user interacts. It may take the form of any type of user interface, such as a Visual Basic application, or (increasingly commonly) a web browser. In ASP applications, the client tier usually takes the form of a web browser.

❑ The **middle tier** (also referred to as the **business tier**) represents most of the logic that makes the application functional. In the case of ASP this is where our ASP pages reside, upon the web server.

❑ The **data tier** represents the storage mechanism used to hold persistent data. This could be a relational database, text-based file, directory, mail server etc.

Let's see how this breaks down diagrammatically:

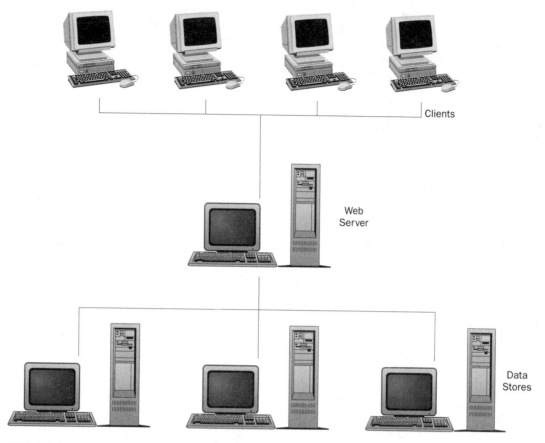

We've only seen one example in this book so far; but how does this diagram relate to it?

The Client Tier

The client browser requests an ASP page from the server, and is presented with an HTML form for entering data about the size of wall and brick. The user then clicks on the Calculate button, which sends the form details to the web server. Later, the client receives the response from the web server and displays the results of the calculation.

The Middle Tier

This is where our web server resides, holding (amongst other things) the ASP pages and our components. When the client requests the form, the web server creates it as HTML using WroxBloxForm.asp. When the user clicks Calculate on the client end, the values are sent to WroxBloxResult.asp. WroxBloxResult.asp creates an instance of the BrickCalculator component, also on the middle tier, which uses the passed parameter values to calculate the number of bricks required, and returns the result to the page. The page then writes this back to the client.

In this case, all of the logic of the application, creating the component, and calculating the number of bricks required, goes on in the middle tier.

The Data Tier

OK, so our example doesn't use the data tier. However, if we needed to collect or store any persistent data in a database, such data would reside in this tier. Busy sites will gain great performance advantages from actually having the database residing on a separate physical server, because databases typically require a lot of system resources. During the design phase, this is not always possible—but the notion of a logical data tier still exists, whether or not the database resides on a separate server.

Building Our First Component

Earlier, we visited our first example of using an ASP component—the `BrickCalc` component—and we promised that we'd return to see how to build the component. The Brick Calculator component is a **Windows Script Component** (WSC), written using the Windows Script Component Wizard and Notepad. WSCs are an ideal way to prototype components, allowing us to write the components using VBScript or JScript, which means that they can be written in a matter of minutes.

If this is the first time you've heard of WSCs, then you might be asking yourself the same sorts of questions I asked myself when I first heard about them. For example, we've already said that a COM object is a binary file—so how does WSC create a COM object using VBSscript or JScript? Moreover, how will we deal with registration and getting a CLSID? How do we get an interface to work with?

A Similar Case

WSCs work in a very similar way to the OLE DB simple providers in Visual Basic. An OLE DB simple provider is a two-tiered component made up of your simple Visual Basic (or C++ or J++ , for example) code and a DLL. The DLL processes the code you've written, and exposes a regular OLE DB programming interface to its consumers.

WSCs (previously known as Scriptlets) work in much the same way. Whenever we register a script-based COM object, the registry entry points to a COM-compliant executable called `scrobj.dll`. Furthermore, any script-based COM object has an extra key in the registry, which points to a script file. This file contains metadata, which defines both the executable code and the interfaces to be made externally available.

Without further ado, let's build our first component for use in ASP. In order to build the component, you'll need to download the WSC kit from http://msdn.microsoft.com/scripting. You'll need to download both the Windows Script Components (Windows Script Version 5) and the Windows Script Component Wizard—both of which are available at this site.

Planning the Brick Calculator Component

The Brick Calculator component has just one task to perform—calculating the number of bricks needed to build a wall. So, the component will implement one method called `HowManyBricks()`. Knowing that we only need one method to perform the required task, we need think about what information we should to supply the method, in the form of parameters, to perform the calculation.

If we were approaching this methodically in the real world, we could work out the size of the wall, check the size of the brick, and then divide the size of the wall by the size of the brick to find out how many bricks we need. To perform this calculation we'd need to know four things

❑　The length of the wall

❑　The height of the wall

❑　The length of the bricks used

❑　The height of the bricks used

We are defining one property of the component, `BrickType`, which will tell the component the type of brick we are using—breezeblock or house brick. This covers the length and the height of the bricks, which are hard coded into the component. We are then left with the length and height of the wall, which we will pass to our component as parameters to the method. Our method now looks like this:

```
HowManyBricks(WallHeight, WallLength)
```

And that's all the information we need to create the shell of the component using the Windows Script Component Wizard—to which we will later add the functionality using script.

Using The Windows Script Component Wizard

This Wizard is made available from the Programs | Microsoft Windows Script option on the Start menu. When you start it up, you should get the following:

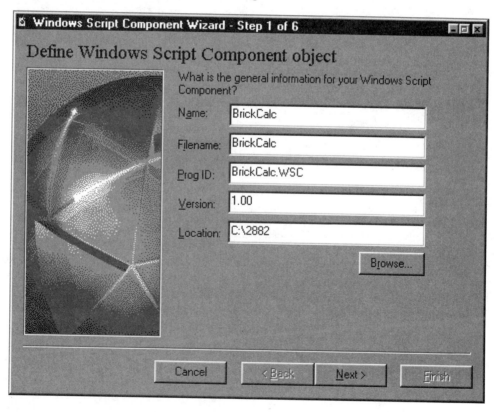

In this screen we've already added a Name for the component we are creating—BrickCalc. As you type in the name of the component, you'll see that the Filename and ProgID are provided for us automatically. We can also provide a Version number and a Location for the component. Having named the component, click on Next, which takes you to the screen where you can provide the characteristics of the component.

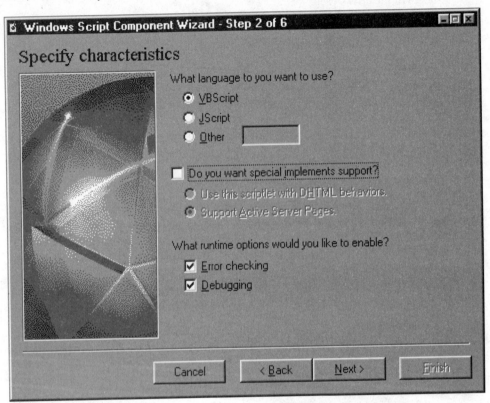

The first option in Screen 2 allows you to specify the script language that you want to use to write the component. We have chosen VBScript. The next option allows you to use the scriptlet with DHTML behaviors (which we do not want to do), or add in support for Active Server Pages. The support for ASP option allows us to access the intrinsic ASP objects from our component. This is not necessary for this component, so you can uncheck the checkbox. The final option is to support Error Checking and Debugging. If you are only prototyping your component, it is helpful to have these options checked—because they provide helpful information if you have not implemented your component correctly. Once you have selected the options that you want, click Next.

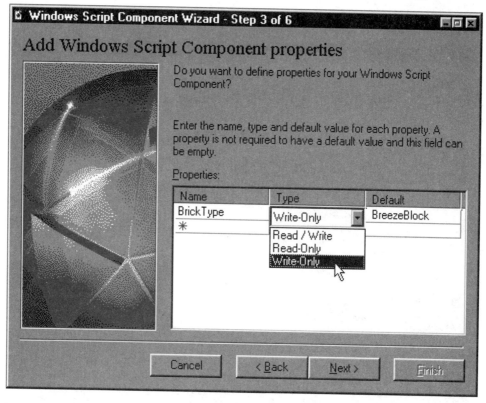

In Screen 3 we enter the properties for our component. Remember that our component only has one property, `BrickType`, which tells the component whether it needs to calculate the number of breeze blocks or normal house bricks needed. We set this to **Write-Only** because we only need to retrieve the value from our ASP page, and we have set a default of **BreezeBlock** (although we don't actually need to set a default). Then we click **Next** to define our methods.

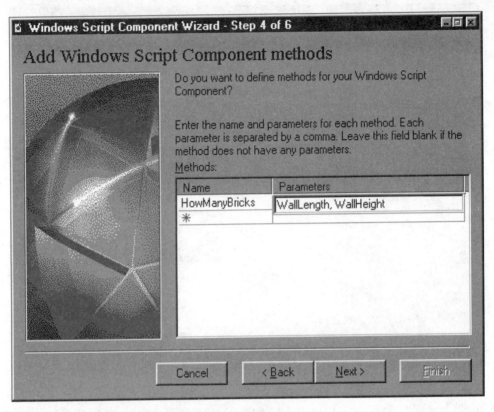

Again, we only have one method: HowManyBricks(). This takes two parameters—WallLength and WallHeight—which the user submits from the form.

When you've completed this hit **Next** to take you to Screen 5, which handles the events in our component. We're not going to use any events, so hit **Next** again for Screen 6.

The final screen gives us a summary of the component we are about to create. If we need to change anything we can use the Back button. Otherwise, we just click the finish button.

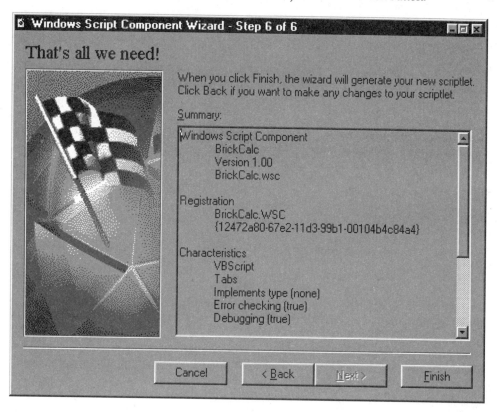

And that should create the .wsc file. This file currently defines the interface of the component; we can now add our script, which will provide the implementation.

The XML File Created by the Wizard

Let's look at the XML file that our component has created (just navigate to the file in Windows Explorer and double-click). Don't worry if you do not understand XML—this will actually show you just how easy the basics of XML are. As you will see, XML looks very similar to HTML.

We start off on the first line with the XML declaration, which any XML file uses. This is followed by a **root** tag, <component>, which surrounds the whole component. Then we have a **processing instruction** (in the tag that starts and ends with question marks) to say that we are supporting error handling and debugging (remember we checked tick boxes for these in the second screen of the Wizard):

```
<?xml version="1.0"?>
<component>

<?component error="true" debug="true"?>
...
```

Next we have the registration details, which include a description of the component, a ProgID, the version number and the CLSID. Note the simplicity of the XML tags that actually describe their contents:

```
...
<registration
    description="BrickCalc"
    progid="BrickCalc.WSC"
    version="1.00"
    classid="{f954a720-67c1-11d3-99b1-00104b4c84a4}"
>
</registration>
...
```

Next we have the properties and methods that the component will expose, nested inside the `<public>` tags, held in tags that say `<property>` and `<method>`:

```
...
<public>
    <property name="BrickType">
        <put/>
    </property>
    <method name="HowManyBricks">
        <PARAMETER name="WallLength"/>
        <PARAMETER name="WallHeight"/>
    </method>
</public>
...
```

Finally we have the block, which will contain the script code that adds the functionality of the component. (And a closing `</component>` tag.) At the moment it is like an interface without any implementation.

```
...
<script language="VBScript">
<![CDATA[
dim BrickType
BrickType = "BreezeBlock"

function put_BrickType(newValue)
    BrickType = newValue
end function

function HowManyBricks(WallLength, WallHeight)
    HowManyBricks = "Temporary Value"
end function

]]>
</script>
</component>
```

Now we have to add in the functionality, using a simple bit of VBScript (note that we have hard-coded values for the size of the bricks):

```
function HowManyBricks(WallLength, WallHeight)
    If BrickType = "BreezeBlock" Then
        TheResult = Int(WallLength / 0.75) + 1
        Result = TheResult * (Int(WallHeight / 0.33) + 1)
        HowManyBricks = Result
    Else
        TheResult = Int(WallLength / 0.35) + 1
        Result = TheResult * (Int(WallHeight / 0.15) + 1)
        HowManyBricks = Result
    End If
end function
```

Once you've done that, save the file—and now we are ready to register our component.

Registering the File

Windows Script Components are very easy to register, as the WSC kit adds options to **Register**, **Unregister**, and **Generate TypeLib** (type library) for a component when you right click on it in Windows Explorer. Don't worry about the type library option for the moment; we'll talk about type libraries later in the book.

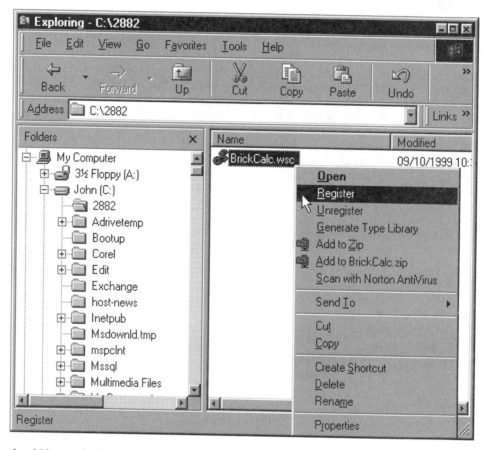

We should be notified that our component registered successfully. This uses the `regsvr32.exe` program to add the necessary references to the registry, including the extra key that points to `scrobj.dll`.

And that's it—we have created our first COM component. To check that it works, try your own version with the ASP pages provided in the `WroxBloxForm.asp`/`WroxBloxResult.asp` example, which are available with all the rest of the code for the book from http://webdev.wrox.co.uk/books/2882/.

WSCs offer far greater functionality than is described here. They have evolved very quickly, and the best way to keep up with them is to check out http://msdn.microsoft.com/scripting/ where there are full tutorials and more examples.

Summary

In this chapter we've highlighted typical software development problems and shown how **componentization** can go a long way to making our applications easier to develop and maintain. We've taken the time to understand some of the concepts behind componentization, including some analogies—such as the telephone operator, the hi-fi separates, and the car component. We understood the difference between interface and implementation, and noted that we can exchange one component in a system with another, provided the new component offers the same interfaces as the old one.

We've shown how the Component Object Model (COM) provides a specification and infrastructure that allows us to develop COM objects and use them in any language that is COM enabled. COM components can use, and be used by, any other COM-enabled language or environment—which makes COM extremely powerful. We've also explained how interface-based programming is central to COM.

We looked at how components are identified—via a GUID or ProgID—and that COM uses the registry to store and access this information. We suggested an informal categorization of components, in order to try to understand more about where componentization can be applicable. We also took a first look at 2-tier and 3-tier architecture. Finally, we saw how to implement a COM component using the WSC, and used within an ASP page.

That's quite a lot for one chapter! In the next chapter, we'll be consolidating our foundation on COM, and components in ASP, and we'll create and deploy our first Visual Basic component for ASP.

Components and Interfaces in Visual Basic

In the last chapter, you saw an introduction to component-based programming from a number of angles. You should now have a fair idea of why components are so important, what problems they can solve, and the influence they can have on the makeup of your applications.

Before we can take a closer look at the benefits of using components in our ASP development, we need to develop a better understanding of how they actually work. The best way to do this is to get our hands dirty and create a component using Visual Basic, the tool used for a large part of this book.

At the end of Chapter 1 we quickly put together a Windows Script Component, and demonstrated how to use it in an ASP page. However, we didn't pay a great deal of attention to designing it because WSCs aren't really ideal for serious component development. Proof of concept is a fine thing, but we need more than that in order to build real commercial quality components. We need something that can produce components that are robust, efficient, quick and scalable—while Windows Script Components are great for prototyping components, they don't stand up well enough in a production environment, so we won't be discussing them any further in this book.

This chapter will build on your knowledge of implementing components and their interfaces by showing you how to create and use a simple component in Visual Basic. We'll also look at some of the issues that you need to be aware of and take into account when building generic components, especially if you intend to host them in an environment other than Visual Basic—Active Server Pages or a web page, for example. More specifically, the chapter will cover:

- ❏ COM interfaces and good design practices
- ❏ COM component and application development issues
- ❏ Implementing a COM component and its interface in Visual Basic
- ❏ A brief look at some of the other features of COM that we need to consider when building components: type libraries, threading models, and state.

We'll start by thinking about the functionality we want from a simple component. The actual example that we will be building in this chapter calculates car insurance premiums. Before we build it, however, we need to consider some of the key points that you will have to look at when designing your own components. Then we will look at the design of our example component. Only once we have looked at these very important processes will we implement it, by which time you will see why it is important to plan your component properly. During the process we'll also uncover some of the other aspects of COM that we haven't yet talked about—where these might otherwise distract us from the task in hand, we'll come back to explain them at the end of the chapter. By the end of the chapter, we'll have built a simple COM component in Visual Basic, tested it in an ASP page, and learnt a lot about the component design process on the way.

Design Issues and Planning Considerations

The first steps down the road to creating a great component are to define precisely what it is that we need our component to do, what role it will play in the architecture of an application, and how its consumers (clients) will access the functionality it contains.

Choosing a Language

As far as languages for writing components in are concerned, the main ones supplied by Microsoft are Visual Basic and Visual C++. The latter does have a slight edge in terms of performance and flexibility, but that comes at a price. In reality, not only must you have experience with the language, you also need a far greater understanding of the inner workings of COM in order to write C++ components. Once you have that understanding, using Microsoft's Active Template Library (ATL) to write components in C++ is almost as quick and easy as doing so in Visual Basic—but you have got a lot of learning to do first.

> *While we appreciate that Visual J++ is also a language in which COM components can be written, we will not be covering it in this book.*

Visual Basic provides an excellent balance, as it allows us to write components quickly, without having to spend so much time learning COM first, and it still gives quite respectable performance. Of course, even in Visual Basic, an understanding of COM will help you optimize your components by understanding why things work the way they do. So, we will introduce more about COM as we go.

Visual Basic is often seen as the natural progression for ASP developers learning to write components, especially as many are used to working with VBScript. We will spend a lot of time developing components using Visual Basic in the first half of this book, before moving on to show how to use C++, which as it happens has more resemblance to JavaScript.

We'll be using Visual Basic 6.0 as our development tool, although for the topics we'll cover there's little difference between this and the earlier version 5.0.

What Do We Want Our Component To Do?

At your place of work, you're likely to be approaching the design of your component from a different direction than the one we're faced with here. You will probably have the task of solving a specific problem or set of problems, and have a definitive list of features and functionality that are required. We don't have such specific direction or requirements, so we will invent a component that fulfills some imaginary requirement, based upon our real world personal experiences of times past. In doing so, we will at least cover a large percentage of the same issues you'll be faced with when developing your first component.

We're going to build a component that is reasonably simple, yet still produces a useful result. Reflecting the increasing number of services being offered on line, we will build a component that can calculate the annual insurance premium for a car driver, based on three criteria:

❑ Details of the car

❑ The driver's age and gender

❑ The driver's past record

Because we want to avoid database access and other complexities in this chapter, we'll implement the functionality of the component using some simple arithmetic. This will enable us to focus specifically on the development and usage of components in general, rather than getting side tracked and potentially confused by the use of a 3rd party component-based technology such as ADO.

The overall aim is to undertake the design and implementation of a very simple component in Visual Basic. As we go along, we will also be examining some of the issues introduced in the last chapter in more detail. We're going to start off by looking at some of the factors that you ought to consider when designing a component—and particularly when designing the component's interface.

Interface Design

As you saw in Chapter 1, the interface or interfaces of a component are the only way for a consumer (that is, an application or ASP page) to interact with it. An interface defines the methods by which a consumer can call upon the functionality of a component (or a set of components if each one implements the same interface). Interfaces describe the way in which this communication between the component and consumer takes place. It details the available functionality, and how that functionality should be called upon—such as what parameters should be passed to each method. In this section we will look at three key areas. The way that COM hides the implementation of the component from its user, how we design the interface, and some guidelines for designing your own interfaces.

Black Box Reuse

The interface does not expose any implementation details, and the consumer is not given any insight into how the functionality it uses is implemented, unless of course that is covered in some accompanying documentation. As a result, a component could be written well, resulting in super efficient operations, or it could be written badly, resulting in less efficient operations. It could be written in Visual Basic or Visual C++. As far as the interface is concerned, none of these things matter. The consumer can use the component however it is written, provided they are given one or more interface definitions, and have a programming tool or application that implements the required COM support. This type of trusted interaction is often termed **black-box reuse**—you can use it, but you can't see inside.

Properties are Just Methods

Interface methods that provide the ability to read and write an object's data (state) are termed properties. They are methods under the covers as you'll see in C++, but in VB you are given the illusion that they are different. The semantics are, so VB is doing a good thing, but the implementation isn't so VB introduces a level of encapsulation that can lead to a misunderstanding.

Interface Factoring

The task of deciding which (and how many) different interfaces to provide on your components, and what members (properties, methods and events) to include in each interface, is called **interface factoring**.

As a general rule of thumb, interfaces usually have at least one method, and at most have one thousand and twenty four—a limit imposed by COM. Exactly how many methods an interface has is a design issue that only you can answer, depending on the situation you face.

We will introduce some guidelines in the next section that will to help you make this decision, although other considerations will crop up throughout the book (especially in Chapter 5).

Interface Guidelines

In many ways, component interface design is a similar problem to user interface design. When considering user interface design, we need to look at what the user will want to achieve by interacting with the interface we provide. From this, it is possible to design a user interface that makes it easy or obvious for the user to see *how* to do what they want, and then to do it. The second part (the actual doing) is the more important.

The difference is that in user interface design, we are dealing with controls such as text boxes and radio buttons, and their layout on one or more forms. With components, we are dealing with properties and methods, and their factoring into one or more interfaces. When designing components, the better we factor the interfaces, the more usable they are by our consumers and the greater the potential for reuse.

Again, like user interface design, component interface design is something of an experience-based process. You might approach a problem one way for one project because it suits the client base, then you might be set a similar task and do it another way because there are specific limiting or enabling technologies available. Either way, there is usually a common goal: keep your client happy.

While we can't give you a perfect set of interface design guidelines for every problem you'll ever encounter, here are some common traits of well-designed interfaces:

- ❑ Ensure that the consumer can use the interface. COM has the ability to define interfaces that are language or application unfriendly—that is, they won't work in all situations. While COM *is* designed to be a binary standard, some langauges have more capabilities than others. COM would not be widely adopted if it limited these languages to the lowest common denominator, so we have to think carefully about interface compatibilty. For example, components that are used extensively in a scripting environment like ASP should always use the `Variant` type for parameters that have to be passed in, modified and passed out. This is a feature of scripting engines, so we have to make sure our interfaces abide by those guidelines for them to work correctly.

❑ Make your interface name (or class module in Visual Basic) and method names descriptive. There is no point in calling an interface `IDoSomething` and having a method called `DoIt()`. The names should always be descriptive, and where possible have a clearly defined meaning in the consumer's problem domain. Take our driving interface example, `IDrive`, from the last chapter. `Accelerate()` is quite a useful method, and a reasonable name. However, if we had used methods like `LocateFoot()`, `PlaceFootOnPedal()`, and `PressPedal()` instead, the usage of the interface would be less obvious, and the semantics have to be explicitly defined. We would have to tell the user that they have to call `LocateFoot()`, then `PlaceFootOnPedal()`, then `PressPedal()`.

❑ Methods should be well factored, logically related, and there shouldn't be too many of them. If you've got an interface called `IDrive`, it shouldn't contain methods that aren't related to driving. For example, if we need a method called `ChangeOil()`, then it should be exposed by an interface called `ICarMaintance`.

❑ A similar approach should be used when defining properties. Properties should also correspond to the types of information they represent.

❑ Interfaces should be strongly typed. Languages like Visual Basic and C++ *are* strongly typed. This means that the variables we typically define are of a specific type, and contain only certain types of data—a number, for example. If somebody then tries to assign a string to the variable, the compiler will raise an error. The benefit of an interface being strongly typed is that its use is simply more explicit: we don't have to guess what types of data a method may be able to process.

Inside the Component

Having seen the public face of the component—its interface—let's take a look at what we need to think about in the design phase regarding its inner workings. Good interface design helps us give consumers a clear picture of how they can use the functionality of our components. What they don't see (and more importantly, what they don't have to worry about) is the implementation—that is solely our responsibility as component designers/builders. Some of the things that do concern us include:

❑ What variables and state (data) the component uses internally

❑ How many functions or subroutines we use

❑ How long each function or subroutine takes

❑ What algorithms we use

❑ Data storage techniques

❑ Function names

Because the implementation of the component is hidden from users, it comes down to us as component writers and application designers to worry about such implementation details. So, we have to consider application design and component design together, along with the overall effect these have on interface design. If we go back to the user interface design analogy we made earlier, the important point was to make the life of the user easier, so that they could perform their operations with minimum fuss and confusion. On the same lines, we should therefore initially focus on interface design to make *our* consumers' life easier, and picture these consumers not only as 3rd parties, but also as other parts of our application.

> Suggesting that we *forget* about implementation details while designing interfaces would be wrong. It would be like designing the perfect car, only to realize we are going to have to wait 20 years before anybody has the technology or capabilities to actually build it—there is little point. We need solutions today, so the trick is to find a good balance: let the implementations sway your interface design, but don't let them dictate it.

In the car insurance example that we'll meet later on, the consumer has to be able to tell our component the values for each variable that affects the premium level in order to get the final premium back. This process of calculating the premium isn't related to interface design—it's application design—but it is actually the most important aspect overall. After all, without it we wouldn't need an interface.

Components Evolve—Interfaces, Once Published, Don't

Whether you think about implementation issues before or after interface design will probably depend partly on your way of working. However, it is worth bearing in mind that while application design and implementation can evolve over time, the interface shouldn't. Once it has been published, the interface should be immutable. If you change an interface once it has been published, client applications that use it are likely to break. So, try to get it right first time and keep yourself and your clients happy.

If you decide to add new functionality to your component, you should really add a new interface to expose it. However, this brings up an interesting issue because scripting clients like ASP are restricted by the interfaces they can access on a component. While Visual Basic and C++ clients can access multiple interfaces, you will probably have to create a second component if it is going to be called though script. We will come back to discuss these issues later in this chapter.

> Always remember: a badly designed interface can give you and your company a bad reputation. And, if you abide by the rules of COM, you'll be stuck with it for a very long time!

Having looked at both the interface and the implementation that COM hides behind the interface, let's see an example of how we would go about designing a component.

A Sample Design Process

Having explained the importance of interfaces, we should respect the fact that *application* design may well be an earlier stage in the process than interface design. This is because you will want to make sure that the interface design allows all the required information to be communicated between the client and the component. The application design tells you what that information is going to be.

Taking this into account, a typical scenario might follow this general outline:

1. Decide exactly what the component is going to do.

2. Decide what information the component needs to perform its task, and what information needs to be returned to the client.

3. Design a good interface that not only takes account of 1 and 2, but is also easy for developers to understand how to use.

4. Map out a way of implementing the methods on the interface.

5. Reiterate steps 1-4 to make sure that the interface is satisfactory, and that it will service the initial task set.

In a more complex component, we may have to think about a number of other issues.

❑ How to get the optimum performance from the component.

❑ If the component is going to require a backend database, you will also need to consider which database is most appropriate for the task in hand, how should you access the database, and how to arrange the data in it.

❑ If the component will be run under Microsoft Transaction Server, that imposes additional restrictions on interface and component design that we will cover in Chapters 6 and 7.

There are some other aspects of component design that we will have to come back to later. These include choice of threading model, and whether the component should be in-process or out-of-process. We will return to look at these nearer the end of this chapter.

There are really no hard and fast rules here, but we can't overemphasize the importance of good interface design. Most programmers who have used COM extensively have at some point experienced problems writing clients that are caused by badly designed interfaces.

The Insurance Premium Calculator

Having seen some of the issues that face us when developing components, we are ready to embark on writing our first COM component in Visual Basic. Along the way, we'll see how many of these considerations affect our component design. We'll start by looking at the task we need our component to achieve, and then take a look at the interface. Once our design phase is complete, we will show you how to implement the component we have designed in Visual Basic. While we're building the component, we'll see the basics of how components are built within the Visual Basic environment. Finally, we will prove that it's a true COM component by demonstrating it being used in an ASP page, and also in a simple Visual Basic client application.

What Does the Component Do?

When writing a component, stay focused on what it is meant to do as an individual unit, and try not to make it do too much or too little. Try and define what it should do clearly, then stick to it. We'll discuss how much functionality to put in each component, along with issues regarding reuse, in more detail in Chapter 5.

As we mentioned at the beginning of the chapter, the component we will be developing is a car insurance premium calculator. Given the details of the drivers that affect the premium, our component will calculate the annual payment required.

Specification of Requirements—Defining the Functionality

Generally speaking, a component will often perform a number of tasks, each of which is exposed through its interface methods. However, to demonstrate the basic principles for now, we are only going to assume one component, one interface, and one method.

In order to design the component, we need to understand how the insurance premium is calculated. For our example component, we will be calculating the premium using the following:

❑ Charge a fixed dollar rate per cubic inch (cu. in.) of engine size. 1 cu. in. is approximately 16 cubic centimeters (cc).

❑ Add on a percentage based on the type of car—Sedan, Coupe, Sports or (Station) Wagon.

❑ Add on a percentage for each claim or accident during the last five years.

❑ Take the age when drivers are at the lowest risk (that is, they have fewest accidents based on past statistics), and add on a percentage for each year of the driver's age above or below this figure. To make life interesting (and to encourage lively debate), we'll assume that this age is different for men and women.

For our component to calculate these premiums, it will need to receive five pieces of information:

Variable	Type
Engine size	`Integer`
Vehicle type	`String`
Number of claims	`Integer`
Driver gender	`String`
Driver age	`Integer`

The output of the component will be the calculated premium:

Calculated premium	`Double`

We've used the `Double` type here so that we can do real number calculations—the resulting value could be something like 49.99. If the component needed to be used in international markets, we may well have decided to use the CURRENCY type instead. This sort of choice affects the interface, so you should consider such things early on in your design process. If we released the component and then decided to change the type, we'd either have to create another interface to expose the new type (however our ASP applications would not be able to use the new interface), or break existing clients. The latter is generally not an acceptable approach, unless you can update all clients once the change is made.

Constant Values

To perform its calculation, our component needs to know how to rate the different types of input, each of which affects the premium. Therefore we define eight constants that set the charges and percentages used by the component based upon the input parameters:

Constant	Description
DOLLARS_PER_CU_INCH	The charge in dollars for each cubic inch of engine size.
ADD_WAGON ADD_COUPE ADD_SPORTS	The percentages to add on for each of the 'non-standard' vehicle types. We'll assume that sedan owners get the standard rate, and we'll give a discount (a negative percentage) for station wagons.
LOWEST_CLAIM_AGE_MALE	The statistical age when men are at lowest risk of an accident.
LOWEST_CLAIM_AGE_FEMALE	The statistical age when women are at lowest risk of an accident.
ADD_PER_YEAR_FROM_LOW	The percentage we'll add on for each year either side of the lowest risk age. We'll use the same value for men and women in our example.
ADD_PER_CLAIM	The percentage we'll add on for each accident or claim made during the last five years.

> For a commercial quality component, constant values would probably be held externally in a database because the rates could change. Since this is a sample project, we'll opt for simplicity here and hard-code the constants.

Designing the Interface

The previous tables define the complete set of values that we'll need for the *one* function of our component, but they don't define the interface, or the method by which the values will be passed in and premium passed out. In COM we use the **Interface Definition Language** (**IDL**) to define components and their interfaces. COM is language neutral, so IDL is the universal way of specifying our functionality.

IDL

Visual Basic shields us from IDL when we are writing components, automatically creating it for us depending upon what functions and properties we add to a class module. Whilst this can save us time, and generally speaking you don't have to worry too much about IDL in VB, it is essential that you realize that IDL is there, and that it plays a *pivotal* role in COM. For example, when using the References and Components dialogs in Visual Basic (which we will meet soon) you are seeing a list of **type libraries**, which are simply a compiled form of IDL that are more efficient to process. Without IDL and type libraries, how else would a Visual Basic Integrated Development Environment (IDE) know what the interfaces and methods written in C++ are? Or how would the VC++ IDE know about Visual Basic interfaces and methods?

> A class module in Visual Basic is just an interface definition combined with the
> implementation code required for each method. If you want to just define an interface
> using VB, you simply write a class module without adding any implementation.

A *detailed* discussion of IDL at this point would be confusing, however we will talk about it more in
Chapter 10.

Let's move on then, to look at some of the possible ways our consumers could use this functionality via
interface in Visual Basic.

Using a Single Method

One way we could expose the functionality of our component is by defining a single **method**. In
accordance with the principle of making our methods descriptive, we could call it something like
GetPremium(). In the interface, the GetPremium() method could accept the five values required to
perform the calculation (engine size, vehicle type, number of claims, driver gender, and driver age) as
parameters. If we implemented our interface like this, the consumer could use the component like so,
returning the result of the method as a Double:

```
Set objInsurance = CreateObject(<ProgID>)
intEngineSize = 175
strVehType = "Coupe"
strGender = "M"
strAge = 26
intClaims = 1
dblPremium = objInsurance.GetPremium(intEngineSize, strVehType, _
                                          strGender, strAge, intClaims)
```

This is a good approach, because the method is clearly defined as requiring five strongly typed
parameters. If we forget one parameter, or specify the wrong type, an error will be raised. The variables
such as intEngineSize are only shown here for clarity. Typically we would not use them, passing in the
actual values instead, like so:

```
Set objInsurance = CreateObject(<ProgID>)
dblPremium = objInsurance.GetPremium(175,"Coupe", "M", 26, 1 )
```

Using a Single Method and Properties

An alternative way to implement the interface might be to define all the pieces of information that were
passed as parameters of the method in the previous example as **properties**. In this case, we would still use
a method, such as CalculatePremium(), to get the resultant premium out:

```
Set objInsurance = CreateObject(<ProgID>)
objInsurance.EngineSize = 175
objInsurance.VehType = "Coupe"
objInsurance.Gender = "M"
objInsurance.Age = 26
objInsurance.Claims = 1
objInsurance.CalculatePremium()
dblPremium = objInsurance.Premium    ' Query the Premium property
```

This approach is generally not advisable for several reasons:

❑ We could easily forget to set one of the properties before calling the `CalculatePremium()` method.

❑ The semantics of the interface are now fuzzy. Additional documentation will have to be provided to clearly define what parameters should be set before calling the function. If the interface has, say, 10 methods and 25 properties, that's a lot of documentation and potential support calls.

❑ It is less efficient. Instead of one method being invoked, seven methods are being invoked: 1 for each property that is set, 1 to calculate the premium, and 1 to get the premium. Depending on the distance between the consumer and the component, this approach could involve several network round trips—that is, calls from one machine to another.

> Remember that a property in COM is retrieved and set using a method, although Visual Basic can give the impression that this is not happening.

Both of these approaches for adding a method to an interface and exposing the functionality of a component are legitimate and practical alternatives, although for reasons of clarity and performance the former is preferable.

Having said that, we will actually implement the second approach in this chapter as our main example. This might sound crazy, given we've just described it as the less desirable approach, but it does actually cover more COM and Visual Basic— such as using properties and methods inside of Visual Basic.

As well as these two approaches for exposing the functionality via our interface, there are a number of 'in-between' versions. For example, we could implement some of the communication through properties, and others through methods. We could even return the calculated premium as a parameter of an event if we wanted to (though this does add unnecessary complexity). All of these approaches are valid to some degree, but ask yourself this question: would you want it to work that way if you were using it?

Implementing the Design

We have got to the point where all that remains is to decide how to implement the component. For something of this simplicity, the 'obvious' way of doing it does rather stand out: don't store or pass any of the input parameters as properties; just pass them all in to a single function called `CalculatePremium()` which then returns the premium:

```
Function CalculatePremium( iEngineSize As Integer, _
                           sVechicleType As String, _
                           iNumberOfClaims As Integer, _
                           sDriverGender As String, _
                           iDriverAge As Integer ) As Double

  Dim dblResult As Double

   ' Do calculations here and store in dblResult

  CalculatePremium = dblResult
End Function
```

For more complex, real world components, you'd probably have to think a lot harder about how to design the implementation—after all, this *is* only a simple demonstration component.

However, as we said, we are going to over-complicate our component for demonstration purposes, so the actual implementation of the function will be more along these lines:

```
Dim iEngineSize As Integer
Dim sVechicleType As String
Dim iNumberOfClaims As Integer
Dim sDriverGender As String
Dim iDriverAge As Integer

Function CalculatePremium() As Double

    Dim dblResult as Double

    ' Do calculations using global variables

    CalculatePremium = dblResult

End Function
```

Rather than passing the parameters into the function, we are going to assume they have already been set up by another means. In choosing this approach for demonstration, we have brought about some interesting issues to consider:

❑   What happens if the user forgets to set one of the property values before calling `CalculatePremium()`?

❑   What if the values specified are inappropriate and invalid? For example, we can safely assume that there are no cars with an engine capacity of 3 cubic inches—100 would be nearer the mark.

❑   How does the component handle invalid entries? And should it try to?

❑   Can we assume the consumer will always do things the right way?

Generally speaking, a component's implementation of a function should guard its parameters. That is, it should be written to ensure that it has the right inputs to work with before doing any type of processing. We'll discuss this in more detail in Chapter 5 when we discuss business rules and *n*-tier design, but for the rest of this chapter we will omit such code and just assume the client performs the necessary validation and correctly sets the various properties before calling `CalculatePremium()`.

Error codes returned from a function aren't strictly part of an interface contract, so they can change should you decide to provide additional validation in subsequent releases of a component. It is, however, common practice to document all error codes returned by a function so that a consumer can take an informed action for given error situations.

For our simple insurance component, we will opt for all error and bounds checking to be done by the client.

In-Process or Out-of-Process

We mentioned in Chapter 1 that components are either in-process (hosted in DLLs) or out-of-process (hosted in EXEs). We need to decide which our component will be. For this sample, we will make our component in-process, because this is the most natural choice for ASP pages. We'll come back to look at the differences between the two later in the chapter.

Other considerations that we will eventually have to account for include the programming language and the threading model of our component. However, we haven't yet covered enough of the theory of COM to examine these issues at the moment—you should just be aware that these choices are waiting to be made. To be practical, one of the prime considerations that will affect your choice of language will be which languages the developers in your team are skilled at.

We've now completed designing the component. It's time to set about actually building it.

Building Our Component

As we said earlier, we're going to build our sample component in Visual Basic. To start off, we fire up the Visual Basic integrated developer environment (VB IDE). Once it has loaded we will be asked to specify the type of project we want to create. For an in-process component, the choice we want is ActiveX DLL:

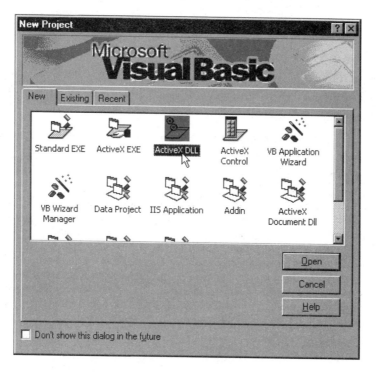

This creates a project containing a single class module (remember that a class module is what Visual Basic calls a component). After this step, you'll see something like this:

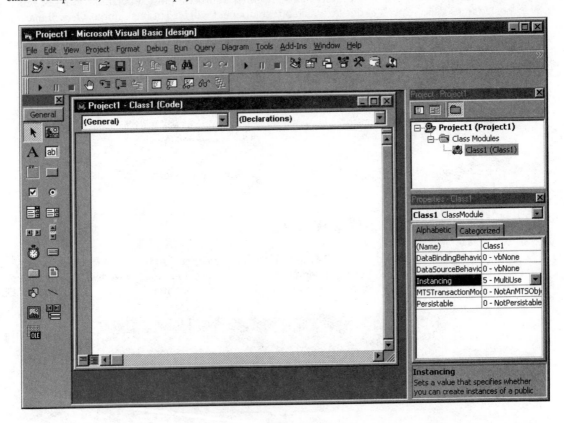

In future screenshots, we've done quite a lot of window-moving in order to emphasize the particular areas of interest, so don't worry if the Visual Basic screenshots you see in this chapter don't look quite like what you get when you start up VB—the same windows are there, just in different places!

Your new component is shown in the **Project** window. You can change the name of your component, and of the project, by clicking on it in this window and then typing the appropriate name in the list view in the **Properties** window.

Here, we'll set the name of the project to WX2882, and the class name to Insurance. (The WX part of the name for the component is short for Wrox, while 2882 is the last four numbers of the ISBN for this book.) We've already discussed that the class name forms the basis for component and interface, but Visual Basic will use it to generate the component's ProgID, which in this case will be WX2882.Insurance. Visual Basic always forms the ProgID by using *ProjectName.ClassName*:

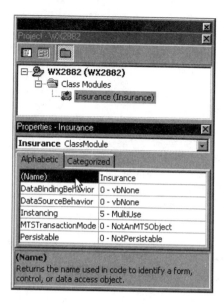

Using the Class Builder

The next step is to define the methods and properties that our interface will expose. We could do this by hand, but Visual Basic provides a nice utility that allows us to do this in a more automated and time saving fashion—it is known as the **class builder**, and you can find it in the Add-Ins menu. If it doesn't appear in the menu, you'll have to select Add-In Manager... and load it by checking the Loaded/Unloaded box. Then reopen the Add-ins menu to fire it up.

Because the Class Builder didn't create the existing class in this project (it was created from the New Project *dialog), it will complain that it can't be used to edit any existing class members. However, as the class is currently empty, this is not a problem.*

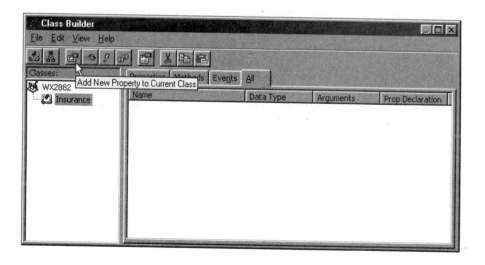

Class builder makes things appear simpler than they really are underneath the covers of Visual Basic, by making it look as though you're adding the methods and properties to the component rather than to an interface. The interface is there; Visual Basic gave the component one behind the scenes when it created the component. It's just Visual Basic's way of hiding the inner workings of COM (again).

Class Builder can be used to create new classes for your projects too, but we'll be using it simply to modify the existing class.

Adding Properties With Class Builder

Click on the class you want to edit, in this case Insurance, so that it is selected. Then, click the toolbar button shown in the previous screenshot to add a new property to the current class. This opens the Property Builder dialog, where we can enter the name for the new property, and select a data type for it. First, we'll create the property that will be used to store the engine size, named EngineCubicInches, and give it a data type of Integer:

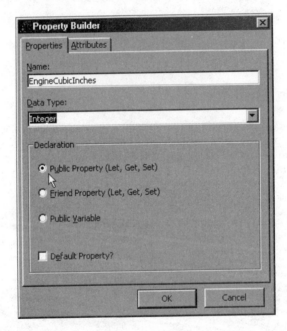

The Property Builder dialog allows us to specify how (and if) the property will be set from outside the class module. It can be a Public property (which is available from outside the component), a Friend property (which is only available from within other classes in the component), or a Public variable (which is available to all applications). These last two options are really intended for use if your class is being written for internal use in your Visual Basic application, rather than primarily as a COM component. Here, we are declaring EngineCubicInches as a Public property by using special functions (Let, Get, Set) to manage the value. We can also control the value ourselves within the component and thereby enforce any business rules that we specify. You'll see more of this soon.

*We can also use this dialog to decide whether this property should be the **default property**. If it were, it could be accessed in code simply by specifying the class name, without using the property name as well. This is what we often do with Visual Basic's integral controls, such as the humble text box. We can use code like* `txtMyText = "This text"`, *when what we actually mean is* `txtMyText.Text = "This text"`. *It works because* `Text` *is the default property. The same is true for the ASP intrinsic objects. When you write* `Session("SomeName") = "some value"`, *the following occurs behind the scenes:* `Session.Value("SomeName") = "some value"`.

The **Property Builder** dialog also contains a page where we can enter a description for the property, and this is another good reason (besides the time it saves) for using the Class Builder. These descriptions go into the type library Visual Basic creates for us, which gives people using our components reminders of what the various methods and properties do (we will talk more about type libraries later in the chapter).

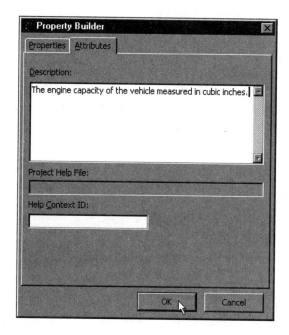

Once you've closed the **Property Builder** *dialog, you can reopen it by double-clicking the property name in the* **Class Builder** *dialog.*

Once you've entered the description, click OK and Class Builder will display the new property:

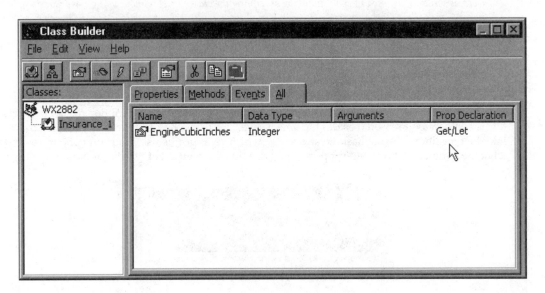

Now we can continue to add the other four properties we need. Afterwards, the Class Builder window should look something like this:

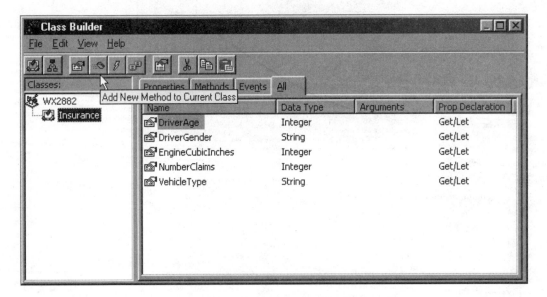

Adding a Method with Class Builder

We decided to give our component a single method to calculate and return the insurance premium. In Class Builder, click the toolbar button to add a new method (it's the one where someone's throwing green erasers). In the Method Builder dialog that appears, enter the method name (GetPremium), and select the return type Double from the drop-down list:

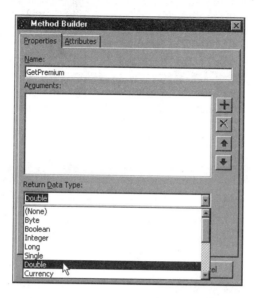

Flip open the Attributes page and enter a description (something along the lines of Calculates the premium), and then click OK to return to the Class Builder window:

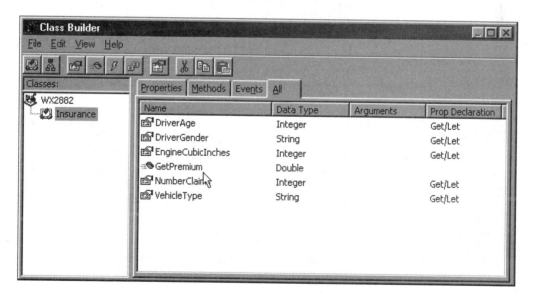

With that, the definition of our class (and therefore the interface of our component) is complete. I should warn you, though, that Class Builder seems sometimes to forget that you've edited the class. Closing the window loses the changes you've made, including those carefully worded descriptions of each item.

> Always use the **File | Update Project** option before closing the **Class Builder** window. Class Builder will update your project, and you can click the **Save** button on the main Visual Basic toolbar to save the result.

Classes and Interfaces in Visual Basic

The previous section of this chapter showed Class Builder at work, creating our COM interface automatically from a few well-chosen dialog entries. So, what did we end up with? This is what the Code window looks like, showing the first part of the code that Class Builder added:

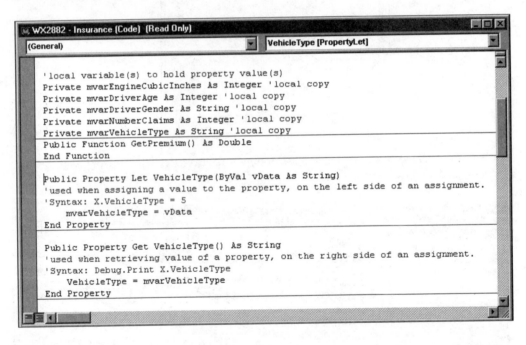

> We've manually added the line `Option Explicit`. This ensures that all variables are defined before they can be used, rather than letting Visual Basic assume that whatever we type is a valid variable name as ASP does.

You should always do this. If you mistype a variable name (say, mvarBechicleAype rather than mvarVehicleType) without this option, Visual Basic will blindly create the varaible mvarBechicleAype and assign the value to it. You'll then be puzzled when mvarVehicleType doesn't appear to be working!

Member Variables and Methods

You can see that Class Builder has created five `Private`, or local, **member variables** that have the same names as the five properties, prefixed with `mvar`. These will hold the property values as the user sets them. However, because they are private, the user will never know that they are there. The information is held within the class and is only accessed by `Property Let` and `Property Get` statements.

After that comes a skeleton for the `Public GetPremium()` function, in which we will implement the functionality of our component's `GetPremium()` method:

```
Public Function GetPremium() As Double
End Function
```

Properties

The two sections after this are the code for `Public` routines of the special type reserved for handling property values in a Visual Basic class. The first is a subroutine that's used to set (or to use Visual Basic's terminology, `Let`) the value of the property by making an assignment to a local variable; it takes a single parameter that will be used as the new value. You can see how the parameter (`vData`) is applied to the internal member variable:

```
Public Property Let VehicleType(ByVal vData As String)
'used when assigning a value to the property, on the left side of an assignment.
'Syntax: X.VehicleType = 5
    mvarVehicleType = vData
End Property
```

The second `Public` routine is used to read the property value. As it did for the `Property Let` routine, Visual Basic knows what data type to use because we specified it in Class Builder. All it has to do is return the value of the member variable as the value of the `Property Get` function:

```
Public Property Get VehicleType() As String
'used when retrieving value of a property, on the right side of an assignment.
'Syntax: Debug.Print X.VehicleType
    VehicleType = mvarVehicleType
End Property
```

The third type of property routine, `Property Set`, is used to set the value of property member variables that hold an object rather than a simple value. This is similar to the situation when we assign values to ordinary variables, where we use `SimpleVariable = NewValue` for simple variables, but `Set ObjectVariable = ObjectReference` for object variables.

Note the significance of these property routines. We mentioned earlier that even though a COM property looks like a variable to the client, it is in fact represented by method calls—and these routines are those methods. Doing it this way allows the component developer the flexibility of not having to store member variables corresponding to the properties, if that's not appropriate. All we need is that the `Get`, `Set` and `Let` routines are implemented in such a way as to make it *look* syntactically to the client as if we are setting variables. The class builder gives us code containing member variables corresponding to the properties, and it is up to us to modify the code if that's not what we want. One example might be a property that gives the height of a control. You'd probably want to modify the code for the `Let` function so that when the client attempted to change the height property, the control actually got redrawn with the new height.

Read and Write Properties

If you explore the rest of the code that Class Builder created, you'll see that there are matching `Property Get` and `Property Let` routines for each of the five properties we specified. This allows the user to read and write the values of all five properties, but you should consider that this might not always be appropriate. You may have properties that you might wish to be read-only (a good example of this would have been the premium, had we implemented it as a property), or write-only (which you might want to use for passwords). If you do want to have a property like this, you just need to remove one of the routines given to you by Class Builder.

As an example, suppose we had decided to implement the calculated premium as a property rather than returning it from a method. Class Builder would have created both a `Property Get` and a `Property Let` routine for it. In the case of our premium, however, a `Property Let` routine makes no sense at all, because the property is calculated within the component—as far as clients are concerned, it should be read-only. Getting this behavior is no problem: we just delete the whole of the `Property Let` routine. Similarly, if we wanted to make a property write-only, we could remove the `Property Get` routine.

One other point is that, if we did implement the calculated premium as a property (rather than as the direct result of a method), we would have to calculate it before we could return it to the user. So, we would have to modify the routine generated by the Class Builder to the calculation in the `Property Get` routine:

```
Public Property Get Premium() As Double
    '----------------------------------------------------------
    'code here to calculate premium in member variable mvarPremium
    '----------------------------------------------------------
    Premium = mvarPremium    'and return it to the user
End Property
```

Validated Property Values

One reason for using the `Property Get` and `Property Let` routines, rather than exposing the internal property values as `Public` variables, is to allow us to control the way they are accessed. For example, we could validate new values before applying them to the internal member variables, and throw away the changes if we don't like them:

```
Public Property Let ColorName(ByVal vData As String)
    'we have an unexplained hatred of all things green
    If InStr(LCase(vData), "green") = 0 Then
        mvarColorName = vData
    Else
        Err.Raise vbObject + 1, "PremiumComponent ", "I don't like green!"
    Endif
End Property
```

As we'll discuss in Chapter 5, some components are positioned in the design of an application to perform this type of validation. The line starting with `Err.Raise` causes a COM error code to be returned to the client. In ASP, you will have encountered and handled such errors by using an `On Error GoTo` handler.

We could also perform validation (as well as, or instead of, calculations) within the `Property Get` routine:

```
Public Property Get Premium() As Double

    If WeekDay(Now) = vbSunday Then
        Err.Raise vbObject + 1, "PremiumComponent", "Not on a Sunday!")
    End If

    Premium = mvarPremium
End Property
```

Calculating a Premium

To finish off our component, we just need to implement the code that will calculate the premium, inside the `GetPremium()` function that Class Builder created for us. We saw the plan earlier on, and part of it involved hard coding the 'constant' values (that is, the charge rates for the calculation) into the component. We'll make it tidy and easy to maintain by using global constants, which we add to the top of the class module after the `Option Explicit` statement:

```
'constants for calculating premium
Private Const DOLLARS_PER_CU_INCH = 1.25
Private Const LOWEST_CLAIM_AGE_MALE = 45       'years old
Private Const LOWEST_CLAIM_AGE_FEMALE = 40     'years old
Private Const ADD_PER_YEAR_FROM_LOW = 0.01     '1 percent
Private Const ADD_PER_CLAIM = 0.35             'plus 35 percent
Private Const ADD_WAGON = -0.15                'minus 15 percent
Private Const ADD_COUPE = 0.25                 'plus 25 percent
Private Const ADD_SPORTS = 0.5                 'plus 50 percent
```

The code to do the actual calculation is relatively simple. Using the values of the member variables, we can calculate the basic premium in dollars, then calculate each 'add-on' percentage in turn and add it to the running total in a local variable called `dblPremium`:

```
Public Function GetPremium() As Double
    Dim dblPremium As Double
    Dim sngExtraPercent As Single

    'calculate base premium depending on engine size
    dblPremium = mvarEngineCubicInches * DOLLARS_PER_CU_INCH

    'add on loading depending on driver gender and age
    If UCase(Left(mvarDriverGender, 1)) = "F" Then
        sngExtraPercent = Abs(LOWEST_CLAIM_AGE_FEMALE - mvarDriverAge) _
                    * ADD_PER_YEAR_FROM_LOW
    Else
        sngExtraPercent = Abs(LOWEST_CLAIM_AGE_MALE - mvarDriverAge) _
                    * ADD_PER_YEAR_FROM_LOW
    End If
    dblPremium = dblPremium + (dblPremium * sngExtraPercent)

    'add on loading for number of accidents or claims
    sngExtraPercent = mvarNumberClaims * ADD_PER_CLAIM
    dblPremium = dblPremium + (dblPremium * sngExtraPercent)

    'add on loading for type or vehicle, using specific letters
    Select Case UCase(Left(mvarVehicleType, 1))
        Case "S": sngExtraPercent = 0
        Case "W": sngExtraPercent = ADD_WAGON
        Case "C": sngExtraPercent = ADD_COUPE
        Case "P": sngExtraPercent = ADD_SPORTS
    End Select
    dblPremium = dblPremium + (dblPremium * sngExtraPercent)

    'assign result to function variable
    GetPremium = dblPremium
End Function
```

Once we've done the calculation, `dblPremium` will contain the final result.

You'll find the source code, and the compiled DLL and application, with the remainder of the samples for this book on our web site at http://webdev.wrox.co.uk/books/2882.

Saving and Compiling the Component

If you haven't already done so, hit the Save toolbar button to save the component source files in the location of your choice—preferably, a new folder. Then, from the File menu, choose the Make WX2882.dll... option to compile the component for the first time.

When you examine the folder where you have saved the component, you'll see a series of files. As well as the new `.dll` file, there is the class file (`.cls`) and project file (`.vbp`) that make up the source code. The other two files (`.lib` and `.exp`) store information about the compiled DLL. These last two files are used by the executable that loads the DLL, and are needed for the process of using a DLL to work properly:

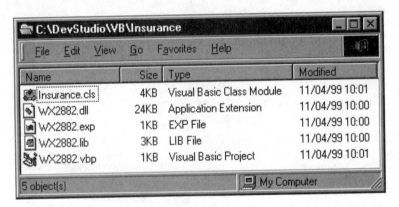

Examining the Component

To see exactly what Visual Basic has produced, fire up the Object Browser from the View menu. The Object Browser is a tool that allows us to examine the registered components. From the project drop-down list, select the new library that has just been created for us by Visual Basic when we compiled the component (WX2882), and then the `Insurance` class. You should be able to see all the public and private members of the class, with the description we provided for each appearing in the status bar when selected:

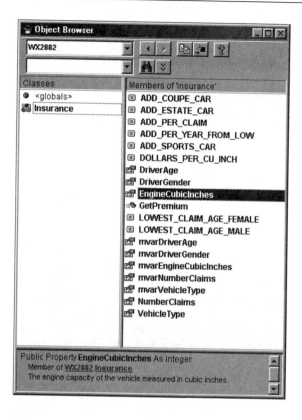

Using Our Component

So, we've finished building our first ActiveX DLL in Visual Basic. Now we should see whether it works. First, we will try it out in an ASP page. Then, to show that it is a true COM component, and to prove that the component can be reused in different environments, we will test it with a simple Visual Basic application that you can download from our web site.

Testing Our Component in Active Server Pages

While we've got our programming hats on, and the web server is humming away quietly in the corner just ready for some action, we'll get to work with testing our component in ASP. However, before we can use our component in an ASP page, we have to make sure that it is registered.

Installing the Component

If we are going to run the component on the same machine as we built it on, then it will already be registered, since Visual Basic registers the component as part of the build process. Often, however, you will have built a component on one machine and will want to install it and run it on another. We could do this by building a setup package using the Visual Basic 6 Package & Deployment Wizard or the Visual Basic 5 Setup Wizard, but if there's only a single component to install, it's easier to do it manually. So, let's look at how we do this.

Copy the component DLL to your web server. It is common to create a new folder with a name such as Components beneath the Winnt\System32\inetsrv\ directory to house all of the components that are installed on a web server. Then, open a DOS Command window, move to the folder where you placed the component, and type:

```
>regsvr32 wx2882.dll
```

And that's all you need to do. The reason this works so easily is because Visual Basic produces what are called **self-registering** components. What this means is that the files in which the components are hosted also contain all the code required to register the components. In the case of components hosted in DLLs, as we have just seen, this code can be called by running a program called regsvr32.exe, supplying the name of the DLL as a parameter. For components hosted in executables, you can run the executable directly, but you must supply the command-line option regserver. In other words, if you have a component hosted in an executable called MyComponent.exe, the following DOS command will register the component.

```
>MyComponent /regserver
```

With the component successfully registered on the web server, we are ready to create our ASP page that will use it.

The ASP Client

In order to test the insurance component, we've written an ASP page that asks the user for the values of the vehicle type and engine size, and the driver's gender, age and number of claims, and uses these values to ask the insurance component for a premium. This is what the page looks like when it's running:

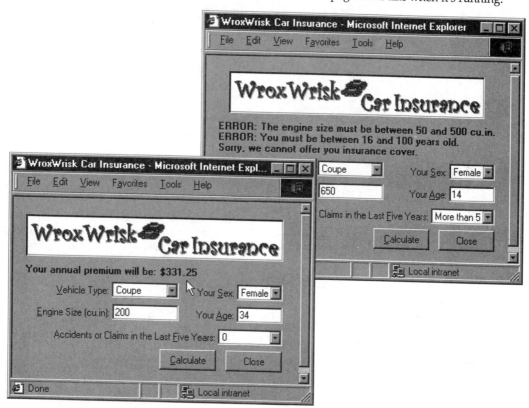

So, our ASP page looks like a standard form. The users can fill in the values for the various input parameters using a couple of text boxes and list boxes, and when they have done so clicking on the **Calculate** button will let them find out their annual insurance premium. The screenshots show one result for which valid data was entered and a premium was calculated, and one result where data was entered that was beyond what the component would accept. This second test was deliberately put in to make sure that the page does trap errors. Since we decided that our component would not perform bounds checking, it is up to our client to do this.

Most of the code for the page is devoted to the form that the users fill in, so the page starts off by declaring the form and displaying the Wrox Wrisk logo:

```
<%@LANGUAGE="VBSCRIPT"%>

<HTML>
<HEAD>
    <TITLE>WroxWrisk Car Insurance</TITLE>
        <STYLE TYPE="text/css">
        BODY,TD,SELECT,INPUT {font-family:MS Sans Serif; font-size:9pt}
        BUTTON {font-family:MS Sans Serif; font-size:9pt; width:70px; height:25px}
        </STYLE>
</HEAD>

<BODY BGCOLOR="silver">
    <FORM ACTION="<% = Request.ServerVariables("SCRIPT_NAME") %>"
                            NAME="frmValues"  METHOD="POST">

<TABLE CELLSPACING="5">
  <TR>
   <TD COLSPAN="2" ALIGN="CENTER">
    <IMG SRC="wwlogo.gif" WIDTH="319" HEIGHT="50" ALT="WroxWrisk Car Insurance">
   </TD>
  </TR>
```

The form uses the http post protocol, so its first task is to check whether it is being displayed in response to some data having been filled in—if so, the premium must be calculated. It checks whether this is the case by examining whether the form contains a vehicle type.

```
<%
strVehType = Request.Form("cboVehType")
If strVehType <> "" Then

  'we got a value from the page, so need to calculate the premium

  CRLF = Chr(13) & Chr(10)  'carriage return
  QUOT = Chr(34)            'double quote character
  blnErrorFound = False     'error flag for any non-legal value

  'start a new table row
  Response.Write "<TR><TD COLSPAN = " & QUOT & "2" & QUOT & "><B>" & CRLF
```

This is followed by some error checking code to make sure that the required input parameters are all there and within a set of limits, or bounds, so that we know it is OK to attempt to calculate the premium.

```
  'see if the vehicle type we've got is legal
  If Len(strVehType) = 0 Then
    Response.Write "ERROR: You must specify the vehicle type.<BR>"
    blnErrorFound = True   'set the error flag
  End If

  'now get the rest of the values from the request
  'and output error messages if they're not legal
  strSex = Request.Form("cboSex")
  If Len(strSex) = 0 Then
    Response.Write "ERROR: You must specify either Male or Female.<BR>"
    blnErrorFound = True   'set the error flag
  End If

  strEngineSize = Request.Form("txtEngineSize")
  If Len(strEngineSize) = 0 Then
    Response.Write "ERROR: You must specify the engine size.<BR>"
    blnErrorFound = True   'set the error flag
```

```
    ElseIf Not IsNumeric(strEngineSize) Then
        Response.Write "ERROR: You must specify the engine size as a number.<BR>"
        blnErrorFound = True     'set the error flag
    Else
        intEngineSize = CInt(strEngineSize)
        If (intEngineSize < 50) Or (intEngineSize > 500) Then
            Response.Write "ERROR: The engine size must be between 50 and 500_
                        cu.in.<BR>"
            blnErrorFound = True     'set the error flag
        End If
    End If

strAge = Request.Form("txtAge")
    If Len(strAge) = 0 Then
        Response.Write "ERROR: You must specify your age in years.<BR>"
        blnErrorFound = True     'set the error flag
    ElseIf Not IsNumeric(strAge) Then
        Response.Write "ERROR: You must specify your age as a number.<BR>"
        blnErrorFound = True     'set the error flag
    Else
        intAge = CInt(strAge)
        If (intAge < 16) Or (intAge > 100) Then
            Response.Write "ERROR: You must be between 16 and 100 years old.<BR>"
            blnErrorFound = True     'set the error flag
        End If
    End If

    strClaims = Request.Form("cboClaims")
    If Len(strClaims) = 0 Then
        Response.Write "ERROR: You must the number of claims.<BR>"
        blnErrorFound = True     'set the error flag
    End If
    If strClaims = "X" Then
        Response.Write "Sorry, we cannot offer you insurance cover.<BR>"
        blnErrorFound = True     'set the error flag
    End If
```

If everything is OK, we can perform the calculation. This is the interesting bit, where the component is actually created.

```
    'see if OK to fetch the final premium
    If Not blnErrorFound Then

        'create our component instance
        Set objWX2882 = Server.CreateObject("WX2882.Insurance")

        'set the properties
        objWX2882.VehicleType = strVehType
        objWX2882.DriverSex = strSex
        objWX2882.DriverAge = intAge
        objWX2882.EngineCubicInches = intEngineSize
        objWX2882.NumberClaims = strClaims

        'then call the GetPremium method and display the result
        dblPremium = objWX2882.GetPremium()
        strMesg = FormatNumber(dblPremium, 2, 0, 0, -1)
        strMesg = "Your annual premium will be: $" + strMesg
        Response.Write strMesg

    End If

    'finally close the table cell and row
    Response.Write "</B></TD></TR>" & CRLF

End If
%>
```

The final part of the ASP page simply consists of displaying all the controls in the form and putting the appropriate values in the list boxes.

```
<TR>
  <TD ALIGN="RIGHT">
   <U>V</U>ehicle Type:
   <SELECT NAME="cboVehType" SIZE="1" ACCESSKEY="V" TABINDEX="1">
     <OPTION>
     <OPTION VALUE="S"
        <% If Request.Form("cboVehType") = "S" Then Response.Write "SELECTED" %>>
        Saloon
<OPTION VALUE="E"
        <% If Request.Form("cboVehType") = "E" Then Response.Write "SELECTED" %>>
        Estate
     <OPTION VALUE="C"
        <% If Request.Form("cboVehType") = "C" Then Response.Write "SELECTED" %>>
        Coupe
     <OPTION VALUE="P"
        <% If Request.Form("cboVehType") = "P" Then Response.Write "SELECTED" %>>
        Performance
   </SELECT>
  </TD>
  <TD ALIGN="RIGHT">
   Your <U>S</U>ex:
   <SELECT NAME="cboSex" SIZE="1" ACCESSKEY="S" TABINDEX="3">
     <OPTION>
     <OPTION VALUE="F"
        <% If Request.Form("cboSex") = "F" Then Response.Write "SELECTED" %>>
        Female
     <OPTION VALUE="M"
        <% If Request.Form("cboSex") = "M" Then Response.Write "SELECTED" %>>
        Male
   </SELECT>
  </TD>
</TR>
<TR>
  <TD ALIGN="RIGHT">
   <U>E</U>ngine Size (cu.in):
   <INPUT TYPE="TEXT" NAME="txtEngineSize" SIZE="14" ACCESSKEY="E" TABINDEX="2"
           VALUE="<% = Request.Form("txtEngineSize") %>">
  </TD>
  <TD ALIGN="RIGHT">
   Your <U>A</U>ge:
   <INPUT TYPE="TEXT" NAME="txtAge" SIZE="9" ACCESSKEY="A" TABINDEX="4"
              VALUE="<% = Request.Form("txtAge") %>">
  </TD>
</TR>
<TR>
  <TD ALIGN="RIGHT" COLSPAN="2">
   Accidents or Claims in the Last <U>F</U>ive Years:
   <SELECT NAME="cboClaims" SIZE="1" ACCESSKEY="F" TABINDEX="5">
     <OPTION>
     <OPTION VALUE="0"
      <% If Request.Form("cboClaims") = "0" Then Response.Write "SELECTED" %>>0
     <OPTION VALUE="1"
      <% If Request.Form("cboClaims") = "1" Then Response.Write "SELECTED" %>>1
     <OPTION VALUE="2"
      <% If Request.Form("cboClaims") = "2" Then Response.Write "SELECTED" %>>2
     <OPTION VALUE="3"
      <% If Request.Form("cboClaims") = "3" Then Response.Write "SELECTED" %>>3
     <OPTION VALUE="4"
      <% If Request.Form("cboClaims") = "4" Then Response.Write "SELECTED" %>>4
     <OPTION VALUE="5"
      <% If Request.Form("cboClaims") = "5" Then Response.Write "SELECTED" %>>5
```

```
      <OPTION VALUE="X"
        <% If Request.Form("cboClaims") = "X" Then Response.Write "SELECTED" %>>
        More than 5
      </SELECT>
    </TD>
  </TR>
  <TR>
    <TD COLSPAN="2" ALIGN="RIGHT">
      <BUTTON NAME="cmdCalculate" ACCESSKEY="C" TABINDEX="6" ONCLICK="doCalculate()">
      <U>C</U>alculate
      </BUTTON>
         
      <BUTTON NAME="cmdClose" TABINDEX="7" ONCLICK="doClose()">
      Close
</BUTTON>
    </TD>
  </TR>
</TABLE>
</FORM>

<SCRIPT LANGUAGE="JScript">
<!-- hide from old browsers

function doCalculate() {
  // submit the form containing the controls to the server
  frmValues.submit();
}

function doClose() {
  window.close();
}

//-->
</SCRIPT>

</BODY>
</HTML>
```

You'll find the source code, and the compiled DLL and application, with the remainder of the samples for this book on our Web site at http://webdev.wrox.co.uk/books/2882.

When we were first talking about COM, we said that a COM component can interact with any other COM component or COM-aware application. So, let's see how this very same component can be run from a Visual Basic application.

Testing Our Component in Visual Basic

Testing our new ActiveX component in Visual Basic is easy. Versions 5 and 6 provide a feature called a **project group**, which can contain more than one project. This allows us to create an ordinary application, or **EXE** project and include within it the ActiveX DLL (or OCX) project as well.

While there is not space to discuss how we implemented the test application in detail here, you can download it from our web site with the rest of the code for the book, if you want to try it yourself. It basically consists of a Standard EXE with the form set to load on start up. The form is then linked to the component, which is made available to the Visual Basic IDE by including it in the Project | References dialog shown in the next screenshot:

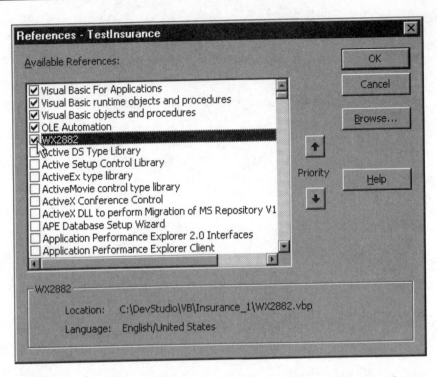

Once you have added a reference to the component, and you have started adding the code into your form, you'll see how the IDE uses the type library, to which it has a reference, so that it can display lists of the available members (we'll come back to look at type libraries in the next section):

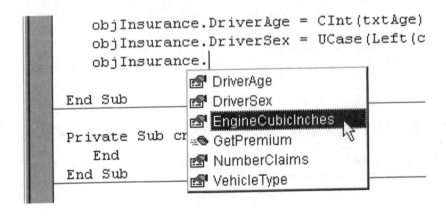

And here you can see our little test application running, and how similar it is to the ASP page that used the same component.

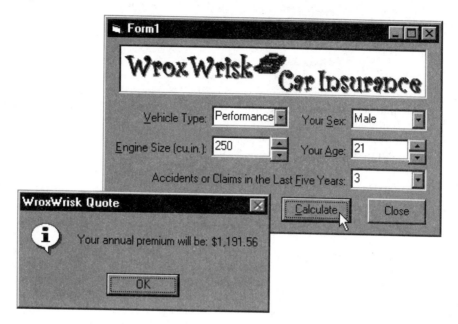

The only bad news is that even our imaginary insurance company won't give us a decent quote on that Ford Mustang...

More About COM

At this point, we have developed a component in Visual Basic, and shown how it can be called from an ASP page. Of course, this is a very simple problem that we could have solved without using components at all—as shown by the fact that our ASP test harness was more complicated than the component itself was! But by using components, we have gained all the potential reuse advantages. If we later decide that we want to carry out insurance calculations from a completely different ASP page, or even from some other application, we don't need to rewrite the component. Alternatively, if we have to modify the algorithm that calculates the premiums, maybe increasing the prices to cover inflation, then we don't need to change any of the ASP pages that call the component. We can simply write and distribute a newer version of the component.

We've also managed to get a long way without having to know that much about COM. But we are now pushing at the limits of what we can reasonably do without understanding a little more of the features of COM. In the last part of the chapter, we will go over a few of the topics that it's useful for us to understand something of. Then we'll have a closer look at some of the options Visual Basic gives you for changing some of your project settings, to see how we can take advantage of these features. In particular, we will look at type libraries, state and scalability, in-process and out-of-process components, threading models, and compilation options for your component.

Type Libraries

Earlier on, when we had built the Insurance project, we took a look at the Visual Basic object browser so we could see that the component was there and registered. At the time we didn't say anything about how this was possible, or from where Visual Basic was able to get all this information about a registered component.

You see, we've already said that COM components are registered using registry entries. However, these registry entries are quite limited in the information they contain. They will tell you the names of the components, and where the files hosting the components are located. They also contain some other information, concerning things like whether the component is in-process or out-of-process and sometimes details of the threading model. But the information in the registry doesn't say anything about what interfaces a given component exposes, or what methods and properties an interface exposes.

That information is supplied in a special file called a **type library**. Sometimes the type library is contained in its own file, which will normally have the extension .tlb. Visual Basic, however, will normally produce DLLs that contain the type library information inside the DLL. So in our insurance example, the DLL itself also serves as the type library.

If you use the Object Browser, located under the View menu in the Visual Basic IDE, it is the type libraries that the browser uses to examine the components. The Object Browser is able to view any components, as long as you tell Visual Basic that the project is going to use them. You can tell Visual Basic which type libraries the project will be using from the Project | References dialog. In this screenshot you can see that the Insurance project has just been added to the references:

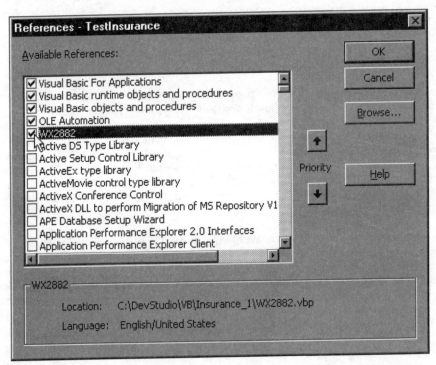

Note that you also need to add the corresponding type libraries to the project references in order to declare variables as being of a type given by an object. VB programmers will be familiar with this, but this will be new to ASP programmers, since it is not possible to define variables typed by specific objects in VBScript.

Now that we've added the insurance component's type library to the references, we can inspect the interfaces and components defined in it using the Object Browser.

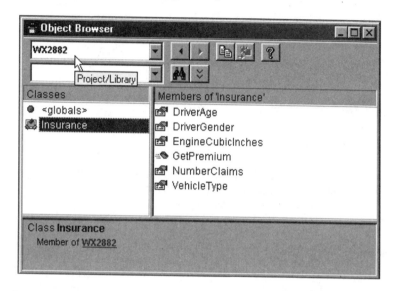

In this screenshot, you can see that the WX2882 type library has been selected in the top left drop down list box, which allows you to select the type library for the Insurance project. The **Classes** list box on the left of the screen shows you the interfaces defined in that type library, while the list box just to the right of that shows you the methods and properties of the selected interface. (Or the global variables defined in the type library if you select <globals>.)

Type libraries are important because Visual Basic clients are only able to talk to components that have been fully defined in a type library. It is possible to register components without their having been defined in a type library, but in that case they will only be able to be used by clients written in C++.

State and Scalability

When we were planning out the interface for the Insurance component, we looked at two designs. The first, which we did not implement, was noted as being better because one method call took all the required data needed to calculate the premium. This approach seemed stronger because it did not require us to store any of the input parameters as member variables. This is significant because it introduces the concept of **state**.

A component is said to have state if it is storing some information that is particular to that instance of the component. What this means is that calling a method on one instance of a component will not necessarily give the same result as calling the same method on another component.

If we created two instances of the insurance component, set the input parameters on one of the instances, but then called the `CalculatePremium()` method on the other instance, we'd expect to get the wrong answer! Such a component has state. On the other hand, if we'd designed our interface so that `CalculatePremium()` took all the input variables as parameters, then we would get the correct answer no matter which instance we used to call `CalculatePremium()` against. Such a component is **stateless**.

So far this probably sounds fairly trivial, and you may wonder why I'm making such a big deal out of it. The reason will become apparent in Chapter 5 when we come to examine MTS. One of the functions of MTS is to make applications that use components more scaleable. However it can only do this if your components satisfy certain requirements. One of these requirements is that your component should be stateless.

If you are intending to use Microsoft Transaction Server, then this is an important consideration when you are designing your interface.

In Process and Out of Process Components

One important decision in the design of your component is whether it should be implemented in-process (that is to say, in a DLL), or out-of-process (in an executable).

This is really an implementation detail of the component—it's not something you need to worry about when designing the interface, because the interface itself doesn't contain any information about the type of component. It is perfectly possible to implement the same interface on different components, some of which may be in-process and others may be out-of-process.

If you choose to place your component in-process, then it will be hosted inside the same process space as the client. This has a big advantage as far as performance is concerned. All method calls against the component will normally execute very quickly as the overhead involved with calling the method is little more than that for calling any other function in Visual Basic. On the other hand, since the component will share the same memory space as the client, a badly designed component that goes wrong could easily start trashing memory that is used by the client. An out-of-process component, however, cannot do that since it occupies a separate process, and so a separate memory space. Set against that, calling methods on the out-of-process component will be a lot slower because the COM runtime will have to sort out passing any parameters between the different processes.

Note that there is no difference between how you call an in-process and an out-of-process component. One of the principles of COM is that the client will not even be aware of where the component has been hosted. That is all handled by the COM runtime. It is quite possible to, say, replace an in-process component by an out-of-process one, or vice versa, that exposes the same interfaces. Furthermore, if it has the same ProgID, your ASP script will not need to be changed at all to use the new component.

Threading Models

Due to restrictions in the abilities of VB, threading will normally only be an area of consideration if you are coding your components in C++. However, at the same time, it is important to be aware of the significance of the different threading models.

A thread can be thought of as the sequence of instructions that your computer is executing. Normally your computer will appear to be doing several things at once. For example, it might be accepting what you're typing into a word document and at the same time continually checking to see if you click on another window to do something else. If you do something like print a document, or any other task that takes a long time, the computer will normally display a Cancel button and have to continually check to see if you've pressed it. Again there are two tasks happening at the same time. Each such line of execution is known as a **thread**.

Setting Compilation Options for Your Component

When we built the Insurance component, we didn't stop to look at any of the different compilation options that VB can give us—we just left everything at its default values. In this section we'll go over some of those compilation options and see how they allow us to take advantage of some of the facilities offered by COM.

The options in question can be found in the Project Properties dialog, which surprisingly enough, you can bring up by selecting Project then Properties from the main menu in the Visual Basic IDE.

The first tab in this dialog is marked General:

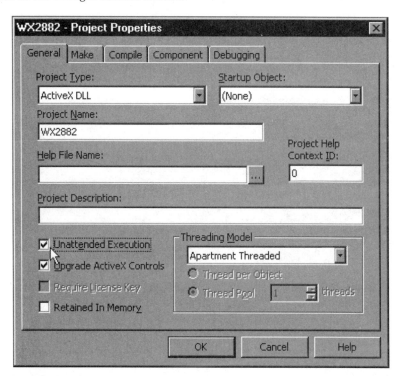

We won't go through all the controls on this page here, since not all of them are relevant at this level, but we will cover the important ones.

The Project Name and Description text boxes have their obvious meanings.

The Threading Model list box is where you can choose the threading model of your component. When we select ActiveX DLL as the project type, the default it is set to Apartment Threaded. The only other option for an ActiveX DLL project is Single Threaded, which as we saw earlier we would only use if we had backwards compatibility issues with Windows 3.1.

If you select ActiveX executable as your project type, so that you compile to a component housed in an executable, then the threaded model will be apartment threaded. However, you will also find that you can change the number of threads in the thread pool, (these controls are disabled for a DLL project). Increasing the number of threads will cause different instances of the component to be created on separate threads. This can improve performance for the case in which your component is called from a multi-threaded client, which creates multiple instances of your component. Again, it's something that's not too relevant if you are expecting your clients to be ASP pages.

The Unattended Execution checkbox is a safeguard that, when checked, prevents the code from being compiled if it contains any interface code (such as a `MsgBox()` statement) or interface objects (such as forms). This is a useful safeguard if we want to make sure that the project does not contain any user-interface code.

In the Make tab, we can enter a name for the component, set the internal version number, and provide other version information. This is mainly useful for documentation purposes. Also, it's always worth entering some text for the File Description, as this will be displayed in the Properties dialog of the component's DLL file (the one that can be selected from the right-click context menu).

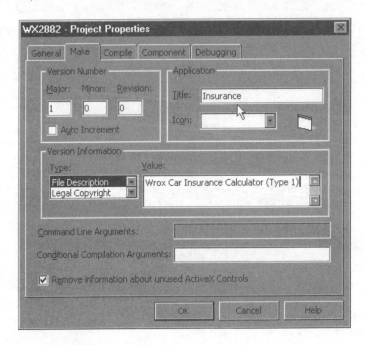

Finally we need to consider the **Component** tab:

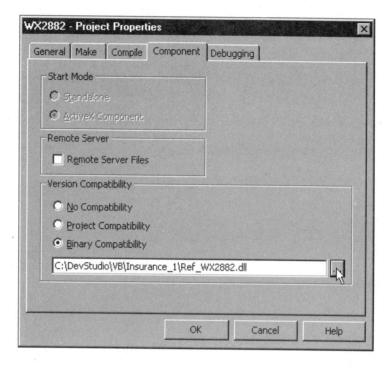

Tucked away here are the **Version Compatibility** radio buttons. These are important, and you should make sure they are set correctly.

You'll recall that every component is identified by a globally unique identifier (a GUID)—and that it is the GUID rather than the ProgID, which really identifies the component. The ProgID is just a friendly name used to refer to the component, although it is not guaranteed to be unique.

If your project is set to **No Compatibility**, then every time you rebuild your project Visual Basic will generate new GUIDs. This means that if you are copying your component on to another machine, you will need to reregister it each time. Clients will only work with whichever compiled version was last registered. Generally, this option is not particularly useful.

With both **Binary** and **Project Compatibilities**, Visual Basic will not keep generating new GUIDs, but will reuse the same ones with each build. With **Project Compatibilities**, you can make your current build the **reference DLL** (the one used to retrieve the GUIDs, and against which all future builds will be compared). In this case, there are a few other steps to follow. Click the button with the three dots to display the **Compatible ActiveX Control** dialog and point it at the folder with your new DLL in it. Right-click on the existing DLL, change its name to Ref_Wrox.dll, select it, and click the **Open** button. Recompile the DLL, and the renamed component file now becomes the reference DLL to which all future builds will be compared (The compiler will now use the same GUIDs as the reference DLL for all future builds of the DLL file.) However, if **Binary Compatibility** has been selected, then the GUIDs will change if you make any changes to the interface definition.

Summary

In this first practical 'hands-on' chapter, we've seen how easy it is to build components using Visual Basic. In version 5, and even more so in version 6, Visual Basic provides lots of useful features that allow us to build high performance, efficient and reusable components quickly and easily. Even if you decide at a later date that you need to implement the component in another language, such as C++, Visual Basic provides a very useful prototyping and testing environment in which to experiment.

So, you've seen some of the issues that are involved in planning and building components. Of course, good planning is key to getting the results you need quickly, and with the minimum of effort. It also gives you a chance to stand back and generally consider the wider picture.

❑ Which internal features of the component should be exposed?

❑ Which extra internal values should be made into public properties?

These kinds of issues can make the difference between components that are single-task specific, and those that are reusable in other applications and by other programmers.

In all, this chapter looked at:

❑ Basic design issues when planning components for use in other applications

❑ How we specify and implement a component's interface in Visual Basic

❑ A step by step example of building a simple component in Visual Basic

❑ Those topics in COM that we didn't cover in chapter 1, and which you need to know in order to write effective components in VB.

In a book like this, we can't guess at the exact requirements you may have for business logic or application components. Instead, all we can do is show you the various ways that you can implement solutions to the common problems and issues that you will most certainly meet. However, the wide range of components that you'll find in this book, together with the case studies, will provide you with plenty of extra help and guidance. With a little practice, you will easily be able to modify your components to more exactly suit your own requirements.

Interfacing With Hosting Environments

Back in Chapter 2, we saw how we can use Visual Basic to build a component that exposes functionality to a VB application using COM. Specifically, the properties and methods of the component were made available via a COM interface—a binary contract that describes the component's behavior, without exposing any details of its implementation.

We exercised our simple component by demonstrating it within an ASP page, but in fact we can use it in any number of other environments. It would be a fairly trivial exercise to write a client Visual Basic application, or a script running within the browser, which instantiated and used the component in a very similar way. In fact, the component can be called in exactly the same way in *any* COM-enabled language or environment.

There are two important characteristics of the component that help to ensure its 'versatility'. First, it is self-contained in terms of functionality—everything that's needed to call the methods of the component is contained within the DLL that we distribute, so all the application client needs to do is create an instance of the registered component and call its methods. Second, the component doesn't pre-suppose any particular features of the calling environment, except that it is a COM-compliant environment.

This chapter introduces two ideas related to these characteristics. First, we'll consider the notion that our COM components can take advantage of other COM components. For example, if our component needs other custom-built components then it makes sense to include and distribute them as part of the same DLL. There are lots of other components around that we can make use of (such as ADO, third-party components, etc). And, in particular, since we're writing components for use in an ASP environment then it sometimes makes sense to take advantage of that environment—using the intrinsic ASP objects within the implementation of the component itself.

Second (and not entirely unrelated), we'll look at the notion that we should consider deployment environment issues. Imagine your manager's face if you and your development team created a solution for a client using IIS4—only to find that the client's system actually runs IIS3. Or that you specialized your client's components to run in an IIS environment—after which they unhelpfully announce that they want to call the components from VB as well. Requirements like these do have an impact on how we write our components, so we need to be aware of what impact these types of changes would have *before* we create a solution.

So here's what we'll see in this chapter:

❑ How to use ASP intrinsic objects in a component, via the `ScriptingContext` object

❑ How IIS, since version 4, provides ASP functionality in components via a Microsoft Transaction Server (MTS) object called the `ObjectContext` object

❑ Employing other COM components within our component

In order to demonstrate the issues raised, we'll also build a couple of sample components, and show them at work.

Aspects of Component Design

As a component developer, you will often find that you are asked to build components for a specific, specialized task. You'll need to ensure that the component runs in a specific environment; and it's likely that your solution will have dependencies on other components that provide additional functionality (such as database access).

The decisions you make during the system design stage will affect the potential reuse of the components written to provide the solution. If you take care during the design stage, you should be able to ensure that your components can be reused in environments other than the one you wrote for, and hence you can reap the rewards of reuse. This can be achieved either by avoiding any dependency upon the hosting environment, or by allowing the component to discover the environment in which it is running so that they can adjust their behavior accordingly. Of course, code reuse is part of our overall motivation for ASP component development in the first place.

What sort of things should we be thinking of during our design phase? Environment issues, component granularity and component dependencies are three areas that are definitely worth consideration. We'll look at component granularity in Chapter 5, and we'll examine what the other two concepts mean in this chapter.

Component–Environment Interactions

If you have a moment sometime, take the components that you've seen so far in this book, and try writing a few applications (in different COM-compliant languages and environments) that call the methods of those components—you shouldn't have too much difficulty in getting them working. In fact, COM provides the infrastructure that enables us to reuse those components within different environments. As the component's developer, all we had to do was write the implementation code, and define the COM interface that would expose the functionality to the client.

There's another factor that makes these components employable within *any* COM-compliant environment. Namely, the components were designed in such a way that they don't interface with any functionality of the hosting environment. We might say that the components are **environment-neutral**.

Perhaps the best way to appreciate what we mean by environment-neutrality is to look at a counter-example. Suppose we're designing a component specifically for use within an ASP page running under IIS. In that case, we might write the implementation of the component so that it takes advantage of the fact that it's only going to be called from within ASP pages. For example, we might ask our component to access cookies or parameters passed to the page, or to send additional cookies back to the client. (For the record, we can do that relatively easily, by working with ASP's intrinsic objects—`Request`, `Response`, `Session`, `Application` and `Server`—within the component's code. We'll see some examples later.) Such a component is not environment-neutral—rather, it's **environment-dependent**. This dependence on the component's calling environment limits its potential reuse outside of IIS.

Environment-dependent components have pros and cons, as do environment-neutral components. A lot of components that incorporate some kind of business logic (such as the insurance calculator that we developed in the last chapter, which encompassed rules about how we calculate premiums) are environment-neutral—by remaining firmly aloof from the hosting container, the component has no reliance on the environment, allowing it to be used more freely in many different types of applications. As component developers, we often favor environment-neutral components, simply because they can allow us a greater opportunity for code reuse—we can save a lot of development-time by avoiding the need to code the same piece of functionality repeatedly into a number of different environment-dependent components.

Components that are environment-dependent, on the other hand, tend to address specific requirements so their reuse outside of a specific environment is often not a consideration we have to worry about. For example, if we were to build a component that displays the internal state of each ASP intrinsic object, we can hardly expect it to function successfully within a standalone VB application, as the component is dependent upon the ASP object model; but the chances are that we'll never use such a component anywhere other than in ASP applications.

One common trait of environment-dependent components is that their dependence is on the object model of the calling environment. These types of components simply cannot function outside of a specific hosting environment.

Component Dependencies

When the implementation of a custom component makes use of the interfaces of one or more other components, we have to give careful consideration to how we re-use that component. For example, in the next couple of chapters we'll develop our own custom components that perform data access operations—and in order to do that they make calls to the methods of a set of components called the ActiveX Data Objects (ADO). When we come to use our custom component in ASP applications or elsewhere, we'll need to ensure that the ADO components are available to our custom component wherever it is used.

> In fact, ADO is pretty much a de-facto standard for data access on Microsoft systems now. Because ADO is found on so many machines, you're unlikely to have a problem—if you do, it's just a case of downloading the ADO DLL from Microsoft's web site *http://www.microsoft.com/data/* and registering it as part of your tasklist for installing the application. One continuing problem to be aware of is using the latest features in a new version of ADO when client machines may have an older version.

Of course, our custom component might also need to interact with other less widespread components, and we'll also need to ensure that those components are installed on the client machine (and that any necessary configuration has been set up). For example, if we are building components to handle email messages automatically then we might well consider making use of a set of Microsoft components called Collaborative Data Objects (or CDO—a series of COM components used to access mail servers and manipulate messages and attachments). Later in this chapter we'll write a custom component that makes use of another third-party component, called RegEx. When you come to use the custom component you'll see some of these issues, because you'll need to make the RegEx component available on your machine too.

Adaptive Components

In the remainder of this book, you'll find many components that are aimed at specific environments and have a number of dependencies. However, even though their purpose and working environment may be highly specific, we should still consider building in as much generality as possible. This is likely to make them more re-usable within that specific environment in different solutions, even if they aren't reusable across other environments.

We'll see an example of this later in this chapter—we'll write a component that runs within ASP, but is sufficiently generic that it can detect the underlying version of IIS and adjust its behavior accordingly. Such components might be referred to as **adaptive components**.

Components for the IIS/ASP Environment

Internet Information Server and Active Server Pages together provide a special environment in which we can use components. This environment does differ between versions of IIS and ASP (and with different script engine versions), but it still provides a common set of objects and collections that we can use. This book is specifically about components for ASP; therefore it makes sense to look at how we can write components that use the ASP intrinsic objects within their implementation.

Why don't we just place our ASP-specific code within ASP pages? Well, if we were only performing a few mundane actions with our ASP code then we probably wouldn't gain much advantage from placing the code within a component. In fact, it'll be easier (and usually more efficient) to place simple ASP scripts within the ASP page. However, if we're writing an application that's ASP-intensive then we can gain a number of benefits from designing components to do the ASP activity for us:

❑   If we're in the business of selling code, then there's a question of security. If we distribute our ASP solutions in text files, then our customers can read our code and copy our ideas for free—they can even write over the code and break it or change the functionality. If we distribute solutions in a compiled DLL, then the implementation is locked into place via COM's binary contract—that means that our VB and VC++ solutions can't be read without the highly intensive effort of reverse engineering the machine code, so it is very unlikely that they would be changed. (It is worth noting that if you were to write your components in Java it would be possible to use a decompiler that converts Java byte code into Java source.)

❑   If we're dealing with long and complex ASP code, then it's worth remembering that an ASP page needs to be compiled by IIS before it's executed, while an ASP COM component's implementation is already compiled. So there's a point at which the cost of runtime code compilation outweighs the cost of instantiating a component to do the job—in other words, you can get better performance by putting long ASP scripts into a component.

❑   If we're planning to reuse the solution, then a DLL is more portable than a set of text files.

❑   If we're planning an *n*-tier solution, then separating the different types of logic (presentation, data-centric, etc.) into a component fits very neatly into such an architecture. There's more about this in Chapter 5.

❑   Compiled languages offer additional functionality that is not possible with VBScript or JavaScript.

Accessing the ASP Objects from Components

When we build our web applications from components ASP acts as a programming 'glue', which we use to bind together the various chunks of code. ASP (in the .asp pages) can interact with the Web server itself to access information about the client request, and create output that is sent back to the client. ASP can also interact with components that run on the server (or on a networked server), and these components can interact with the other Windows services and applications as required. Of course, ASP can also interact directly with these Windows services and applications itself.

But, the clever part is that the same interface used by ASP to communicate with the Web server (IIS) is *also* available to our components (assuming the component is created within the ASP environment) because it uses COM. This means it is possible for the component to interact directly with the ASP interpreter to create output in the page being sent back to a client and collect values from the intrinsic objects.

The request from the client is received by IIS, and is used to fetch the page from the server's disk. If the page has a file extension that identifies it as being an ASP page (such as .asp or .asa), it is passed to the ASP script interpreter. To help you see what we mean, look at the next diagram.

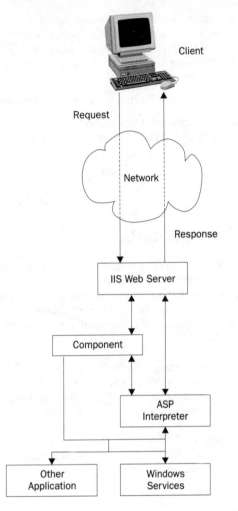

The page may include script that creates an instance of our component. The created component can then interface with almost any service or application on the local server, or on any available networked system provided security is configured correctly.

In the remainder of this section we'll first remind ourselves of the ASP object model; then we'll take a look at a simple component that implements an ASP solution.

The ASP Object Model

In this book, we're assuming that you are reasonably familiar with Active Server Pages and the object model and collections, properties and methods that it provides. What we will do, however, is briefly summarize the common objects that are available in all versions, and which we'll be using in our components.

For a more complete reference overview of the ASP object model, see Appendix A.

The ScriptingContext Object

The effective root of the ASP object model is an object called the `ScriptingContext`. This represents our interface to the ASP interpreter, and acts as a gateway to the five intrinsic ASP objects—`Request` and `Response`, which contain information about the client's request to the server and the server's response to the client, and the `Server`, `Session` and `Application` objects that provide extra support:

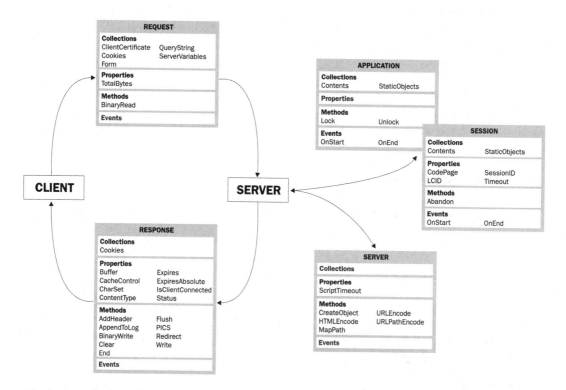

We don't need to use the `ScriptingContext` in traditional ASP pages—we can access the ASP intrinsic objects directly there. In component code, however, we can't access the ASP objects directly and the `ScriptingContext` object is one way to gain access to them.

The Request Object

The `Request` object contains all the details of the request that a client sends to the server when an ASP page is accessed. It provides one method and one property. It also has five collections that contain information from particular sections of the request:

❑   `Request.Cookies` is a collection of all the cookies sent by the client with the request.

❑   `Request.ClientCertificate` is a collection of all the fields of the client certificate (if any) submitted by the client with the request.

❑   `Request.Form` is a collection of all the control name/value pairs for all HTML controls on a `<FORM>` that the user has submitted.

- ❏   `Request.QueryString` is a collection of all the name/value pairs in any query string that is appended to the URL, following a question mark '?' character.

- ❏   `Request.ServerVariables` is a collection of all the HTTP variable name/value pairs sent by the client browser.

The Response Object

The `Response` object provides access to the page that is created and sent back to the client, as the ASP script interpreter is generating it. It has more properties and methods than the `Request` object, and just a single collection—the `Cookies` collection.

The Server Object

The `Server` object provides access to the basic tasks involved in serving Web pages to the client. This includes escaping characters that form part of a URL or HTML page, and creating COM objects from within an ASP page.

The Session Object

The `Session` object provides access to a user's ASP session. The session is created when a user first accesses a web site, and is subsequently destroyed when the user is no longer using it. The object can be used to store values on the server that are available only to an individual user during their current session (hence the term **session-scope**).

The Application Object

The `Application` object provides access to the global ASP application, or a specific application within a subdirectory. An ASP application provides a way to store variables that are global to every user for every page within that application (hence the term **application-scope**). An ASP application's lifetime does not begin until a client requests a page from the application; thereafter, the application's life continues until the web service is stopped.

A Note About MTS's ObjectContext Object

The `ScriptingContext` object is available in all versions of IIS, and we can use it in our components to access the ASP intrinsic objects—`Request`, `Response` etc. Indeed, for IIS version 3.0 and earlier the `ScriptingContext` object is the only way to access the ASP object model. However, Microsoft has deprecated the scripting context object over recent versions of IIS. Since IIS version 4.0, it is also possible (and *essential* for some types of transactional components) to access the ASP objects using the `ObjectContext` object.

> *The `ObjectContext` object is a very important feature that has arrived as part of the integration of Microsoft Transaction Server (MTS) into IIS. You can think of it like a global object variable that is always available from every instance of a component that you develop for IIS4 onwards. MTS itself is a transaction manager and component broker, that helps components work in unison to create scalable applications. The* main *purpose of the* `ObjectContext` *object is to assist the component in its tasks by containing information about the environment and the object within which an object is running.*

So the `ObjectContext` object has an important role to play in terms of making the ASP objects available within our components. We'll create two components in this chapter. The first uses the `ScriptingContext` object only, because (although it is deprecated) it still allows us to use our components in ASP pages run in older environments such as IIS3, as well as in test environments such as Personal Web Server. The second component in this chapter is an adaptive component, which detects the calling environment and uses the `ObjectContext` if it's available—resorting to the `ScriptingContext` object only if necessary.

A Component that Uses the ASP Objects

We've done a lot of talking in this chapter so far; let's write a simple component that demonstrates some of the concepts we've discussed. As we mentioned, the component will use a reference to the `ScriptingContext` object to make the ASP components available; and we'll demonstrate it in action by using a couple of the ASP intrinsic objects within the implementation of the component.

The component's job is to retrieve two quantities of beans from a form, calculate the total, and write some text back to the browser. In the process, we'll make use of the `Request`, `Response` and `Session` objects. It's not what the component does that we're interested in here; it's the way that it's done.

We'll create the component in Visual Basic, so fire up the VB IDE. Change the name of the project: select **Project | Project1 Properties** and in the **Project Name** field, overwrite the default project name (Project1) with the name of our project—**Calculator**.

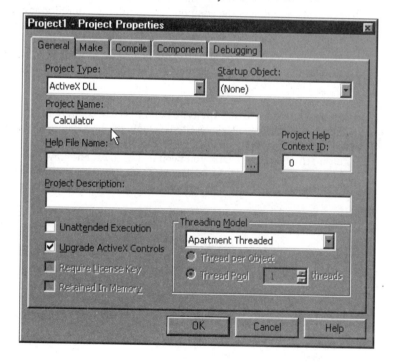

The DLL, `Calculator.dll`, will contain the implementation of a single component, which is to be called `BeanAdder`. Before we begin the implementation of the component, change the name of default class module. You can do this in the Properties pane of your Visual Basic IDE (select View | Properties Window if it's not there). Just overwrite Class1 with BeanAdder, as shown here.

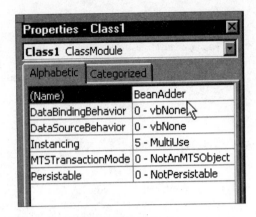

Adding an ASP Type Library Reference to the Visual Basic IDE

In order to use the ASP objects within our component, we need to make the functionality of those objects available to the component. Visual Basic works best (well, makes our life simpler!) if we add a reference to the appropriate type library to the VB Integrated Development Environment (IDE). This de-compiles the type library and makes the component and interface definitions contained within directly available to us inside the IDE. (This includes the pop-up lists of members and syntax help, thanks to IntelliSense.)

In this case, we want to be able to reference the built-in objects, and declare variables as being of the various ASP object types. In particular, we want to be able to declare a variable that will hold the ASP `ScriptingContext` object.

Adding a reference to the ASP type library is easy enough. In Visual Basic 6.0, the ASP DLL is provided for you (in the Microsoft Visual Studio\Common\IDE\ folder) and is already contained in the list of references that you can add to a project. In Visual Basic 5.0, you will have to copy the relevant DLL onto your machine first. The DLL you need is `asp.dll`, and it will probably be in the Winnt\system32\inetsrv\ folder on your server. Open the References... dialog from the Project menu, and select Microsoft Active Server Pages Object Library. If it's not in the list, you can click Browse... and go off to find it:

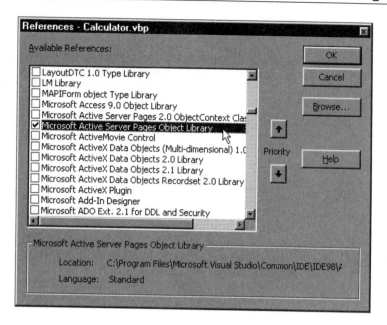

There is also a reference to the Microsoft Active Server Pages 2.0 ObjectContext Class Type Library, which is used to provide context information across an ASP application running under MTS.

The ScriptingContext Object

When we program directly in ASP script (in any scripting language), the methods and properties of the ScriptingContext object are globally available, so we don't have to explicitly qualify references to them using the typical *object.method* notation—we can just write *method*. So rather than using:

```
ScriptingContext.Response.Write "Some text to send back to the client"
```

we can just use:

```
Response.Write "Some text to send back to the client"
```

in the manner you will be used to using from your scripts. Each method and property is just like any other global function that we would define and use. This type of object is called an **application object**, and is common in most VBScript/VBA enabled environments, such as Microsoft Word, Microsoft Access, ASP (of course) and even Visual Basic.

An application object only has meaning inside of the application that created it, and can only be implicitly used within certain contexts over which it has complete control, such as interpreting and executing ASP script.

Inside of a component—even one that is instantiated using the `Server.CreateObject()` method—we are operating outside the logical confines of the application (and hence of the application object). This means that the `ScriptingContext` object is not immediately available. If you want to use the `ScriptingContext` object, we have to obtain a reference to it, and then qualify references to it explicitly using the normal *object.method* notation with the *object* being the name of the variable that holds the object reference.

In order to access the ASP interpreter and use the ASP objects like `Request` and `Response` in our component, we have to find a way to get a reference to them. In this example we're going to do it through the `ScriptingContext` object; here's how.

In IIS3 onwards, when an ASP page creates an instance of a component using `Server.CreateObject()`, the ASP interpreter will determine whether that component supports a method called `OnStartPage()`. If `OnStartPage()` is supported, the ASP interpreter will invoke the `OnStartPage()` method and will pass in a reference to the `ScriptingContext` object. To prepare for this in the component, all we have to do is declare a global variable that will hold a reference to the `ScriptingContext` object, and then set it to the reference that ASP passes as a parameter of the `OnStartPage()` event:

```
Dim gobjContext As ScriptingContext          ' create a global variable

Sub OnStartPage(objSC As ScriptingContext)   ' this method is invoked
                                             ' when the page starts

  'save the scripting context reference
   Set gobjContext = objSC                    ' set the global variabel using objSC
End Sub
```

> Note that the ASP page only invokes `OnStartPage()` if the component instance is created using `Server.CreateObject()`. A VBScript `CreateObject()` function call from the ASP page does not have the same effect. This is because `CreateObject()` calls go straight to the COM runtime while `Server.CreateObject()` calls will be processed by IIS.

Once we've made this reference available, we can use it to access any of the child ASP objects and their members. Effectively, we've created a reference to the `ScriptingContext` **interface**—this interface contains a number of properties (`Request`, `Response`, etc.) that expose each of the ASP intrinsic objects. So, within the component, accessing an ASP-intrinsic object simply requires using one of the `ScriptingContext` object's properties:

```
gobjContext.Response.Write "This code is contained in the component's interface"
```

> As we mentioned earlier, we're using the `ScriptingContext` object here because it's available in all versions of IIS. However, its use is no longer encouraged by Microsoft—if you're using IIS4 or later then use of the `ObjectContext` object is recommended instead. We're covering it here because you still have to use `ScriptingContext` in applications running on IIS3/undetermined environments. We'll be covering the `ObjectContext` object in the next example in this chapter.

The BeanAdder Component

Now that we know how to get a reference to the `ScriptingContext` object, we can use it to access the ASP child objects and their members from our components. Here's the full implementation of our `Calculator.BeanAdder` component. It contains just two methods: the `OnStartPage()` method that we've just seen and a method called `DisplayBeansSum.()`

```
Option Explicit
Dim gobjContext As ScriptingContext

Sub OnStartPage(objSC As ScriptingContext)
    'save the scripting context reference
    Set gobjContext = objSC
End Sub
```

```
Public Sub DisplayBeansSum()
    Dim intVal1 As Integer
    Dim intVal2 As Integer
    Dim strUName As String

    intVal1 = 0
    intVal2 = 0

    If IsNumeric(gobjContext.Request.Form("AmtL")) Then
        intVal1 = gobjContext.Request.Form("AmtL")
    End If
    If IsNumeric(gobjContext.Request.Form("AmtR")) Then
        intVal2 = gobjContext.Request.Form("AmtR")
    End If
    strUName = gobjContext.Session("UserName")
    gobjContext.Response.Write "<HR>" & _
        "Well, " & strUName &_
        ", here's the result of your most recent calculation: <BR>"
    gobjContext.Response.Write intVal1 & " beans and " & intVal2 & " beans is " & _
        intVal1 + intVal2 & " beans.<BR>"
End Sub
```

The functionality itself is pretty trivial, but it makes direct two-way interaction with the ASP page that will call it, reading the content of the `Request` object's `Form` collection and a `Session` variable called `UserName`; and also using the `Response` object to write text which will appear directly on the browser.

With this code in the Calculator.BeanAdder (Code) window, you're ready to compile the component (by selecting File | Make Calculator.dll).

Testing the Component

To test the component, we'll use two pages. The first, `Welcome.htm`, is simply a vehicle for assigning a value to the `Session` variable, `UserName`:

```
<HTML>
<HEAD><TITLE>Accessing ASP Objects via the ScriptingContext Object</TITLE></HEAD>

<BODY>
<H2>The Personalized Bean Counter</H2>
<HR>

<FORM NAME="GetName" ACTION="BeanAdder.asp" METHOD="POST">
Welcome. Please type your name here: <INPUT TYPE="TEXT" NAME="UserName"><BR><BR>
<INPUT TYPE="SUBMIT" VALUE="Enter">
</FORM>
</BODY></HTML>
```

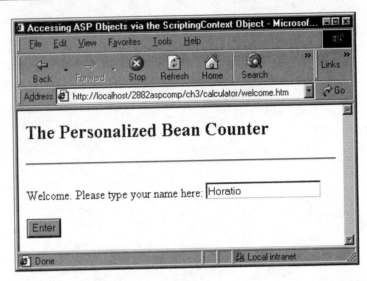

The name entered into the text box is passed to BeanAdder.asp when you hit the Enter button. Here's BeanAdder.asp:

```
<HTML>
<HEAD><TITLE>Accessing ASP Objects via the ScriptingContext Object</TITLE></HEAD>
<BODY>

<%
  If Request.Form("UserName") <> "" Then
    Session("UserName") = Request.Form("UserName")
  End If

  Dim intAmtL
  Dim intAmtR
  intAmtL = Request.Form("AmtL")
  intAmtR = Request.Form("AmtR")
%>

<FORM NAME="MyForm" ACTION="BeanAdder.asp" METHOD="POST">
Number of beans in left hand: <INPUT TYPE="TEXT" NAME="AmtL" VALUE="<%=intAmtL%>"><BR>
Number of beans in right hand: <INPUT TYPE="TEXT" NAME="AmtR"
                               VALUE="<%=intAmtR%>"><BR><BR>
<INPUT TYPE="SUBMIT" VALUE="Add Beans">
</FORM>

<%
  If Request.Form.Count > 1 Then      ' integers entered, so perform the calculation
    Dim objBAdder
    Set objBAdder = Server.CreateObject("Calculator.BeanAdder")

    objBAdder.DisplayBeansSum
    Set objBAdder = Nothing
  End If
%>
</BODY></HTML>
```

The code comes in four parts, but the first time the user visits the page, the first and third sections are the only relevant parts. In the first part, we populate the Session-level variable UserName with the value given by the user in Welcome.htm. In the third part—the HTML form—we ask the user to input a couple of integers:

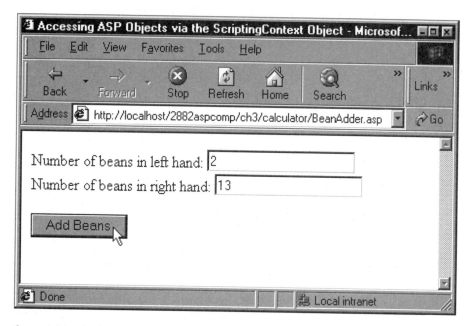

When the user hits the **Add Beans** button, the page is reloaded. This time, the second, third and fourth parts of the code are relevant. The variables intAmtL and intAmtR are populated using values from the Request object's Form collection (for use in populating the text boxes) and the form is displayed again. But the interesting bit is in the last part.

Assuming the user has entered the necessary details and therefore populated the `Request.Form` collection sufficiently, we can now perform the calculation. In the ASP page, this simply involves instantiating a copy of the `Calculator.BeanAdder` component and calling the `DisplayBeansSum()` method from its interface, which is going to do all the work and display the results:

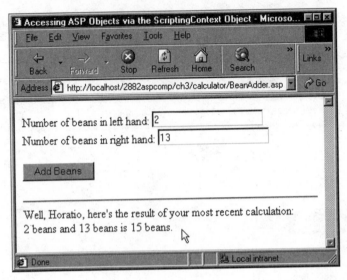

How It Works

When the component loads, the ASP script engine checks for the existence of an `OnStartPage()` method within the component's interface, and invokes it. In this component, `OnStartPage()` simply declares a global variable, `gobjContext`, and assigns it a reference to ASP's `ScriptingContext` object:

```
Sub OnStartPage(objSC As ScriptingContext)
    'save the scripting context reference
    Set gobjContext = objSC
End Sub
```

Now we can use `gobjContext` to reference the other ASP intrinsic objects within the component's interface. For example, we use it to get values from the `Request` object's `Form` collection:

```
If IsNumeric(gobjContext.Request.Form("AmtL")) Then
    intVal1 = gobjContext.Request.Form("AmtL")
End If
If IsNumeric(gobjContext.Request.Form("AmtR")) Then
    intVal2 = gobjContext.Request.Form("AmtR")
End If
```

In fact, these lines (from the component's implementation of `DisplayBeansSum()`) are assigning values to `intVal1` and `intVal2` from the `Request.Form` collection—just as we accessed the same collection when assigning values in the `BeanAdder.asp` ASP page itself:

```
Dim intAmtL
Dim intAmtR
intAmtL = Request.Form("AmtL")
intAmtR = Request.Form("AmtR")
```

What else is happening inside the component? Well, we've gratuitously included usage of a `Session` variable, just to prove that we can:

```
strUName = gobjContext.Session("UserName")
```

And we also write text to the browser. This is quite useful, because it means that we can give entire components over to writing text if we wanted to:

```
gobjContext.Response.Write "<HR>" & _
    "Well, " & strUName &_
    ", here's the result of your most recent calculation: <BR>"
gobjContext.Response.Write intVal1 & " beans and " & intVal2 & " beans is " & _
    intVal1 + intVal2 & " beans.<BR>"
```

The main thing to notice is that we can use the ASP intrinsic objects within the component almost as if they were written in the page. All we need in the component is the reference to the `ScriptingContext` object.

Concluding Thoughts

So, when we instantiate our component within the ASP page, the component instance can access the functionality and state (i.e. the methods, properties and collections) of the ASP objects—almost exactly as though we were using these methods and properties in the page itself. In particular, note that we didn't need to pass ASP objects from our ASP script via properties, or as parameters into methods of the component—all we needed is a reference to the ASP page's `ScriptingContext` object in the component.

As a result, the ASP script is tidier, our code is more secure, and (if the ASP code performs a lot of actions) there will usually be a performance benefit because compiled code within a component will process the object collections much more quickly than interpreted ASP code could.

Of course, we've made a concession in order to achieve this. Because we're using the ASP objects within our component's implementation, the component has become environment-specific. It's only of use to us when called from an ASP page—if we tried to use it's functionality within a client-side script, or from a stand-alone Visual Basic component, the component would fail.

In this case, it's a straight trade-off—our component isn't reusable across environments, but it does do the job of encapsulating the presentation logic of our application.

Detecting the Calling Environment

When we talk about environment-dependent components, we need to appeal to common sense. The fact is that, if your customer asks you to write a component that calculates car insurance premiums, and you name it appropriately, then they're unlikely to try to use the same component in the airline reservations project that they're also working on—because they'll know it's the wrong component to use.

By the same count, a component written specifically for use in an ASP environment—given careful naming, documentation and handling—is unlikely to be used in unsuitable environments. Of course, there's no accounting for folk—someone will try it—and so it's worth designing your component so that it closes down gracefully instead of crashing the system, if it can't find the environment resources that it needs to execute correctly.

In this section, we'll write a component that does that—it's another component that uses ASP objects within its implementation. But not only will our component detect whether or not it's being invoked by an Internet Information Server or Personal Web Server environment, it will examine the program group (i.e. IIS or PWS) and the version, and will adapt its behavior accordingly. It's a classic example of an adaptive component.

ScriptingContext and ObjectContext

Our motivation for this example is that we need to tackle an important issue that was left hanging in the first part of the chapter: namely, that the BeanAdder component above accesses the ASP objects via a reference to the ScriptingContext object. The great thing about ScriptingContext is that (at the time of writing) it is common to all versions of IIS from version 3, and all versions of PWS. This means that we don't need to worry about versioning issues on the calling web server—our component will work in any ASP-supporting version of IIS3, IIS4, IIS5 and PWS.

The bad news about the ScriptingContext object is that, in IIS5, it is considered obsolete. Even in IIS4, ScriptingContext is considered secondary to using the ObjectContext object. What is ObjectContext, and why is it important?

The ObjectContext Object and MTS

The ObjectContext is a very important feature that arrived with IIS4, because it was built using Microsoft Transaction Server (MTS) technology. You can think of it like a global object variable, and one is always available for each instance of a component that you develop for IIS4 onwards. MTS itself is a transaction manager and component broker, helping components to work in unison to create scalable applications. The *main* purpose of the ObjectContext is to assist an object running under MTS in its tasks by containing information about the environment within which an object is running.

> *Microsoft Transaction Server (MTS) is a Microsoft service that acts as a transaction manager and object broker. COM+ is the embodiment of Microsoft's decision to integrate MTS with COM—in preparation for a future that they believe demands stateless environments and increasingly scalable applications. COM+ is introduced as part of Windows 2000. We'll see more about MTS (and a little of COM+) in Chapters 6 and 7.*

When to use ObjectContext

Microsoft is suggesting that ScriptingContext should only be used in legacy ASP applications. ObjectContext is a more natural choice as part of Microsoft's long-term plan for COM, and therefore they recommend that ObjectContext be used in IIS4- and IIS5-specific code, although ScriptingContext is still *supported* in IIS versions 4 and 5. Microsoft's strategy suggests that we can't be sure that ScriptingContext will be available in future versions of IIS.

So what we'll do is build a component that is able to adjust to its calling environment. In IIS4 and IIS5, we'll use the ObjectContext in the implementation, as recommended by Microsoft. In IIS3, and in PWS, we'll use the ScriptingContext. The trick is in detecting the environment, and we'll show you how to do that too.

An ASP Component that Detects its Environment

The component that we're going to create is called **ASPCollections**. This component will be able to iterate through any of the five collections of the `Request` object, and will write the contents of these collections into the page currently being generated by ASP. We'll come to the specific code that we'll use to implement this functionality shortly. First we'll take a look at how we'll detect the environment.

In this component, there are really two things that we need to know. We need to check whether the component has been called from an ASP page and if so, we need to know which web server (and which version) is hosting that web page.

Are We Running Under ASP?

The first question we should address is how we detect whether we are running under ASP. This might seem a little strange, since we know we're building an ASP component but as we mentioned a little earlier, it's worth looking into if we're in the business of selling our components. If a user tries to instantiate this component in a browser, it would be a little more professional if the object were able to, for example, display a warning—instead of just dying in the page.

In fact, it's easy to detect whether or not we're running under ASP. Remember the `OnStartPage()` method that we used in the `BeanAdder` component earlier? When the component is instantiated (within the ASP page, using `Server.CreateObject()`), ASP looks for the `OnStartPage()` method in the component's interface and invokes the method if it's found—passing a reference to the `ScriptingContext` object as the method's only argument. Within the `OnStartPage()` method, we can capture that reference in a variable—the global variable `gobjSContext` in this case—and then we can use it within the component's implementation:

```
Private gobjSContext As Object       'global ScriptingContext object reference

Public Sub OnStartPage(objContext As Object)
    'executed by ASP when it loads the page and starts to execute it
    Set gobjSContext = objContext 'the context passed by ASP
    Call SetGlobalObjects
End Sub
```

Even though we don't always use `OnStartPage()` in IIS 4.0 and above, it's still there to support legacy components—and it's likely to continue to be supported in new versions of ASP for the foreseeable future.

> *Again, it's worth mentioning that `OnStartPage()` is only invoked if the component is instantiated using `Server.CreateObject()`. The VBScript `CreateObject()` method doesn't have the desired effect.*

Then, elsewhere within the component we can check to see whether our global object reference really does point to a valid object. If it does, we can conclude that we must be running under ASP:

```
If Not gobjSContext Is Nothing Then        ' gobjSContext is populated then ...
    ' ... we're running under ASP
    ...
Else
    ' ... no ScriptingContext object, so we aren't running under ASP
    ...
End If
```

If So, Which Version?

OK, so assuming we're running in an ASP environment, how do we find out which Web server software is underlying? One way to find out is by parsing the contents of the `Request` object's `ServerVariables` `collection`: the `ServerVariables("SERVER_SOFTWARE")` value contains a value such as **Microsoft-IIS/4.0** (for ASP pages hosted on IIS4 or PWS4) or **Microsoft-IIS/3.0** for IIS3. This solution would work but in order to implement it we'd need to access the `Request.ServerVariables` collection via the `ScriptingContext` object, which rather defeats the point of the exercise. We're trying to avoid using `ScriptingContext` if `ObjectContext` is available.

Instead, we'll find out the necessary information by accessing the registry, which contains a range of reliable values about the host system. The IIS/PWS program group and version number are stored under the following key in the registry:

`HKEY_LOCAL_MACHINE\Software\Microsoft\InetStp\`

The information we want is that of the **IISProgramGroup** and **MajorVersion** values:

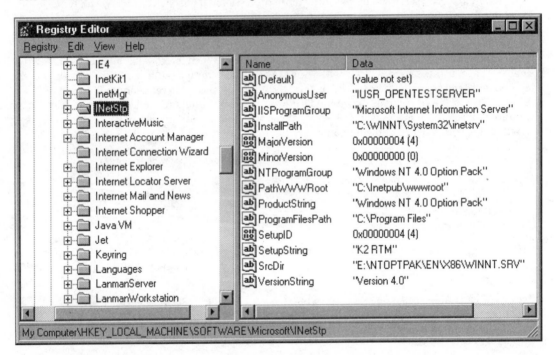

The value of **IISProgramGroup** will be either Microsoft Internet Information Server or Microsoft Personal Web Server (both fairly self-explanatory). The value of **MajorVersion** value will be 3 for IIS3/PWS1, 4 for IIS4/PWS4, and 5 for IIS5.

Accessing the Registry

There are also many other useful entries here. However, reading these extended registry values is not an elementary task. Unfortunately, the registry access functions in Visual Basic can't get at this part of the Registry. We could resort to hitting the Windows API directly, but we won't. Instead, we'll use a commercial component that can read the registry directly, and this makes it a simple task. The component we've used is called RegEx—this literally allows us to sub-contract the hard part of our task.

> *The DLL that hosts this component is downloadable from http://webdev.wrox.co.uk/books/2882/. The version that we've made available is a 60-day trial version of a component that has been made available by Stonebroom Software (http://www.stonebroom.com). Note that Microsoft has also released a free registry component, called Registry Access 1.0, which will also perform the task of querying the registry for you. At the time of writing, Registry Access 1.0 is available at http://www.microsoft.com/NTServer/nts/downloads/archive/IISRegistryAccess/default.asp.*
>
> *Windows API programming requires some care—if you're writing your own Windows API functions then you're well advised to save your work on a regular basis, as mistakes can cause your machine to crash. Windows API programming is beyond the scope of this book; if you want to learn more about using the Win32 API from Visual Basic, try Visual Basic 6 Win32 API Tutorial (Wrox, ISBN 1-861002-43-2).*

The way we use RegEx within our component to access the registry is easy. First, we create the object instance using CreateObject():

```
Set objRegEx = CreateObject("Stonebroom.RegEx")
```

Having instantiated this object, we only use one of its methods: GetRegExValue(). This method has four parameters. The first two are input parameters that tell the method where to look in the registry for the data (in registry terms these are known as the hive and the subkey). The third is another input parameter, which specifies the element that we're searching for in that part of the registry. The fourth is an output parameter, which records the data type of the parameter. We use the method twice, to retrieve the program group and version number:

```
strValueName = "MajorVersion"
varMajorVersion = objRegEx.GetRegValueEx(HKEY_LOCAL_MACHINE, _
                  strSubKey, strValueName, varValueType)
strValueName = "IISProgramGroup"
strProgGroup = objRegEx.GetRegValueEx(HKEY_LOCAL_MACHINE, _
                  strSubKey, strValueName, varProgGroupType)
```

Once we've received those values, we can destroy the RegEx instance (because we've finished with it). Then we can compare the retrieved values with those that we expect to find, and set a Boolean flag blnIsIIS4 accordingly:

```
Set objRegEx = Nothing
If (varValueType = REG_DWORD) And (IsNumeric(varMajorVersion)) And _
 (varProgGroupType = REG_SZ) And _
 (InStr(strProgGroup, "Microsoft Internet Information Server") <> 0) Then
   blnIsIIS4 = (CLng(varMajorVersion) >= 4)
End If
```

Then, the value of blnIsIIS4 will determine how the object behaves for the rest of its life. If blnIsIIS4 is true then we'll get a reference to the ObjectContext object, and access the ASP intrinsic objects from there. If blnIsIIS4 is false then we'll assume that ObjectContext is unavailable, and we'll proceed with legacy code, using a reference to the ScriptingContext object to access the ASP intrinsic objects instead.

Again, we could spend all day debating which is the better solution for accessing host machine information: via the Request.ServerVariables collection (which depends on the ScriptingContext) or using a third-party component such as RegEx (which means that we have to distribute RegEx with our own component). We've decided to go for the latter, because it gives us the opportunity to show one component's interface being made available within another component's implementation. It also gives us a chance to notice that there's a wealth of useful information available in the registry.

Putting It All Together

Start by installing and registering stnregex.dll onto your machine. This DLL is the host for the RegEx component that we'll be using in the component.

Next, fire up the Visual Basic IDE: change the default project name from Project1 to WroxCollections and the default class name from Class1 to ASPCollections. Now set up the type library references, using the References dialog from the Project menu. You'll need to add three references to the component—the Microsoft Active Server Pages Object Library (for ScriptingContext), the Microsoft Transaction Server Type Library (for ObjectContext) and the Stonebroom library (for RegEx):

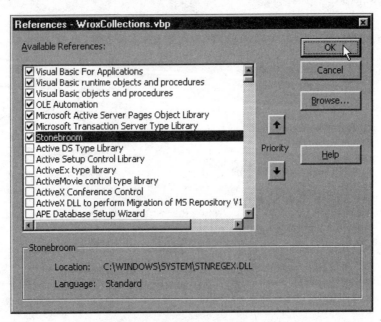

Global Variables

Now we can add the code to the component. We'll list all of the code over the next few pages, and we'll step through it as we go. First, here are the global variables:

```
Option Explicit

Private gobjSContext As Object    'global ScriptingContext object reference
Private gobjRequest As Object     'global Request object reference
Private gobjResponse As Object    'global Response object reference
```

We have three global variables in our component:

- ❏ gobjSContext will hold a reference to the ScriptingContext object (this is the same technique we used in the BeanAdder function earlier

- ❏ gobjRequest will hold a reference to the ASP Request object

- ❏ gobjResponse will hold a reference to the ASP Response object

The OnStartPage Method

gobjSContext is initialized when OnStartPage() executes, just as we saw in the BeanAdder component earlier in the chapter:

```
Public Sub OnStartPage(objContext As Object)
   'executed by ASP when it loads the page and starts to execute it
   Set gobjSContext = objContext 'the context passed by ASP
   Call SetGlobalObjects
End Sub
```

In this component, the OnStartPage() method performs an extra action. We can't initialize the other two global variables immediately, because we first need to establish whether we'll use the ScriptingContext or the ObjectContext. For that we need to determine the calling environment, and that's done by calling SetGlobalObjects().

The SetGlobalObjects Method

The SetGlobalObjects() private function is where our environment detection code lives. SetGlobalObjects() is called from OnStartPage(), which means that the environment detection code will run each time we instantiate a component from an ASP page using Server.CreateObject():

```
Private Sub SetGlobalObjects()
   Dim blnIsIIS4 As Boolean  'we'll set this to true if running under IIS4+
   blnIsIIS4 = False         'assume not IIS4 to start

   If Not gobjSContext Is Nothing Then
      'variable and constants for RegEx component
      Const HKEY_LOCAL_MACHINE = 2
      Const REG_SZ = 1
      Const REG_DWORD = 4
      Dim objRegEx As Object
      Dim strSubKey As String
      Dim strValueName As String
      Dim varValueType As Variant
      Dim varMajorVersion As Variant
      Dim strProgGroup As String
      Dim varProgGroupType As Variant
```

Here's where we create the `RegEx` object, and use it to establish information about the calling environment, as we saw earlier:

```
    'try and instantiate the RegEx component
    Set objRegEx = CreateObject("Stonebroom.RegEx")
    If Not objRegEx Is Nothing Then
        'get the IIS major version number (if any)
        strSubKey = "Software\Microsoft\InetStp"
        strValueName = "MajorVersion"
        varMajorVersion = objRegEx.GetRegValueEx(HKEY_LOCAL_MACHINE, _
                          strSubKey, strValueName, varValueType)
        strValueName = "IISProgramGroup"
        strProgGroup = objRegEx.GetRegValueEx(HKEY_LOCAL_MACHINE, _
                          strSubKey, strValueName, varProgGroupType)
        Set objRegEx = Nothing
        'see if we got a version, and check if it's 4 or later
        If (varValueType = REG_DWORD) And (IsNumeric(varMajorVersion)) And _
          (varProgGroupType = REG_SZ) And _
          (InStr(strProgGroup, "Microsoft Internet Information Server") <> 0) Then
            blnIsIIS4 = (CLng(varMajorVersion) >= 4)
        End If
    End If
```

Now the value of the Boolean, `blnIsIIS4`, dictates whether we set the global variables `gobjRequest` and `gobjResponse` via a `ObjectContext` reference or a `ScriptingContext` reference:

```
    'now we can use the version information to see which way to handle context
    If blnIsIIS4 Then
                            ' IIS4 or later, so we can get the MTS ObjectContext
        ' get a reference to ObjectContext
        Dim objLocalContext As ObjectContext
        Set objLocalContext = GetObjectContext()

        ' set global object references
        Set gobjResponse = objLocalContext("Response")
        Set gobjRequest = objLocalContext("Request")
    Else
                            'not IIS4 or later, so we can't use ObjectContext
        ' set global object references
        Set gobjRequest = gobjSContext.Request
        Set gobjResponse = gobjSContext.Response

        ' use the global object context passed to the OnStartPage
        ' routine to write the result to the page
    End If
  End If
End Sub
```

The Private Helper Functions

Before we look at the component's single public method, it makes sense to take a look at the private helper functions. First, we have five functions—`ShowForm()`, `ShowQueryString()`, `ShowClientCertificate()`, `ShowServerVariables()` and `ShowCookies()`—each of which is responsible for displaying the contents of one of the `Request` object's five collections. Here are four of them (we'll see the fifth in a moment):

```
Private Sub ShowForm()
   IterateCollection gobjRequest.Form
End Sub
```

```
Private Sub ShowQueryString()
   IterateCollection gobjRequest.QueryString
End Sub
```

```
Private Sub ShowClientCertificate()
   IterateCollection gobjRequest.ClientCertificate
End Sub
```

```
Private Sub ShowServerVariables()
   IterateCollection gobjRequest.ServerVariables
End Sub
```

To iterate through each of these collections, we use a private helper function called
`IterateCollection()`:

```
Private Sub IterateCollection(colThis As Object)
   Dim objItem As Variant
   Dim intLoop As Integer
   'loop through the specified collection
   For Each objItem In colThis
      'loop through each subkey in each item
      For intLoop = 1 To colThis(objItem).Count
         gobjResponse.Write objItem & " = " & _
                                 colThis(objItem)(intLoop) & "<BR>"
      Next
   Next
End Sub
```

This subroutine accepts any one of the ASP collection objects as a parameter. Note that these are not the
same as the generic VBScript collections, so we declare the parameter as being of type `Object` rather than
`Collection`. Inside the subroutine, we iterate through each member of the collection with a `For Each`
construct. This is because the ASP collections can contain items that are themselves arrays of name/value
pairs (in other words, a collection can have sub-keys), and so we also need to iterate through these, using a
second nested loop.

Once we've got each sub-key (or the single key for that item) we can write it into the page in much the
same way as we do in ASP script—using the `Write()` method of the `Response` object. The only
difference is that the method we're calling is `gobjResponse.Write()`—that is, we're calling the
`Write()` method through the global reference to the `Response` object that we created in the
`SetGlobalObjects()` method.

The one case where this simple formula won't work is with the `Request.Cookies` collection, which is
specially designed to hold the values of all the cookies sent to the server from the client. These may
contain more than just a simple name/value pair so to cope with this specific format, each item in the
collection is itself a collection (rather than a simple array). Each item also has a `HasKeys` property, which
is `true` if there is a collection of cookies for that item, rather than a single cookie.

So, to display the contents of the `Cookies` collection, we use this subroutine:

```
Private Sub ShowCookies()
   Dim objItem As Variant
   Dim objItemKey As Variant
   'loop through the Request.Cookies collection
   For Each objItem In gobjRequest.Cookies
      If gobjRequest.Cookies(objItem).HasKeys Then
         'use another 'For Each' to iterate all keys of dictionary
         For Each objItemKey In gobjRequest.Cookies(objItem)
            gobjResponse.Write objItem & "(" & objItemKey & ") = " & _
                        gobjRequest.Cookies(objItem)(objItemKey) & "<BR>"
         Next
      Else
         'print out the cookie string as normal
         gobjResponse.Write objItem & " = " & _
                     gobjRequest.Cookies(objItem) & "<BR>"
      End If
   Next
End Sub
```

Of course, our page won't be able to detect cookies that were supplied to the client by other servers. So when we come to test our component, we'll supply a few cookies in advance.

The Public ShowCollections Method

We'll add a single method to the component's interface—the ShowCollections() method can be called by the client, and will itself call some or all of the five Show… helper functions that we just saw:

```
Public Sub ShowCollections()
  If Not gobjSContext Is Nothing Then
    If gobjRequest.Form("chkForm") = "on" Then
      gobjResponse.Write "<H3>The Request.Form collection</H3>"
      ShowForm
      gobjResponse.Write "<HR>"
    End If
    If gobjRequest.Form("chkQString") = "on" Then
      gobjResponse.Write "<H3>The Request.QueryString collection</H3>"
      ShowQueryString
      gobjResponse.Write "<HR>"
    End If
    If gobjRequest.Form("chkCCert") = "on" Then
      gobjResponse.Write "<H3>The Request.ClientCertificate collection</H3>"
      ShowClientCertificate
      gobjResponse.Write "<HR>"
    End If
    If gobjRequest.Form("chkCookies") = "on" Then
      gobjResponse.Write "<H3>The Request.Cookies collection</H3>"
      ShowCookies
      gobjResponse.Write "<HR>"
    End If
    If gobjRequest.Form("chkServerV") = "on" Then
      gobjResponse.Write "<H3>The Request.ServerVariables collection</H3>"
      ShowServerVariables
      gobjResponse.Write "<HR>"
    End If
  Else
    MsgBox "Sorry: this component is for use in an ASP environment only! " & _
           Chr$(10) & _
           "Ask your administrator to consult the component's documentation."
  End If
End Sub
```

It's essentially a set of five If…End If statements—one for each of the Request object's collections. It reads each of the five variables in the Request.Form collection, and decides (based on the values of those variables) which of the collections it will display. The thing to notice about this public function and all the helper functions is that they can access ASP's intrinsic objects through the global variables that we set when the object was created in the page.

There's one more thing to do before you compile the
component. Because we're may be using the
ObjectContext object, we need to set the
MTSTransactionMode to 1–NoTransactions, so that the
object may be registered within MTS:

This ensures that the object is not transactional, but does make the ObjectContext available where
necessary. You'll see more of this in the MTS chapters, later in the book.

Now you can compile the component as normal—select File | Make WroxCollections.dll. When you've
compiled, select Project | WroxCollections properties and choose the Component tab. Here, change the
Version Compatibility property to Binary Compatibility—this ensures that if you recompile, certain
properties of the component (e.g. the CLSID) don't change. This is useful if you're using the CLSID
directly (as we'll do later on)—and we'll see it used again in this book.

Using the ASPCollections Component

Here's a simple page, Show_Collections.asp, that uses the component. The page contains five
checkboxes that allow you to select which collections you want to display, and a button to start off the
process by submitting the form back to the server:

```
<%@LANGUAGE="VBSCRIPT"%>
<%
'create some cookies on the client
Response.Cookies("simplecookie") = "testvalue"
Response.Cookies("testcookie")("value1") = "testvalue1"
Response.Cookies("testcookie")("value2") = "testvalue2"
%>

<HTML>
<HEAD>
<TITLE>Reading ASP Collections - in IIS 3.0, 4.0 or 5.0</TITLE>
</HEAD>
<BODY>
<FONT FACE="Tahoma,Verdana,Arial,sans-serif" SIZE="2">
This page allows users to browse the contents of the Request object's collections.
<BR>
In <B>IIS3</B>, the component accesses the ASP object model via the
<B>ScriptingContext</B> object. <BR>
In <B>IIS4 and later</B>, the component accesses the ASP object model via MTS's
<B>ObjectContext</B> object. <BR>
<HR>

<H3>Select the collections to display:</H3>
<FORM METHOD="POST"
    ACTION="<%=Request.ServerVariables("SCRIPT_NAME")%>?value1=dummy&value2=test">
<INPUT TYPE="CHECKBOX" NAME="chkForm">
```

```
                            <B>Request.Form</B> collection<P>
<INPUT TYPE="CHECKBOX" NAME="chkQString">
                            <B>Request.QueryString</B> collection<P>
<INPUT TYPE="CHECKBOX" NAME="chkCCert">
                            <B>Request.ClientCertificate</B> collection<P>
<INPUT TYPE="CHECKBOX" NAME="chkCookies">
                            <B>Request.Cookies</B> collection<P>
<INPUT TYPE="CHECKBOX" NAME="chkServerV">
                            <B>Request.ServerVariables</B> collection<P>
<INPUT TYPE="SUBMIT" VALUE="Show">
</FORM>

<%
On Error Resume Next

If Request.Form.Count > 0 Then
  'create the component instance
  Set objWroxCol = Server.CreateObject("WroxCollections.ASPCollections")
  If IsObject(objWroxCol) Then                  'see if it was created OK
  objWroxCol.ShowCollections
  Else
    'couldn't create the component instance
    Response.Write "ASP could not create the object on the server.<HR>"
  End If
  Set objWroxCol = Nothing
End If
%>
<FONT FACE="Tahoma,Verdana,Arial,sans-serif" SIZE=1>
<P>&copy;1999 Wrox Press Limited, UK and USA</P></FONT>
</BODY>
</HTML>
```

This is what we get when we first load the page. We've selected two collections that we want to view:

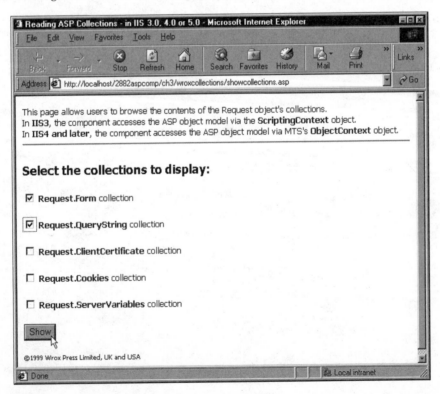

Populated Collections

When you hit the **Show** button, the page is reloaded. Just to populate the `QueryString` collection, the URL specified in the form's `ACTION` attribute also adds a couple of querystring parameters:

```
<FORM METHOD="POST"
    ACTION="<%=Request.ServerVariables("SCRIPT_NAME")%>?value1=dummy&value2=test">
    ...
</FORM>
```

The `Form` collection will contain the values that we `POST` to the server from the form, so there will be something to see there and the `ServerVariables` collection will have plenty of content because the browser fills it with a whole range of values automatically for every request.

If you want, you can arrange to put some dummy values into the `Cookies` collection by adding a little ASP code right at the start of the page:

```
<%@LANGUAGE="VBSCRIPT"%>
<%
'create some cookies on the client
Response.Cookies("simplecookie") = "testvalue"
Response.Cookies("testcookie")("value1") = "testvalue1"
Response.Cookies("testcookie")("value2") = "testvalue2"
%>
...
```

Note that cookies (along with any other HTTP variables you need) are transmitted to the browser as part of the HTTP headers. Therefore, they should be created *before* you send any other output (such as text or HTML) back to the browser.

The `ClientCertificate` collection could still be empty. We can't do much about that unless we deploy a certificate on the client, install the ASP page into a secure directory, and enable SSL so we can then access the page with `https://`.

Executing the Component's ShowCollections Method

The block of ASP at the end of the page contains the code that instantiates the component that we've just created, and calls the `ShowCollections()` method, which in turn calls whichever `Show...` methods were requested—which depends on which checkboxes were set when the page was submitted:

```
If Request.Form.Count > 0 Then
  'create the component instance
  Set objWroxCol = Server.CreateObject("WroxCollections.ASPCollections")
  If IsObject(objWroxCol) Then                    'see if it was created OK
  objWroxCol.ShowCollections
  Else
    'couldn't create the component instance
    Response.Write "ASP could not create the object on the server.<HR>"
  End If
  Set objWroxCol = Nothing
End If
```

Here's the result, showing the contents of the `Form` and `QueryString` collections. The ASP code you've just seen is placed after the `<FORM>` section of the page, so that the results of the previous submission are shown at the foot of the page. The form can then be resubmitted to view other collections:

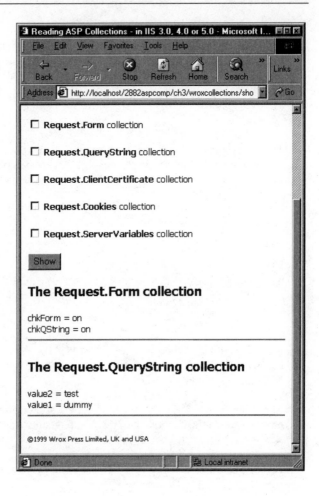

The ServerVariables Collection

The other really useful collection that the `Request` object provides is the `ServerVariables` collection. Although the name doesn't sound very exciting, you've already seen how we used one member, the `SCRIPT_NAME` variable, in our example page. The following screenshot shows the result of executing the sample page for the `ServerVariables` collection on our server and with our browser—the results *you* get will be different:

There's a lot of useful information here. It's all available for use in ASP code, and is extracted using a line like the following:

```
strHeader = gobjRequest.ServerVariables("SERVER_PORT")
```

In this case we're using the global reference to the `Request` object to access the value of the server port.

Closing Down Gracefully

The `ASPCollections` component is very environment-dependent—if it's not called from an ASP scripting environment, then there is no `ScriptingContext` object and certainly no `ObjectContext` object, so it won't function. Indeed, it's unlikely that anyone would try to use it in a non-ASP situation, because it's not applicable to such a situation, but we've put in a little mechanism to help things not to break down horribly if they do.

To demonstrate, try using the object client-side on a pure HTML page like the following:

```
<HTML>
<HEAD>
<TITLE>Testing WroxCollections.ASPCollections in a Browser</TITLE>

<SCRIPT LANGUAGE="JavaScript">
<!--
function TestComponent() {
  var objObject = document.all("ASPCollObject");
  objObject.ShowCollections();
}
//-->
</SCRIPT>
</HEAD>

<BODY>
<FONT FACE="Tahoma,Verdana,Arial,sans-serif" SIZE="2">
This page demonstrates that the <B>WroxCollections.ASPCollections</B> component
will close down gracefully when called client-side.<P>
<HR>

<!-- create the WroxCollections.ASPCollections object -->
<!-- you'll need to consult the registry to check your object's CLSID -->
<OBJECT CLASSID="clsid:11A2De20-5D8B-11D3-99B1-00104B4C84A4" ID="ASPCollObject">
</OBJECT>

<CENTER>
<INPUT TYPE="BUTTON" VALUE="Test ASPCollections Component"
       ONCLICK="TestComponent()">
</CENTER>
<HR>
<FONT FACE="Tahoma,Verdana,Arial,sans-serif" SIZE=1>
<P>&copy;1999 Wrox Press Limited, UK and USA</P></FONT>
</BODY></HTML>
```

You'll need to browse to this page using a machine that has the `WroxCollections.ASPCollections` DLL installed and registered on it, because the browser is going to instantiate the object client-side. The `<OBJECT>` tag creates an instance of the object specified by the CLSID. The CLSID of the component may be different from the one shown here—you'll be able to find the CLSID in the registry by running `RegEdit.exe` and navigating to \HKEY_CLASSES_ROOT\WroxCollections.ASPCollections\Clsid:

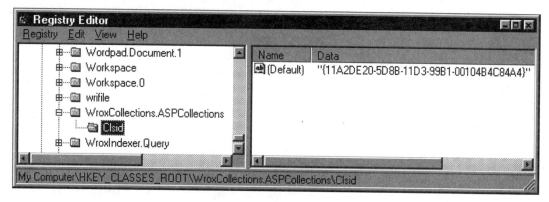

Here's what the page looks like:

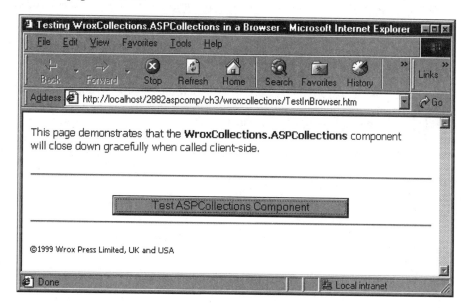

When you hit the **Test ASPCollections Component** button, it calls the JavaScript `TestComponent()` function—which assigns the object to a variable, and then uses that to call the object's `ShowCollections()` function. The component recognizes that there's no `ScriptingContext`, and therefore it's not being called within an IIS environment. So it politely apologizes to the end-user accordingly.

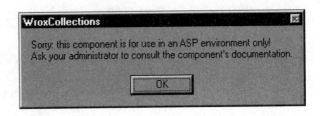

Summary

We began this chapter by considering some component design issues (more design issues will be covered in Chapter 5), but we focused in particular on how we can write components that interact with other components and elements of the calling environment. Writing components that interact with IIS is of particular interest to us as ASP component writers.

Generally (and with the exception of some task-specific components that implement business rules), we'd like our components to be as reusable as possible. There are levels of reusability. Our component might be reusable only within a specific environment (for example, the `BeanAdder` and `ASPCollections` components in this chapter are reusable within any IIS environment—but they make specific and valuable use of the environment's functionality). Other components are employable within a far wider range of environments (such as the components we saw in the first two chapters of the book).

We implemented two components, both of which were able to interact with the ASP objects provided by the IIS calling environment. The ASP objects were made available within the component's implementation via a reference to either the `ScriptingContext` object or the `ObjectContext` object. The `ASPCollections` component was adaptive, in that it was able to detect information about the calling environment and adjust its behavior accordingly.

In the next chapter, we'll take a look at a subject that lies at the heart of very many web applications—data access.

Universal Data Access Through ADO and COM

Take a look around the Web and you'll see that a great many sites are there specifically to deliver information—news stories, pictures, statistics, the list is endless. Look at the average intranet system and you'll find that the same principle holds—perhaps your company's intranet is able to deliver customer information, account details, employee records, business reports…

The point is that all this information has to be stored somewhere—and increasingly, data is stored in many different locations and formats. When an end-user requests the information, the infrastructure needs to be in place that can locate the data, retrieve it from its native format, and return it to the page.

Microsoft has a vision of universal access to all types of data. This vision encompasses two sets of COM components—Object Linking and Embedding Database (OLE DB) and ActiveX Data Objects (ADO). Because they're COM objects, they integrate naturally into our objective for creating ASP applications using components. In this chapter, we'll look at how these two technologies fit into Microsoft's data access solution, and we'll focus in particular on using ADO to access different data sources. Throughout, we'll be using the COM concept of component interfacing to connect our components and applications together.

So, in this chapter, you'll see:

- ❑ What the concept of Universal Data Access actually means, and what it involves
- ❑ The relationship between ADO and OLE DB, and how they provide data access
- ❑ How ADO provides the interface between components and various types of data store
- ❑ How disconnected recordsets are important in component development
- ❑ A component that uses ADO to access a database
- ❑ A component that uses ADO to index a web site
- ❑ Demonstrations of these components from ASP pages and via RDS components

We start off with a look at how ADO creates and implements a universal data access environment for our components.

Universal Data Access

What is **Universal Data Access (UDA)**? Is it just another acronym to confuse the programmer? Is it another set of strict rules to be followed when developing programs? Luckily, it is neither. UDA is a Microsoft strategy—a well-defined set of state of the art technologies. The objective of UDA is that you should be able to use a *single* device to access *any* type of data.

When you consider the way in which computers are changing the way we work, you can see that this is no bad thing. With the rise of the microcomputer, developers have found two new problems to contend with. First, data is more widely distributed about the organization; gone are the days when all data was held centrally on a mainframe. Second, data is being stored in a variety of different formats. Relational databases have become the norm in many companies, but relational databases are not the only source of data. There are spreadsheets, Web pages, graphics, mail systems, and so on—they all contain data too.

It seems unreasonable to expect programmers to use a different method to access different forms of data in different locations, but this is exactly what they have to do. UDA is designed to overcome this by promoting a system that allows all forms of data to be accessed in the same way.

OLE DB and ADO

In order to achieve the dream of UDA, Microsoft have given us two different (but related) technologies—called **Object Linking and Embedding Database (OLE DB)** and **ActiveX Data Objects (ADO)**. The general idea is that you call the data access layer (ADO or OLE DB) from your application, and let it handle the data from the data source. This allows you to use a single method for accessing data—whatever the type of data.

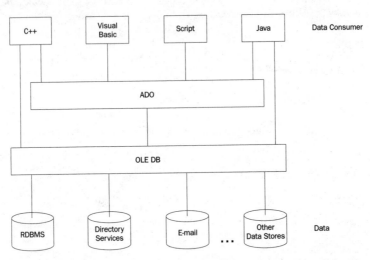

OLE DB is a set of COM objects that provide a common set of functionality for accessing data. OLE DB is relatively low-level, and is really only accessible through lower-level languages such as C++. OLE DB is not designed to be accessed directly from Visual Basic, due to its complex interfaces.

By contrast, **ADO** is a higher-level model of OLE DB—which means that it's somewhat easier to use but allows a little less overall control. Visual Basic and scripting languages use ADO to talk to OLE DB, and hence access data.

> *In this early part of the book, we're focusing on Visual Basic and ASP: therefore, a discussion of direct OLE DB usage would be really out of place in this chapter. We'll defer it until Chapter 12 instead. However, it's important to know that OLE DB is there, so that we can get a proper understanding of how ADO works in relation to OLE DB.*

ADO provides us with a level of usability that we're used to—we create ADO objects, and call their methods and properties. And because ADO objects are ActiveX objects, they can be used from *any* language that supports COM—including Visual Basic, VBA, scripting languages, Visual C++, and so on.

ADO and OLE DB are available in a single install, as part of a product called **Microsoft Data Access Components** (**MDAC**). At the time writing, MDAC version 2.1 is the most recent release. MDAC 2.5 will ship with Windows 2000, and will also be available as a separate download for use on other platforms.

Data Providers and Data Consumers

When dealing with ADO and/or OLE DB, it's important to understand the difference between the supplier of the data and the user of the data:

❑ A **data provider** is (unsurprisingly) something that provides data. Note that the data provider isn't the physical source of the data—rather, it's the *mechanism* that connects us to the physical data store. This means that there will be a data provider for each different type of data store.

❑ A **data consumer** is something that uses (or consumes) data. The consumer is usually something like an application, a Web page, or a component. Strictly speaking, ADO is actually a consumer, because (as we just saw in the diagram) it uses data provided by OLE DB.

ADO (indirectly through OLE DB) and OLE DB are designed to use data providers to access different types of data. We have to stop thinking solely about databases—because the source of the data might be something other than a database. Consequently, we often use the term **data store** because it gives a much clearer indication that we're referring to the store of data itself (rather than the way in which the data is stored).

OLE DB uses a specific data provider to access a specific type of data source. The following is a list of the *initial* set of providers that ships with MDAC 2.1. Looking down the list of providers, you can begin to get an idea of the number of different data types out there:

OLE DB Provider	Description
Jet 4.0	For Microsoft Access databases. This allows access to standard Access databases, including linked tables. (ADO 2.0 shipped with the Jet 3.5 provider.)
Directory Services	For resource data, such as Active Directory. This becomes more important with the release of Windows 2000, because the Directory Service will allow access to user information as well as network devices.
Index Server	For Microsoft Index Server. This will be particularly useful as web sites grow, allowing us to index the data on our site and even create dynamic query forms.
Site Server Search	For Microsoft Site Server. Again for use with web sites—especially large complex sites which are maintained with the help of Site Server.
ODBC Drivers	For existing ODBC drivers. This ensures that legacy data is not omitted as part of the drive forward.
Oracle	For Oracle databases. Connection to Oracle data stores has never been particularly easy with Microsoft products in the past, but a native driver will simplify access to existing Oracle data stores.
SQL Server	For Microsoft SQL Server, to allow access to data stored in SQL Server data stores.
Data Shape	For hierarchical recordsets. This allows drilling down into detailed data via creation of master/detail-type recordsets.
Persisted Recordset	For locally saved recordsets and recordset marshalling.
OLAP	For accessing On Line Analytical Processing data stores.
Internet Publishing	For accessing web resources that support Microsoft FrontPage Server Extensions or Distributed Authoring and Versioning (DAV). For more information on DAV check out the WebDAV Working Group home page at http://www.ics.uci.edu/~ejw/authoring/.
Remoting Provider	For connecting to data providers on remote machines.

You don't need to know about all these now—the point is that there are very many types of data, and that ADO and OLE DB can allow you to handle most of them. This is just the list of standard data providers supplied by Microsoft with MDAC 2.1; other vendors are actively creating their own. For example, most database suppliers have released OLE DB providers for their own databases.

OLE DB Providers and ODBC Drivers

Some data providers get the data directly from the data store—others may go through a third party product to get to the data store. A data provider can even use other data providers as the source of data, and provide added value along the way.

For example, OLE DB can use **Open Database Connectivity (ODBC)** to access existing relational databases. ODBC predates OLE DB, and was designed to provide a common set of data access functions in a similar way to OLE DB. It was designed as a cross-platform, database-independent method for data access, and used **drivers** to do the work. However, ODBC was more complex to use than OLE DB, and it was also more limited in that it was targeted specifically at relational databases.

So, if OLE DB is the panacea for data access, why is ODBC still relevant? Well, although OLE DB can talk directly to some relational databases, it can only do this if an appropriate data provider exists. If there is no data provider, but there's an ODBC driver that does the job, then OLE DB can use the ODBC driver to access the data. This means that you can immediately start using ADO to access any existing data store that supports ODBC—even if it isn't supported by an OLE DB provider yet.

Here's how OLE DB providers relate to ODBC drivers. Effectively, the ODBC standard is being encapsulated within the all-encompassing OLE DB vision via the **OLE DB Provider for ODBC Drivers**. Take a look at the following diagram:

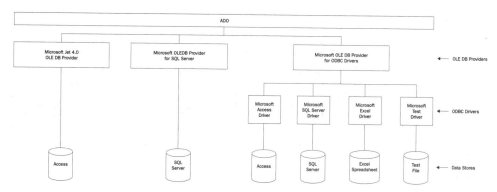

This distinctly shows the two layers at work. OLE DB providers can be used to access data sources, including ODBC data sources. This allows OLE DB to access data for which there is an ODBC driver, but no native OLEDB provider.

> **Let me just reinforce the terminology: OLE DB uses providers, and ODBC uses drivers.**

The ADO Objects

In this section we'll meet the objects that ADO provides, and we'll look at the essentials that we'll need in order to start building data access components for our ASP applications. Before you can understand some of the features of ADO, you need to know what it actually provides you with. There are three main objects:

❏ A Connection object represents a connection to a data store. In addition, it allows us to interrogate the data store to see what facilities it supports, and gives us the ability to run commands against the data store.

❏ A Command object represents commands that can be run against the data store. In many cases, a command can be a SQL query, or another type of query that returns a set of data. Although this facility is inherent in the Connection object, the Command object allows more complex commands, such as those with parameters.

❏ A Recordset object represents a recordset: a vessel for holding data. Often, we'll use a recordset to contain the data retrieved as the result of a command; we can also create and populate our own 'stand-alone' recordsets that exist without a data store in the background. With a Recordset object, we can also read and manipulate the data contained in the recordset.

There are four subsidiary objects:

❏ A Field object represents an individual field (or column) in a recordset.

❏ A Error object represents details of a single error that may have occurred during a command.

❏ A Parameter object represents the details of a single parameter for a stored procedure or stored query (that is, a pre-compiled procedure or query that resides in the data store itself).

❏ A Property object represents a provider-specific property. ADO can talk to many different types of providers, and it is by use of the Property object that the provider can indicate any special facilities that it provides.

ADO also provides four collections—Fields, Errors, Parameters, and Properties. Each of these holds a collection of associated subsidiary objects (for example, the Properties collection holds zero or more Property objects). The relationship between all these objects and collections is shown in the diagram:

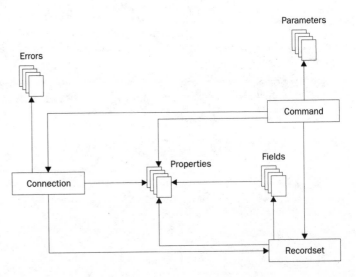

Connection Strings

In order to connect to a data store, we need to tell ADO a few essential pieces of information: for example, the name of the data store, where to look for it, and which data provider to use. We use a **connection string** to provide these details. By their very nature, connection strings are an important part of connecting through ADO.

A Connection String for a SQL Server Database

The following is an example connection string that gives all the information that ADO needs to connect to a Microsoft SQL Server data store:

```
"Provider=SQLOLEDB; Data Source=Tigger; Initial Catalog=pubs; User Id=sa; Password="
```

You can see that each nugget of information here is contained in an expression of the form *connection_property=value*. The properties are:

Connection Property	Description
Provider	The name of the OLE DB provider. In the example above, we've chosen SQLOLEDB, which is the OLE DB Provider for Microsoft SQL Server data stores.
Data Source	The supplier of the data. In this case we've put Tigger, which is the name of my SQL Server.
Initial Catalog	The source of the data. The example above selects pubs, which is the name of one of the sample databases supplied with SQL Server.
User Id	The name or ID of the user with which to connect to the data store. The example above, we'll connect to the data store using the sa account.
Password	The password for the user. We've specified the zero-length password here.

The exact form of your connection string will depend on which OLE DB data provider you're using. If you're using a SQL Server data store, and therefore the SQLOLEDB data provider should suit you fine. Here are a few other examples.

A Connection String for an Access Database

If you're accessing a Microsoft Access database via the OLE DB Provider for Microsoft Access, then your connection string might look like this:

```
"Provider=Microsoft.Jet.OLEDB.4.0; Data Source=C:\data\MyDataBase.mdb"
```

Connection Strings for ODBC Data Sources

To connect to a data source via OLE DB and ODBC, you need to specify the OLE DB Provider or ODBC Drivers (curiously named MSDASQL), the name of the ODBC driver, and the name and location of the data source. For example, for an Access database:

```
"Provider=MSDASQL;Driver={Microsoft Access Driver (*.mdb)};DBQ=C:\data\MyDataBase.mdb"
```

127

Accessing other data stores in this way requires a similar technique. You'll find ODBC driver names in the **ODBC Data Sources** dialog, on your **Control Panel** (select the **System DSN** tab and hit **Add...**).

For a more detailed look a connection strings, as well as other aspects of ADO, take a look at *ADO 2.1 Programmers Reference* (Wrox Press, ISBN 1-861002-68-8).

Using ADO in Components

So far we've covered a lot of background on ADO, but not much practice. This section will show you how to use ADO in components, and discuss some of the issues arising from the use of ADO. Before you can use ADO in a Visual Basic component you need to make a reference to the ADO type library, from the standard **References** dialog:

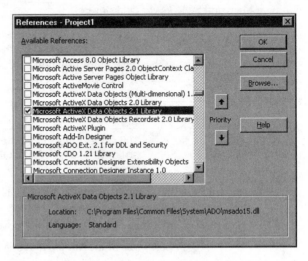

Is ADO on your Machine?

We've already mentioned that ADO comes as part of the Microsoft Data Access Components (MDAC). You could use **References** dialog of Visual Basic now, to check whether you have a version of ADO on your development machine. If you can't find the **Microsoft ActiveX Data Objects 2.*x* Library** in the list of **Available References**, the hit the **Browse...** button and search for `msado15.dll`.

If it's not there then you'll need to download MDAC from the Microsoft web site. In fact, if you don't have the most recent version of MDAC on your machine then you might consider updating your MDAC installation anyway. At the time of writing, the most recent (and therefore recommended) release is MDAC version 2.1. As we mentioned earlier, MDAC 2.5 will be released with Windows 2000, and will be available as a separate download for other Windows platforms.

> *Note that MDAC version numbers and ADO version numbers coincide—so you'll make ADO 2.1 available by installing MDAC version 2.1.*

We're not going to give blanket coverage of ADO in this chapter. Instead we'll take a look at some practical examples which demonstrate some of the features that make ADO useful in components. In the first of the examples that follow we'll use a component to display a recordset on the browser; then we'll adapt it so that we can edit the recordset and update the data store; then we'll use Index Server to create an index of our website.

Disconnected Recordsets

When dealing with ADO in components, we generally deal with disconnected recordsets. Put simply, a **disconnected recordset** is one that doesn't have a permanent connection to a data store. This means that we create a set of data that exists independently of its data store, allowing us to pass it around between other components. We can even save the recordset to disk, as a file.

When you think about the stateless nature of the Web, this is exactly what's required. We can create Web applications that use data that exists on the Web server, or even on the client. A disconnected recordset can also allow changes: we can make changes to the recordset while it's disconnected from the data store, and later on, we can use a single operation to send all those changes back to the data store. Thus, the application *appears* to hold a continuous direct connection to the data store, but *in fact* the data store connection is only open for as long as it takes to send or retrieve data.

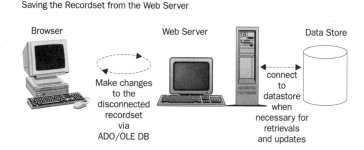

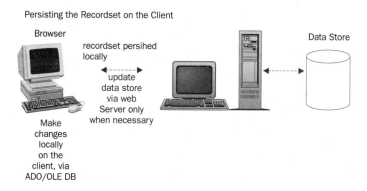

If we plan to persist data in recordsets on the client machine, then we can use a technology called **Remote Data Services** *(RDS). We'll take a look at some RDS examples later in this chapter.*

Creating a Recordset

Our first attempt at a component that creates a normal (that is, *not* disconnected) recordset via a function might look something like this. First, global objects for the connection string, a `Connection` object and a `Recordset` object:

```
Private Const strConnection As String = "Provider=SQLOLEDB; " & _
            "Data Source=Tigger; Initial Catalog=pubs; User Id=sa; Password="
Dim g_objConn As New ADODB.Connection       ' create a Connection object
Dim g_objRec As New ADODB.Recordset         ' create a Recordset object
```

Then a function to retrieve the data. The `Connection` object uses the connection string to connect to the data store, and the `Recordset` object uses the `Connection` object to retrieve data:

```
Public Sub GetAuthors()
    g_objConn.Open strConnection                    ' open the connection
    g_objRec.Open "authors", objConn, adOpenKeyset, adLockOptimistic, adCmdTable
                                                     ' open the recordset
End Sub
```

This simply creates and opens a recordset containing data from the `authors` table of SQL Server's `pubs` sample database. We can call the `GetAuthors()` method from an ASP page:

```
<%
...
    objMyCustomObj.GetAuthors
%>
```

At this stage in the ASP page, the recordset that we've created is still connected to the data store—so as you update the recordset's data within the page (using other methods of the component), the changes will be directly reflected in the data store:

```
<%
...
    objMyCustomObj.ChangeData(parameters)
%>
```

Remember, though, that the Web is a stateless model, so once the completed Web page is returned to the browser, the objects created within the page are lost and so we lose the connections to the Web server and the data store. This means that we can't retrieve data on one page and update it on another—unless we consider the option of session- or application-level objects, which brings a potentially high resource cost to the Web server. To get around this problem you can use a disconnected recordset.

Disconnecting the Recordset

We can create a recordset that is populated with data from the data store but is disconnected from it:

```
Private Const strConnection As String = "Provider=SQLOLEDB; " & _
            "Data Source=Tigger; Initial Catalog=pubs; User Id=sa; Password="
```

```
Public Function GetAuthors() As ADODB.Recordset
    Dim objConn As New ADODB.Connection
    Dim objRec As New ADODB.Recordset

    objConn.Open strConnection
    objRec.CursorLocation = adUseClient
    objRec.Open "authors", objConn, adOpenKeyset, adLockBatchOptimistic, adCmdTable
    Set objRec.ActiveConnection = Nothing
    Set GetAuthors = objRec
    objConn.Close
    Set objRec = Nothing
    Set objConn = Nothing
End Function
```

The most obvious change here is that we can give the Connection and Recordset objects function scope, instead of global scope within the component—it makes sense to free those objects' resources at the end of the function.

However, that's not the important point here. There are three other more significant changes between our first version of GetAuthors() and this one. It's these three changes that have the effect of creating a disconnected, updateable recordset. Let's have a look at them.

Cursor Location

The first thing to note is the use of the CursorLocation property. When a recordset is created, it gets a cursor. Unless you specify otherwise, that cursor is located in the data store—which means that the data store has control over the records in the recordset. Clearly this is unsuitable for a disconnected recordset, which (by definition) isn't connected to the data store. Therefore, we must use a client cursor (specified by adUseClient):

```
    objRec.CursorLocation = adUseClient
```

This means that ADO itself will provide the handling of records.

> *Don't be confused by the use of the term 'client' here—it refers to the client of the data store. Thus, depending on where the recordset is stored, 'client' could mean the Web server or the browser.*

Batch Updating

The second change is in the locking argument of the Open method of the recordset. For the majority of connected situations it's common to use optimistic locking (adLockOptimistic). Optimistic locking has two key features:

❑ Changes to the recordset are updated in the data store whenever the cursor moves off the edited record

❑ The record in the data store is locked just before changes are written to the data store, and unlocked again just afterwards

The first of these features makes optimistic locking unsuitable for disconnected recordsets, because we will probably want to change a number of different records before re-connecting to the data store. So instead, ADO offers us the batch optimistic locking (adLockBatchOptimistic) option, which instructs ADO to contact the data store to update records *only* when explicitly told to do so.

With our batch-updating disconnected recordset, the changes we make to our records will not be immediately reflected in the data store—because the recordset isn't connected to the data store. To update the data store with changes, we need to re-connect the recordset to the data store and then update all of the changes:

```
objRec.ActiveConnection = strConnection   ' reconnect using global connection string
objRec.UpdateBatch
```

This simply reconnects the recordset to the data store, and then updates the data store with all changes from the recordset.

Closing the Connection

The third difference is the use of the recordset's ActiveConnection property. This property contains the details of the connection that the recordset is using to communicate with the data store. For a client-based cursor, the act of setting ActiveConnection to Nothing has the effect of disconnecting the recordset from the data store.

An Example Component using Disconnected Recordsets

So let's create a real component that encapsulates the data access functionality that we discussed above. It will feature two public functions—one to retrieve a recordset from a data store, and another to commit updates to the data store. It'll also have some error-handling capability.

We'll put the whole component first, and then we'll look in more detail at how it works.

Setting up the DLL

To build the sample component you can follow the procedures that you've used before. First, create a new ActiveX DLL project; change the project name from Project1 to PubsDataAccess. Change the name of the ready-created class from Class1 to AuthorDataAccessor.

Make sure that the project has a reference to the ADO type library (select Project | References... and check the Microsoft ActiveX Data Objects 2.1 Library checkbox).

If you can't find this type library in the References dialog then you'll have to browse for the DLL (or possibly install MDAC onto your machine). We discussed this a few pages back.

The Implementation of the AuthorDataAccessor Component

Now add the following code to the PubsDataAccess – AuthorDataAccessor window. We'll start by creating the connection string (you'll recall that we discussed connection strings earlier in this chapter). You'll need to change this to a string that's suitable for your own data store:

```
Private Const strConnection As String = "Provider=SQLOLEDB; " & _
           "Data Source=Tigger; Initial Catalog=pubs; User Id=sa; Password="
```

The `AuthorDataAccessor` component will have two methods. The first is called `GetAuthors()`:

```
Public Function GetAuthors() As ADODB.Recordset
    Dim objConn         As New ADODB.Connection
    Dim objRecAuthors   As New ADODB.Recordset

    objConn.Open strConnection
    objRecAuthors.CursorLocation = adUseClient
    objRecAuthors.Open "authors", objConn, adOpenKeyset, _
                        adLockBatchOptimistic, adCmdTable
    Set objRecAuthors.ActiveConnection = Nothing
    Set GetAuthors = objRecAuthors
    Set objRecAuthors = Nothing
    objConn.Close
    Set objConn = Nothing
End Function
```

When we call this method from our ASP page, it will connect to the pubs database, return a recordset containing the contents of the `authors` table, and close down the connection.

`AuthorDataAccessor`'s second method, named `UpdateAuthors()`, accepts a disconnected recordset and updates the data store with any changes:

```
Public Function UpdateAuthors(ByRef recA As ADODB.Recordset) As String
    On Error GoTo UpdateAuthors_Err

    Dim strError    As String           ' error string for return value
    Dim fldF        As ADODB.Field

    recA.ActiveConnection = strConnection
    recA.UpdateBatch

    UpdateAuthors = ""                          ' no errors: return empty string

UpdateAuthors_Exit:
    Exit Function

UpdateAuthors_Err:
    strError = "Errors occurred whilst updating the data. " & _
            "The details are shown below: " & vbCrLf
    recA.Resync adAffectAll, adResyncUnderlyingValues
    While Not recA.EOF
      If recA.Status <> adRecUnmodified Then
        strError = strError & vbCrLf & StatusDesc(recA.Status) & vbCrLf
        For Each fldF In recA.Fields
          If fldF.OriginalValue <> fldF.UnderlyingValue Then
            strError = strError & "  Field: " & fldF.Name          & vbCrLf & _
                    "  Your value: "      & fldF.Value          & vbCrLf & _
                    "  Original value: " & fldF.OriginalValue & vbCrLf & _
                    "  Database value: " & fldF.UnderlyingValue
          End If
        Next
      End If
      recA.MoveNext
    Wend
    UpdateAuthors = strError                         ' return error info
    Resume UpdateAuthors_Exit
End Function
```

This looks quite complicated, but in fact most of the processing goes on in the first six lines. The remainder of this method is error-handling code, which we'll examine later in the chapter.

The Implementation of the Descriptions Module

We're going to add a module to the project. This module is called Descriptions, and it is included specifically to provide written descriptions for the errors that may occur during the data store update process. The Descriptions module will contain a single method, called StatusDesc(), and the concept behind it is simple: it reads the Status property of a record in the recordset, interprets that value, and translates it into a more comprehensible message.

Although we won't discuss this in detail until later in the chapter, we'll place it within out component now. We'll be using the component a number of times throughout this chapter.

Here's how to add the Descriptions module to the project. First, we need to add a new module—select Project | Add Module, select Module from the dialog and hit OK. Now, in the Properties window for the new module, change the module's name from Module1 to Descriptions.

Now add the following code for the StatusDesc() method to the AuthorDataAccessor – Descriptions window. It's quite long, but it's essentially simple code:

```
Function StatusDesc(lStatus As Long) As String
    Dim strStatus        As String
    If lStatus = adRecOK Then
        StatusDesc = "The record was successfully updated."
        Exit Function
    End If
    If (lStatus And adRecNew) = adRecNew Then
        strStatus = strStatus & "The record is new."
    End If
    If (lStatus And adRecModified) = adRecModified Then
        If strStatus <> "" Then strStatus = strStatus & vbCrLf
        strStatus = strStatus & "The record was modified."
    End If
    If (lStatus And adRecDeleted) = adRecDeleted Then
        If strStatus <> "" Then strStatus = strStatus & vbCrLf
        strStatus = strStatus & "The record was deleted."
    End If
    If (lStatus And adRecUnmodified) = adRecUnmodified Then
        If strStatus <> "" Then strStatus = strStatus & vbCrLf
        strStatus = strStatus & "The record was not modified."
    End If
    If (lStatus And adRecInvalid) = adRecInvalid Then
        If strStatus <> "" Then strStatus = strStatus & vbCrLf
        strStatus = strStatus & _
                "The record was not saved because its bookmark is invalid."
    End If
    If (lStatus And adRecMultipleChanges) = adRecMultipleChanges Then
        If strStatus <> "" Then strStatus = strStatus & vbCrLf
        strStatus = strStatus & _
            "The record was not saved because " & _
            "it would have affected multiple records."
    End If
    If (lStatus And adRecPendingChanges) = adRecPendingChanges Then
        If strStatus <> "" Then strStatus = strStatus & vbCrLf
        strStatus = strStatus & _
            "The record was not saved because it refers to a pending insert."
    End If
    If (lStatus And adRecCanceled) = adRecCanceled Then
        If strStatus <> "" Then strStatus = strStatus & vbCrLf
        strStatus = strStatus & _
                "The record was not saved because the operation was canceled."
    End If
```

```
If (lStatus And adRecCantRelease) = adRecCantRelease Then
        If strStatus <> "" Then strStatus = strStatus & vbCrLf
        strStatus = strStatus & _
                    "The new record was not saved because of existing record locks."
    End If
    If (lStatus And adRecConcurrencyViolation) = adRecConcurrencyViolation Then
        If strStatus <> "" Then strStatus = strStatus & vbCrLf
        strStatus = strStatus & _
            "The record was not saved because optimistic concurrency was in use."
    End If
    If (lStatus And adRecIntegrityViolation) = adRecIntegrityViolation Then
        If strStatus <> "" Then strStatus = strStatus & vbCrLf
        strStatus = strStatus & _
            "The record was not saved because " & _
            "the user violated integrity constraints."
    End If
    If (lStatus And adRecMaxChangesExceeded) = adRecMaxChangesExceeded Then
        If strStatus <> "" Then strStatus = strStatus & vbCrLf
        strStatus = strStatus & _
            "The record was not saved because there were too many pending changes."
    End If
    If (lStatus And adRecObjectOpen) = adRecObjectOpen Then
        If strStatus <> "" Then strStatus = strStatus & vbCrLf
        strStatus = strStatus & _
            "The record was not saved because " & _
            "of a conflict with an open storage object."
    End If
    If (lStatus And adRecOutOfMemory) = adRecOutOfMemory Then
        If strStatus <> "" Then strStatus = strStatus & vbCrLf
        strStatus = strStatus & _
            "The record was not saved because the computer has run out of memory."
    End If
    If (lStatus And adRecPermissionDenied) = adRecPermissionDenied Then
        If strStatus <> "" Then strStatus = strStatus & vbCrLf
        strStatus = strStatus & _
            "The record was not saved because the user has insufficient permissions."
    End If
    If (lStatus And adRecDBDeleted) = adRecDBDeleted Then
        If strStatus <> "" Then strStatus = strStatus & vbCrLf
        strStatus = strStatus & _
                    "The record was not saved because " & _
                    "it violates the structure of the underlying database."
    End If
    If (lStatus And adRecPermissionDenied) = adRecPermissionDenied Then
        If strStatus <> "" Then strStatus = strStatus & vbCrLf
        strStatus = strStatus & _
                    "The record has already been deleted from the data source."
    End If
    StatusDesc = strStatus
End Function
```

As you can see, it begins with an empty string and appends more substrings onto the end of the string, based on the value of the integer parameter. When we pass the record's Status property into this method, we'll get easy-to-read details of the record's status.

We've used a set of If...Then statements because a simple Select Case structure won't do the job we want. The Status property works on a bitwise-integer principle—its value can reflect a combination of characteristics. If the record updates successfully, then its Status value is 0. Otherwise, the Status reflects the reason(s) that the record was not modified. We use a set of If...Then statements to ensure we capture all of those characteristics.

Compiling the DLL

You can build the component as normal—by selecting File | Make PubsDataAccess.dll.

Using the Component to Display Data

First, we'll test the component by having it return a recordset that will be stored on the Web server and used to write a page to the browser. Here's the code for the ASP page, ReadRS.asp:

```
<!-- line below references the ADO type library -->
<!-- METDATA TYPE="typelib"
FILE="C:\program files\common files\system\ado\msado15.dll" -->

<HTML>
<HEAD>
<TITLE>Creating a Disconnected Recordset on the Web Server</TITLE>
<STYLE TYPE="text/css">                              ' a little formatting
    BODY {font-family:Tahoma,Arial,sans-serif; font-size:12px; font-weight:bold}
    TD   {font-family:Tahoma,Arial,sans-serif; font-size:12px; font-weight:normal}
    TH   {font-family:Tahoma,Arial,sans-serif; font-size:12px; font-weight:bold}
</STYLE>
</HEAD>
<BODY>

<%
    Dim objAuthors
    Dim objRS

    Set objAuthors = Server.CreateObject("PubsDataAccess.AuthorDataAccessor")
                                                     ' create the object
                                                     ' retrieve the recordset
    Set objRS = objAuthors.GetAuthors                ' destroy the object
    Set objAuthors = Nothing

    ' display the contents of objRS
    Response.Write "<TABLE><THEAD>" & _
                   "<TH>ID</TH>" & _
                   "<TH>First Name</TH>" & _
                   "<TH>Last Name</TH>" & _
                   "<TH>Phone</TH>" & _
                   "<TH>Contracted?</TH>" & _
                   "</THEAD>"
    While Not objRS.EOF
        Response.Write "<TR><TD>" & objRS("au_id")    & "</TD>     " & _
                       "   <TD>" & objRS("au_fname") & "</TD>     " & _
                       "   <TD>" & objRS("au_lname") & "</TD>     " & _
                       "   <TD>" & objRS("phone")    & "</TD>     " & _
                       "   <TD>" & objRS("contract") & "</TD></TR>"

        objRS.MoveNext
    Wend
    Response.Write "</TABLE>"
    Set objRS = Nothing                              ' destroy objRS
%>
</BODY>
</HTML>
```

To run this page, you'll need to register the component on your Web server machine, by selecting Start | Run and typing:

regsvr32 <file_path>\PubsDataAccess.dll

Alternatively, you can select Project | Properties and place the URL for this page as your choice for debugging the component:

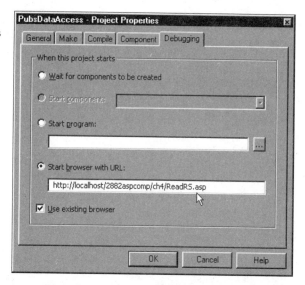

When you call this in your browser (or run it using Run | Start in Visual Basic), you should see something like this:

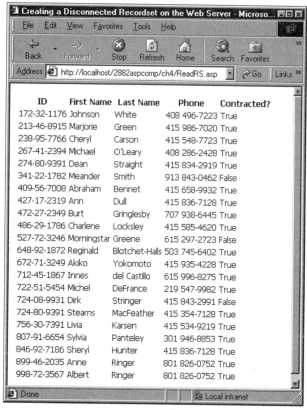

How It Works

In the ASP page itself, we only need two variables to achieve our goal:

```
Dim objAuthors
Dim objRS
```

We set `objAuthors` to an instance of our new `AuthorDataAccessor` component, and then we call the object's `GetAuthors` method:

```
Set objAuthors = Server.CreateObject("PubsDataAccess.AuthorDataAccessor")
                                                    ' create the object
Set objRS = objAuthors.GetAuthors                   ' retrieve the recordset
```

The `GetAuthors` method encapsulates quite a few steps: connecting to the data store, retrieving the records and closing the connection again. It can do all that because, in the component, we gave the recordset has a client-side cursor. Having assigned the recordset to the `objRS` variable, and closed the connection, `objRS` actually represents a disconnected recordset which sitting on the Web server.

Our `AuthorDataAccessor` component has done its job now, so we can release it:

```
Set objAuthors = Nothing                            ' destroy the object
```

The remainder of the page takes care of writing some of the contents of our disconnected recordset to the browser. Then, having finished with the disconnected recordset, we can destroy that too:

```
Response.Write "<TABLE><THEAD>" & _
...
While Not objRS.EOF
    Response.Write "<TR><TD>" & objRS("au_id")      & "</TD>      " & _
                 ...
                 "    <TD>" & objRS("contract") & "</TD></TR>"
    objRS.MoveNext
Wend
Response.Write "</TABLE>"
Set objRS = Nothing                                 ' destroy objRS
```

What else could we have done on this ASP page? Well, we could have provided the end-user with some facility for editing the recordset, and an **Update** button which called the `AuthorDataAccessor` object's `UpdateAuthors` method. In fact, we're going go further than that in the next example—because we're going to dispense with holding on the recordset on the Web server and use our component client-side.

Remote Data Services

Building the `GetAuthors()` method into a component and using that in an ASP page is quite simple, but what do you do then? We've created an HTML table, showing the details of the authors, but this isn't really very 'active'. In this section we'll look at how we can use the data on the Web client, allowing the user to browse around the records, make changes, and so on. **Remote Data Services** (**RDS**) is the solution.

RDS is the client-side equivalent of using ADO on the Web, designed for use with Microsoft Internet Explorer. So far you've seen plenty of examples of using components on ASP pages, but RDS is different because RDS uses both server and client components, and allows you to transfer and manipulate recordsets between the server and the client, and vice versa. There are several components involved in the use of RDS. The following diagram shows how they all fit together:

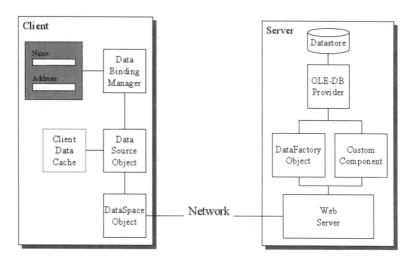

At the server, you have a component that creates the data. You can use either the
RDSServer.DataFactory component, or a custom component. The RDSServer.DataFactory is the
default business object on the server, and provides a simple way to execute SQL queries from the client. If
you need more functionality then you can use a custom component in its place, and it's this that we'll be
looking at.

On the client, the RDS.DataSpace component provides the way in which we invoke business objects on
the server—whether we invoke the RDSServer.DataFactory or a custom datafactory component. Once
the DataSpace receives the data, it can be stored in a local object variable, or placed in a **Data Source
Object** (DSO), which allows us to bind the data to HTML elements. It is this binding method that we'll be
using.

Note that RDS is a Microsoft technology and only works in Microsoft Internet Explorer.

An Example Using Disconnected Recordsets and RDS

If we're going to use recordsets on the client, then they'll need to be disconnected—because we won't have
a connection to the server. The PubsDataAccess.AuthorDataAccessor component that we
developed in the previous section deals in disconnected recordsets, and happily we'll be able to test it out
by using it as the 'custom datafactory' component in an RDS example. Its two methods provide just the
functionality we'll need: GetAuthors() will create disconnected recordsets from the data store, and
UpdateAuthors() will take a disconnected recordset and updated the data store from it.

The process of registering the PubsDataAccess.AuthorDataAccessor component as an RDS custom
datafactory component is somewhat different what we've seen so far in this book. First, you must ensure
that the component is registered on the Web server machine, using regsvr32.exe as we've seen many
times already (or using MTS, as we'll see in later chapters).

Second, you must also instruct IIS that this component can be called by the RDS.DataSpace in place of the RDSServer.DataFactory object. (This is a deliberate security policy by Microsoft, and ensures that *only* registered components can be instantiated on the Web server. Otherwise it might be possible to call any server component through IIS.)

To perform this second part of the registration process, you need to modify the registry of your Web server machine. From the Start menu, select Run and type regedit.exe.

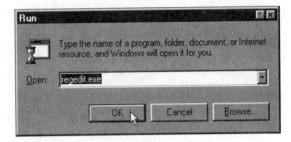

The registry window will appear. In the left-hand pane, you need to navigate to the following path:

HKEY_LOCAL_MACHINE\SYSTEM\CurrentControlSet\Services\W3SVC\Parameters\ADCLaunch\

Right-click on ADCLaunch and select New | Key. Then right-click on the new key, select Rename and type PubsDataAccess.AuthorDataAccessor. You can leave the value of the key empty.

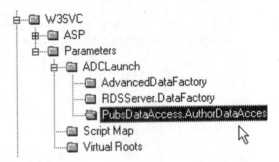

Using the Component

Since we're using the component from the client, we can't create it in the ASP script. Instead it has to be created in HTML, using client side scripting. Here's the code for our web page, RDSSingle.asp:

```
<!-- line below references the ADO type library -->
<!-- METDATA TYPE="typelib"
FILE="C:\program files\common files\system\ado\msado15.dll" -->

<HTML>
<HEAD>
<TITLE>Using the RDS Objects</TITLE>
<STYLE TYPE="text/css">                              ' a little styling
BODY  {font-family:Tahoma,Arial,sans-serif; font-size:12px; font-weight:bold}
TD    {font-family:Tahoma,Arial,sans-serif; font-size:12px; font-weight:normal}
TH    {font-family:Tahoma,Arial,sans-serif; font-size:12px; font-weight:bold}
</STYLE>
</HEAD>
<BODY>

<!-- this is the normal RDS DataControl object with no parameters set -->
<OBJECT id="dsoAuthors"
    classid="clsid:BD96C556-65A3-11D0-983A-00C04FC29E33" height="0" width="0">
</OBJECT>
```

```html
<!-- this is the client-side RDS DataSpace object -->
<OBJECT id="dspDataSpace"
     classid="CLSID:BD96C556-65A3-11D0-983A-00C04FC29E36" height="0" width="0">
</OBJECT>

<TABLE id="tblAuthors" BORDER="0">
  <TR>
    <TD>ID</TD>
    <TD><INPUT DATASRC="#dsoAuthors" DATAFLD="au_id" ></INPUT></TD>
  </TR>
  <TR>
    <TD>First Name</TD>
    <TD><INPUT DATASRC="#dsoAuthors" DATAFLD="au_lname" ></INPUT></TD>
  </TR>
  <TR>
    <TD>Last Name</TD>
    <TD><INPUT DATASRC="#dsoAuthors" DATAFLD="au_fname" ></INPUT></TD>
  </TR>
  <TR>
    <TD>Phone</TD>
    <TD><INPUT DATASRC="#dsoAuthors" DATAFLD="phone" ></INPUT></TD>
  </TR>
  <TR>
    <TD>Contract</TD>
    <TD><INPUT DATASRC="#dsoAuthors" DATAFLD="contract" ></INPUT></TD>
  </TR>
</TABLE>
<P>
<button id="cmdFirst" title="First Record"
    onclick="dsoAuthors.recordset.MoveFirst()"> |&lt; </button>
<button id="cmdPrevious" title="Previous Record"
    onclick="if (!dsoAuthors.recordset.BOF) dsoAuthors.recordset.MovePrevious()">
     &lt; </button>
<button id="cmdNext" title="Next Record"
    onclick="if (!dsoAuthors.recordset.EOF) dsoAuthors.recordset.MoveNext()">
     &gt; </button>
<button id="cmdLast" title="Last Record"
    onclick="dsoAuthors.recordset.MoveLast()"> &gt;| </button> 
<button id="cmdDelete" title="Delete This Record"
    onclick="dsoAuthors.recordset.Delete()">Delete</button> 
<button id="cmdAddNew" title="Add New Record"
    onclick="dsoAuthors.recordset.AddNew()">Add</button> 
<button id="cmdCancelAll" title="Abandon All Changes"
    onclick="dsoAuthors.CancelUpdate()">Cancel</button> 
<button id="cmdUpdateAll" title="Save All Changes"
    onclick="updateAuthors()">Save</button>


<SCRIPT LANGUAGE="JavaScript">
   function window.onload()
   {
     <%
      ' Create a client-side variable with the name of the Web server in it
      Response.Write "   strServer = 'http://" & Request("server_name") & "'"
     %>
     // first we create a DataFactory object, specifying the server to use:
     myCustomObject =
          dspDataSpace.CreateObject("PubsDataAccess.AuthorDataAccessor", strServer);
     // now we create a recordset from the custom object using a custom method:
     myRecordset = myCustomObject.GetAuthors();
     // finally, assign the returned recordset to the DataControl object:
     dsoAuthors.SourceRecordset = myRecordset;
   }
```

```
    function updateAuthors()
    {
      var sError;
      // get a reference to the client-side recordset:
      objRs = dsoAuthors.recordset;
      // tell the recordset to only send back changed records:
      objRs.MarshalOptions = 1;    // adMarshalModifiedOnly
      // then call the method in our custom business component:

      sError = myCustomObject.UpdateAuthors(objRs);
      if (sError == '')
        alert("Changes were successfully applied.");
      else
        alert(sError);
    }
</SCRIPT>
</BODY>
</HTML>
```

When you run this in your browser, you should get something like this:

How It Works—Creating the RDS Objects

The first thing that we do is create the DSO and the RDS.DataSpace object, both of which can be done using the HTML OBJECT tag:

```
<OBJECT id="dsoAuthors"
    classid="clsid:BD96C556-65A3-11D0-983A-00C04FC29E33" height="0" width="0">
</OBJECT>
```

```
<OBJECT id="dspDataSpace"
    classid="CLSID:BD96C556-65A3-11D0-983A-00C04FC29E36" height="0" width="0">
</OBJECT>
```

Each of these controls has its own unique ID, which allows us to reference it in the client script. We can then use the RDS.DataSpace to create our server-side datafactory component. The best place to do this is in the onload() event for the browser's window object—so that the component is created as the HTML page loads:

142

```
function window.onload()
{
  <%
    Response.Write "    strServer = 'http://" & Request("server_name") & "'"
  %>
  myCustomObject =
    dspDataSpace.CreateObject("PubsDataAccess.AuthorDataAccessor", strServer);
  myRecordset = myCustomObject.GetAuthors();
  dsoAuthors.SourceRecordset = myRecordset;
}
```

There are only four lines of code here. The first is the only bit of ASP in the page—it creates a client-side variable, `strServer`, which contains the name of the Web server. This is instead of hard-coding the Web server name into the page—we don't have to change the server name every time we move the page onto a different server.

The second line uses the `RDS.DataSpace` object declared in our `<OBJECT>` tag. The `DataSpace` has a method called `CreateObject`, which creates server-side custom components—in this case, we've created an instance of our custom datafactory, `PubsDataAccess.AuthorDataAccessor`, on the Web server. The third line calls the component's `GetAuthors()` method, which (as we know) returns a disconnected recordset to the client. The fourth line uses the DSO, setting the source of its data to the newly returned recordset.

How the Data Binding Works

Having a DSO on its own on the client is not a great deal of use—we really need to show the data to the end-user. To this end, we use a technique called **data binding**. Many HTML elements allow themselves to be bound to a DSO. This is achieved using the `DATASRC` and `DATAFLD` tags of the HTML element. In this case, we've bound data from some of the fields from the recordset to a set of HTML `<INPUT>` elements:

```
<INPUT DATASRC="#dsoAuthors" DATAFLD="au_id" ></INPUT>
<INPUT DATASRC="#dsoAuthors" DATAFLD="au_lname" ></INPUT>
<INPUT DATASRC="#dsoAuthors" DATAFLD="au_fname" ></INPUT>
<INPUT DATASRC="#dsoAuthors" DATAFLD="phone" ></INPUT>
<INPUT DATASRC="#dsoAuthors" DATAFLD="contract" ></INPUT>
```

The `DATASRC` attribute specifies the name of the DSO—note that you must put a hash sign (#) in front of the DSO name. The `DATAFLD` attribute specifies the field in the recordset that the element is to be bound to. We've added a little descriptive text, and formatted the data in a `<TABLE>`, and you can then see the effect this has in the Web page:

ID	172-32-1176
First Name	White
Last Name	Johnson
Phone	408 496-7223
Contract	True

Remember that RDS requires Microsoft Internet Explorer.

How the Navigation and Recordset-Editing Buttons Work

Behind these five textboxes is a DSO, and behind that is an ADO recordset. That means that you can use the **navigation methods** built into the recordset to move around the records. You can add some buttons that do this for you. Here's the code for the first four buttons:

```
<button id="cmdFirst" title="First Record"
    onclick="dsoAuthors.recordset.MoveFirst()"> |&lt; </button>
<button id="cmdPrevious" title="Previous Record"
    onclick="if (!dsoAuthors.recordset.BOF) dsoAuthors.recordset.MovePrevious()">
     &lt; </button>
<button id="cmdNext" title="Next Record"
    onclick="if (!dsoAuthors.recordset.EOF) dsoAuthors.recordset.MoveNext()">
     &gt; </button>
<button id="cmdLast" title="Last Record"
    onclick="dsoAuthors.recordset.MoveLast()"> &gt;| </button> 
```

These buttons simply call the navigation methods of the underlying recordset:

- ❏ The `MoveFirst` method takes you to the first record in the recordset

- ❏ The `MovePrevious` method takes you to the record immediately before the currently displayed record

- ❏ The `MoveNext` method takes you to the record immediately after the currently displayed record

- ❏ The `MoveLast` method takes you to the last record in the recordset

Note that, before we call `MovePrevious`, we check that we're not currently looking at the first record in the recordset. We do this by checking the recordset's `BOF` (beginning of file) property, which is `true` if and only if we're on the first record. There's a similar check for the value of `EOF` (end of file), before calling the `MoveNext` method.

In fact, we can use this method to add more buttons, giving even more functionality to the users:

```
<button id="cmdDelete" title="Delete This Record"
    onclick="dsoAuthors.recordset.Delete()">Delete</button> 
<button id="cmdAddNew" title="Add New Record"
    onclick="dsoAuthors.recordset.AddNew()">Add</button> 
```

These two buttons call the recordset's `Delete` and `AddNew` methods, which allow the end-user to delete records and to add new records. You might also want to add another, as we've done here, to allow the user to cancel any changes they've done so far:

```
<button id="cmdCancelAll" title="Abandon All Changes"
    onclick="dsoAuthors.CancelUpdate()">Cancel</button> 
```

The code behind this button is a little different from the others, in that it *doesn't* use a method of the recordset. Instead, it calls `CancelUpdate`, which is a method of the DSO itself.

All together, these first seven buttons now give us a usable Web page—we can navigate around the recordset and make changes to it. There's just one thing we haven't dealt with: namely, updating our changes back on the data store.

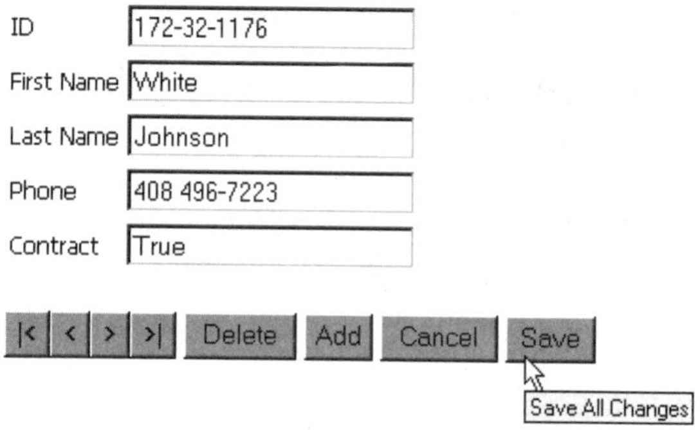

ID	172-32-1176
First Name	White
Last Name	Johnson
Phone	408 496-7223
Contract	True

`|<  <  >  >|  Delete  Add  Cancel  Save`

Save All Changes

How It Updates the Data Store

Updating the data store is not so difficult, and can be achieved with a few lines of code. First, the code to create the **Save** button to call our update function (on the far right of the screenshot above) is this:

```
<button id="cmdUpdateAll" title="Save All Changes"
    onclick="updateAuthors()">Save</button>
```

Now here's the `updateAuthors()` function:

```
function updateAuthors()
{
    var sError;
    objRs = dsoAuthors.recordset;
    objRs.MarshalOptions = 1;    // adMarshalModifiedOnly

    sError = myCustomObject.UpdateAuthors(objRs);
    if (sError == '')
      alert("Changes were successfully applied.");
    else
      alert(sError);
}
```

In the first line, we're setting a recordset object (`objRs`) to the recordset that underlies the DSO. This is the opposite of what we did in the `windows.onload()` function earlier:

```
        dsoAuthors.SourceRecordset = myRecordset;
```

Then we set the `MarshalOptions`. This dictates which records will be sent back (or **marshaled**) to the data store. A value of 1 (`adMarshalModifiedOnly`) indicates that the update will take the records that have changed and marshal them back to the data store—no other records will be marshaled.

> Note that the default value for the `MarshalOptions` property is for all records to be marshaled; marshaling changed records only ensures that we're using less network resources.

Finally, we pass this recordset into the `UpdateAuthors` function of our custom datafactory object (the `PubsDataAccess.AuthorDataAccessor` object, `myCustomObject`). So it's the `AuthorDataAccessor` component that actually updates the data store.

There's one more thing outstanding, that we haven't looked at yet—the error handling code.

How the Error-Handling Code Works

You may recall from earlier in the chapter that, on completion, the object's `updateAuthors()` method returns a string. If `updateAuthors()` succeeds in updating the data store then the returned string is an empty string. By contrast, if there's any failure in the update process then the returned string will be a non-empty string, containing error details.

Let's return to the code in our `AuthorDataAccessor` component, to take a look at how this error handling works.

> *The technique that we'll outline here is an important one in terms designing components for data access—because it's essential to ensure that your users have as much information as possible when an error occurs.*

The first thing to observe is in the component's `updateAuthors()` method. If there's an error in the processing of this function, then execution must go immediately to the `UpdateAuthors_Err` mark:

```
On Error GoTo UpdateAuthors_Err
```

If an error occurs, we'll handle the error by telling the user what has happened. We begin with some text that tells the user that an error has occurred:

```
UpdateAuthors_Err:
    strError = "Errors occurred whilst updating the data. " & _
               "The details are shown below: " & vbCrLf
```

Next we use the recordset's `Resync` method to get the underlying values from the database:

```
recA.Resync adAffectAll, adResyncUnderlyingValues
```

The `Resync` method uncovers hidden depths to the recordset. Until now, when we've used the data contained in the recordset we've only been using the `Value` property of each recordset field. In fact, each field actually has *three* properties, which hold three different types of value:

Property	Description
Value	The current value of the field in the recordset.
OriginalValue	The value of the field when it was read from the data store.
UnderlyingValue	The value of the field currently in the data store.

When you first open a recordset, the values of these three properties will all be the same. When you change a value of a field in the recordset, you only change its `Value` property. However, between the time you open the recordset and the time you change a field, another user might already have changed the same field. You can't immediately see changes made by other users—so you have to use the `Resync` command to resynchronize the values in your recordset with the values in the data store. Using the constant `adResyncUnderlyingValues` ensures that only the `UnderlyingValue` property is overwritten with the new values.

After we have resynchronized the recordset, the `UnderlyingValue` property contains the latest values from the data store. Now we want to loop through all of the records in the recordset, checking each field. However, we don't really want to check each field for every record, because not all of the records have changed. So, we use the `Status` property of each record to identify whether or not any changes have taken place on that record:

```
While Not recA.EOF
    If recA.Status <> adRecUnmodified Then
```

The `Status` property indicates the status of the current record. If the record has not been modified then its `Status` will be `adRecUnmodified`—we are interested in all other records. When we find one, we use a function `StatusDesc` to convert its `Status` value into a description:

```
strError = strError & vbCrLf & StatusDesc(recA.Status) & vbCrLf
```

Now we can loop through the fields of the record, checking its values. We only want fields where the `UnderlyingValue` is different from the `OriginalValue`, because this means that the field value has changed since we read it from the data store:

```
For Each fldF In recA.Fields
    If fldF.OriginalValue <> fldF.UnderlyingValue Then
```

If the field value has changed, we just add the various values, including the field name, to a string:

```
        strError = strError & "  Field: " & fldF.Name          & vbCrLf & _
                   "  Your value: "        & fldF.Value          & vbCrLf & _
                   "  Original value: " & fldF.OriginalValue & vbCrLf & _
                   "  Database value: " & fldF.UnderlyingValue
        End If
    Next
    End If
    recA.MoveNext
Wend
```

Finally, we return this string full of error information back to the calling routine.

```
UpdateAuthors = strError                        ' return error info
```

If another user happens to change a record at the same time as you, you'll get a message like this:

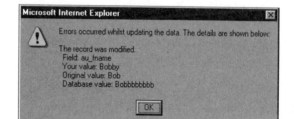

This shows that I tried to modify the first name field to **Bobby**. The original value of the field, when the recordset was opened, was **Bob**. Between the time I opened the recordset and the time I tried to change the field, someone else (me again, on another window!) changed the value to **Bobbbbbbbb**.

At the end of all this, we have a component that returns a disconnected recordset, and allows that recordset to be updated. If any errors occur during the update process, we get a full list of information back to the user.

Another Example—Binding Data to Tables

If you want to give a grid-like appearance to your Web page, you can do so by binding an entire table to a DSO. In this case, you specify the DATASRC attribute in the TABLE element, and the DATAFLD in each table cell.

The architecture of this example is almost exactly the same as that of the previous example—the PubsDataAccess.AuthorDataAccessor component acts as data factory (on the Web server) again, and we use the RDS DSO and DataStore objects on the client.

To set this up, copy the code from RDSSingle.asp into a new file, RDSTable.asp. Now we need to make two changes to the code. First, replace the existing table (i.e. everything between the <TABLE> and </TABLE> tags) with the following:

```
<TABLE id="tblAuthors" DATASRC="#dsoAuthors" DATAPAGESIZE="10" BORDER="0">
  <THEAD>
    <TH>ID</TH>
    <TH>First Name</TH>
    <TH>Last Name</TH>
    <TH>Phone</TH>
    <TH>Contracted?</TH>
  </THEAD>
  <TR>
    <TD><INPUT DATAFLD="au_id"></INPUT></TD>
    <TD><INPUT DATAFLD="au_lname"></INPUT></TD>
    <TD><INPUT DATAFLD="au_fname" ></INPUT></TD>
    <TD><INPUT DATAFLD="phone" ></INPUT></TD>
    <TD><INPUT DATAFLD="contract"></INPUT></TD>
  </TR>
</TABLE>
```

The DATASRC and DATAFLD attributes work much as they did in the previous example. One advantage of this technique is that it allows us to partition our recordset into smaller units, called **pages**, for easy viewing. We use the DATAPAGESIZE attribute to set the number of records that will be displayed on a single page—in this case we'll display a maximum of 10 records on a page. If you don't specify a value for DATAPAGESIZE then all records are shown, and this could lead to quite a large table.

Second, we need to change the logic behind the first four buttons:

```
<button id="cmdFirst" title="First Page"
    onclick="tblAuthors.firstPage()">
     &lt;&lt; </button>
<button id="cmdPrevious" title="Previous Page"
    onclick="tblAuthors.previousPage()">
     &lt; </button>
<button id="cmdNext" title="Next Page"
    onclick="tblAuthors.nextPage()">
     &gt; </button>
<button id="cmdLast" title="Last Page"
    onclick="tblAuthors.lastPage()">
     &gt;&gt; </button>
```

In each case, we've changed the underlying logic so that the buttons move from page to page—rather than from record to record. This uses the firstPage, previousPage, nextPage and lastPage methods of the table.

All this gives a Web page that looks like an editable grid:

ID	First Name	Last Name	Phone	Contracted?
172-32-1176	White	Johnson	408 496-7223	True
213-46-8915	Green	Marjorie	415 986-7020	True
238-95-7766	Carson	Cheryl	415 548-7723	True
267-41-2394	O'Leary	Michael	408 286-2428	True
274-80-9391	Straight	Dean	415 834-2919	True
341-22-1782	Smith	Meander	913 843-0462	False
409-56-7008	Bennet	Abraham	415 658-9932	True
427-17-2319	Dull	Ann	415 836-7128	True
472-27-2349	Gringlesby	Burt	707 938-6445	True
486-29-1786	Locksley	Charlene	415 585-4620	True

`<<` `<` `>` `>>` Delete | Add | Cancel | Save

Next Page

A One-Stop Index-Creation Component Using Index Server

Indexed web sites are becoming increasingly common on the Web. By providing an index to your site, the end-user can more easily find what they're looking for—and that makes for an altogether less stressful experience. Microsoft's Index Server service is a tool that helps us to index a web site easily.

> We won't explain Index Server in detail here—Microsoft provides a full overview and demonstration at http://www.microsoft.com/ntserver/web/default.asp.

Microsoft does supply some sample ASP pages that perform Index Server queries using both the Index Server components and ADO. However, if you look closely at these samples you'll notice that they run on the Web server and just return a page of results. If the end-user wants to move from page to page within the index, each new page request will result in another trip to the Web server. It would be better if we had an RDS situation in which the results of the search are available on the browser—allowing paging without repeated trips to the server.

There's a simple solution to this. We can build a component that encapsulates the search functionality, and install this component on the Web server that's hosting Index Server. Then, we can call this component from Web pages using the RDS `DataSpace` object, or in ASP script, or from other applications. The advantage is that we have a central component that can be used from many different places.

To keep our component simple, we'll concentrate on just searching for a particular phrase. Index Server uses an extended form of SQL for its queries. We're not going to cover this here—it's well-explained in Microsoft's Index Server documentation. The idea, however, will be familiar—you select columns from an index catalog.

So, with that in mind we might start by trying to build our component in a similar way to the `AuthorDataAccessor` component above. However, this first attempt is going to cause us some problems:

```
Public Function Search(ByVal Phrase As String) As ADODB.Recordset
    Dim sConn       As String
    Dim sSearch     As String
    Dim oConn       As New ADODB.Connection
    Dim oRec        As New ADODB.Recordset

    sConn = "Provider=MSIDXS; Data Source=Web"    'open the recordset of the query
    oConn.Open sConn
    sSearch = "SELECT DocTitle, characterization, vpath, size" & _
              " FROM SCOPE()" & _
              " WHERE CONTAINS('" & Phrase & "') > 0"
    oRec.CursorLocation = adUseClient
    oRec.Open sSearch, oConn, adOpenKeyset, adLockBatchOptimistic, adCmdUnknown
    Set oRec.ActiveConnection = Nothing
    Set Search = oRec
End Function
```

The structure should look familiar. This uses the **Index Server Data Provider** (`MSIDXS`), and runs a query that returns the document title, the characterization (abstract), the virtual path of the document, and the document size—for all documents that contain a given phrase. Note that it uses a *client-side* cursor, and then tries to disconnect the recordset by setting the `ActiveConnection` to `Nothing`.

It would be great if things were that simple. However, we said that there would be problem with this solution, and there is: namely, the OLE DB Provider for Index Server *doesn't* support client-side cursors. This means we can't create a disconnected recordset directly from an Index Server query. Instead, we'll have to create a recordset using a server-side cursor, and then copy the data from this recordset into a manually-created client-side recordset.

The good news is that ADO allows us to create new, empty, disconnected recordsets that have no connection to a data store, and then populate them using data from elsewhere. So that's the technique we'll use for our component.

Creating the WroxIndexer.Query Component

We'll create a project called `WroxIndexer` which contains a single component called `Query`. The `WroxIndexer.Query` component will have a public function called `Search()`.

Fire up your Visual Basic IDE, create a new **ActiveX DLL** project and change the project name from the default (**Project1**) to **WroxIndexer**. Change the name of the default class that's been created from **Class1** to **Query**. Don't forget to create a reference to the **Microsoft ActiveX Data Objects 2.1 Library** set, using the **Project | References** dialog.

The only thing we'll declare outside of the functions is this:

```
Option Explicit
```

The Search() Function

Now we're ready to insert the implementation of the component. Here's the implementation of the public function, `Search()`, that we'll use in the finished component:

```
Public Function Search(ByVal Phrase As String) As ADODB.Recordset
    On Error GoTo Search_Err
    Dim sConn       As String
    Dim sSearch     As String
    Dim oConn       As New ADODB.Connection
    Dim oRec        As New ADODB.Recordset
    Dim oRecNew     As New ADODB.Recordset

    sConn = "Provider=MSIDXS; Data Source=Web"     ' open the recordset of the query
    oConn.Open sConn
    sSearch = "SELECT DocTitle, characterization, vpath, size" & _
            " FROM SCOPE()" & _
            " WHERE  CONTAINS('" & Phrase & "') > 0"
    'Allow the recordset to take a server-side cursor (this is the default)
    oRec.Open sSearch, oConn, adOpenKeyset, adLockBatchOptimistic, adCmdUnknown

    Set oRecNew = RecordsetDuplicate(oRec)      ' duplicate the recordset
    Set Search = oRecNew                        ' return the newly created recordset

    If oRec.State = adStateOpen Then                    ' tidy up
        oRec.Close
    End If
    Set oRec = Nothing
    If oConn.State = adStateOpen Then
        oConn.Close
    End If
    Set oConn = Nothing

Search_Exit:
    Exit Function

Search_Err:
    Set Search = Nothing
    Resume Search_Exit
End Function
```

This function takes a single argument, `Phrase`, which represents the string the end-user is searching for. Then it makes a connection to the data store (via the OLE DB Provider for Index Server). The recordset `oRec` (with a *server*-side cursor) queries the data store; then we use a private function called `RecordsetDuplicate()` to create another recordset, which also contains the content of the query but has a *client*-side cursor. This duplicate recordset is assigned to the variable `oRecNew`. Note that `oRecNew` is a *disconnected* recordset—it has a client-side cursor and is not connected to a data store. It's this recordset that we return to the client—and that's the end of the component's task.

The Private RecordsetDuplicate() Function

The `Search()` function needs some supplementary functionality—we need to create the `RecordsetDuplicate()` function. `RecordsetDuplicate()` will copy the contents of a server-side recordset into a client recordset. Because it's only used from within the `Search` method, we'll make it a private function—we don't want this function to be part of the component's interface.

Here's our first attempt at the code for `RecordsetDuplicate()`. It gives the general idea for the logic we'll use for this function (although again, there's a technical problem with it, which we'll deal with in a moment):

```
Private Function RecordsetDuplicate(oRec As ADODB.Recordset) As ADODB.Recordset
    Dim oCR     As New ADODB.Recordset
    Dim oFld    As ADODB.Field
    Dim lType   As Long
    Dim lSize   As Long

    oCR.CursorLocation = adUseClient        'use a client-side cursor
    With oCR
        For Each oFld In oRec.Fields        'create the new fields
            .Fields.Append oFld.Name, oFld.Type, oFld.DefinedSize
                                            ' append the field to the new recordset
        Next
        .Open                               'open the new recordset
        While Not oRec.EOF                  'append the existing data
            .AddNew
            For Each oFld In oRec.Fields
                .Fields(oFld.Name).Value = oFld.Value
            Next
            .Update
            oRec.MoveNext
        Wend
    End With
    Set RecordsetDuplicate = oCR
End Function
```

It might look quite complex but it's actually very simple, and hinges around the fact that ADO allows us to create our own new, empty recordsets and then populate them with fields and records. For this we define a new recordset called oCR, set the cursor location to client-side (`adUseClient`), add some fields, and then open the recordset, but without specifying a source of data or a data store.

To make this routine generic we set the fields of the new recordset (oCR) using the `Fields` collection of the existing recordset (oRec—the recordset we passed in as a parameter to this function). A recordset's `Fields` collection contains the details of each field in the recordset. We can use this to loop through all of the fields in oRec and generate identical fields in oCR using the same details.

At least, that's what I thought would happen when I first built this component. If you compile this component using the `Search()` and `RecordsetDuplicate()` functions given above, it'll work perfectly when called from Visual Basic programs; but it will fail when used in RDS.

Further investigation revealed the problem—some fields (specifically the `DocTitle` and `characterization` fields) *refer* to text that is only returned when the field is accessed. These fields don't contain the data itself—instead they contain a pointer that tells the application where to find the data. (Consequently, the size of these fields doesn't relate to the size of the data itself—instead it relates to the size of the pointer.) RDS, it seems, cannot cope with these fields. What we really need to do is replace each of these fields with a character field whose size is large enough to contain the data. To achieve this, we'll create another function that will search through all records to find the record with the largest amount of text in it, and we use that value to assign the size of our new character field.

So, instead of just duplicating the fields exactly, we have to do several things:

❑ Convert variant fields to character fields.

❑ Find out the maximum length of data in these fields.

❑ Ensure that null values are catered for

With this in mind, our duplication function is more complex, but provides a recordset that works with RDS. Here's the implementation of `RecordsetDuplicate()` that we'll use:

```
Private Function RecordsetDuplicate(oRec As ADODB.Recordset) As ADODB.Recordset
    Dim oCR     As New ADODB.Recordset
    Dim oFld    As ADODB.Field
    Dim lType   As Long
    Dim lSize   As Long

    oCR.CursorLocation = adUseClient      ' use a client side cursor

    With oCR
        For Each oFld In oRec.Fields       ' create the new fields
            If oFld.Type = adVariant Then    ' convert variants to chars
                lType = adVarWChar
            Else
                lType = oFld.Type
            End If

            'If the field may 'defer' (i.e. it may only be fetched when
            'it's directly accessed) then it's likely to be a pointer
            'to long data, and it's size will reflect the size of the
            'pointer rather than the data. So get the actual field size
            If (oFld.Attributes And adFldMayDefer) = adFldMayDefer Then
                lSize = GetFieldSize(oRec, oFld.Name)
            Else
                lSize = oFld.DefinedSize
            End If
            .Fields.Append oFld.Name, lType, lSize    ' append field to new recordset
        Next
        .Open                                'open the new recordset
        While Not oRec.EOF                   'append the existing data
            .AddNew
            For Each oFld In oRec.Fields
                ' For Variants and Chars, append an empty string
                ' This has the effect of converting nulls to empty strings
                If oFld.Type = adVariant Or oFld.Type = adVarWChar Then
                    .Fields(oFld.Name).Value = Trim$(oFld.Value & "")
                Else
                    .Fields(oFld.Name).Value = oFld.Value
                End If
            Next
            .Update
            oRec.MoveNext
        Wend
    End With
    Set RecordsetDuplicate = oCR
End Function
```

The routine still has the same structure as the first attempt, but just converts fields that contain deferrable data into fields with the actual data. To find the length of the text fields, we use another private routine called `GetFieldSize()`:

```
Private Function GetFieldSize(oRec As ADODB.Recordset, sField As String) As Long
   Dim lSize       As Long            ' largest size so far
   Dim lS          As Long            ' current size
   Dim oRC         As ADODB.Recordset ' clone of the recordset

   If oRec.EOF Then            ' return same size if no rows
      lSize = oRec(sField).DefinedSize
   Else
      Set oRC = oRec.Clone    ' clone the recordset so we can do our own positioning
      While Not oRC.EOF       ' loop through the records finding the largest size
         If Not IsNull(oRC(sField)) Then
            lS = Len(oRC(sField))
            If lS > lSize Then
               lSize = lS
            End If
         End If
         oRC.MoveNext
      Wend
   End If
   Set oRC = Nothing
   GetFieldSize = lSize
End Function
```

This simply searches through the recordset, checking a specific field, and finding the length of the data in that field. It returns the length of the largest data found.

To summarize: your complete component should contain a single class called `Query`, which has one public function called `Search()` and two private functions called `RecordsetDuplicate()` and `GetFieldSize()`. You should be ready to compile the component now (select File | Make WroxIndexer.dll).

This component provides very simple searching of Index Server. You could easily extend it to search for other criteria, such as document creation times, document sizes, and so on. The Microsoft Samples supplied with Index Server (under `inetpub\iissamples\ISSamples`) include an ASP page that uses ADO for advanced searching (`advsqlq.asp`). You could easily use this as a basis for extending the component.

Testing the WroxIndexer Component in an ASP Page

Now that we have a component to do Index Server searching, we can build a Web page to use it. Here's an ASP page called `ASPSearch.asp`:

```
<%@ LANGUAGE=VBSCRIPT %>
<!-- METADATA TYPE="typelib"
FILE="c:\program files\common files\system\ado\msado15.dll" -->
<HTML>
<HEAD>
<TITLE>The Wrox Press Intranet</TITLE>
<STYLE TYPE="text/css">
  BODY {font-family:Tahoma,Arial,sans-serif; font-size:10pt}
    .heading {font-family:Tahoma,Arial,sans-serif; font-size:14pt; font-weight:bold}
    .cite {font-family:Tahoma,Arial,sans-serif; font-size:8pt}
  TR.title {font-weight:bold; background-color:darkgray}
</STYLE>
</HEAD>
```

```
<BODY BGCOLOR="#FFFFFF">
<SPAN CLASS="heading">Welcome to the Wrox Press Intranet</SPAN><HR>
<!----------------------------------------------------------------------->

<%
  Dim sQuery
  sQuery = Request.Form("SearchString")
%>

<FORM NAME="QueryForm" ACTION="ASPSearch.asp" METHOD="POST">
Search for
<INPUT TYPE="TEXT" NAME="SearchString" VALUE="<%=sQuery%>">
<INPUT TYPE="SUBMIT" VALUE="Search">
</FORM>

<%
if sQuery <> "" Then
    Dim oQuery
    Dim oRec

    Set oQuery = Server.CreateObject("WroxIndexer.Query")
    Set oRec = Server.CreateObject("ADODB.Recordset")
    oRec.CursorLocation = adUseClient
    Set oRec = oQuery.Search(sQuery)

    oRec.MoveFirst
    While Not oRec.EOF %>
        <TABLE>
          <TR CLASS="title">
            <TD>Title</TD><TD><%=oRec("DocTitle")%></TD>
          </TR>
          <TR>
            <TD>Abstract</TD><TD><%=oRec("characterization")%></TD>
          </TR>
          <TR>
            <TD> </TD><TD><A HREF=<%=oRec("vPath")%>><%=oRec("vPath")%></A></TD>
          </TR>
          <TR><TD> </TD><TD> </TD></TR>
        </TABLE>
        <%
        oRec.MoveNext
    Wend

    oRec.Close
    Set oRec = Nothing
    Set oQuery = Nothing
End If
%>
<!----------------------------------------------------------------------->
<HR>
<SPAN CLASS="cite">&copy;1999 <A CLASS="cite" HREF="http://www.wrox.com/">
Wrox Press</A></SPAN>
</BODY>
</HTML>
```

It uses an instance of our component on the Web server, so you'll need to ensure that `WroxIndexer.dll` is registered on the Web server machine. And don't forget that this will only work if you have Index Server installed on the Web server too!

When you fire this up, and enter a search term, you should get something like this:

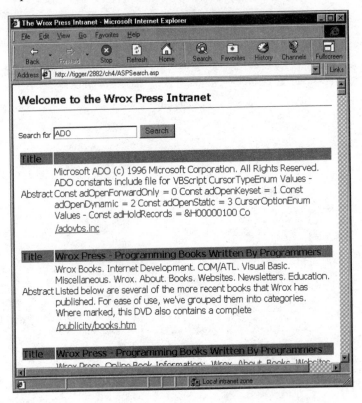

How It Works

The first time you call this, you should get a simple message asking you for a search term. It's just a simple form that creates this:

```
<FORM NAME="QueryForm" ACTION="ASPSearch.asp" METHOD="POST">
Search for
<INPUT TYPE="TEXT" NAME="SearchString" VALUE="<%=sQuery%>">
<INPUT TYPE="SUBMIT" VALUE="Search">
</FORM>
```

When you hit the **Search** button, the page is reloaded and your search term passed as part of the `Request.Form` collection. Its value is assigned to a page-level variant, `sQuery`:

```
sQuery = Request.Form("SearchString")
```

If this string is non-empty, then we set about searching the web site and displaying the results of the search. First, we create an instance of the `Query` component and an ADO `Recordset`. We ensure that the recordset has a client-side cursor, and then we populate it using the `Query` component:

```
if sQuery <> "" Then
    ...
    Set oQuery = Server.CreateObject("WroxIndexer.Query")
    Set oRec = Server.CreateObject("ADODB.Recordset")
    oRec.CursorLocation = adUseClient
    Set oRec = oQuery.Search(sQuery)
```

We've finished with the `Query` component now, so we can destroy that component instance and release its resources:

```
Set oQuery = Nothing
```

Now it's just a case of writing the contents of the recordset to the browser, using a combination of HTML and ASP. The only slightly tricky part is the third line of the table, where we've used an anchor tag `<A>` to give the end-user a click-through to the indexed pages. Finally, we release the recordset's resources:

```
  oRec.MoveFirst
  While Not oRec.EOF %>
    <TABLE>
      <TR CLASS="title">
        <TD>Title</TD><TD><%=oRec("DocTitle")%></TD>
      </TR>
      <TR>
        <TD>Abstract</TD><TD><%=oRec("characterization")%></TD>
      </TR>
      <TR>
        <TD> </TD><TD><A HREF=<%=oRec("vPath")%>><%=oRec("vPath")%></A></TD>
      </TR>
      <TR><TD> </TD><TD> </TD></TR>
    </TABLE>
    <%
  oRec.MoveNext
  Wend
  oRec.Close
  Set oRec = Nothing
End If
```

Testing the WroxIndexer Component via RDS

In order to use the `WroxIndexer.Query` object as a custom datafactory object for RDS we follow the two-step registration process that we used for `PubsDataAccess.dll` earlier in the chapter. First, register the component on the Web server by using `RegSvr32.exe` at the command prompt:

```
regsvr32 WroxIndexer.dll
```

Second, instruct IIS that this component can be used as a custom component instead of the `RDSServer.DataFactory` object. To do this, run `RegEdit.exe`, and in the registry window navigate to the following path:

```
HKEY_LOCAL_MACHINE\SYSTEM\CurrentControlSet\Services\W3SVC\Parameters\ADCLaunch\
```

Right-click on **ADCLaunch** and select **New | Key**. Then right-click on the new key, select **Rename** and type **WroxIndexer.Query**.

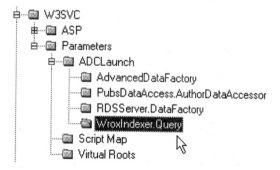

To test this, we'll use the following web page, called `RDSSearch.asp`:

```
<!-- line below references the ADO type library -->
<!-- METDATA TYPE="typelib"
FILE="C:\program files\common files\system\ado\msado15.dll" -->

<HTML>
<HEAD>
<TITLE>Using RDS and Components for Index Server Searching</TITLE>
<STYLE TYPE="text/css">
TR.title {font-weight:bold; background-color:darkgray}
</STYLE>
</HEAD>
<BODY>

<!-- this is the normal RDS DataControl object with no parameters set -->
<OBJECT id="dsoResults"
    classid="clsid:BD96C556-65A3-11D0-983A-00C04FC29E33" height="0" width="0">
</OBJECT>

<!-- this is the client-side RDS DataSpace object -->
<OBJECT id="dspDataSpace"
    classid="CLSID:BD96C556-65A3-11D0-983A-00C04FC29E36" height="0" width="0">
</OBJECT>

Search For
<INPUT TYPE="text" ID="txtSearch"></INPUT>
<BUTTON ID="cmdSearch" onclick="Search()">Search</BUTTON>
<P>
<P ID="lblNoResults" STYLE="display:none">No matching documents found</P>
<button id="cmdPrevious1" title="Previous Page" STYLE="display:none"
    onclick="tblResults.previousPage()">
     &lt; </button>
<button id="cmdNext1" title="Next Page" STYLE="display:none"
    onclick="tblResults.nextPage()">
     &gt; </button>
<P>

<TABLE id="tblResults" DATASRC="#dsoResults"
                      DATAPAGESIZE="10" BORDER="0" STYLE="display:none">
  <TR CLASS="title">
    <TD>Title</TD><TD><A DATAFLD="vpath"><SPAN DATAFLD="DocTitle"></SPAN></A></TD>
  </TR>
    <TR><TD>Abstract</TD><TD><SPAN DATAFLD="characterization"></SPAN></TD></TR>
    <TR><TD> </TD><TD><A DATAFLD="vpath"><SPAN
DATAFLD="vpath"></SPAN></A></TD></TR>
    <TR><TD> </TD><TD> </TD></TR>
</TABLE>
<P>
<button id="cmdPrevious2" title="Previous Page" STYLE="display:none"
    onclick="tblResults.previousPage()">
     &lt; </button>
<button id="cmdNext2" title="Next Page" STYLE="display:none"
    onclick="tblResults.nextPage()">
     &gt; </button>

<SCRIPT LANGUAGE="JavaScript">

  function Search()
  {
    <%
      ' Create a client side variable with the name of the Web server in it.
      ' This means you don't have to change the server name of you move this
      ' page onto a different server
      Response.Write "    sServer = 'http://" & Request("server_name") & "'"
    %>
```

```
    // first we create a DataFactory object, specifying the server to use:
    myCustomObject = dspDataSpace.CreateObject("WroxIndexer.Query", sServer);

    // now we create a recordset from the custom object using a custom method:
    myRecordset = myCustomObject.Search(txtSearch.value);

    if (myRecordset.EOF)
    {
      lblNoResults.style.display = "inline"
      tblResults.style.display = "none"
      cmdPrevious1.style.display = "none"
      cmdNext1.style.display = "none"
      cmdPrevious2.style.display = "none"
      cmdNext2.style.display = "none"
    }
    else
    {
      lblNoResults.style.display = "none"
      tblResults.style.display = "inline"
      cmdPrevious1.style.display = "inline"
      cmdNext1.style.display = "inline"
      cmdPrevious2.style.display = "inline"
      cmdNext2.style.display = "inline"

      // finally, assign the returned recordset to the DataControl object:
      dsoResults.SourceRecordset = myRecordset;
    }
  }
</SCRIPT>

</BODY>
</HTML>
```

When you fire this up in your browser, you should get a page like this:

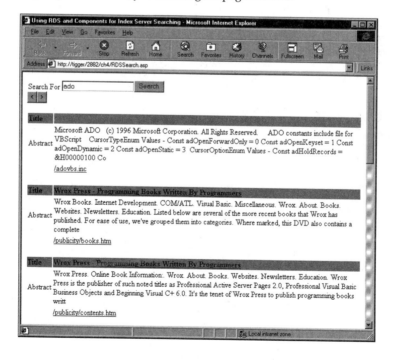

The screenshot shows the result I got when searching for the term **ADO**. You can use the paging buttons to move through the pages of results, without returning to the server. Also notice that although the first two documents do not have titles, you can still use the URL to access them. All in all, this is a fairly simple component and Web page, but it offers great possibilities. The full set of code is available from the supporting Web site. Let's focus in on how it works.

How It Works

The first things to include in the page are the RDS objects:

```
<OBJECT id="dsoResults"
    classid="clsid:BD96C556-65A3-11D0-983A-00C04FC29E33" height="0" width="0">
</OBJECT>

<OBJECT id="dspDataSpace"
    classid="CLSID:BD96C556-65A3-11D0-983A-00C04FC29E36" height="0" width="0">
</OBJECT>
```

We need a table to view the results:

```
<TABLE id="tblResults" DATASRC="#dsoResults"
                        DATAPAGESIZE="10" BORDER="0" STYLE="display:none">
  <TR CLASS="title">
    <TD>Title</TD><TD><A DATAFLD="vpath"><SPAN DATAFLD="DocTitle"></SPAN></A></TD>
  </TR>
  <TR><TD>Abstract</TD><TD><SPAN DATAFLD="characterization"></SPAN></TD></TR>
  <TR><TD> </TD><TD><A DATAFLD="vpath"><SPAN
DATAFLD="vpath"></SPAN></A></TD></TR>
  <TR><TD> </TD><TD> </TD></TR>
</TABLE>
```

This table has three rows, for the title of the document, the abstract, and the URL. In our previous data-binding example, RDSTable.asp, we used input fields bound to the data, but here we only want to display the data, so we use different HTML elements depending upon what we are trying to achieve. For the document title and URL, we use <A> tags, since we want people to be able to click these fields and jump directly to the document. For the abstract we use a <SPAN> tag. You can't bind data directly to a table cell (<TD>) so we have to use another tag, and a <SPAN> fits well.

Now we need some way for the user to specify the phrase to search for:

```
Search For
<INPUT TYPE="text" ID="txtSearch"></INPUT>
<BUTTON ID="cmdSearch" onclick="Search()">Search</BUTTON>
```

And finally, the client-side Search() function, which actually runs the search:

```
function Search()
{
  <%
    Response.Write "    sServer = 'http://" & Request("server_name") & "'"
  %>
  myCustomObject = dspDataSpace.CreateObject("WroxIndexer.Query", sServer);
  myRecordset = myCustomObject.Search(txtSearch.value);
```

So far, this code is very similar to our previous examples. It uses the `DataSpace` object to create our custom component, and then calls the method to perform the search. If the recordset returned has no records, then some text indicating that the search found no matches is made visible:

```
if (myRecordset.EOF)
{
  lblNoResults.style.display = "inline"
  tblResults.style.display = "none"
  ...
}
```

If the returned recordset is not empty, then the recordset is assigned as the source of the Data Source Object, and the table is displayed:

```
else
{
  lblNoResults.style.display = "none"
  tblResults.style.display = "inline"
  ...
  // finally, assign the returned recordset to the DataControl object:
  dsoResults.SourceRecordset = myRecordset;
}
}
```

ADO Future

ADO is a technology under continual development. Version 2.1 is supplied with Internet Explorer 5, and with Office 2000, and is available for free download from the Microsoft Web site (http://www.microsoft.com/data), where the latest version is available for download.

Windows 2000 will ship with ADO version 2.5, which extends the features that ADO provides. At the time of writing, we expect the most noticeable extensions to be:

❑ The ability to access Internet resources. This will, for example, allow you to create recordsets that contain files retrieved from a Web server; ADO will also provide the ability to manage those files. You'll be able to open, edit, move, and delete documents on remote Web servers, allowing you to build Web management tools.

❑ An OLE DB provider for the next version of SQL Server, allowing better transformation of data between SQL Server and clients.

❑ An OLE DB provider for the next version (6.0) of Exchange Server, allowing full ADO access to Exchange resources, such as mailboxes, public folders, and so on.

❑ Improved support for XML, allowing recordsets to be easily converted to XML.

Some of these features have yet to be confirmed, but they will provide great opportunities for component builders. With these features, the objective of UDA to become closer to reality.

Summary

In this chapter, we began with the idea that ADO and COM provide a level of abstraction that allows us to use similar techniques in quite widely differing situations. For example, ADO uses the same three intrinsic objects (Connection, Command, and Recordset) to access all kinds of data sources—from all types of relational databases to Microsoft Index Server and Microsoft Exchange.

In the same way, by building components that abide by the rules of COM, we can use them in a variety of situations. This might be on the client in a Web page, on the server in an ASP page, or wrapped up in another custom component or compiled application. In some circumstances, these components can even be created by simple text files containing script code.

We've seen that:

❑ The object of Microsoft's Universal Data Access strategy is to provide access to multiple data formats in multiple locations

❑ ADO is a set of high-level COM components that we can use in COM-compliant languages to access data

❑ ADO's disconnected recordsets have an important role to play in data access via components

❑ We can components to encapsulate server side data access to different data stores

❑ We can easily create components to create data that is persisted on the browser machine (via RDS) or on the Web server (via ASP pages)

In the next chapter, we'll take a look at granularity in components, and we'll study a data access problem in order to illustrate some of the issues involved.

In subsequent chapters we'll begin to tackle Microsoft Transaction Server (MTS)—a collection of services that includes transaction management but actually provides a whole lot more. MTS is going to be an integral part of COM+ in Windows 2000—which reflects the power that MTS can give us in terms of component management. We'll also be returning to the subject of data access, with an example that combines the flexibility of ADO and the capabilities of MTS as a transaction server.

Application Architecture and ASP Component Design

The first and golden rule of writing any application holds equally true when building your components. Planning in advance will save you time in the long run. If you have to visit a friend and you have no idea where they live, you don't just get in your car and drive aimlessly hoping you might find them, you look at a map and plan your journey. Even if your deadline to develop an application seems impossibly tight, planning your implementation first will save you time in the long run. This chapter covers some of the issues you should look at when planning your applications and where you should be when using components.

Often, the best way of solving a problem is to break it up into pieces. Figure out the answer to each individual part, and how they piece together to form a solution. This approach works, and it just so happens to be a good way to implement a component-based system—write lots of individual components that individually don't really do too much, yet are interrelated and integrated so that when orchestrated together (perhaps with a little ASP glue) form a solution to the problem.

If we design our components right, we'll be able to reuse them time and time again either in different projects or even within our applications, repeatedly using them to solve similar problems. However, for a component to achieve this level of reuse we have to make sure that it doesn't do too much, at the same time as making sure it doesn't do too little. The last thing we want to do is spend all our time writing the glue code to hold the components together, if it's quicker to write bigger components and have a solution that consists of larger pieces.

In this chapter we will look at some of the issues (not *yet* covered) that confront us when we are designing components. Firstly, we will expand the notion of 3-tier architecture which we met in Chapter 1, and introduce the concept of **n-tier** applications. While we are looking at *n*-tier structures we will come across another term for some components: **business objects**. After this, we will go over several points that you must consider when deciding how much functionality to put into each component.

> We have already come across several design issues in this book already. In particular, we met a number of interface design considerations in Chapter 2, and looked at when we should consider taking advantage of the environment in which our component may be run, in Chapter 3. The discussion on component design in this chapter will build upon what we have seen already. One issue is that we will be paying particular attention to how much functionality we put into each component.

Some of the *n*-tier and business object concepts we will be explaining in the first half of this chapter may be new to a lot of web developers. They have, however, been successfully employed by many programmers implementing component-based solutions, and as we shall see they are particularly relevant in the distributed environment of the Web.

Of course, we could never claim to provide a definitive answer on how to design each and every component you will ever build—not even in a series of books, let alone one chapter. What we will do, however, is show you many of the points that you need to consider when looking at your specific problem. By taking these points into consideration when you are designing your components you will be in a position to determine the most appropriate solution for your particular problem.

In this chapter we will see:

❑ The difference between 3-tier and *n*-tier artchitectures

❑ How application architecture can affect the benefits of componentization

❑ How 'business objects' can be used to model real world situations

❑ Some generalized component design issues

❑ Points to consider when deciding how much functionality to put into your component

> **Different people have their own views on how architecture should be described, Object Oriented programmers, Visual Basic developers and web programmers often talk about system architecture in different ways. Rather than concerning yourself with using the correct terminology, for the moment, understanding the issues you need to be concerned with is far more important.**

Understanding the Problem Domain

We have already said that splitting up a problem into distinct pieces helps us solve problems. Before you can get started on planning your web applications, you must make sure that you are clear on what you are trying to achieve. When approaching building a web application your first task is to understand the **problem domain**, understanding the goals you have to achieve. When you know what the real aim of the application is, you can look at how you are going to provide an application with the necessary functionality to achieve the goal set.

If you remember back to Chapter 2, we developed a component that calculated the insurance premium for cars. Now consider the situation where you're working for an insurance company who want to give out quotes on the web, and they ask you to implement this as one feature of the whole web site. In order to implement these calculations, you'll need to understand the company's **business rules**.

These may include:

- The prices charged for different types of car—sports cars may cost more than family cars

- Different multipliers based upon engine size—the larger the engine size the more that may be charged

- The discounts that are available on these rates for different customers—women may be charged a certain percentage less than men

- When you will not offer insurance—maybe to a young male who has a powerful sports car

Business rules are important because they define how a business functions—in a sense they are the fabric from which a business is built. They are also vital to the design of the application, as you have to offer a solution that models these rules in code.

These are the types of rules we had to encapsulate into the component we built in Chapter 2. However, if we were implementing a system for the insurance company, we might have to take this application further and allow some people to offer insurance based on these quotes. Or, we might like to allow insurance to be taken out over the Web, in which case we would have to look at a lot more of the business rules and perhaps develop several more components.

When we are trying to understand the problem domain, if we have several tasks to perform, it is often wise to create several components. Each component can then model a particular part of the business. For example, we might have an object that represents the customer, one that validates the customer's credit card and starts the transfer of funds from their account to the company's, one that makes sure the customer is sent a receipt and a certificate, etc. When each component models a part of the business in this way they are referred to as **business objects**. Of course, it is not always possible, or indeed wise, to follow this structure, but we will come back to a discussion on what each component should achieve after we have had a look at application architecture.

3-Tier and N-Tier Application Architecture

In order to learn about component design, we have to look at application architecture. I was once told by an architect working for a well-known company which offered web solutions that, when teaching ASP, they used to tell their programmers to use JavaScript on the client, but to use VBScript on the server. While this practice is not uncommon, their reason for teaching it this way was that many of the web programmers had difficulty understanding where each bit of script was running. Was it on the client or on the server?

As distributed applications started to take off, programmers introduced the idea of tiers in applications to help them devise better solutions. Because the Web is inherently distributed, we can learn a lot from these architectural concepts, and as ASP developers we can use them to help understand how we can model our ASP applications, which in turn helps us with our component design.

In Chapter 1 we introduced the idea of 3-tier architecture, where you have a client application, a middle tier where your web server resides, and a data tier holding your persistent data.

Here we should note two points:

❑ There is no universal definition of how a tier is distinguished—different people use the term in slightly different ways.

❑ There is a very important distinction between logical and physical tiers. Logical tiers help us think about the different parts of the application conceptually, while physical tiers are the physical machines that each section of code resides on. In reality the physical tiers may reside on any number of machines (possibly only one in the development environment), while the logical tiers may span more than one physical tier).

The three tiers we described earlier break down as follows:

❑ The **presentation tier** (also referred to as the client tier) is the front-end tool with which the end user interacts. It contains all the presentation logic: the code responsible for displaying data to the end user, and also for retrieving information from the end user.

The presentation tier of a 3-tier application may take the form of any type of user interface, such as a Visual Basic application, or (increasingly commonly) a web browser. In ASP applications, the client tier usually takes the form of a web browser. In any case, applications and components in the presentation tier run on the client's machine, and therefore consume the client's resources.

> As we shall see later in the chapter, this does not particularly fit the case of ASP applications as the ASP pages in the middle tier generate the code that the user interacts with. However, we will continue with this breakdown of tiers for the moment.

❑ The **middle tier** is where the business rules come in and where you'll find a collection of business objects (or, more accurately, business components) that model one or a set of those rules. As you may realize, these objects make up the greater part of the application's functionality and also account for a big percentage of its size too.

The client tier collects information required from the user so that the middle tier can perform whatever processing is neccesary to achieve the task the application is intended to perform. Sometimes this will require additional information from a data store, or it may require information to be written to some form of persistent storage. The data transactions, however, are handled by the third tier.

> Because the middle tier is where the business rules are enforced, it is often called the 'business tier'.

❑ The **data tier** represents the storage medium used to hold persistent data. As we keep more and more data in electronic formats, this tier encompasses an ever growing number of storage formats, not only relational databases, but also text-based files, directories, mail servers, speadsheet files etc.

Each tier is responsible for providing a specific type of service. Indeed, you'll often hear of these tiers being referred to as **presentation services**, **business services** and **data services**, and these terms are generally used interchangeably with the terms above.

We can represent the three tiers of a distributed application visually, where each tier is on a different machine or different physical tier, in such a way that the logical relationship between them is clear. In the diagram below, each tier is a 'client' to the tier on its right, and a 'server' to the tier on its left. The client on the presentation tier has a user interface that allows it to ask for a list of customers, perhaps based upon some criteria such as customers that have bought something within the last year, or customers that have spent over $200 in the past six months. The middle tier includes a component called by an ASP page to retrieve the list of customers from the data tier, where the actual details of the customers reside.

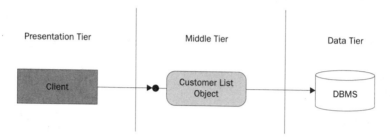

We will come back to this example in various points throughout this chapter. But here you can see that the client application (in the presentation tier) contacts the customer list object (in the middle tier) and requests customer information. In order to service this request, the customer list object uses the services of the data store (in the data tier) to supply the actual data (in the form of a recordset, in this case). The customer list object then presents the data in the appropriate form to the client, and then the client can deal with the presentational issues involved in displaying the data to the end user.

The Presentation Tier

The presentation tier has two key characteristics:

❑ The presentation tier only contains presentation logic—it does not concern itself with the inner workings of the application (that logic is isolated within the business tier, as we'll see shortly).

❑ The presentation tier does not access a data source directly. In order to access data, it must pass requests to the business tier, which performs data access on the client's behalf.

This level of separation and encapsulation is important, because it shields the browser (or other client tool) from the complexity of our application's inner workings. As a consequence, we can make changes in the middle tier without having to update the client. For example, we could change the business rules; we could add new servers to enhance performance; we could even add or change databases. This is one of the main advantages of three-tier systems, as we'll discuss later when we talk about the scalability of *n*-tier systems.

There is a parallel here with the components that we are developing. In the same way that the presentation tier shields the user from the things that are going on in the middle and data tiers, components can shield the implementation code behind the component from the user, just exposing its methods and properties through an interface in the same way that a user interface may expose functionality of the application through form fields and other methods for gathering data.

The Middle Tier

We have already said that the middle tier is where most of the applications logic resides. As we said earlier, there is an intention that this should model the real business that it is representing. It is composed of business components that represent real-world things or concepts that are meaningful within a specific problem domain.

> *If you find yourself wanting to use business components regularly in your ASP application's development, after your introduction to using components from ASP in this book, then Visual Basic 6 Business Objects and Visual Basic 6 Distributed Objects published by Wrox Press (ISBN 1-861001-07-X and 1-861002-07-6) both provide more coverage on how to model and implement VB Business Objects.*

Let's look at another example to make sure that we understand this concept; think about a sales-ordering system. A customer, order, delivery, product, or invoice could each be represented using a business component, because each of these components represents a real world concept, and can have similar interactions.

Think about how you could order a copy of this book in the real world over the phone. The customer phones up and gives someone at the other end of the phone the details of the book they want, the quantity, where it should be delivered and how they will pay. This is like the presentation tier. But what happens then once the order is placed?

❑   An order form would be created and filled in. This would contain details about the books ordered, who they are for, and how they will be paid for.

❑   The payment has to be verified and collected

❑   The order has to go to the warehouse for dispatch

❑   The warehouse has to send it to the customer

❑   Stocks have to be updated

These are all distinct tasks. In an automated on-line bookselling system it might be a little different. The user fills in a form on the Internet using a browser, then:

❑   An instance of the customer component could create an order object with the details collected from the form

❑   A credit card validating component can be used to check that the payment details given are correct and start the transfer of funds

❑   The order object, once payment has been verified can be passed to the warehouse for dispatch

❑   The order object can also be used to update the stocks residing on the data tier using a data access component

In the on-line version we have modeled the physical situation using an instance of each component. The individual objects take the place of a task from the phone-based scenario. By modeling our applications on real world concepts and relationships, it makes the application itself easier to design and to understand.

The concepts also follow the general rules by which the business operates: the business rules. Business components just put the ordinary everyday business rules into programming logic. We always need to know the title of a book and the quantity ordered, whether the book is ordered over the phone or online, just like we need to know the person's name, address, and payment details in addition to the order so that we can fulfill it. We also need to keep a record of our stock so we don't sell items we haven't got, so we need to decrement stock numbers each time we fulfill an order. Following the business rules is a way of ensuring that the data of the application maintains **integrity**.

By isolating the rules in the business components, no matter where the objects are used, the same business rules will be enforced. This is important as it ensures consistency throughout our distributed application. We can even allow different types of clients access to our business objects—web browsers or Visual Basic applications—but our business integrity will not be violated because the same objects will always be used. Furthermore, because each component has modeled a part of the real business rules, should one area of the task change, we only have to alter one component rather than finding all of the appropriate changes that would need to be made in a linear application.

The Data Tier

As we saw in the last chapter, there are many sorts of data that may need to be accessed. In addition to the relational databases that are often used as examples in ASP books, we may need to interact with directories (we will see how to do this in Chapter 9 on ADSI), with Index Server (as we saw in the last chapter), text-based files (as we will see in Chapters 15 and 16), the list goes on. Again, we separate this out from the implementation of the business rules that reside in the middle tier. This enables our applications to accept data from any number of sources without concern for their type or location.

Exceptions to the Rule

Like all good attempts at rigid classification, there are a couple of fairly common examples that are not so easy to categorize, and at least one of them is directly relevant to us here. The lines between the tiers begin to blur when we examine stored procedures and—you guessed it—Active Server Pages.

Stored Procedures—Business Logic in the Data Tier

There are many cases where operations such as queries are performed on a frequent basis. Rather than have a database interpret these instructions each time, most modern databases allow some means of saving these instructions in the database, so that they can be accessed quickly. These are known in some databases as **stored procedures**, or in the case of Access, **QueryDefs.**

Both can search through, retrieve, create, update and destroy data, but while QueryDefs can hold just the one query, stored procedures can hold several to be run consecutively, just as a procedure or function does in Visual Basic or C++. These stored procedures are actually compiled as execution plans, which further reduce the work that needs to be done on each call. These complied execution plans save the database from having to interpret the SQL statement and build an access map at runtime.

Access maps are essentially the route a SQL engine takes to retrieve rows for a SQL query depending upon available indexes and other optimizations.

In the case of stored procedures, a lot of the processing can be done on the server hosting the database, which effectively means that the processing is occurring within the data tier. So, while they give SQL-intensive applications a great performance boost, they do not fit neatly into our physical 3-tier model.

At a very minimum, using stored procedures in SQL Server usually shows a 25% increase in overall scalability of a system, but much higher improvements can be achieved depending upon the complexity of the database schema and the individual queries used.

Whilst it might initially sound as though we are putting business rules into the data tier, we've still got the logic isolated in one location (although it could be spread through many different stored procedures), and the performance factor alone is a reasonable trade off to make. The only time you have to question using stored procedures is when you've got an *n*-tier system that makes use of multiple databases on different servers, in which case stored procedures may be duplicated.

ASP Pages—Middle Tier or Presentation Tier?

We mentioned earlier that ASP does not fit easily into the physical three-tier model. As ASP developers, our business tier will encompass the ASP-dependent and ASP-independent components we write, and also the ASP pages themselves. But this statement presents us with something of a paradox, because the ASP pages are responsible for creating visual output for a client, which means they have presentation elements. So, why do we say that ASP pages live in the middle tier?

In physical tier terms, the presentation tier is effectively the client machine, and Active Server Pages are clearly not part of this presentation tier, although they do have a tendency towards it. Because having both visual and non-visual elements as part of a single tier is confusing, the middle tier of ASP applications is subdivided into two tiers: the **user-centric** and **data-centric** tiers. This gives a typical, well-designed ASP application four tiers, leading us nicely on to a discussion of *n*-tier applications.

The user-centric and data-centric tiers are not specific to IIS and ASP. They are generic concepts that are used when a business tier contains different components that have different focus.

N-Tier Applications

There need be no mystery behind the term '*n*-tier application'—it's simply a generic way of referring to applications that have three or more tiers. The case where we are splitting up the middle tier to incorporate user-centric and data-centric tiers is an ideal example of an *n*-tier application.

User-Centric and Data-Centric Tiers

The user-centric tier of an ASP application contains the ASP pages and environment-dependent ASP components that help render HTML pages to the presentation tier. As we discussed in Chapter 3, environment-dependent ASP components generally make use of the ASP object model, so they are effectively tied to the user interface in some fashion—generating HTML, accessing and creating cookies, etc. These components generally enforce basic business rules that are unlikely to change, such as validating the contents of the Request object to ensure that a user has correctly logged on.

The data-centric tier contains the components that do not depend upon the ASP environment. These are responsible for performing database manipulation, such as adding, deleting, querying and updating records in a table. These components are in no way dependent upon the ASP environment.

Four Tiers

If we re-consider the situation where we were retrieving a list of customers, which we met at the beginning of the section on 3-tier application architecture, we can see how it would fit better into an *n*-tier architecture. We will split the middle tier into two logical tiers. We now have an ASP page, residing on the user-centric tier that provides an interface for the user on the client browser. It also collects the information from the user interface on the client and passes it to the data-centric tier, which is responsible for accessing data from the database. The return values are then passed back to the ASP so that they can be formatted for the client to see.

In this case, the ASP component responsible for creating the HTML page resides in the user-centric tier, whilst the customer list component resides in the data-centric tier, as shown in the following diagram:

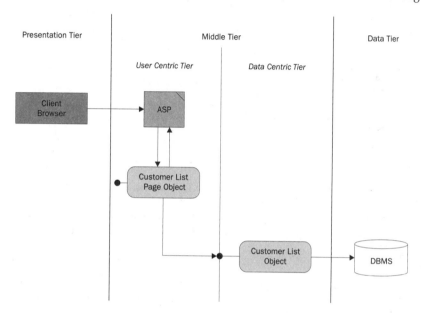

Because our customer list object does not rely on the ASP object model (the form values are passed through the ASP page), there is no reason why our distributed application can't have different types of client interfaces. Rather than always using a web browser, we could decide that a Visual Basic application is better for some clients.

Also, consider the possible scenario that we have to change our database—perhaps we are upgrading from Access to SQL Server as more people are using our application. If all of the code that uses the database is kept in a data-centric component, we only need to change that one part of our application.

The middle tier can even be split up into three rather than two, if we separate out the ASP pages from the user-centric objects, so the n in n-tier is now effectively five tiers:

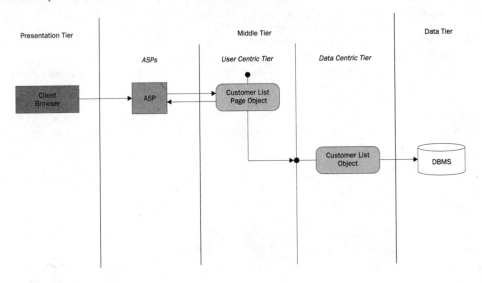

Thin and Fat Clients

Now consider a slightly more diverse client base, with a Visual Basic client as well as a web-based client, as shown in the figure below. The Visual Basic application accesses the objects located in the data-centric tier *directly*. This is important because it emphasizes that tiers are only a logical construct. It is possible for the presentation tier to access the data-centric tier without going through the user-centric tier.

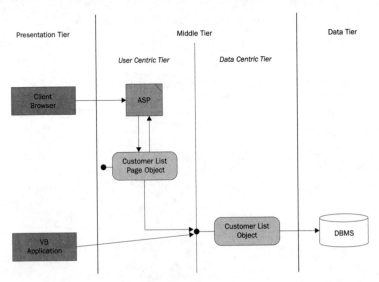

As ASP developers, we generally create **thin clients**, so called because most of the application processing and business logic is actually on the server in the form of Active Server Pages and possibly one or more additional components.

Thin Clients

The main benefit of thin clients is that all of the presentation code, application code and business logic is effectively centralized in one location, so we can completely redesign the look and feel of our application, correct business logic errors or add new business rules without having to go around and physically update each and every client. Instead, we just change the ASP and/or components (which are stored in a central location), and that's it! In addition, thin clients should be faster to download and run, and there are fewer dependencies upon the environment.

The main disadvantage of thin clients is that they do not make use of the considerable computational power that most clients now have. We can of course achieve this with some browser-based solutions, by packaging up components into CAB files and having them automatically downloaded and installed. Alternatively we could use ActiveX controls, scriptlets, or Java applets. We then just use JScript or VBScript on the client side to carry out more client-side processing. The only problem here is that CAB files, ActiveX controls and scriptlets are not browser-neutral, and generally only work well with Internet Explorer 4 and above.

Fat Clients

The alternative to thin clients is **fat clients** (also known as intelligent clients), in which some Active Server Pages on the server are essentially replaced by more code on the client in the shape of an application. The advantages of fat clients are that less CPU time on the server is consumed, and they tend to be more visually rich. Reduced CPU consumption per client results in much more scalable systems, with the trade off being increased maintenance of clients. In theory, fat clients could be quite attractive for systems that have larger numbers of users, and/or business objects that perform operations consuming a large amount of CPU time.

The main disadvantage of fat clients is that, should we decide to change the style of the user interface (or need to fix bugs), each and every client has to be updated. Even if we have used a component to contain our business logic, we still have to update that component on every single machine. At one extreme, some updates could require a manual process that involves somebody going around and upgrading each machine, and as such it's expensive and time consuming. At the other, you could invest in a tool that automates this update or create an auto-installer for the update which could be downloaded automatically.

So, which should you opt for? The answer comes down to a choice between having to update 2,000 clients each time we find a bug, and upgrading a single isolated location but having to invest more money in servers. The ultimate decision is yours, but generally speaking the maintenance overhead for fat-client based, solutions outweighs their benefits, so most people plump for thin clients and ensure their server-side systems and network are meaty enough to cope. This means you have to make sure that the server side can scale, and has the potential to be deployed across 10, 20 or even 30 servers. Is that realistic using Microsoft technologies? Well, take a look at microsoft.com, which gets a little over *43 million* page impressions a day. That's quite a large system, and it's built using Microsoft technologies.

When you have some spare time, go to http://www.microsoft.com/backstage *and read about the systems that run the Microsoft site. Although the designers say it's a modest configuration, I think you'll agree that twenty-nine servers hosting general web content, twenty-five servers hosting SQL Server, and thirty other servers in distributed data centers is a reasonably large n-tier system! Then again, maybe I just don't get out much?*

Scalability and N-Tier Systems

An *n*-tier system is scalable because it can service a large number of clients by distributing each logical tier across one or more physical machines. Typically, each client of the system will have the presentation tier running on their machine, in the form of a web browser viewing HTML created by an ASP-based solution.

The number of machines used to host the business and data tiers is pretty much unlimited. The more servers we add to the business and data tiers, the more scalable it should become, because each machine can share the requests made by the client machines. The sign of a badly designed 3-tier application is when performance reduces as it is distributed over more machines.

Physical Deployment of an N-Tier Application

In a typical *n*-tier system, we generally have at least *three* machines, as shown in the following diagram. The client machine runs the user interface; this can be a Visual Basic application, a C++ application, a web browser, etc. The application server hosts the business objects, which are essentially the main part of our application. The database server is responsible for holding and servicing requests for data—a duty typically performed using a database such as SQL Server or Oracle.

The idea of talking about anything other than a browser-based UI may seem a little strange to some web programmers; however, ASP is not only used by those who deal with browser-fronted applications. It is not uncommon to see a Visual Basic UI interact with ASP in web-based applications.

Physical Machines	Logical Tiers
Client Machine	Presentation Tier
Application Server	Business Tier
Database Server	Data Tier

In small installations, the business and data tiers are often hosted on the same machine. During development, you can even have all three tiers on the same machine. Hosting the business and data tiers on the same machine is fine for small applications that are not database intensive, but any database-intensive application will run much better if the data tier is given its own, dedicated machine. This is simply because heavy database access consumes a lot of machine resources—memory, CPU and disk access. This has an adverse effect on the business tiers and slows down the rest of the application, making the whole system less responsive.

The next figure shows the typical logical and physical structure of tiered ASP applications. The difference from the previous model is that the client machine is now called the web browser, the application server is now called the web server, and we've divided the middle tier up into the three logical sections we discussed earlier.

Physical Machines	Logical Tiers		
Web Browser	Presentation Tier		
Web Server	Middle Tier	ASP's	
		User Centric Objects	
		Data Centric Objects	
Database Server	Data Tier		

As an example of the flexibility of *n*-tier systems, consider the next figure that introduces another physical machine—the application server, which is responsible for running data-centric objects. The term "Application Servers" is used to indicate explicitly that we can easily deploy our data-centric objects on more than one machine. By using more than one machine to host our business objects, we improve our application's ability to service more clients, because we have more resources available to service their requests. Of course, the more machines we add, the more network traffic we introduce and the more time we must spend administering those servers, so we have to ensure that this is not a limiting factor.

Physical Machines	Logical Tiers		
Web Browser	Presentation Tier		
Web Server	Middle Tier	ASP's	
		User Centric Objects	
Application Servers		Data Centric Objects	
Database Server	Data Tier		

The Data Tier Across Multiple Machines

Hosting the data tier on more than one machine requires a lot more pre-planning than doing the same thing for the business tier. It is not something that can be done easily once a system has been deployed.

The data tier for average *n*-tier applications consists of a single database. As such, splitting that across more than one machine is not really feasible. Although SQL Server and other databases have replication features that allow them to be mirrored to another machine, that is only useful for backup purposes. It is not designed to allow simultaneous updates to both machines, synchronizing any changes made.

To host the data tier on multiple machines requires multiple databases, each database being located on a single machine, as shown below. This is a relatively easy scheme to implement in an n-tier system—our business objects encapsulate the database, so the client application doesn't know (or need to know) where the data source resides. In a 2-tier system, this would require major changes to any existing applications, as each would have to be updated with the new location of the database.

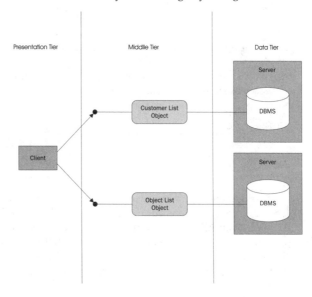

177

The factors we have to consider when using multiple databases in an n-tier application are integrity and consistency. How do we perform atomic updates across them? This is actually an extremely difficult task to implement ourselves, but fortunately Microsoft Transaction Server can do it for us, as we'll discuss in Chapter 7.

Conclusions on Architectural Considerations

In the first section of the chapter we have seen how we can expand on the client-server model that we are used to thinking about when using ASP. The concepts described here may be new to many of you. Hopefully you will see why they are particularly useful to us when planning our component deployment and application design, especially as we are now component developers.

In some ways the architecture of an application helps solve many of the considerations regarding how the individual parts of our problem can be orchestrated to provide a single solution. We still need the ASP 'glue' to stick it all together however—the placement of the component and ASP pieces allow the jigsaw to take shape.

There is just one thing to say before we move on; the person who told me that his company trains its programmers to use JavaScript on the client and VBScript on the server to help them understand where the script was executing also told me that programming books never appreciate the real world enough when talking about architecture. Splitting up the logical and physical tiers of an application is a goal any design should try to achieve. It's very useful when planning an application and even more so to translate this split strictly when you are implementing large or busy applications. In smaller systems when time is against you, it is not always possible or practical to maintain these distinctions. They are without a doubt very helpful for any programmer to know, but there are times when a system does not require such segmentation or when you have to cross the boundaries.

Component Design

In the second half of this chapter we will look at some of the issues surrounding the design of your components. As the uses for components are so wide and varied, it is not possible to cover all of the possible design issues that you will meet. Indeed, we have already met many concepts in passing while introducing COM and building our first components. In Chapter 2 we looked at a number of interface design considerations. In Chapter 3 we had a discussion about interacting with the environment in which a component should be used, and we will see more that crop up as we go through the book. What this section covers, however, are some of the key **general** design issues that relate to architecture.

> There are a number of other considerations that we have to take into account when designing components that will partake in transactions, but we shall meet those in the next two chapters, which cover Microsoft Transaction Server. They will also address the issue of holding state or data in objects.

As we said at the beginning of the chapter, often the best way of solving a problem is to break it up into pieces. Figure out the answer to each individual part, and how they piece together to form a solution. If you think of an ASP application as 'the problem', then some of the little pieces will be ideally solved by components. So, one of the big questions is how to break the problem up. Of course, not every part of the problem will require a component to solve it; there will be parts such as forms, presented as user interfaces, which will still be written using plain ASP. So we also need to think about when to use a component.

The decision of whether to use a component can be influenced by a number of factors, including whether:

❑ There is already a component commercially available that will do the job you require

❑ The particular part of the task is something that you regularly need to do and you could re-use the component that implements that part in other applications

❑ The same piece of code would otherwise have to be repeated within the application for different parts of the code to call

❑ A part of the script code is particularly complex, causing the interpreter to use a great deal of processor resources. Would it execute faster if it were written as a component in a compiled language?

❑ You need to distribute the code, but it contains sensitive business rules that you do not want to expose to the public, so you need to hide this logic using a compiled language

❑ Script is not adequate for the job in hand and you need the functionality offered by a programming language such as Visual Basic or C++

❑ You are working on a multi-author project, and want someone else to write a distinct section that can be incorporated into the application

These tie in quite neatly with the benefits of components that were discussed in Chapter 1. However, once you have decided where you are going to use a component to solve one of the problems, you then have a number of other things to consider about the design of the component itself.

The main key area we shall look at is how to decide how much functionality should be contained in each component, although we will also mention some points you should consider to make your components as re-usable as possible first.

Enabling Re-use

If we want to be able to re-use our components in different situations, there are two key issues to consider here:

❑ Environment dependency

❑ Maintaining the interface

So, let's take a quick look at each of these in turn.

Environment Dependency

We have already had a discussion of environment-dependent components in Chapter 3, when we looked at creating a component that interacted with the ASP object model. If one of our primary reasons for creating the component is that it will be re-usable in different situations, we would rather it not be environment-dependent. However, this is something that you need to assess for each component that you develop—there is no easy rule that says you should use environment-dependent components in x, y and z situations and you shouldn't in a, b and c.

Maintaining the Interface

As we gain more experience with writing components, we may decide that we want to add a little bit of extra functionality to an existing component. The result is an updated version of a component. The programs that use these components, however, are dependent upon the component's interface remaining the same.

Up to now, we haven't mentioned the **interface contract**—but it is a most important topic. When you release or publish a component, the COM guidelines say that the interfaces it provides should be absolutely **immutable**. They should never change again. You should think of the interface definition as a contract between you and the users of your component. Users will build applications and other components that interact with the published interface. If you change this in the future, their applications are liable to break. And it will all be your fault.

Here are some general rules that can maintain an interface used by ASP:

- ❑ Don't publish an interface until you're happy with it

- ❑ If you do change an existing interface, recompile all client applications

- ❑ Remember that VB hides a lot of interface information from you, so that when you modify a class module you are modifying the default interface.

- ❑ Visual C++ users, don't change any part of an interface once it has been published. This includes the order of methods, parameter types etc. Visual Basic users, your chosen language hides all this detail from you, so don't worry about this.

Version Numbering

As an aside, if you are updating your components, don't be tempted to include a version number in the names of your classes or component filenames. This generally causes confusion, even though (providing the registry is properly updated) it doesn't actually break applications. Take, for example, the ADO DLL, `msado15.dll`. While the DLL name suggests that you have ADO version 1.5 installed, you may find that you've actually got version 2.0, 2.1 or even 2.5:

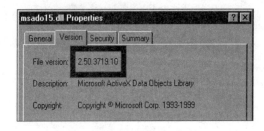

On the other hand, do remember to include a version number in the ProgID of your class. After all, how else would the registry know you want to install a newer or older version of your component?

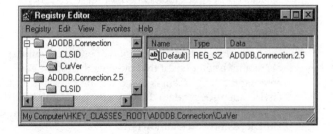

Fine-Grained and Coarse-Grained Components

One aspect of component design we haven't yet considered is how much functionality should we place within each component. It's an issue that raises itself during the secondary stages of an application's design phase. Having conceptualized the problem domain there's a point at which we get down to identifying the best ways to abstract the key players and functionality into objects—it's one of the most interesting parts of the design cycle. This is the issue of **component granularity**.

Component granularity relates to the way we factor out certain elements of functionality into smaller pieces—and the amount of functionality contained in each of those pieces. In looking at this we will see how some of our earlier discussion about architecture can be implemented.

As we mentioned when talking about architecture, one of the fundamental rules of component design is that the component should really reflect some part of the problem domain. This may be a real-life entity (such as a customer), or some abstract entity (such as a recordset) and the component's interface will then include methods that represent the functionality that we want the entity to be capable of performing. However, as we will see, this is not always practical.

If our entities are truly distinct, then it might be easy to dissect the functionality required by each entity. But what if we had a number of similar (but not identical) entities that had similar (but not identical) functionality? In that case, the dissection of functionality becomes blurred, and the 'correct solution' is not so clear-cut. Let's look at an example.

Dissecting the Problem Domain

Suppose we're designing an ASP intranet application that will be used by all the employees of a company, to access and update business-related data contained in a data store. To illustrate the point, suppose that the company implements access restrictions upon their system, and that the employee's rank determines to what extent they can change the information on the database. The three main positions in the company are clerks, managers, and the boss, and the system restrictions are such that we only allow staff the permissions they *need* to use the database.

How do we model this? Well, we could have three components—Clerk, Manager, Boss—and implement the functionality of each of these components individually. This is how we would approach the problem if we were trying to create an object for each real-life business entity. The interfaces of these components might have the following methods:

Clerk:

The clerks do all the work, so they are permitted a great deal of 'write' functionality:

```
ReadAccounts()
ReadCustomerData()
WriteAccounts()
WriteCustomerData()
WriteSalesCompleted()
```

Manager:

The managers only have to change a few things, and mostly have read-only access:

```
ReadAccounts()
ReadCustomerData()
ReadSalesCompleted()
WriteSalesCompleted()
```

Boss:

The boss is always at the golf club and therefore doesn't have access to the data store at all:

```
ReadProfitMargin()
ReadSalesCompleted()
```

In all, we've had to implement 11 methods here. The thing to notice is that some of the methods are used by more than one type of employee—and there are actually only 7 methods that we need to write. So, you could argue that it doesn't make sense to write the three components in this 1-dimensional way. Instead, it makes more sense for us to write two helper components responsible for the related sub-tasks of reading data from and writing it to the database. These can then be shared among the three employee components:

DataReader:

```
ReadAccounts()
ReadCustomerData()
ReadProfitMargin()
ReadSalesCompleted()
```

DataWriter:

```
WriteAccounts()
WriteCustomerData()
WriteSalesCompleted()
```

Then we'll make these helper components available to the three employee components:

Clerk:

Component	Methods allowed
DataReader	ReadAccounts() ReadCustomerData()
DataWriter	WriteAccounts() WriteCustomerData() WriteSalesCompleted()

Manager:

Component	Methods allowed
DataReader	ReadAccounts() ReadCustomerData() ReadSalesCompleted()
DataWriter	WriteSalesCompleted()

Boss:

Component	Methods allowed
DataReader	ReadProfitMargin() ReadSalesCompleted()

That's better. Careful componentization will allow us to reuse the code in the form of the helper components. And if our company expands, we've got a lot less work to do in order to implement any new employee ranks that are created within the company's hierarchy. For example, we may need to add an accountant component:

CompanyAccountant:

Component	Methods allowed
DataReader	ReadAccounts() ReadProfitMargin()
DataWriter	WriteAccounts()

Comparing Approaches

Here we have a good example of creating business components. We have the role components representing the various positions in the company, and the helper components representing two common tasks. There are three main advantages to the second approach:

❑ Increased re-usability

❑ The design makes the system easier to extend

❑ Easier to maintain

The new helper components increase code re-use, as we have cut down the number of methods from eleven to seven. The Clerk, Manager, and Boss components reflect the various roles within the company, while the helper components reflect the tasks that have to be performed, several of which are common tasks.

Rather than designing all of our objects to fit in with the real world, which often means that we have to maintain state for a prolonged period of time, we are writing objects that fit in with our requirements for processing data. The approach of modeling components around the processing of data is referred to as process oriented, so components that exhibit this behavior are called process-oriented components.

In addition, by being flexible, we have an overall design that is more **extensible**, because we can easily add a new role component—such as CompanyAccountant—and allow them to use the existing helper components. To create the new role we simply need to decide what functions they need to perform and allow access to the relevant component, there is no need to write the necessary functions that enable the roles to perform their tasks.

Finally, if you need to change the actual implementation of one of the methods, such as the ReadAccounts() method, you only need to change the one helper component, rather than edit each of the various role components.

There are, however, trade-offs in choosing this approach. The main disadvantage being that, in order to achieve the same ends, we need to create a greater number of component instances. Since each component instance takes time and occupies server resources, the resulting performance is likely to be fractionally worse.

In the end, the decision is up to you, but the advantages of business components that don't model purely real-life parts of the business/problem domain are clearly re-use, extensibility, and ease of maintenance. You could even say that it is a more logical and easy-to-understand approach.

Granularity

How does granularity fit into this discussion? You could say that granularity refers to the entire application, rather than to individual components: it is a reflection of the size of the pieces (or components) into which we have broken down the application's solution.

Granularity is the term used to describe how functionality is factored out into one or more components. The more we separate and logically divide functionality and dependencies between components, the more likely we are to be able to use some of those components to help solve other problems.

So how do we describe the granularity of our application? We can refer to a component as being **fine-grained** if, for example, the component performs a single task, or a small set of related tasks—such as enforcing a business rule. By contrast, a **coarse-grained** component is one that is capable of performing a number of (not necessarily related) tasks—often, though not always, by using one or more fine-grained components.

So the measure of granularity is not discrete: rather, granularity might be measured on a continuous scale with 'fine-grained' components at one end and 'coarse-grained' components at the other. Usually, we won't want to get too close to either end of the scale.

If our design is too fine-grained it means:

- ❑ There are more components to instantiate
- ❑ The design may be too fiddly to be worth turning into a component anyway (a component needs to encapsulate a set of related functionality—there's no point (to be extreme) in encapsulating each method call into a single component

If our design is too coarse it means:

- ❑ The components do not capture the logical architecture of our application
- ❑ We don't gain the benefits of componentization

With reference to the last point, we could encapsulate an entire application into a single component, and just instantiate it in the ASP page (the one component could do all the data access, business calculations and ASP output for us)—but what would be the point of that? It may execute faster than an ASP page, but we'd get no value from reuse because the component would be specialized to solving just that single problem.

So, in each application that we solve, we need to find a happy medium in terms of granularity. Not too fine and fiddly; not too coarse and bulky.

Example of Granularity

To help us consider some of the issues related to component design, we'll run through a basic example of component granularity. First we will look at the situation for which we are developing our component, then a number of solutions.

The Problem Statement

We've been asked to write a simple application that allows an end-user to view customer information using a web browser. The customer information is stored in a central database. No update capabilities are required, and all the end-user requires is basic summary information such as the customer name and telephone number.

A Traditional Non-Component Based Solution

A non-component based solution to this problem would be simple, but brutal; write a series of ASP pages, each of which uses ADO to access the database and then creates the HTML content using some basic VBScript. This approach is undoubtedly the quickest to build and therefore cheapest way of creating a solution for the customer.

The basic sequence of events for creating each page would look like this:

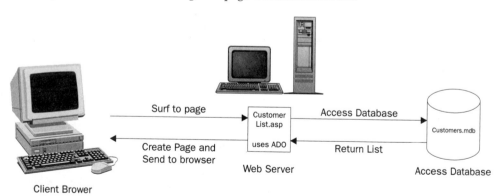

In this scenario, the ASP is generated as normal when a client requests the customer information page by typing its URL into their browser. IIS parses the page and each line of code is executed. If all goes well, the HTML page is created and sent back to the client.

Code for our Non-Component-Based Solution

Assuming we've got the customer information in an access database, we could access and display the information using the following ASP code, using something along the lines of the code shown below:

```
<HTML>
<BODY>
<%
   'Create and Open Connection Object
   Set objConn = Server.CreateObject("ADODB.Connection")
   objConn.Open "Provider=MSDASQL;DSN=Customers"        ' access data

   'Create and Open Recordset Object
   Set objRS = Server.CreateObject("ADODB.Recordset")
   objRS.ActiveConnection = objConn
   objRS.Source = "Customer"

   ' place data from data store into recordset
   objRS.Open

   ' create page and send back to browser
   Response.Write "<H1>Customer List</H1><HR>"
   While Not objRS.EOF
      Response.Write objRS.Fields("ID") & "  " & objRS.Fields("Name") & "<BR>"
      objRS.MoveNext
   Wend
   Set objRS = Nothing
   Set objConn = Nothing
%>
</BODY>
</HTML>
```

This page is called getcustomers1.asp. To use the example, you will need to make the database Customers.mdb available (which is provided with the download code for this chapter). This ASP page accesses the database via a data source name (DSN) whose name is set to Customer. The result is a simple list like this:

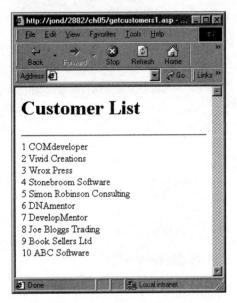

A First Attempt at a Component-Based Solution

The easiest and most obvious way to approach this (although not the most subtle) would involve simply moving the logic from the ASP page and placing it within the implementation of a single component. The component would therefore access the database using ADO, and use the ASP Response object from within Visual Basic to generate the page.

This effectively introduces an extra step, because the sequence of events for each page request would look like this:

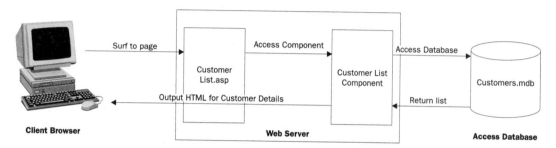

You can see that the ASP page has been relieved of both responsibilities: the data access and the HTML page creation. All of this is done within our single, rather coarse-grained component. Here's the code—you can recreate this if you want.

Code for our First Attempt at a Component-Based Solution

The code for this component (located in the GetCustomers directory for Chapter 5) is very similar to the ASP code we have just seen. The only difference is that we use late binding for most of the interfaces. In terms of component design, it's not very subtle and it's not the best approach—but it is quite illustrative.

To create the component, fire up Visual Basic and create a new ActiveX DLL. Change the project name from Project1 to GetCustomers, and the class name from Class1 to CustomerPage. You'll need to add two references, one for the ASP Object Library and one for the ADO library—select Project | References and check the Microsoft Active Server Pages Object Library and the Microsoft ActiveX Data Objects 2.1 Library checkboxes (then hit OK).

Now place the following code in the GetCustomers – CustomerPage (Code) window:

```
Dim g_objSC As ScriptingContext

Sub OnStartPage(objSC As ScriptingContext)
    Set g_objSC = objSC
End Sub

Sub CreatePage()
    Dim objConn As New ADODB.Connection
    Dim objRS As New ADODB.Recordset

    objConn.Open "Provider=MSDASQL;Data Source=Customers"
    Set objRS.ActiveConnection = objConn
    objRS.Source = "Customer"
    objRS.Open
```

```
    g_objSC.Response.Write "<H1>Customer List _
                            (via a Visual Basic component)</H1><HR>"
    While Not objRS.EOF
        g_objSC.Response.Write objRS.Fields("ID") & "   " & _
                               objRS.Fields("Name") & "<BR>"

        objRS.MoveNext
    Wend

    Set objRS = Nothing
    Set objConn = Nothing
End Sub
```

Note that the `ScriptingContext` interface is established using the `OnStartPage` function called when the component is first created on the ASP page. The component also uses the DSN to the `Customers` database so you'll need to set that up if you haven't already.

Finish up by compiling the component (select **File | Make GetCustomers.dll**). With this component, the role of the ASP page is reduced to the output of the HTML page header/footer, and creating the object. You can test the component using the following ASP page, `getcustomers2.asp`:

```
<HTML>
<BODY>
<%
    Set objComponent = Server.CreateObject("GetCustomers.CustomerPage")
    objComponent.CreatePage
    Set objComponent = Nothing
%>
</BODY>
</HTML>
```

Comparing our Non-Component-Based and Component-Based Solutions

From the end-user's point of view, this component-based solution (`getcustomers2.asp`) gives the same result as the ASP-based solution (`getcustomers1.asp`) that we presented a few pages back. Indeed, in both cases the implementation details are hidden from the browser. So which of the solutions is better? Let's consider the characteristics of each.

The only real difference between the solutions is the location of the main program logic—in the first case it's in VBScript within an ASP page, while the second case uses a coarse-grained Visual Basic component. The component-based solution has the advantage that it might execute quicker than the VBScript version—there are two reasons for this:

❑ The component's code is already compiled, so the ASP within will run faster. Consequently, this also means that there is less un-compiled ASP for IIS to interpret as well, making that interpretation faster too.

❑ The component uses early binding (by creating the objects using the `New` keyword)—this means that calls to the ADO components will be quicker.

However, there's an overhead introduced—namely, the cost of loading the component's DLL and creating the object. This (coupled with the fact that most of the processing time is actually spent on the database connection) means that the overall performance of both solutions is pretty much identical.

In contrast to the ASP-based solution, the main disadvantages of our ASP component are fairly apparent:

- ❑ It takes longer to develop than the ASP/VBScript version
- ❑ It gives a greater maintenance overhead (because we have to manage and maintain the Visual Basic program, which is more complicated than an ASP page)

So if the component-based solution offers no real performance advantage, we would probably conclude that the ASP-based solution is the better of these two options.

> **Note that simply converting the VBScript of an ASP into VB code to create an ASP component is rarely a good way to approach any solution.**

Secondly, we have hardcoded details of the connection to the database into the component, rather than using a global variable. While this is not really important for a component this size, if it were a larger component that used the connection string more often, were we to utilize registry settings, it would not be necessary to change the values several times in the component if we change the data store, making it easier to maintain.

The Drawbacks with our First Effort

Let's look more closely at the GetCustomers component, and see how we might implement the solution in a different way.

The first point to note is that the component we have developed is environment-dependent. It uses the ASP object model to help generate the page—which means that the component can't be used outside of IIS.

Secondly, the component's single method creates the HTML output *as well as* performing the data access. This means that whenever we use the data access part of the component, the HTML output part is inextricably linked to it—we can't use one without the other. This is a severe limitation to the reuse potential of the component, and highlights one of the pitfalls of developing coarse-grained components— that unrelated functionality cannot be separated and reused.

If we had several pages that displayed the database content in different ways, we would have to duplicate the database access part of the component for use in the pages that display the information in different ways.

For the sake of simplicity, let's assume that we're developing an IIS-specific component—and therefore we'll keep the ASP code inside of the component. But let's approach the problem in another way. We will use two finer grained components; one for generating the page, one for providing access to the customer information. By taking this approach, we end up with an environment-neutral component for accessing customer information that we can potentially reuse time and time again in many different environments whenever we need to access this information, and a second component in which we isolate the environment-dependent code.

An Improved Component-Based Solution

Having seen the drawbacks with our first attempt at a component-based solution to our problem, we need to rethink our strategy, just as you may well have to when designing your first component-based application. It would be possible to revamp our solution as follows:

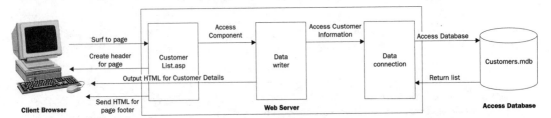

The customer list component is now *only* responsible for the application's data-centric business logic—accessing the database and making the customer information available—so we shall rename this `DataConnection`. This isolates the environment-dependent ASP page-creation code and user-centric logic in another component—which is responsible *only* for creating portions of the ASP page from the database and will be called `DataWriter`. As a result of this, the new `DataConnection` component becomes one that we can **reuse** in other ASP pages (and potentially within other types of application)—because it isn't tied to, or dependent upon, the page-writing code.

Code for our Improved Component-Based Solution

We're going to create a second class module in our Visual Basic project, effectively creating a second component. The first, `DataConnection`, is responsible for data access. The second, `DataWriter`, is responsible for instantiating `DataConnection` and asking it to fetch the data, and then for writing the resulting data to the ASP page. The code will look rather similar to before—but the levels of granularity are clearly different.

To create this component, fire up Visual Basic and create a new ActiveX DLL. Change the project name from Project1 to GetCustomersNTier. Create a new class (select Project I Add Class Module). Now change the default class names from Class1 and Class2 to DataConnection and DataWriter. Again, you'll need to add references to the Microsoft Active Server Pages Object Library and the Microsoft ActiveX Data Objects 2.1 Library checkboxes, using select Project I References.

Now place the following code in the GetCustomersNTier – DataConnection (Code) window:

```
Public Function GetData() As Object
    Dim objConn As New ADODB.Connection
    Dim objRS As New ADODB.Recordset

    objConn.Open "Provider=MSDASQL;Data Source=Customers"
    Set objRS.ActiveConnection = objConn
    objRS.Source = "Customer"
    objRS.CursorLocation = adUseClient
    objRS.Open "SELECT * FROM Customer", objConn
    objRS.Close

    Set GetData = objRS

    Set objRS = Nothing
    Set objConn = Nothing
End Function
```

The function must be Public, *because it is going to be called by the* DataWriter *component. Also, there's an extra line that sets the recordset's* CursorLocation *to* adUseClient. *This basically means that the recordset can be disconnected from the data store once we've captured the data, and can exist independently. We looked at disconnected recordsets in more detail in Chapter 4.*

Now place the following code in the GetCustomersNTier – DataWriter (Code) window:

```
Dim g_objSC As ScriptingContext
```

```
Sub OnStartPage(objSC As ScriptingContext)
    Set g_objSC = objSC
End Sub
```

```
Public Sub WriteData()
    Dim objDataSupply As New DataConnection
    Dim objRS As New ADODB.Recordset

    Set objRS = objDataSupply.GetData

    g_objSC.Response.Write _
            "<H1>Customer List (via a Visual Basic component)</H1><HR>"
    objRS.Open
    While Not objRS.EOF
        g_objSC.Response.Write objRS.Fields("ID") & "   " & _
                objRS.Fields("Name") & "<BR>"
        objRS.MoveNext
    Wend
    objRS.Close
    Set objRS = Nothing
    Set objDataSupply = Nothing
End Sub
```

The DataWriter component uses a method called WriteData() to send the data collected from the DataConnection component to the client. It collects the recordset generated by the DataConnection component using the method GetData().

Compile the component (select File | Make GetCustomersNTier.dll). You can test the component using the following ASP page, getcustomers3.asp:

```
<HTML>
<BODY>
<%
    Set objComponent = Server.CreateObject("GetCustomersNTier.DataWriter")
    objComponent.WriteData
    Set objComponent = Nothing
%>
</BODY>
</HTML>
```

And just to prove that our class modules act as separate components, we'll write `getcustomers4.asp` which uses the `DataConnection` component independently of the `DataWriter` component:

```
<HTML>
<BODY>
<%
   Dim objDataSupply
   Dim objRS
   Set objDataSupply = Server.CreateObject("GetCustomersNTier.DataConnection")

   Set objRS = objDataSupply.GetData
   Set objDataSupply = Nothing

   Response.Write "<H1>Customer List (via DataConnection)</H1><HR>"
   objRS.Open
   While Not objRS.EOF
      Response.Write objRS.Fields("ID") & "   " & objRS.Fields("Name") & "<BR>"
      objRS.MoveNext
   Wend
   objRS.Close
   Set objRS = Nothing
%>
</BODY>
</HTML>
```

Granularity and Architecture

The granularity of components and the architecture of an application are inextricably linked. The advantages of choosing the *n*-tier architecture we presented at the end of the first section of this chapter are mirrored by the advantages of aiming for optimum granularity in the 'pieces' that we are using to solve our problem.

Let's look at the way our third solution comes together in terms of granularity and *n*-tier architecture:

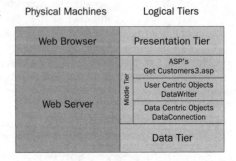

In the physical middle tier we have:

❑   The ASP page that calls the components

❑   The user-centric object that is responsible for displaying the page

❑   The data-centric object that is responsible for retrieving the content from the database.

This example is quite simplistic compared with the ones that you will probably develop for real-world applications. You may have a more complex user-interface, more attractive presentation, and more flexibility in the data you access. Nevertheless we can see some of the advantages in using components, especially in this type of situation, and the advantages of implementing an *n*-tier architecture.

Our first component-based solution to this problem involved mixing the database and presentation code (which also happened to be environment-dependent), so what have we gained by splitting the two up?

❑ If we have to change the formatting of the results, we need only alter the user-centric object

❑ If we want to display the contents of different databases with the same formatting, we can keep the same user-centric object with a different data-centric object

❑ If we change databases, we only need to alter the data-centric object

❑ If we want to use the data-centric component in other applications we can, because it has been separated from environment-dependent presentation logic

I think you will agree that, particularly when you start implementing larger ASP applications, design and architecture become increasingly important.

It Takes Time

Component design, more specifically system design, is not an easy task. It is something that you will get better at as you develop more components, are involved in more problem domains, and simply spend more time thinking, designing and coding. And you will not achieve this by going on any training course.

It's not difficult actually to program and implement components once you've got an idea what you're doing, it's just difficult to actually think ahead to other solutions you might implement in the future, deciding what is a good way of factoring functionality that will lead to better reuse of your components in the longer term, and understand what is a bad way of doing it—which would result in increased development times with no long term return.

Even well-seasoned component developers learn something new from most projects they work on. In many ways this quirk of component design is similar to traditional object-oriented analysis, design and programming. In both cases two experts designing and implementing the same system would probably come up with completely different system implementations.

> The best way of testing a system design is by implementing a prototype.

If you are able to prototype your solutions, you might like to take another look at the Windows Script Components we introduced in Chapter 1. They are ideal for prototyping components that may later be implemented in other languages, as they can be created quickly and are COM-compliant. For a further discussion of Windows Script Components either visit http://msdn.microsoft.com/scripting/ or pick up a copy of *Windows Script Host Programmer's Reference* from Wrox Press (ISBN 1-861002-65-3).

Summary

In this chapter we have addressed two issues which overlap in certain areas: architecture and general component design issues. Our look at architectural models showed how the client-server split (that ASP developers often talk about) can be expanded upon, to help us piece together the jigsaw we have created. While the granularity discussion looked at how we split the problem up into pieces that maximize the advantages that components offer us.

We have seen:

❑ The difference between 3-tier and *n*-tier architectures

❑ How application architecture can affect the benefits of componentization

❑ How 'business objects' can be used to model real world situations

❑ Some generalized component design issues

❑ Points to consider when when deciding how much functionality to put into each component

In the next five chapters we will expand upon what we have learned so far regarding designing and building components. We will look at the practical side of using components alongside a number of the technologies that we regularly use when developing ASP applications. In particular, we will introduce MTS and transactional components, MSMQ and ADSI.

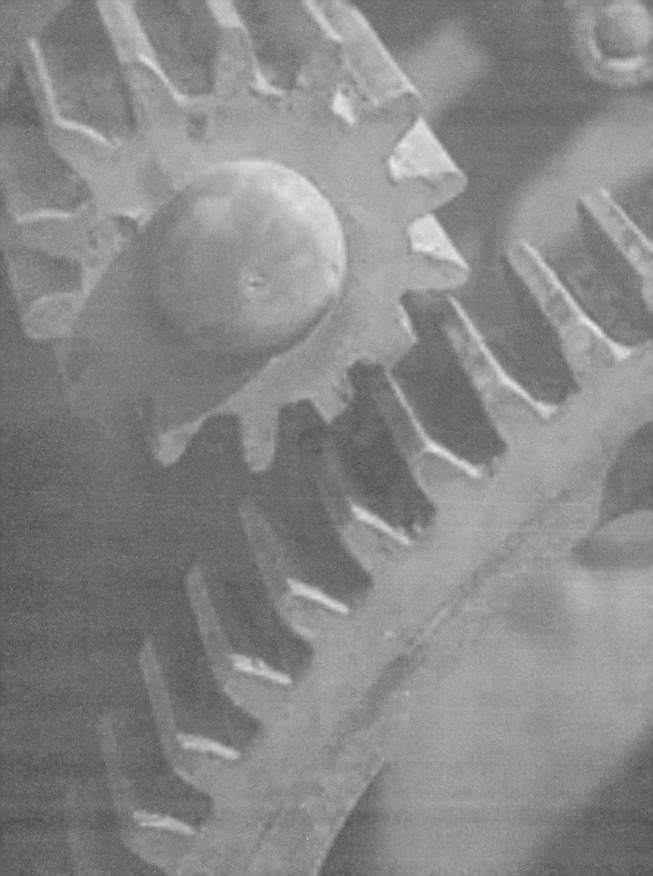

Introducing MTS

So far in this book we've taken a good look at how COM underlies our components. We've developed some components using Windows Script Host, and then using Visual Basic, and we've taken a good look at how the design of our components can affect their behavior and reuse.

When it comes to deploying our components for use in a 'real-life' production application, there are more questions that we need to ask ourselves. For example, suppose we're writing our component as part of an ASP application that will attract hundreds or potentially thousands of users. We need to think about the consequences that such a demand might have on our Web server, our ASP pages, and our components. Here are some simple scenarios:

❑ The content of our ASP pages and configuration files (such as `global.asa`) will affect the load on our Web server. For example, suppose we have a component that requires 10k of memory to execute, and we have an estimated 5000 active sessions during peek times. If we store that component instance at the session level, we'll need at least 5000 * 10k = 50,000k (or around 49Mb) just to support that *single* component at peak times. Sure, memory is a cheap resource; but we need to consider whether we should manage the server resources more carefully.

❑ If we have an ASP page that uses a data source (such as the example that we saw in Chapter 4), we'll need to be sure that we have enough connections to service each user request. The memory requirements for 5000 users, each using their own SQL Server connection, would be around 5000 * 37k = 185 000k; and in any case, most database management systems (DBMSs) support only a limited number of connections. There needs to be an effective way of sharing these connections around.

❑ Most importantly, we need to consider issues that are inherent in multi-user systems. For example, what happens when two or more users try to update the same data at the same time? We've got to be sure that users are protected from the risk of leaving inconsistent information on the data store, and no user's updates are lost.

So, in this chapter and the next one, we're going to discuss how we can ensure that our ASP applications *are* scalable, robust and secure, and can cope with the demands put on them by our users. To achieve this we are going to get a little help from **Microsoft Transaction Server** (MTS).

MTS builds on the COM architecture. In this chapter we'll discuss the basic concepts behind MTS, its architecture, and how it generally helps in the development of scalable applications. We'll start with a discussion of transactions, because they give a good route into the whole technology. However, we'll see that MTS isn't just about transactions—it's a complete infrastructure for simplified component development and deployment.

At the end of the chapter we'll develop and deploy a simple component in MTS, essentially using MTS as a super-surrogate—that is, as a container for our components. And in Chapter 6 we'll focus in on the concept of **resources** and **scalability**; we'll pay particular attention to the importance of transactional components in data access applications, and look at how transactions are created and managed under the cover by the Microsoft Distributed Transaction Coordinator (MS DTC).

In this chapter, we will cover:

❑   What transaction processing is all about

❑   The basic architecture of MTS

❑   The benefits of using MTS

❑   How MTS effectively extends and improves COM

❑   Using MTS and the MTS Explorer (or Component Service Explorer)

❑   Developing an MTS object in Visual Basic, for use in an ASP page

We'll analyse the concept of a transaction and explain the characteristics of transactions. If you've got a database background, you may already be familiar with the principles of transactional processing. As you'll see in this chapter, the notion of transactions extends beyond databases, and the concept of a transaction is generic.

MTS is a powerful tool. It's quite easy to use once you understand the basic principles, but we can't pretend that it's possible to cover the full set of capabilities in two chapters. We will try and outline the fundamental features, but if you want a more detailed discussion of each feature, especially the technical underpinnings, I suggest you look at *Professional Visual Basic 6 MTS Programming* (Wrox, ISBN 1-861002-44-0). Another truly technically detailed book for C++ developers is *Professional Visual C++ 6 MTS Programming* (Wrox, ISBN 1-861002-39-4).

> *MTS is best suited for Enterprise development—as such, you really need to be using Windows NT to get the best out of MTS. It is possible to run MTS on a Windows 9x platform, but it has reduced functionality, several key features are missing, and the MTS Explorer looks different. Under Windows 2000, MTS (version 3.0) is an integral part of the operating system, under the guise of COM+.*

What is a Transaction?

The very word *transaction* conjures up images of financial exchanges. Merriam–Webster (http://www.m-w.com/) gives a couple of clues in its definitions of *transaction*:

> *"an exchange or transfer of goods, services, or funds"*
> *"a communicative action or activity involving two parties or things that reciprocally affect or influence each other"*

That's a good start—a transaction involves communication between two (or more) entities and some form of exchange. But if you look more closely at the characteristics of a financial transaction—or any other kind of business transaction—you'll see that they're rather more formalized than these definitions would lead us to believe. In Chapter 7 we'll implement a transaction that manipulates author details in a SQL Server database; here, though, we'll just consider something a little lighter—the coffee machine in your office.

A Coffee Purchase Transaction

There's nothing like a refreshing cup of coffee when things aren't going too well at work. Unfortunately, the coffee's not free—the management imposes a small charge of 25c per cup to cover the maintenance of the machine. So, there's a two-stage process involved before you get your cup of coffee. First, you have to come up with the money and insert it into the machine. Second, if all goes well, the machine presents you with your cup of coffee.

These two stages form a **transaction**—an atomic action that either takes place as a whole, or not at all. The coffee machine transaction is only semi-automated, but the principles of transactions are all there.

If Something Goes Wrong

If either part of the transaction fails, then the entire transaction will **fail**:

❑ If you *don't come up with the money* (e.g. you put the wrong coins into the machine), then the machine recognizes this: it will return the coins to you and it won't present any coffee.

❑ If you make the correct payment, then the machine holds your coins temporarily in a 'holding bay'. Then, if the machine *doesn't deliver the coffee*, the machine has failed its part of the transaction. In this case, you're instructed to make a telephone call to your company's Services department, who will open up the machine, retrieve the coins from the holding bay and return them to you.

Note that when the transaction fails, everything returns to the state it was in before the transaction began: you get your money back and you're still thirsty! This is true whichever part of the transaction failed. The act of returning everything to its original state is called **rollback**.

If Everything Goes Right

If both parts **complete** successfully, then the transaction itself will have successfully completed. The completion is triggered mechanically when you lift the coffee from the dispenser. When you do this, the machine can **commit** the sale, by transferring the coins from the holding bay to the internal cashbox, and (being a state-of-the-art model) writing details of the successful transaction to its high-tech built-in accounting and coffee-inventory database!

Formalizing Transactions

In our coffee machine scenario above, we've seen a (relatively) real-life example of a transaction. But what, in more general terms, are the characteristics that make it a transaction? What we need is an identification and formalization of the characteristics—then we will be able to assure ourselves that these characteristics are in place *whenever* we use transactions in our applications.

Transaction Outcome

After performing its work, each party involved in a transaction must cast its vote as to the overall outcome of the transaction. Each party can vote to **commit** (or **complete**) the transaction (if its portion of work was carried out successfully) or it can vote to **abort** the transaction (if its work was not completed for some reason).

> There are only two possible outcomes for a transaction: either it completes successfully, or it fails. There are no intermediate states, so a transaction can never 'partially' complete.

For a transaction to complete successfully, the voting from *all* parties must be **unanimous**. It is not *democratic* discussion—so any **single** vote to abort a transaction will cause it to fail, and any work will be rolled back.

The ACID Test

The official definition of a transaction comes in the form of the **ACID** properties. ACID stands for Atomicity, Consistency, Isolation, and Durability—and any self-respecting transaction *must* satisfy all four properties.

Atomicity

A transaction meets the requirement of being **atomic** if it executes either completely or not at all. If the transaction makes updates to a system, then they too should be completed (if the transaction is committed) or rolled back to their original state (if any part of the transaction fails). If the process breaks down in the middle, based on atomicity, everything that occurred before the breakdown should be rolled back.

In our coffee machine example, the coffee-purchase transaction is atomic—if you pay the money and receive the coffee then the transaction is complete. If any part of the transaction fails, then any changes that were made are rolled back—you get your money back and the machine does not write to its records.

Consistency

A transaction meets the requirement of being **consistent** by ensuring that the business rules of the system are reflected in the data that is being manipulated. The data (or state) was consistent when the transaction was begun, and it must also be consistent at the end.

Returning to the coffee-machine example, the system is consistent if the amount of money contained in the cashbox is equal to 25c times the number of coffee sales made. Since the placement of coins in the cashbox is triggered when you lift the coffee from the dispenser, the state will always be consistent. If there's an error in the transaction, then there's no coffee delivered, and no money is placed in the cashbox.

Isolation

A transaction meets the requirement of being **isolated** if it does not effect (and is not affected by) other concurrently-executing transactions. This means that each transaction is unaware of what all concurrent transactions are doing—thus each transaction thinks it has exclusive use of the system. This is an important characteristic, because we want the end point of the transaction to be independent of the outcome of other concurrent transactions.

During the course of a transaction's execution, the state of the system may not be consistent (the consistency property ensures that the system is consistent at the *end* of the transaction, but not necessarily *during* the transaction). If a transaction was not running in isolation, then other transactions on the system might make decisions based on data that is current being manipulated by another transaction, and therefore in an inconsistent state. Transaction isolation prevents this from happening, by effectively serializing access of data.

What about our coffee dispenser? Let's stretch the example a little and suppose that the coffee machine has *two* coin slots and *two* coffee dispensers—and hence can support two simultaneous users. However, the machine has a single supply of coffee that supports both dispensers. If you and your colleague each request a coffee at the same time, the machine will need to check that there's enough coffee in the supply to provide both cups of coffee.

To do that, and hence ensure transaction isolation, the machine will need to appeal to its internal database (which records how many servings have been made, and therefore also knows how much coffee remains in the supply). The machine will deal with one request at a time:

❑   First, it will read the database to confirm that there's enough for one of the requests—and will update the database when that cup of coffee is being processed. during this process, the database is briefly locked so that the second reqest can't access it.

❑   Then, it will repeat the same procedure for the second request.

The locking technique means that the machine can ensure it's able to handle the first request before it starts to deal with the second. By handling the two concurrent transactions separately, the machine ensures that it won't assign the same serving of coffee to more than one user.

Durability

A transaction meets the requirement of being **durable** if, once it has been successfully completed, all of the changes made to the system are stored in a permanent or durable device before it reports success. If a transaction fails, there are safeguards that will prevent the loss of information, and rollback all changes made. Rollback is achieved by logging the steps that the transaction performs, so the state of the system can be recreated even if the hardware itself has failed (e.g. through system power failure). The durability property means that the completed transaction is a permanent part of the system, regardless of what happens to the system later on.

Our coffee dispenser rather obligingly provides durability by writing the result of each completed transaction to its whizzy internal database. The database is used to record the number of servings made, and also to indicate the remaining coffee supply (as we saw above)—enabling isolation and also allowing our Services guys to check (at the touch of a button) whether the machine needs refilling.

What, you mean you don't have a coffee machine with an internal database in your office?

Transactions in ASP Applications

It's clear that we can enhance the robustness of applications by using transactions. But the task of writing code that can keep track of what each user is doing (and can undo all the changes made when just one part of the transaction fails) is extremely complex—even for relatively simple applications. At the very minimum we would have to co-ordinate each party involved by passing information about the transaction between them, and ensure that the voting for a transaction outcome is implemented and policed correctly. Whilst implementing transactions inside of a single component or ASP page is not that difficult, co-ordinating transactions that span multiple components is difficult, especially so if we are utilising third party components.

The alternative to co-ordinating transactions ourselves is to use a purpose-built transaction environment—such as Microsoft Transaction Server. MTS can track and control our transactions for us, allowing us to focus on other aspects of our application. In fact, MTS offers much more than transaction management. Moreover, MTS is probably already loaded onto your machine—you get it automatically when you install IIS 4. We'll come to the details of installation later in the chapter. Let's look at MTS now.

What is MTS?

Microsoft Transaction Server is essentially a component-based run-time environment that provides the infrastructure required for writing n-tier applications that are scalable, robust, transactional and secure. It provides us with many services that as component developers free us from writing 'component plumbing', than would otherwise take around 40-50% of our development time. A lot of this component plumbing can only be implemented in C++, so MTS also makes it possible for us to write scalable applications using languages like Visual Basic.

Using MTS allows us to focus on solving business problems. This means that our components are smaller and easier to write, simpler to understand by other developers, and less error-prone because they are not complicated by typical distributed application plumbing, such as synchronization.

MTS is the New Generation of COM

MTS 2.0 is built around COM, and you should think of it as an extension of the existing functionality that COM provides. Indeed, in COM+ under Windows 2000, MTS (version 3.0) is integrated directly into the COM runtime.

MTS builds on the experience of 30 years of transactional systems in other environments, object request brokers that have been around since the early 1980s, and (of course) some of Microsoft's own systems.

MTS Functionality

The name Microsoft Transaction Server is somewhat misleading: MTS does rather more than just deal in transactions, although that is a very important aspect.

Microsoft describes MTS as **middleware**—software that generally makes the development of scalable distributed applications easier. MTS's functionality is a combination of two main capabilities (although there are a few extra bits thrown in). First, as the name suggests, MTS is a **transaction monitor** (TM). Second, and less obviously, MTS is an **object request broker** (ORB).

Transaction Monitors

MTS's transaction monitor is called the **distributed transaction coordinator** (or **MS DTC**). As a transaction monitor, the MS DTC has two main functions. First, it enables business applications to scale by sharing system resources (such as processes and threads). For example, a process under Windows NT needs a fair amount of memory—about 540 kB. So if we had 1000 clients and each needed its own system process to perform an operation, the operating system would require around 540 MB of memory just to create the processes, and probably a lot more to perform something useful.

Whilst today's memory prices mean that it's not unrealistic for our servers to have large amounts of memory, it's fairly wasteful and inefficient. Windows NT would spend a lot of CPU time just managing the processes—and that would degrade the overall performance of our applications. We can achieve a more efficient approach by **sharing** processes among our clients. So instead of supporting one process for each client, we might consider supporting only 50 processes. If we had 1000 simultaneous clients, then each process would service 20 clients. With this approach, there are fewer processes available to clients, but the operating system requires far less CPU time to manage those processes—so overall, each client should receive equal (or better) service.

> *This basic concept of sharing a resource between multiple clients can also be applied to threads, database connections and many other types of resources. The notion of resource sharing generally makes for a more scalable system. In some cases, it's our only choice—for example, if we're dealing with a very limited resource such as database connections. We'll tackle this issue in Chapter 7, when we talk about MTS resource dispensers and resource pooling.*

The second main function of the transaction monitor is to use **transaction protocols** to ensure that work is executed correctly and the results are recorded accurately—effectively enforcing the principles of ACID. Transaction protocols essentially coordinate the work being done by different elements of a system. This means that we don't need to put transaction management logic in the client code, and that our transactions are all handled in a robust way via a central location.

> *We'll meet the MS DTC again later in these chapters.*

Object Request Brokers (ORBs)

In its role as an ORB, MTS creates objects for clients; it knows where objects are located and how to create them, and it generally provides the basic plumbing and services required to perform such tasks by using code that is separate from the components you develop. As an ORB, MTS can also enable the deployment of distributed applications, and can generally make the development process of component software easier.

MTS does this by intercepting the client's `Server.CreateObject` call, and using COM components to manage the lifetime of the requested object.

Where to Get MTS

Microsoft originally made a $2000 charge for the privilege of using MTS, in the days when it was part of Back Office (code named Viper) in late 1996. The arrival of MTS version 2.0 saw a change in policy—they decided to give it away as part of the Windows operating system. This change of heart is a result of the fact that MTS is part of a strategy for distributed development introduced in September 1997, known as Windows DNA.

> *Windows Distributed interNet Application Architecture (DNA) is Microsoft's framework for developing internet/intranet based n-tier applications with all the features they typically need: high performance, maintainability, extensibility, scalability, security, and reusability. The services that DNA supports are provided by products like MTS, MSMQ and IIS.*

MTS 2.0 is available in all versions of Windows NT. Currently, MTS is included with Windows NT Workstation 4.0 Edition and Windows NT 4.0 Enterprise Edition (though not the standard edition). It also comes with the Windows NT 4.0 Option Pack. There's even a reduced-functionality version available with Windows 9x when you install Personal Web Server from the Windows NT 4.0 Option Pack. Microsoft says that MTS will ship with every operating system that they release from now on.

> *The Windows NT 4.0 Option Pack is licensed as part of the operating system, and is downloadable from http://www.microsoft.com/com/.*

In Windows 2000, the COM and MTS programming models are unified, bringing the features of MTS directly into the COM runtime. This unification is probably one of the most important features of Windows 2000, and it means that your investment in MTS today won't be wasted with the advent of the next generation of Windows operating systems. COM under Windows 2000 is called COM+ to reflect both this integration, and many other new features.

Installing MTS

As we already mentioned, MTS is installed as part of IIS 4 (in fact, you could install MTS independently of IIS 4 if you wanted to). Should you need to install it on another machine (maybe you want to spread the workload of the business tier across multiple servers as we discussed in Chapter 5) you need to make sure it meets the following minimum requirements:

- ❑ It's running Windows NT Server or Windows 9x (ideally the former)
- ❑ At least 30MB of free disk space for the MTS files
- ❑ At least 64MB of memory

In addition to hardware requirements, you should be aware of a few software issues before installing MTS:

- ❑ If you're using Windows NT 4.0 Server, you should install Service Pack 5 (available at http://www.microsoft.com/ntserver/), which resolves a number of installation problems

- ❑ If you plan to install MTS, and you also plan to install any version of SQL Server 6.5, then the order of installation is important. This is because SQL Server 6.5 has a tendency to overwrite the registry setting for the Distributed Transaction Controller (MS DTC)—a fundamental part of MTS that we'll meet later. So, you'll need to install SQL Server 6.5 (and all the service packs) first, and MTS second.

   This problem does not arise when installing SQL Server 7.0 and MTS on the same machine.

- ❑ If you plan to use an Oracle 7.3.3 or greater database, contact Oracle Technical Support (http://www.oracle.com/) for an available patch.

- ❑ In Windows 2000, there are no special installation procedures (because MTS is an integral part of COM+ in Windows 2000).

Using MTS

MTS's configuration information is contained in something called the **MTS Catalog**. This contains information on components, security settings, and all sorts of other things. Managing the information in the MTS Catalog is fairly simple—Microsoft has provided a handy graphical interface to help us to do this. In Windows NT 4, the primary tool for administering MTS is a GUI called the **MTS Explorer** (or **Transaction Server Explorer**). With COM+ in Windows 2000, things are a little different—so the tool for administering MTS/COM+ in Windows 2000 is the **Component Services Explorer**.

The MTS Explorer and Component Service Explorer both look fairly similar to the Windows NT Explorer. Through these GUI tools, the administrator can work with components on any machine that is a part of the application.

Before we learn more about how MTS works, we'll familiarize ourselves with some of the architecture of MTS by taking a tour of the MTS Explorer.

Touring the MTS Explorer

For this tour, we're going to assume that you're working in Windows NT4. If you're in Windows 2000, things will look slightly different, but we'll try to highlight the differences as we go. If you're in Windows 9x, you won't be able to see all these features, because MTS on Windows 9x has considerably reduced functionality.

The Microsoft Management Console

In order to use the MTS Explorer (or Component Services Explorer), we make use of the **Microsoft Management Console** (MMC). Essentially, the MMC is a common management environment—which just means that it allows us to access different service management tools (such as IIS Explorer, MTS Explorer and others) from a single user interface. The MMC allows us to administer these services via **snap-ins**—the administration components of the services.

The MMC is nothing more than a *host* that contains management snap-ins—MMC doesn't have any management properties of its own. If you're using Windows NT and you installed MTS from the Windows NT 4.0 Option Pack, MMC will already be installed. Otherwise, if you want to use the MMC in Windows NT or Windows 9x then you can install it from the Windows NT 4.0 Option Pack or download it from Microsoft's web site. In Windows 2000, the MMC is a standard feature.

From the Start menu, select Run and type mmc. This will open an empty Microsoft Management Console session, which looks something like this (you should see the splash screen first):

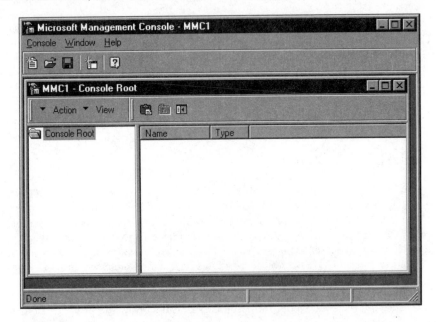

The MTS Explorer is the snap-in for MTS, and we run it inside the MMC. From the toolbar, select Console | Open—you'll be presented with an Open dialog. In Windows NT4, you'll need the MTS Explorer, which has been conveniently encapsulated for us in the file mtxexp.msc (you should find it in a folder such as C:\Program Files\MTS):

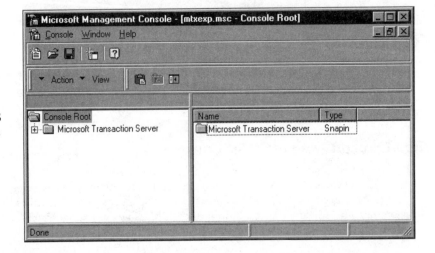

In Windows NT4, you an also get this far from the Start *menu by selecting* Programs / Windows NT4.0 Option Pack / Microsoft Transaction Server / Transaction Server Explorer. *This will launch the MMC with the MTS Explorer snap-in already set up.*

In Windows 2000, you'll need the Component Service Explorer (the snap-in for COM+)—in this case you'll need to open the file comexp.msc *(you should find it in the* C:\WINNT\system32\com *folder). Alternatively, you can choose* Start / Programs / Administrative Tools / Component Services—*this will fire up the* Component Services *window.*

The Distributed Transaction Controller (MS DTC)

From the MTS Explorer (or Component Services Explorer), select the Console Root folder in the left pane and double-click to open all the folders in the left-pane. (You can also achieve this by highlighting the folder and pressing the asterisk key on the numberpad of your keyboard.)

Once you've had a play opening the various branches available, close the folders to match the screen shot below. Before you go clicking around in the explorer again, highlight My Computer:

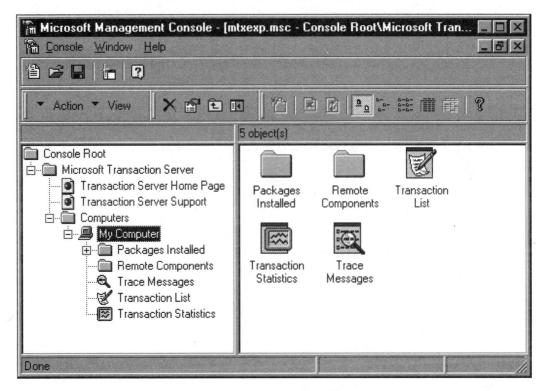

In the Windows 2000 Component Services *window, things will appear rather differently. In this case, open things up so that you can see the contents of the* Console Root / Component Services / Computers / <computer_name> *folder.*

First, notice the little **My Computer** icon in the left-pane. The color of the icon's tiny screen indicates the state of the Distributed Transaction Controller (MS DTC) service. If the icon has a bright-green glow, it indicates that the MS DTC services are running. Conversely, if the icon has a dull-gray color, it means that the MS DTC services are not running.

You can try stopping and starting the MS DTC by selecting **Action | Stop MS DTC** and **Action | Start MS DTC** (assuming you're not going to disrupt any other applications that are currently being served from your machine!). When the MS DTC services are starting you may be lucky enough to briefly notice the icon turn yellow.

Note that the icons are slightly different in Windows 2000.

Note that the **A**ction menu shows different options depending on what's highlighted in the main part of the window. You can get a similar menu by highlighting an icon and clicking the right mouse button.

Packages

Now go back to the items in the left pane. Directly under **My Computer** is a folder called **Packages Installed** (in Windows 2000, you'll want the **COM+ Applications** folder instead). Open up that folder:

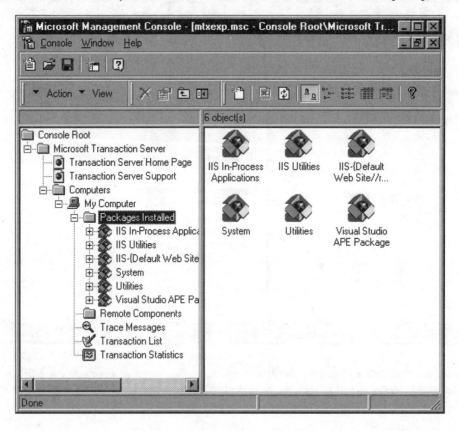

We'll talk about packages in more detail later in this chapter; for now, all you need to know is that a package is made up of a group of (usually related) components that execute in the same server process. In the screenshot above, you can see the list of packages that are installed on my local machine. These packages are not necessarily the same as the default packages that will automatically be installed on your machine. (You can see that a number of packages begin with the string IIS. That's because IIS is built on MTS technology—these packages contain components that provide parts of IIS's functionality.)

We can add new packages to MTS by highlighting the **Packages Installed** folder in the left-pane and right-clicking (or using the **A**ction menu)—we'll see that later in this chapter. Deleting a package is all-too-easy, if it's allowed (highlight the package and hit the *Delete* key, or right-click and select **Delete**).

> *Deleting a package from the MTS Explorer (or Component Services Explorer) does not delete the component from disk; it only removes it from the MTS catalog. Furthermore, you can easily reinstall a component back into the same package or a different package, as we'll see in a moment.*

You can take a look at the properties for each package by highlighting a particular package and right-clicking. A tabbed pop-up form will display each property listed. Here, I've opened the properties for the **IIS Default Web Site** package:

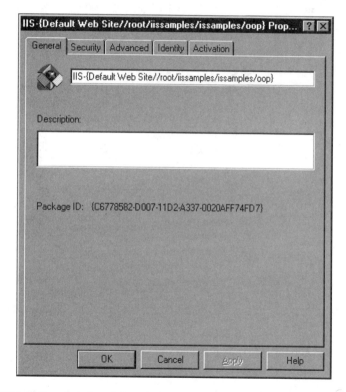

The **Package ID** shown is a unique GUID assigned to the package when it is first created. We'll see some of the other tabs as we progress through this chapter and the next.

Components and Roles

Close the Properties dialog; now highlight a package and press the * key to expand the next few levels. You'll see two folders underneath that: Components and Roles. The Components folder contains all the components for a particular package:

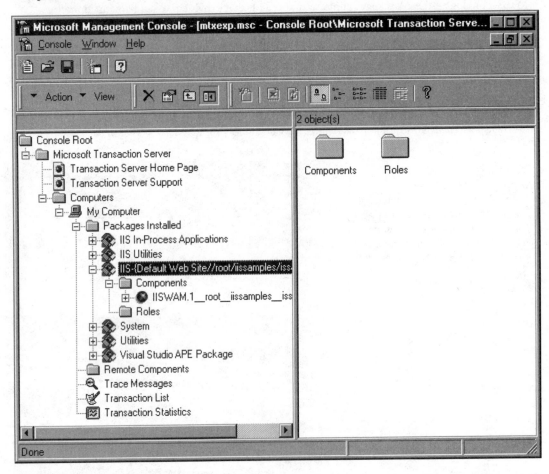

There's a little round icon with a cross for each component within the package. We can configure each component to run with different settings. The package above contains a single component—the web application manager (WAM) component of IIS4.

We can add components to (and delete components from) your packages by highlighting the Components folder in the left-pane and right-clicking. Clicking New | Component will take you to a menu screen. Installing, deleting, and importing components is similar to working with packages. You can also export components to other machines as well as manage general and security properties (though we won't be doing that here).

Interfaces

If you expand one of the component folders, you'll find more sub-folders. Clicking open the Interfaces folder lists the interfaces implemented by the component. The default IIS package we've seen so far doesn't show any interfaces, so we've used a different package to show you an example:

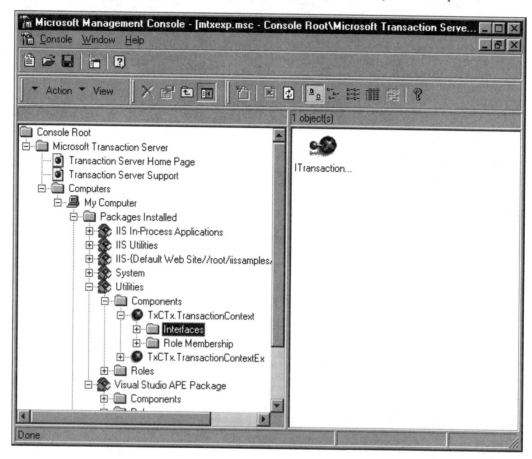

Methods and Role Membership

Double click on an interface icon in the right pane:

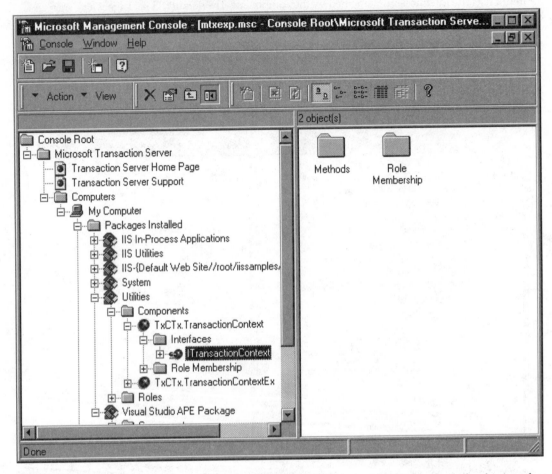

Believe it or not, there are two more folders! The Methods folder contains the methods for this interface. The Role Membership folder contains a list of roles supported at the interface level. A **role** is a symbolic representation of users' access privileges. In the example above, this folder is actually empty (though I haven't shown that here). If a list were present, it would allow you to go down another level to a Role object that signifies a specific role. And yes, it's possible to go even deeper with a Users folder that houses specific users.

Now go back to the **Methods** folder and open it. The right-pane displays each method that is used with the component:

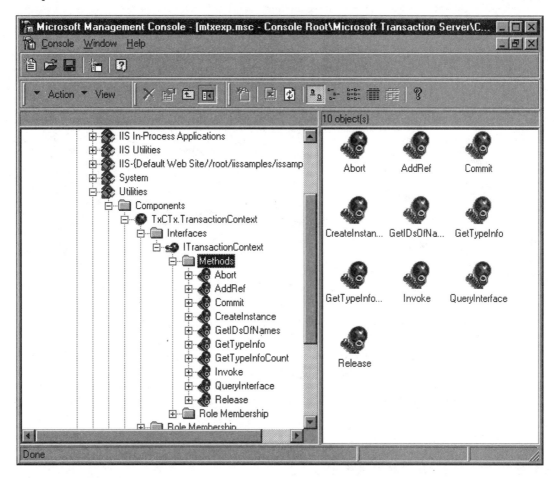

Transaction Monitoring

We've just toured the **Packages Installed** (or **COM+ Applications**) folder, which is the one we'll work with in these chapters. Let's just quickly take a look at a couple of other things of interest.

Highlight **Transaction List** in the left-pane (in Windows 2000 you'll find it under the | **COM+ Applications** | **Distributed Transaction Coordinator** node). This allows you to view active transactions for components on the server that you've selected to monitor. In this example, selecting the **Transaction List** would allow you to monitor transactions for **My Computer**.

The Transaction Statistics node displays MS DTC information. If your machine isn't executing any transactions at the moment, it probably looks a little unexciting. However, when you're executing transactions through the MS DTC, you'll see all kinds of activity that provides statistics for MS DTC, such as current, aggregate, and status information:

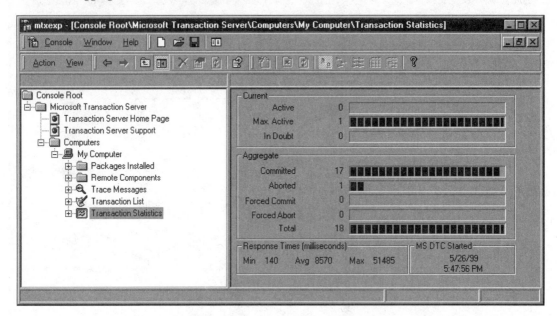

So that's a fairly brief visual tour of the MTS Explorer snap-in running in the MMC console, but we haven't covered the whole thing. Try clicking around using both left and right mouse buttons and pay attention to the different type of menus and features that are offered. Remember that deleting a package or a component from MTS Explorer does not actually delete the item from the system. You can easily reinstall the package or component.

The Architecture of MTS

Any object can be configured to run inside of MTS; but in order to develop components that genuinely benefit from MTS we have to understand more about the underlying concepts and how they're implemented.

In this section, we'll begin to get under the skin of MTS and find out how it works. We will gradually build up a picture of the architecture, by looking at the features MTS provides and how it implements them. The main point we'll try to emphasize during this discussion is that MTS builds on the COM architecture by introducing a 'stateless' programming model to enforce good transaction management and allow scalable application design. (In fact, the word 'stateless' isn't entirely accurate; but as we'll see, MTS *does* affect the way we manage state inside of our components.)

The Relationship between MTS and COM

You should picture MTS as a logical extension to COM—it has a number of services and features that effectively extend COM making it much better. However, MTS is not an integral part of COM. That is, the COM runtime is not aware of MTS, and you as a programmer have to take on board some of the responsibility of ensuring that MTS and COM work well together. This is something of a burden, but it's not a complicated responsibility.

Under Windows 2000 you'll find that the name MTS has disappeared, because the functionality of MTS (3.0) now forms part of COM+. As we mentioned, COM+ is essentially COM plus MTS, with a few other nice features (such as In-Memory Database). Because the two are now integrated, MTS programming under Windows 2000 means that you have to take on fewer of the MTS responsibilities.

So what capabilities does MTS bring to our component development routine? Here's a list of some of the functionality that MTS 2.0 provides over and above COM. We've seen evidence of some of these facilities in the MTS Explorer tour—you'll find that some other terminology here is new. We'll be going over many of these terms during the next chapter-and-a-half:

❑ Context-aware components and interception

❑ Just-in-time activation of COM objects and as-soon-as-possible deactivation of COM objects

❑ Declarative programming and transactions

❑ Automatic component-based transactions

❑ Fault tolerance (Failsafe)

❑ Resource pooling and thread pooling

❑ Concurrency management—multi-user support

❑ Role-based security

❑ Static load balancing

❑ Statistics and activity monitoring

Declarative Attributes

Don't worry if these terms don't mean anything just yet. These features are pieces of compiled code (written by Microsoft) that provide significant functionality, which can easily be used to enhance components. The best thing is that we can benefit from many of these services without programming our components any differently—we can simply add them once the component is compiled.

This is achieved using **declarative attributes**. In MTS/COM+, an attribute is simply a piece of information (or metadata) that describes runtime properties for a component. By associating one or more of a component's attributes, we can affect its runtime behavior *without any need for additional programming or recompiling*. An administrator can adjust a component's declarative attributes, using a simple GUI, to achieve the desired behavior from his compiled components. This is the ultimate level of code re-use.

Contexts

In the next few pages we will focus on two objects that are central to MTS—the **context wrapper object** and the **context object**. We'll also discuss the **object control** interface and the object context interface.

The context wrapper object is the object that the caller gets to see when they create an instance of an MTS component—it 'pretends' to the caller that it's the object that was requested. Meanwhile, the context object is essentially used by MTS as an 'information holder'. For example, it contains security information that allows the context wrapper to determine whether a caller is *allowed* to invoke the methods that it has requested.

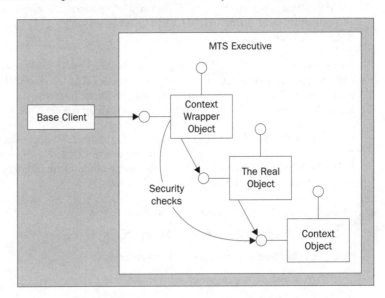

The context object is the single most important feature that MTS brings to COM. The context object is itself a COM object, which enables the MTS Executive to store information about our component that describes its execution environment. With this extra information, MTS is able to make an isolated stand-alone object transparently form part of a distributed application—with synchronized concurrency, distributed transactions and role-based security, without any additional effort on the part of a developer.

> The **MTS Executive** is the 'plumbing' that makes MTS work. You'll be seeing more of it in this chapter and the next.

As we saw in Chapter 3, IIS stores information in the context object—such as the references to the ASP intrinsic objects. This makes them available to a component at any point, without having explicitly to pass them in any way. When we're dealing with MTS objects generally, MTS employs the same technique—using the object context to hold information that it needs about our component.

Let's study each of these objects in greater depth—starting with the context wrapper.

The Context Wrapper Object

MTS is not an integral part of COM. So somehow, it has to get involved in the creation of a COM object so that it can work its magic and create the object context. It achieves this simply by modifying the registry information for a component, which COM uses when creating a component. Let's look at an example.

The following is the registry for the string manipulator component we'll see later in the chapter. It's a standard ActiveX DLL, and as such the following information is stored:

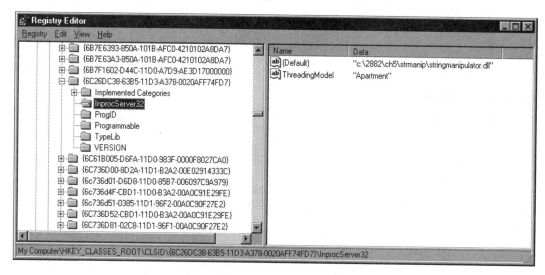

The screenshot shows that the DLL containing the string manipulator component is StringManipulator.dll. Now, suppose we go away and install this component into an MTS package, and then return to look at its registry settings again. You'll see that they have changed, to reflect the fact that the component has been installed into MTS:

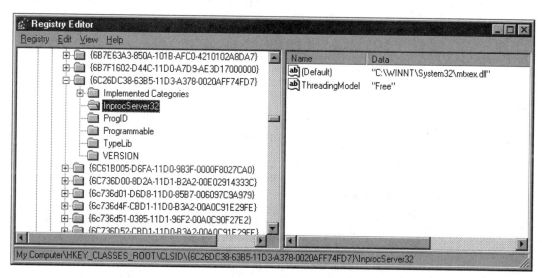

MTS has modified the registry, and you can see that here. Now, when an application requests an instance of our component, the instantiation will be intercepted by MTS—and what *actually* gets loaded is an MTS DLL called `mtxex.dll`—the MTS Executive. This **interception** allows MTS to gain complete control of the creation of our object.

> *MTS also provides `mtx.exe`, which is responsible for creating packages with an extra degree of isolation. When we create a package, we can specify it as **server**—this would create the package as a new process, and hence provide that extra isolation. Such a package is called a **surrogate**, and can be responsible for hosting your DLLs.*

As a result of MTS's interception, the calling application doesn't get the object it asked for. Instead, MTS gives it an MTS object known as the **context wrapper**.

Visualizing the Context Wrapper Object

MTS describes the client who creates a COM object as a **base client**. As we've just seen, when a base client first creates an object hosted in MTS, the client does not get a reference to the real object. Instead, it gets a reference to a **context wrapper** object:

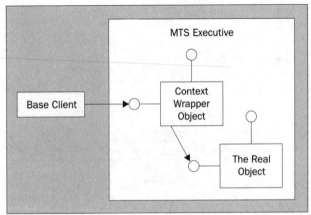

The white box (in the figure above) represents the MTS Executive. It's the MTS Executive that provides the run time services that MTS components use.

> *Here's a word on terminology. In MTS terms, a client outside of MTS that uses an object hosted inside of MTS is known as a **base client**. An client object inside of MTS that uses another object inside of MTS is simply referred to as a **client**. So when you see 'base client', think 'runs outside of MTS'.*

Let's look at that a bit more closely. When the application creates an instance of an MTS component, MTS effectively intercepts the `CreateObject` call. Instead of creating the object immediately, MTS takes a look at the component's interface and creates the context wrapper object, in the image of the component's interface. The client then receives a reference to the context wrapper. The real server object itself (i.e. the requested object) isn't activated until the calling application first calls one of the object's methods.

This entire process is invisible to the calling application—it all happens without their knowledge. It means that the client application never knows that it's not referencing the real object itself. This entire process means that MTS can delay the physical activation of the real object until the last possible moment—i.e. the first method call from the client. This is called **just-in-time activation**.

MTS Object Activation and Deactivation

Just-in-time (JIT) activation—the concept that a component instance is not activated until the first method of an interface is invoked—means any initialization code is delayed until it is really needed. This means that the server's resources aren't consumed unless and until it's absolutely necessary. This is a nice idea, because it means that a client can create a component earlier on in an application's life, and use it much later, without having to worry about resources being consumed prematurely.

By the same principle, MTS deactivates objects as soon as possible. **As-soon-as-possible deactivation** enables MTS to release the memory and resources consumed by the object—while allowing the client to believe that it still has a reference to the real object, without knowing that it has been destroyed. That's right, the real object is destroyed! It's all related to statelessness—a concept that we'll come back to in a moment.

The *real object* is deactivated under either of the following conditions:

❑ The object has been involved in a transaction that has just been completed or aborted

❑ An ASP page (or other base client) has released the last outstanding reference to the context wrapper, which will always cause the real object to be destroyed even if a transaction has not been completed.

The *context wrapper* is only destroyed when the base client releases its last reference to the object.

A Word about Object Pooling

You may have noticed that the terminology has changed subtly—we've been using the terms *activation* and *deactivation*, rather than *creation* and *destruction*, when referring to the real object. This is because there's a very definite difference between the two concepts.

The terms 'create' and 'destroy' are related to the physical creation and destruction of the real object. By contrast, the terms 'activate' and 'deactivate' are related to the process of assigning the real object to the client's call, and initializing any data (or state) required for the duration of that call. The difference is brought to life by the existence of **object pooling** in MTS 3.0. An object pool is a collection of objects that aren't currently being used. When a client requests an object, the idea is that MTS can look in the pool—if there's a suitable object there, MTS can borrow it and use it. Each of the objects in the pool has been created (but not activated).

In MTS 2.0, there is no object pooling. Therefore, when a client requests an object, the real object is created and then activated, so it can be used. When the client has finished with the object, it is deactivated and destroyed.

MTS 3.0 *does* implement object pooling. In MTS 3.0, the client's method call doesn't necessarily mean that we'll need to create an object and destroy it again afterwards—because it may be able to take an object from the pool. That means that we only need to activate the object for use, and then deactivate it again afterwards.

The lifetime of the real object is itself an interesting point. Depending on the transactional nature of the application and the existence (or otherwise) of object pooling, the real object's lifetime might be the duration of an ASP page's execution; or the duration of a transaction; or the duration of a single method call. If this sounds complex, don't worry—we'll tackle the issue in some depth now, and more in the next chapter.

Scalability and Stateless Components

As we've already noted, the signal for JIT activation is fairly clear—it's the time at which the ASP page (or other client) makes its first method call to the object. The signal for ASAP deactivation is rather less clear. Do we deactivate immediately after each method call? To be a good transactional MTS component that is genuinely scalable, the answer is 'yes'.

That might sound surprising—because if there are a number of method calls, it will introduce a degree of overhead in that the server has to keep deactivating and re-activating the object. However, MTS caches the DLL in its own memory—so the activation–deactivation process isn't actually that expensive. In fact, it makes server applications potentially more scalable—because it allows server resources to be used more efficiently.

It might also sound surprising because, if the object is deactivated between method calls, there's no way to maintain the object's state (e.g. the values contained in its properties). But this can actually be a good thing, because we are encouraged to write **stateless** objects—and this will help us to ensure that the data in our application remains consistent.

Stateless objects help us to enforce the ACID properties—specifically the property of isolation. When a transaction is completed or aborted, the member variables inside of our object will contain transaction-sensitive information. If our component aborted a transaction for any reason, we must ensure nobody uses the contained data. To ensure that somebody accessing this data does not violate the isolation of our component data, MTS deactivates the real object, destroying the state data contained therein—and re-activates it when the next method of our component is called.

This is why you'll often hear people say that MTS introduces a stateless programming model. Objects still have state—but the state doesn't last very long. Any information that has to be retained across method calls has to be stored elsewhere, such as in a database; or passed to the method using parameters.

The Context Object

JIT activation, ASAP deactivation, transaction monitoring and statistics are just some of the features enabled by the **context object** in conjunction with the MTS Executive and the context wrapper. The context object is very different to the context wrapper object:

❑   The context object holds information that is used by the environment to determine how your component interacts with it

❑   The context wrapper object is responsible for pretending to be your object, so that MTS can activate and deactivate the real object in the background while the client still maintains a reference to a valid COM object

The context object is responsible for maintaining information implicitly associated with an object hosted inside of MTS. So, it contains information about the object's execution environment—including information such as the identity of the object's creator, security information, and, optionally, the transaction encompassing the work of the object if one is active. The context object is sometimes referred to as the real object's **shadow** or **guardian angel**, because every MTS object has one.

So, the base client interacts with a context wrapper, and the real object interacts with the context object. Let's extend the picture:

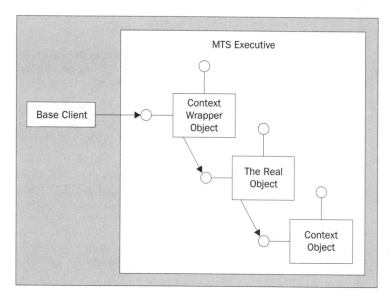

The ObjectContext Interface

A context object implements the `ObjectContext` interface (or `IObjectContext` in C++). We can easily access this interface from within any MTS object by calling the `GetContextObject()` function:

```
Dim objContext As ObjectContext
Set objContext = GetObjectContext()
```

We saw this syntax briefly in Chapter 3, when we looked at how the object context gave us access to the IIS ASP intrinsic objects. Since IIS 4 is part of the environment, and built on MTS technology, this is a logical way of accessing the ASP objects.

Being a COM object, you won't be surprised to learn that the object context object supports a number of methods. Here's a list of the methods supported by the `ObjectContext` interface—we'll see some of them in action later:

Method	Description
CreateInstance()	Creates another MTS object within the activity of the calling application. We will discuss activities shortly.
DisableCommit()	Changes the object's internal state, to indicate that it has not finished its current work and that its transactional updates are in a potentially inconsistent state.
EnableCommit()	Changes the object's internal state to indicate that its work isn't necessarily finished, but its transactional updates are in a consistent state. This is the default state for a newly-created object.
IsCallerInRole()	Indicates whether the object's direct caller is in a specified role (either directly or as part of a group).

Table Continued on Following Page

Method	Description
IsInTransaction()	Indicates whether the object is currently executing within a transaction. This method can be used to enforce the transaction requirements of a component.
IsSecurityEnabled()	Indicates whether security is enabled. MTS security is enabled unless the object is running in the client's process (when configured as a library package), or MTS is running under Windows 9x.
SetAbort()	Declares that the object has failed to complete its work and can be deactivated once the currently-executing method has returned. It should be called to indicate that transactional updates are in an inconsistent state or that some sort of unrecoverable error occurred. This means that the transaction (in which the object was executing) must be aborted. If any object executing within a transaction returns to its client after calling SetAbort, the entire transaction is doomed to abort.
SetComplete()	Declares that the object has completed its work and can be deactivated once the currently-executing method has returned. For objects that are executing within the scope of a transaction, it also indicates that the object's transactional updates can be committed. When an object that is the root of a transaction calls SetComplete, MTS attempts to commit the transaction on return from the current method.

It's worth noting now that an object shouldn't pass its ObjectContext to another object. Doing so invalidates the reference—because the object context is tied to the real object and has no meaning to third parties. It's also worth noting that a real object shouldn't pass a reference to itself—otherwise it could be called directly, rather than by its context wrapper.

Controlling the Lifetime of the Real Object with ObjectControl

As we've already mentioned, the creation, activation, deactivation and destruction of an MTS object is done transparently to our ASP page (or other client), but this does require a certain amount of participation from the component hosted in MTS.

Any *good* component under MTS implements a custom interface called ObjectControl. This interface is used by MTS to inform our object that it is being activated (or re-activated) and deactivated. The object should respond to these events, initializing any state that will exist for the duration of the object's life.

The ObjectControl Interface

This `ObjectControl` interface (or `IObjectControl` in C++) has just three methods:

Method	Description
Activate()	Called when this object is activated or re-activated.
Deactivate()	Called when this object is deactivated.
CanBePooled()	Called when an object is deactivated to see if it can be pooled. Object pooling is not implemented in MTS 2.0—so in MTS 2.0, the `CanBePooled()` method always returns `false`. MTS 3.0 does implement object pooling.

The `Activate()` method is called by the MTS Executive, the first time a client invokes a method exposed by one of the object's interfaces (that's the JIT activation we discussed earlier in the chapter). We can write the code for the `Activate` function at the time we write our component—it's in this method that an MTS object should perform any useful initialization that is global to all of the object's methods.

For example, if we were writing a component whose methods all required the same database connection, and if the component is intended always to execute within a transaction, then we could use the `Activate()` method to allocate the connection and perform any error handling.

At the end of the transaction, we would want to free the connection—and we'd use code in the `Deactivate()` method to do that. The `Deactivate()` method is called when the real object is destroyed (or returned to the pool).

> If your component's methods perform a considerable amount of work, you should consider allocating resources and freeing them inside of the method. The quicker you release resources, the quicker somebody else can use them. That means greater scalability due to improved concurrency.

The `CanBePooled()` method is called just after MTS has called the `Deactivate()` method. `CanBePooled()` returns a Boolean value, which indicates whether or not MTS is permitted to re-use the object in future creation requests by other clients. In theory, the cost of pooling already-created objects is much less than the cost of creating objects on demand using the COM runtime. Note that MTS 2.0 (the version available with Windows NT4) does not currently implement object pooling, but COM+ (with MTS 3.0) does implement this feature.

Class_Initialize and Class_Terminate

A class has two events called `Class_Initialize` and `Class_Terminate` that are called when an object is (respectively) created and destroyed. These should *not* be used for MTS objects. Instead, all of your initialization code (which would normally go in `Class_Initialize`) should be placed inside the `ObjectContext_Activate` handler instead. Similarly, all of your clean-up code (which would normally go in `Class_Terminate`) should be placed inside of `ObjectContext_Deactivate`.

A similar rule applies for C++ developers—for MTS objects, don't put the initialization and destruction code into the class's constructor and destructor.

There are a number of reasons for this, and I'll discuss a couple here. First, when an MTS object is first used inside of a package, MTS needs to run a check to find out whether or not it's a Java object. To do that, it quickly creates the object and destroys it again. On this occasion, there is no point initializing the object and then cleaning it again, because it has only been created for MTS's test purposes—so, just in this test situation, MTS chooses not to call Activate or Deactivate.

What does this mean for your initialization code? Well, MTS still calls Class_Initialize—so if your initialization code is there then your object will be initialized anyway (which is a potentially expensive waste of resources). However, if your initialization code is contained in the ObjectContext_Activate handler, then the test object won't get initialized this time round—which is what we want.

Second, in the longer term, we'll have Windows 2000—which does implement object pooling (only for C++ components at this point in time), and that means that which means your objects can be recycled. It works because the object can be stored in the object pool once it has been deactivated; and it will potentially improve the overall efficiency of MTS for some types of component that take a while to initialize. The point here is that the ACID **isolation** property demands that object state *must* be reset between method calls—and that requires that clean-up code is contained in the ObjectContext_Deactivate handler, and initialization code in the ObjectContext_Activate handler.

> *Before we move on, let me just point out that the lifetime of the context wrapper and context object is identical to that of any other COM object—that is, it is destroyed when the last client reference to it is released.*

Activities

When a base client creates an object running under MTS, an **activity** is created to host it. Each base client has its own activity, and each object is associated with *one* activity:

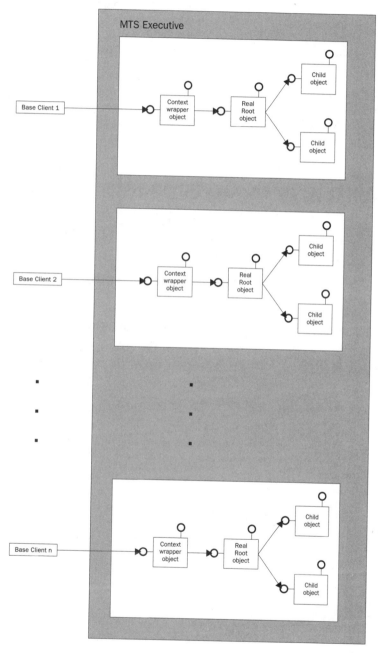

An activity is essentially an object container that hosts one or more objects. The first object created within an activity is known as the **root object**. Any child objects created by the root object's `ObjectContext.CreateInstance` function are created within the same activity.

Activities are all about maintaining consistency and isolation at the object level. The root object's children aren't necessarily located in the same package as the root object (or each other)—this means that the objects might actually reside in different processes. Objects contained in different processes are capable of running at the same time—this means that we might get a root object and/or various child objects running concurrently. Now, here's the problem: if these related objects are running concurrently, and are also trying to access and change the same piece of data, then there is a danger of inconsistency in the resulting data.

So, as objects interact inside of MTS, MTS tracks the flow of execution through each activity, and prevents any two objects hosted in the same activity from being active at the same time. Thus, an activity effectively results in a single logical thread of execution (through one or more packages, potentially distributed across several machines). This synchronization ensures the integrity of the application's state (i.e. the consistency of its underlying data).

Writing MTS Components with Visual Basic

When we write components for use with MTS, we should write them as if they are going to be used by a single user. MTS provides the infrastructure that allows our components to be deployed for use by (potentially) thousands of clients.

Before we can write some components for use in MTS we need to understand a few things about how we create MTS objects.

Creating MTS Objects from Visual Basic

Visual Basic provides two ways of creating objects: the New keyword and the CreateObject() method. MTS works differently with each of these ways, and also introduces a third method— CreateInstance()—through the ObjectContext object.

The New Keyword

The New keyword acts just like CreateObject() when creating an object from another ActiveX server, but it actually bypasses some COM processing when it creates an instance of a class within the same COM server. This because Visual Basic knows how to construct the object, so it doesn't need to invoke the COM runtime.

> The term **COM server** is used to refer an ActiveX DLL. So classes contained within the same COM server are simply components hosted by the same DLL.

Using the New keyword only creates a *private* instance of the object—that's why we must use it for creating instances of classes whose Instancing property is 1 – Private or 2 – PublicNotCreatable.

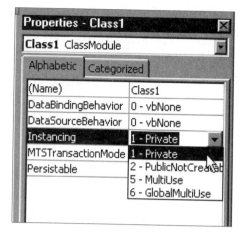

Since it's private, MTS won't know anything about it—this means that no context object will be created and it won't be able to be involved in any transactions. It will simply run as a traditional COM object—which may or may not be the behavior you're looking for.

The CreateObject Method

The CreateObject() method is almost the exact opposite of the New keyword—it always uses COM to create an instance of the class, regardless of whether the class is in the same COM server or not.

If an MTS object is created using CreateObject(), MTS will treat it as if it had been created by a client—i.e. it will get its own context object. This means that the new object won't contain any information about the context of the component that created it, and so will be outside of the current transaction.

The CreateInstance Method

The CreateInstance() method of the context object is the way to create objects within MTS that work together within a transaction. CreateInstance() works like CreateObject(), except that it performs a bit more work behind the scenes.

When a new object is created with CreateInstance(), MTS copies the context information of the creating object to the new object's context object. This means the new object will inherit the same security and transactional environment from its creator, and run within the same activity.

Creating MTS Objects from ASP

In an ASP we can create objects in two ways, both of which you've probably seen before—here, we'll try to explain the important differences in relation to MTS. First, the VBScript CreateObject() function:

```
Dim objAccount1
Set objAccount1 = CreateObject("Bank.Account")
```

The VBScript CreateObject() function results in a direct call to the COM runtime—which means that neither IIS or MTS are involved. Microsoft's IIS documentation recommends that you should never use this function in ASP scripts.

Second, and more interesting with regard to MTS, is the `CreateObject()` method of the ASP intrinsic `Server` object:

```
Dim objAccount1
Set objAccount1 = Server.CreateObject("Bank.Account")
```

If your page is marked as transactional then this method will use the `ObjectContext`'s `CreateInstance()` method to create the object (see above). Moreover, if the ASP page is transactional, `Server.CreateObject()` will enlist the new object into the same transaction as the ASP page.

If you `CreateObject()` instead of `Server.CreateObject()`, the new object will run in its own activity and (if it's transactional) in a separate transaction—thereby defeating the point of transactional ASP pages. We'll discuss this more in the next chapter.

> I've done some research on the usage of `CreateObject()` in ASP scripts, and talked to Microsoft's IIS team. It turns out that it is safe to use `CreateObject()` in ASP scripts, but only to create instances of any apartment-threaded COM component that is not installed in MTS and is never stored at the `Session` scope. It's not a simple rule to remember—if you can remember it, use `CreateObject()` at your own risk! You'll be safer using `Server.CreateObject()`.

Building an ASP Component for use in MTS

Now that we've seen the basics behind creating MTS compatible components with Visual Basic, let's go ahead and write one of our own. We'll build a simple component that takes a character string, performs a little manipulation on it and returns a different string.

The exact function of the component isn't important—what we'll focus on here is the fact that we're designing it to take full advantage of the MTS environment that we've described in the preceding pages. As you'll see, preparing our component for the MTS environment takes very little extra effort over building a regular COM component.

Setting up the Component

Fire up your Visual Basic IDE and create a new ActiveX DLL project. Select Project | Project1 Properties and change the name of the project to StringManipulator:

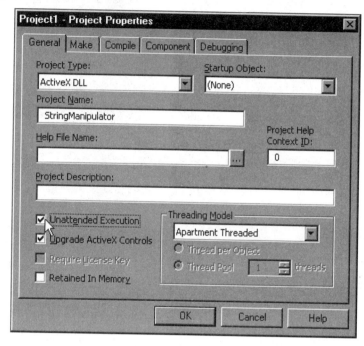

We're not going to include a user interface, so we can specify Unattended Execution (which ensures that any normal run time functions, such as messages that normally result in user interaction, are written to an event log). Notice that this causes the Retained In Memory option to become available. Leave that option off.

Retained In Memory is an interesting option. If you check it, Retained In Memory will cause a project (DLL) to be cached in memory until the process that loaded it exits—so there's a potential improvement in performance because the DLL doesn't have to load repeatedly. On the other hand, you have an object that won't destroy itself when references are set to 0, and this can generate errors. On balance, MTS provides the caching facility for us, and even allows us to specify a timeout value, so in this case we'll choose not to check it.

Next comes the first step that relates directly to tailoring the component for MTS. In order for our objects to use the `ObjectContext` and the `ObjectControl` objects, we need to add a reference to the MTS type library. Using the Project | References dialog add a reference to the Microsoft Transaction Server Type Library (for Windows 2000 you'll need a reference to `comsvcs.dll`—the COM+ Services Type Library):

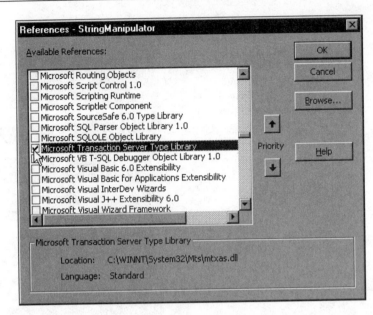

Our component will contain a single class called the `CStringReverser`. It will contains a single method, `ReverseString()`, which performs (you'll never guess!) string-reversing.

So set up the first class by changing the existing class name from Class1 to CStringReverser (as shown in the screenshot).

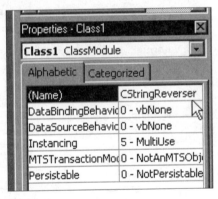

Now add the following code to the `CStringReverser` code window:

```
Option Explicit
Implements ObjectControl
Private mobjContext As ObjectContext
Private bActivated As Boolean
Private lCallCount As Long

Function ReverseString(SubjectStr As String) As String
    ' Setup error handler
    On Error GoTo MTSErrorHandler

    Dim intLength As Integer
    Dim strResult As String
    Dim intCounter As Integer
    Dim strCharacter As String
```

```
      lCallCount = lCallCount + 1
      intCounter = 0
      intLength = Len(SubjectStr)

      ' Ensure the object context is available
      If mobjContext Is Nothing Then
         Err.Raise vbObject + 1, "CStringReserver", "Object must run inside of MTS"
         Exit Function
      End If

      ' Reverse the string
      Do Until intCounter = intLength
         strCharacter = Mid$(SubjectStr, (intLength - intCounter), 1)
         strResult = strResult & strCharacter
         intCounter = intCounter + 1
      Loop

      ' Give caller result
      ReverseString = strResult

      ' Indicate to MTS we can be deactivated and that we're happy with the transaction
      mobjContext.SetComplete
      Exit Function

MTSErrorHandler:
      ' Indicate to MTS we want the transaction to be aborted
      mobjContext.SetAbort

      ' Pass on the original error
      With Err
         .Raise .Number, .Source, .Description
      End With
End Function

Private Sub ObjectControl_Activate()
   bActivated = True
   Set mobjContext = GetObjectContext
End Sub

Private Function ObjectControl_CanBePooled() As Boolean
   ObjectControl_CanBePooled = False
End Function

Private Sub ObjectControl_Deactivate()
   Set mobjContext = Nothing
End Sub

Function CallCount() As Long
   CallCount = lCallCount
End Function
```

We'll examine the code more closely in a moment. We'll force the component to require a transaction by having it tell MTS that our objects work with transactions. This is easily done by changing the MTSTransactionMode property for the `CStringReverser` to 2 – RequiresTransaction.

Now you can compile the DLL by selecting File | Make StringManipulator.dll.

How It Works

We haven't seen it working yet, but we can analyse the aspects of this component that are different from the other components we've seen so far.

Adding the **Microsoft Transaction Server Type Library** reference allows us to employ the MTS object `ObjectContext` and implement the `ObjectControl` interface in our code. In order to implement the interfaces of the `ObjectControl` object, we need to add the following line to the global code for each class:

```
Implements ObjectControl
```

We'll also be using the `ObjectContext` object, and for that we'll set a reference to that object. We'll be needing a couple of other global variables, and they're declared here also:

```
Private mobjContext As ObjectContext
Private bActivated As Boolean
Private lCallCount As Long
```

We need an implementation for each of the three methods offered in the `ObjectControl` interface—`Activate()`, `Deactivate()`, and `CanBePooled()`. First, here's `Activate()`:

```
Private Sub ObjectControl_Activate()
    bActivated = True
    Set mobjContext = GetObjectContext
End Sub
```

As soon as the object is activated, `Activate()` does two things. First, it sets the global `Boolean` variable to `True`—we can use this later to indicate that the object was indeed activated at some point. Second, it creates a reference to the `ObjectContext` object (via the `GetObjectContext()` method), so that we can use methods like `SetComplete()` and `SetAbort()` within the component. We could put other code in there that we want to execute on activation—such as event logging or reports.

Here's `Deactivate()`:

```
Private Sub ObjectControl_Deactivate()
   Set mobjContext = Nothing
End Sub
```

This is just common sense resource management. We release the resources occupied by the `ObjectContext` object when the object is deactivated.

This line is not strictly mandatory because the reference will be destroyed anyway.

Finally, here's `CanBePooled()`:

```
Private Function ObjectControl_CanBePooled() As Boolean
   ObjectControl_CanBePooled = False
End Function
```

As we explained earlier, `CanBePooled()` is called automatically when the object is deactivated—it simply returns a Boolean that indicates whether or not the object is set up for object pooling. MTS in Windows NT4 doesn't support object pooling, so we'll specify it as `False` for now. Even in Windows 2000, object pooling is not currently supported for components written using Visual Basic.

Finally, let's look briefly at some aspects of the functions' implementation. We won't talk about the detail of the string manipulation itself—that's quite straightforward. However, we are using the `SetComplete()` and `SetAbort()` methods that are made available to us by the `ObjectContext` object, stored in `mobjContext`. The following line tells the component that it must jump to the `MTSErrorHandler` marker if an error occurs:

```
On Error GoTo MTSErrorHandler
```

If no errors occur, then the method performs normally. In this case, we'll eventually reach this line near the end of the method:

```
mobjContext.SetComplete
```

Reaching this line is subject to all other components saying they were successful. It's this line that tells MTS that this part of the transaction has completed successfully, and that it can deactivate and destroy our object when the transaction completes. If there were a database involved, this would commit any database changes.

On the other hand, if an error occurs during the execution of the method, the execution jumps straight to here:

```
MTSErrorHandler:
   ' Indicate to MTS we want the transaction to be aborted
   mobjContext.SetAbort

   ' Pass on the original error
   With Err
     .Raise .Number, .Source, .Description
   End With
```

This will also result in our object being deactivated and destroyed, but as we discussed earlier, the "I'm not happy" vote will cause the whole transaction to be rolled back.

Usefully, we've also arranged for details of the error to be made available to the base client.

Preparing the Component for Installation into MTS

Once the DLL is compiled, bring up the project properties, select the Component tab, and set the Version Compatibility from Project to Binary. This is quite important, because MTS stores certain information about our components, such as the CLSID. If we do not select this option and we recompile the component at some time then Visual Basic will regenerate the CLSID, and MTS will no longer recognize it.

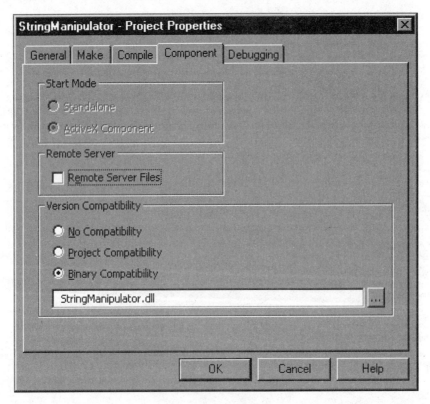

Now we have the DLL set up to run under MTS, we need to get MTS to recognize its existence. Installing a component in MTS permanently changes the way that the component is referenced within Windows—at least until you remove it from MTS. MTS makes these changes to enable it to intercept the creation of your COM component. This gives MTS complete control over the object creation process, and enables MTS to return a reference to a context wrapper object (rather than a reference to the real object) to our ASP page.

MTS Packages

Under Windows NT4, we host a component in MTS by installing it into a package. A **package** is a set of one or more components that have been grouped together so that they can be easily set up and managed together. Packages make it easier to distribute, administer and deploy groups of components.

A package can be configured to host objects in their own process space (by setting it to run as a **server package**). Alternatively it can be configured to create components in the process space of the calling base client, (by setting it to run as a **library package**). We make this configuration choice using the package's Properties dialog, as we'll see shortly.

An important feature of both types of packages is that unnecessary component loading and unloading can be prevented, with components being quickly created and destroyed. An MTS package can be configured to stay loaded for a period of time, even when there are no clients using it. This enables MTS to reduce unnecessary loading and unloading of the DLLs. The default period is three minutes.

> *Packages can only contain DLLs. You can't put an ActiveX EXE into a package.*

Installing the Component in MTS

We shall first see how to get our objects running under MTS on a local machine and then see how to export them to be used from a remote client. We'll step through this using MTS on Windows NT4 (using the MTS Explorer within the MMC as we saw earlier). If you're using Windows 2000, the procedures for this example are fortunately quite similar to those described here—but you'll be using the Component Services Explorer, comexp.msc, instead.

First, we need to register the component on the Web server! Select Start | Run and type the following, where *folderpath* is the path from the root directory to your DLL:

```
RegSvr32 folderpath\StringManipulator.dll
```

> *If your development machine and the web server are one and the same you do not need to run this command.*

235

Open the MTS Explorer (Start | Run and type mmc, then Console | Open mtxexp.msc) and browse to the Packages Installed node.

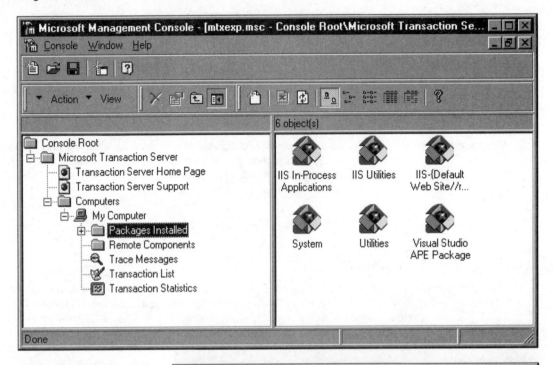

We need to add a new package so choose Action | New | Package option from the toolbar. MTS will bring up a wizard that guides us through the process of adding a package. The first page asks whether we are creating a new empty package or importing an existing one. Since we haven't placed our DLL into MTS previously, we need to Create an empty package.

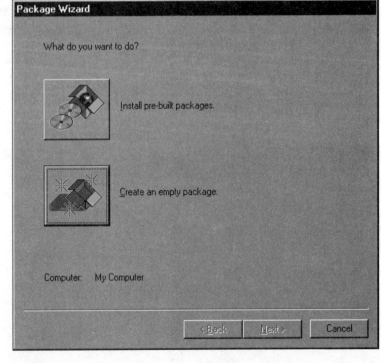

Provide a name for our new package. We'll call it **StringManipulator**, just like the DLL.

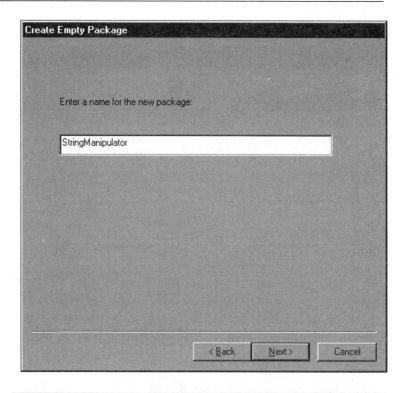

Finally, we need to provide MTS with information about the user under which the component will be running (this page doesn't appear under the 9x version). We can either supply a specific user account or use the currently logged-on user. Typically, you'd want to use a specific account, or you might want to get the ASP page to authenticate the user and then run the component under the **Interactive user** (i.e. under the security context of the authenticated user). But for simplicity, we'll just use the **Administrator** account here.

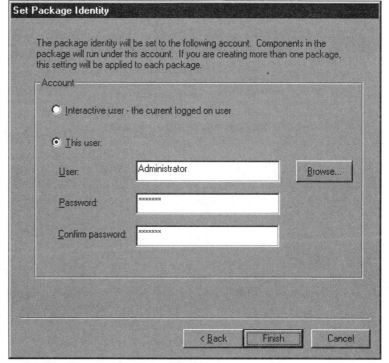

Now when we click Finish, MTS will add our new packages to the list of installed packages:

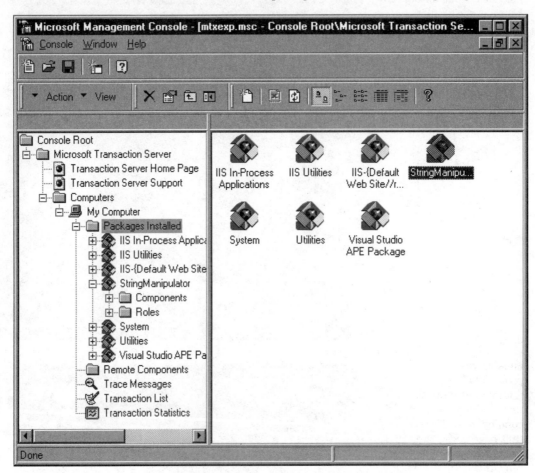

There's one more thing to do, to complete the setup of the package. By default, MTS creates a **server package**—which means that the package will run in its own process space. In this case, we'll allow our component to run in the caller's process space—so we'll change the package's properties to turn it into a **library package**. To do this, simply right-click on the StringManipulator icon and select Properties; then choose the Activation tab and ensure the Library Package option is selected.

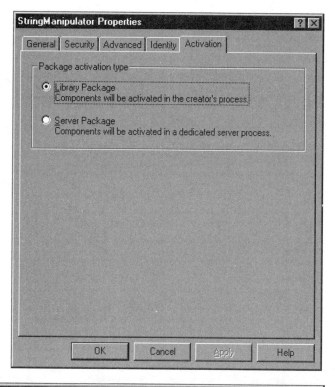

So far we've only created an empty package. We need to get the objects from our DLL into the package. This is simpler than even creating the package. It's merely a matter of dragging and dropping. Expand our package until you can see the empty Components folder:

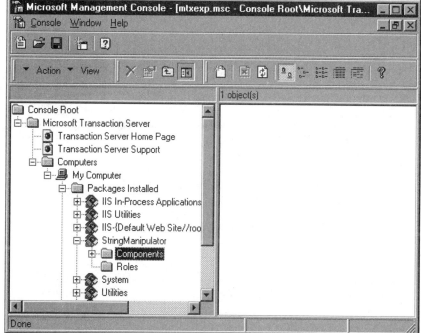

Then, using Windows NT Explorer, simply drag and drop the `StringManipulator.dll` file into the empty **Components** folder. When you've done this, you'll see a listing of all the classes contained in the DLL shown as components of this package:

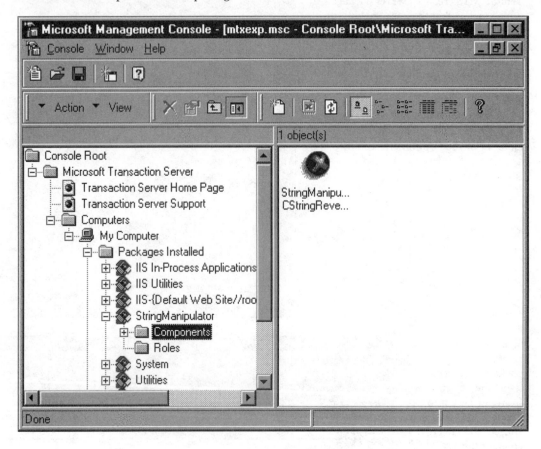

*Earlier, we saw that the installation of the component into a Library package in MTS changes the registry's **InProcServer32** key from **StringManipulator.dll** to **mtxex.dll** (and that allows MTS to intercept calls to the component).*

*In Windows NT4, if you recompile your component, you'll uncover a problem related to this, which stems from the fact that COM and MTS are not integrated. By recompiling the component, the changes that MTS made to the registry will be lost. To ensure that MTS is involved again, you have to select the **Refresh All Components** option from the context menu of **My Computer** in the MTS Explorer.*

That's all we need to do to install our objects into MTS. Now we can build the ASP page that will test the component.

Testing the Component Locally

Here's a really straightforward ASP page to test the component. All we do is create the component, and invoke the ReverseString() method four times, after which we invoke the component's CallCount method to return the global counter (which is incremented inside the component, each time the ReverseString() method is called).

You'll need to ensure that the page is being served from the same Web server that you're running MTS on at this point, because we've not discussed the remote creation of objects. Here's the ASP:

```
<HTML>
<HEAD><TITLE>Testing the MTS Component</TITLE></HEAD>
<BODY>
<%
Dim objMTSObject
Set objMTSObject = Server.CreateObject("StringManipulator.CStringReverser")

Response.Write objMTSObject.ReverseString ("HELLO MTS") & "<BR>"
Response.Write objMTSObject.ReverseString ("HELLO MTS") & "<BR>"
Response.Write objMTSObject.ReverseString ("HELLO MTS") & "<BR>"
Response.Write objMTSObject.ReverseString ("HELLO MTS") & "<BR><BR>"

Response.Write "At the time this line was written, " & _
               "we've called the ReverseString method " & _
               objMTSObject.CallCount & _
               " times since the component was last deactivated. <BR>"
%>
</BODY>
</HTML>
```

It should produce the following output:

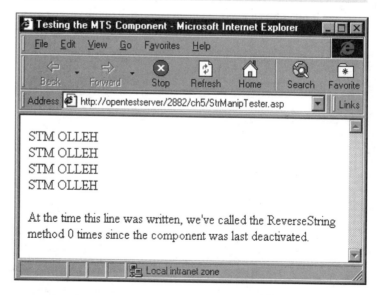

As you can see the string has been reversed and displayed four times. The interesting point to note is that the call count is zero. The call count variable is incremented by 1 each time the method executes, but (as we've discussed) that state is lost, because we invoked the SetComplete() function to indicate that we have completed our work, and MTS therefore destroys our object instance after the method call.

An Experiment

As an experiment, you could remove the `SetComplete()` call from the method's implementation, and recompile the component.

If you try this, don't forget that the MTS-specific registry settings will be lost when you recompile the component—so don't forget to refresh the registry data using the **Refresh All Components** option in MTS Explorer, we mentioned a few pages back. Once you've done that, you'll see the call count return value of 4.

So what's different in this case? We didn't call `SetComplete()`, so MTS didn't deactivate the object. Therefore, the object still exists when execution of the ASP page reaches the following line:

```
Response.Write "At the time this line was written, " & _
               "we've called the ReverseString method " & _
               objMTSObject.CallCount & _
               " times since the component was last deactivated. <BR>"
```

The state has been maintained throughout the four method calls, and is output as expected.

MTS and IIS 4.0

IIS4 is built on MTS technology. The object responsible for interpreting and executing an ASP page is an MTS object, which means it is possible to involve the ASP page itself, and any objects it creates, within a single transaction. That is, the ASP page as a whole can succeed or fail.

We'll cover this integration in greater detail in the next chapter, but to demonstrate the integration between an ASP and a component, change the ASP earlier to look like this:

```
<%@TRANSACTION=REQUIRED%>
<%
Sub OnTransactionCommit()
  Response.Write "<STRONG>Transaction Committed</STRONG>"
End Sub

Sub OnTransactionAbort()
  Response.Write "<STRONG>Transaction Aborted</STRONG>"
End Sub
%>
<HTML>
<HEAD><TITLE>Testing the MTS Component</TITLE></HEAD>
<BODY>
<%
Dim objMTSObject
Set objMTSObject = Server.CreateObject("StringManipulator.CStringReverser")

Response.Write objMTSObject.ReverseString ("HELLO MTS") & "<BR>"
Response.Write objMTSObject.ReverseString ("HELLO MTS") & "<BR>"
Response.Write objMTSObject.ReverseString ("HELLO MTS") & "<BR>"
Response.Write objMTSObject.ReverseString ("HELLO MTS") & "<BR><BR>"

Response.Write "At the time this line was written, " & _
               "we've called the ReverseString method " & _
               objMTSObject.CallCount & _
               " times since the component was last deactivated. <BR>"
%>
</BODY>
</HTML>
```

The top of this ASP page specifies the @TRANSACTION=REQUIRED directive, to indicate that the page is transactional. The attribute value REQUIRED is used to tell MTS that a transaction must be started when the ASP page begins its execution.

When the @TRANSACTION directive is used, ASP will invoke one of two event handlers, depending upon the outcome of the transaction. If the transaction is successful, the OnTransactionCommit event handler is called, and the message **Transaction Committed** (as seen in the figure on the right) will be seen at the bottom of the page. Typically we can use this handler to tell the user the good news, or maybe redirect to another page. If the transaction fails, the **Transaction Aborted** message will be seen instead.

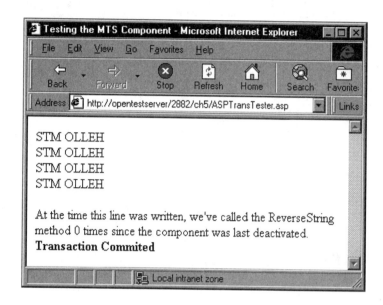

Another Experiment

To prove that the ASP will catch failed transactions, and to demonstrate the relationship between IIS and MTS, we can change the StringReverser component to abort a transaction. The quickest way to demonstrate this is to raise an error and add a SetAbort() method call at the start of the ReverseString() method, like this:

```
...
On Error GoTo MTSErrorHandler
Err.Raise vbObject + 1, "CStringReverser", _
         "Error: Just a pretend error, for demo purposes"
mobjContext.SetAbort
Dim intLength As Integer
...
```

When you recompile the component, don't forget also to **Refresh All Components**.

*You might get a **Permission denied** message when you try to recompile the component. If you do, that's because MTS is still using the DLL. In order to avoid this, you need to force MTS to unload the component—by stopping and restarting the WWW Service. From the **Start** menu, select **Programs | Administrative Tools | Server Manager**, then the **Computer | Services...** option. In the list, select **World Wide Web Publishing Service** and hit the **Stop** button. Restarting the service is a similar process—select the service and hit **Start**.*
*Note that this will stop and restart **all** webs, so use it wisely in a production environment!*

If we refresh the browser and view the page again, the transaction will be aborted, and ASP will invoke the handler as shown below:

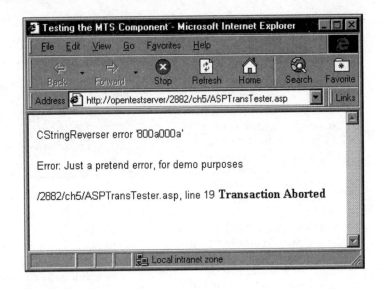

Summary

In this chapter we learned how MTS can help to make COM components more scalable, functional, and reliable. MTS provides us with many features—like database connection pooling, just-in-time activation, thread pooling, and more—without us having to write a lot of plumbing code or calling a complex API.

We discussed how transactions worked and how they should adhere to the ACID principles of Atomicity, Consistency, Isolation, and Durability. We also saw how MTS changes the COM programming model to enforce these properties.

We also saw how to build an MTS component and install it into MTS—using it from an ASP, and taking compensating action depending upon the outcome of the transaction.

Microsoft has made a commitment to MTS. It will be enhanced, extended and integrated into the next releases of the Windows operating system and will be thought of more as a service than an application. Indeed, when COM+ finally hits the streets you will see how MTS is a fundamental part of it.

If you or your company are building distributed COM applications, I suggest you read on to find out more about this interesting tool, and see if you can save yourself a lot of development effort.

Transactions, Scalability, and Resource Management

As we've already hinted, MTS has the potential to assist any application that requires one or more of the following characteristics: scalability, support for localized or distributed transactions, activity monitoring, secure access to components, multi-user support and/or concurrent access to components, and easy deployment of remote client installation. There is not space to discuss all of these problems in detail here, as some of them require fine detail and are highly specialized. But we can talk about some of the more *general* benefits that MTS brings to our component design.

One of the most important areas is the relationship between transactions, statelessness and scalability. In MTS, these three concepts are intricately related. Essentially, by controlling the lifetime of our components, and minimizing the amount of state that the system is required to store, we can achieve much greater efficiency with the available resources—and before we know it we'll be well on the road to genuinely scalable applications. When we come to look at the resource sharing that's available in MTS 2.0 (and the object pooling that's coming up in COM+, which contains the next incarnation of MTS), we can gain an even better advantage.

In this chapter we're going to develop a simple application based around a database, which will benefit greatly from the features provided by MTS 2.0. We will see how transactions are essentially all about lock management, and how careful lock management increases the scalability of the application.

> To save typing MTS 2.0 or even MTS 2.0 service pack one, we'll just stick with the term MTS from here on to mean MTS 2.0 and above.

In this chapter we will cover:

- ❏ Pooling resources to gain greater scalability
- ❏ Using lock management to ensure that our data is consistent
- ❏ How careful use of lock management prevents the issue reducing scalability
- ❏ How the MS DTC is responsible for creating and managing transactions
- ❏ How we can ensure transactions maintain consistency over multiple data sources
- ❏ One way of sharing data between components

We'll be giving particular attention to database-driven applications in this chapter. At the present time, it's probably true to say that most applications using MTS are database oriented, however it's certainly not true to say that MTS is a database application-specific product. With the right development, *any* application that wants better concurrency, multi-user functions and a simplified development model can benefit from MTS.

Resource Management and Pooling

Part of the power of MTS is that the basic principles of transaction processing can apply to any number of data sources of varying types on one or more machines. For example, it's possible to have a transaction whose success depends on the completion of all of the following actions:

❑   Update a database table that's hosted on machine A

❑   Create and modify a number of files that are hosted on machine A

❑   Update some more database tables that are hosted on machine B

In fact, it's both possible and quite acceptable to have a single transaction take responsibility for making changes to many different data sources, in many locations. So, how does MTS manage the committal or abortion of the transaction when so many different data sources are involved? The answer lies in **resource managers** and **resource dispensers**.

Resource Managers and Resource Dispensers

The role of a **resource manager** in MTS is to implement transactions over a specific data source, such as a database. Resource managers are responsible for managing **durable** data—or persistent data. It's a resource manager's job to keep this durable data in a **consistent** state when it's used and manipulated by an object. In order to do this, they implement transactions—which, as we saw in the last chapter, implement consistency as part of the ACID contract.

What does a resource manager look like? Well, SQL Server and Oracle are examples of resource managers—they are capable of managing their data in a transactional way. However, not all data stores can be classed as being resource managers, because they don't all *manage* their data in the way we're talking about—although they can all be classed as durable data. The important factor about an MTS resource manager is that it participates in MS DTC (Microsoft Distributed Transaction Coordinator) transactions, which we'll expand upon in more detail in the later part of this chapter.

Durable data includes (but isn't limited to) databases. In fact, a resource manager can be written for any type of data stored in any type of data source. For example, Microsoft Message Queue (MSMQ) can perform transactions over a message queue. Using MSMQ, we could provide a transaction that:

❑   Adds a sales order to a database

❑   Sends a message to the sales manager to ensure that he is aware of the sale

Resource dispensers are closely related to resource managers. A resource dispenser's job is to manage (and sometimes pool) the **non-durable** shared resources (such as database connections) that are needed by an object to manipulate the durable data maintained by a resource manager. Resource dispensers can work outside of the scope of transactions (and indeed resource managers), and can also maintain their own transient data.

The transient resources managed by a dispenser do not have to be those provided by a resource manager. For example, MTS provides a shared property manager that enables state to be shared within an MTS package by a number of components—as we will see at the end of the chapter. The resource dispenser maintains the state and is not dependent upon a resource manager.

> Resource dispensers are known as **singleton** objects, because only one instance of the object is created per process.

Resource Pooling and Scalability

Together, resource managers and resource dispensers are major players in the scalability game. Resource dispensers enable this by sharing limited resources efficiently between clients. It does this by **pooling** these resources, which means it holds the resources in a pool when they're not being used, and allocates them to clients when they are needed.

When a client requests a resource from a resource dispenser (for example, when it creates an ADO connection object within the scope of an MTS transaction) one of two things happen:

- ❑ If a resource exists matching the requirements of the client, it is marked as 'in use' and then returned it to the client.

- ❑ If a suitable resource is not found, a new resource is created and returned to the client.

In both of these cases when the client releases the resource it is returned to the pool, so it can then be recycled and used by another client. Pool sizes are not generally limited, but resources within the pool are typically freed after a period of idle time. For example, OLE DB pooling of database connections frees resources after 60 seconds.

How does that compare with more traditional, non-scalable systems? Typically, clients using a non-pooled system would request the resources they need at the start of the application, and once allocated a resource they would hold onto the resource for the entire lifetime of the application. For precious resources such as database connections (which are often in limited supply) this severely limits the number of clients that an application can support, because such a system can't support more clients than there are available database connections.

MTS uses resource pooling to enable many clients to share a relatively small pool of resources. Instead of allocating resources at the start of the application, MTS listens to clients' demands for resources and provides these resources to each client only for as long as it is needed during the lifetime of the application—then releases the resource as soon as the client has finished with it.

Resource Pooling in More Detail

The following diagram shows how resource dispensers pool and re-use the resources they give out to objects in order to aid performance and scalability:

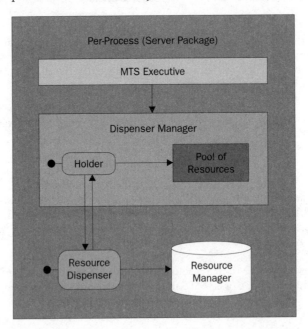

In this diagram we have a **resource dispenser manager**, which is actually responsible for providing access to pooled resources. Despite the name it is not a combination of a resource dispenser and a resource manager; so in order to try and dispel the confusion over terminology we'll refer to this as the **DispMan**. Individual resource dispensers register themselves with the DispMan, which creates a **holder** object to manage resources for each dispenser.

When an MTS object requests a resource, such as a database connection, the following process takes place:

❑ First, the MTS Executive asks the DispMan to provide the resource

❑ Second, the DispMan consults its resource pool to find out whether one or more of the requested resources has already been created and exists is in the pool. If the resources do exist and are currently free, then the DispMan will ask the associated resource dispenser to rate the resources for suitability

❑ Third, if a suitable candidate is found within the pool, it is returned to the client—and the resource dispenser marks the resource as being 'in use'. Suitability of a resource varies, but two overriding considerations are transactional status, and security. Some clients temporarily free their resources, while still in the transaction. In this case, only clients within the same transaction can pick up the resource. If the security attributes (context) of a free resource would allow the client to do more than they would normally be allowed to do, and therefore comprise the expected security, they cannot re-use the existing resource, and one has to be created for them with the appropriate context.

❑ If (in the third step) a suitable resource is *not* found, the DispMan will ask the resource dispenser to create a new resource. The new resource will be added to the pool and then returned as in the third step.

This sequence of events is a pattern that is pretty typical for any type of pooling. For example, when using an ADO connection inside of a Visual Basic application, connection pooling (or session pooling in OLE DB parlance) is actually implemented in this way by **OLE DB services**. OLE DB services is part of OLE DB that adds common services to all providers without each provider having to effectively implement and provide the same code. OLE DB services doesn't actually use the resource pooling provided by DispMan but the techniques it uses are based on the same principles. OLE DB services also provide auto-transaction enlistment as we'll discuss shortly.

Resource Rating

In the second step of the pooling process described above, the resource dispenser is required to **rate** the available resource before it is returned to a client. The reason for this is that, while a resource might be available, it might still be in an incompatible state for client consumption. Each resource has four possible states:

❑ **Unenlisted inventory**—the resource is not in use and is not enlisted in a transaction.

❑ **Enlisted inventory**—the resource is not in use but it is enlisted in a transaction

❑ **Unenlisted use**—the resource is being used but is not enlisted in a transaction.

❑ **Enlisted use**—the resource is being used and is enlisted in a transaction.

The bottom line is that although a resource may be free, it could be enlisted in a transaction—and such resources can only be released to a client object if the object requesting the resource is contained within the same transaction.

Transaction Propagation—the Scope of Transactions

When a resource is returned from the DispMan MTS will enlist the resource into the current transaction—if one is active. This auto-enlistment means that transactions are automatically propagated to include returned resources without any interaction on our behalf.

Let's consider how and when is propagation will occur, by examination of four distinct situations.

No Transaction

First, consider the following ASP code:

```
<%
  ' Create a new connection
  strConn = "Data Source=your_server_name;Provider=SQLOLEDB;" + _
            "Initial Catalog=pubs;User ID=sa"

  set objConn = CreateObject("ADODB.Connection")
  objConn.Open strConn
  '...
%>
```

We've seen examples similar to this in Chapter 4. In this case, the ASP page is not transactional, and there are no transactional objects involved, so there's no transaction scope to consider:

ASP Creates a Transaction

Second, consider this very similar ASP page:

```
<%@TRANSACTION=REQUIRED%>
<%
    ' Create a new connection
    strConn = "Data Source=YOUR_SERVER_NAME;Provider=SQLOLEDB;" + _
              "Initial Catalog=pubs;User ID=sa"

    set objConn = CreateObject("ADODB.Connection")
    objConn.Open strConn
    '...
%>
```

When the page is executed a new MTS transaction is started—because the page is marked as being transactional through the @TRANSACTION=REQUIRED directive. The call to the Connection object's Open method will result in a call to the underlying OLE DB provider, SQLOLEDB. (You may recall from Chapter 4 that SQLOLEDB is the OLE DB provider for SQL Server Databases.) The OLE DB provider acts as a resource dispenser, and will either create a *new* connection or will use an *existing* one. Either way, the returned resource will be enlisted within the transaction created by the page as shown below:

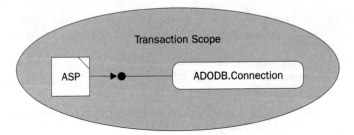

Here, both the ASP and the ADO Connection object are contained in the scope of the transaction. We use the term **transaction scope** to define the extent to which objects are included within a transaction. All of these objects together determine the actions taken as a whole, and vote on the outcome of the transaction. Another term for transaction scope is **transaction stream**—a transaction that flows across one or more objects.

Non Transactional ASP Creates a Transactional MTS Object

Third, consider the case where we have a non-transactional ASP that creates a transactional MTS object:

```
<%
    ' Create a new non-transactional object
    set objNonXActObject = CreateObject("WroxObjects.NonXactObject")
    objNonXActObject.UsefulMethod
    '...
%>
```

In this case, the transaction scope does not encompass the page, but it does encompass any ADO connection objects created by the MTS object's methods:

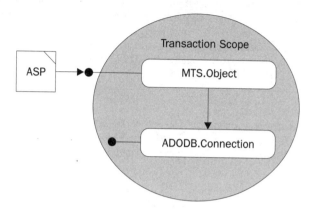

Here, only the MTS object and the ADO Connection object are involved in the transaction.

Transactional ASP and Transactional Component

Fourth and finally, consider when the ASP is transactional and it creates and uses an instance of an MTS component:

```
<%@TRANSACTION=REQUIRED%>
<%
    ' Create a new non-transactional object
    set objNonXActObject = CreateObject("WroxObjects.NonXactObject")
    objNonXActObject.UsefulMethod
    ' ...
%>
```

Then, the transaction would encompass everything:

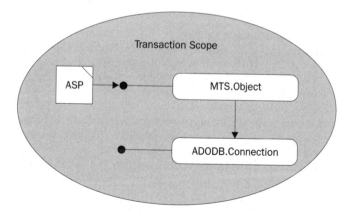

Here the ASP page, the MTS object and the ADO Connection object are held within the scope of the transaction.

> Many people often get confused about the real technical difference between `Server.CreateObject` and `CreateObject`. The truth of that matter is that the only difference between them is that `Server.CreateObject` calls the `CreateInstance` nethod of the `ObjectContext` object (and does some basic registry checks) and the `CreateObject` doesn't. There are no unexpected side effects from using `CreateObject`, it simply means transactions will not be propagated. In IIS5 `CreateObject` will propagate transactions.

The real beauty of resource management in MTS is that it's all done *transparently* and *automatically* for you—thanks to the MTS Executive. This means you don't have to do anything other than use MTS (or if you are running under Windows 2000 COM+) for its magic to work.

Are You Running Under A Transaction

A common question (and topical at this point) is how does ADO, for example, know whether or not a transaction is active, and then enlist a newly created connection in to it? The solution lies within OLE DB services as we saw earlier. As well as providing session pooling, OLE DB services provide auto MTS transaction enlistment, when the underlying provider is actually a resource manager proxy—an interface to a resource manager. If it is, when a connection is first opened, OLE DB services will determine if an MTS transaction is active (exactly how this done is detailed later), if so, it will ask resource manager proxy to enlist the connection into the current transaction being returned it to the client.

Thread Pooling in MTS

MTS provides another type of resource management, called **thread pooling**. We haven't discussed the concept of threads in great detail so far in this book—essentially because, when programming ASP components in Visual Basic, we don't have a great deal of control over them. There's a detailed discussion of the issues involved in Chapter 12. However, threads form an essential part of any scalable system, especially in MTS, so let's bite the bullet and tackle the subject now.

Put simply, you can think of a thread as a lightweight process. But unlike a process, threads do not actually own the system resources they use. The operating system will create a process when you start an application (e.g. NotePad) under Windows, in which the application executes. This process will have its own address space, and will be isolated from other processes—such that if the application goes seriously wrong, the integrity of other applications in the system is maintained.

Inside of a process you always have at least one thread, known as the **main thread**. A thread is the basic entity to which the operating allocates CPU time. So, if we have 10 processes, each with a thread that is doing some intensive work, the operating system will give each thread 10% of the overall available CPU time. A percentage of this time will actually be spent managing the thread switching, so the overall time given to your process for executing *your* code may be slightly less, say 9.5%.

A process can contain multiple threads that run concurrently. Each thread shares the system resources owned by the process, such as its virtual address space. This means that threads can execute the application's code, access global memory and other resources such as files, while not consuming too much additional resources.

Because threads are 'cheaper' than processes, truly scalable systems will always use one-thread-per-client, rather than one-process-per-client, because the resource saving is great. Depending upon how the system is partitioned, the system might use multiple processes for different applications, with a thread per-client. MTS takes this approach by enabling each package to be configured to run in its own process—these are the **server packages** that were briefly mentioned in the previous chapter.

MTS takes care of threads for you by pooling them, just like the resource dispenser does with database connections, and it does this very efficiently. When the thread pool is exhausted, MTS arranges for components to share threads in a round robin fashion. For example, if we had a thread pool size of 5, the sixth component created would share the first thread; the seventh component would share the second thread; and so on. Again, because MTS manages the threading for us, there's no need for us to write custom thread managers within our code.

> *We cover threads in more detail in Chapter 12. MTS allows a maximum of 100 threads for each process it creates. The thread limit for MTS can be modified by changing the registration for a package. By default IIS 4 reduces the limit to 25. In IIS 5, the pool is dynamically managed based upon load.*

Object Lifetimes, Transactions and Statelessness

We've seen that we can manage resources with the help of DispMan and thread pooling so that we can support multiple users and make applications scalable, without the need to write complicated code manually to take care of these processes. This greatly improves our scalability. But scalability means more than just having the resources to handle many simultaneous users. We've also got to be sure that the data accessed by each of these concurrent users is consistent data, in a state that reflects our business rules.

So, transactions are intricately related to scalability in more than one way—because the ACID properties of consistency and isolation combine to ensure that data is carefully protected when being accessed and manipulated simultaneously by two or more parties. Note that we're not only referring to database transactions here, but to MTS transactions in general—transactions that span one or more machines containing potentially different types of data sources.

Under the covers, the lifetime of MTS objects—and specifically transactional objects—is somewhat different to the lifetime of normal COM objects.

> *The lifetime of an object is the duration of time for which it exists and consumes resources. Its life starts when it is created. Its life ends when it is destroyed.*

The Stateless Programming Model

We can think of a COM object as having three main characteristics—**identity, behavior**, and **state**. An MTS object has all of these properties too, but it is important to understand that, if the object is involved in a transaction, then the lifetime of the object's state is short. The context wrapper and object context exist while a client still holds a reference to 'what it thinks' is the real object, thus abiding by the rules of COM. But typically, the real object (which is created on demand by the context wrapper) is created and activated when needed, then deactivated and destroyed when the transaction it is involved in completes.

When a transaction is committed or aborted in MTS (the outcome is determined by a call to the SetComplete or SetAbort method of each object involved in the transaction), all of the objects that formed part of the transaction are deactivated and destroyed. This ensures that resources consumed by those objects, including the objects' state, are freed, although the context wrapper and object context live on. You can control the lifetime of objects that you create inside of your transaction (such as database connections) and destroy them as soon as you like, but you cannot directly control the lifetime of **root object** that started the transaction. The root object is that name given to the object that is created by the context wrapper when a base client invokes a method of a component. You can signal that the root object should be destroyed, by calling SetComplete or SetAbort, but it is actually the MTS executive that destroys it, via the context wrapper.

This de-activation model means that any transient state that was manipulated and held within the objects during the transaction is lost when it completes. Of course, the important durable state is maintained inside of the resource manager and will live on. This destruction of transient state might seem strange and not very object oriented, but transactions have to maintain ACID properties. As the object's state is transaction sensitive, MTS has to destroy it when a transaction completes (whatever the outcome) to ensure consistency and isolation.

> *People often talk about using MTS for non-transactional objects. While these follow the same principles and can be created, activated, deactivated and destroyed using the object context interface, you have to consider if this is actually benefically before you do it. The context wrapper and object context consume quite a lot of resources. Unless your object consumes at lot more resources than these objects, and can live with the so called stateless model, don't use MTS for them.*

To understand why the objects are destroyed consider a familiar scenario.

Ensuring Consistent State

A banking system uses an Account object to represent your bank balance during a financial transaction. The balance is initially read from a central bank database (running SQL Server)—on this particular occasion, by the application using the object. The Account object is set to reflect your current balance of $1,000. In order to pay the bank your mortgage for the month, a transaction removes $200 from the account, and places this amount into the bank's account, updating the central database to reflect this. However, at the very last moment a problem occurs in the bank's system, and the transaction is aborted—this happens *after* the account balance in your Account object has been reduced to $800, which has also modified the durable state in the central bank database. Because the transaction has aborted, your account should still contain $1000, as the database should have rolled back the changes, but the account object may still contain the value $800.

Now, what if the `Account` object weren't destroyed by the application at this stage, and was used again later? In that case, the object's state won't be modified again to the correct value: the `Account` object still exists, and is in an inconsistent state with a balance amount of $800. At this stage, the central database will still contain the true value of your account balance—$1000—because the database will maintain a transaction log, which would have been used to undo any changes when the transaction aborted. (In theory, `Account` object could keep its own transaction log and rollback changes, but that would mean a lot of work for the component designer! We'll discount that possibility, because it's impractical.)

When the bank's system is up and running again, another new transaction is started to deduct $100 for your electricity bill. This new transaction uses the same account object that currently exists in an inconsistent state, so your balance value for this second transaction starts at the incorrect value of $800. This new transaction completes its task of deducting $100 for your electricity bill successfully, and so updates the central database with the final (incorrect) balance of $700. Effectively, you've lost $200—all because that first `Account` object maintained its state after the transaction finished.

Of course, the reverse could happen—you might *gain* money as a result of an inconsistency. But MTS isn't happy with either type of inconsistency, so it avoids such inconsistencies by always destroying an object as soon as a transaction is completed. The consequence of this is that the state is recreated afresh for every new transaction—so the chances of inconsistencies are pretty much non-existent, unless the central database itself contains invalid information.

This is a fairly simplistic example, but hopefully it brings across the fact that maintaining state in two places (the central database and the account object) can lead to problems if the two are not always kept synchronized, and the account object does not always refresh its state to ensure consistency *before* starting a new transaction.

Assisting Concurrency

You might be thinking that if a transaction succeeds, there really is no need to destroy the object. That's true, but in that case there's still another issue to consider which relates to the multi-user situation—the notion of **concurrency**. What if we had two simultaneous transactions that each created an object to contain and manipulate your balance at the same time? Or a large company where one account is potentially updated thousands of times a day as invoices are paid? How could we ensure that objects containing and/or manipulating the balance always contained the same value? That the outcome of one transaction in one object that changes the balance, notified all the other objects that the data they contain is now out of date? And that they shouldn't use it as a start point for a new transaction?

The simple answer is that we can't, and if we restricted systems to only ever creating one instance of a specific object we compromise concurrency, as only one transaction at a time would safely be able to access and manipulate any piece of data, and each request to the data would have to be serialized. What we have to do is allow multiple objects to exist, but **guarantee** that all objects always access and retrieve an accurate, consistent balance before starting a new transaction.

For all of these reasons and a lot more, the MTS approach of deactivating and destroying objects is good. It simplifies the whole transaction processing model, and it helps enforce the most important aspect of any system—accuracy and consistency of data. However, this model has a large degree of overhead, so method calls will be in the region of 2 or 3 times slower. But, of course, the larger objective of scalability is at work here.

By destroying objects when a transaction completes MTS forces us to store state in a central location such as a database. This should in theory result in better consistent and better performance for a large number of users. However, it doesn't solve all of our problems. If we've got better concurrency, two or more objects are more likely to try and update the same piece of information (our balance) at the same time, so how do we ensure consistency then? As we'll discuss shortly, implementing a careful locking strategy is the solution.

We've covered a lot of very important issues here regarding consistency and concurrency, and we will shortly discuss locking as method of enforcing consistency when there is a large degree of concurrency. Before this, we need to fully understand the lifetime of object inside of MTS, and discuss how we can share state between so called stateless component.

Transaction Lifetimes

Recapping from the last chapter the object context and context wrapper are used when accessing an object inside of MTS. So for the `Account` object we've just discussed any client using it (such as an ASP) would actually be holding a reference to the context wrapper:

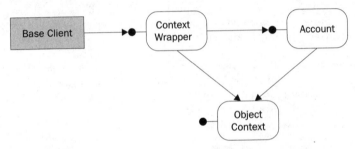

The context wrapper is responsible for just-in-time (JIT) activation of an object when a method is invoked from the base client. The object context contains "environment" details about the object such as the current transaction.

When our object is deactivated the base client just holds onto the context wrapper which references the object context:

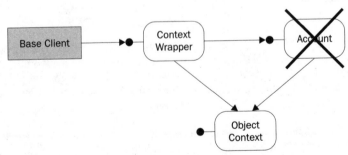

No DLL Load Thrashing

When an MTS object is destroyed by a base client, the COM server (DLL) containing the component is not immediately unloaded, even if there are no objects of the type supported by the COM server currently in use. In normal COM this would typically happen.

However, because the components in an MTS package are typically used in high-demand systems, objects are generally created time and time again, 24 hours a day. Imagine if a DLL was immediately unloaded from memory every time the last object originating from it was it destroyed. Then imagine that a single object was created and destroyed 1000 times in quick succession. Would we really want to load and unload the DLL 1000 times? Of course, not. We'd want to load it once, and then when no more object requests are coming in unload it. This is the approach adopted by MTS.

A DLL (or more specifically a package) is only unloaded once all context wrappers have been released by all base clients, and the unload timeout specified for the package containing it—shown in the following figure as being 3 minutes—has expired. Unloading the DLL immediately, or even after 10 seconds, would lead to thrashing—repeated and unnecessary loading and unload of a DLL. This has a negative effect on performance because of the increase disk activity.

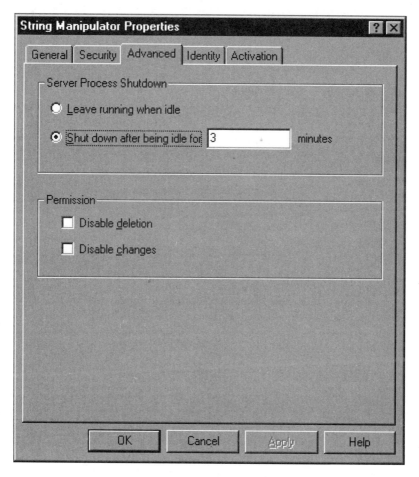

How Long Does An Object's State Live For?

So, the key point to remember is that an MTS object does have state, but that its state generally only lasts for a short period of time—the duration of a transaction. If an ASP page is transactional and all other transactional objects are created using `Server.CreateObject`, then the duration of the transaction and the lifetime of all objects is equal to the time taken to render the page.

If an ASP is not transactional and an MTS object is created using `CreateObject` or `Server.CreateObject` the lifetime of the object is tied to the duration of one method call from an ASP page to the object. So, in the following piece of code, the real object is recreated by the context wrapper when the `SomeCall` method is called, and destroyed when the `SomeCall` method returns:

```
' Create Object Context object and Context Wrapper Object

set oMTSObject = Server.CreateObject("MTS.Object")
oMTSObject.SomeCall    ' Object created and destroyed
oMTSObject.SomeCall    ' Object created and destroyed
oMTSObject.SomeCall    ' Object created and destroyed
```

> **When using transactional ASP pages, components installed in an MTS package should be called using `Server.CreateObject` rather than `CreateObject`.**

This is because each object created using `CreateObject` will start its own transaction and will therefore run inside of its own activity, meaning that is will also use its own thread.

Hopefully, so far we've made it clear that transactions are a very important part of MTS, and when combined with the other features it adds, MTS provides a strong and solid infrastructure upon which we can build scalable applications, with or without IIS4. Remember, IIS4 uses MTS to provide a large degree of its functionality, but that same functionality can be used in your applications and components.

Having seen this, we now need to look at how we guarantee that two objects are not trying to alter the same things at the same time, which would compromise the consistency of the data.

Locking

When we talk about transactions it is important to understand one very important concept behind them: **locking**. If one transaction is modifying data, such as our bank balance, we have to ensure that other transactions are prevented from modifying the same data. This is done using a lock; the transaction responsible for modifying the data holds a **lock** to prevent other transactions from accessing the data until it has either committed or aborted, at which point it releases the lock. Once the lock is released, the next transaction can use the data and hold the lock. If we don't do this both transactions could attempt to update the same data at the same time producing inconsistent results.

If we think back to the bank example, we have to lock the data every time we want to alter the bank balance, and hold that lock until the transaction is completed. We are not only concerned about the objects responsible for the data during the transaction, but also the data sources holding the durable data. We can therefore say **locks** provide the isolation part of ACID, and therefore they are *very* important.

There are two types of locks:

- ❑ **Read Locks**—applied within a transaction when data is read
- ❑ **Write Locks**—applied within a transaction when data is updated

We need to have a strong understanding of locks and their relationship to transactions if we are to have any chance of writing a scalable system. Apply too many locks in the wrong places and the overall concurrency of a system is comprised, because everybody is always waiting for locks. Apply too few locks and consistency of data is comprised.

Locks are applied during a transaction as data is accessed. Depending upon the type of access a read or write lock is applied.

Read Locks

In MTS a read lock (also called a **shared** lock) is a way for one transaction reading a piece of data to prevent any other transactions from updating it. Several transactions can all read the same data at the same time, each can apply their own read lock.

The motivation behind applying read locks within a transaction is that they enable the same piece of data to be read many times during the same transaction, while ensuring that each read will consistently return the same value, knowing that nobody else can update it until you release the lock. For example, imagine two transactions T1 and T2 where we don't use read locks:

T1 reads the number of free seats for the latest blockbuster film showing at Rock Cinemas. It sees that 1 seat is free, and based on that assumption performs another action to sell the seat.

Meanwhile, before T1 has actually sells the seat T2 starts. Because there is no read lock, T2 takes the number of the seats available to be 1. T2, however, involves a customer returning 4 tickets, making the total number of seats available 5.

If T2 completes before T1 sells the ticket, when T1 completes, the number of seats available will be zero, because T1 has sold the remaining seat that was available when it read the data. This leaves the 4 returned seats unaccounted for.

If T1 had created a read lock for the free seat number data, T2 would not have been able to update it until the read lock was released. This is where a problem occurs, because you cannot create a write lock while read locks are pending. So, if T2 had also applied a read lock that would have prevented T1 from completing also. This is known as a dead lock—neither process can complete because each own one lock, and each lock is also required by the other process to complete. When this happens SQL server breaks the dead lock and aborts both transactions.

Dead locks can be avoided by using **pessimistic locking** when reading data. Rather than applying a read lock for data that is read, a data source will always apply a write lock. This prevents any other transaction from reading the same data until the lock is released. While this is essential, we should be aware that it does reduce concurrency within the system—if you obtain the write lock too early, people will be unnecessarily kept from reading it.

Using ADO you set pessimistic locking by setting the LockType property to adLockPessimistic as shown in this VB code:

```
sConn = "Data Source=YOUR_SERVER_NAME;" + _
        "Provider=SQLOLEDB;" + _
            "Initial Catalog=pubs;" + _
            "User ID=sa"
set oConn = CreateObject("ADODB.Connection")
oConn.Open sConn

set oRS = CreateObject("ADODB.Recordset")
oRS.LockType = adLockPessimistic
oRS.Open "select * from authors", oConn
```

Write Locks

In MTS, applying a write lock (sometimes also called an **exclusive** lock) means a transaction reading a piece of data has exclusive access to the data until it releases the lock. It prevents anybody else from reading or updating the data as we've just discussed.

A write lock cannot be applied while there are any outstanding read locks, unless the transaction trying to create the write lock also created the original read lock, in which case the lock type will simply be changed.

The isolation level that MTS uses when applying locks is called SERIALIZABLE. As the name suggests, the effect of using this level of lock is that, locks are applied in such a way that transactions behave as if they are executing one after another. The serializable isolation level is therefore a natural choice for MTS because it attempts to simplify the programming model to a single user.

Outside of MTS though there are other isolation levels you should be aware of:

Isolation Level	Description
Read Uncommitted (also called **Browse**)	Data is always read irrespective of any applied locks that have been applied. This means that a transaction can read 'dirty' data. For example, the first read of a balance within a transaction could be $800, the next read could be $200 and so forth.
Read Committed (also called **Cursor Stability**)	You cannot read the data until it is committed by a transaction, so the read will block until any write lock is release. A read lock is applied while reading the data, but it is released after the read completes, it does not last for the duration of a transaction.
Repeatable Read	You cannot read data until it is committed by a transaction, so the read will be blocked until any write lock is released. A read lock is created when reading the data, and is kept until the transaction that read the data completes. This means that any data read or re-read within a query will always produce the same values.

Isolation Level	Description
Serializable (also called Isolated)	As per repeatable read, but the scope of repeatable reads is extended to a level guarantees that all concurrent transactions interact only in ways that produce the same results as if each transaction were entirely executed one after the other. For example if T1 determined the number of rows in a table, T2 would not be able to add rows to that table because the results of same query performed a second time would be different.

In ADO these levels can be selected using the `IsolationLevel` property of the connection objects. To apply the same locking strategy that MTS uses you would write the following VB code:

```
sConn = "Data Source=YOUR_SERVER_NAME;" + _
        "Provider=SQLOLEDB;" + _
            "Initial Catalog=pubs;" + _
            "User ID=sa"
set oConn = CreateObject("ADODB.Connection")
oConn.IsolationLevel = adXactSerializable
oConn.Open sConn
oConn.BeginTrans

do something with the data

oConn.CommitTrans
```

Locks and MTS Component Granularity

It's important to understand that if one transaction implements a read lock on a piece of data, then it will delay other transactions from being able to create a write lock. For example, imagine a transaction component that:

❑ Runs an SQL query to retrieve a list of all authors

❑ Updates a single author's details, based upon some criteria

❑ Does some other processing that lasts for 2 seconds

Such a transaction would have a fairly significant impact on scalability. The first part of the transaction will apply a read lock to *all* customers—thereby preventing all other transactions in the system from updating author's details (they can only read the data, using another read lock). Since the third step takes two seconds to complete, and our transaction's read lock is not released until the transaction completes, we've got a serious scalability problem.

This type of problem can occur with or without components, because such statements can also be executed within a transaction when only using the @TRANSACTION directive. So, we have to ensure that our components and ASP pages use the correct transaction attributes, and ensure we consider what data will get what types of locks. We will demonstrate this with an example.

Managing Locks

Any page or component enlisted in a transaction will fall under the scope of that transaction. Therefore it will inherit the locking mode for the scope of the transaction. So, you can either: a) divide your transaction scope to fit in with this inherited locking mode or b) turn up the locking level if it is not specific enough for you

An Example of Locking

To see how locking works in an example application, we'll write a scalable system for maintaining author details. We'll begin by demonstrating the issues involved using a page-based ASP application, and then we'll port the entire situation to a component-based solution. In the process, we'll show how a simple mistake can prevent the whole application from scaling.

The system will consist of three pages:

❑   List_Authors.asp—shows a complete list of authors. Each author edit has an edit button that invokes Edit_Author.asp

❑   Edit_Author.asp—shows the details for a single author and allows them to be modified

❑   Update_Author.asp—performs the process of updating of the author details. It is called using the post action of the form used in Edit_Author.asp.

To demonstrate the issues with locking, we are going to make Update_Authors.asp transactional.

List_Authors.asp

The List_Authors.asp page displays a list of all the authors that are held in our system. As you can see, there is no @TRANSACTION directive, so List_Authors.asp will not form part of a transaction. This means that no read locks will be created while the data is read. Here's the code for this page:

```
<%
' Create an object that lets us pause for x milliseconds

set oWait = CreateObject("BegASP.Sleeper")

' Building the DB connection string

sConn = "Data Source=YOUR_SERVER_NAME;" + _
        "Provider=SQLOLEDB;" + _
            "Initial Catalog=pubs;" + _
            "User ID=sa"

' Create and open the connection

set oConn = CreateObject("ADODB.Connection")
oConn.Open sConn

' Create the recordset and open the cursor

set oRS = CreateObject("ADODB.Recordset")
oRS.Open "select * from authors", oConn

%>
  <HTML>
   <HEAD>
     <TITLE>Author List</TITLE>
```

```
        <STYLE TYPE="text/css">
            BODY {font-family:Veranda,Tahoma,Arial,sans-serif; font-size:10pt}
            TD {font-family:Veranda,Tahoma,Arial,sans-serif; font-size:10pt}
        </STYLE>
</HEAD>
<BODY BGCOLOR=WHITE>
 <H1>Author List</H1>
    <HR>
    <P>The following authors are currently defined in the pubs database:

 <TABLE cellspacing="2" cellpadding="0">
    <TR>
        <TD bgcolor="#3AC2EF"><STRONG>ID</STRONG></TD>
        <TD bgcolor="#3AC2EF"><STRONG>Last Name</STRONG></TD>
        <TD bgcolor="#3AC2EF"><STRONG>First Name</STRONG></TD>
        <TD bgcolor="#3AC2EF"><STRONG>Contact No.</STRONG></TD>
    </TR>
    <TR>
    </TR>

 <%
  ' Process each row
    while oRS.EOF = false
 %>

    <TR>
        <TD bgcolor="#FFFF6C"><%=oRS("au_id")%></TD>
        <TD bgcolor="#FFFF6C"><%=oRS("au_lname")%></TD>
        <TD bgcolor="#FFFF6C"><%=oRS("au_fname")%></TD>
        <TD bgcolor="#FFFF6C"><%=oRS("phone")%></TD>
        <TD bgcolor="#3AC2EF">

            <FORM NAME="A" METHOD="POST" ACTION="edit_author.asp?au_id=_
                <%=oRS("au_id")%>"><input type="SUBMIT" value="Edit" name="B1" />
            </FORM>
        </TD>
    </TR>
<%
  ' Sleep for a number of milliseconds, as specified by Wait
  oWait.WaitMS Request.QueryString("Wait")
  oRS.MoveNext
  wend
%>

    </TABLE>
  </BODY>
</HTML>
```

Remember to add the name of your server to the connection string for the database.

This ASP page connects to the SQL Server `pubs` sample database, and produces a list of authors by reading the `authors` table. The output of the ASP page is shown in shown in following screenshot. For our demonstration we'll just use four of the fields in the `authors` table.

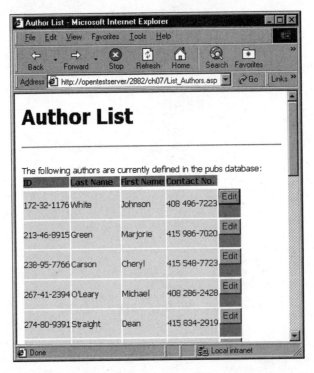

There are two important points to note. Firstly, the ASP is *not* marked as requiring a transaction (there is no @TRANSACTION directive). Second, we're using a third party object called BegASP.Sleeper, which allows us to artificially slow down the page generation. We are doing this so that we can load two separate instances of the page in two different processes. This in turn enables us to simulate more than one user accessing the data at the same time as the first page is executing, enabling us to demonstrate issues with locking the data.

> *BegASP.Sleeper was written in C++ and we have provided the compiled DLL with the source code for the book. Remember you will have to register it on your machine before you can use it. We have also supplied the source code if you are familiar with C++ for you to see how this simple component works.*

We slow down the page generation by employing the following line between each row that is written from the database to the list page (we'll see *why* we need this in a moment):

```
oWait.WaitMS Request.QueryString("Wait")
```

The call to the WaitMS function pauses the list creation for a specified number of milliseconds. This is how we delay the page loading, so that we can load another instance of the same page in another browser window—simulating two simultaneous users. List_Authors.asp is written so that we can specify the parameter of the WaitMS function as a query string, within the URL. Using this, we'll create one page that takes a long time to load, like this:

```
http://127.0.0.1/chapter6/asp/list_authors.asp?wait=1000
```

And while that's loading, we'll create another page in another user session, which loads rather more quickly like this:

```
http://127.0.0.1/chapter6/asp/list_authors.asp?wait=0
```

The Sleeper object itself is created within the ASP page as follows:

```
set oWait = CreateObject("BegASP.Sleeper")
```

You'll find the source code and hosting DLL for this component in the downlaod files with the rest of the cod e for this book at http//webdev.wrox.co.uk/books/2882/.

By slowing down the creation of the page, we can exaggerate the load on the system, and indeed the duration of the lock that is applied. There should be around 20 records to write, giving us about 20 seconds after the first session request to start another browser and perform the second session request. On your marks...

Edit_Author.asp

The Edit buttons next to the authors in List_Authors.asp allow the user to edit the details for that author. By clicking the button, the user brings up the Edit_Author.asp page, shown in this screenshot:

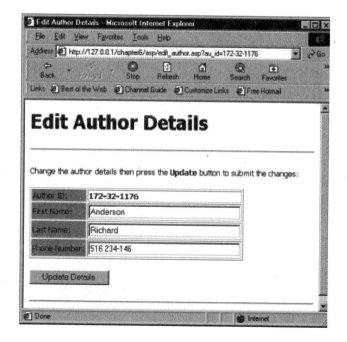

`Edit_Author.asp` is not transactional and the ASP is fairly elementary. We will look at the interesting parts after we have seen the code:

```
<%
sConn = "Data Source=YOUR_SERVER_NAME;" + _
        "Provider=SQLOLEDB;" + _
           "Initial Catalog=pubs;" + _
           "User ID=sa"

' Create a new connection
set oConn = CreateObject("ADODB.Connection")
oConn.Open sConn

' Create the recordset and open the cursor. This time we only select a single author
set oRS = CreateObject("ADODB.Recordset")
oRS.Open "select * from authors " & _
           "where au_id = '" & request.QueryString("au_id") & "'", oConn

%>

<HTML>
  <HEAD>
    <TITLE>Edit Author Details</TITLE>
      <STYLE TYPE="text/css">
             BODY {font-family:Veranda,Tahoma,Arial,sans-serif; font-size:10pt}
             TD {font-family:Veranda,Tahoma,Arial,sans-serif; font-size:10pt}
      </STYLE>
  </HEAD>
  <BODY BGCOLOR=WHITE>
      <H1>Edit Author Details</H1>
        <HR>

  <%
     if oRS.BOF = true then
  %>

  <P>The customer ID <STRONG> <%=Request.QueryString("ID")%> </STRONG>
             does not appear to be valid.</P>
  <P><A HREF="list_customers.asp">Back to customers list</A></P>

  <%
     else
     sAction = "update_author.asp?au_id="
     sAction = sAction + Request.QueryString("au_id")
  %>

  <P>Change the author details then press the <strong>Update</strong> button to
     submit the changes:</P>

<FORM NAME="CUSTINFO" ACTION="<%=sAction%>" METHOD="POST" BORDER="1">

  <TABLE border=1>
      <TR>
          <TD bgcolor="#3AC2EF">Author ID:</TD>
          <TD><strong><%=oRS("au_id")%></strong></TD>
      </TR>
      <TR>
          <TD bgcolor="#3AC2EF">First Name:</TD>
          <TD><INPUT TYPE="TEXT" NAME="new_au_fname" SIZE="35" VALUE="
                  <%=oRS("au_lname")%>" /> </TD>
      </TR>
      <TR>
```

```
                <TD bgcolor="#3AC2EF">Last Name:</TD>
                <TD><INPUT TYPE="TEXT" NAME="new_au_lname" SIZE="35"
                    VALUE="<%=oRS("au_fname")%>" /> </TD>
        </TR>
        <TR>
                <TD bgcolor="#3AC2EF">Phone Number:</TD>
                <TD><INPUT TYPE="TEXT" NAME="new_phone" SIZE="35"
                    VALUE="<%=oRS("phone")%>" /> </TD>
        </TR>
    </TABLE>

    <p />
        <INPUT TYPE="SUBMIT" VALUE="Update Details" />
    <%
        end if
    %>
        <P />
        <HR />
    </FORM>
    </BODY>
    </HTML>
```

In this page, we retrieve the details for a specific author that is identified via the `au_id` query string:

```
oRS.Open "select * from authors " & _
        "where au_id = '" & request.QueryString("au_id") & "'", oConn
```

Then we generate a form to allow the user to change the details. Submitting the form loads the `Update_Author.asp` page, a transactional ASP for updating the details:

```
sAction = "update_author.asp?au_id="
    sAction = sAction + Request.QueryString("au_id")
```

Update_Author.asp

`Update_Author.asp` is a transactional ASP page that displays the SQL query used to update the author information. It also displays the start time and end time for the transaction. In this following screenshot we can see that this transaction took less than one second:

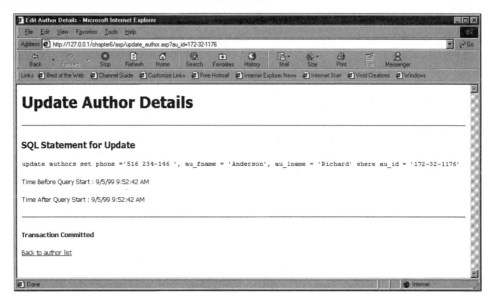

Here is the code for the `Update_Authors.asp` page:

```
<%@TRANSACTION=REQUIRED%>
<HTML>
    <HEAD>
        <TITLE>Edit Author Details</TITLE>
        <STYLE TYPE="text/css">
            BODY {font-family:Veranda,Tahoma,Arial,sans-serif; font-size:10pt}
            TD {font-family:Veranda,Tahoma,Arial,sans-serif; font-size:10pt}
        </STYLE>

    <BODY BGCOLOR=WHITE>
        <H1>Update Author Details</H1>
            <HR>

<%
' Setup the connection string
sConn = "Data Source=YOUR_SERVER_NAME;" + _
    "Provider=SQLOLEDB;" + _
        "Initial Catalog=pubs;" + _
        "User ID=sa"
    sConn = "Data Source=YOUR_SERVER_NAME; Provider=SQLOLEDB; Initial _
            Catalog=pubs; User ID=sa"

' Create a new connection
set oConn = CreateObject("ADODB.Connection")
oConn.Open sConn
' Create the recordset and open the cursor
set oRS = CreateObject("ADODB.Recordset")

sQuery = "update authors set phone ='"
sQuery = sQuery + Request.Form("new_phone")
sQuery = sQuery + "'"
sQuery = sQuery + ", au_fname = '"
sQuery = sQuery + Request.Form("new_au_fname")
sQuery = sQuery + "'"

sQuery = sQuery + ", au_lname = '"
sQuery = sQuery + Request.Form("new_au_lname")
sQuery = sQuery + "'"

sQuery = sQuery + " where au_id = '"
sQuery = sQuery + Request.QueryString("au_id")
sQuery = sQuery + "'"
%>

<h3>SQL Statement for Update</h3>
    <pre><p><%=sQuery%></p></pre>

<P>Time Before Query Start : <%=now%></P>
    <%oRS.Open sQuery, oConn%>
<P>Time After Query Start : <%=now%></P>

    </FORM>
    </BODY>
</HTML>

<%
    ' Called if the transaction succeeds
    Sub OnTransactionCommit()
        Response.Write "<hr />"
        Response.Write "<p><strong>Transaction Committed</strong></p>"
        Response.Write "<p><a href='list_authors.asp'>Back to author list</a></p>"
    End Sub
```

```
' Called if the transaction fails
   Sub OnTransactionAbort()
       Response.Write "<hr />"
       Response.Write "<p><strong>Transaction Aborted</strong></p>"
       Response.Write "<p><a href='list_authors.asp'>Back to author list</a></p>"
   End Sub
%>
```

In this page, we build the SQL query that will be used to update the database, based upon the parameters passed in from the Edit form:

```
sQuery = "update authors set phone ='"
sQuery = sQuery + Request.Form("new_phone")
sQuery = sQuery + "'"
sQuery = sQuery + ", au_fname = '"
sQuery = sQuery + Request.Form("new_au_fname")
sQuery = sQuery + "'"

sQuery = sQuery + ", au_lname = '"
sQuery = sQuery + Request.Form("new_au_lname")
sQuery = sQuery + "'"

sQuery = sQuery + " where au_id = '"
sQuery = sQuery + Request.QueryString("au_id")
sQuery = sQuery + "'"
```

Then we write the time to the client, and execute the query using the oRS.Open method, and write the time again once it has executed:

```
<P>Time Before Query Start : <%=now%></P>
<%oRS.Open sQuery, oConn%>
<P>Time After Query Start : <%=now%></P>
```

Testing the System

The only transactional page is Update_Author.asp, so we are not using any read locks in the other ASP pages. The database's resource manager will actually be implementing the write locks for us, on behalf of MTS. We only need to specify the @TRANSACTION directive in the Update_Author.asp page, so MTS will ensure that the database update succeeds making changes to the author details.

Let's prove this. Start two copies of Internet Explorer. In the first instance, enter the URL of the list authors ASP, specifying a delay of 1000 milliseconds:

http://127.0.0.1/chapter6/asp/list_authors.asp?wait=1000

The Wait command will pause 1 second (1000 ms) between each author detail line it writes back to the browser. Therefore the page should take about 21 seconds to generate a list of 21 authors. While the page is being rendered, bring the second copy of Internet Explorer to the front and enter the following URL there:

http://127.0.0.1/chapter6/asp/list_authors.asp?wait=0

This page specifies no delay between each author detail line, so this page should be generated well before the generation of the page within the first browser instance is complete.

Select any author entry from the second browser instance and edit it by clicking the Edit button. When the edit screen appears, change some details and then press Update. After a very short delay you should get a message saying that the transaction has completed.

What does this show? Mainly, that the first browser instance isn't applying any read locks to the author data that it's reading. Our first user can happily view the author details while the second user is busy updating them. This indicates we've got good concurrency in our system.

Changing the Locking

What would have happened if we *had* applied read locks to List_Authors.asp and/or Edit_Author.asp? We could find out by adding @TRANSACTION=REQUIRED directive at the top of the List_Authors.asp page:

```
<%@TRANSACTION=REQUIRED %>
<%
' Create an object that lets us pause for x MS

set oWait = CreateObject("BegASP.Sleeper")
...
```

Try it out by adding this line and repeating the experiment.

> *You can run both ASP sessions from the same physical client machine, but you must create a completely new process for the second Internet Explorer instance—so that two distinct ASP user sessions are created. To do this, either use the Start|Programs|Internet Explorer option or a shortcut if you have on set up. If you just use File | New | Window to create the second browser instance from the first (in the same process), only a single ASP session is created and the example will fail.*

In the event, you should see a long delay in the update process. That's because the Update_Authors.asp page has to wait for a very long time (up to 20 seconds) before being able to obtain a write lock—because it can't obtain the write lock until all the read locks have been released. The first user's read lock (implemented by our slowed-down List_Authors.asp) isn't released until the page is completely rendered—so the second user's update page is delayed for as long as it takes for the first user's page to be rendered. That's not good for concurrency.

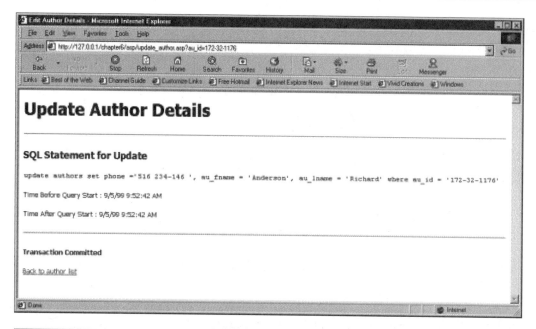

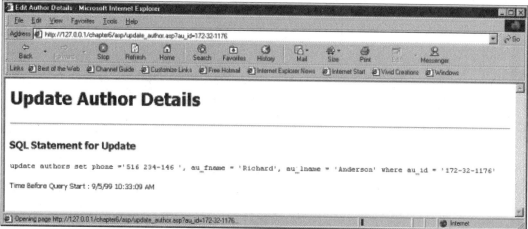

The result of this test shows us what happens if we are not very careful when placing read locks on data that we are not going to update: we lose concurrency, which affects the scalability of the application. We must remember, when an ASP page or component is within an MTS transaction, a read lock is created for any data it reads, and a write lock is obtained for any data it updates. Therefore we should be very careful about the scope of any transaction and be aware of the effect it can have upon concurrency, and therefore scalability.

Component Based Author System

Now let's turn to have a look at creating a component based version of the application we have just seen. We'll be creating two components for this example. The first will read the list of authors from the database, while the second will allow us to update the authors' details.

Create the new ActiveX DLL Project

To start off, create a new Visual Basic ActiveX DLL project. Rename the default created class from **Class1** to **AuthorList** and change the **MTSTranactionMode**, listed in the **Properties** window, to `NoTransactions`. We will discuss the various options for MTSTranactionMode after we have built and tested our components, you might recognize that they are similar settings to the ASP pages in the first example. This AuthorList component will retrieve the authors' details from the database.

Then add another class module, and change its name to **UpdateAuthor**. This time set its MTSTransactionMode property to `Requires Transaction`. We'll come back to discuss the MTSTransactionMode options after we have built and tested our components. This component will be used to update the details in the database.

You will also need to add a reference to the Microsoft ActiveX Data Objects 2.0 Library using the **Project | References** dialog, which will be used to connect to the database.

Compile the project, then bring up the project properties and set the version compatibility to **Binary**. This setting instructs Visual Basic to ensure that the unique identifiers it assigns to components (the CLSID) within the DLL are the same as in previous versions. It does this by reading the values from an existing DLL. So, the DLL has to exist before we change the setting. It is important we do this because MTS remembers these identifiers. It they change, we have to delete and re-add our components to the package. We don't want to do that every single time we compile, so this option should always be used.

Author List Component

The author list component will be used by `list_authors.asp` and `edit_author.asp`. It has five different methods:

Methods	Description
OpenList()	Initializes the list with all the authors in the authors table
OpenListFilter()	Initializes the list with all a single authors' details given an au_id— author ID
CloseList()	Closes the ADODB connection
IsEOF()	Determines if there are any authors left to be returned
NextAuthor()	Returns the next author. Should only be called if IsEOF returns false

Here is how they are implemented in the component. Remember, you will need to update the connection string to point to your database.

OpenList() Function

The `OpenList()` function is not only used when the list first needs creating, but will also allow us to see the updated list of authors when we have edited them.

```
Dim oConnection As ADODB.Connection
Dim oRS As ADODB.Recordset

' Open the connection and the recordset

Sub OpenList()

Set oConnection = New ADODB.Connection
Set oRS = New ADODB.Recordset

oConnection.Open "Data Source=YOUR_SERVER_NAME;" + _
        "Provider=SQLOLEDB;" + _
        "Initial Catalog=pubs;" + _
        "User ID=sa"

oRS.Open "select * from authors", oConnection

End Sub
```

OpenListFilter() Function

`OpenListFilter()` selects an authors details using a SQL select statement. We will be using this function to generate the details of the author once the user has clicked on the button next to the authors name in the ASP page.

```
Sub OpenListFilter(id As String)

Set oConnection = New ADODB.Connection
Set oRS = New ADODB.Recordset

oConnection.Open "Data Source=YOUR_SERVER_NAME;" + _
        "Provider=SQLOLEDB;" + _
        "Initial Catalog=pubs;" + _
        "User ID=sa"

oRS.Open "select * from authors where au_id = '" & id & "'", oConnection

End Sub
```

IsEOF() Function

`IsEOF()` simply checks that we have reached the end of the list of authors in the database.

```
Function IsEOF() As Boolean

IsEOF = oRS.EOF

End Function
```

NextAuthor() Function

The special point to note here is that ByRef parameters, which in COM speak are [in,out] parameters which have to be of type Variant. We have to define out parameters that way because the VBScript engine deals only deals with this type internally. It is used to fetch the next author in the list.

```
Sub NextAuthor(id As Variant, _
               fname As Variant, _
               lname As Variant, _
               phone As Variant)


id = oRS.Fields("au_id")
fname = oRS.Fields("au_fname")
lname = oRS.Fields("au_lname")
phone = oRS.Fields("phone")

oRS.MoveNext

End Sub
```

CloseList() Function

CloseList() simply closes the record set containing the list and closes the connection to the database.

```
' Close the list

Sub CloseList()

' Close the record set

If Not (oRS Is Nothing) Then
    If oRS.State = adOpen Then
        oRS.Close

End If
    Set oRS = Nothing
End If

' Close the connection

If Not (oConnection Is Nothing) Then
    oConnection.Close
    Set oConnection = Nothing
End If

End Sub
```

So, this first component provides us with the ability to read author information from the database. It is designed for use in non-transactional pages, so that the list of authors can be read without implementing locks that would have a negative impact on the concurrency of the system.

Update Author Component

Now let's take a look at the other component which is created in the AuthorUpdate class module. This only has two methods:

Method	Description
UpdateAuthor()	Allows us to update the details of the author in the database
ObjectControl_Activate()	Used to implement the ObjectControl interface

Let's see the code for each of these.

UpdateAuthor() Function

For updating an author we add the following function to the UpdateAuthor class module:

```
Function UpdateAuthor(id As Variant, _
                fname As Variant, _
                lname As Variant, _
                phone As Variant) As Boolean


Dim oConnection As ADODB.Connection
Dim oRS As ADODB.Recordset
Dim sQuery As String

On Error GoTo Abort

' Build the query string

sQuery = "update authors set phone ='"
sQuery = sQuery + phone
sQuery = sQuery + "'"
sQuery = sQuery + ", au_fname = '"
sQuery = sQuery + fname
sQuery = sQuery + "'"

sQuery = sQuery + ", au_lname = '"
sQuery = sQuery + lname
sQuery = sQuery + "'"
sQuery = sQuery + " where au_id = '"
sQuery = sQuery + id
sQuery = sQuery + "'"

Set oConnection = New ADODB.Connection
Set oRS = New ADODB.Recordset

oConnection.Open "Data Source=YOUR_SERVER_NAME;" + _
        "Provider=SQLOLEDB;" + _
        "Initial Catalog=pubs;" + _
        "User ID=sa"

' Execute the update

oRS.Open sQuery, oConnection

UpdateAuthor = True

oObjectContext.SetComplete

Exit Function

Abort:

oObjectContext.SetAbort

Err.Raise Err.Number, Err.Source, Err.Description, Err.HelpFile, Err.HelpContext

End Function
```

ObjectControl_Activate()

Of course, to be a good MTS object we implement the `ObjectControl` interface. In this implementation we grab the object context in the active event and place it in the global variable `oObjectContext`:

```
Implements ObjectControl

Dim sObjectContext As ObjectContext
```

at the top of the page, then we release it in the deactivate event. This is a pretty standard implementation of the technique which we discussed in the last chapter:

```
Private Sub ObjectControl_Activate()

Set oObjectContext = GetObjectContext

End Sub

Private Function ObjectControl_CanBePooled() As Boolean

CanBePooled = False

End Function

Private Sub ObjectControl_Deactivate()

Set sObjectContext = Nothing

End Sub
```

And that is all there is to our `Update Author` component. You can save and compile the project, so that we can use the components in our ASP pages.

Using the List Authors Component

In order to see how we use the components we have just created, we need to modify the original ASP pages to use the component. The changes are fairly minor, so rather than going through each page in detail I'll just highlight the differences:

List_authors.asp

`List_authors.asp` is the page that lists the authors and allows us to select the one we want to edit. Therefore it will make use of our `AuthorList` component.

```
<%
    set oWait = CreateObject("BegASP.Sleeper")

    ' Create a author list object
    set oAuthorList= Server.CreateObject("BegASP.AuthorList")
%>
```

```html
<HTML>
<HEAD>
<TITLE>Author List</TITLE>
<STYLE TYPE="text/css">
  BODY {font-family:Veranda,Tahoma,Arial,sans-serif; font-size:10pt}
  TD {font-family:Veranda,Tahoma,Arial,sans-serif; font-size:10pt}
</STYLE>
</HEAD>
<BODY BGCOLOR=WHITE>
<H1>Author List</H1>
<HR>
<P>The following authors are currently defined in the pubs database:

<TABLE cellspacing="2" cellpadding="0">
<TR>
   <TD bgcolor="#3AC2EF"><STRONG>ID</STRONG></TD>
   <TD bgcolor="#3AC2EF"><STRONG>Last Name</STRONG></TD>
   <TD bgcolor="#3AC2EF"><STRONG>First Name</STRONG></TD>
   <TD bgcolor="#3AC2EF"><STRONG>Contact No.</STRONG></TD>
</TR>
<TR>
</TR>

<%
   Dim sID
   Dim sFirstname
   Dim sLastname
   Dim sPhone

   ' Initialize the list
   oAuthorList.OpenList

   ' Process each author
   while oAuthorList.IsEOF = false
      oAuthorList.NextAuthor sID, sFirstname, sLastname, sPhone
%>

<TR>
   <TD bgcolor="#FFFF6C"><%=sID%></TD>
   <TD bgcolor="#FFFF6C"><%=sFirstname%></TD>
   <TD bgcolor="#FFFF6C"><%=sLastname%></TD>
   <TD bgcolor="#FFFF6C"><%=sPhone%></TD>
   <TD bgcolor="#3AC2EF">
      <FORM NAME="A" METHOD="POST" ACTION="edit_author.asp?au_id=<%=sID%>">
         <input type="SUBMIT" value="Edit" name="B1" />
      </FORM>

   </TD>
</TR>

<%
   oWait.WaitMS Request.QueryString("Wait")
   wend
%>

</TABLE>
</BODY>
</HTML>
```

Edit_author.asp

`Edit_author.asp` is the page that we use to provide a form in which the user can edit the details of an author. So, again it will use the AuthorList component, this time using it to collect the details of the selected author.

```
<%

set oAuthorList = Server.CreateObject("BegASP.AuthorList")
oAuthorList.OpenListFilter request.QueryString("au_id")

%>

<HTML>
<HEAD>
<TITLE>Edit Author Details</TITLE>
<STYLE TYPE="text/css">
   BODY {font-family:Veranda,Tahoma,Arial,sans-serif; font-size:10pt}
   TD {font-family:Veranda,Tahoma,Arial,sans-serif; font-size:10pt}
</STYLE>
</HEAD>
<BODY BGCOLOR=WHITE>
<H1>Edit Author Details</H1>
<HR>

<%
   if oAuthorList.IsEOF = true then
%>

<P>The customer ID <STRONG> <%=Request.QueryString("ID")%> </STRONG> does not appear
to be valid.</P>
<P><A HREF="list_customers.asp">Back to customers list</A></P>

<%
   else
%>

<%
   Dim sID
   Dim sFirstname
   Dim sLastname
   Dim sPhone

   oAuthorList.NextAuthor sID, sFirstname, _
                     sLastname, sPhone

   sAction = "update_author.asp?au_id="
   sAction = sAction + Request.QueryString("au_id")
%>

<P>Change the author details then press the <strong>Update</strong> button to submit
the changes:</P>
<FORM NAME="CUSTINFO" ACTION="<%=sAction%>" METHOD="POST" BORDER="1">
```

```
<TABLE border=1>
<TR><TD bgcolor="#3AC2EF">Author ID:</TD><TD><strong><%=sID%></strong></TD> </TR>
<TR><TD bgcolor="#3AC2EF">First Name:</TD><TD><INPUT TYPE="TEXT" NAME="new_au_fname"
SIZE="35" VALUE="<%=sFirstname%>" /> </TD> </TR>
<TR><TD bgcolor="#3AC2EF">Last Name:</TD><TD><INPUT TYPE="TEXT" NAME="new_au_lname"
SIZE="35" VALUE="<%=sLastname%>" /> </TD> </TR>
<TR><TD bgcolor="#3AC2EF">Phone Number:</TD><TD><INPUT TYPE="TEXT" NAME="new_phone"
SIZE="35" VALUE="<%=sPhone%>" /> </TD> </TR>
</TABLE>
<p />
<INPUT TYPE="SUBMIT" VALUE="Update Details" />


<%
   end if
%>

<P />
<HR />
</FORM>
</BODY>
</HTML>
```

Update_author.asp

Update_author.asp is the page that introduces the transaction, here we need to actually write to the database, and update the authors' details, so we will use the UpdateAuthor component. As we did in the first ASP example, we only want to make this one component transactional. This means that we do not affect the concurrency of the application in the way that we would if we were to make all pages transactional, however we ensure the consistency of the data by making this operation of updating author details isolated.

```
<%@TRANSACTION=REQUIRED%>

<HTML>
<HEAD>
<TITLE>Edit Author Details</TITLE>
<STYLE TYPE="text/css">
  BODY {font-family:Veranda,Tahoma,Arial,sans-serif; font-size:10pt}
  TD {font-family:Veranda,Tahoma,Arial,sans-serif; font-size:10pt}
</STYLE>
<BODY BGCOLOR=WHITE>

<H1>Update Author Details</H1>
<HR>

<P>Time Before Query Start : <%=now%></P>
<%
set UpdateAuthor = Server.CreateObject("BegASP.UpdateAuthor")
UpdateAuthor.UpdateAuthor Request.QueryString("au_id"), Request.Form("new_au_fname"),
Request.Form("new_au_lname") , Request.Form("new_phone")
%>
<P>Time After Query Start : <%=now%></P>

</FORM>
</BODY>
</HTML>

<%

' Called if the transaction succeeds
```

```
Sub OnTransactionCommit()
  Response.Write "<hr />"
  Response.Write "<p><strong>Transaction Committed</strong></p>"
  Response.Write "<p><a href='list_authors.asp'>Back to author list</a></p>"
End Sub
' Called if the transaction fails

Sub OnTransactionAbort()
  Response.Write "<hr />"
  Response.Write "<p><strong>Transaction Aborted</strong></p>"
  Response.Write "<p><a href='list_authors.asp'>Back to author list</a></p>"
End Sub

%>
```

Install the Component Inside MTS

The final step is to install the components into MTS. Open the MTS Explore, and navigate down to the Packages Installed folder. To create the new package choose Action | New | Package from the toolbar. Name the new package Authors and drag the .dll into the package from Windows Explorer. Remember, if you make any changes to the components you have to refresh the component information MTS, by using the Refresh all components option located on the My Computer tab.

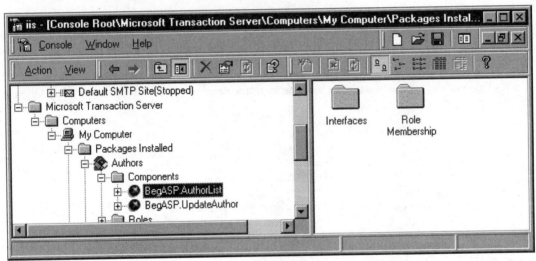

Once you have done this you need to modify the properties for each component. You get to the Properties window by right clicking on the component, a pop-up menu gives this option. For the AuthorList component, select the Transaction tab and make sure that Does not support transactions is selected. This should already be done for you as we specified it in Visual Basic using the MTSTransactionMode option.

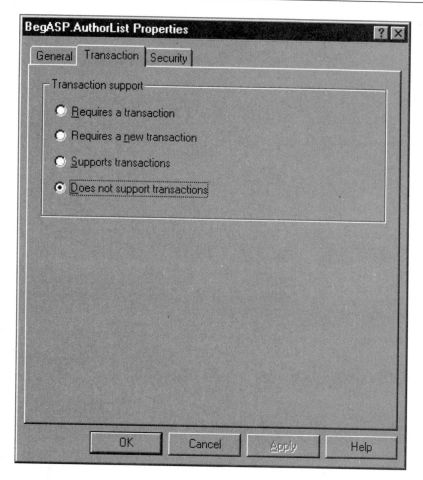

Then, for UpdateAuthor, make sure that Requires a transaction is selected. Again, this should have been done for you by Visual Basic when you changed the MTSTransactionMode property.

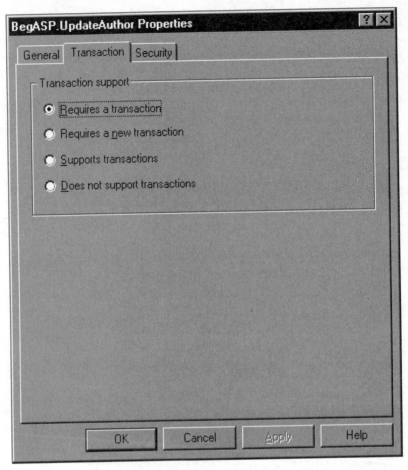

Now, if you retry the test we did earlier, you should see the system working in an identical fashion, except this time it's component based.

Making Objects Support Transactions

MTS can host any COM component contained in an ActiveX DLL. However, if you simply install a couple of components into MTS and hope for the best, then you might be disappointed.

Visual Basic 6 makes it very easy for us to specify whether our objects are to be used in MTS or not. Each public class now has an **MTSTransactionMode** property, which we used earlier, which is used by MTS to determine how the object wants to handles transactions:

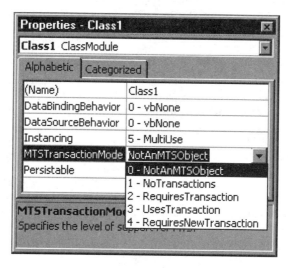

These settings are associated with the component in the type library. When you add your component to an MTS package, MTS will see these attributes and import them, so when you use the MTS Explorer, the setting will initially reflect the setting selected by the programmer. You can alter these settings in the **Properties** dialog for the component in MTS Explorer (right-click on the component and select **Properties** from the pop-up menu).

- ❑ **NotAnMTSObject** specifies that the object will not be involved with MTS. This is the default option.

- ❑ **NoTransactions** specifies that the component will not support transactions. An object context will still be created, but it will not participate in any transactions. This value is useful for when you are just using MTS as a central repository for a component class. With this value, there will not be a transaction as part of the class.

- ❑ **RequiresTransactions** mandates that the object must run within a transaction. When a new instance of the object is created, if the client has a transaction already running then the object context will inherit the existing transaction—the transaction scope will encompass the newly created object and any others that previously existed within the same scope. If that client does not have a transaction associated with it, MTS will automatically create a new transaction for the object.

❑   UsesTransactions indicates that should a transaction be available when the object is created, then it will use the existing transaction. If no transaction exists then it will also run but without any transactional support.

❑   RequiresNewTransaction indicates that the object will execute within its own transaction. When a new object is created with this setting, a new transaction is created regardless of whether the client already has a transaction.

When you change the transactional attributes (or any configuration of a package generally) of a component you have to stop and restart the package if it is already running.

Process Oriented Objects

The net result of using MTS to contain objects is that we have to effectively change the way we program. We can't depend on an object holding onto state beyond the lifetime of a transaction, so we have to always re-read state from a data source each time a method is invoked, or pass the required state into the method by parameters.

Modeling components around the processing of data is referred to as **process oriented**, therefore, components that exhibit this behavior are called **process oriented components**. This is the model that has to be followed to create truly scalable applications in MTS. Rather than designing objects to fit in with the real world that contain state for a prolonged period of time, we are writing objects that fit in with our requirements for processing data. In the example we have been looking at, we don't want read locks to be applied when reading author details so we have to create a non-transactional component. We do want locks to be applied when updating data so we create another component that is transactional. What this boils down to is yet more granularity in our objects. We have created one for the reading of author details and one for updating them, rather than creating one single author list object to model the list as a whole.

Long Lasting Locks

Although our ASP application is now scalable because we didn't fall into the trap of making list_authors.asp transactional, we've still got a problem. (One that we cannot go into detail about here as it is beyond the scope of this book, but we'll look at it briefly.)

When edit_author.asp is viewed no locks are applied. Even if write locks were applied, after the page is rendered the locks would be destroyed anyway as the connection object or component would go out of scope, so locks would serve no real purpose. This means it is possible for two people to view and edit the details at the same time, as shown in the following screenshot. The only solution to this problem that still permits scalability is to perform a check that the data hasn't been changed before you perform an update. If the data has changed you fail the request. This technique and many others are discussed in great depth in *Enterprise Application Architecture* by Joseph Monitz (ISBN 1-861002-58-0) published by Wrox Press.

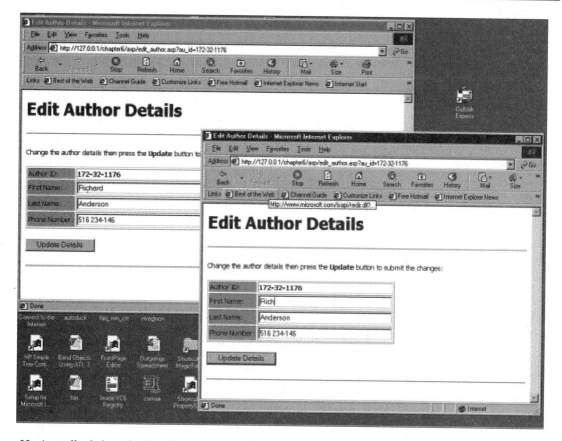

Having talked about locking in transactions, let's look at locking in database resource managers because, as we have seen, databases are a vital part of transactions.

Lock Granularity

There are different types of locks that a resource manager will apply during transactions depending upon different optimizations. For example, SQL Server 7 has three main lock types: **table**, **page**, and **row**. A table is comprised of a number of pages, and a number of rows live within a page. Pages are 2k in SQL Server 6.5 and 4k in SQL Server 7.0. Depending upon the size of each row you can roughly calculate the number of rows per page. Let's look at each of these in terms of lock granularity.

Table Level Locks

If a query spans every row in a table SQL server can optimize the locking by just creating a single page level lock. This lock type uses fewer resources than locking each row individually would, and is therefore quicker to acquire and check for. However, it is obvious that locking a table will have serious effects on concurrency. Depending upon the lock type, it might be that nobody else will be able to read or update the table!

A table lock will be applied when a transaction performs an operation like "select * from authors" or "select count(*) from authors".

Page Level Locks

Page level locks are better, because they take up less of the database, but still, a page lock could result in a number of unnecessary rows being locks, or if there are a large number of individual pages that need to be locked, then it makes more sense to lock the table to save on resources.

Row Level Locks

Row level locks can be applied when a single row is manipulated by a transaction. This has the highest overhead, because there could potentially be millions of rows in a table. Maintaining millions of locks for each row is very expensive, so generally speaking page level locks are applied. While this is generally better overall, it does mean that a number of rows are locked needlessly.

As a rule general rule, the resource manager will always lock as little data as is possible to ensure consistency. Conversely, it will use the next level lock up, if it would otherwise have to lock each of the lower level locks.

> For full coverage of lock management and other internal functions of SQL Server take a look at *Inside SQL Server 6.5 ISBN 1-572313-31-5 (or Inside SQL Server 7.0 0-735605-17-3) published by Microsoft Press.*

The following screenshot shows you how you can view locks in SQL Server by using the sp_lock stored procedure.

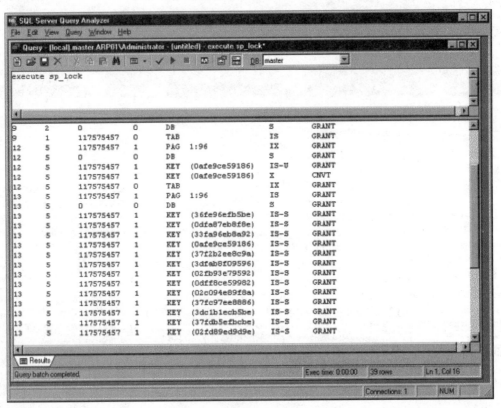

Microsoft Distributed Transaction Coordinator

Up until now we've discussed the duration and scope of transactions along with lock management. However, we've not really discussed how transactions are created, how their lifetime is coordinated, and how we can ensure that transactions over a number of diverse resource managers (such as databases or message queues) responsible for the holding of consistent durable data are committed or rolled back correctly—even when they are potentially located on different machines.

> *Remember, a resource manager is something that manages the data held within a data source. There are no restrictions on what or where that datasource can be.*

The creation and management of a transaction is the job of a **transaction monitor** (**TM**). MTS's transaction monitor is the **Microsoft Distributed Transaction Coordinator** (**MS DTC**). MS DTC has the following responsibilities:

❑ It enables applications to perform distributed transactions across one or many heterogeneous data sources, that can be located on one more or machines across a network

❑ It uses transaction protocols to co-ordinate and monitor the work performed by each resources manager under the influence of the MS DTC transaction

❑ It provides the infrastructure that enables each resource to manager to vote and determine the outcome of the distributed transaction, and the co-ordinates the commit or abort process that is local to each resource manager

It is the responsibility of each individual resource manager to ensure that its work is executed correctly within a **localized transaction**, and that the results are recorded accurately and effectively enforcing the principles of ACID. The MS DTC orechestrates the all encompassing **distributed transaction** and acts as the negotiator between resource managers to ensure that all of the work performed by each resource manager is committed or aborted as a whole.

So it is the MS DTC that creates the distributed transactions, and then it watches over them to ensure that they either succeed and complete, or abort and roll back. The transaction protocol used by the MS DTC essentially coordinates the work being done by different elements of a system across the network. This means that we don't need to put transaction management logic in the client code to achieve this impressive management feat, and that our transactions are all handled in a robust way via a central location—effectively under MTS. This saves us a lot of development time!

MS DTC is an NT Service that runs on each machine that has one or more resource managers that want to take part in distributed transactions. The service was originally created as part of SQL server to co-ordinate transaction across one or more *different* installation of SQL servers.

You should think of the term 'distributed transaction' as meaning a transaction that spans one or more resource managers. Each resource manager can be located in different processes on different machines anywhere across a network. A local or localized transaction is the transaction created by a resource manager to coordinate its work across its data. Because resource managers don't necessarily know the inner workings of other resource managers, they cannot coordinate individual localized transactions to give the facade of a single transaction. Somebody else has to do that, and that's the MS DTC.

> A distributed transaction effectively encompasses one or more localized transactions within resource managers. It hides those localized transactions, making it seem to all intents and purposes that there is only one transaction.

We won't cover transactions spanning multiple machines in much detail in this text, but the MS DTC is capable of coordinating them, and it is something you will have to do when building enterprise scalable systems where MTS and SQL Server (or other XA compliant databases) are running on different machines.

So, let's have a look at how we manage the lifetime of a distributed transaction, from its creation to the end result: success or failure—remembering that, whether it succeeds or fails, the system (therefore each resource manager) must maintain consistent reliable data. This involves the creation of a transaction object followed by a two-phase commit process. The two phases are required so that the data can be set, ready for commitment by each resource manager involved in a distributed transaction, then if the participating resources all agree, all of the work can be committed.

In the process we will see:

❑ How MS DTC starts a transaction by creating a transaction object

❑ How simple it is to create a distributed transaction using SQL Server

❑ How to MTS handles transaction objects

❑ Ensuring that multiple database updates commit or abort together

❑ How to share data between components in transactions

But let's start with how the transaction object is created by the transaction manager: MS DTC.

The Transaction Factory

So, you can think of MS DTC as the factory from which all distributed transactions originate, and the entity which ensures that they are correctly committed or aborted. But how is the transaction started in the first place? When an MTS object (or any other client) needs to start a new transaction it asks the MS DTC to create one, by invoking the `BeginTransaction()` method of the `ITransactionDispenser` interface that the MS DTC supports (although the process actually goes through a proxy) as shown in the following diagram:

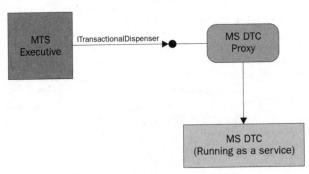

The MS DTC proxy shown is returned by a call to the function DTC function `DtcGetTransactionManager`.

In IIS, a distributed transaction is created when an ASP is requested, and it has been marked as transactional using the `@TRANSACTION` directive. IIS4 installs an MTS based web application manager (WAM) object for each web server or virtual directory you create. When this object is created to process an ASP request, IIS sets the transactional attributes of this object and then creates it. IIS5 does the same thing under Windows 2000, but IIS3 and before do not do this.

When MS DTC creates a transaction it returns to MTS (or any other client—same as a base-client inside of VB) a COM-*like* object with two interfaces: `ITransaction` and `IGetDispenser`, as shown in the following diagram.

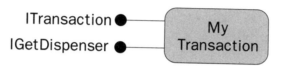

ITransaction

The `ITransaction` interface has three methods:

- ❏ `Commit()`—Commits the transaction
- ❏ `Abort()`—Aborts the transaction
- ❏ `GetTransactionInfo()`—Returns information about the transaction, such as the isolation level.

These methods are called on behalf of an MTS base client to control the outcome of a distributed transaction. How and when these methods are called is up to the discretion of the MTS executive. However, we directly affect that by the way we use `IObjectContext`, and the `SetComplete()` and `SetAbort()` methods.

Take a simple scenario outside of IIS:

- ❏ A base client creates an object hosted inside of MTS
- ❏ A method is invoked, that performs some work, and then calls `SetComplete()` using `IObjectContext`

The first step will involve the client getting a reference back to the context wrapper, although for all intense and purposes it thinks it is the real object. We know the real object doesn't actually exist yet, we saw this in the last chapter. Next, the base client calls a method, which as we know will actually go via the context wrapper. The context wrapper will create the real object, and if it is marked as requiring a transaction (configured from within the MTS explorer), it will create the real object, create a distributed transaction, make a note that a transaction is active in the object context, and finally invoke the real method implemented by the real object.

By the time a method is created the distributed transaction is always created. Now, the client uses ADO to create a database connection. As we've discussed, OLE DB services will determine if a distributed transaction is active, and, if it is supported by the OLE DB provider that created the connection, it will ask underlying the resource manager to enlist the newly created connection into that transaction.

The method will then use the connection and perform some database work. All of this work will be tracked by the resource manager, as the method uses the various ADO objects, all of which eventually map down into resource manager functions. (They actually do this through the resource manager which really only sits on top of a data source.)

When method is about to complete it should call either SetComplete() or SetAbort(). These functions actually have two real purposes:

❑   They tell the context wrapper it can destroyed the real object when the method ends and control is returned back to the base client

❑   It indicates if any transactional work should be completed or aborted

Depending upon what method you call, the context wrapper (part of the MTS executive) will make the call to either commit or abort the transaction.

So, that's how the magic of distributed transactions, MTS, ADO and OLE DB works. Simple, right ? Well no it isn't, but that's the whole point. As programmers we use it like it's a trivial little API, but should we have to implement in ourselves it *would* takes many years of development, and could only be done using C++. Just as well Microsoft have already done it for us, and that they give it away for free!

Transaction Types

As a small note MS-DTC supports two types of distributed transaction:

❑   OLE Transactions—COM based

❑   XA transactions—a more global industry standard

As an IIS/MTS developer XA transactions are only of interests when using non-Microsoft products. Support was added for them in MTS 2.0 to allow MTS to work with Oracle and other systems in larger enterprises. The real benefit of OLE Transactions (read OLE = COM) is that they are, for the most part, COM based (remember you don't actually have to initialize COM to use them), and they can support multi-threaded applications.

Is a Transaction Object really a COM object ?

The transaction object created by MS DTC to represent and manage a distributed transaction is a COM object, but it doesn't require the COM runtime to be initialized before it can be used, or any of the other MS DTC COM objects and interfaces. This might sound a little strange, but it works this way for a number of reasons:

❑   Not all resources manager are COM enabled. Resource managers like ODBC do not use COM internally and therefore do not initialize the COM runtime. To force them to use COM would prevent them from using MS DTC, as they would most likely have to be re-written.

❑ MS DTC doesn't actually need any of the services provided by the COM runtime. It manages the creation of all objects, it has no concurrency requirements, it provides the communications between machines and so on.

The fact the COM runtime doesn't actually have to be used is just an interesting thing to know, and doesn't really make that much difference. It is still COM, because the binary semantics of an object and interface are the same, but not all of the COM services (like marshalling and remoting) are used.

IGetDispenser

As a transaction object is passed around, various entities involved in a distributed transaction need to talk to the MS-DTC that created it. The `IGetDispenser` interface supported by the transaction object provides this facility.

Creating a Transaction

Before getting any more technical, let's see how we can create a transaction object without using MTS. This will demonstrate the fact that the MS DTC is actually an individual service that was originally shipped with SQL Server 6.5 to enable it to perform distributed transactions.

A resource manager like SQL Server can expose MS DTC functionality however it likes, and doesn't have to involve MTS, e.g.:

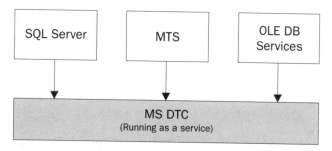

After all, creating a transaction only requires a couple of function calls:

❑ Get the COM object/interfaces that represents the MS-DTC using `DtcGetTransactionManager()`

❑ Create the transaction object by calling the `BeginTransactions()` method of `ITransactionDispenser`

SQL server exposes the MS DTC and its functionality via its Transact-SQL (or T-SQL, a dialect of SQL specific to SQL Server) commands that can be executed using ISQL (SQL Server 6.5) or the Query Analyzer (QA - SQL Server 7.0)—the tools are effectively the same, they just changed names. Both are installed as part of the client side installation of SQL Server. In order to take a look at how easy it is to create a transaction, we will create one using the SQL Server 7.0 query analyzer.

Before creating a transaction, you need to stop and start the MS DTC service to see the same screens that you'll see here. This can be done in the MTS Explorer. To stop the MS DTC service, right click on the My Computer icon (as shown in the following screen shot) and select the option Stop MS DTC. When it has been stopped, just right click again and start it using the Start MS DTC option.

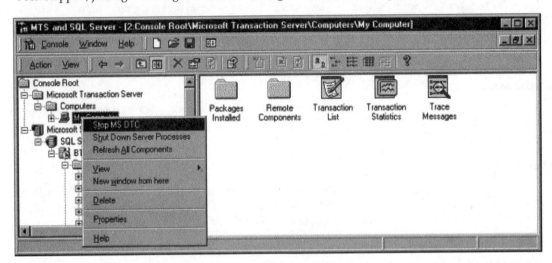

Run the query analyzer (Start | Programs | Microsoft SQL Server) so you can execute T-SQL commands. Connect to your local server, enter the following command and press F5 to run it:

```
Begin distributed transaction
```

If you get the error "MSDTC on server is unavailable" as shown in the following screenshot, double check that the MSDTC has really been started.

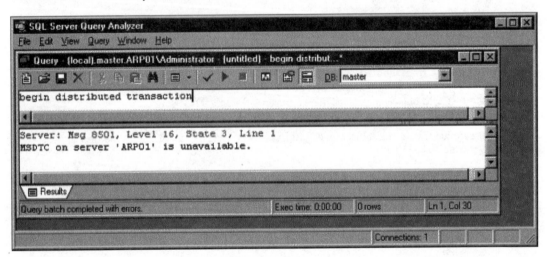

You can confirm that the MS DTC is running by looking at the Services on your machine via the Control Panel.

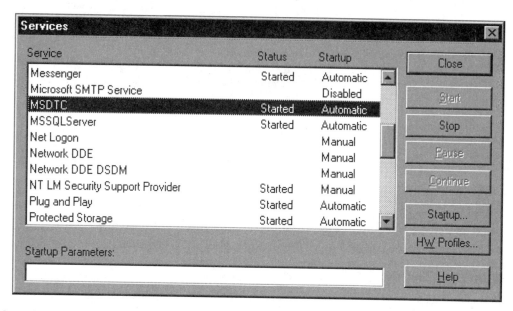

Once the `begin distributed transaction` command executes successfully, bring up the MTS Explorer and navigate down to the Transaction List item. If you wait about 10-15 seconds and you should see a new item in the list as shown in the next screenshot:

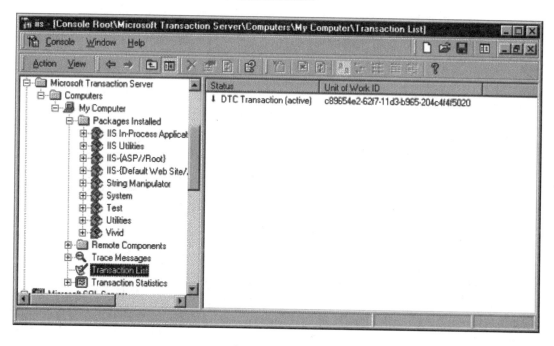

The list has two fields: Status, and Unit of Work ID. The first one, Status, is a composite that shows two items: the transactions' status in brackets, with some descriptive text as a comment assigned by the resource manager to the left of it. Using SQL Server 7.0 as I have for this example, you'll see DTC Transaction for the description. For MTS objects you'll see the ProgID being used as the descriptive text. The second field, Unit of Work ID, is the GUID that the MS DTC assigned when it created the transaction object. This is used to uniquely identify it across the network.

To create a transaction and then make it commit you can use the following Transact-SQL commands in ISQL/W or Query Analyzer—whichever you are using:

```
begin distributed transaction
commit transaction
```

To create a transaction and then make it abort you can use the following Transact-SQL commands:

```
begin distributed transaction
rollback transaction
```

And, that's all there is to creating a transaction. So, let's see how this process differs when we re-introduce MTS into the equation.

What Does MTS Do with Transaction Objects ?

OK, we've seen how MS DTC creates a transaction object for us in the first part of this section, so what does MTS do with them?

Once MTS has created a transaction object for a transactional component, or associated a component with a transaction that is already active, the MTS executive asks the resource dispenser manager to enlist any returned resource to the transaction. As we said earlier, in the case of a transactional ASP page creating an ADO connection, the transaction will encompass the newly created resource:

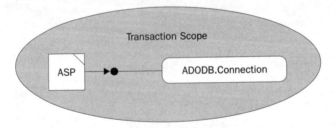

A resource, such as a database connection, is enlisted by the API or library used to return the object (e.g. ADO, OLE DB, MSMQ etc). There is no magic, so the ADO library will do the following:

- ❏ Create the ADODB.Connection Object
- ❏ When the open method is called determine if a transaction is active
- ❏ If a transaction is active, associate the connection object with the transaction

The code that performs this process is known as the resource manager proxy—it is effectively a friendly interface (such as ADO) to the underlying resource manager. When MTS asks the resource dispenser manager (DispMan) to enlist a resource, the DispMan asks the resource dispenser that created the resource to enlist it. The resource dispenser then either ignores the request if its resources are not transactional, or forwards the resource and the transaction into which the resource should be enlisted, to the underlying resource manager. The resource manager performs the association, and registers an *interest* in the transaction with the MS DTC by calling the `Enlist()` method exposed by `IResourceManager`.

MS DTC and Resource Manager Setup

The resource manager and the MS DTC communicate via a MS DTC RM Proxy Object. This object is created by MS DTC to represent the unique resource manager. When a resource manager such as SQL Server first starts it registers with the MS DTC, and this interface pointer is given back to it:

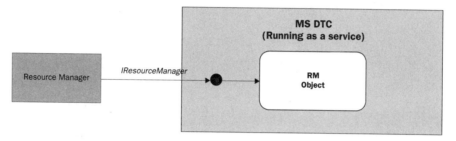

The returned object supports the `IResourceManager` interface, which has the following methods that the RM can use to communicate with MS DTC:

Methods	Descriptions
`Enlist()`	Enlists a resource manager in a specific transaction. The method accepts amongst other things a pointer to the `ITransaction` interface passed down by the resource dispenser.
`Reenlist()`	Re-enlists a resource manager in a transaction after a recovery was been performed.
`ReenlistmentComplete()`	Notifies MS DTC to forget about any obligations to *any* transactions.
`GetDistributedTransactionManager()`	Obtains an interface on the MS DTC proxy.

Now, the key point to remember is that it is the **resource manager** that finally gets associated with the MS DTC and the transaction, and not the resource dispenser. It's the resource manager which is involved in the 2 phase commit proceedings, which begin when somebody (e.g. MTS) calls the `Commit()` method of `ITransaction` as discussed earlier.

2 Phase Commit

The great thing about MS DTC transactions is that they can span multiple data sources. So, as discussed earlier we could have a transaction that flows across SQL Server and MSMQ:

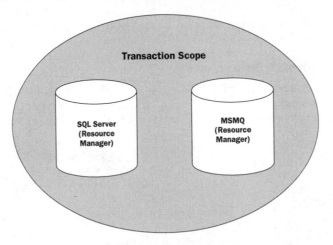

Now, from our definitions of a transaction in the last chapter we know that it either commits or aborts as an atomic unit of work (e.g. all or nothing!) and has ACID properties. From our discussion earlier we know each resource manager maintains a local transaction that abides by these rules, and that each of these local transactions is effectively controlled by the distributed transaction, so that every local transaction is committed or aborted as a whole. This is a very complex task to achieve especially when multiple processes and machines are involved. We are talking about a seriously clever infrastructure that we don't have to write.

Because resource managers can be implemented in different processes, and potentially on different machines, we need to ensure that one resource manager does not make any changes performed within a local transaction persistent if the other transaction within other resource manager could fail for some reason, maybe the process containing the RM crashes.

To achieve this MS DTC uses a two-phase commit:

❑   Each resource manager is asked to prepare to commit

❑   If successful, each resource manager is then asked to commit

Phase 1—Prepare

The prepare phase tells each resource manager that a distributed transaction is in its final stages. That is, the client who has requested all the work (changes in state) won't be doing anything else. The resource manager should get ready to commit the changes made during the transaction, but not actually make them. As part of this phase the resource manager must make a permanent record, if one doesn't already exist, of all the changes made under the transaction, and only indicate a successful prepare phase if it can absolutely guarantee the commit phase will work.

After the prepare phase (all locks are still held at this point), if all resource managers indicated success the commit phase commences. If any resource manager fails, each resource manager is told to abort and the transaction fails.

Phase 2—Commit

Once the prepare messages have successfully been sent to all resource managers the commit phase is almost a formality. Each resource manager has promised it can commit the work, so when it receives the final request to commit it, the changes it has recorded under the duration of the transaction are finalized, and any locks are released. Once all resource managers have done this, the transaction is committed.

MS DTCs Across the Network

When a transaction spans machine boundaries, each machine has its own local copy of MS DTC, and the MS DTC responsible for creating the transaction is called the global commit coordinator, because it is responsible for overseeing the 2 phase commits sequence.

As shown in the following diagram, each MS DTC that creates a transaction propagates that transaction across machines and resource managers. The MS DTC that creates the transaction is called the global commit coordinate and is responsible for talking to all subordinate MS DTCs involved in a transaction when a transaction is committed.

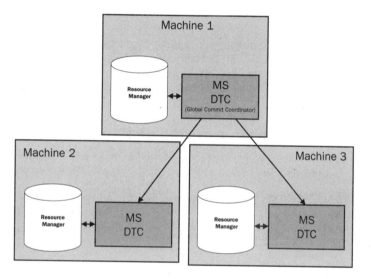

Sharing Data Between Components in MTS

When creating MTS-hosted components, you should make them stateless, because, as we just discussed, objects within transactions are deactivated and destroyed between each call to the root object by the base client. However, there will be cases when we need to maintain state in the ASP application across transaction components, so how do we achieve that?

Well, assuming we generally want to pass data around within a single web site or virtual directory, we've got a number of options, such as storing and sharing information in the application or session object, but for MTS components we are far better of using the Shared Property Manager (SPM). In the final section of the chapter, we shall see exactly how this is done with an example that uses a counter.

The SPM is designed for sharing state between components that reside within the same package (process). It groups shared state into *named* property groups as shown in the following diagram. Each group generally contains one or more named properties that a component can create, manipulate and share with other components.

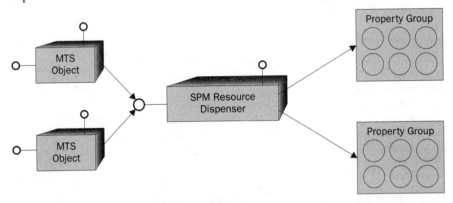

The MTS on-line help suggests that property groups can be used for things like web page counters. Whilst this is a reasonable suggestion, a non-transient counter would have to be read from a database or file when it is *initially* created so that value doesn't always start from zero, and we would have to persist its value on a regular basis so that if the web server crashed for any reasons we wouldn't lose too many counts.

Creating a Counter Component using the SPM

Using the SPM in a component is fairly easy. You just need to include the Shared Property Manager type library in the references to your Visual Basic component, as show in the next screenshot:

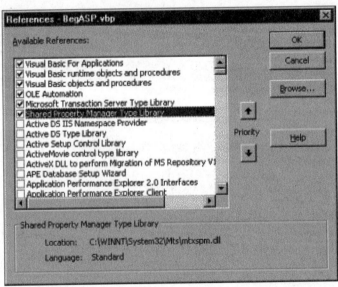

You can then make use of three components it implements:

- ❑ **Shared property group manager**—responsible for creating and opening groups
- ❑ **Shared property group**—represents one or more properties
- ❑ **Shared Property**—used to hold a value

To demonstrate the SPM we are going to create a counter component. It will enable us to create a named counter that increases each time we call the `GetNextCounter()` method specifying its name. We'll actually create more than one named counter to illustrate the point.

Creating the Component

Start off as usual by opening up Visual Basic and creating a new ActiveX DLL project. Rename the project `BegASP` and change the class name to `SimpleCounter`. Don't forget to add the **Shared Property Manager Type Library** reference.

Open the class module for `SimpleCounter` and add the following function:

```
Function GetNextCounter(name As String) As Long

    GetNextCounter = 1

    Dim bExists As Boolean
    Dim oSPM As SharedPropertyGroupManager
    Dim oGroup As SharedPropertyGroup
    Dim oProperty As SharedProperty

    Set oSPM = New SharedPropertyGroupManager

    If oSPM Is Nothing Then
        Err.Raise vbObject + 1, , "Failed to create SPAM"
    End If

    Dim IsolationLevel As Long
    Dim LifeTime As Long

    IsolationLevel = LockSetGet
    LifeTime = Process

    Set oGroup = oSPM.CreatePropertyGroup("MyCounters", _
                        IsolationLevel, LifeTime, bExists)
    If oGroup Is Nothing Then
        Err.Raise vbObject + 1, , "Failed to create Group"
    End If

    Set oProperty = oGroup.CreateProperty(name, bExists)
    If oProperty Is Nothing Then
        Err.Raise vbObject + 1, , "Failed to create Property"
    End If

    GetNextCounter = oProperty.Value

    oProperty.Value = oProperty.Value + 1
End Function
```

The component is very simple, so that's all the code we need to add. Now you can compile it.

Next, bring up the **Project | Properties** dialog, and from the **Component** tab change the compatibility option to **binary**. Remember, MTS uses the CLSID to track the component, and Visual Basic will generate a new one each time you recompile the component, breaking the link, unless you choose binary.

Once the component is compiled, create a new MTS package called **Counter** using the MTS explorer, and add your new component to the package. Then right click on the new package and select the properties. From the **Advanced** tab, change the **Server Process Shutdown** option to **Leave running when idle**. By selecting this option the package will never be unloaded unless stopped manually, so the shared property manager group will not be destroyed when nobody is using it. This could occur during idle periods and the counters would simply restart, you don't want this to happen because otherwise the memory count would get destroyed.

Finally, use `spm.asp` to test the component. Here is the code:

```
<%
' Create the object
Set oPageCount = Server.CreateObject("BegASP.SimpleCounter")
%>

<HTML>
<HEAD>
<TITLE>Page Counter</TITLE>
<BODY BGCOLOR=WHITE>

<H1>Current Count</H1>

<p>Counter 1 next value is <%=oPageCount.GetNextCounter("counter1")%></p>
<p>Counter 1 next value is <%=oPageCount.GetNextCounter("counter1")%></p>
<p>Counter 1 next value is <%=oPageCount.GetNextCounter("counter1")%></p>
<p>Counter 1 next value is <%=oPageCount.GetNextCounter("counter1")%></p>
<p>Counter 2 next value is <%=oPageCount.GetNextCounter("counter2")%></p>
<p>Counter 2 next value is <%=oPageCount.GetNextCounter("counter2")%></p>

</BODY>

</HTML>
```

When you view the page, you should see the object as shown in the following screenshot. If you refresh the page, and even view it from multiple instances of your browser you'll see the counter just keeps on increasing. The values of the counters are being held in the shared property manager, and being accessed and updated by the component.

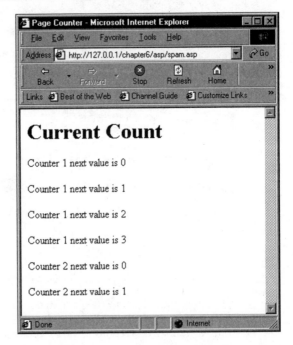

So, let's review the SPM code and take a closer look. The first few lines create an instance of the shared property group manager. If the creation fails we raise an error:

```
Set oSPM = New SharedPropertyGroupManager

    If oSPM Is Nothing Then
        Err.Raise vbObject + 1, , "Failed to create SPAM"
    End If
```

Next we create the shared property group. This is given the name `MyCounters`. We could have created a group for each counter, but, generally speaking, a group contains a number of related counters so we've just got the one that holds all of the counters:

```
    Dim IsolationLevel As Long
    Dim LifeTime As Long

    IsolationLevel = LockSetGet
    LifeTime = Process

    Set oGroup = oSPM.CreatePropertyGroup("MyCounters", _
                        IsolationLevel, LifeTime, bExists)
    If oGroup Is Nothing Then
        Err.Raise vbObject + 1, , "Failed to create Group"
    End If
```

The `LockSetGet` specified as the second parameter, `IsolationLevel`, specifies the isolation level for the group. The value used indicates that nobody else can access the shared properties we are using, much like a write lock. We could have used the parameter `LockMethod` to lock the entire group, but doing so would affect scalability. If you wrote a reset function to reset another value as an atomic action you could use this value.

The third parameter, `LifeTime`, indicates the lifetime of the shared property group. `Standard` means it is destroyed when nobody has a reference to it, much like a normal COM object. `Process` indicates that it should only be destroyed when the process that created it ends.

The fourth parameter, `bExists`, is set to `true` when the method returns if the call created the group, and `false` if it didn't. If `false` is returned, the `IsolationLevel` and `LifeTime` parameters will contain the values used by the original creator of the group. These can be check to ensure that they match specific requirements.

Finally, we create/access the shared property using the name passed into the function:

```
Set oProperty = oGroup.CreateProperty(name, bExists)
    If oProperty Is Nothing Then
        Err.Raise vbObject + 1, , "Failed to create Property"
    End If


    GetNextCounter = oProperty.Value
    oProperty.Value = oProperty.Value + 1
```

Once again the `bExists` values indicate whether we are the first person creating the property. If we are, we could initialize it to some specific value. The default will be zero.

Although the SPM doesn't manipulate durable resources, and is not transactional in any way, locking is still an issue. When we create an SPM object, we are effectively creating an object that does two things:

- ❑ Gives access to functionality—create groups, values etc
- ❑ Locks out others depending upon the isolation level specified for the group

For the second reason you shouldn't hold on to the SPM objects for too long. Remember, the quicker you release locks, the quicker another user can acquire them.

Resource dispensers, like SPM, that don't manipulate durable data generally don't need MTS. Try using it in a component that is not registered in MTS and you'll find it works just as well.

Summary

In this chapter we've seen two crucial aspects of scalability: **concurrency** and **pooling**. Both are important in two particular areas that are involved with a transaction: within MTS, and in databases.

We've looked at how pooling enables us to efficiently share and recycle a finite set of resources, such as database connections, between a large number of users. The resource dispenser manager provides the pooling, while the resources themselves are provided by resource dispensers. We also discussed that resource managers are responsible for managing durable state and enforcing ACID when transactions occur.

Then we went on to look at how locking is needed to ensure the consistency of the data within a transaction or database. However, locking affects concurrency. By careful forethought and consideration of how transactions create read and write locks we can increase concurrency levels. Resource managers create locks during transaction that manipulate their durable state.

Having looked at these areas we saw how the whole operation from creating the transaction to ensuring that the data is either committed or rolled back is managed by the MS DTC. The role of the MS DTC pulled the discussion together and illustrated how we ensure consistency in transactions.

Finally, we briefly looked at the Shared Property Manager (SPM) that can be used within MTS to share state between objects.

Next we shall continue our look at practical uses for components within our ASP applications, by showing how components can interact with Microsoft Message Queue Server.

Interacting with Microsoft Message Queues

In the last chapter, we saw how to create ASP components that take advantage of the transactional capabilities of Microsoft Transaction Server. We used MTS to help us with scalability issues by making more efficient use of system resources.

Another approach to scalability is asynchronous messaging. Rather than making a method call and waiting for a response, the client simply sends a **message** to a server. When the server performs the desired task, it sends a message back to the client. In addition to allowing the client to proceed with other work, messaging servers permit messages to be queued up and processed as the server becomes available.

Microsoft's messaging product is called **Microsoft Message Queue Server (MSMQ)** which we'll be looking at in some detail in this chapter. So we will cover:

- ❑ What MSMQ is and what can it do
- ❑ What COM objects are available with MSMQ and what they offer
- ❑ How components can be built to interact with MSMQ
- ❑ How to use MSMQ from components in an ASP application

To get us started, let's take a look at what message queuing technology is all about.

What is Message Queuing?

> **Message queuing is a system that allows different applications to communicate with each other using a 'store and forward' process.**

These applications can be on the same or different physical platforms. The platforms can be located in the same room, on the same LAN, or at any locations that are electronically connected. This connection does not even need to be permanent or reliable. In addition to this, the platforms can even be running different operating systems.

This sounds like a very heterogeneous system. Different applications, wide geographic locations, different connection types, and different operating systems are all characteristic of the Internet-connected world that we are living in today. Being able to move data between these systems has always been a goal of those who preach about connectivity.

Technologies such as SQL, ODBC, FTP, and HTTP all provide different mechanisms for data to be moved between systems in this heterogeneous environment. The principal drawback is that these technologies are oriented to particular types of applications. We'd like to have an application-neutral technology that lets us exchange data between heterogeneous platforms as they become available. The format of the data exchanged and the rules of the platform-to-platform interaction should be left to specific applications. The technology should simply be a communications channel. The fact that large numbers of systems have been created using these systems doesn't mean that there isn't a more efficient method of communication.

Messaging middleware systems are well-known in the mainframe community, where they have been a fixture of high-volume transaction processing applications for years. There are a number of messaging technology products for PCs, but we will concentrate on MSMQ as it is well-integrated with Visual Basic and ASP.

Messaging Middleware Features

There are two primary components that make up a message queuing system. One of these is, of course, a **message**:

> **A message is a piece of information that is sent between two applications.**

The format and content of the information is specific to the application. As far as the messaging system is concerned, it's simply an arbitrary body of data to be passed between systems. The other component of the system is the **queue**:

> **A queue is a container that can hold messages.**

Applications can then either put messages into a queue or read messages from a queue.

Messages

A message is made up of a number of different parts, the main one being its content, which can be either in text or encoded as binary data. The actual content is not examined by the message queuing system itself and there is no explicit standard method for formatting the content of a message. This means that the format of the content can be freely determined by the two applications that are passing the message.

A message can also include implementation-specific information about, for example, who the sender and the receiver are, a timestamp saying when it was sent, and even an expiration date, after which if it has not been read, it will be deleted. We'll examine the features of MSMQ messages later.

Queues

A **message queue** is where a message lives until it is picked up by the destination application. In this case, the message queue is similar to a post office box; messages will queue up until the destination application explicitly asks for them.

There can be more than one queue in a system – as we'll see later, MSMQ supports vast hierarchies of connected systems. However, on any particular machine, a **queue manager** manages all of the queues resident on that machine. Typically, this will consist of all the queues destined to receive messages for applications on that machine. This need not always be the case. Most messaging products permit you to directly address queues hosted on remote machines provided the network administrator has configured the remote queue manager appropriately. It is up to the queue manager to determine if the destination of a message is a local queue or not. If it is local, it simply drops the message in its destination queue. If it is not local, then it locates the machine where the destination queue is by using a directory server. It then negotiates the transfer of that message with the destination machine's queue manager. Once the destination queue manager receives the message, it then deposits it in the destination queue.

Message Queuing vs. E-Mail

Doesn't this sound a lot like e-mail? Both e-mail and message queue systems have messages, with senders and receivers. An e-mail system has mailboxes and a message queue system has queues, but in general they are similar. The queue manager functions much like an e-mail server in that it will forward messages to their proper destinations. So what is the difference?

You can think of e-mail as *person-to-person* communications. The information that is sent has to be readable and interpreted by humans. Message queue messages, on the other hand, are for *application-to-application* communications. The applications have to be able to programmatically interpret the results of the message. This is more than just interpreting the body of the message. If a message cannot be delivered, then the human can generally figure out why from the text in the response that was added by the e-mail server. A message queue message has to provide this type of information in a standard way that the application reading the message can understand.

In the body of an e-mail message, the content is understandable by anyone who can understand the language it is written in. In a message queue message, the content is only understood by the sending application and the receiving application. This means that intercepting a message between two systems is useless unless you know exactly how to interpret the message. Another by-product of this is that the message can be made very concise. The information can be in shorthand known by the two applications, rather than in verbose text that has to be understood by humans. You might think of the contents of a message as being a data structure particular to an application.

A message queue system also has more safeguards in place to ensure that a message arrives at its destination. With e-mail, especially over the Internet, reliable delivery is not something you can count on. Message queuing systems have the capability to ensure that a message arrives at its destination. Queue managers typically coordinate transmission and receipt so that both queue managers know when a message has been received. Messaging systems also have another reliability mechanism. If performance is an issue, the message queue may be held entirely in memory, thereby avoiding the overhead of writing a message to the comparatively slow hard disk. If reliability is more important than raw performance, messages may be written to disk when they are queued for transmission. That way, should the transmitting computer fail before the message is sent, the queue manager can recover the message from the disk and complete the transmission when the machine is restored.

Why use Message Queuing?

Now that we better understand what message queuing is, we need to look at why systems of today might require this technology. In order to define this, we need to examine what other technologies exist that perform the same role as message queuing, when message queuing should be used instead, and what benefits and limitations this will incur. This is really an artifact of the changing system architectures we see today.

Distributed Systems

In the early days of computing, users were limited to one (usually shared) machine. As machines became less expensive (and more powerful), you would find multiple machines, each performing different tasks. Pretty soon these systems became connected together, and users could access data on any of these systems, usually via a dumb terminal. This was the beginning of the 'network'.

As more and more applications were being developed, and as different types of computers were running these applications, the systems evolved from a centralized storehouse of business information to a more distributed system. As the processing and the data in a system become distributed, you have to start worrying about how the systems are connected together. In many instances, the connection may not be permanent. You may have to dial-up, or even physically dock your machine in order to connect and exchange information. These connections can be unreliable, and at times the system that you are trying to communicate with may not even be running. It is these types of distributed systems where message queuing can provide great advantages.

Specifically, application servers can queue messages for delivery to applications until the system they run on is again available. When that system becomes available, the queued messages can be sent and processed. This support for distributed applications makes message queuing technology an important technology in creating tomorrow's business applications.

Speed vs. Availability

In general, messaging middleware is regarded as a technology for improving availability and scalability. This should not be confused with speed. Messaging will always be slower than a low level method of inter-process communication like sockets or named pipes. Messages, after all, eventually use those methods for their transmission. The middleware technology adds all the overhead of negotiation and notification to the basic performance of the communications protocol. How can messaging be a scalability solution if this is the case? Wouldn't we want the fastest possible communication?

Messaging middleware acknowledges that no matter how fast a technology may be, it will never be fast enough. This includes processors as well as communications. Unless a machine can handle an infinite load in zero time, you can always overwhelm it. That's where messaging middleware comes in.

First, by introducing asynchronous communications into the process, clients are freed for other tasks while awaiting a response to a message. Since queue managers place incoming messages into a buffer – the queue – the receiving server doesn't have to be fast enough to handle the heaviest possible levels of traffic. It merely needs to be 'sized' for the average amount of traffic in the system. Extra messages coming in during spikes will back up in the queue, only to be cleared when traffic eases. A system that must synchronously process messages as they arrive will fail – poor availability – while an asynchronous messaging system remains available for service.

> Thus, messaging is a scalability solution in the sense that a system with asynchronous messaging can handle more traffic without failure, not in the sense that it handles lots of traffic faster.

This should illustrate the value of adding additional features to a low level protocol. Messaging middleware offers an array of features important to enterprise systems in exchange for some additional overhead:

- ❏ It improves availability, as we have seen
- ❏ It allows for the inclusion of occasionally disconnected computers, which basic protocols will not allow
- ❏ It allows both sender and recipient to know that a given message was received, and was received exactly once

As we go forward in this chapter, remember that raw speed is seldom the most important factor in building a scalable enterprise system.

Messaging vs. Synchronous Communication

So, should you *always* use message queuing to communicate between applications? This isn't the case either. If your business environment requires some activities be carried out synchronously, then a communication method such as DCOM or CORBA is better suited to perform this type of processing. If everybody using the application is always connected to the LAN, and all of the application servers are connected over fast, local, reliable links, then messaging may not be the answer either. In addition, for many developers message queuing is a new and unfamiliar technology that they may not be willing to invest in.

A few short guidelines of when to use message queuing can help to clarify the decision to use it or not:

- ❏ If the application you are communicating with is not guaranteed to be running at the same time as your application
- ❏ If the message is important and will cause problems if it is lost
- ❏ If your application is not always connected to the receiver application, but still needs to be functional
- ❏ If you perform many communication tasks with other applications asynchronously, and may or may not care about their response

Introduction to Microsoft Message Queues

Microsoft Message Queue Server (MSMQ) is part of the Microsoft BackOffice line of technologies. MSMQ is included as part of Windows NT Server/Enterprise Edition in a complete implementation. A more limited implementation is available on the regular Windows NT Server. MSMQ is also integrated into Windows 2000 Server, and there are clients available for every Windows platform. MSMQ provides the technologies to allow the transmission of messages over network connections, management of these messages as they are grouped into queues, and a programmatic API that allows developers to access all of the functionality of this technology.

MSMQ also provides a COM object model with interfaces that give programmers complete access to all aspects of the messaging system. Through these, we can handle all our messaging needs from any language that supports COM. This helps promote close integration between MSMQ and IIS, ASP, and MTS. MSMQ can also be enabled to understand the relative costs of connections, and thereby choose the most efficient routing method for messages within a network infrastructure. As with many of the other tools that are part of the BackOffice family, MSMQ provides a graphical management application called the Microsoft Message Queue Explorer that provides centralized management facilities for even the most widely distributed systems.

System Architecture

The primary parts of the MSMQ system architecture are the messages, the queues, the queue managers, and the interface that allows programs to access the information. The system operates transparently with respect to physical location. This means that an application can be sending a message to another application without having to worry about how the message actually gets there. MSMQ provides the facility for programmatically searching the set of queues available throughout a system. Once the application finds the queue it is interested in, it can send messages to it without worrying about how the message will actually get there. MSMQ handles the route taken by the message, and can (if necessary) *guarantee* that it gets to its final destination.

Features and Benefits of MSMQ

Microsoft Message Queue Server provides a number of key benefits to developers because of its close integration with other Microsoft technologies. We have already touched on one key benefit, which is the integration of MSMQ and COM. The use of the MSMQ COM components allow any application development environment that supports COM to use the features of message queuing in their applications. These development environments include Visual C++, Visual Basic, Visual J++, and scripting hosts that support COM. Both VBScript and JavaScript as implemented on Windows support this. It is this ability to use MSMQ both from VBScript and within ASP Components that allows for integration with Active Server Pages.

Delivery Options

Microsoft Message Queue Server supports three options for the delivery of messages. Each of these delivery options provides different advantages to the transmission of messages. Likewise, they each have associated trade-offs. The three types of delivery options are:

- ❑ Memory-based
- ❑ Disk-based
- ❑ Transactional-based

Memory-based Delivery

In this delivery type the message remains in the system memory as it moves from queue manager to queue manager through the message queue system. If there is a problem in the network and the queue manager that is currently processing the message cannot contact the next queue manager in the network, then the message will be held until the connection can be restored. Memory-based delivery is very fast, since the message is never transferred from system memory to disk storage. While this type of message will survive a failure in the network connection between two queue managers, it will not survive a failure of the machine that it is currently on. This is the price you must pay to get the speed advantage of memory-based delivery.

Disk-based Delivery

Alternatively, as the message moves from queue manager to queue manager, it can be written to permanent disk storage on each machine. When the message is transferred off to the next machine, it will be removed from the previous machine's disk storage as soon as the sending machine finishes its transmission. Since this message has to be written to disk on every machine that it passes through it will take the message much longer to reach its destination than with memory-based delivery. Disk I/O, after all, is several orders of magnitude slower than RAM. The benefit here is being able to recover the message in the event of system failure. Since this delivery method means that each queue manager the message passes through writes every message sent with this delivery method to disk, a system failure would not destroy the message. This is reliant on the use of a recoverable file system, such as NTFS, for the installation of the MSMQ server.

Transactional Delivery

Finally, the progress of each message from sender to receiver can be considered a transaction. Since transactions support the ACID properties, this means that a transactional delivered message will be atomic, consistent, isolated, and durable.

> To be durable, a transactional message uses the disk-based delivery method of writing every message to permanent storage as it moves through the system. The atomic characteristic means that the message will be delivered exactly one time, and in the same order it was sent.

Transactional messages use the transaction control features of MTS to provide the transactional characteristics of the message's delivery. A notable benefit of this delivery method is that MSMQ messages can participate in transactions with database operations. This permits the creation of complex transaction rules in applications that use MSMQ.

MSMQ Server Types

In a large enterprise, a message queuing network is made of three primary types of servers:

- ❑ Primary Enterprise Controller
- ❑ Site Controller
- ❑ Message Router

The **Primary Enterprise Controller**, or **PEC**, is responsible for maintaining the configuration of the entire enterprise system. There is only one PEC within an enterprise-wide installation. This system is responsible for holding the certification keys, which are used to validate messages in the system.

A **Site Controller** has information about the computers and queues that are at one site. A site is considered to be a group of computers that are connected together via a fast network.

Fast in this definition means 10Mbit Ethernet speeds and faster.

A specialized Site Controller is not necessary in the site where the PEC is located; the PEC doubles as a site controller.

A **Message Router** supports the routing of messages from one site to another. The Message Routing server is the system that holds the messages as they are moving from sender to receiver. If using memory-based delivery, the messages will be stored in the Message Router's system memory. For disk and transactional-based delivery, the messages will be stored on this system's hard drive. Site Controllers and Enterprise Controllers function as Message Routers as well. Since every site has at least one PEC or Site Controller, then every site will by default, have a Message Router. Additional Message Routers can be added to a site if a particular site generates a great deal of traffic.

MSMQ Client Types

An enterprise with MSMQ also must have one or both types of MSMQ clients:

- ❑ Independent client
- ❑ Dependent client

An **Independent client** has its own queues. If a message cannot be sent, it will be held in a local queue until transmission is possible. This is obviously useful for reliability, but is most commonly used for mobile users. The typical example is a traveling salesman application. The salesman will periodically dial in to his home server to receive messages pertaining to product updates and to send messages detailing orders he has sold. His laptop would be configured as an independent client. The application would create messages and direct that they be sent. MSMQ, acting as an independent client, would hold these messages until the next dial in session.

A **Dependent client**, by contrast, has no local queues of its own. It is *totally dependent* on a server for queue storage. These are ideal for thin-client systems where local resources are at a premium.

Windows NT servers have a fixed upper limit of four gigabytes for all queue storage, however, so we must be careful not to assign too many dependent clients to the same server.

Routing Types

In addition to there being types of delivery, servers and clients, there are also two possible methods of routing the message:

- Dynamic routing
- Static routing

Dynamic routing means that there does not have to be a single planned path between the sender and the receiver of a message.

This differs from **static** routing, where the routing tables along the way ensure that there is at most one path between two points.

Multiple Paths

When configuring an enterprise installation of MSMQ, you determine the 'cost' of the links between two message routers. This cost can be based on any factors that you determine as relevant. Things such as speed of link, available bandwidth on link, and actual monetary usage cost of the link can go into computing the 'cost' for a link. When performing dynamic routing, MSMQ will compute the 'cheapest' link between the sender and the receiver and send the message that way. This makes the configuration of an MSMQ enterprise much simpler, as static routes do not need to be explicitly created. It also allows MSMQ to route around breaks in the network topology, thereby increasing availability of messaging services.

Working with Queues and Messages

MSMQ implements a robust queuing system. It permits users and applications to specify the delivery priority of a message, as well as designating the privacy status of the message. Queues, in turn, use the priority of messages in the delivery of messages, and can be configured for privacy issues as well. Let's take a brief look at these topics.

> *Additionally, queues have journal queues associated with them. Much like a database journal, this allows retrieved messages to be archived for analysis and recovery.*

Message Priority

Messages can be given a priority for delivery. Higher priority messages are inserted into queues ahead of lower priority messages. Messages with the same priority are placed according to their time of arrival. MSMQ uses a simple numeric priority numbering scheme ranging from zero to seven, where zero is the lowest priority and seven is the highest. If you do not explicitly set the priority of a message, MSMQ will assign a default of 3. Transacted messages automatically receive a priority of zero, and the transaction itself ignores the message's priority property.

Message Privacy

Privacy is a matter of encrypting the body of a message. A public message is one in which the body is sent in plain text, i.e., unencrypted. If you want privacy, you are able to set a message property (PrivLevel) to control encryption. The encryption is end-to-end and transparent to applications. Once MSMQ gets a private message for transmission, it encrypts it prior to sending it. The message body remains encrypted until arrival, at which time the receiving queue manager decrypts the message. The receiving application retrieves the body without having to perform any additional steps to decrypt it.

> *The header information attached to a message must remain clear text so that MSMQ can perform routing and delivery.*

There is an additional issue to consider with privacy. Queues may be set up to respect privacy levels. A queue may be configured to accept only private messages, only public messages, or any message (public or private). An application trying to send a message with a conflict between the message privacy level and the queue privacy configuration will receive an error.

MSMQ Object Model

There is a set of COM objects that you can use to interact with the MSMQ system. There are objects representing individual queues and messages as well as utility objects. These objects allow you to look up queues from MSMQ servers, manage the messages for those queues, and administer those queues. You can access these objects from Visual Basic by adding a reference to the Microsoft Message Queue Object Library.

The full list of MSMQ objects is as follows:

Object	Usage
MSMQApplication	Supports obtaining the machine identifier
MSMQCoordinatedTransactionDispenser	Obtains an MS DTC object
MSMQEvent	Implements an event handler that may support events on multiple queues
MSMQQuery	Used to locate a collection of queues (uses Active Directory in Windows 2000)
MSMQQueueInfos	Collection of information about queues returned by the MSMQQuery object
MSMQQueueInfo	Information about a single queue in the MSMQQueueInfos collection
MSMQQueue	Object allowing you to interact with a specific queue itself
MSMQMessage	Object corresponding to a message in a queue
MSMQTransaction	A transaction object. The object may be obtained from an external source, or may be created internally by the application

Next, we will look at how to use these objects to perform the basic interactions with MSMQ that you need to deal with messages.

Queue Operations

It is surprising how easy it is to support message queues in your components, given the power and flexibility that MSMQ provides. You can perform two primary operations with a message queue:

- ❏ You can open or close the queue
- ❏ You can send or receive a message to or from a queue

In addition, you can also search for queues, create or delete queues, and manage the properties of existing queues.

Obtaining a Queue

The first thing that you will need to do is obtain the queue to send your messages to. There are two ways to do this:

- ❏ You can create a new one
- ❏ You can search for an existing one

Let's first look at the case where you create a new queue.

Creating a New Queue

To create a new queue, you need to use the `Create` method of the `MSMQQueueInfo` object.

Before you call `Create` you need to set the `PathName` property of the `MSMQQueueInfo` object. This property indicates three things about the queue:

- ❏ The machine the queue is located on
- ❏ Whether the queue is public or private
- ❏ The name of the queue

The format of the queue name is `machinename\queuename` for a public queue, or `.\PRIVATE$\queuename` for a private queue. Private queues can only be created on the local machine, so a machine name is not needed in this case. For example, in Visual Basic you could set the pathname using:

```
Dim QInfo As MSMQ.MSMQQueueInfo

Set QInfo = CreateObject("MSMQ.MSMQQueueInfo")

QInfo.PathName = "NT4_Server\TestQueue"
```

Once the queue has been named, other properties can be set, shown in the above table. Once you've done this, you can create the queue using the `Create` method:

```
QInfo.Create
```

We just used the `Create` method with its default parameters. This is sufficient in non-transacted cases where only the queue owner is receiving messages from the queue.

> *If we wish to create a queue for use with transactions, we must set the first parameter of the method to `True`. If we want users other than the queue owner to be able to read messages in this queue, we must supply a second parameter of `True`.*

Accessing an Existing Queue

If you know that the queue you are interested in already exists, you can look up a reference to it using the `LookupQueue` method of the `MSMQQuery` object. This is the only method of this object, and will return a collection of queues based on criteria that you set via its parameters, in the form of an instance of the `MSMQQueueInfos` object. The syntax of this method is as follows:

```
queryObject.LookupQueue([QueueGuid] [, ServiceTypeGuid] [, Label] [, CreateTime]
                        [, ModifyTime] [, RelServiceType] [, RelLabel]
                        [, RelCreateTime] [, RelModifyTime])
```

The first five parameters specify the properties to search for in available queues:

Parameter (Optional)	Type	Value
QueueGuid	String	Identifier of queue
ServiceTypeGuid	String	Type of service provided by the queue
Label	String	Label of queue
CreateTime	Variant Date	Time when queue was created
ModifyTime	Variant Date	Time when queue properties were last set (both when the queue was created and the last time Update was called)

You can also set Boolean operators for each of these parameters (except `QueueGuid`, which makes sense when you think about it). The default value for these operators is `REL_EQ`, which simply means that the query will return a collection of queues whose properties exactly match the parameters you specify. These operators can be chosen through the last four parameters of `LookupQueue`, the names of which are simply the names of the associated property preceded by `Rel`:

Relationship Parameter	Corresponding Criteria Parameter
RelServiceType	ServiceTypeGuid
RelLabel	Label
RelCreateTime	CreateTime
RelModifyTime	ModifyTime

The possible values for these parameters are:

Relation Parameter	Means
REL_EQ	Equal To
REL_NEQ	Not Equal To
REL_LT	Less Than
REL_GT	Greater Than
REL_LE	Less Than or Equal To
REL_GE	Greater Than or Equal To
REL_NOP	Ignore this parameter

To call the `LookupQueue` method, you would do something like the following:

```
Dim objQuery As MSMQ.MSMQQuery
Dim QInfos As MSMQ.MSMQQueueInfos
Dim QInfo As MSMQ.MSMQQueueInfo

Set objQuery = CreateObject("MSMQ.MSMQQuery")
Set QInfos = objQuery.LookupQueue(Label:="Bill")
```

This will return a collection of queues, all of which have a `Label` value of `Bill`. The collection is represented by an `MSMQQueueInfos` object containing one `MSMQQueueInfo` object for each queue found. This facilitates searches across queues. If you need to differentiate between queues with the same label, you can look at the `PathName` property in each `MSMQQueueInfo` object.

> **While this return value is a collection, it is not navigable using the same methods as other collections.**

Instead, there is a `Reset` method to move to the beginning of the collection, and a `Next` method to get the next entry in the collection. To navigate through each entry in the collection, you can use this format:

```
Dim objQuery As MSMQ.MSMQQuery
Dim QInfos As MSMQ.MSMQQueueInfos
Dim QInfo As MSMQ.MSMQQueueInfo

Set objQuery = CreateObject("MSMQ.MSMQQuery")
Set QInfos = objQuery.LookupQueue(Label:="Bill")

QInfos.Reset

Set QInfo = QInfos.Next

Do While Not QInfo Is Nothing
 ' Do something with this queue
   Set QInfo = QInfos.Next
Loop
```

This completes our discussion of the two methods you can use to retrieve a queue. Once you have retrieved a reference to the queue that you want, the next step is to open it.

Opening a Queue

The MSMQQueueInfo object that was returned when you created a queue, or found one using LookupQueue, is merely *information* about a queue. To actually work with a queue (use it to send and receive messages) you have to *open* it. You can open a queue with the Open method of the MSMQQueueInfo object, the return value of which is an MSMQQueue object.

The Open method takes two parameters: the first parameter will determine what you are doing with the queue, and the second will determine what others can do with it while you have it open.

When you have an open queue in your application, there are three operations that you can perform on it. The first parameter determines whether you can:

❑ Send messages to the queue (MQ_SEND_ACCESS)

❑ Retrieve messages from the queue (MQ_RECEIVE_ACCESS)

❑ Peek at messages in the queue (MQ_PEEK_ACCESS or MQ_RECEIVE_ACCESS)

The cases where you will be reading and writing messages are self-explanatory. Peeking at a message in the queue means 'looking at the contents of a message in the queue without removing it from the queue'.

You also need to set how other people can interact with the queue when you have it open. This is controlled by the second parameter of the Open method, ShareMode. The setting for this parameter is dependent on the Access method you specified in the first parameter:

❑ If you have opened the queue for sending or peeking, then the only valid setting for this parameter is to allow others to fully interact with the queue (MQ_DENY_NONE)

❑ If you have opened the queue for receiving, then you can either: allow others full access to the queue (MQ_DENY_NONE), or prevent others from receiving messages from the queue (MQ_DENY_RECEIVE_SHARE).

Even if you set this flag to one of these values, other applications can still send messages to the queue and peek at messages in it.

Once you have determined the parameter settings for your queue, you can issue the open call. The format for this call is:

```
MSMQInfoObject.Open(AccessMethod, ShareMode)
```

So, to open a queue for sending messages to it, you would:

```
Dim objQueue As MSMQQueue
Dim QInfo As MSMQ.MSMQQueueInfo

Set QInfo = CreateObject("MSMQ.MSMQQueueInfo")
QInfo.PathName = "NT4_Server\TestQueue"

Set objQueue = QInfo.Open(MQ_SEND_ACCESS, MQ_DENY_NONE)
```

The value of the first parameter, MQ_SEND_ACCESS, establishes that we are opening the queue solely to send it messages. The value of the second parameter, MQ_DENY_NONE, tells MSMQ that we want the queue to be available to other users while we are working with it.

Now that you have a queue open for writing, the next step is to create a message that can be sent to that queue.

Creating Messages

To send a message, you will need to create an instance of the MSMQMessage object. This object encapsulates everything you need to create and send a message. There are a number of properties that you can set when sending a message; including both what are considered core properties (such as the body of the message), and others that allow you to modify certain secondary message characteristics (such as how the message is delivered).

The primary parameter for the MSMQMessage object is the Body parameter. This holds the actual contents of the message, and can be a string, or any type of binary data. The maximum size of a message body is 4 MB.

Let's take a look at an example that will create a message, set its properties, and set its content. This will be everything that needs to be done to get the message ready to send:

```
Dim msgSent As MSMQ.MSMQMessage

Set msgSent = CreateObject("MSMQ.MSMQMessage")

msgSent.Label = "My Message"
msgSent.Body = "Test message with acknowledgment."
msgSent.Ack = QMSG_ACKNOWLEDGMENT_FULL_RECEIVE
msgSent.MaxTimeToReceive = 60

Set msgSent.AdminQueueInfo = QInfoAdmin
```

This will create a new Message object and set its Label and Body. When it is retrieved from its destination queue, the queue manager will send an acknowledgement to the QInfoAdmin queue. This parameter is a reference to an MSMQQueueInfo object that points to the acknowledgement queue. If the message is not retrieved within 60 seconds, it will be deleted from the destination queue, and a negative acknowledgement will be sent.

The last step is to actually send the message to its destination queue.

Sending Messages

To send a message, you will need both a queue that is open for sending, and a Message object that has been properly configured. The Send method is actually a method of the Message object, not the Queue object. The destination queue is passed as a parameter to the Send method. To send the message we created in the last section to the queue we opened in the section before you would use:

```
msgSent.Send QInfo
```

The message is now on its way to its destination queue. Once it arrives there, it will wait for 60 seconds. If no application retrieves it within that time, it will delete itself from the queue and send the appropriate negative acknowledgement.

Retrieving a Message

Now that there is a message sitting in this queue, we need to be able to retrieve it and use its contents in another application. There are two ways of retrieving messages from a queue:

❑   A queue can be read synchronously, where all program execution will be blocked until a message is available in the queue, or a timeout value is reached

❑   A queue can also be read asynchronously, where a queue will fire events as messages arrive, and these events can be handled by the receiving application

In the web-based application world, the majority of message retrieval will be done using synchronous reads. At first glance, it may seem like this would adversely affect system performance – after all, we went to asynchronous messaging to gain improved availability. In reality, we can specify a timeout value when we retrieve messages. This interval should be set to the lowest possible value consistent with the expected latency of your network. You should structure your application so that it looks for messages when it expects them to be there rather than using the timeout interval to wait for a message to arrive. If you are sending messages to local queues, the timeout interval will cover the delay in sending the message between processes. Otherwise, use this as a measure of error tolerance. If you expect long delays, poll for messages at intervals using a multi-threaded application.

Let's assume that we've sent a message to a queue with the label of `Bill`. We can use the technique detailed earlier to find this queue from within our receiving application, but this time we'll open the queue for read access:

```
Dim objQuery As MSMQQuery
Dim QInfos As MSMQQueueInfos
Dim QInfo As MSMQQueueInfo

Set objQuery = CreateObject("MSMQ.MSMQQuery")
Set QInfos = objQuery.LookupQueue(Label:="Bill")

QInfos.Reset
Set QInfo = QInfos.Next

Set QInfo = FindQueue(QInfos)
QInfo.Open(MQ_RECEIVE_ACCESS, MQ_DENY_NONE)
```

The `FindQueue` routine will apply some application specific logic to inspect the individual queue information structures and locate the queue in which we are interested should there be more than one queue with the label `Bill`. This code uses the `MQ_RECEIVE_ACCESS` flag to indicate that this queue will be used to retrieve messages.

```
Dim msgDest As MSMQMessage

Set msgDest = QInfo.Receive(ReceiveTimeout:=100)
```

This will retrieve the first message in the queue. If, after 100 milliseconds (1/10th of a second), there are no messages then this method will return `Nothing`. So, to check if a message was found, you just need:

```
If Not msgDest Is Nothing Then
  ' Valid message found
Else
  ' No message found
End If
```

You can then get the information that this message contained by examining the contents of its body:

```
Debug.Print msgDest.Body
```

Once you have read this message from the queue, you can close the queue, freeing the resources used by the MSMQQueue object. The message object that you retrieved will still be valid, even after you close the queue. To close the queue, you simply use the Close method:

```
QInfo.Close
```

Now that we've looked at the steps to work with messages and queues, let's take a look at how to build some components that will help us work with MSMQ from within ASP applications.

MSMQ Component Example

Now that we have seen the basics of using the COM interface to work with MSMQ, let's put this into practice. In our example, we'll look at the ordering and shipping department of a book publisher. For this example, we will be using the pubs database that comes with SQL Server. The functionality that we will be looking at will include:

- Sending order information from the user to the ordering department
- Order department validation of order, and generation of shipping notice and merchandise pick slip
- Warehouse retrieval of merchandise pick slip
- Shipping department creation of packing slips

This will be an ASP-based application, using components written in Visual Basic to handle the business logic and interactions with the database. It will be considered part of a larger application that provides full e-commerce functionality for the book publisher. We will be looking at components to handle these four aspects of the commerce pipeline.

Workflow

In this application, we will be using the pubs database to hold the list of books that can be purchased, and track orders and other information using MSMQ. This will allow us to route the appropriate information to the appropriate application. It also gives us the MSMQ advantage of inter-application communication without multiple applications being active at any one time. At each step in the process we will generate an MSMQ message based on information from the user (possibly combined with information from the previous step as sent in another message) and send it to the appropriate queue. The next step will retrieve that information from the queue and perform its processing. The workflow is implemented as a series of ASPs that in turn make use of some components we will build to perform the messaging tasks needed to communicate with the next application in the workflow. Pages with a user interface typically call an ASP that uses the relevant business component to format and send a message. The results returned by the component are presented to the customer as HTML.

A simple html page, default.html, is provided that offers links to each step in the process. If you wish to follow a typical order from start to finish, you will want to start with OrderEntry.asp. As always, all the sample code for this application is available from the Wrox web site.

There are four steps in our process:

1. The first step will be to take the information supplied by the customer in `OrderEntry.asp`. This includes the titles and quantities desired as well as the shipping information. This information will be packaged into an XML-formatted block of data and sent to a `PendingOrder` queue by an instance of the `OrderPage` component.

2. The second step is the order validation step, implemented in `ValidateOrder.asp`. Here we will take the pending orders from the `PendingOrder` queue and present the information for validation by an order processor. This processor is the `OrderValidation` component. This order processor will be responsible for generating the order number and passing the information to the next step. The `OrderValidation` component passes order information to the next step of the workflow by sending two messages:

    ❑ The first will be sent to an `OrderPicking` queue, and will contain details of the books required for this order

    ❑ The second will contain the shipping information and will be sent to the `PackingSlip` queue for generation of a packing slip

3. The packing slip will only be finalized once the order has been filled at the warehouse, so a message will be sent to an `OrderReady` queue once the merchandise has been picked for shipping. Warehouse staff use the application embodied in `PickList.asp` to perform this task. That page uses an instance of the `Warehouse` component, which is responsible for sending the message.

4. It will be the responsibility of the `Shipping` component to wait until both messages for a single order – the one sent by the `OrderValidation` component to the `PackingSlip` queue and the one sent by the `Warehouse` component to the `OrderReady` queue – are waiting, in order to generate the pick slip. This happens in `Shipping.asp`, which generates HTML by applying an XSL style sheet to the XML contained in the bodies of the messages. This page uses the `Shipping` component to retrieve the messages needed by the application.

If you are not familiar with the Extensible Markup Language (XML), do not worry. All you really need to know for the purposes of this sample is that it is an open standard that allows data to be marked up with descriptive information similar to the way HTML marks up content. We will also make use of a technology stemming from XML, the Extensible Stylesheet Language (XSL), that allows for data-driven formatting of XML data into HTML for presentation to users.

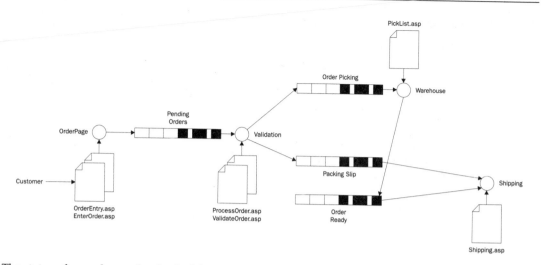

The status of an order can be checked from Status.asp, which uses the OrderStatus component to monitor the messages in each queue. This component peeks at all four queues and reports on the messages found in each.

> *Given the focus of this chapter on queued messages, this sort of status is sufficient, even useful for those who want to focus on the queuing aspect of the application. In an actual production system, however, you will be more interested in the status of orders and will want to hide the queues from the customer.*

Each component in this application will be an MTS-aware component. It is implemented as a class module, which is used to create a separate DLL for each component. To support MTS, we are going to implement the ObjectControl interface, which was examined in detail in the last chapter. The methods we need to implement the interface will appear at the beginning of each class module. As we saw in the last chapter, we'll also keep a modular reference to the current ObjectContext reference. We'll also set the class' MTSTransactionMode property to 1-NoTransactions so that we can access the Context object:

```
Option Explicit
```

```
Implements ObjectControl

Private mobjContext As ObjectContext
```

```
Private Sub ObjectControl_Activate()

  Set mobjContext = Nothing

End Sub
```

```
Private Function ObjectControl_CanBePooled() As Boolean

  ObjectControl_CanBePooled = True

End Function
```

```
Private Sub ObjectControl_Deactivate()

  Set mobjContext = Nothing

End Sub
```

We will also be using a BAS module in all the components to hold some constants to return messages back to the user based on the results of using a message queue:

```
Public Const cQueueEmpty = "Queue Empty"
Public Const cPackQueueEmpty = "Packing Queue Empty"
Public Const cQueueError = "Queue Error"
Public Const cQueueOK = "Queue OK"
Public Const cQueueNotFound = "Queue Not Found"
```

The OrderPage Component

The `OrderPage` component is the primary entry point for the user. The `OrderEntry.asp` builds the user interface and allows the user to select the quantity per title of a book and fill in their shipping information:

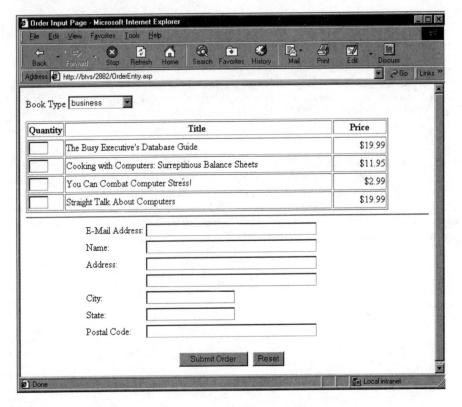

You can find the ASP pages for these application in the source code available for download.

The script code that uses the OrderPage component is quite simple and just calls a single method of the component:

```
<%

  Dim objOrder
  Dim blnOK As Boolean

  Set objOrder = Server.CreateObject("OrderPage.Order")
  blnOK = Order.ASPProcessOrder

  If blnOK then
      Response.Write "Order Placed Successfully"
  Else
      Response.Write "Order Placement Failed"
  End If

  Set objOrder = Nothing

%>
```

The responsibility of the OrderPage component is to process the information that was posted as part of the request. This information will need to be placed into an XML-formatted message and then sent to the PendingOrders queue.

The structure of the XML message calls for a <BOOKORDER> element to be composed of multiple <ITEM> elements. Each <ITEM> element represents one book in the order. The <ITEM> element contains two elements: <BOOK_ID> contains the ID number of the book and <QUANTITY> contains the number of those books in the order. So the constructed hierarchy for the message will be:

```
<BOOKORDER>
   <ITEM>
       <BOOK_ID>BU1032</BOOK_ID>
       <QUANTITY>1</QUANTITY>
   </ITEM>
   <ITEM>
       <BOOK_ID>BU1111</BOOK_ID>
       <QUANTITY>3</QUANTITY>
   </ITEM>
</BOOKORDER>
```

We will also be passing the customer's shipping information in an XML format. The structure of the customer message is even simpler. There will be root <CUSTOMER> element followed by the shipping properties as sub-elements:

```
<CUSTOMER>
   <EMAIL>JSmith@ISP.COM</EMAIL>
   <NAME>Mr J Smith</NAME>
   <ADDR1>12 Main St</ADDR1>
   <ADDR2>The Burbs</ADDR2>
   <CITY>Cityville<?CITY>
   <STATE>ZZ</STATE>
   <ZIP>12345</ZIP>
</CUSTOMER>
```

These two elements are enclosed by the generic <ORDER> and </ORDER> tags. The elements <BOOKORDER> and <CUSTOMER> will be generated by two functions private to the components which we'll examine shortly.

Now we know what the component will be doing let's look at it's code. The `OrderPage` component is a simple ActiveX DLL with a single class module called `Order`. It has references to:

- ☐ Microsoft Transaction Server Type Library
- ☐ Microsoft Active Server Pages Object Library
- ☐ Microsoft Message Queue Object Library

The class module contains the MTS code we saw earlier but the main body of the work is performed in the single `Public` function `ASPProcessOrder`. We start by declaring all our variables and setting a refernce to the Context object and the `Request` object for that context:

```
Public Function ASPProcessOrder() As Boolean

  Dim objReq As ASPTypeLibrary.Request
  Dim coll As Variant
  Dim colBookQuantity As New Collection
  Dim colBooks As New Collection
  Dim strVal As String
  Dim strBkID As String
  Dim strQuantity As String
  Dim strXMLData As String
  Dim objQuery As MSMQQuery
  Dim QInfos As MSMQQueueInfos
  Dim QInfo As MSMQQueueInfo
  Dim objQueue As MSMQQueue
  Dim msgOrder As MSMQMessage

  On Error GoTo ErrorProcessOrder

  Set mobjContext = GetObjectContext

  Set objReq = mobjContext("Request")
```

Then we create a local collection for the books the user has selected to buy by testing the `Form` collection of the passed in `Request` object. We can identify the relevant controls because they will be prefixed with the characters "bk_":

```
For Each coll In objReq.Form

    strVal = CStr(coll)
    strQuantity = CStr(objReq.Form(coll))

    If Left(strVal, 3) = "bk_" And strQuantity <> "" Then ' Book Quantity
        strbkID = Mid(strVal, 4, Len(strVal))
        colBooks.Add strBkID
        colBookQuantity.Add strQuantity, strBkID
    End If

Next
```

Once we've built up the local collections, we pass them to a local function to turn them into XML data:

```
strXMLData = "<ORDER>" & BuildOrderXML(colBooks, colBookQuantity)
strXMLData = strXMLData & BuildCustomerXML(objReq) & "</ORDER>"
```

Now that we have the XML content that we need to place an order, our next step in `ASPProcessOrder` is to send the order information as an MSMQ message to the appropriate message queue, which we'll first have to locate. We'll do this as we saw earlier, through the `MSMQQuery` object:

```
Set objQuery = mobjContext.CreateInstance("MSMQ.MSMQQuery")
Set msgOrder = mobjContext.CreateInstance("MSMQ.MSMQMessage")
```

We need to locate the queue named "PendingOrders" in the MSMQ system. This is accomplished by using the `LookupQueue` method of the `MSMQQuery` object.

We will assume that we have only one queue with this name on the local machine. Remember that this method returns a collection of MSMQQueueInfo objects, but the collection cannot be iterated through by standard means. We need to reset the pointer to the first object in the queue with the Reset method, then retrieve a reference to it with the Next method:

```
Set QInfos = objQuery.LookupQueue(Label:="PendingOrders")
QInfos.Reset
Set QInfo = QInfos.Next
```

If the collection returned by the `LookupQueue` query is empty, then the value returned by the `Next` method will not be an object. This means that the particular queue could not be located on the system. If this is the case, we need to return an error to the calling ASP script by passing a return value of `False` from the function:

```
If Not IsObject(QInfo) Then
    ASPProcessOrder = False
    Exit Function
End If
```

Once we have a valid queue, we can open it by using the `Open` method, and as we are adding messages to this queue, we want to open it using the `MQ_SEND_ACCESS` parameter. Since we also want to allow other users to add information to the queue, we open it with `MQ_DENY_NONE` access:

```
Set objQueue = QInfo.Open(MQ_SEND_ACCESS, MQ_DENY_NONE)
```

With the queue properly opened, we can now set to work with the message itself. We will set the message label to correspond to the order number for this order, and the body will contain the XML information that was created earlier. Once the information in the message is set correctly, we can send it to the queue that was opened earlier:

```
msgOrder.Label = CStr(CreateOrderNumber)
msgOrder.Body = strXMLData
msgOrder.Send objQueue
ASPProcessOrder = True

Exit Function
```

Finally, we need to deal with any errors that occur in the processing of the method – remember we set up an error handler at the beginning of the method that directed any errors to the `ErrorProcessOrder` label. To deal with errors in this method, we will simply return a value of `False` to the calling script:

```
ErrorProcessOrder:

  ASPProcessOrder = False

End Function
```

Now we have the main routine we can take a look at the two helper routines used to format the XML message.

The BuildOrderXML Function

The first of the two XML formatting functions builds the <BOOKORDER> element based on a collection of book IDs and quantities. These functions are actually very simple. All they do is loop through the book collections and use string concatenation to build the XML string:

```
Private Function BuildOrderXML(colBkList As Collection, _
                                 colBkQuan As Collection) As String
  Dim strXML As String
  Dim varBk As Variant

  strXML = "<BOOKORDER>"

  For Each varBk In colBkList
      strXML = strXML & "<ITEM>" & vbCrLf
      strXML = strXML & "<BOOK_ID>" & varBk & "</BOOK_ID>" & vbCrLf
      strXML = strXML & "<QUANTITY>" & colBkQuan.Item(CStr(varBk)) & _
               "</QUANTITY>" & vbCrLf
      strXML = strXML & "</ITEM>" & vbCrLf
  Next

  strXML = strXML & "</BOOKORDER>" & vbCrLf

  BuildOrderXML = strXML

End Function
```

The BuildCustomerXML Function

This function does little different from BuildOrderXML except that it gets its data from the Request object:

```
Private Function BuildCustomerXML(objReq As Request) As String

  Dim strXML As String

  strXML = "<CUSTOMER>"
  strXML = strXML & "<EMAIL>" & objReq.Form("Email") & "</EMAIL>" & vbCrLf
  strXML = strXML & "<NAME>" & objReq.Form("Name") & "</NAME>" & vbCrLf
  strXML = strXML & "<ADDR1>" & objReq.Form("Address1") & "</ADDR1>" & vbCrLf
  strXML = strXML & "<ADDR2>" & objReq.Form("Address2") & "</ADDR2>" & vbCrLf
  strXML = strXML & "<CITY>" & objReq.Form("City") & "</CITY>" & vbCrLf
  strXML = strXML & "<STATE>" & objReq.Form("State") & "</STATE>" & vbCrLf
  strXML = strXML & "<ZIP>" & objReq.Form("PostalCode") & "</ZIP>" & vbCrLf
  strXML = strXML & "</CUSTOMER>" & vbCrLf

  BuildCustomerXML = strXML

End Function
```

There is one more twist we have to take care of before we are done with this component.

Numbering Orders

Since this is the first time that the order is entered into the system, it will need to have an order number assigned. In this example, we are just going to create a random order number. In a real-life application, you may retrieve the next order number from a database. If a unique identifier is preferable to a sequential ID a GUID might be generated. In either case, the generating code goes in the `CreateOrderNumber` helper function:

```
Private Function CreateOrderNumber() As Long

  Randomize
  CreateOrderNumber = CLng(Rnd * 1000000)

End Function
```

If you refer back to the `ASPProcessOrder` function from earlier, you can see that we assigned the result of this number to the `Label` of the Order message:

```
msgOrder.Label = CStr(CreateOrderNumber)
```

The OrderValidation Component

The `OrderValidation` component is responsible for retrieving the orders from the `PendingOrders` queue. The validating application, `ValidateOrder.asp`, will use XML data from the message together with an XSL style sheet to display validated order results to the user:

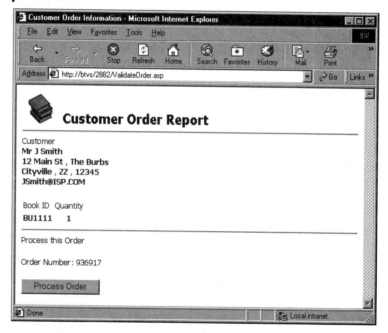

The syntax and capabilities of XSL is beyond the scope of this chapter. For our purposes, it is sufficient to say that the style sheet provides rules that map each XML element into some HTML fragment. When we apply the style sheet rules to the XML document in the message body, the result is HTML that we can pass on to the user. For further information on XSL, please see XML Applications (Wrox Press, ISBN 1-861001-52-5).

This page would be used by associates responsible for the validation of orders that have been placed by customers. After the associate reviews and approves the order, the component is then responsible for passing the order information on. There are two branches in the next step in the order process. The order needs to be sent both to the warehouse, so that the items in the order can be picked from stock, and the shipping department, so that a shipping manifest can be generated.

The `OrderValidation` component is again an ActiveX DLL with a single class module called `GetNextOrder`. It also has the same references as the `OrderPage` component. It also contains the same BAS module and MTS code.

Posting Messages

One action that we will need to carry out in multiple places in this component, as well as in other components in this example, is the sending of a message to a queue. We have taken nearly the same code as we saw in the previous component and put it into a `Private` function in each of our components. This is a good approach for a simple sample application such as ours. As it is, our MSMQ tasks are very simple, requiring only a thin layer over the MSMQ objects themselves.

We have made some simplifying assumptions based on our knowledge of the application and queue configuration. If we were building a large number of applications in a production setting that required MSMQ messaging, we would need to develop the error checking and handle cases such as multiple queues with the same name. In general, we would need to make the processing more robust. At that point, it might be worthwhile to create a separate component solely for the purpose of posting messages.

> For an introductory look at what such a component might look like, please see Designing Distributed Applications (Wrox Press, ISBN 1- 861002-27-0).

The only specific pieces of information needed to use this function are the order number and XML data, as well as the name of the queue that we are sending the information to. These values are passed as parameters to this function:

```
Private Function PostQueueMessage(strQueue As String, OrderNum As Variant, _
                        strXML As Variant) As String

    Dim objQuery As MSMQ.MSMQQuery
    Dim QInfos As MSMQ.MSMQQueueInfos
    Dim QInfo As MSMQ.MSMQQueueInfo
    Dim objQueue As MSMQ.MSMQQueue
    Dim msgOrder As MSMQ.MSMQMessage

    On Error GoTo ErrorPostQueueMessage

    Set mobjContext = GetObjectContext

    Set objQuery = mobjContext.CreateInstance("MSMQ.MSMQQuery")
    Set msgOrder = mobjContext.CreateInstance("MSMQ.MSMQMessage")
```

The primary change to the code in our helper function from what we looked at earlier is in the `LookupQueue` method. This is where we specify the name of the actual queue that we are interested in. This value is one of the parameters that is passed to the function and stored in the `strQueue` variable:

```
    Set QInfos = objQuery.LookupQueue(Label:=strQueue)
```

One other difference in this function is in the way that we return error messages. Rather than returning simply `True` or `False` indicating success or failure, we will be returning descriptive strings to indicate what happened. The descriptive strings are actually stored as constants, in a module file that is included into all of our components:

```
QInfos.Reset

Set QInfo = QInfos.Next

If Not IsObject(QInfo) Then
   PostQueueMessage = cQueueNotFound
   Exit Function
End If
```

The last difference in this function is the way that general error information is returned. The `Err` object contains descriptive information about the error that caused the error handler to fire. This descriptive information is appended to the standard error message and then passed back to the caller:

```
Set objQueue = QInfo.Open(MQ_SEND_ACCESS, MQ_DENY_NONE)

msgOrder.Label = CStr(OrderNum)
msgOrder.Body = strXML
msgOrder.Send objQueue

PostQueueMessage = cQueueOK

Exit Function

ErrorPostQueueMessage:

PostQueueMessage = cQueueError & " " & Err.Description

End Function
```

Transmitting Order Information to the Queues

This component exposes two public methods that are used to transmit order information to various queues. The `CreatePickSlip` method will send the order information to the `OrderPicking` queue while the `CreatePackingSlip` method will send the order information to the `PackingSlip` queue. You can see that by using a helper function like `PostQueueMessage` these public methods become very short and straightforward:

```
Public Function CreatePickSlip(xmlOrder As Variant, _
                          OrderNum As Variant) As Variant

   CreatePickSlip = PostQueueMessage("OrderPicking", OrderNum, xmlOrder)

End Function
```

```
Public Function CreatePackingSlip(xmlOrder As Variant, _
                            OrderNum As Variant) As Variant

   CreatePackingSlip = PostQueueMessage("PackingSlip", OrderNum, xmlOrder)

End Function
```

Retrieving Orders from the Queue

The other public method of this component will retrieve an order from the `PendingOrders` queue and return it to the ASP page for processing. The value returned by the `PullNextOrder` method will be used to indicate the success or failure of the method. The information will actually be returned via the two parameters that are passed by reference. In passing by reference, the method receives a pointer to the actual data location, rather than a copy of the data. Any changes it makes to the data using this reference will be automatically reflected in the data in the calling application.

> *As with posting messages, a real-world, production-grade application would require much more involved checks and tests. This function, suitably enhanced, would be the logical complement to the hypothetical messaging component we discussed earlier.*

```
Public Function PullNextOrder(ByRef strXML As Variant, _
                              ByRef OrderNum As Variant) As Variant

  Dim objQuery As MSMQ.MSMQQuery
  Dim QInfos As MSMQ.MSMQQueueInfos
  Dim QInfo As MSMQ.MSMQQueueInfo
  Dim objQueue As MSMQ.MSMQQueue
  Dim msgDest As MSMQ.MSMQMessage

  On Error GoTo ErrorPullNextOrder

  Set mobjContext = GetObjectContext
```

The first thing that we need to do is find the queue that we are interested in retrieving messages from. The queue is located using the same steps we used when sending messages. The difference comes in the way that the queue is opened. Since we are going to be retrieving messages from the queue, we need to open it for receive access by passing the `MQ_RECEIVE_ACCESS` parameter:

```
  Set objQuery = mobjContext.CreateInstance("MSMQ.MSMQQuery")

  Set QInfos = objQuery.LookupQueue(Label:="PendingOrders")
  QInfos.Reset
  Set QInfo = QInfos.Next

  If Not IsObject(QInfo) Then
     PullNextOrder = cQueueError
     Exit Function
  End If

  Set objQueue = QInfo.Open(MQ_RECEIVE_ACCESS, MQ_DENY_NONE)
```

We can use the `Receive` method of an `MSMQMessage` object to check for the presence of a message using a timeout interval. If there are no messages at the end of the interval, we will set an error code. Otherwise, we can pass the label of the message to a variable for the order number, and the body of the message to a variable for the XML information. After doing this, we can indicate that the message was successful by setting the `cQueueOK` value for the return and exiting the function:

```
  Set msgDest = objQueue.Receive(ReceiveTimeout:=100)

  If msgDest Is Nothing Then
     PullNextOrder = cQueueEmpty
     Exit Function
  End If
```

```
OrderNum = msgDest.Label
strXML = msgDest.Body

PullNextOrder = cQueueOK

Exit Function
```

Finally, we need to deal with any errors that occur in the processing of the method. We set up an error handler at the beginning of the method that directed any errors to the `ErrorPullNextOrder` label. In this error handler, we will be passing more detailed information back to the calling application. We will be combining the `cQueueError` error string along with the Visual Basic error message that is contained in the `Err.Description` property:

```
ErrorPullNextOrder:

  PullNextOrder = cQueueError & Err.Description

End Function
```

The Warehouse Component

In the warehouse, the information about the order needs to be retrieved and a merchandise pick slip generated. This is a printed form that the stock clerk can walk around with and retrieve the appropriate items for an order. Once the pick slip is generated, the order is ready for the final step, which is the generation of the shipping manifest, or packing slip. The application that creates the pick slip and sends a message to the shipping manifest application is `PickList.asp`, which uses the Warehouse component for its business logic:

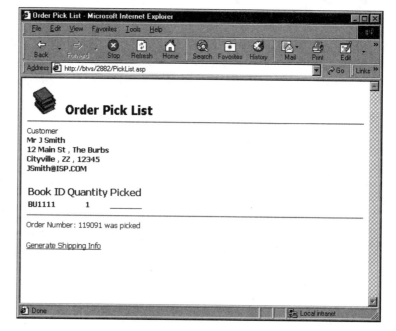

This component, as have the other ones we have created in this application, will use the standard MTS plumbing to make the component MTS-aware. The `PostQueueMessage` method is also exactly the same as in the previous component. It is a single DLL with a class module called `PickList`. As well as the same references as the previous components, the Warehouse component also contains a reference to Microsoft XML, version 2.0.

The component includes a `Generate` method that is responsible for retrieving the order information from the `OrderPicking` queue and then creating and outputting the pick slip for the warehouse associate. We will be using an XSL style sheet to convert the XML information stored in the message into HTML that can be displayed by the browser. In order to do this, we need to tell this method what style sheet file we wish to use by passing it in as a parameter.

The message retrieval follows the same steps as we have seen in the previous component. In short, the steps to follow are:

❑ Find the Queue

❑ Open the Queue

❑ Retrieve the message

❑ Read the information from the message

The information that is read from the message is saved into the `OrderNum` and `strXML` parameters. Since these are passed by reference, the information stored in them will be available to the calling application when the method has returned. Once that has been accomplished, the information is ready to be converted into displayable HTML using the XSL style sheet:

```
Public Function Generate(ByRef strXML As Variant, ByRef OrderNum As Variant, _
                    strStyleFile As Variant) As Variant

   Dim objQuery As MSMQ.MSMQQuery
   Dim QInfos As MSMQ.MSMQQueueInfos
   Dim QInfo As MSMQ.MSMQQueueInfo
   Dim objQueue As MSMQ.MSMQQueue
   Dim msgOrder As MSMQ.MSMQMessage
   Dim msgDest As MSMQ.MSMQMessage
   Dim StyleFile As String
   Dim docSource As MSXML.DOMDocument
   Dim docStyle As MSXML.DOMDocument
   Dim strResult As String

   On Error GoTo ErrorGenerate

   Set mobjContext = GetObjectContext

   Set objQuery = mobjContext.CreateInstance("MSMQ.MSMQQuery")
   Set msgOrder = mobjContext.CreateInstance("MSMQ.MSMQMessage")

   Set QInfos = objQuery.LookupQueue(Label:="OrderPicking")
   QInfos.Reset
   Set QInfo = QInfos.Next

   If Not IsObject(QInfo) Then
      Generate = cQueueNotFound
      Exit Function
   End If

   Set objQueue = QInfo.Open(MQ_RECEIVE_ACCESS, MQ_DENY_NONE)

   Set msgDest = objQueue.Receive(ReceiveTimeout:=100)

   If msgDest Is Nothing Then
      Generate = cQueueEmpty
      Exit Function
   End If

   OrderNum = msgDest.Label
   strXML = msgDest.Body
```

We first create the appropriate query and message objects, then look for the OrderPicking queue. We must check to see if the queue was found and exit the function if it was not. Assuming the proper queue was located, we open it for receive access without denying any other users access to the queue:

```
Set objQueue = QInfo.Open(MQ_RECEIVE_ACCESS, MQ_DENY_NONE)
```

Next, we retrieve the next message in the queue, checking to be sure a message was retrieved. If so, we extract the message label and body for processing:

```
Set msgDest = objQueue.Receive(ReceiveTimeout:=100)
If msgDest Is Nothing Then
    Generate = cQueueEmpty
    Exit Function
End If

OrderNum = msgDest.Label
strXML = msgDest.Body
```

The name of the style sheet file is passed as a string. We will need to read this file from the server's disk directly. In order to do this, we need to convert from the virtual path name to a physical path on the server's disk. The MapPath method of the ASP Server object will do this conversion for us. To use this method, we will access the intrinsic ASP Server object through our reference to the ObjectContext:

```
StyleFile = mobjContext("Server").MapPath(strStyleFile)
```

The conversion from XML to HTML using an XSL style sheet will be performed by the XML document parser that is part of IE5. In order for this to work, the server must have IE5 installed on it.

For more information on using XML, you can check out a number of Wrox Press books, including Alex Homer's XML IE5 Programmer's Reference (1-861002-57-6).

We created two variables to hold object references of the XML DOMDocument object. One will be used to represent the XML information and the other will represent the XSL file.

We will create an instance of the Microsoft.XMLDOM object using the CreateInstance method of the ObjectContext, and assign that reference to the source variable we created earlier. We will then use this object's loadXML method to read the XML information that we retrieved from the message into the object. We will add the proper XML header to beginning of the file by simply adding it to the string when it is passed in.

```
Set docSource = mobjContext.CreateInstance("Microsoft.XMLDOM")
docSource.loadXML "<?xml version=""1.0""?>" & strXML
```

To load the XSL information, we will need to retrieve it from the file. This was the file name that we passed into the method, which we then converted into a physical path using the MapPath method. Before loading this file we will set the async property of the DOMDocument object to False. This tells the object to load the file completely before returning control back to the application, ensuring that the file is ready to go when we continue processing. The load method performs the same function as the loadXML function did earlier, except it reads the information from a file on disk rather than from a string in memory:

```
' Load the XSL
Set docStyle = mobjContext.CreateInstance("Microsoft.XMLDOM")
docStyle.async = False
docStyle.load StyleFile
```

With both the XML and XSL information properly loaded, we can now apply the XSL to the XML in order to generate the HTML that can be displayed in the browser. We will create a string to hold the string that is generated when the style sheet is applied. The transformNode method of the XML document object will accept an XSL object as a parameter and then apply that style sheet to the data it represents. The results of this are the return value from the method, which we will hold in the strResult variable. Once this has been done, we can send this information directly back to the browser by using the Write method of the intrinsic ASP Response object:

```
On Error Resume Next

strResult = docSource.transformNode(docStyle)

mobjContext("Response").Write strResult
```

Once that has been completed, we can end our method in the same way that we have ended the other ones in the example. If everything works OK, we can return the cQueueOK string, if an error occurs, then the error handler will be called, and we can return the cQueueError string along with the information from the Visual Basic Err object's Description property:

```
Generate = cQueueOK

  Exit Function

ErrorGenerate:

  Generate = cQueueError

End Function
```

After the user validates that the generated pick slip is OK, they will need to notify the system that the books are actually being picked. This notification is performed by sending the order information to the OrderReady queue. This order information consists of the order number and XML description of the order. The ASP page will call the public OrderPicked method, which in turn uses the standard PostQueueMessage function to actually add the message to the OrderReady queue:

```
Public Function OrderPicked(xmlOrder As Variant, OrderNum As Variant) As Variant

  OrderPicked = PostQueueMessage("OrderReady", OrderNum, xmlOrder)

End Function
```

Shipping Component

The final step in the process is to generate a packing slip (manifest) for the order, which will be included with the shipment going to the customer. Once this has been done, the order is ready to go out the door. This step can only be accomplished when the order has been picked and a packing slip is ready to be generated. The application that performs this task is `Shipping.asp`:

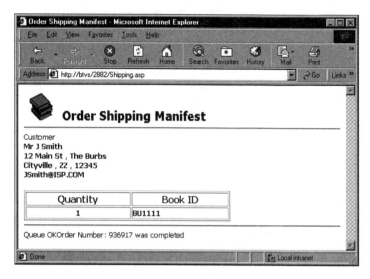

The `Shipping` component contains a single class module called `Manifest` and has the same references as the `Warehouse` component, i.e. it also references Microsoft XML.

The `Generate` method of this component has a similar parameter list to the `Generate` method we looked at for the `Warehouse` component. We'll pass in the XML data from the message, the order number, and the XSL style sheet name to the method. The `strXML` and `OrderNum` variables are passed by reference so that we can use them to return the information to the calling application:

```
Public Function Generate(ByRef strXML As Variant, ByRef OrderNum As Variant, _
                         strStyleFile As Variant) As Variant
```

The business requirements of this component are a bit different than the ones we have looked at already. In order for an order to be processed, it has to be in both the `OrderReady` queue and the `PackingSlip` queue. We will therefore need `MSMQQueue` objects to handle both queues at once:

```
Dim objQuery As MSMQ.MSMQQuery
Dim QInfos As MSMQ.MSMQQueueInfos
Dim QInfo As MSMQ.MSMQQueueInfo
Dim objQPicked As MSMQ.MSMQQueue
Dim objQPacking As MSMQ.MSMQQueue
Dim msgPicked As MSMQ.MSMQMessage
Dim msgPackSlip As MSMQ.MSMQMessage
Dim StyleFile As String
Dim docSource As MSXML.DOMDocument
Dim docStyle As MSXML.DOMDocument
Dim strResult As String

On Error GoTo ErrorGenerate

Set mobjContext = GetObjectContext()

Set objQuery = mobjContext.CreateInstance("MSMQ.MSMQQuery")
```

We will first open the `OrderReady` queue for receive access. If this queue is not found, then we will return an error message to the calling application that indicates that the queue named `OrderReady` was not found. Since we will be peeking for a message first, then want to retrieve that same message later, we need to make sure that no other applications remove messages from the queue. Passing the `MQ_DENY_RECEIVE_SHARE` parameter to the `Open` method does this:

```
Set QInfos = objQuery.LookupQueue(Label:="OrderReady")
QInfos.Reset
Set QInfo = QInfos.Next

If Not IsObject(QInfo) Then
    Generate = cQueueNotFound & ": OrderReady"
    Exit Function
End If

Set objQPicked = QInfo.Open(MQ_RECEIVE_ACCESS, MQ_DENY_RECEIVE_SHARE)
```

The `PackingSlip` queue will be opened using the exact same steps as we used to open the `OrderReady` queue. We again limit share access with `MQ_DENY_RECEIVE_SHARE` to prevent another user from retrieving messages. We will be peeking at messages in the queue to locate the one that matches the order from the `OrderReady` queue and we do not want that order to be disturbed before we can retrieve the message:

```
Set QInfos = objQuery.LookupQueue(Label:="PackingSlip")

QInfos.Reset
Set QInfo = QInfos.Next

If Not IsObject(QInfo) Then
    Generate = cQueueNotFound & ": PackingSlip"
    Exit Function
End If

Set objQPacking = QInfo.Open(MQ_RECEIVE_ACCESS, MQ_DENY_RECEIVE_SHARE)
```

The first step is to peek to see if there is a message waiting in the `OrderReady` queue. If there are no messages in that queue, we know that we can't complete any orders at this time, so we will exit the method:

```
Set msgPicked = objQPicked.Peek(ReceiveTimeout:=100, WantBody:=False)

If msgPicked Is Nothing Then
    Generate = cQueueEmpty
    Exit Function
End If
```

If there is a message waiting in the queue, the next step is to check to see if a message with the same order number is in the `PackingSlip` queue. Since the message `Label` is the same value as the order number, this is very easy to do.

We will want to loop through the contents of the `PackingSlip` queue until we find the message that matches our order number. In order to loop through the queue, we need to have a way to look at the messages in order. Just as with a database cursor, we can use a cursor to move through the message queue. The `PeekCurrent` method will look at the first message in the queue and set the cursor at that point. Since all we are interested in is the message label and not the body, we set the `WantBody` parameter of this method to `False`. This tells MSMQ not to retrieve the contents of the body, thereby speeding up the retrieval.

If there is nothing in this queue, then the loop will be skipped, and the function will be exited with an error message that states that the `PackingSlip` queue is empty. If there is a message in the queue, then we check its `Label` against the `Label` of the message in the `OrderReady` queue. If they match, then we can exit the loop since we have the two messages that we need. If they don't match, we need to peek at the next message in the queue. The `PeekNext` method will move the cursor to the next message and then peek at it. Again, we only want the message label, so the `WantBody` property is set to `False`. This will continue until we find the message that matches, or until we run out of messages in the queue:

```
Set msgPackSlip = objQPacking.PeekCurrent(ReceiveTimeout:=50, WantBody:=False)

Do While Not (msgPicked Is Nothing)
   If msgPackSlip.Label = msgPicked.Label Then
      Exit Do
   Else
      Set msgPackSlip = objQPacking.PeekNext(ReceiveTimeout:=50, WantBody:=False)
   End If
Loop

If msgPicked Is Nothing Then
   Generate = cPackQueueEmpty
   Exit Function
End If
```

Now that we have the two messages that we are interested in, we can retrieve them both from their respective queues. Since the message in the `PackingSlip` queue may not be at the top of the queue, we need to retrieve it from the current cursor position. The `ReceiveCurrent` method will do that for us. With the messages retrieved, their order number and XML data can be assigned to the parameters that were passed into this message. This makes the information available to the calling application.

I'm going to take a slight shortcut in the code. Since I know no physical process is going on in a real warehouse, I will simply take the information from the packing slip message. I know the information originated from the same source. In the real world, mistakes will be made in fulfilling the order, so a production application should check the data from the Order Ready queue to ensure that the books pulled for packing match what is in the packing slip, as the packing slip reflects the placed order.

```
Set msgPicked = objQPicked.Receive(ReceiveTimeout:=10)
Set msgPackSlip = objQPacking.ReceiveCurrent(ReceiveTimeout:=10)

OrderNum = msgPackSlip.Label
strXML = msgPackSlip.Body
```

The final step is to output the information directly to the web browser. We will use the same XSL conversion of XML data into HTML that we looked at in the last section. The primary difference is that we will use a different XSL file to perform the conversion. This file name is passed as a parameter to the method, and stored in the `strStyleFile` variable. This variable is then used to determine the name of the physical file on the server so that it can be loaded:

```
StyleFile = mobjContext("Server").MapPath(strStyleFile)

Set docSource = mobjContext.CreateInstance("Microsoft.XMLDOM")
docSource.loadXML "<?xml version=""1.0""?>" & strXML

' Load the XSL
Set docStyle = mobjContext.CreateInstance("Microsoft.XMLDOM")
docStyle.async = False
docStyle.Load StyleFile

On Error Resume Next

strResult = docSource.transformNode(docStyle)

mobjContext("Response").Write strResult
```

Once all of the processing has been done, we can successfully exit the function. If any error occurs along the way during the function, the code in the `ErrorGenerate` section will be executed. This will return an error message the to calling application, along with more information about the error:

```
  Generate = cQueueOK
  Exit Function

ErrorGenerate:

  Generate = cQueueError & Err.Description

End Function
```

The OrderStatus Component

As the orders flow through the system of queues that make up this application, it would be nice to have a way to view the status of all of the orders at once. To do this, we need to display information about the items in each of the queues in the application. This information could be retrieved at any time, and should not affect the contents of the queue when doing so. `Status.asp` exists as a tool for viewing the contents of the queues at any given time:

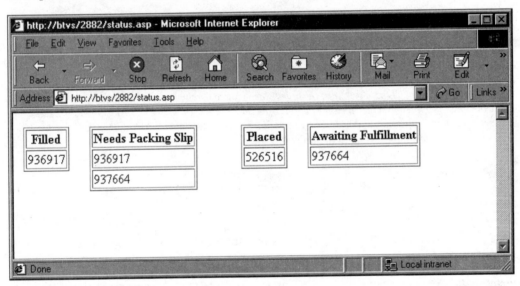

It uses the `OrderStatus` component consisting of a single class called `Status`. By now you should be familiar with how to set it up. All its functionality is contained within a single function:

```
Public Function Display() As Variant

  Dim objResp As ASPTypeLibrary.Response
  Dim objQuery As MSMQ.MSMQQuery
  Dim QInfos As MSMQ.MSMQQueueInfos
  Dim QInfo As MSMQ.MSMQQueueInfo
  Dim objQueue As MSMQ.MSMQQueue
  Dim objMsg As MSMQ.MSMQMessage
  Dim avarQueues As Variant
  Dim varQueueName As Variant
  Dim strStatus As String
```

```
On Error GoTo ErrorDisplay

Set mobjContext = GetObjectContext

Set objResp = mobjContext("Response")

Set objQuery = mobjContext.CreateInstance("MSMQ.MSMQQuery")
```

In the display method, we will be working with the message queues that make up our application. We will also be directly sending the information to the browser through the intrinsic ASP `Response` object. This object is retrieved through the `ObjectContext` reference and stored in a local variable named `objResp`:

```
avarQueues = Array("OrderReady", "PackingSlip", "PendingOrders", "OrderPicking")
```

We will want to look at each queue individually to see which messages are in that queue. Since the code to peek at the messages is identical for each queue, we will want set up one code segment that can look at each queue individually. To do this, we will need an easy way to look at each queue one-by-one. By setting up an array of the queue names, we can then iterate through this array and execute our code for each entry. If we wanted to look at orders in terms of MSMQ queues, we could simply use the MSMQ Explorer. In addition to providing access to this information via a browser, then `Shipping.asp` should provide the user with more descriptive information:

```
objResp.Write "<TABLE WIDTH=95%><TR>"

For Each varQueueName In avarQueues

    Select Case varQueueName

        Case "OrderReady"
            strStatus = "Filled"

        Case "PackingSlip"
            strStatus = "Needs Packing Slip"

        Case "PendingOrders"
            strStatus = "Placed"

        Case "OrderPicking"
            strStatus = "Awaiting Fulfillment"

        Case Else
            strStatus = "Unknown"

    End Select

    objResp.Write "<TD valign=top><TABLE BORDER=1><TR><TH>" & strStatus & _
                "</TH></TR>" & vbCrLf
```

Our presentation will use a table within a table display. The outermost table will span the width of the page and each column in that table will have the table of messages for the particular queue. The `For Each` statement will loop through each element in the `avarQueues` array and set the current value to the `varQueueName` variable. Rather than display the queue name in the table, we assign a slightly more descriptive label to the `strStatus` variable based on the name of the queue using the `Select Case` statement.

This application is focused on learning the use of MSMQ from within an ASP. An interesting step toward building a robust customer service application would be to obtain the queue status as we do here, then sort the information according to the order number. That way, an order that has a message in the Packing Slip queue as well as either the Order Picking or Order Ready queue could display the complete status of the order, e.g., "Order 1: Filled, Awaiting Packing Slip". For simplicity, we'll stick to displaying order status by queue rather than by order.

```
Set QInfos = objQuery.LookupQueue(Label:=varQueueName)
QInfos.Reset
Set QInfo = QInfos.Next

If Not IsObject(QInfo) Then
    Display = cQueueNotFound
    Exit Function
End If

Set objQueue = QInfo.Open(MQ_PEEK_ACCESS, MQ_DENY_NONE)
```

The queues will be opened with the access parameter set to MQ_PEEK_ACCESS since all we are interested in is peeking at the messages in the queue, not retrieving them:

```
Set objMsg = objQueue.PeekCurrent(ReceiveTimeout:=100, WantBody:=False)

If objMsg Is Nothing Then
    objResp.Write "<TR><TD>Queue Empty</TD></TR>" & vbCrLf
Else

    Do While Not (objMsg Is Nothing)
        objResp.Write "<TR><TD>" & objMsg.Label & "</TD></TR>" & vbCrLf
        Set objMsg = objQueue.PeekNext(ReceiveTimeout:=50, WantBody:=False)
    Loop

End If

objResp.Write "</TABLE></TD>" & vbCrLf

Next

objResp.Write "</TR></TABLE>" & vbCrLf
```

We will use a loop that is very similar to the one we looked at in the previous section. The first step is to do a PeekCurrent to look at the first message in the queue. If there is no message found, then we can output that the queue is empty. If there is a message there, then we will want to loop through outputting the message label to the Response object and then checking for the next message. This will continue until there are no more messages in the queue. Once that has happened, we will need to move onto the next queue name in the avarQueues array:

```
Display = cQueueOK

Exit Function

errorDisplay:

Display = cQueueError & Err.Description

End Function
```

Finally, we will notify that the function was completed successfully. If any errors occurred and are trapped by the error handler, then the standard cQueueError message, along with the Visual Basic description will be passed back to the calling application.

That's it for the components themselves. Compile the DLLs and place them in an MTS package. However, before we can test our components we need to set up the queues themselves on our server.

Setting up the Queues

Adding the necessary queue is very straightforward. We know that we need to add four queues to our MSMQ server:

- ❑ PendingOrders
- ❑ OrderPicking
- ❑ OrderReady
- ❑ PackingSlip

To add a queue, open the Microsoft Message Queue Explorer:

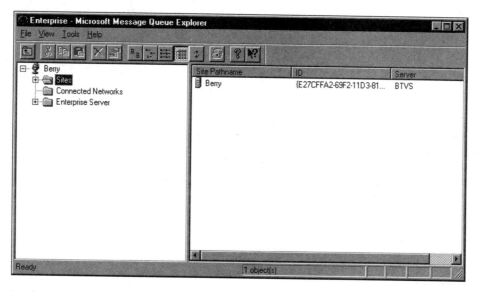

For simplicity's sake, we will add all the queues locally, although it is more likely that you would have them dispersed across the network.

Expand the Sites node until you reach your defined MSMQ Server (in my case Berry) and right-click the node. This will bring up a pop-up menu:

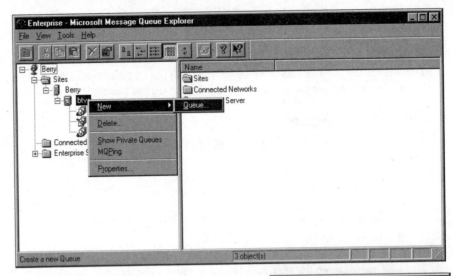

Select New | Queue... from the pop-up menu and a dialog box will appear asking you to specify the queue's name:

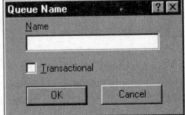

Enter Pending Orders, leave the Transactional check box empty, and press OK. This will add the PendingOrders queue to the list of queue on your computer:

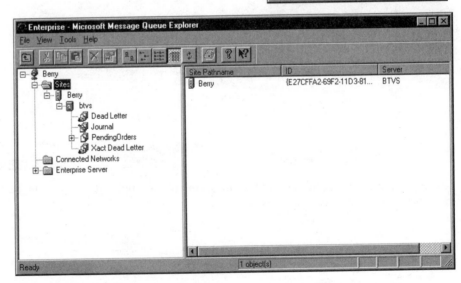

Follow the same steps for the other queues.

Trying it out

The components that we have created here can be combined together to create the sample application. The steps in the application itself include:

- ❑ Use the `OrderEntry.asp` page to place an order.
- ❑ You can then process the order validation by using the `ValidateOrder.asp` page.
- ❑ This will take you on a series of links where you generate a merchandise pick list (`PickList.asp`)
- ❑ Then you generate the shipping information (`Shipping.asp`)
- ❑ At any time you can display the contents of the queues (`Status.asp`)

Summary

In this chapter, we have taken a look at the Microsoft Message Queue Server system. MSMQ allows us to communicate between applications even when those applications are not running at the same time or the connection between applications is unreliable. The easiest way to think of it is as e-mail for applications. The MSMQ system allows for an interconnected network of systems that can pass messages back and forth between them. The system figures out where a message needs to go, and makes sure that the message gets there. MSMQ is directly usable from ASP as well as ASP components through its COM interface.

In this chapter, we specifically looked at:

- ❑ What MSMQ is and what it can do
- ❑ Why you should use messaging technology in your application, and when you shouldn't
- ❑ How to interact with MSMQ using COM objects
- ❑ How components can be built to interact with MSMQ
- ❑ How to use MSMQ components in an ASP application

In the next chapter, we will be looking at other types of components and elements. There are many other types of data sources and systems that we can interact with using components. Some of these include Microsoft Exchange, the Active Directory through ADSI, Microsoft Site Server, and even more XML. The integration of these types of systems with ASP through components will give your web applications even greater flexibility and functionality moving forward.

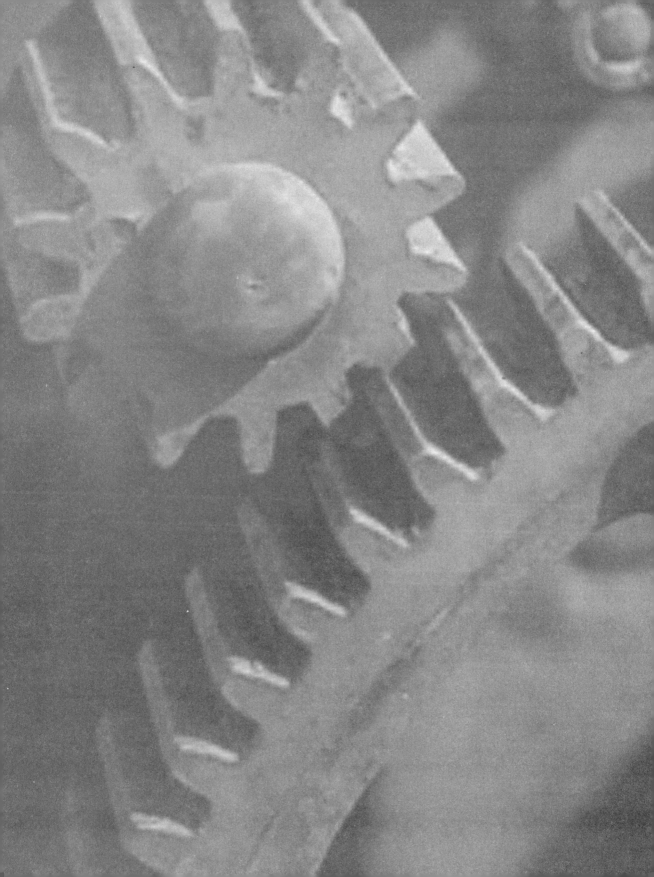

Interacting with Directories via ADSI

In Chapter Four, we discussed the way that Microsoft's **Universal Data Access** initiative provides us with access to many different kinds of data and information. This is achieved via the **Microsoft Data Access Components** kit (MDAC), using the common interface technology of **ActiveX Data Objects**, or **ADO**. However, ADO is a general-purpose library designed to allow access to any information store—particularly relational stores. As such it is not that well suited to directories, which tend to have a more tree-like, **hierarchical** structure. In this chapter, we're going to look at how to use ADSI, the Active Directory Services Interfaces, which is similar to ADO but designed to access hierarchical directories. In particular, it is ADSI that you will normally use to read or modify the new **Active Directory**, a directory service that is introduced with Windows 2000.

Although the focus of this chapter is on ADSI rather than Active Directory, we're going to start with a brief look at what the Active Directory actually is, since that will also give us a better idea of what directories are and how directories differ from databases. Then we'll see how we can build components that use ADSI to access directories and perform real work. The two samples we will develop in this chapter are designed to browse the available directories and perform searching.

So, this chapter covers:

- ❑ An introduction to directories and directory services, in particular the Active Directory (AD)
- ❑ A look at what the Active Directory Service Interfaces (ADSI) are and how they work
- ❑ Some examples of how ADSI is used within components, and the things we can do with ADSI
- ❑ Two sample components that help us to understand and work with ADSI

We'll start with a look at what the Active Directory is, and why it is so important.

What is the Active Directory?

The **Active Directory** (AD) sounds like a super, new technology. However, it is really only a long-awaited implementation of a technology that has been in use on other operating systems and in different environments for some time. I don't mean to belittle the efforts that Microsoft has made to get to their current position with AD—as we'll see shortly, Windows evolved along a path that started from a very different place than the other enterprise-level operating systems.

To begin, let's consider some basic questions, in an attempt to make some sense out of all these new acronyms and phrases. We need to answer four questions:

- ❏ What is a Directory?
- ❏ What is a Directory Service (DS)?
- ❏ What is the Active Directory (AD)?
- ❏ What are the Active Directory Service Interfaces (ADSI)?

All About Directories

To answer these questions about directories, we'll take a couple of real-life examples. We'll talk about phone books and company accounts.

What is a Directory?

The simple answer is that a **directory** is somewhere to keep information – primarily information that is useful (though it doesn't have to be). So, that large cardboard box you keep next to your desk into which you toss all the invoices, statements, delivery advice notes and other papers, is a directory. It stores useful and valuable information about your business.

However, a directory itself is really only useful if you can retrieve the information it stores, and preferably retrieve it quickly and efficiently. A telephone directory is an obvious example of a good directory model. It's easy to access and retrieve the information as long as you know the person's name and at least part of their address. On the other hand, our cardboard box isn't a good example—especially if the papers you want are somewhere near the bottom of the pile.

That's the simple answer to what a directory is—but it's probably left you wondering what the difference is between a directory and a database. After all, isn't a database also an information store that is only useful if you can retrieve the information it stores?

In reality, the difference between a directory and a database isn't that precise. And to some extent it's probably not worth worrying about it too much. What we need to know is that there are some data stores (such as Microsoft Access and SQL Server) which you will need to use ADO to access, and other data stores (such as Active Directory and the Exchange Server Directory) for which ADO is not really suitable, or for which there is no OLE DB provider.

For these other data stores, which have a tree-like, hierarchical structure, if there is an ADSI provider available for it, you should use ADSI because it assumes a hierarchical directory structure. An ADSI provider, by the way, serves a similar purpose as an OLE DB provider. It's the set of COM objects which expose the ADSI interfaces, and which are used to access a particular directory.

Having said all that, there are some general characteristics that tend to distinguish directories from relational databases. Apart from the fact that directories tend to be hierarchical, some of the other characteristics are listed below.

- ❑ In directories, it tends to be more obvious what the objects are that information is being stored about—e.g. computers and resources on the network, or employees of a company. The whole structure of the directory is based on these objects.

- ❑ Directories are usually optimized to be read more often than they are written to. A phone directory is a good example of this: people look up phone numbers a lot more often than phone numbers are changed. (If that wasn't true, paper phone directories wouldn't be very useful!)

- ❑ Directories often have quite sophisticated search facilities—for example Active Directory is perfectly well able to handle a request for all the users with account names that begin with d or e and which haven't logged in since last Tuesday.

- ❑ Directories are often replicated (the telephone company usually prints lots of copies of the phone books) for easier access. It also doesn't matter too much if some replicas get out of synch with others for a short time, as long as all copies are eventually updated. (There may be some out-of-date phone books circulating but that doesn't matter too much as people can always ring directory enquiries if they are stuck.)

- ❑ Directories don't usually have sophisticated transaction processing, in the way that relational databases often do.

I should stress, however, that these differences are guidelines only, not rigid rules. 'Directory' and 'database' aren't the sort of terms that you can give rigid, absolute, definitions of, and there are going to be many information stores in existence that have some directory characteristics and some database characteristics. Whether you use ADSI, ADO, or some other tool, to access those information stores will depend on what tools and providers are available.

You'll notice that I've used the example of the phone directory several times. There's a good reason for this; phone directories are an excellent example of a prototypical directory, and you will find that the computer-based directories we are going to explore share much of their behavior with the basic, paper-based, phone book.

Directory Design Fundamentals

Of course, designing a good directory means that you need to know up front what kind of access will be required. For example, if we know a phone number, and want to find the matching address, a normal phone book isn't any help at all. In this situation, it's about as much good as our cardboard box. So, simply putting things in alphabetical order isn't always the best option.

If we're going to sort out our company paperwork problem, we probably need to file the papers in separate files for each month, each arranged in alphabetical order by supplier. That way, we stand a chance of finding a specific item given a month or a supplier name, without having to look at every item.

Indexing Directories

Ideally when using a directory, you would be able to find any item, given any of the different bits of information it contains. In our office paperwork example we would like to be able to search by date, by supplier, by product, by value, etc. For directories stored on bits of paper, this type of capability means that we have to resort to **indexing** our directory. For directories stored on a computer, we need to provide software that can search through the directory. This searching will normally be a lot more efficient if the directory is once again indexed in some way.

Take a look at the simple diagram that follows. This shows one way that we can provide a search facility for an item of stored information.

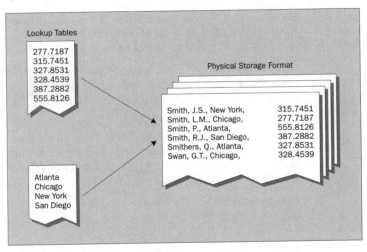

This is, of course, how most relational databases store information already. They can therefore provide the basis for a computerized directory system quite easily. However, we're not really interested in the way that this is implemented internally, only in the perceived structure and access that is exposed to us when we come to use it.

In terms of our earlier phonebook analogy, we could provide, say, a lookup table for towns and cities. This would allow users to obtain a list of all the pages that contained entries for a particular town or city. Of course, this would probably be a waste of time because of the huge amount of information stored on each page of a phone book. Taken to the extreme, it would be like including an alphabetical index in a dictionary.

So, a directory requires careful design, based on knowledge of both the **type** and **volume** of information it will store, and the way that it will be **searched** and **accessed**. In some cases, a directory differs from other types of data stores in that there are few or no indexes maintained on it, and so finding information depends on using the physical order of the entries or relying on the computer to do a brute force search. In the case of a residential phone book, this order is the alphabetic order of the subscriber's last names. Microsoft's Active Directory is a lot more sophisticated in this regard, because it indexes quite a large number of properties.

What is a Directory Service?

So, now that we know what a directory is, what is a **directory service** (DS)? Well, calling the phone company's directory enquiries line to get a phone number is a perfect example of using a directory service. You get someone else to do the searching for you. In this example, we are carrying out a **synchronous** search. It's no good putting the phone down after giving the name and address of the person we're looking for—we have to wait for the operator to come back with the number.

However, if we dump our cardboard box containing the office paperwork in the back of the truck and take it to the accountant each month, we can just phone them when we want to retrieve some item of information from it. Best of all, we can get them to call us back once they've found it. This is a perfect example of an **asynchronous** directory searching service (although it would probably cost a lot of money in accountant's fees).

As you've probably guessed, in computing terms a directory service is a software layer that provides access and search features for a computer-based directory of information. Sometimes the directory service includes the directory itself, other times you might write a software layer to extract information from some data store that already exists. Examples of directory services include the new **Active Directory** from Microsoft, the existing **Novell Directory Services** (NDS), and **StreetTalk** from Banyan. All three provide an implementation of a directory to store information about the computer and its environment, and software to access and maintain that directory.

Besides allowing convenient access to the information in a directory, a directory service might also provide suitable security around the data, ensuring the users are only able to read or modify data where they have been authorized to do so and have supplied appropriate credentials.

Of course, most networks already contain other types of directory. For example, most will contain a messaging and collaboration application such as Microsoft Exchange, Microsoft Mail, Lotus Notes, Domino, or cc:Mail. All of these products contain their own directories of recipients, users, mailing lists, etc. in their own specific formats. They also all tend to have their own directory services that make the information available to the correct people or applications in the correct format. Unfortunately, here, the 'correct' format often means some proprietary format that makes it hard for other users to write applications to access the data. It also makes it more difficult to code up applications that need to access more than one directory, as you need to learn more than one proprietary format in order to do so.

What is the Active Directory?

In this chapter we'll be taking a closer look at Microsoft's implementation of their new **Active Directory** (AD) and the associated **Active Directory Services Interfaces**. These are only just becoming available on Windows, despite that fact that other operating systems have used directory services for many years. The main reason for this is the way in which Windows has evolved from a simple graphical environment in its early years, to an enterprise-level operating system with Windows NT and Windows 2000.

Active Directory is a directory that stores all the information that controls the operation of a domain. This includes which computers are members of a domain, all of the domain users' accounts with their security permissions, trust relationships, etc. You might wonder what is so revolutionary about that, after all NT4 stores all the security and user account information in a directory. The answer is that NT4 used a proprietary directory that was only accessible using the relevant Windows API functions. By contrast, Active Directory is compliant with the LDAP standard. LDAP is an industry-wide standard protocol that specifies how access to a directory is performed. If a directory is LDAP-compliant then it can be accessed using any one of the numerous standard LDAP SDKs, and it is possible to write clients that can access the directory without a detailed knowledge of any API specific to that directory—all you need is a knowledge of LDAP. LDAP also requires that directories should have some fairly sophisticated functionality. For example, they must support searching, even if a client specifies quite complex search queries.

The other key new feature about Active Directory is that as well as being *the* directory of network resources and of your domain, it doubles up as a general-purpose directory. In other words, you can add any other information to it that you feel might usefully be stored there.

Besides this, Active Directory does significantly improve the domain model, for example by implementing Kerberos security (an industry-wide standard that is considered superior to NTLM's security mechanisms), and by allowing the formation of treelike hierarchies of domains.

> By this point you'll have noticed the similarity between the names 'Active Directory' and 'Active Directory Service Interfaces'. Although these sound very similar, remember that they are different. ADSI is a standard set of COM interfaces and objects that implement these interfaces, which allow access to a number of different directories. Active Directory is a particular directory which can be accessed using ADSI.

Why is Active Directory Only Just Appearing?

When Windows first appeared, it was designed to provide a graphical file management service and a 'desktop' paradigm on single-user machines. The early PC was predominantly a single-user, stand-alone system, and it was only over time that they began to be networked together. Then, Windows 3.1 evolved into Windows for Workgroups (3.11), which included the first rudimentary networking features built into Windows.

At the same time, Microsoft and IBM were working on a project to create an enterprise operating system with a graphical user interface, based on Posix®. This project went through many changes, and finally surfaced as IBM's OS/2 and Microsoft's **Windows NT**. However, being developed from a workgroup concept, it used the **domain** model to provide a security and management boundary. While domains *can* be linked together, the core information about each domain (and hence the network within that domain) is still stored only within the domain.

This is totally unlike many other operating systems, particularly those with a history of being used in a network environment, which tend to store the core information about each machine on that machine, while information about the network itself is stored in servers around the network. These servers residing on the network contain a directory of the network and its resources, and replicate the information between each other, making it available to all the machines on the network. This is the concept of a **network directory**, like that which is provided by Novell as part of the Novell Directory Services.

So, adding Active Directory to Windows does, to some extent, imply a change in the networking model, which is why it is only now starting to appear as part of Windows 2000 (formerly Windows NT5). Windows 2000 can still operate in a domain that is controlled by NT4 domain controllers, but in order to run and get the full benefits of Active Directory you need domain controllers that are running Windows 2000.

What Does the Active Directory Store?

The next point to consider is what *kind* of information we want to store in our directory. Obviously, if we are going to replace NT4's proprietary domain database with Active Directory, then Active Directory will need to store all the things that are no longer stored by what was the **Primary Domain Controller** (PDC). Active Directory becomes *the* data store for domain setup, holding all of the domain user and group account information, and their policies and rights within the network. I should emphasize here that Active Directory is specifically a domain-based directory. That is to say, it stores information related to the domain as a whole. By default it doesn't store much information that is local to the member workstations of the domain, such as *local* user/group account details. These are still stored on individual machines. Having said that, we've indicated that AD is also a general-purpose directory, so you can add any information you want to it, and you might choose to replicate local machine information in AD. You may, for example, wish to do so in case a machine fails, so that you can easily recover such information.

Keeping these details in a directory also makes it easier for other machines to locate resources. For example, if a program running on one machine wants to use the services of a component that it doesn't have installed locally, it can use the directory to find out which machine has the component and request it from there. If we store user profiles (such as desktop settings and preferences) in the directory, users can log on to any machine and retrieve their profile automatically.

Finally, the directory should also be able to store messaging and collaboration information, as held in any of the mail or workgroup applications (such as Lotus Notes or Microsoft Exchange). For example, it could provide access to all users' e-mail addresses. At the time of writing Microsoft's Exchange Directory is an LDAP-compliant directory, but is a separate directory. Microsoft have, however, made it clear that they intend to release a new version of Exchange Server, in which the Exchange Directory will become a part of Active Directory. It's the same story for the Site Server membership and personalization directory (which since Site Server 3.0 has been a separate LDAP directory).

What are the Active Directory Services Interfaces (ADSI)?

In addition to the Active Directory, Microsoft has released the Active Directory Services Interfaces. These are a set of COM interface definitions, which are designed to allow access to any directory service. There are also some system DLLs and several COM components that are needed to make the whole thing work.

By any directory service, I'm not talking just about LDAP-compatible directories, but—in principle—any directory at all. For example, in a typical network administration duties will involve more than just managing the domain's groups and users. You may also administer the web server, ftp server, mail or workgroup server, etc. ADSI is a set of definitions that permit you to access these different services using a series of components and interface method calls, much in the same way that ADO provides a set of objects for interacting with data stores of different varieties.

Of course, the interface definitions alone aren't enough. We also need implementations of the interfaces. In other words we need some components. Here ADSI works in much the same way as ADO/OLE DB—using providers. An ADSI provider is a set of components that expose the ADSI interfaces and which allow access to a particular directory or set of directories.

ADSI is very much a client side API (in the sense that it can be used in components or programs, but these are still clients of the directories that they are accessing). The ADSI components that you create are all in-process components. Internally, these COM components will contact the directory service—which may involve going across the network. This means that, rather than having to physically sit in front of each of these servers to access information from them or administer them, ADSI allows you to access their data remotely. More importantly, ADSI also makes all of these facilities available to other programs. This becomes increasingly important with the rise in popularity of distributed applications.

Most importantly of all, the fact that ADSI comprises one **common** set of interfaces designed to access any directory means that you can write a client application, for example an Active Server Page, which can get information from multiple directories using ADSI, only using the one single API. You do not have to learn a separate API for each directory.

When we consider the number of directories that are already available on many networks, including details for the operating system users and groups, mail servers, and groupware products, it's easy to see the advantages that ADSI provides by unifying these in one set of interfaces.

> **ADSI helps solve problems such as users having multiple logons and different user interfaces, and administrators having to manage (or cope without much of the functionality of) these different directories and services.**

This versatility is provided via ADSI **providers**, of which there are many available. As you'll have gathered, these are essentially COM objects implementing interfaces, and which allow communication between a client and a particular directory service. It is these components that handle all the communication with the directory service—they sit between you and the directory service, and in effect pretend to be the directory service, while passing any requests you make to the components on to the directory service. You communicate with the component using the ADSI interfaces. The component communicates with the directory service using whatever API that directory service uses—and which you now, as the writer of the clients, do not need to know.

ADSI permits this functionality because there are a standard set of COM properties and methods that all ADSI objects must expose through the usual ADSI interfaces, which allow navigation and management of the directory tree and of the objects in it. (These are similar to, though not the same as the properties exposed by individual directory objects, which we meet later.)

Although I said that in principle ADSI should allow access to any directory, you can only access directories for which an ADSI provider is available. Microsoft has written several ADSI providers, and third parties may also write their own in order to allow access to their own directories using ADSI. The diagram illustrates how the process works with the providers Microsoft have written.

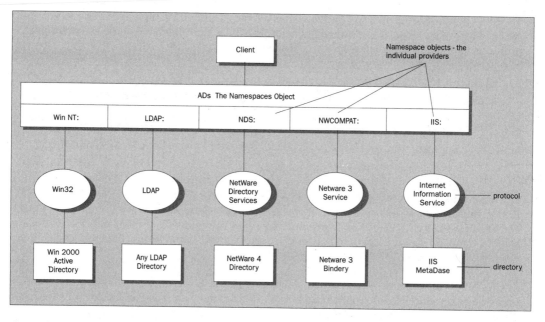

Beneath the client, we can see a level that exposes a number of providers. This is referred to as the **Namespaces** object, although you may also see it referred to as the **ADSI router**. It has the pathname ADs: It is not associated with a particular directory; rather it contains all the ADSI providers installed on your computer as children. By this means, it's possible to some extent to extend out the directory hierarchy so that all the directories with ADSI providers on your system can appear as branches of an apparent super-directory. It is beneath the Namespaces object that we see the different ADSI providers; these are the individual **Namespace** objects that permit access to the directories.

The three main ADSI providers that we'll meet in this chapter are the LDAP, WinNT and IIS providers. We'll take a look at these next.

LDAP

The LDAP provider allows you to access any LDAP directory. This is particularly important to us as both Active Directory and Exchange are accessed through LDAP. LDAP stands for Lightweight Directory Access Protocol, and its purpose is as a protocol to define how directories should be exposed to the outside world—thereby unifying directory access. So, "why do we need ADSI?" I hear you cry. Well, to a large degree the concepts behind LDAP and ADSI are very similar. It's how they're implemented that varies.

The major difference between ADSI and LDAP is that ADSI is defined using COM, and is a relatively high level SDK. ADSI can be accessed from any language that supports COM (Visual Basic, VC++, ASP, etc.) and is object oriented in its approach. The LDAP API, however, is a set of C function calls. While it is an open standard (approved by the Internet Engineering Task Force, the IETF), these lower level C function calls are harder to access from other environments, so Microsoft created a wrapper around them. This wrapper is the ADSI LDAP provider, and is perfect for those who don't want to make the lower level calls.

The other difference is that ADSI is a client-side API, the ADSI COM components that you will use are, as we've already mentioned, in-process components. LDAP, on the other hand, deals with the actual protocols for sending information around the network.

> The ability to connect to the Active Directory using LDAP C function calls can confuse some people, and the ability to do this is completely separate from the facilities provided by ADSI.

In addition, there are also other ADSI providers for directories that are not LDAP compliant.

WinNT

Having met the LDAP provider, we can now see an obvious problem. While Active Directory and Exchange may be exposed using LDAP, if you are running a network based on Windows NT4 there is no equivalent to the Active Directory. In this case, the WinNT provider allows you to access information about computers, user accounts and network resources as if they were maintained in a single directory, despite the directories not being LDAP compliant.

In effect, the WinNT provider looks round your network and gathers information from all the machines on it. It then presents this information to the ADSI client as if it were a single directory. By this means, you can administer NT4 networks as if they have a directory similar to Active Directory. While it is limited in functionality compared with Active Directory, the WinNT provider does allow basic administration for an NT4 domain. In fact, even in Windows 2000 the WinNT provider does play a role, since it allows access to some local machine information and resources, such as NT Services and local user accounts, which are not stored by default in Active Directory.

IIS

Now we've looked at the LDAP and WinNT providers, you can probably guess that the IIS provider allows you access to resources within Internet Information Server. It permits the control of web management tasks, such as the specifying the permitted number of concurrent users, which services start at start up, log files and directory browsing options.

IIS uses a Jet style database file called the **metabase** to store much of the Web, FTP and other site configuration information. It is the IIS ADSI provider that makes the contents of the metabase available through ADSI.

Other ADSI Providers

There are additional ADSI providers, not covered here, that make other directory information available. These include one for Novell NetWare Directory Services, Novell Directory Services and one for X500 compliant directories. Here is a sneak preview of a page from the sample application you'll see later in the chapter, showing a typical list of ADSI providers installed on a machine. This screenshot was taken on a machine running Windows 2000 beta 3 but the same providers will normally be present on NT4.

In this chapter, we're going to be using the WinNT and LDAP ADSI providers for our examples, since these are the providers that you'll probably find yourself using most often. However, the only provider we'll look at in any sort of detail is the WinNT provider but all the principles of ADSI apply to any provider, so you will find that once you know how to manipulate directory objects using the WinNT and LDAP providers, you'll be able to do the same for any other directory.

> *The WinNT provider, incidentally, is the one standard provider that you'll find you'll be able to use on just about any machine in an NT4 or W2K domain that is running Windows 9x, NT4 or W2K, and has ADSI installed. Note also that the LDAP provider will be present on NT4, but you won't be able to use it unless you have an LDAP directory installed. If you are running a Windows 2000 domain controller, then that's not a problem since Active Directory will be installed. Otherwise, you'll only be able to use the LDAP provider if some other LDAP directory is present—such as the Exchange Server Directory, the Site Server membership directory or Netscape Directory Server. However, we won't be covering these directories in this chapter.*

To see what's really involved we need to look a bit deeper at the actual structure of accessing the data from a Windows NT machine using this provider. While we are at it, we'll also briefly look at how we can access other directories as well for the sake of completeness.

Interfaces Syntax

the Active Directory Service Interfaces allow us to unify the many
ory systems that may already exist. We have also seen how Windows 2000
rectory instance (the Windows 2000 Active Directory) to hold Windows-
can be accessed using LDAP or the ADSI LDAP provider.

ADSI object: **container** and **leaf** objects. To help understand these, we can compare
s file system. A container object is an object that contains other objects, in the same
an contain specific files or other folders. The leaf objects are like the files themselves in
contain other objects. However, here the analogy breaks down, in that—unlike folders—
er objects can additionally store their own information. So in one way, an ADSI container
e a folder and a file combined together.

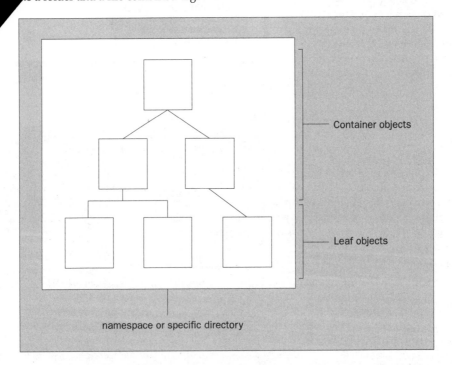

Starting from the ADSI router at the top of the tree, ADs:, we can burrow down into any of the directories
to extract and (in most cases) modify the information that directory contains. In this sense, it's rather like
working with the familiar ActiveX Data Objects (ADO), where we have a common interface model that
can access all kinds of different data sources. The one major difference between ADSI and ADO being that
the ADSI interface locates an item in any of the directories using a string called the **ADsPath**, while ADO
normally uses some SQL syntax to effectively search for an object given the values of certain fields. The
ADsPath is just analogous to pathname of a file.

Using this path we are able to gain access to the objects and manipulate them, just like we could in DOS or Windows. So, for example, going back to the file system metaphor, this chapter you are reading is stored under the following pathname on my computer:

```
c:\wrox\writing\aspcomponents\chapter10\finalversion.doc
```

My C: drive is the equivalent to the appropriate namespace, WinNT:, LDAP:, or IIS:, and by going through the folders—which are like container objects—wrox, writing, aspcomponents and chapter10, I can get to the leaf object, which is finalversion.doc.

Just to make life a little harder, however, each of the directory services can have a different syntax. For example, to access Windows NT4 (or Windows 2000, without LDAP) we use the WinNT provider, so the ADsPath for a user (another leaf object) will be in the format:

```
WinNT://domain_name/user_name
```

So, for example, at Wrox I might be:

```
WinNT://wrox/alexh
```

However, the LDAP provider uses the common X400 naming protocol within a URN format, so the ADsPath to a mail server account will be of the form:

```
LDAP://servername/uid=user_id,ou=organizational_unit,o=organization
```

For example, my mail account on the Wrox1 mail server is followed by my account details, which include the user id of alexh, in the webdev group, within the Wrox.com domain:

```
LDAP://wrox1/uid=alexh,ou=webdev,o=wrox.com
```

> Note that the LDAP provider, following the LDAP standard, uses a construction for the pathname that is completely different from the WinNT provider. They are organized in different orders of specificity. The path gets more specific from left to right in WinNT, while it gets less specific in LDAP.

To learn more about ADSI, why not pick up a copy of one of the following books from Wrox Press ADSI CDO Programming with ASP *(ISBN 1-86001-90-8),* ADSI ASP Programmer's Reference *(ISBN 1-861001-69-x), or* Professional ADSI Development *(ISBN 1-861002-262).*

ADSI Schemas

The standard set of COM properties and methods that all ADSI objects must expose through the usual ADSI interfaces allow navigation and management of the directory tree and of the objects in it. (We shall come to these shortly.) Unfortunately, since ADSI supplies a standard set of interfaces intended to be used by any directory, we have a problem: there is no way that the people who designed those interfaces could have anticipated every property that might ever need to be stored in a directory object. For example, one of the interfaces is IADsUser. This defines automation properties for a lot of the information that might want to be stored for a user—such as full name, department, telephone number, time of last login, etc. However, if you run a publishing company and you have user accounts for all your authors, you might want to store a list of books written by each user, and IADsUser would not define that. So, we need a way that we can add new properties other than the standard ones defined by the interfaces. There are two parts to this. Firstly, we need a method that let's you get at any named property. There are a couple of methods aimed at this: Get(), GetEx(), Put() and PutEx() are exposed by the IADs interface—a basic interface that is exposed by all ADSI directory objects. Secondly, we need some way of finding out what the properties that are available for a certain type of directory object actually are. That's where the **schema** comes in.

The schema is a set of objects in the directory that describe what properties can be stored in other objects. We're not going to go into schemas in too much detail, but you'll normally find all the schema objects in a special container in the directory known as the schema container. There are class objects, which expose the interface IADsClass, and which give details of the classes of object that can be stored in the directory (eg. users, computers, etc.) There is one class object for each class, and it gives a list of the properties that objects of that class can implement. There are actually two such lists—one for **mandatory properties** and one for **optional properties**. As you might guess, mandatory properties are ones that must have a value in every instance of that class, while optional properties mean that instances can, but do not have to, have a value for the property.

Also in the schema container, you'll find **property objects**, which expose the interface IADsProperty, and **syntax objects**, which expose the interface IADsSyntax. These objects give details of how information is stored for each property—for example they might tell you that a list of books is an array of strings, while a photo property must contain a bitmap.

The great thing about schemas is that they make ADSI a very flexible environment. Some providers support something known as **schema extension**, which means that we can change the values in a schema object in exactly the same way as we can in any of the ordinary item objects. This means that we can programmatically change the type of information that is allowed to be stored in the directory. Active Directory stores schema extensions, although there are some fairly strong restrictions to stop you from accidentally invalidating the data that's already in the directory, however the WinNT provider does not offer this support. We won't be considering schema extension in this book, though it is important to be aware that it is possible.

By the way, one thing you might notice from the above explanation is that we've started using the term *property* in two different senses. Firstly, in the sense that components have automation properties, which you will get to by using statements like Object.PropertyName in your code. Secondly, in the sense that items in directories have properties—which are not necessarily exposed as automation properties by any COM component. This might seem confusing, but usually it'll be obvious which meaning of 'Property' we are using.

The Property Cache

We've indicated that when using ADSI you may be talking to a directory that resides on another computer on your network. If every time you try to read or set some piece of information (normally a property on one of the objects in the directory), a call had to go out over the network, the performance of client applications would be pretty bad. To get round this, each ADSI COM object that wraps a directory object has something called a **property cache**. This is a local copy of all the data for the corresponding directory object. It means that most of the time you will simply be reading or writing to this local data, which is held in-process, so access is very fast. Then every so often, you can copy the entire cache back to the directory in one go, or update the cache from the directory when you want. When we come to look at the IADs interface we'll see that it has methods to allow you to do this.

ADSI Versions

At the time of writing, ADSI is at version 2.5. If you are running Windows 2000, you will have ADSI supplied with the operating system (though if you are running a beta of Windows 2000 it may be a beta of ADSI too). If you are running Windows NT4 or Windows 9x, you can download ADSI from

```
http://www.microsoft.com/ntserver/nts/downloads/other/ADSI25/default.asp
```

If you want to develop VB or C++ code that uses ADSI, you will also need the ADSI SDK, available from the same URL.

The ADSI Interfaces

Each container or object in a Namespace exposes one or more interfaces, which we can use when programming in any COM-enabled language. In Visual Basic, we treat these as normal **automation server** objects, and we use them as we do any other OLE Automation interface.

All objects within the directory expose an interface named IADs. This provides every object with six properties and seven methods that provide some basic information about this object.

ADSI 2.5 IADs Interface Properties

Property Name	Description
Name	The name of the object.
ADsPath	A string that describes the path to the object. The ADsPath is in most cases unique and serves to identify this object
Class	A string containing the class type (object type) of this object.
GUID	A unique identifier for the class type of this object. This property is not always implemented.
Parent	A string containing the ADsPath of the parent container of this object
Schema	A string containing the ADsPath of a class schema object which contains information describing the class of this object

ADSI 2.5 IADs Interface Methods

Method Name	Description
GetInfo()	Retrieves the values of the attributes of the object and puts them into the local property cache where they can be read and, in the case of read/write properties, changed.
GetInfoEx()	Similar to GetInfo() but allows optimization of performance: you can specify which particular values you want instead of just getting all of them.
SetInfo()	Updates the contents of the directory with the values in the property cache, including any changes that have been made to read/write properties.
Get()	Retrieves the value of a single property for an object from the local property cache.
GetEx()	Similar to Get() but retrieves the value in a slightly different format
Put()	Sets the value of a single property for an object in the property cache. Note this only affects the local cache. You also need to call SetInfo() to copy the changes back to the directory itself.
PutEx()	Similar to Put(), but contains more options appropriate to multi-valued properties, for example you can use PutEx() to add a value to or remove a value from the list of values already present

Container objects also support a second interface, IADsContainer. This helps manage tasks related to navigating down the directory tree, as well as to the object lifecycle, such as creating, deleting or moving objects—this is usually done by calling the methods of the IADsContainer interface on the relevant parent object. IADsContainer adds two more properties and five more methods (in addition some Container objects will have a third property Count):

ADSI 2.5 IADsContainer Interface Properties

Property Name	Description
Filter	Allows you to restrict the results from enumerating children of this object to those children of certain classes. The filter value is an array of strings that defines each class to include. For example, a filter value of Array("Computer", "User") will limit the retrieved objects to only **Computer** and **User** objects. The default value of " " causes all objects to be returned.
Hints	Allows optimization of network access by indicating that we are only interested in certain properties on objects, so only these properties need to be loaded.
Count	Returns the number of children of the container that are of class given by the Filter property. Note that this property is not always implemented.

ADSI 2.5 IADsContainer Interface Methods

Method Name	Description
GetObject()	Returns an interface pointer to the ADSI object for which the ADsPath and the Class name of the object were supplied as parameters.
Create()	Creates a new object of a specified type within the current container of the directory.
Delete()	Deletes the specified object or container from the directory.
CopyHere()	Copies an object or container as specified by an ADsPath to the current container, as long as it is within the same directory namespace.
MoveHere()	Moves an object or container as specified by an ADsPath to the current container, as long as it is within the same directory namespace. This method can also be used to rename an object that is a child of the container.

There are many other interfaces provided by ADSI, specific to the different types of objects in a namespace. For example, in the WinNT provider, each User object exposes the IADsUser interface as well as the default IADs interface. Likewise, each NT Service object (such as the Content Indexer service) exposes the IADsService, IADsServiceOperations and IADs interfaces, while each Computer object (one for each machine on the network) exposes the IADsComputer, IADsComputerOperations and IADs interfaces. Computer objects also expose IADsContainer since in both WinNT and Active Directory the directory structure puts computers as the parent of some of the objects that represent items on that computer. Each of these item-specific object interfaces provides properties and methods suitable for that item.

For a detailed list of the interfaces, properties and methods for ADSI, check out the documentation on the MSDN Web site at http://msdn.microsoft.com/. Alternatively, there are SDKs available for download from the same sources as the ADSI runtime code. There are also several books available that detail the ADSI object models, such as those noted earlier.

Inside the WinNT: Directory Namespace

Although the Namespaces container is the 'top level' container of the Active Directory Service Interfaces—acting as the main root to all the other ADSI providers—each of the directory services has its own 'root' as well. In this case, the root is WinNT:. The reason why this is important is that once we move into the WinNT: section of the directory the ADs: part of ADsPath is replaced with just WinNT:. You'll see this as we look at some samples later on.

So, the ADsPath for the root of our WinNT Namespace is simply:

```
WinNT:
```

Before we get into ADSI programming issues, we'll look at a broad outline of the structure of the directory exposed by the `WinNT:` ADSI Namespace, which allows you to access objects on computers on your local network. Recall that this is really a fictitious directory as the WinNT provider simply gathers information from the computers on your network and presents the information as if it is a directory. Nevertheless, the structure we describe here is the structure that any ADSI client programs that use the WinNT provider will see.

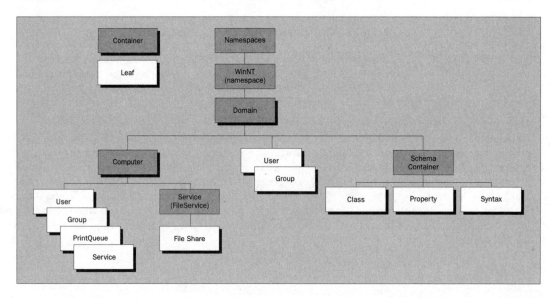

The structure is as shown in the diagram. Directly beneath the `WinNT:` namespace are the domains on your network. The computers all appear as children of the domain of which they are members, while users, groups, services etc. appear as children of the relevant computer object. Domain users and groups also appear as children of the corresponding domain, while each domain object contains one schema container, which contains the objects that describe the WinNT schema.

You will notice that users and groups can appear in this tree both under computer and under domain objects. In fact, local machine user and group accounts appear in `WinNT:` as children of the corresponding computer object, while domain user and group accounts each appear more than once, under the computer object for the domain controller and under the domain object. These duplicate objects do still represent the same accounts. The fact that they appear twice is just a peculiarity of this particular ADSI provider.

Getting Started with ADSI

Programming with ADSI is much like any other tree-walking programming technique. Once we have a reference to a container object, we can use this to get a reference to its parent or child objects. We can also reference individual items directly if we know the path to them. We'll have a look at some of these basic techniques now.

Binding to Objects

We start by obtaining a reference to a specific object or container within the tree using Visual Basic's `GetObject()` function. `GetObject()` is a function generally available to VB, it's not specific to ADSI. It gives you a reference to a particular instance of a COM component where you supply the name of the instance itself rather than the name of the type of component, a process which is know as **Binding** to the object. This process involves locating the object in question, where appropriate starting it (if it has not already been started), and returning an interface pointer to the object. You can get an interface pointer to any ADSI object by passing the ADsPath of the object to `GetObject()`. So, to get a reference to the root of the `WinNT:` tree using Visual Basic or VBScript, we can execute the code:

```
Set objThis = GetObject("WinNT:")
```

> Note that the namespace names (such as `WinNT:` and `LDAP:`) are case sensitive. For most providers however, including WinNT and LDAP, any subsequent text in the ADsPath is not case sensitive.

To get a reference to an object inside the WinNT namespace, we do the same sort of thing:

```
Set objThis = GetObject("WinNT://MyDomain/MyGroup/ThisUser")
```

Browsing down the tree is easy. In Visual Basic, once we have a reference to an object that is a container, we can use a `For Each` construct to enumerate all of its children. The objects returned in the `For Each` loop are references to the child objects:

```
For Each objChild in objThis          'iterate through a container
   Debug.Print objChild.Name          'display the name of each object
Next
```

Navigating up the tree is also simple. The `IADs` interface also exposes the `Parent` property, which gives the ADsPath of the parent of the current object or container. Note that, since this obtains the ADsPath, rather than a reference to the parent object itself, obtaining the parent is a two-stage process. We need to use the ADsPath to actually bind to the object.

```
objParentPath = objThis.Parent          'get the parent's ADsPath string
Set objParent = GetObject(objParentPath) 'and get a reference to it
```

Using the Class Name with the WinNT Provider

Within any container, the name of each object should normally be unique, which implies that the complete ADsPath to an object should also always be unique. Unfortunately, the design of the directory tree exposed by the WinNT provider means that you occasionally find objects with the same ADsPath. This happens in the situation where we have a machine within a domain that has the same name as a user account within that domain. This should not normally occur in a 'real world' situation if the domain has been well designed, or at least be very unlikely, but it does occur in the test domain that we are using in this book.

The result of this is that when we iterate through the `Domain` container, we will get an object of type `User` for the user account and an object of type `Computer` for the machine. The `Name` properties of both will be the same, and so will the ADsPath string. Of course, they are different objects of different types, but the fact that they have the same ADsPath is going to give us problems when we try to reference any of them. This is a fairly unusual situation and only happens with the WinNT provider.

Fortunately, Microsoft anticipated this problem and specified that for names in the WinNT provider only, it is OK to add the name of the class to the ADsPath, separated from the rest of the ADsPath by a comma. Like this:

```
Set objThis = GetObject(strADsPath & "," & strClass)
```

For example, to get the `Computer` object name `SUNSPOT`:

```
Set objThis = GetObject("WinNT:/SUNSPOT,Computer")
```

Restricting Browsing to Certain Classes of Objects

Quite often when browsing a directory, we know we are only interested in certain objects. For example, we might want to know about all the computers on our network, or about all the NT services on a computer. In that case we would like to restrict the objects returned when we enumerate the children of a container to just those classes of object.

The way we do this is to apply a **filter** to the container after we bind to it. For example, to get a list of the NT services within the `Computer` folder of a machine (again called `SUNSPOT`), we could use:

```
Set objThis = GetObject("WinNT://SUNSPOT ")
objThis.Filter = Array("Service")
For Each objService in objThis          'iterate through the container
    Response.Write objService.Name      'display the name of each service
Next
```

> *Remember that the `Filter` property accepts an array of strings that contains the object class names to be included in the filtered collection, rather than a single string. This allows us to obtain any combination of classes when browsing, rather than being restricted to any one class.*

More About the ADSI Property Cache

Once we bind to any ADSI object and access any of its properties, then all the properties of that object are copied from the directory and placed in a local property cache for the object.

The ADSI property cache is an important concept, as it reduces the number of network calls made. There is a property cache for each directory object, stored client-side. In effect, copies of all of the object's properties are made in the cache, so that all operations can be made upon the local copy of the object. Once the user has finished with the object, the `SetInfo()` method of the `IADs` interface should be called. This method copies the property cache into the directory. So, one call can affect several properties on the one object, without making several trips across the network. There are also `GetInfo()` and `GetInfoEx()` methods, which retrieve the object's properties in case they are out of date, or to initialize the cache. `GetInfo()` retrieves all the properties in the cache, while `GetInfoEx()` retrieves only the named properties, and so can work more efficiently if you know you only need certain properties.

The following code gets a reference to the object that wraps the domain SUNSPOT, and then explicitly loads all the properties of the domain object into the ADSI property cache:

```
Set objThis = GetObject("WinNT:/SUNSPOT")
objThis.GetInfo
```

You should always call SetInfo() after modifying data. It is not necessary to call GetInfo() or GetInfoEx() unless you specifically need refresh some properties after using the cache, since GetInfo() is called implicitly for you the first time you access the property cache, if it hasn't already been called.

Getting Property Values

As we have just seen, the values of each object's integral properties, such as Name, Class, ADsPath and Parent, can be obtained by simply referencing them as we would any other object property, using the GetObject() call:

```
Set objThis = GetObject("WinNT:/SUNSPOT")
strName = objThis.Name
strClassName = objThis.Class
strPath = objThis.ADsPath
strParentPath = objThis.Parent
```

However, most objects that describe actual entities, such as users, account groups, services, computers, etc. have a set of extra properties that are defined in the schema for that object.

Because we don't actually know the names of each property in each of these collections, we can't refer to them using the normal syntax that we do for standard properties. Instead, we use the Get() or GetEx() methods of the object, which are part of the standard IADs interface for all objects. Get() and GetEx() will be implemented internally in the component so that they look up the appropriate class schema object in order to retrieve the information. You should also explicitly use the class schema object to find out the names of the mandatory and optional properties, if you don't already know the names of the properties you need.

The next code example shows how we could get the value of each property from the MandatoryProperties and OptionalProperties collections in turn, implicitly loading all the properties of the object into the cache if GetInfo() hasn't already been called:

```
Set objThis = GetObject("WinNT:/SUNSPOT")    'get the object reference
strSchemaPath = objThis.Schema               'get the path of its schema
Set objSchema = GetObject(strSchemaPath)     'get a reference to the schema

For Each strPropertyName In objSchema.MandatoryProperties
    Response.Write strPropertyName & " = " & objThis.Get(strPropertyName) & "<BR>"
Next

For Each strPropertyName In objSchema.OptionalProperties
    Response.Write strPropertyName & " = " & objThis.Get(strPropertyName) & "<BR>"
Next
```

Setting Object and Container Property Values

In order to set or change the values of properties, we first have to load the object or properties into the local property cache, as we did in the previous section. Then we can change them by simply assigning new values to them. However, this change only affects the instance of the object or property in the cache. To make it permanent in the directory we have to call the `SetInfo()` method of the `IADs` interface after updating the properties:

```
Set objThis = GetObject("WinNT://SUNSPOT/MyUserName")
    objThis.Put("Description", "This is my cool user account")
    objThis.SetInfo
```

Browsing the ADSI Providers: The ADSIExplorer Sample

OK, that's enough theory. Let's get on now and build a component that uses ADSI. Something that would be really useful would be a component that we could use to explore the contents and structure of the various directories on any machine. We'll aim to do that.

> You can download all the code for this example, along with the rest of the code for this book, from our website at `http://webdev.wrox.co.uk/books/2882/`. This includes the source code for the component and the ASP page that uses it.

Designing a Directory Explorer Component

The plan is to create web page that allows you and other users to walk through the various namespaces available through ADSI and examine the contents on the way. This also helps you to get a feel for how the directories are structured, and what they contain. The component will work on both NT4 and Windows 2000, although you won't be able to use it to browse the LDAP namespace on NT4.

The page will be called `ADSIExplorer.asp`, and this is what the page looks like when you first start it up:

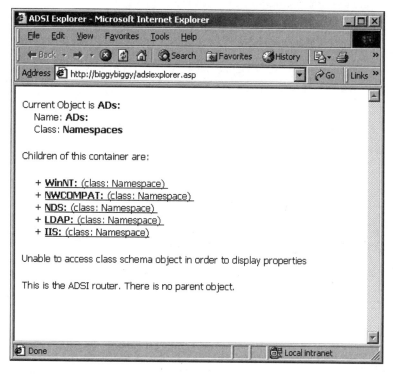

Like most tree-walking routines, we follow a reasonably standard process. First we get the root 'element' of the tree, and then iterate through its child elements. We will show each one of the child elements as a link, so that the user can move to that element to view its contents. In the previous screenshot, when we've just opened the web page, we are shown the ADSI router, and given a list of its children—the ADSI namespace objects installed on your machine.

The ADSIExplorer page also usually displays the mandatory and optional properties, along with a hyperlink to the parent object where available, and if none are present a message is displayed to this effect.

The plus signs in front of the names of the child objects indicate that they are containers.

We can see our web page at work if we use it to actually browse into a directory by clicking on a link. In the next screenshot, we've browsed into the WinNT provider down to the level of a group, and we are examining the Domain Admins group on my machine, BiggyBiggy.

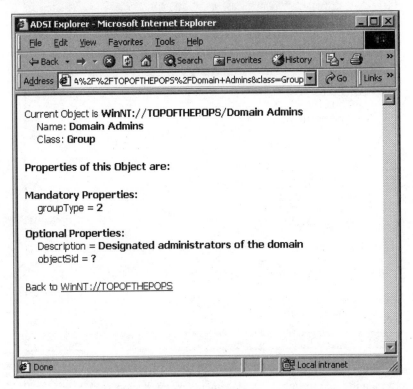

The group object is a leaf rather than a container, so it does not have any children to list. The ADSIExplorer.asp page has detected this and not attempted to display the children. On the other hand, we do now have a working class schema object, making it possible to display the mandatory and optional properties. Groups don't have many properties in WinNT. The group type is an integer that gives general information about the nature of this group, including whether it is a local or global group. The description is a human-readable string that describes the group, while the objectSid is a binary value that contains security information. Since it is a binary value, it is not possible to display it.

Similarly, in Windows 2000 we can look at Active Directory by browsing into the LDAP provider:

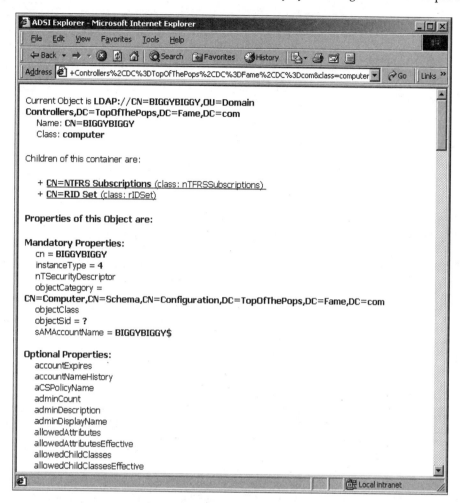

Here I've browsed into my Active Directory installation, and navigated down to look at the object that represents my domain controller, **BiggyBiggy**. Computers in Active Directory (and in the WinNT provider) are containers, with their children being objects that refer to objects hosted on the computer. Notice how the Active Directory ADsPath shows the lowest level object first, and works up to the top level, DC=com, in a manner which is similar to URLs but the opposite to how the WinNT works. Also notice that there are a large number of mandatory and optional properties defined but very few of them have values assigned. This is because Active Directory has been designed as a general-purpose directory. So it has been given a very extensive schema, just in case administrators wish to make use of it by storing some of the defined properties—but most of the properties are by default not filled in when Active Directory is installed.

The meanings of the different properties shown in the screenshot is beyond the scope of this book. Here I just want to give you a feel for the sort of information that Active Directory can contain. If you want more information about both Active Directory and ADSI, you might want to look at Professional ADSI Development (ISBN 1-861002-62), also published by Wrox.

So that's what the web page does. Before I show you the code, let's quickly run through what the page has to do:

- Bind to the requested object
- Get and display the class, ADsPath and name of this object
- Attempt to get the class schema object—and if succeessful then look up the mandatory and optional properties
- Check whether it is a container or a leaf object
- If this is an ADSI container object then list its children
- If we did succeed in getting the schema object, display the mandatory and optional properties
- Finally, display the link to return to the parent object

Building the Directory Explorer Component

Since this is a book about components, we will use a component here, and so take advantage of code reusability, as well as the fact that this means we will be able to write the code in the component in the more powerful VB instead of VBScript.

There are two ways of working this. The component could contain a method that returned the list of child objects as a `Variant` array, or as a delimited string. This leaves a lot of the work to the calling ASP page. Alternatively, the component could do virtually everything, including displaying the results and links to other objects, itself. This means that the ASP page is reduced to a few lines to basically call up the component.

I've chosen the last of these as an interesting option, because it allows us to exert complete control over the layout of the results from within our component code. Of course, you may be building more generic components that are designed for use in several environments, and so you may prefer to return the results in another form, such as XML, and allow the ASP code in the calling page to format them as required.

When we create a reference to a type library in the Visual Basic IDE, using the **References** dialog, we automatically get access to any named constants in that type library. This means that, instead of explicitly defining the constant values in our ASP pages or using the actual values in our code instead, we can simply use the named constants.

Using the Directory Explorer Component

First, let's look at the ASP page that we use to instantiate and execute our new custom component. The page works by taking the ADsPath and classname of the object to be viewed as additions to the URL, hence using the HTTP Get procedure to pass the data to the server. If these fields are blank, the component will assume that we want to look at the ADSI router.

The component returns a value which will either be the URL to the parent object or text to indicate there is no parent object. This is probably not how you'd design the component in real life since it links it rather closely to this particular client, but it is fine for an example.

Notice how the value returned from our component is used to create the hyperlink back to the parent object, providing no error has occurred:

```
<%@LANGUAGE="VBScript"%>
<HTML>
<HEAD>
<TITLE>ADSI Explorer</TITLE>
<STYLE TYPE="text/css">
  BODY {font-family:Tahoma,Arial,sans-serif; font-size:10pt}
</STYLE>
</HEAD>
<BODY BGCOLOR=#FFFFFF>

<%
strStart = Request.QueryString("path")
strType = Request.QueryString("class")
If Len(strStart) = 0 Then strStart = "ADs:"

On Error Resume Next
Set objADSI = Server.CreateObject("WX2882ADSI.Explorer")
strHRef = objADSI.ListADSIMembers(strStart, strType)

If Err.Number = 0 Then
   Response.Write "<P>" & strHRef & "</P>"
Else
   Response.Write "<P>Error: " & Err.Number & "<BR>" _
   & Err.Description & "<BR>Source: " & Err.Source & "</P>"
End If
%>

</BODY>
</HTML>
```

Creating the ADSI Explorer Component

OK, let's actually create the component now. Fire up Visual Basic and select the option to create a new ActiveX DLL. Then change the name of the project to WX2882ADSI, as this will be the name of the DLL.

Setting Up a Reference to ADSI in Visual Basic

In order to use the integral objects and constants that are part of ADSI, and at the same time benefit from the pop-up syntax help, we need to create a reference to the ADSI runtime DLL within the Visual Basic IDE. The only file we need is the Active Directory type library file activeds.tlb. You'll find this in the Winnt\System directory on your NT/Windows 2000 Server machine or in Windows\System in Windows 9x.

375

Copy this file to your development machine and, using the VB Project | References dialog, add the type library—named Active DS Type Library—to a new ActiveX DLL project. Make sure that the Microsoft Active Server Pages Object Library is selected as well:

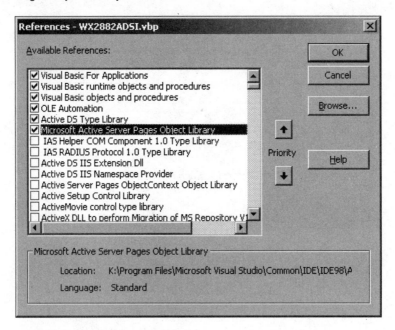

Referencing the Scripting Context

Our component will need to store a reference to our ASP page's ScriptingContext object. We're doing this the 'old-fashioned' way (without using the ObjectContext object), as we're only going to be using it to write some output with the Response object. As usual we will use the OnStartPage() method to grab this interface reference.

```
Dim objScript As ScriptingContext

Sub OnStartPage(objContext As ScriptingContext)
    Set objScript = objContext
End Sub
```

The ListADSIMembers Function

Our component contains a VB Class named Explorer, which itself contains just a single method that creates the list of contents or properties for a specific ADSI object. The function, named ListADSIMembers(), takes two Variant parameters and returns a Variant value:

```
Function ListADSIMembers(ADSIStartPath As Variant, _
                     Optional ADSIClassName As Variant = "") _
                     As Variant
```

The first parameter, ADSIStartPath, is the ADsPath string of the object within the ADSI namespace where the listing should begin. The second parameter is the Class name (as a string) of the object that we want to list. As pointed out earlier, this is useful for the WinNT provider only when we have duplicated ADsPath strings in a container. The return value of the function is a string that we can use to create the return hyperlink, which allows the user to navigate back up (or down) the directory tree towards the root.

We used Variant *parameters because we intend to use the component only within ASP (it depends on the ASP* ScriptingContext *to work).* Variants *make passing values in and out of components easier, as ASP uses only* Variant *type variables.*

The code for the ListADSIMembers() method is quite long, we will see it all here so you can get an overview of how it works, then we'll go through all the interesting bits of it.

```
Function ListADSIMembers(ADSIStartPath As Variant, _
Optional ADSIClassName As Variant = "") _
As Variant

'-------------------------------------------------------------------
'Lists the members of the directory of type ADSIClassName (if
'specified)in the path ADSIStartPath and returns the path to the
'previous container if there is one, or an empty string if not.
'-------------------------------------------------------------------

    On Error GoTo FNSML_Err

    Dim objStartObject As IADs
    Dim strObjectClass As String
    Dim strObjectName As String
    Dim strObjectADsPath As String
    Dim strSchemaPath As String
    Dim strChildClass As String
    Dim strChildName As String
    Dim strChildSchemaPath As String
    Dim strParentPath As String
    Dim strPath As String
    Dim strHRef As String
    Dim QUOT As String
    Dim bIsContainer As Boolean
    Dim bChildIsContainer As Boolean

    Dim objSchema As IADsClass
    Dim objChildSchema As IADsClass
    Dim objChild As IADs
    Dim strPropName As Variant

    QUOT = Chr(34)
    strHRef = objScript.Request.ServerVariables("SCRIPT_NAME")

    'get the current start object from the directory
    If Len(ADSIClassName) And Left(ADSIStartPath, 8) = "WinNT://" Then
        'specify the class name in case two different types of object have
        'the same name, otherwise we will only get the first one in the list
        Set objStartObject = GetObject(ADSIStartPath & "," & ADSIClassName)
    Else
        'class name (type) not specified
        Set objStartObject = GetObject(ADSIStartPath)
    End If

    'get the class and name of this object
    strObjectClass = objStartObject.Class
    strObjectName = objStartObject.Name
    strObjectADsPath = objStartObject.ADsPath
    objScript.Response.Write "Current Object is <B>" & strObjectADsPath & "</B>"
    objScript.Response.Write "<BR>    Name: <B>" & strObjectName & "</B>"
    objScript.Response.Write "<BR>    Class: <B>" & strObjectClass & "</B>"

    On Error Resume Next
    ' list children of this object if it is a container
    bIsContainer = GetWhetherContainer(objStartObject)
    If bIsContainer Then
```

```
            objScript.Response.Write "<P>Children of this container are:<P>" & vbCrLf
        For Each objChild In objStartObject
            strChildClass = objChild.Class
            strChildName = objChild.Name
            strPath = objChild.ADsPath
            bChildIsContainer = GetWhetherContainer(objChild)

            'display a + sign if child is a container
            If bChildIsContainer Then
                objScript.Response.Write "    <B>+</B> "
            Else
                objScript.Response.Write "       "
            End If

            'put object name as a hyperlink:
            objScript.Response.Write "<A HREF=" & QUOT & strHRef _
            & "?path=" & objScript.Server.URLEncode(strPath) _
            & "&class=" & strChildClass & QUOT & ">"
            objScript.Response.Write "<B>" _
            & strChildName & "</B> (class: " & objChild.Class & ") </A><BR>" & vbCrLf
        Next

    End If


    'create a list of schema-defined properties for this object

    On Error Resume Next
    strSchemaPath = objStartObject.Schema
    Set objSchema = GetObject(strSchemaPath)
    If (Err.Number = 0) Then
        objScript.Response.Write "<P>"
        objScript.Response.Write "<B>Properties of this Object are:</B><P>" & vbCrLf
        objScript.Response.Write "<B>Mandatory Properties:</B><BR>"
        For Each strPropName In objSchema.MandatoryProperties
            objScript.Response.Write "    " & strPropName
            objScript.Response.Write " = <B>" & objStartObject.Get(strPropName)
            objScript.Response.Write "</B><BR>" & vbCrLf
        Next

        objScript.Response.Write "<BR><B>Optional Properties:</B><BR>"
        For Each strPropName In objSchema.OptionalProperties
            objScript.Response.Write "    " & strPropName
            objScript.Response.Write " = <B>" & objStartObject.Get(strPropName)
            objScript.Response.Write "</B><BR>" & vbCrLf

        Next
    Else
        objScript.Response.Write "<P> Unable to access class schema object" _
            & " in order to display properties<BR>" & vbCrLf
    End If



    'display link to the parent
    'do not need to include a class name in this case
    objScript.Response.Write "<P>"
    strParentPath = objStartObject.Parent
    If strParentPath = "" Then
        ListADSIMembers = "This is the ADSI router. There is no parent object."
    Else
        ListADSIMembers = "Back to <A HREF=" & QUOT & strHRef _
        & "?path=" & objScript.Server.URLEncode(strParentPath) _
        & QUOT & ">" & strParentPath & "</A>"
    End If

    Exit Function
```

```
'- - - - - - - - - - - - - - - - - - - - - - - - - - - - - - - -
FNSML_Err:
    objScript.Response.Write "Unable to display this ADSI object<BR>"
    objScript.Response.Write "error " & Err.Number & "<BR>" & Err.Description

    Exit Function
End Function
```

Declaring our Variable Requirements

The `ListADSIMembers()` function first sets up an error handler and then declares most of the `variables` that we'll need later. These variables give us the chance to see some of the ADSI interfaces in action. We'll use `IADs` and `IADsContainer` on the object we are looking at, and `IADsClass` to examine the schema information for the object. The `QUOT` variable is used to store the double quote character—we'll need it these quotes characters in the strings we construct to send back to the HTML page.

Discovering the Correct Variable Data Types

If you aren't sure about the data type of an object when you come to declare it, you have two options. You can simply define it as being of type `Object`, and leave the binding of an appropriate object type until run-time. This is an example of late binding, as we discussed in more detail in Chapter 5 when we looked at how we can get a reference to the scripting context. Alternatively, if you prefer early binding (which is more efficient at run-time) you can use the VB **Object Browser** to view the object definitions:

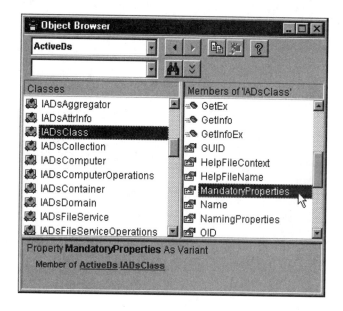

Late Binding has one advantage in that it allows your code to select the object at runtime depending on the settings in the host machines Registry for a ProgID (such as `ObjectName.ClassName`). This can prevent DLL version problems where incompatible data types exist in different versions of an installed object.

Because of the advantages of vtable binding(which we will see in the next chapter), there is really no reason not to use it, in a component, so we declare all of our object variables using the specific interface type.

Getting the Root Object for the Listing

The first real task for our function is to get a reference to the object that we'll be listing the contents of—in other words our 'start object'. We have an ADsPath provided for this as the first parameter of our function, and we may also have the optional class name in the second parameter. We use whatever is available to build the path to our start object, and then bind to it using the GetObject() method:

```
'get the current start object from the directory
If Len(ADSIClassName) And Left(ADSIStartPath, 8) = "WinNT://" Then
    'specify the class name in case two different types of object have
    'the same name, otherwise we will only get the first one in the list
    Set objStartObject = GetObject(ADSIStartPath & "," & ADSIClassName)
Else
    'class name (type) not specified
    Set objStartObject = GetObject(ADSIStartPath)
End If
```

This code would be a lot simpler if we were not taking account of the problem that sometimes occurs in the WinNT provider, when we need to supply a class name as well as the ADsPath. If we weren't bothered about that, or were fairly sure that we had a system that had did not have any global users or groups having the same names as computers, then we could replace the above code by the single line

```
    Set objStartObject = GetObject(ADSIStartPath)
```

The next few lines simply get the name, class and ADsPath of the object and display them

```
'get the class and name of this object
strObjectClass = objStartObject.Class
strObjectName = objStartObject.Name
strObjectADsPath = objStartObject.ADsPath
objScript.Response.Write "Current Object is <B>" & strObjectADsPath & "</B>"
objScript.Response.Write "<BR>    Name: <B>" & strObjectName & "</B>"
objScript.Response.Write "<BR>    Class: <B>" & strObjectClass & "</B>"
```

Iterating Through a Container's Children

We've now established that we are able to bind to the object and print basic information about it. So, we change the error handling to Resume Next, since if any errors occur in displaying any one property or listing any one child we don't want that to stop us listing everything else.

We only want to list the children if our object is actually a container. To determine this our class has another function, GetWhetherContainer(), which takes an object and checks whether it exposes the IADsContainer interface. We'll cover how we've implemented this function later.

We actually use the GetWhetherContainer() function at two points in the code—once to check whether we should attempt to display any children, and again inside the loop, to check whether each child is a container. If it is, we will display a + sign next to that child to indicate it is a container.

Beyond that, the code to list all the children shouldn't need any explanation. We add HTML tags around the ADsPaths of the children to ensure that they get displayed as hyperlinks:

```
On Error Resume Next
' list children of this object if it is a container
bIsContainer = GetWhetherContainer(objStartObject)
If bIsContainer Then
```

```
            objScript.Response.Write "<P>Children of this container are:<P>" & vbCrLf
      For Each objChild In objStartObject
          strChildClass = objChild.Class
          strChildName = objChild.Name
          strPath = objChild.ADsPath
          bChildIsContainer = GetWhetherContainer(objChild)

          'display a + sign if child is a container
          If bChildIsContainer Then
             objScript.Response.Write "    <B>+</B> "
          Else
             objScript.Response.Write "       "
          End If

          'put object name as a hyperlink:
          objScript.Response.Write "<A HREF=" & QUOT & strHRef _
          & "?path=" & objScript.Server.URLEncode(strPath) _
          & "&class=" & strChildClass & QUOT & ">"
          objScript.Response.Write "<B>" _
          & strChildName & "</B> (class: " & objChild.Class & ") </A><BR>" & vbCrLf
      Next

   End If
```

An Aside: Don't Forget that Scripting Context

Notice how the `Request.ServerVariables` collection and the `Server.URLEncode()` method in the previous code are prefixed with the object variable that holds a reference to the ASP `ScriptingContext` object. If you forget to add this then, in most cases, the compiler will complain and prevent you from creating your component. However, there is one particularly dangerous point where you must take extra care.

The `Server.CreateObject()` method is used in ASP when you want to create an instance of an object from a component such as an ActiveX DLL on the server. In a VB component, it is possible to use this method by prefixing it with your usual `ScriptingContext` object variable:

```
Set objNewObject = objScript.Server.CreateObject("NewObject.ClassName")
```

However, the `CreateObject()` method of the ASP `Server` object is specially designed to ensure that objects are created properly in ASP, not within a component. It's far better and far safer to use Visual Basic's own internal `CreateObject()` method if you want to create an object through late binding. Alternatively, create the object directly using early binding with the syntax:

```
Dim objNewObject As NewObject.ClassName
```

Or:

```
Dim objNewObject As New NewObject.ClassName
```

Displaying the Properties of an Object

Because each type of high-level leaf object may have a different structure (and probably will), we won't know up front what properties are available—if any.

Remember that we originally defined the object variable `objStartObject` type as simply `IADs`, so that it would be correct for all types of object. Recall also that the names of the mandatory properties are contained in the `MandatoryProperties` collection of the class schema object that describes the class of object we are looking at, while the names of the optional properties are contained in the `OptionalProperties` collection of the same object.

So, we check for properties by binding to the schema object. Once we have the name of each property, we can use the Get() method of the IADs interface to retrieve its value. Note that we need to test for an error after we have attempted to bind to it, because some objects (such as the namespace object) are not described by a schema object.

Once those principles are understood, the code to display the mandatory and optional properties should be fairly clear.

```
On Error Resume Next
   strSchemaPath = objStartObject.Schema
   Set objSchema = GetObject(strSchemaPath)
   If (Err.Number = 0) Then
       objScript.Response.Write "<P>"
       objScript.Response.Write "<B>Properties of this Object are:</B><P>" & vbCrLf
       objScript.Response.Write "<B>Mandatory Properties:</B><BR>"
       For Each strPropName In objSchema.MandatoryProperties
           objScript.Response.Write "    " & strPropName
           objScript.Response.Write " = <B>" & objStartObject.Get(strPropName)
           objScript.Response.Write "</B><BR>" & vbCrLf
       Next

       objScript.Response.Write "<BR><B>Optional Properties:</B><BR>"
       For Each strPropName In objSchema.OptionalProperties
           objScript.Response.Write "    " & strPropName
           objScript.Response.Write " = <B>" & objStartObject.Get(strPropName)
           objScript.Response.Write "</B><BR>" & vbCrLf

       Next
   Else
       objScript.Response.Write "<P> Unable to access class schema object" _
           & " in order to display properties<BR>" & vbCrLf
   End If
```

There are a couple of potential problems here that may be caught by the On Error Resume Next command. Firstly, we don't know beforehand if there will be *any* properties at all. If a collection is empty (meaning that the MandatoryProperties or OptionalProperties property is Null), the For Each...Next construct will cause an error, but in our code that is now harmless.

Also, a property might either not have any value defined, or the value might be in some binary format which cannot be displayed. Notice how, in the above code, we've been careful to separate the displaying of the actual value into a different line of code from the lines that print all the other information, such as the property name. This ensures that if the property value is absent or unprintable, the name still appears, as you can see on the earlier screenshot from Active Directory.

Creating a Link to the Parent Container

At the bottom of each page, we want a link that will open the previous page, and go back towards the root of the tree again. We can get the ADsPath of the parent container from the Parent property of the current 'start' object. If this is blank, we know that we are at the top (ADs:) level, and if not we can use this ADsPath to create a link to the parent object. We use the path of the current ASP page that's hosting our component, and again remember to URLEncode the value of the ADsPath variable in the query string:

```
'display link to the parent
'do not need to include a class name in this case
objScript.Response.Write "<P>"
strParentPath = objStartObject.Parent
If strParentPath = "" Then
ListADSIMembers = "This is the ADSI router. There is no parent object."
Else
```

```
    ListADSIMembers = "Back to <A HREF=" & QUOT & strHRef _
    & "?path=" & objScript.Server.URLEncode(strParentPath) _
    & QUOT & ">" & strParentPath & "</A>"
    End If

    Exit Function
```

Rather than put the hyperlink into the page directly, we've chosen to return it as the value of the `ListADSIMembers()` function.

However there is another problem here. Notice that we aren't including a container type in the hyperlink URL, as we did when building the list of links earlier in the page. The reason for this is that we don't definitely know what the container type will be. As we discussed earlier, it is possible that when using the WinNT provider we might have two entities with the same `ADsPath`, a `Computer` container and a `User` object for example. If the `Parent` property of the current object returns such an `ADsPath` we will get the first occurrence of the path string, which may well be the wrong object (in this example the `User` object instead of the `Computer` container). So, querying the object type (`Class`) of the parent object is no help, because we may have the wrong parent object anyway. For this reason, we have omitted the class name altogether from the URL in this link.

Checking Whether an Object is a Container

I mentioned earlier that we used a helper function, `GetWhetherContainer()`, that checked whether an object was a container. Here's the code that does it.

```
Function GetWhetherContainer(objObject As IADs)

On Error Resume Next
    Dim objContainer As IADsContainer
    Set objContainer = objObject
    If (Err.Number = 0) Then
        GetWhetherContainer = True
    Else
        GetWhetherContainer = False
    End If

End Function
```

How it works is fairly simple. We try to find out if the object exposes the `IADsContainer` interface by declaring an `IADsContainer` variable and setting it to the object. If we don't get an error, we know that we are dealing with a container, which may, in principle, contain children.

Notice that this piece of code is a good example of a reason for using components. It would simply not be possible to write this kind of code in VBScript, where we cannot explicitly type object references. If we had wanted to find out if an object was a container directly using an ASP page, we would have needed to look up the `Container` property of the corresponding class schema object, which would return `true` if the object is a container. However, that is only possible if the object has a corresponding schema object.

And that is our Directory Explorer component finished. We can save the project, compile the DLL, and register it on the machine hosting our Web server, ready for use by our ASP pages.

Exploring the WinNT Namespace

In this section we'll have a closer look at the structure of the WinNT namespace, as seen through ADSI.

If we use the **ADSIExplorer** sample to examine the WinNT namespace, we'll find the domains beneath the namespace object. On my machine I have only one domain, **TOPOFTHEPOPS**. (Believe me, I did have a good reason for giving it that name. If you ever happen to read the book *Professional ADSI Development*, published by Wrox, you'll find out the reason—it fits in with the sample ADSI provider that gets written in that book).

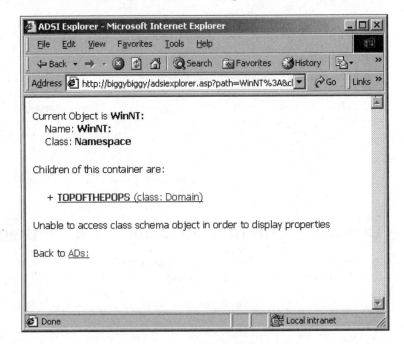

As we've remarked, the namespace object isn't described by a schema. The **ADSIExplorer** page has detected this.

As the next screenshot shows, inside the **TOPOFTHEPOPS** domain we find that the children of the domain object are the various global users and groups in the domain, as well as the computers. The WinNT provider simply mixes up domain controllers and workstations so you'll have to believe that the computer **BIGGYBIGGY** is the domain controller, while **CRASHLOTS** is a member workstation. OK, so it's a very small domain. There's also an object named Schema, which is the schema container:

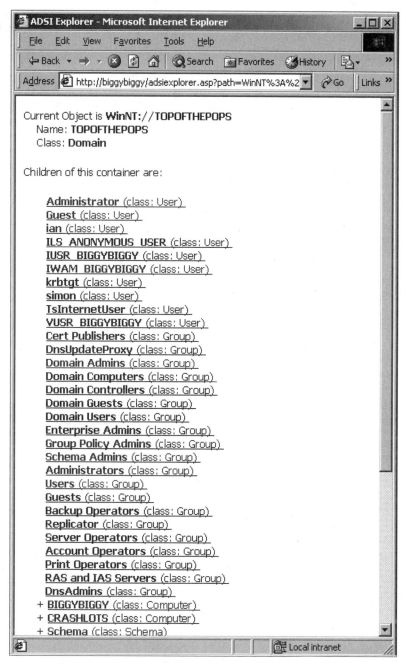

The domain object does have some properties to display, but we can't see them without scrolling because there are so many default user and group accounts!

Selecting the computer **BIGGYBIGGY**, we get a long list of users, account groups, and other children. Amongst these are all the Windows NT Services that are available on that machine. In the next screenshot, we're selecting the **World Wide Web Service** (W3SVC) object. The screenshot also shows that the computer object has a number of optional properties, although no values have been set for them.

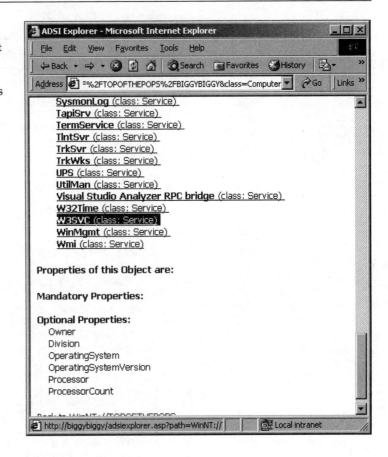

By clicking on this service, our ADSIExplorer page shows us the information about this service, because it is a leaf object on an NT4 machine. You can see several properties that look familiar, or have familiar values:

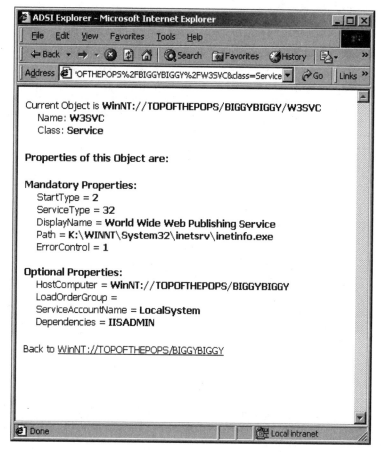

The World Wide Web service is the service that handles requests for web pages that arrive at this computer.

> *If you haven't encountered NT services before, just think of them as special applications which are controlled by the system, and which can often start automatically without a user having to double click on a file to start them. NT services are often used to perform tasks in the background that need to be performed even when no-one has actually logged in to that computer—and responding to browser requests for web pages is a good example of that.*

We can start to see more of the power of ADSI here in that it allows us to examine (and modify) properties of NT services—for example we can see here, amongst other properties, which user account the world wide web service runs under, and which file the executable code actually lives in. Although we won't go into the details in this chapter, there are a couple of other ADSI interfaces, IADsService and IADsServiceOperations, which between them allow you to do things like start or stop services.

Searching

So far we haven't done any searching in the sample code, although I emphasized at the start of the chapter that searching is an extremely important thing to be able to do in a directory. The **ADSIExplorer** is a specifically a browsing sample, which means that you can use it to look in any particular container to see what objects are there. It wouldn't be too hard to modify the code to set a filter in objects so that you only browse for certain classes of object. However, that is still not the same as being able to search. A search would be something like 'find all the users with usernames beginning with 'A', not matter where they are in the directory.

As it happens, the ADSI interfaces do include an interface, `IDirectorySearch`, for search requests. However, it is not possible to call up `IDirectorySearch` from ASP pages, or for that matter from any scripting language. This is because `IDirectorySearch` is a custom rather than a dual interface.

In fact, `IDirectorySearch` is intended for use by C++ clients. So, if we're writing clients in VB, VBScript or JavaScript then we need to take a slightly different approach. What we do is use ADO. Yes I did say that right; we use ADO instead of ADSI. The idea of ADO is that you can access any data source for which there is an OLE DB provider installed on your machine, and Microsoft has written an OLE DB provider for ADSI. In other words, we can use an OLE DB provider that hooks up to the ADSI components installed on your system, and can hence access any directory that can be accessed through ADSI. This provider is quite restrictive, because it is read-only, however Microsoft has promised that a future version of ADSI will include a read-write provider for OLE DB. Still, this provider is able to call up the `IDirectorySearch` interface, so you can use it to search a directory that is exposed through ADSI. In fact, at the moment, that is the only purpose for which you can use the provider.

> Note that it is not possible to search any ADSI directory, since not all providers implement the `IDirectorySearch` interface. In particular it is not possible to do searching using `WinNT:`.

There is a good reason for the limitations on searching. Recall that the WinNT provider works by gathering information from around the network, this means there isn't a directory behind the WinNT provider with the infrastructure necessary to support searching. So, the WinNT provider simply doesn't bother. The LDAP provider, however, does implement `IDirectorySearch`, so you will be able to search against Active Directory, or against any other directory exposed using the LDAP provider. This shouldn't come as a surprise to anyone familiar with LDAP, since the ability to support searches is a fundamental part of the LDAP specification.

So, our search sample will be tested against Active Directory in Windows 2000. If you are running NT4, you can use any other LDAP directory installed on your machine, if you have one, to try out the sample.

LDAP Search Concepts: Base, Scope and Filters etc.

Before we actually do some searching, we need to explain some of the concepts behind how search requests work in LDAP. Notice I've deliberately said in LDAP rather than ADSI. That is because ADSI has pretty much taken its implementation of searching entirely from LDAP. So, how searching works in LDAP and how searching works in ADSI are virtually the same thing—perhaps not surprisingly when the main directories that you might search using ADSI are all LDAP directories.

When you request a search to be carried out through an ADSI provider, you must supply four items of information: search base, search scope, search filter, and attributes required.

Search Base

The **search base** is the ADsPath of the object at which the search starts. Searches may take place over all of a directory or only a part of it, but there is always one object somewhere in the tree from which the search starts. The search is always confined to the object at which the search starts, plus the portion of the tree below that object—how much of this portion is searched is determined by the search scope.

Search Scope

The **search scope** says how far below the search base we should search. There are three possible values: `base`, `onelevel`, and `subtree`.

Value	Use
base	Only the base object will be searched. This might sound nonsensical, but in LDAP there is no concept of browsing directories, or of looking at one object. Doing a search in which the scope is set to `base` is the way you normally get hold of the data for one chosen object in the directory. Since we are using ADSI rather than LDAP directly, it's easier for us to use the `IADs::Get()` and `IADs::GetEx()` methods to do this.
onelevel	Only direct children of the base object will be searched. This is LDAP's equivalent to enumerating the children of a container, however it is more powerful because we can set a fairly sophisticated search filter.
subtree	The entire portion of the directory below and including the base object will be searched. This is the normal option you will choose if you want to find certain objects, and you do not know whereabouts in the directory they are. If you specify a search base of the namespace object and a search scope of `subtree`, you will search the entire directory.

Search Filter

The **search filter** is a string that says what objects you want to find. There is a fairly precise syntax for it, which is described in Request for Comments (RFC) 2254, but it's probably easiest to see how this syntax works by giving a few examples:

```
(sAMAccountName=s*)
```

This search filter is asking for any objects that have a value for their property, sAMAccountName, that begins with an s. The sAMAccountName is just the name you use to login to your account—so effectively this search filter will return any object (presumably user accounts) that begin with s.

```
(&(objectCategory=person)(sAMAccountName=s*))
```

This is like the previous search filter but explicitly states that we only want people. If there happen to be any other types of object that have a value set for the sAMAccountName property, then we're not interested. So this search filter would be the standard way of asking for any user accounts beginning with s.

```
(objectClass=*)
```

This asks for all objects in the portion of the directory tree that we've specified using the search base and search scope. It works because in LDAP all objects have a property called objectClass, which indicates the type of object this is an instance of. It's similar to objectCategory, but gives slightly more specific information. This query literally says 'give me any object that has any value in the objectClass property'—which effectively means everything.

```
(|(Description=*p*)(Description=*n)(sAMAccountName=simon))
```

This is our first example of the OR operator, |. This request asks for all objects that satisfy at least one of the following: either the description contains a p somewhere, or the description ends in n, or the username is simon.

Finally, a more complicated example to show just what you can do if you're willing to start doing things like nesting brackets:

```
(&(!(sAMAccountName=Administrator))(|(objectClass=Computer)
                                      (ObjectClass=Person))))
```

This will probably take a bit of thinking about. If you carefully expand out the brackets, you should be able to convince yourself that this request is asking for any object that is either a user account or a computer account, but we are specifically excluding any account named Administrator from the search (the exclamation mark means NOT).

These examples should hopefully convince you of how powerful search filters can be. You'll probably also have picked up a fairly good idea from these examples of how the syntax works. The basics of it follow.

A search filter consists of a number of conditions. Each condition indicates the value that a certain property must have—though wildcards may be used in the value. Each condition must be surrounded by round brackets (), as must the filter itself. You can combine as many conditions as you want, using the logical operators AND (&), OR (|) and NOT (!). However, these operators must always precede all the conditions to which they apply. For example, we wrote

```
(|(Description=*p*)(Description=*n)(sAMAccountName=simon))
```

And not

```
((Description=*p*)|(Description=*n)|(sAMAccountName=simon))
```

This latter form looks more intuitively appealing, but would not be recognized as a valid search filter.

Brackets are used in their normal logical way to denote the order in which conditions should be evaluated. There is no limit to how many times you can stick brackets inside other brackets.

Note that you should not put any excess white space anywhere in the search filter, and you should not put quote marks around any of the values of properties that you want to test against.

If you want to test something like whether some property has the value ")", then you have a problem, since the normal way to do this would be

```
(SomeProperty=))
```

Unfortunately the closing bracket) has a special meaning in search filters as marking the end of the condition—so this search filter will not be understood. It's the same story for any other characters that have a special meaning in search filters. To get round this, it is possible to use an escape sequence to represent such characters in property values. The escape sequence takes the form of the backslash character, \, followed by the ASCII code for the character in question, expressed in hexadecimal. So our example should read:

```
(SomeProperty=\29)
```

That's covered the basics of search filters. There are some more advanced things you can do with them, so if you need to use them extensively, it's probably worth your while checking up RFC2254.

We have one other bit of information we haven't covered, which we need to supply with a search request. We've now given all the information necessary to specify which objects we want to search for. What we haven't done is say what information we want from those objects. Do we want all the properties of them, or just certain named ones? This is supplied by a list of attributes. The list can either be the string, * to indicate everything, or a comma-separated list of the names of the properties required, e.g.:

```
"Description, ADsPath, sAMAccountName"
```

Notice that here the ADsPath is treated as just another attribute that we may ask for explicitly.

I've started changing terminology from properties to attributes here. The two terms are equivalent, but the ADSI documentation usually uses properties, whereas LDAP uses attributes.

I should mention that there are some other search preferences that can optionally be set, that cover things like whether you want the results sorted in any particular order and whether the search should be done synchronously or asynchronously, but that's starting to get too advanced for this book (you can find out more about them in *Professional ADSI Development* ISBN 1-861002-26-2 from Wrox Press).

The ADSISearch Sample

This sample works in much the same way as the ADSIExplorer sample—to the extent that most of the functionality is buried in a component written in VB, while an ASP page is used to call up the component. The ASP page is slightly longer than the one for the ADSIExplorer sample, since it requires a form with several text boxes in order to find out all the options the user wishes to specify for the search. Here's what it looks like when you first start up the page

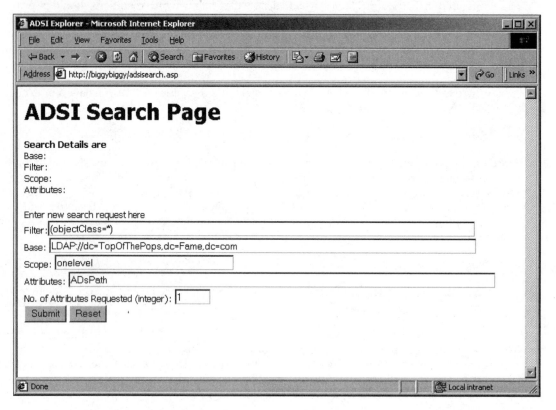

Initially the page doesn't attempt a search because no search parameters have been supplied. However, it has attempted to fill in some useful default values for your request. Submitting these values will result in a search for all objects located one level below the Active Directory root on my computer, and will return the ADsPath will be returned. These default search parameters are hardcoded into the ASP page—you'll probably want to change the Base to match your computer if you run this sample.

There is one extra piece of information requested on the form on the page, which we haven't covered. No. of attributes requested is what it says—the number of attributes that should be displayed for each object. I've put this in as a separate parameter for this sample to simplify the code a bit, it saves the component that does the search and prints the results from having to work out from the attribute list and results how many columns of data must be displayed in the table of results. Obviously, if writing a more commercial sample, you'd probably want to get your application to work this out rather than relying on the user to tell you.

Let's actually try a search. For this one, I've modified the filter and scope to request a search for all users anywhere in the directory tree. I've also requested that the login name (sAMAccountName) and the ADsPath should be returned from the query. Here's the results:

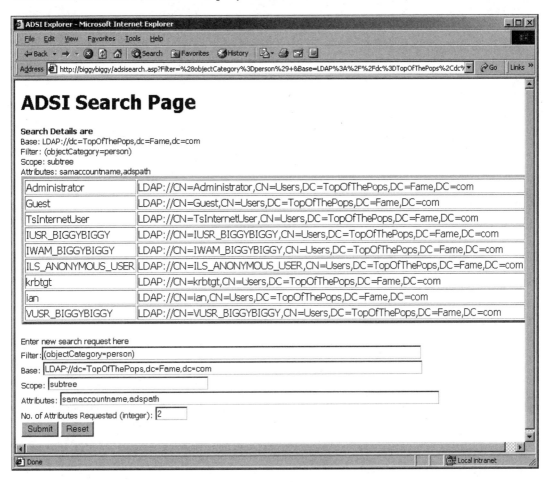

Notice that the asp page has intelligently reused the values for the previous search request as the defaults for the next request—making it easy for you to modify values to make a slightly different search. For this one, I've asked for only those users that have an n somewhere in their name.

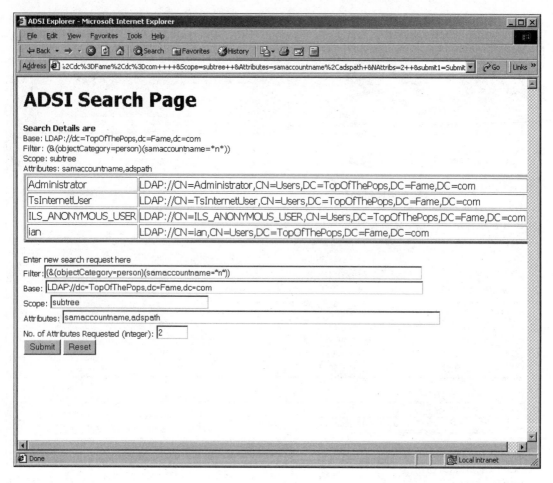

The ASP Page

So that's what the page does. Let's see the ASP code. We start off with the normal headers, then grab and display the current values that were submitted from the search request form. The first time we call up the page these values will be blank.

```
<%@LANGUAGE="VBScript"%>
<HTML>
<HEAD>
<TITLE>ADSI Search</TITLE>
<STYLE TYPE="text/css">
  BODY {font-family:Tahoma,Arial,sans-serif; font-size:10pt}
</STYLE>
</HEAD>
<BODY BGCOLOR=#FFFFFF>

<H1> ADSI Search Page </H1>

<%
```

```
' get the details of the search request
strBase = Request.QueryString("Base")
strFilter = Request.QueryString("Filter")
strScope = Request.QueryString("Scope")
strAttributes = Request.QueryString("Attributes")
iNAttribs = Request.QueryString("NAttribs")

Response.Write "<STRONG> Search Details are </STRONG>"
Response.Write "<BR>Base: " & strBase
Response.Write "<BR>Filter: " & strFilter
Response.Write "<BR>Scope: " & strScope
Response.Write "<BR>Attributes: " & strAttributes
```

Next comes the key part of the page, we create the component that performs the searching (we'll see this next—it's called `WX2882ADSI.Searcher`), and call the `Search()` method on it, supplying all the search options as parameters. Note that we only attempt to perform the search if there appears to be a valid search request—detected by the requested search base not being empty.

```
On Error Resume Next

if not (strBase = "") then
      Set objADSI = Server.CreateObject("WX2882ADSI.Searcher")
      objADSI.Search  strBase, strFilter, strScope, strAttributes,iNAttribs
end if
```

The rest of the page is there simply to set up the form asking for the next search request, and to place default values in all the text boxes.

```
' make sure there are some reasonable default values for the search request
if strBase = "" then
      strBase = "LDAP://dc=TopOfThePops,dc=Fame,dc=com"
end if
if strFilter = "" then
      strFilter = "(objectClass=*)"
end if
if (not(Trim(strScope) = "onelevel") and not (Trim(strScope) = "subtree")_
            and not (Trim(strScope) = "base")) then
      strScope = "onelevel"
end if
if (strAttributes = "") then
      strAttributes = "ADsPath"
end if
if (iNAttribs = "") then
      iNAttribs = 1
end if

%>


<P>
<FORM action = "adsisearch.asp" method = "get" id=form1 name=form1>
Enter new search request here<BR>
Filter:<INPUT type="text" id=Filter name=Filter size = 100 value = "
<% Response.Write strFilter %> "><BR>
Base: <INPUT type="text" id=Base name=Base size = 100 value = "
<% Response.Write strBase %> "><BR>
Scope: <INPUT type="text" id=Scope name=Scope size = 40 value = "
<% Response.Write strScope %> "><BR>
Attributes: <INPUT type="text" id=Attributes name=Attributes size = 100 value = "
<% Response.Write strAttributes %> "><BR>
No. of Attributes Requested (integer):
<INPUT type="text" id=NAttribs name=NAttribs size = 5 value = "
<% Response.Write iNAttribs %> "><BR>
<INPUT type="submit" value="Submit" id=submit1 name=submit1>
<INPUT type="reset" value="Reset" id=reset1 name=reset1><BR>
</FORM>

</BODY>
</HTML>
```

The Searcher Component

So far the code hasn't been particularly interesting, since all we've seen is the routine stuff around displaying the web page appropriately. We haven't seen how the search is actually carried out using ADO.

In fact, this part is very easy, as it's pretty standard ADO stuff. We simply create a Command object, and call its Execute method, to return a Recordset that contains the search results. The provider that we need to specify to ADO is "ADsDSOObject", while the command string to be supplied to the execute command looks like this:

```
<Search Base>;Filter;Attribute List;Scope
```

Where Search Base, Filter, Attribute List, and Scope, should be replaced by their actual values, and all other characters appear literally in the string. So, for example, in our request to retrieve all users, the command string will read:

```
<LDAP://dc=TopOfThePops,dc=Fame,dc=com>;(objectCategory=person);samaccountname,adspath
; subtree
```

The only point to watch is that you shouldn't put any extraneous spaces anywhere in this string—in my experience extra whitespace hopelessly confuses the ADSI provider.

So with all that, the code to actually do the search can be summarized as:

```
oConnection.Provider = "ADsDSOObject"
oConnection.Open "Active Directory Provider"
Dim strCommand
strCommand = "<" & Trim$(strBase) & ">;" & Trim$(strFilter) & ";" & _
    Trim$(strAttributes) & ";" & Trim$(strScope)
Set oRecordset = oConnection.Execute(strCommand)
```

Where strBase, strFilter etc. are the variables that contain the relevant strings. Notice the careful use of the Trim$ function to remove leading and trailing whitespace from the strings—just to be safe.

Writing the Component

Now we're ready to look at the complete code for the WX2882.Searcher component. First up, as usual, we store a reference to the ASP ScriptingContext object.

```
Option Explicit

Dim objScript As ScriptingContext

Sub OnStartPage(objContext As ScriptingContext)
    Set objScript = objContext
End Sub
```

When the Search() method is called, we start off by executing the search, pretty much as described above, except there's some extra error checking.

```
Public Function Search(strBase As Variant, strFilter As Variant, _
        strScope As Variant, strAttributes As Variant, iNAttribs As Variant)

On Error Resume Next
```

```
Dim oConnection As New Connection
Dim oRecordset As Recordset
Set oRecordset = Nothing

oConnection.Provider = "ADsDSOObject"
oConnection.Open "Active Directory Provider"

Dim strCommand
strCommand = "<" & Trim$(strBase) & ">;" & Trim$(strFilter) & ";" & _
    Trim$(strAttributes) & ";" & Trim$(strScope)

Set oRecordset = oConnection.Execute(strCommand)
If oRecordset Is Nothing Then
    objScript.Response.Write "<p>Execution of search failed"
    Exit Function
End If
```

Finally, we display the results as a table, with each row being used to display the details of one object (record) from the search. It is in forming this table that that iNAttribs parameter—the number of attributes requested from the user—is used.

```
Dim i As Integer
objScript.Response.Write "<TABLE border = 4>"
While Not oRecordset.EOF
    objScript.Response.Write "<TR>"
    For i = 0 To iNAttribs - 1
        objScript.Response.Write "<TD>"
        objScript.Response.Write oRecordset.Fields(i).Value
        objScript.Response.Write "</TD>"
    Next
    oRecordset.MoveNext
    objScript.Response.Write "</TR>"
Wend
objScript.Response.Write "</TABLE>"

End Function
```

Authenticating to Directory Objects

We'll finish this chapter with a quick look at security and authenticating. Up to now we've bound to all ADSI objects using Visual Basic's GetObject() function. This is a very versatile function, but does have the disadvantage that it does not allow you to supply any authentication credentials. You will end up bound to the ADSI object using default credentials, which usually means you will be bound with the credentials of the account you've logged in as. This is potentially serious for ASP developers, since the ASP pages will often be running under the Internet Guest Account—so if we can't assume some higher privileges we will very quickly come up against some access denied errors, most likely as soon as we try to actually modify an ADSI object.

If you want to authenticate to an object, the procedure is to start by binding to the namespace object of the appropriate provider (e.g. WinNT: or LDAP:). The namespace object always exposes an additional interface, IADsOpenDSObject, which defines one method, OpenDSObject(). OpenDSObject() works like GetObject(), except that it allows you to supply a username and password. You will then have access to that ADSI object (and automatically to future ADSI objects that you bind to) as if you'd bound to it using the account whose username and password you supplied.

In VB it works like this. Say I wanted to bind to the object that describes my account, as the administrator, and the administrator's account has the password MyPassword. Then I'd do it using this code.

```
Dim oNamespace As IADsOpenDSObject
Set oNamespace = GetObject("WinNT:")

Dim oUser As IADs
Set oUser = oNamespace.OpenDSObject( _
    "WinNT://BiggyBiggy/Simon", "Administrator", _
    "MyPassword", 0)
```

Whereas if I hadn't wanted to use default authentication then this code would have done the job:

```
Dim oUser As IADs
Set oUser = GetObject("WinNT://BiggyBiggy/Simon")
```

By the way, don't worry about that extra 0 in the parameter list to OpenDSObject(). That gives additional information about how we want security to be implemented, but a value of 0 will normally be sufficient.

Summary

In this chapter, we spent quite a lot of time looking at how to integrate the way we work with different directories using ADSI.

We saw how the overall structure of the Active Directory Service Interfaces allows us to work with the different directory systems distributed across the network in a coherent way. This effect of spending more and more time looking at the target technology, rather than how to actually create a component, is going to become increasingly common as you start to explore Windows, COM and componentization in general. The technique of creating the components to interact with the increasing number of features and technologies that Windows encompasses means that we have to spend time familiarizing ourselves with the target object model and the programming techniques that it exposes.

In this chapter, we looked at:

❑ An introduction to directories and directory services, in particular Active Directory.

❑ A look at what the Active Directory Service Interface (ADSI) is, and how it works

❑ How to use the ADSI interfaces to browse directories and retrieve information about the objects in them

❑ How to use ADO with OLE DB's provider for ADSI to search an ADSI-compliant directory that supports searching.

Clearly we've only been able to scrape the surface of ADSI and Active Directory in this chapter, but you should now have the grounding you need to be able to perform simple operations against any directory service using ADSI.

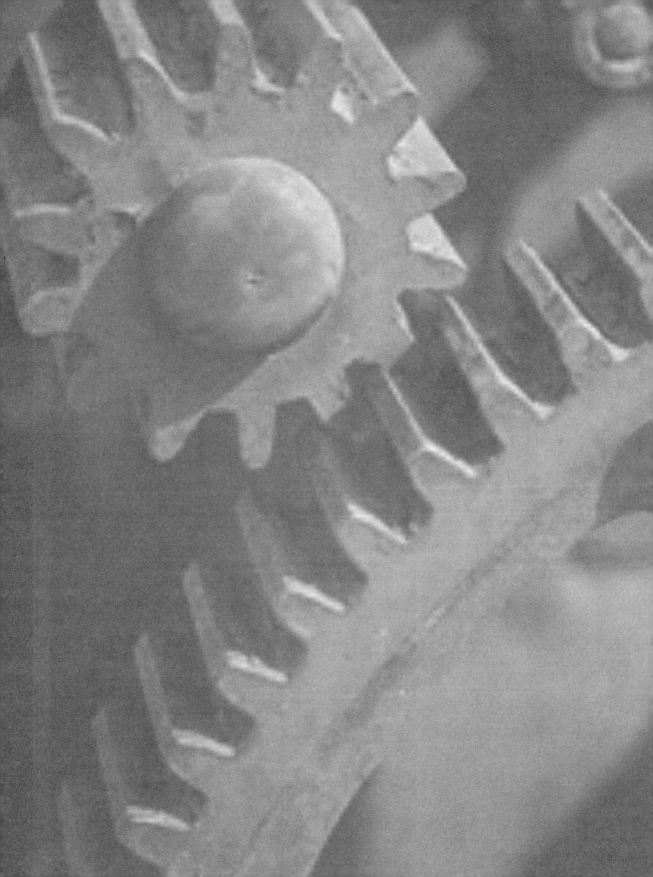

Writing C++ Components Using the Active Template Library

Welcome to Part Two of the book, which begins with a little admission. Everything you've read in the chapters so far has been true, but occasionally it hasn't been the *whole* truth. Visual Basic has been designed very deliberately to make COM programming as easy as possible by hiding some of the trickier details, and we've taken advantage of that fact to skirt around some potentially awkward issues. When you program COM with C++, however, you find yourself much closer to the metal, and some of the things that Visual Basic tucks away come right out into the open.

We're not about to tell you that the facts you've learned about COM are untrue. Components *do* expose their functionality through interfaces. Broadly speaking, interfaces *do* contain methods, properties and events (although you've already seen that properties and events are really just methods that have been marked as properties and events). COM objects *can* be run in-process (in a dynamic-link library) or out-of-process (in an executable application or service). COM components and their clients *can* be written in many different languages, including Visual Basic, C++, Delphi and scripting languages. However, we haven't yet examined the mechanisms by which COM operates in any great detail.

If we're to write components with Visual C++, we need to start understanding more about how components and COM work under the surface. In fact, it's a good idea to understand a bit more about how COM is designed if we're to produce efficient components and clients that make the best use of COM in *any* language, but it's especially important when you're using C++.

COM Under the Hood

On several occasions in this book we have described COM as a **binary standard**, in reference to the fact that the COM specification describes at a very low level how the methods of an interface are called by its clients. Now that we can talk freely in the terms that C++ uses, we can be a lot more specific about the way COM works, and what the binary standard really means.

For example, a COM interface actually has a very specific structure: it is an array of pointers to the implementations of the functions it contains. Because the implementation of each function in the interface is accessed by a pointer in an array, the precise order of the items in that array is an important part of the interface's definition. As you'll see later in the chapter, when you access an interface in C++, you use a pointer to that interface to do so. We end up, then, with a situation like this:

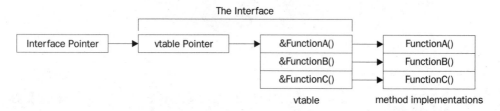

The array of function pointers associated with an interface is usually known as a **vtable** *because it has the same structure as that produced by most compilers for the virtual function table of a C++ class.*

When you program with COM in Visual Basic—whether it's client- or server-side code—you're never exposed to this structure. This is because Microsoft is making every effort to make COM and Visual Basic work seamlessly together. Knowledge of COM is built into Visual Basic itself, and the programmer is thereby insulated from its complexities, as we have seen. Visual C++ and ATL provide some facilities that can make COM programming a little easier, but the pointers you see above are never far away.

Vtables and Inheritance

Let's look a little more closely at that table of function pointers. As indicated beneath the diagram, its structure is exactly the same as that of the vtables produced by C++ compilers, and of course this is no coincidence. It means that if you write some C++ code that contains a class, and provided that class satisfies certain conditions, almost any compiler will compile it into a structure in the object code that exactly matches the structure required of a COM interface. The member functions of the class then correspond to the methods and properties of the interface.

We can take this one step further and consider the situation where we have a C++ class that contains nothing but pure virtual methods—in other words, definitions of methods without any accompanying implementations. In order to be instantiable, any class inheriting from an abstract class like this one would be compelled to implement all the methods it defines, and this is exactly the state of affairs in C++ COM programming. The C++ classes that map to COM components inherit from the interfaces they will implement.

When a C++ class inherits from another one, the composite vtable of the derived class is formed by adding pointers to the methods it defines to the end of the base class's vtable, and this idea also extends to COM. When one *interface* derives from another, the complete definition of the derived interface includes the methods of the base interface.

To see how this works, take a look at the following diagram, in which we have an object implementing an interface called `IDerived` that inherits from another called `IBase`. You can also see how a client is able to call methods of the object that implements the interface:

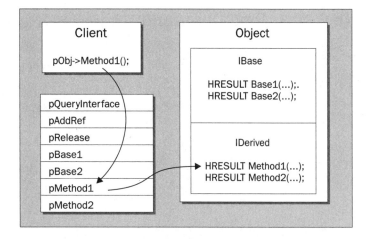

The vtable in the diagram contains three methods that appear in neither the `IBase` nor the `IDerived` interface. These are the methods of the `IUnknown` interface that *all* COM interfaces *must* derive from. We will see why this is important a little later on.

Interfaces in Visual Basic

In COM, clients *only* program against interface pointers. There is no such thing as a pointer to a COM object. Unfortunately, Visual Basic's 'friendly' syntax can make it *look*—incorrectly—as if you're dealing with an object directly, but it's not what's really happening.

When you create an ActiveX DLL in Visual Basic, the methods and properties that you add to the class module are *also* being used to define a COM interface like the ones we've described above, but in such a way that the programmer is protected from what's going on. The interface defined in this fashion is given the same name as the class module, but with a leading underscore that causes it to be invisible in the Visual Basic IDE. When you program COM in C++, however, there's no hiding place.

How Components are Instantiated

All that talk of pointers and vtables has been a little abstract, but we can learn more by examining how different languages instantiate COM components. Once again, COM lays down some guidelines for how instances of a component are created, and because COM is language-neutral, the techniques used to create components in Visual Basic and Visual C++ must eventually amount to the same thing. In this section, we're going to see what happens when you ask COM to supply an instance of a component for you, and in the process we'll discover a lot about how COM works.

Instantiating Components in Visual Basic

What exactly is going on when you make that call to create a new object in Visual Basic? From what you've seen so far, you should already have a pretty good idea of the things that need to be done, but let's consider what they are with reference to a new, very brief example that uses the WX2882.Insurance component we created back in Chapter 2. Here's the complete listing for a standard Visual Basic application called Quote whose form consists of a single label with the name lblQuote:

```
Private Sub Form_Load()
    Dim objInsurance As Insurance
    Dim intQuote As Integer

    Set objInsurance = New Insurance
    objInsurance.DriverAge = 25
    objInsurance.NumberClaims = 2
    objInsurance.EngineCubicInches = 300
    objInsurance.VehicleType = "S"
    objInsurance.DriverGender = "M"

    intQuote = objInsurance.GetPremium
    lblQuote = intQuote
End Sub
```

In order to compile this application, you'll need to go to the Project | References... *dialog and add a reference to* WX2882, *which maps to the* WX2882.dll *file that houses the* WX2882.Insurance *component. Once you've done that, you should be able to build an application called* Quote.exe *that produces a result like this:*

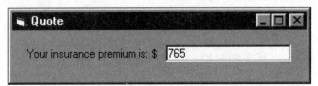

That Dim/Set objInsurance combination hides a *lot* of action. It looks for all the world as if we're just declaring a variable and setting it to a type given by the name of the component, but you know that's not true. In the previous section, you discovered that when you create ActiveX DLLs with Visual Basic, what you get is an object that implements a single, default interface whose name is (but for a leading underscore) the same as the name of the component. What's happening here is that a new Insurance object is being created, and a reference to its _Insurance interface is being stored in objInsurance so that the client can call the methods on that interface.

But that isn't the end of the story, because the object of type Insurance wasn't the only thing we had to add to our project in order to make COM work. We were also required to insert a reference to WX2882.dll in Visual Basic's Project | References... dialog, so that the IDE knew about the Insurance type. Even here, though, all is not quite as it seems. In its eagerness to make things easy for us, Visual Basic runs the risk of pulling the wool over our eyes yet again.

Identifiers and Type Libraries

Although it's certainly true that WX2882.dll contains the COM component we want to use, that's not *really* the reason why Visual Basic is interested in it here. As you saw in Chapter 2, when Visual Basic creates a COM DLL, it puts the type library in there as well.

You already know that the type library contains data about the components in the DLL—their interfaces, and the methods and properties of those interfaces. This is the information that's used by the Visual Basic IDE to implement its IntelliSense feature, and by the compiler to allow early or late binding. However, the type library also contains the GUIDs that get stored in the registry when Visual Basic compiles the DLL. As a reminder, here you can see how the WX2882.Insurance ProgID is linked to our component's CLSID:

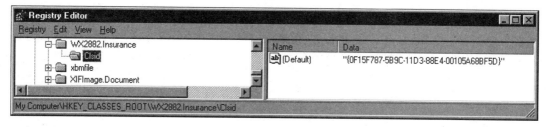

And by cross-referencing under the HKEY_CLASSES_ROOT\CLSID key, you can see that the location of our DLL is safely stashed away:

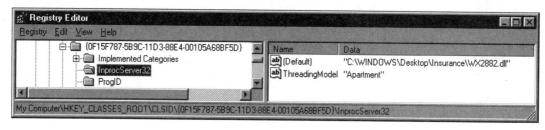

The CLSID on your machine will be different from the value you see here, but the principle of being able to use the ProgID or the CLSID to discover the location of the DLL containing the component will remain the same.

When Visual Basic creates your client (Quote.exe in our case), the identifiers (GUIDs) of the entities it uses are compiled into the executable file. This means that you're completely free to move the DLL around your system, provided that you always remember to re-register it in its new location. Once the application has been created, there is *no* dependency on the location of *any* COM components it uses. It can always use their identifiers to find them.

Instantiating Components in Visual C++

We now have a fairly clear idea of the sequence of actions that must take place in order to get into a position where calls can be made to the methods on an interface of a given object. Whatever language we're using, we need to be able to:

❑ Determine the location of the file containing the component

❑ Cause that file to be loaded into memory

❑ Create an instance of the component in question

❑ Get a way of calling methods on the interface we want to use

To perform operations like this, COM provides a number of C API functions. Visual Basic calls these functions internally, but in C++ we get to use them directly. Let's take a look at some C++ code that is essentially equivalent to the Visual Basic listing above in all but the way it displays its results—it's a console application, so the output goes to the command line.

> Note that this program contains no error checking at all, something that would be completely unacceptable in production code. You'll learn how to check for errors in C++ code that uses COM later in this example.

```
#include <iostream>
#import "c:\windows\desktop\insurance\wx2882.dll"

int main()
{
    CoInitialize(NULL);

    WX2882::_Insurance* pIns = NULL;
    double Premium = 0;

    CoCreateInstance(__uuidof(WX2882::Insurance),
                     NULL, CLSCTX_INPROC_SERVER,
                     __uuidof(WX2882::_Insurance),
                     reinterpret_cast<void**>(&pIns));

    pIns->put_DriverAge(25);
    pIns->put_NumberClaims(2);
    pIns->put_EngineCubicInches(300);
    pIns->put_VehicleType(L"S");
    pIns->put_DriverGender(L"M");
    pIns->raw_GetPremium(&Premium);
    pIns->Release();

    std::cout << "Premium is: $" << Premium << std::endl;

    CoUninitialize();
    return 0;
}
```

If you wish, you can execute this code to prove that it works (making sure that you amend the path to the WX2882.dll file in the second line). If you run it from within the Visual C++ IDE, you should see something like this:

However, seeing that something works is no substitute for understanding *how* it works, and we need to examine this code much more closely. In time, we'll examine the whole program, but at first our attention will be focused on the opening few lines, in which the four steps we outlined at the start of this section are dealt with.

The #import Directive

In an earlier section, you saw how the Visual Basic IDE uses the data in a type library to give your client applications information about the nature and (indirectly) the location of the components they use. Then, the means of performing this feat was the **References** dialog. In Visual C++, we can do the same trick with the **#import** directive:

```
#include <iostream>
#import "c:\windows\desktop\insurance\wx2882.dll"
```

When you provide it with the path of a type library file (or, as here, a file containing a type library), the #import directive will de-compile it and process the information it contains in a way that's similar to Visual Basic's machinations. In this particular case, it will associate GUIDs for the component and the interface with C++ structures called `Insurance` and `_Insurance` respectively, and it will generate definitions for the interface methods so that they may be called from C++ code. In keeping with C++'s policy of openness, you can see these definitions for yourself: the #import directive actually creates a `.tli` and a `.tlh` file in the build (that is, `Debug` or `Release`) directory of your client project.

> The #import directive also generates definitions for some functions that "wrap" calls to the interface methods and make them easier to use, rather as Visual Basic does. However, we're not going to use those here—we're deliberately laying bare COM's inner workings.

CoInitialize() and CoUninitialize()

Before we go any further with our client code, we have to initialize the COM runtime and inform it that this thread wants to use its services, which allows all operations involving COM to take place. It is an absolute requirement that you should call one of these functions once (and only once) on each thread from which you use it—a small detail that Visual Basic spared us from having to worry about. In our code, we perform this task with a call to `CoInitialize()`:

```
int _tmain()
{
    CoInitialize(NULL);

    // The rest of the code

    CoUninitialize();
    return 0;
}
```

It is similarly important that the COM runtime should be uninitialized when all COM work on a thread is complete, and this is the duty of the call to `CoUninitialize()` that appears before the final `return` statement in the listing above.

CoCreateInstance()

With the COM runtime safely initialized, we can at last turn our attention to creating an instance of the Insurance component and getting a pointer to its `_Insurance` interface, so that we can call methods on it. Thanks to the #import directive, `_Insurance` is defined as a type in our project, so we're free to declare variables of type "pointer to `_Insurance`", as we have here:

```
    CoInitialize(NULL);

    WX2882::_Insurance* pIns = NULL;
    double Premium = 0;
```

Notice the use of the scope resolution operator (::). The #import directive has placed all the entities it defines inside a namespace called WX2882, so resolving the name here is essential. The alternative to this technique would have been to apply a using namespace *directive at the top of the file.*

This line is broadly equivalent to the Visual Basic statement "Dim objInsurance As Insurance", in that it prepares a variable to be used as a way of accessing an interface. All that remains then is to fill this variable, which we do with a call to a COM API function called CoCreateInstance():

```
CoCreateInstance(__uuidof(WX2882::Insurance),
                NULL, CLSCTX_INPROC_SERVER,
                __uuidof(WX2882::_Insurance),
                reinterpret_cast<void**>(&pIns));
```

CoCreateInstance() takes five parameters, all of which are dealt with transparently by the compiler when you're using Visual Basic—"Set objInsurance = New Insurance" encapsulated this functionality in our VB client. In C++, the definition of CoCreateInstance() looks like this:

```
STDAPI CoCreateInstance(REFCLSID  rclsid,
                        LPUNKNOWN pUnkOuter,
                        DWORD     dwClsContext,
                        REFIID    riid,
                        LPVOID*   ppv);
```

The essence of CoCreateInstance()'s operation is that you pass it identifiers for the component you want to instantiate and the interface on that component whose methods you wish to call. In return, it will locate the component, create an instance of it ("The clue's in the name!"), and provide you with a pointer to that interface. Looking at our call to the function in that context, you can probably already guess that the first, fourth and fifth parameters are the chief players in this game.

The second parameter becomes relevant when the component being instantiated is involved in **aggregation***; this is a subject we won't be covering until Chapter 12, and it's quite safe to pass* NULL *if you know it's not going to be an issue in this project. The third parameter is used to specify whether the object is to be created in or out of the client process; our component is housed in a DLL, so* CLSCTX_**INPROC**_SERVER *is the right choice. Were the component in an EXE, this value would change to* CLSCTX_**LOCAL**_SERVER. *For more information about this aspect of* CoCreateInstance(), *consult the MSDN library.*

The __uuidof() operator is another Microsoft extension to the C++ language, and in our project it works in tandem with the #import directive. You'll remember that the latter associated GUIDs with Insurance and _Insurance in the files it generated. __uuidof() returns the GUID of the entity it receives as an argument. In our code, then, we're passing the CLSID of the Insurance component as the first parameter to CoCreateInstance(), and the IID of the _Insurance interface as the fourth parameter, exactly as is required.

That brings us to the final parameter, in which we have passed the *address* of the variable that we want to be filled with a pointer to the _Insurance interface, cast to a void**. This type is used because in general, CoCreateInstance() will be used to return pointers to many different interfaces. With correct use of casting, a void** is able to accommodate all of them. The technique of using a pointer parameter of a method to return a value is a very common one in COM programming; as you'll soon see, the "real" return value of the method is frequently otherwise engaged.

Deeper and Down

By examining the creation process in C++, we've seen much more detail than was exposed to us by Visual Basic, and you'll doubtless have your own opinion as to whether that's a good thing. It may come as some surprise, then, to discover that even `CoCreateInstance()` is not the most fundamental function in operation here. To find what lurks beneath the surface of that call, we're going to have to dig deeper still.

You've already seen how the CLSID makes it possible for a function such as `CoCreateInstance()` to locate the file containing a component, but what happens next depends on the type of the object, on some settings in the registry, and (sometimes) on whether the object is already running. We're not going to treat all the possibilities here, but we'll certainly explore how the process works in our particular case.

The `Insurance` component is an in-process component, so the next thing the COM runtime must do is actually load up the DLL into the client process. COM then attempts to call a function in the DLL called `DllGetClassObject()`—it is a requirement of COM that this function *must* be present in a DLL that contains COM components. You might think that this function is responsible for actually creating an instance of the component and returning an interface pointer, and you'd be close—but not quite right.

In COM, creating an instance of a component is actually a two-stage process. The DLL or executable that hosts the component will also host another COM object, known as a **class object** or **class factory**. The class object exposes an interface (usually a standard interface called `IClassFactory`, hence the name) whose methods have the purpose of creating instances of the component you actually want. These methods are called by the COM runtime, the object you originally requested is created, and eventually a pointer to the interface you asked for bubbles back up to `CoCreateInstance()`. The whole process is illustrated in this figure:

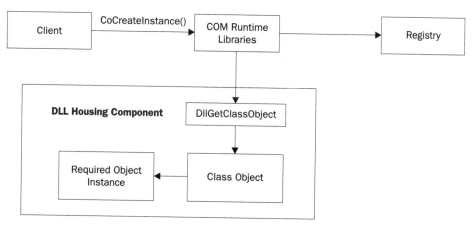

The reasons for this seemingly complex way of doing things are all about performance and flexibility. If you need many instances of the same component, for example, it's possible to write a custom class object that handles more of the initialization process, taking the burden away from the client. However, these are topics beyond the scope of this book, and we will discuss them here no further—Visual Basic and ATL both hide the intricacies of dealing with class objects from the developer. It's good to know that the facilities are there if you need them, though, isn't it?

Calling Methods on a Component

Having acquired a pointer to the _Insurance interface through a means that looked simple but actually turned out fairly complex, our C++ client code goes on to call interface methods in the lines highlighted below:

```
      pIns->put_DriverAge(25);
      pIns->put_NumberClaims(2);
      pIns->put_EngineCubicInches(300);
      pIns->put_VehicleType(L"S");
      pIns->put_DriverGender(L"M");
      pIns->raw_GetPremium(&Premium);
      pIns->Release();
```

The first thing to notice here, of course, is that these *are* all quite definitely method calls, unlike the equivalent lines of code in the Visual Basic client, in which properties appeared to be set by assignment—another of its little ruses. We're using an actual interface pointer to call actual vtable methods, using definitions that were created for us by #import when it processed the type library. Mirroring Visual Basic's (and, as we shall see, ATL's) implementation of the interface, each property is represented by a put_ and/or a get_ method, depending on whether the property is writable, readable, or both. Our code only uses the former, but get_ methods are available too.

> *The name of the interface's single "real" method has been prefixed with the string raw_ to indicate that it's not one of the wrapper methods that #import also generates. If you don't want the wrapper methods, you can add the qualifier raw_interfaces_only to the #import directive. This would also result in the in the "real" method being generated with the name GetPremium().*

Although it doesn't look quite as natural as assignment, the arguments being passed to the property put_ methods here are not difficult to understand. The first three methods' parameters have been defined as short, while those of the fourth and fifth are of type BSTR, a string type that you'll meet in the next chapter. The wide character strings we've passed here are compatible with BSTRs, so they do the job for now.

raw_GetPremium() follows the pattern established earlier by CoCreateInstance(), in that the value we want comes back via a pointer parameter rather than a return value. We're supplying the method with a memory location in which we know it to be completely safe for a value to be placed, and you'd have seen the same system in operation had we used one of the property get_ methods. We promised earlier to explain this mysterious reticence of a COM method to use a return value, and we will... right after we've explained the last important line of our C++ client application.

Object Lifetime and IUnknown

In our discussion about interfaces and vtables earlier in the chapter, we spoke about the importance of the IUnknown interface. That makes the last call through our interface pointer particularly interesting—it's the first time we've seen one of the IUnknown methods in use:

```
      pIns->put_DriverGender(L"M");
      pIns->raw_GetPremium(&Premium);
      pIns->Release();
```

COM specifies that components are responsible for controlling their own lifetimes, although you may find that your definition of "control" is not the same as that of the specification's authors. The rule is that every object should keep a **reference count** of how many clients are using each of its interfaces. As long as there is at least one client using at least one of its interfaces, the object must remain in existence. When that condition is no longer true, the object is free to unload itself—that's what's meant by "control".

The reference count is managed by the `IUnknown` methods `AddRef()` and `Release()`. Any function that returns an interface pointer must call `AddRef()` to ensure that the interface has a reference counted on it, so that it doesn't disappear before the client gets a chance to use it. Similarly, any time an interface pointer is copied, there must be an accompanying call to `AddRef()`. When any copy of the interface pointer has been finished with, clients should call `Release()` to say that they no longer require it. In this way, the status quo is maintained.

In our client application, `CoCreateInstance()` provided us with a pointer to the `_Insurance` interface, and it's safe to assume that `AddRef()` was called during the course of that operation. To be good COM citizens, it's down to us to call `Release()` on that pointer when we've finished using it.

Because the rules for calling `AddRef()` *and* `Release()` *are well-defined, it's possible for compilers to handle reference counting automatically—none of our Visual Basic code has featured calls to either of these methods, because it's all done behind the scenes. Furthermore, Microsoft has written a couple of C++* **smart pointer** *classes that deal with reference counting, and we'll meet those in the next chapter.*

QueryInterface

The third member of the `IUnknown` interface is `QueryInterface()`, which enables a client to establish at runtime what interfaces a COM object exposes. We've said a number of times that a single component can expose *several* COM interfaces, and `QueryInterface()` is the means by which it's possible to get from one to another in your client code.

It works like this: because all interfaces inherit from `IUnknown`, they all provide access to an implementation of `QueryInterface()`. A client that holds a pointer to an interface on a given object can find out whether that object supports another interface by calling `QueryInterface()` and passing the identifier of the interface in which it's interested. If the interface is supported, the client will receive a pointer to it (which will of course have had a reference count made on it). If not, the client will receive a NULL pointer.

All objects must expose the `IUnknown` interface, so we can demonstrate using `QueryInterface()` by making a couple of small amendments to our existing C++ client. Instead of asking for a pointer to the `_Insurance` interface, we can ask `CoCreateInstance()` for a pointer to `IUnknown`, and then query for the interface we really want. The changes you need to make look like this:

```
IUnknown* pUnk = NULL;
WX2882::_Insurance* pIns = NULL;
double Premium = 0;

CoCreateInstance(__uuidof(WX2882::Insurance),
                 NULL, CLSCTX_INPROC_SERVER,
                 __uuidof(IUnknown),
                 reinterpret_cast<void**>(&pUnk));
```

```
        pUnk->QueryInterface(__uuidof(WX2882::_Insurance),
                        reinterpret_cast<void**>(&pIns));

    pIns->put_DriverAge(25);
    pIns->put_NumberClaims(2);
    pIns->put_EngineCubicInches(300);
    pIns->put_VehicleType(L"S");
    pIns->put_DriverGender(L"M");
    pIns->raw_GetPremium(&Premium);

    pIns->Release();
    pUnk->Release();
```

Notice that we now need to make two calls to `Release()`: once for the pointer to `_Insurance`, as before, and once for the pointer to `IUnknown`.

HRESULTs and Error Handling

We've now dissected our C++ and Visual Basic clients line-by-line, and it's about time for us to be good to our word and explain what's going on with the return values of COM method calls. In fact though, if you recall the dire warning we made at the time about our C++ client code containing no error checking, you can probably make a pretty good guess about what they're used for.

In general, COM requires a lot of things to be set up "just so". Components must be registered; entries in the registry must contain the *correct* locations of components; components must implement the interfaces they claim to implement—and we haven't even begun to mention what happens when we start using server and clients on different machines. The point is that there's an awful lot that can go wrong, and COM needs a well-structured way of dealing with the consequences when something does.

The problem is further compounded by the fact that the system used can't be language-specific—it must work regardless of the languages that the client and component are written in. The solution implemented by COM is for almost all functions—APIs *and* interface methods—to return values of type HRESULT.

HRESULT

An HRESULT is a 32-bit value that can contain a code providing information about what happened when a method was executed. There are a good many standard HRESULTs, and you can find a complete list of them in the `winerror.h` header file. We've chosen our words carefully here (rather than just saying, "An HRESULT is a error code," which you'll often see) because while *most* HRESULTs represent failure of some kind, there are dozens of success codes as well. HRESULTs can provide information about *why* a function call failed, or *how* it succeeded.

There are a huge number of different HRESULT values that Microsoft has defined to represent different reasons why a method call might fail. Furthermore there are ranges of values that have been deliberately left for you to define your own HRESULTs for use in your own code. Two common values that you're likely to meet a lot are:

❑   0x00000000, which has the symbol S_OK, and means that your method call succeeded

❑   0x80004005, which has the symbol E_FAIL, and means that the method call failed for some unspecified reason

In this example, we're not going to manipulate HRESULTs very carefully (that can wait for the next chapter), but that leaves us with something of a problem. We're still interested in whether a call succeeds or fails, but with so many possible return values, how do we decide what to test for? Happily, there are a couple of macros that you can use in this situation: when applied to an HRESULT value, SUCCEEDED() and FAILED() will return Boolean values that can be used in tests for success and failure.

Error Handling

Armed with this new information, we can rewrite our client code so that it's rather more robust in the face of potential errors. There are a number of C++ constructs that you could use to implement this functionality (if...break is another that comes to mind); here's the one we've chosen:

```
int main()
{
    CoInitialize(NULL);

    WX2882::_Insurance* pIns = NULL;
    double Premium = 0;

    HRESULT hr = CoCreateInstance(__uuidof(WX2882::Insurance),
                                  NULL, CLSCTX_INPROC_SERVER,
                                  __uuidof(WX2882::_Insurance),
                                  reinterpret_cast<void**>(&pIns));
    if(FAILED(hr))
        std::cout << "Error in object creation" << std::endl;
    else
    {
        if(SUCCEEDED(pIns->put_DriverAge(25)))
            if(SUCCEEDED(pIns->put_NumberClaims(2)))
                if(SUCCEEDED(pIns->put_EngineCubicInches(300)))
                    if(SUCCEEDED(pIns->put_VehicleType(L"S")))
                        if(SUCCEEDED(pIns->put_DriverGender(L"M")))
                            if(SUCCEEDED(pIns->raw_GetPremium(&Premium)))
                                std::cout << "Premium is: $" << Premium << std::endl;
        pIns->Release();
    }

    CoUninitialize();
    return 0;
}
```

In our particular circumstances, the first test is probably the most important. Of all the calls here, CoCreateInstance() is the most likely to fail (perhaps the DLL has been moved but not re-registered), and if that happens we don't want to start making calls against an uninitialized pointer.

Once the object has been created successfully, and since we're dealing with a DLL server, it's quite unlikely that future calls against it will fail. Nevertheless, in the else block we diligently ensure that every method call has succeeded before making the next one, and call _Insurance::Release() whatever else happens. Were we communicating with the server across a network, it would be possible for the connection to break at any time, and checks like these would become vital.

Of course, you'll have realized that this is not how things appear to happen in Visual Basic at all. There, calls to COM methods calls don't return HRESULTs —they appear to return the actual values. C++ code like this:

```
pIns->raw_GetPremium(&Premium)
```

Translates to Visual Basic code like this:

```
intQuote = objInsurance.GetPremium
```

The premium appears as the return value (rather than as a parameter passed to the function), while the HRESULT is nowhere to be seen! Well, in fact the HRESULT *has* appeared. It has become the Number property on the **error object**, Err.Number.

What happens is that Visual Basic takes the returned HRESULT and checks it automatically. If it's a success value, that's fine. If it's an error value, Visual Basic will raise an exception, which is why you need to have On Error statements around to catch them. In *either* case, Visual Basic will place the HRESULT in the error object. If we had an error, it will also check to see whether there is a corresponding description (if it's a standard Microsoft error there surely will be) and add that to the error object too.

Scripting Clients and IDispatch

Before we leave this discussion of client-side code behind and develop our first C++ COM component, we need to look at a subject that has little to do with C++, but everything to do with ASP. So far, we've talked about component instantiation with CoCreateInstance() in C++ and New in Visual Basic, and how under the surface, both techniques amount to the same thing. When we come to ASP pages, however, we have a problem.

The fundamental difficulty is this: scripting languages are simply incapable of using the vtables that we have been talking about as being essential to the operation of COM. Because of this, they no means of recognizing that there are different interfaces around, being exposed by the various components available. This must mean that scripting clients need a different mechanism to be able to call the methods of an object.

> *The discussions here also apply if you are coding in Visual Basic and choose to* Dim *a variable as being of type* Object, *rather than as being a particular interface type.*

Scripting clients call methods through a standard COM interface called IDispatch. Communication with this interface is handled by the environment that processes your script code, and it's set up when you call CreateObject() (or the equivalent object creation function) from script. Thereafter, all communication between your script code and the object goes through a method of the IDispatch interface called Invoke(). For historical reasons, this method of communicating with COM objects is known as **Automation**.

Dispatch Interfaces

Of course, all of these technical niceties are hidden from the programmer writing the script code, who can just set object properties and call methods in a way that's eerily similar to the way Visual Basic can talk to vtable interfaces. In fact, what's going on is that every time an Automation-compatible object is used from script code, a plethora of COM calls take place between the scripting environment and the object before the "actual" call can occur. When it finally does take place, the call is not to a vtable interface, but to a **dispatch interface**.

The methods and properties in a dispatch interface do not have to appear in a vtable. Rather than being identified by their position in such a structure, they are instead distinguished by a simple integer called a **dispatch identifier**, or **DISPID**.

When a script client calls a method in a dispatch interface, the scripting environment will call a method on the IDispatch interface of the COM object called GetIDsOfNames(). The implementation of this method will then check to see whether a function with the requested name appears in the dispinterface it manages, and if it does, it will return the DISPID of the requested method. Next, the scripting environment will call IDispatch::Invoke(), passing the DISPID it just discovered. Any results of calling the method will come back via the other parameters of Invoke(), and will eventually find their way back to the script code.

This is obviously an abbreviated discussion of the process that takes place, which can become even more convoluted if the method being called takes parameters. However, you can probably already appreciate that this process will cause a considerable performance loss, and it's the main reason why you should always try to give explicit types to the objects in your Visual Basic source code. It is also one of the reasons why scripting languages run so much more slowly than compiled languages when COM components are being used.

Early and Late Binding

One way of improving the efficiency of calls through IUnknown is to cut out the need to ask the dispinterface for the DISPIDs of the methods it contains by making the DISPIDs available to the client before it makes the call. That way, it can cut straight to calling Invoke() without the overhead of intervening calls.

It turns out that this feat can be performed using the same source of information that the implementation of GetIDsOfNames() usually uses: the type library. Type libraries can be used to describe dispinterfaces as well as vtable interfaces, and this description includes the DISPIDs of all the methods they contain.

This more efficient technique of using Automation is known as **early binding**, while its slower partner is usually called **late binding**, to reflect the different times at which the DISPIDs of the methods become known to the client. Unfortunately, however, there is no support in the current generation of scripting languages for referencing a type library in the way that (say) Visual Basic does, and so late binding is the only option at their disposal.

Dual Interfaces

You've already seen examples of the same COM object being called in apparently the same way using vtable *and* dispinterface techniques. Given the above discussion, you'd be forgiven for wondering how this can take place. In fact, by default, the interfaces generated by both Visual Basic and (as we shall soon discover) ATL are **dual interfaces**.

A dual interface derives from IDispatch rather than IUnknown (of course, the former derives from the latter), and the methods in the vtable are also given DISPIDs. This means that client languages that can cope with the vtable can use it just as they normally would, but scripting clients can still use the object that exposes the interface using the less efficient technique of Automation. In this way, the components that we create in Visual Basic and Visual C++ can be used in our ASP pages.

Creating a Component in Visual C++

If all that theoretical discussion seemed difficult, here's the section in which you'll get your reward for persevering. We're going to see just how easy it is to create a COM component using C++ and the Active Template Library (ATL).

In fact, in order to get a direct comparison with Visual Basic, we're going to do something really sneaky: we're going to create a car insurance premium component that does exactly the same thing as the one we wrote in Chapter 2. To begin, close the console application project that we were experimenting with in the first part of the chapter and select File | New... to create a new project. From the list available, select an ATL COM AppWizard project and name it CppInsure:

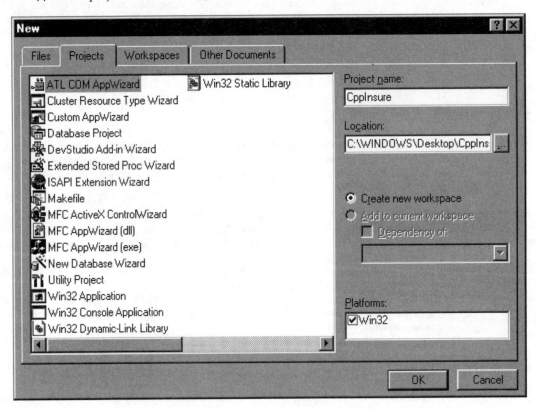

The next dialog then asks us for some more details about the type of component we want to create:

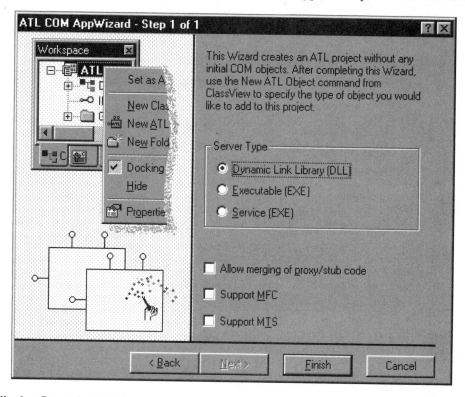

We'll select <u>D</u>ynamic Link Library, as we want this component to run in process. If we had selected <u>E</u>xecutable, we'd have got something that would run out-of-process, and if we'd selected <u>S</u>ervice, we'd have got something that would run as a special type of process known as an NT service. As it happens, we won't be developing any components that are executables in this book, although the techniques involved are the same. If you select EXE rather than DLL here, the code that the Wizard gives you will be different, but that has no effect on the code that you add to it. Services are beyond the scope of this book.

> The **Allow merging of <u>p</u>roxy/stub code** *option can give better performance in some situations, but it's strictly for advanced programmers who know COM inside out—and it's beyond the scope of this book. If the* **Support <u>M</u>FC** *box is checked, we'll end up with some extra includes and code that let us take advantage of some of the user interface classes provided by MFC, but it will have no effect on the component itself.* **Support M<u>T</u>S** *is self-explanatory; we'll cover ATL components that support MTS in Chapter 14. We'll leave these three options unselected for this example.*

Click on the <u>F</u>inish button, and we have our project; the AppWizard has completed its task. However, it's important to understand that we *don't* yet have a component. The ATL COM AppWizard has given us a project that when compiled will be a DLL that is capable of hosting components. It's also given us some C++ boilerplate code that handles some generic COM requirements, like registering the DLL. Remember that multiple components can be housed in the same DLL or EXE file.

The ATL Object Wizard

We need to create the actual component, which we do with the ATL Object Wizard. To start this up, go to the Insert menu of Visual C++ and select the New ATL Object... item in it. This brings up a dialog box asking what kind of component we want:

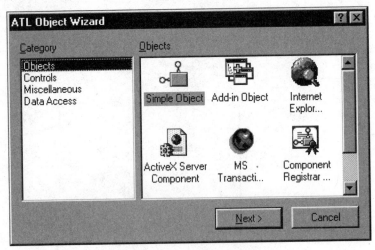

Notice that even Visual C++ gets its terminology muddled here, variously calling the things it adds to your project "objects" and "components".

Select Simple Object from the Objects category, and then click on Next. The resulting dialog box asks us about the properties of the component we want to create. It's a tabbed dialog, and the first tab just asks us for the name of our component. We'll call it CalcPremium:

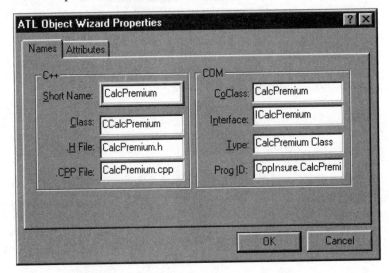

There are a lot of text boxes here, but in fact the only one you need to fill in is the first, labeled <u>Short</u> Name. The Wizard will automatically fill in the other boxes as you type, based on the name you supply here. (For example, it will prefix the interface name with I, and the name of the C++ class that implements this component with C, both in accordance with the usual conventions.) If you don't like what the Wizard gives you for any of the other names, you can change the contents of the other edit boxes as you see fit.

The second tab is more intriguing. It lets us select some of the characteristics of the component, and it's the first dialog box we've encountered that reveals some of the additional flexibility we gain by using C++ instead of Visual Basic:

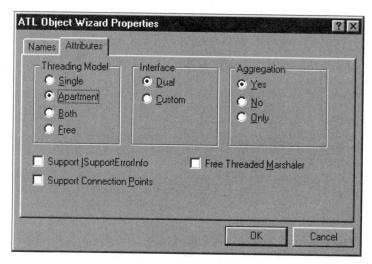

For example, where the Visual Basic Class Builder gave us the option of choosing 'single' or 'apartment' for the threading model, the ATL Object Wizard offers all four currently available models—and we'll be examining the impact this has in Chapter 12. We also get the option of implementing a Dual or a Custom interface, although there's little point in choosing the latter unless you know your object will *never* be accessed from scripting clients. In the third frame, you can choose whether your object is **aggregatable.** This is another subject we're going to touch upon in Chapter 12, but for the time being the default setting will be fine.

Looking beneath the frames, ISupportErrorInfo is a standard COM interface that provides a way of reporting extended error messages (that is, more than just an HRESULT) to the client if anything goes wrong, and we'll see how they work in the next chapter. Supporting connection points enables your component to fire events (that is, to call methods in the client), a feature we won't require in any of our sample projects. For this first example, you can leave *all* the settings on this dialog with their default values, and click OK to proceed.

Implementing Methods and Properties

With that, the Object Wizard is finished, and you have your new class. However, *we* are not yet finished. All the C++ code for the component is now in place—there's a component called CalcPremium that exposes an IDispatch-derived interface called ICalcPremium. The trouble is, ICalcPremium doesn't yet have any methods or properties of its own. We want to add the same methods and properties that were available on the _Insurance interface of the WX2882.Insurance component.

The #import directive we used in our C++ client application had the useful side effect of revealing the equivalent C++ types of the WX2882.Insurance component's methods and properties. As a reminder, the properties were VehicleType (a BSTR), NumberClaims (a short), DriverAge (a short), DriverGender (a BSTR), and EngineCubicInches (a short). The single method GetPremium() returned a value of type double.

It will no doubt come as some relief that where Visual Basic had the Class Builder to assist with adding methods and properties, Visual C++ has Wizards that it makes available via the ClassView:

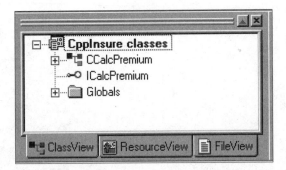

To add the GetPremium() method to the ICalcPremium interface, you need to begin by right-clicking on its name in the ClassView (you can see that it's marked by a COM lollipop). From the resulting context menu, select Add Method.... That brings up the following dialog:

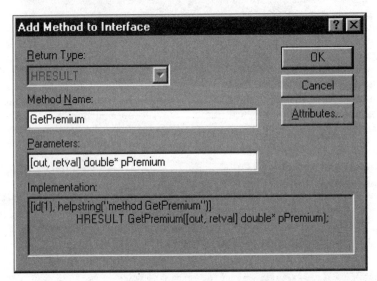

The screenshot shows the details that you need to provide to this Wizard, and the four controls on the left of the dialog all contain interesting information. First, the return type of the method is fixed as HRESULT, in keeping with our discussion about error handling earlier in the chapter. Second, the method name is specified as GetPremium, so there's not really much to talk about there. It's in the third control that things start to become a little trickier.

The right-hand part of the Parameters edit control is simple enough: you've already seen how the HRESULT return type mandates that any other values returned from a function must come back via pointer parameters, so the double* type should come as no surprise. Something else you've already seen is that Visual Basic can make this additional "return value" look like the *actual* return value, and that (in part) is what's being set up by the strange-looking string [out, retval].

Attributes and IDL

[out] and [retval] are examples of **attributes** that can be applied to parameters in definitions of COM interfaces' methods and properties (among other things). This chapter is not the place for a dissertation on the subject, but if you intend to use ATL to create components, some understanding of how attributes work is required.

Here are some basic rules for applying attributes to method parameters in this dialog:

❑　If a parameter will be used for passing values into a method, mark it [in]

❑　If a parameter will be used for returning values from a method, mark it [out]

❑　If a parameter will be used for passing values to and from a method, mark it [in, out]

❑　If an [out] parameter will be used as the "return value" in Visual Basic or script code, you should also mark it [retval]. Only one parameter can have this attribute.

It is important to point out that attributes do not affect your C++ code. Rather, they have an impact on our old friend, the type library. In Visual C++ ATL projects, the type library is generated from a file with the extension .idl that you'll find in the project folder; its name is in deference to the fact that the file contains a description of all the components in your project written in the **Interface Definition Language**, or **IDL**.

The Implementation box on the Add Method to Interface dialog shows the code that will be added to the IDL file (and ultimately to the type library) when you hit the OK button. Apart from the minor chore of applying attributes in this dialog, however, we will not need to concern ourselves with the IDL file in any of the projects we develop in this book. Each time you compile the project, the IDL file will quietly be processed to produce a type library.

You can see attributes being used again in the dialog below, in which we're adding the first of the five properties to our ICalcPremium interface. This Wizard can be summoned by selecting Add Property... from the right-click context menu. We're defining DriverAge as a property of type short, and the Implementation box shows [out, retval] and [in] attributes being applied to parameters of the 'Get' and 'Put' methods respectively:

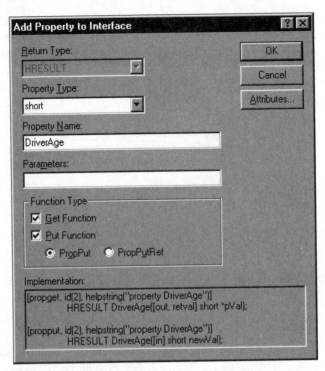

Attributes aside, this is another place where ATL's Wizard scores over Visual Basic's Component Builder, since it offers you the choice of whether you want the property to be readable and/or writable. If you want to disallow either, just uncheck the corresponding box. In Visual Basic, you always get both methods, and have to delete one from your code if you don't want it. The radio buttons that ask whether you want to do a PropPut or a PropPutRef are equivalent to Visual Basic's Let and Set options.

If you add all five properties in this way, we'll get to the point at which we are ready actually to edit the code that has been generated for us.

Looking at the Wizard-Generated Code

The Wizard has given us a lot of C++ code, but as we've remarked a few times already, we're actually going to ignore most of it. All we need to do here is implement the methods that were added to our class by the Wizard.

This is one place where we have a bit more work to do than we had in Visual Basic. Then, the Component Builder made an attempt to fill in the get and put property methods by setting or retrieving the value of an appropriate variable. Of course, if getting or setting a property for our particular component involved more work, we'd still have to edit that code, but at least we had a start. By contrast, the ATL Wizards have given us completely empty functions.

The code for the implementations of the method calls is in the file CalcPremium.cpp. As an example, this is what we've been given for the DriverAge:

```
STDMETHODIMP CCalcPremium::get_DriverAge(short *pVal)
{
   // TODO: Add your implementation code here

   return S_OK;
}

STDMETHODIMP CCalcPremium::put_DriverAge(short newVal)
{
   // TODO: Add your implementation code here

   return S_OK;
}
```

The STDMETHODIMP declaration for the function type is just a macro that's been defined using the #define preprocessor command. It defines the function to return an HRESULT, and signals the compiler to create a COM compatible method. While this macro is very important, it's not very nice to look at!

The functions have been defined as members of the class CCalcPremium, whose name was one of the things that got generated automatically when we specified the component name. We'll be adding all the code that implements the methods and properties we defined to CCalcPremium, despite the fact that it isn't *actually* the class that implements the COM object. *That* class is derived from CCalcPremium, and it's defined using templates as CComObject<CCalcPremium>. For what we're going to do in this chapter, however, that needn't concern us.

A basic definition of CCalcPremium has been written for us by the Object Wizard and placed in the file CalcPremium.h. Here it is:

```
class ATL_NO_VTABLE CCalcPremium :
   public CComObjectRootEx<CComSingleThreadModel>,
   public CComCoClass<CCalcPremium, &CLSID_CalcPremium>,
   public IDispatchImpl<ICalcPremium, &IID_ICalcPremium, &LIBID_CPPINSURELib>
{
public:
   CCalcPremium()
   {
   }

DECLARE_REGISTRY_RESOURCEID(IDR_CALCPREMIUM)

DECLARE_PROTECT_FINAL_CONSTRUCT()

BEGIN_COM_MAP(CCalcPremium)
   COM_INTERFACE_ENTRY(ICalcPremium)
   COM_INTERFACE_ENTRY(IDispatch)
END_COM_MAP()

// ICalcPremium
public:
   STDMETHOD(GetPremium)(/*[out, retval]*/ double* pPremium);
   STDMETHOD(get_DriverAge)(/*[out, retval]*/ short *pVal);
   STDMETHOD(put_DriverAge)(/*[in]*/ short newVal);
   STDMETHOD(get_DriverGender)(/*[out, retval]*/ BSTR *pVal);
   STDMETHOD(put_DriverGender)(/*[in]*/ BSTR newVal);
   STDMETHOD(get_EngineCubicInches)(/*[out, retval]*/ short *pVal);
   STDMETHOD(put_EngineCubicInches)(/*[in]*/ short newVal);
   STDMETHOD(get_NumberClaims)(/*[out, retval]*/ short *pVal);
   STDMETHOD(put_NumberClaims)(/*[in]*/ short newVal);
   STDMETHOD(get_VehicleType)(/*[out, retval]*/ BSTR *pVal);
   STDMETHOD(put_VehicleType)(/*[in]*/ BSTR newVal);
};
```

Now, at first glance, Wizard-generated ATL code can look a little bewildering, but in fact most of this is just more macros defined by Microsoft. You can always tell Microsoft macros because they're invariably named using uppercase letters. To prove it's not as bad as it looks, let's go through the class definition in more detail. First, the declaration:

```
class ATL_NO_VTABLE CCalcPremium :
    public CComObjectRootEx<CComSingleThreadModel>,
    public CComCoClass<CCalcPremium, &CLSID_CalcPremium>,
    public IDispatchImpl<ICalcPremium, &IID_ICalcPremium, &LIBID_CPPINSURELib>
```

The `ATL_NO_VTABLE` macro allows the linker to perform some optimizations, but it doesn't affect how the class works.

Next, you can see that ATL is making use of multiple inheritance. `CCalcPremium` is derived from three base classes. To make things a little more interesting, all three are template classes whose behavior can be customized according to their template parameters. As far as we're concerned, the important one is `IDispatchImpl<>`, which provides a complete implementation of the `IDispatch` interface—this pattern of a class inheriting from the interfaces it implements is a common one in C++, and you should be on the lookout for further examples of it as we progress. `CComObjectRootEx<>` is responsible for the `IUnknown` interface, while `CComCoClass<>` is responsible for sorting out class objects and instantiating the object.

In other words, these three lines are complex, but they tell us that Microsoft has already written boilerplate C++ code that does a lot of the work for us. By the way, if you want to find these base classes, you won't find their definitions anywhere in your project. They are buried away in the header files supplied with Visual C++. Have a look at `atlbase.h` and `atlcom.h` if you're interested.

```
{
public:
    CCalcPremium()
    {
    }

DECLARE_REGISTRY_RESOURCEID(IDR_CALCPREMIUM)

DECLARE_PROTECT_FINAL_CONSTRUCT()

BEGIN_COM_MAP(CCalcPremium)
    COM_INTERFACE_ENTRY(ICalcPremium)
    COM_INTERFACE_ENTRY(IDispatch)
END_COM_MAP()
```

Next, we get a default constructor for the class that does nothing, followed by a couple of macros that need not trouble us here. The set of macros beginning with `BEGIN_COM_MAP` are known as the **COM map**, and they expand into C++ code that creates an array of structures which detail all the interfaces implemented by the component. This list is used by ATL's implementation of `IUnknown`—specifically, by its implementation of `QueryInterface()`. If an interface that you implement is to be available via `QueryInterface()`, it must appear here—and the ATL Wizards will generally ensure that it does.

```
    // ICalcPremium
public:
    STDMETHOD(GetPremium)(/*[out, retval]*/ double* pPremium);
    STDMETHOD(get_DriverAge)(/*[out, retval]*/ short *pVal);
    STDMETHOD(put_DriverAge)(/*[in]*/ short newVal);
    STDMETHOD(get_DriverGender)(/*[out, retval]*/ BSTR *pVal);
    STDMETHOD(put_DriverGender)(/*[in]*/ BSTR newVal);
    STDMETHOD(get_EngineCubicInches)(/*[out, retval]*/ short *pVal);
    STDMETHOD(put_EngineCubicInches)(/*[in]*/ short newVal);
    STDMETHOD(get_NumberClaims)(/*[out, retval]*/ short *pVal);
    STDMETHOD(put_NumberClaims)(/*[in]*/ short newVal);
    STDMETHOD(get_VehicleType)(/*[out, retval]*/ BSTR *pVal);
    STDMETHOD(put_VehicleType)(/*[in]*/ BSTR newVal);
};
```

Finally, you can see the declarations of all the functions we need to implement. These are the functions that actually get called when a method call is made on one of the component's interfaces. The STDMETHOD() macro is similar to the STDMETHODIMP one used in the source file, and indicates that the function is virtual and returns an HRESULT. (It also gives the compiler some information that optimizes the way the function is called).

Adding Functionality

At long last, we're ready to add some functionality to our component. As a first step, we need some member variables to store the property values:

```
    STDMETHOD(get_VehicleType)(/*[out, retval]*/ BSTR *pVal);
    STDMETHOD(put_VehicleType)(/*[in]*/ BSTR newVal);

private:
    short m_lEngineCubicInches;
    short m_lDriverAge;
    short m_lNumberClaims;
    CComBSTR m_bstrDriverGender;
    CComBSTR m_bstrVehicleType;
};
```

CComBSTR is a type defined by ATL to make the potentially difficult task of handling BSTRs easier, and we'll be examining it properly in the next chapter. One of the services it provides is automatic initialization, something we don't have for our short variables, and which we should therefore do in the constructor's initializer list:

```
public:
    CCalcPremium()  : m_lEngineCubicInches(0),
                      m_lDriverAge(0),
                      m_lNumberClaims(0)
    {
    }
```

As well as implementing all the functions, we'll need to define the same constants that were used in the Visual Basic implementation of the premium calculator component. We've chosen to put the constants in the CalcPremium.cpp file, since that's the only file in which they are used. Here's the complete file listing, with all the changes you need to add. Although it's quite long, it's not really hard to follow.

```
// CalcPremium.cpp : Implementation of CCalcPremium
#include "stdafx.h"
#include "CppInsure.h"
#include "CalcPremium.h"
```

```
const double DOLLARS_PER_CU_INCH =      1.25;
const short  LOWEST_CLAIM_AGE_MALE =      45;    //years old
const short  LOWEST_CLAIM_AGE_FEMALE = 40;       //years old
const double ADD_PER_YEAR_FROM_LOW =    0.01;    //1 percent
const double ADD_PER_CLAIM =            0.35;    //plus 35 percent
const double ADD_WAGON =               -0.15;    //minus 15 percent
const double ADD_COUPE =                0.25;    //plus 25 percent
const double ADD_SPORTS =               0.5;     //plus 50 percent

//////////////////////////////////////////////////////////////////////
// CCalcPremium

STDMETHODIMP CCalcPremium::get_VehicleType(BSTR *pVal)
{
    *pVal = m_bstrVehicleType;
    return S_OK;
}

STDMETHODIMP CCalcPremium::put_VehicleType(BSTR newVal)
{
    m_bstrVehicleType = newVal;
    return S_OK;
}

STDMETHODIMP CCalcPremium::get_NumberClaims(short *pVal)
{
    *pVal = m_lNumberClaims;
    return S_OK;
}

STDMETHODIMP CCalcPremium::put_NumberClaims(short newVal)
{
    m_lNumberClaims = newVal;
    return S_OK;
}

STDMETHODIMP CCalcPremium::get_DriverGender(BSTR *pVal)
{
    *pVal = m_bstrDriverGender;
    return S_OK;
}

STDMETHODIMP CCalcPremium::put_DriverGender(BSTR newVal)
{
    m_bstrDriverGender = newVal;
    return S_OK;
}

STDMETHODIMP CCalcPremium::get_DriverAge(short *pVal)
{
    *pVal = m_lDriverAge;
    return S_OK;
}

STDMETHODIMP CCalcPremium::put_DriverAge(short newVal)
{
    m_lDriverAge = newVal;
    return S_OK;
}

STDMETHODIMP CCalcPremium::get_EngineCubicInches(short *pVal)
{
    *pVal = m_lEngineCubicInches;
    return S_OK;
}
```

```
STDMETHODIMP CCalcPremium::put_EngineCubicInches(short newVal)
{
    m_lEngineCubicInches = newVal;
    return S_OK;
}

STDMETHODIMP CCalcPremium::GetPremium(double *pPremium)
{
    double dlbExtraPercent = 0;

    // Calculate base premium depending on engine size
    double dblPremium = m_lEngineCubicInches * DOLLARS_PER_CU_INCH;

    // Add on loading depending on driver gender and age
    if(towupper(m_bstrDriverGender[0]) == L'F')
        dlbExtraPercent = abs(LOWEST_CLAIM_AGE_FEMALE -
                                        m_lDriverAge) * ADD_PER_YEAR_FROM_LOW;
    else
        dlbExtraPercent = abs(LOWEST_CLAIM_AGE_MALE -
                                        m_lDriverAge) * ADD_PER_YEAR_FROM_LOW;

    dblPremium += dblPremium * dlbExtraPercent;

    // Add on loading for number of accidents or claims
    dlbExtraPercent = m_lNumberClaims * ADD_PER_CLAIM;
    dblPremium = dblPremium + (dblPremium * dlbExtraPercent);

    // Add on loading for type or vehicle
    wchar_t cVehicleFirstChar = towupper(m_bstrVehicleType[0]);
    switch(cVehicleFirstChar)
    {
    case L'S':
        dlbExtraPercent = 0;
        break;
    case L'W':
        dlbExtraPercent = ADD_WAGON;
        break;
    case L'C':
        dlbExtraPercent = ADD_COUPE;
        break;
    case L'P':
        dlbExtraPercent = ADD_SPORTS;
        break;
    default:
        _ASSERTE(false);
    }

    dblPremium = dblPremium + (dblPremium * dlbExtraPercent);

    // Assign result to function variable
    *pPremium = dblPremium;
    return S_OK;
}
```

Most of this is really quite straightforward—these are just regular C++ functions—although there are a few things that are worthy of note. First, there's the `towupper()` function, which converts Unicode characters to uppercase. Second, we're using `wchar_t` because that defines a Unicode character—and COM uses Unicode strings. Finally, `_ASSERTE()` is a way of making the application throw an assertion in the event of a problem, something that would be unacceptable in production code.

Incidentally, I wrote the `GetPremium()` *function by pasting in the code from the Visual Basic sample in Chapter 2, then changing all the lines from Visual Basic format to C++ format!*

And that's our component finished. All that remains is to compile the project and test it. When you build the project, it will also automatically get registered, ready for clients to use.

Testing CalcPremium

Since we've written a component that does exactly the same thing as our Visual Basic component in Chapter 2, it makes sense to use the same client to test it. So, our test harness is the same ASP page as we had in Chapter 2, with a single change: we need to make sure it calls up our C++ component, rather than the Visual Basic one.

To do that, all we have to do is change the line in the script code to use the ProgID of our C++ component—that is, CppInsure.CalcPremium:

```
'create our component instance
Set objWX2882 = Server.CreateObject("CppInsure.CalcPremium")

'set the properties
objWX2882.VehicleType = strVehType
objWX2882.DriverGender = strGender
objWX2882.DriverAge = intAge
objWX2882.EngineCubicInches = intEngineSize
objWX2882.NumberClaims = strClaims
```

We are now ready to test our component. To make sure everything really does work just as it did before, we'll see what we get offered for the same car as we gave the Visual Basic component:

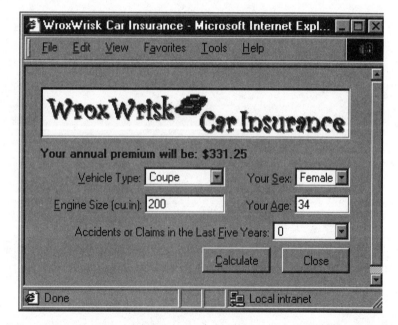

That's exactly the same number we got last time! We may have changed the implementation, but sadly the quote hasn't changed at all.

Summary

In this chapter, we've begun to examine COM programming using Visual C++ rather than Visual Basic, with the ultimate aim of knowing when and how it can be a better tool for ASP component development. Over the next few chapters, we'll be looking carefully at the extra flexibility that using C++ can give us. In this one, however, we've had to return to some basic COM programming issues, this time with a C++ perspective. You've seen that:

❏ The binary structure that COM interfaces conform to is an array of pointers to functions that's known as a vtable in C++ programming.

❏ The C++ classes that implement COM components derive from the interfaces that those components will expose. All COM interfaces derive (directly or indirectly) from `IUnknown`.

❏ When you create an ActiveX DLL in Visual Basic, the properties and methods of the class module you create are also the properties and methods of a COM interface.

❏ In C++, we can get access to the information in a type library by using the `#import` directive, which creates definitions of a COM component's interfaces and identifiers that can be used from your C++ programs.

❏ When you want to use COM in a C++ program, you must initialize it on every thread from which you want to use it, and uninitialize it on every thread after you've finished using it.

❏ The methods of the `IUnknown` interface (`QueryInterface()`, `AddRef()` and `Release()`) are used for discovering what interfaces an object exposes and controlling an object's lifetime respectively.

❏ When you use COM from scripting languages, you're always using Automation. That is, you're always calling methods of dispatch interfaces via the standard COM interface `IDispatch`.

❏ By default, both Visual Basic and Visual C++ (using ATL) generate COM components with dual interfaces that can be called either through their vtables or by using Automation.

The final part of the chapter demonstrated how to create your first COM component using ATL, and we were able to test it successfully in the same ASP page we used back in Chapter 2 for our first Visual Basic component.

In the next chapter, we will look more closely at how ATL works, examine what specific support the ATL Object Wizard provides for writing ASP components, and explore some further assistance that Visual C++ supplies for COM programmers.

Developing An ASP Component Using C++

In the last chapter, we looked at how COM works under the hood and created a very basic COM component using ATL. In this chapter, we'll develop a more sophisticated component, explain some more ATL/COM classes, and examine some issues you need to be aware of in order to develop good components for ASP using C++.

By the end of this chapter, we will have developed a small, commercial quality ASP component designed for storing and manipulating a simple list of values. It may not be the most exciting component in this book, but the development of it will cover a lot of important ground and techniques that you need to understand when working in C++. We will use the Object Wizard to create the initial shell of our component, and then discuss in some detail what the Wizard does for us and why. We'll then extend the functionality of the component using the Standard Template Library, and cover a couple of good reasons why C++ can be better for developing some types of ASP component.

This chapter will deal with the following topics:

- ❑ A tour of the ATL Wizard for creating ASP components
- ❑ Accessing the ASP intrinsic objects from a C++ component
- ❑ Error handling and implementing more than one interface
- ❑ Helpful ATL utility classes: CComBSTR, CComVariant, CComPtr<>, and CComQIPtr<>
- ❑ Using the Standard Template Library
- ❑ The pros and cons of using C++ for developing ASP components using C++

The List Component

As good component writers, we shouldn't start coding a component until we've got a clear description of the problem or task we are trying to address, and a basic idea of the functionality we need. This isn't a chapter about component design per se, so we'll briefly look at the functionality of the component and then cover the methods, although we will of course fully implement the component by the end of the chapter.

The List component is really designed as a teaching tool rather than something you'd use on your web site, but I'm sure that as you read this chapter, you'll think of many potential applications for it, or come up with other ideas for similar components that could be equally as useful. For example, the list component could be used to track all the ASP pages a user visits, saving that information to a database when the user session ends, or just letting the user view the list via another ASP page.

The component is designed to allow a number of values to be stored in a list and then manipulated. Each item added to the list can be accessed using a zero-based index, and the list as a whole can be written to the client browser using the Dump() method, which demonstrates using the ASP Response object.

The Component's Methods

The List component will support the following methods:

Method	Description
Add()	Adds a new value to the list
Count()	Returns the total number of items in the list
Item()	Return an item using a zero-based index
Clear()	Removes all values from the list
Dump()	Writes the contents of the list directly to an ASP page using the Response object.
OnStartPage()	Invoked when the component is first used within a page
OnEndPage()	Invoked when the page hosting the component is closed

As you can see from this list, our proposed component does not have very much functionality. But if you added some more methods to it (to remove individual elements, perhaps) then you would have the basis of something that would be great for manipulating any kind of array of data in an ASP page—and because it is compiled code, it would do so more efficiently than plain VBScript functions could have.

By calling our component a "list", we are using the term in its vague, everyday sense: it's a set of elements. The internal implementation of our List component is actually based on an array, via the STL vector<> class. In computer science, the term "list" is often reserved to indicate specifically a linked list data structure—this is not our intention here.

Creating the Component: Using ATL ASP Objects

Having discussed the basic functionality of the list component, let's get on and create it. To get the ball rolling, you need to create a new ATL project. Just as you did in the last chapter, open Visual C++ and select the File | New... menu item to create a new project. Make sure the Project tab is active, then select the ATL COM AppWizard and enter a project name of BegASP before pressing OK.

On the next page, leave all the options at their default settings and press the Finish button. Finally, click OK to close the New Project Information dialog.

We've now got the boilerplate code for a dynamic-link library that can host COM components, to which we can add the shell of the List component. To add the component, we'll use the ATL Object Wizard that we first saw in the previous chapter. Bring up the Wizard and select the ActiveX Server Component in the right-hand list view:

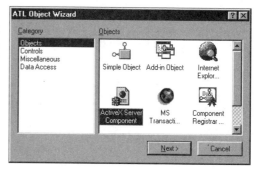

Click the Next button, and enter a short name of List in the Names tab, leaving all the other fields to be filled out automatically.

If you check out the Attributes tab, you'll see that it's identical to the Attributes tab for a simple object, with the exception that the interface type *must* be dual—the Custom option has been disabled. This makes sense because our component is going to be called from scripting languages, so the interface methods must always be callable through IDispatch. We can leave all the settings on this tab with their default values.

You'll have noticed by now that a new ASP tab has been added to the Wizard. Select that tab, and you should see a page like this:

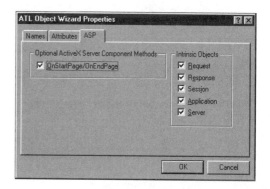

The page has two sets of related options. The Optional ActiveX Server Component Methods frame allows you to support the OnStartPage() and OnEndPage() methods in your component. These methods are called when a component is first used on a page and when a page is subsequently destroyed respectively. If a component is stored in the Session object and accessed from many pages, these methods will be called for each page that uses the component.

If you deselect the **OnStartPage/OnEndPage** option, you will find that the options in the **Intrinsic Objects** frame on the right hand side are disabled. This occurs because the `OnStartPage()` method is the key to accessing ASP intrinsic objects using the `IScriptingContext` interface—this is the default interface of the `ScriptingContext` object we've seen earlier in the book.

The `OnStartPage()` method has a single parameter (a pointer to an `IUnknown` interface) that can be queried for `IScriptingContext`, which then gives us access to the intrinsic objects. If the `OnStartPage()` method is not called, the objects cannot be accessed, and so the option makes no sense.

Leave all the options selected, and press **OK**. We now have a COM component hosted in an in-process server that has access to the ASP intrinsic objects. To see what the Wizard has done, go to ClàssView and expand the tree. You should see something like this:

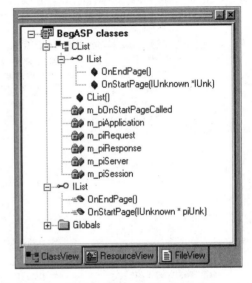

By asking Object Wizard for an ASP component, we've been given an object whose default interface (`IList`) already implements the `OnStartPage()` and `OnEndPage()` methods that will be called by IIS. There are also some member variables used to store references to all the available ASP objects, and a `BOOL` flag to indicate that those references are valid. This flag is set to `TRUE` when `OnStartPage()` is called, and `FALSE` when `OnEndPage()` is called. Let's take a closer look at what the Wizard has actually done for us.

OnStartPage()

The implementation of the `OnStartPage()` method provided by the Wizard looks like this:

```
STDMETHODIMP CList::OnStartPage (IUnknown* pUnk)
{
    if(!pUnk)
        return E_POINTER;

    CComPtr<IScriptingContext> spContext;
    HRESULT hr;

    // Get the IScriptingContext Interface
    hr = pUnk->QueryInterface(IID_IScriptingContext, (void **)&spContext);
    if(FAILED(hr))
        return hr;
```

```
         // Get Request Object Pointer
         hr = spContext->get_Request(&m_piRequest);
         if(FAILED(hr))
         {
             spContext.Release();
             return hr;
         }

         // Get Response Object Pointer
         hr = spContext->get_Response(&m_piResponse);
         if(FAILED(hr))
         {
             m_piRequest.Release();
             return hr;
         }

         // Get Server Object Pointer
         hr = spContext->get_Server(&m_piServer);
         if(FAILED(hr))
         {
             m_piRequest.Release();
             m_piResponse.Release();
             return hr;
         }

         // Get Session Object Pointer
         hr = spContext->get_Session(&m_piSession);
         if(FAILED(hr))
         {
             m_piRequest.Release();
             m_piResponse.Release();
             m_piServer.Release();
             return hr;
         }

         // Get Application Object Pointer
         hr = spContext->get_Application(&m_piApplication);
         if(FAILED(hr))
         {
             m_piRequest.Release();
             m_piResponse.Release();
             m_piServer.Release();
             m_piSession.Release();
             return hr;
         }
         m_bOnStartPageCalled = TRUE;
         return S_OK;
}
```

Validating the Input Parameters

The first part of the OnStartPage() method ensures that the IUnknown pointer passed in is valid. This check is commonly performed in methods that have [in] or [out] parameters, just in case there's a problem in the host container (the client) that has caused a NULL value to be passed. If a NULL value *has* been passed in, it's not possible for the method to access the intrinsic objects, so the E_POINTER error code is returned. This is a failed HRESULT, of the kind we discussed in the previous chapter.

Accessing IScriptingContext

Next, the `IScriptingContext` interface is queried for, via the `IUnknown` pointer that's held in the `pUnk` parameter. If the interface is not supported, the failed `HRESULT` is returned (this will generally be `E_NOINTERFACE` if a call to `QueryInterface()` fails); otherwise the returned interface pointer is stored in the smart pointer `spContext`:

```
// Get the IScriptingContext Interface
hr = pUnk->QueryInterface(IID_IScriptingContext, (void **)&spContext);
if(FAILED(hr))
    return hr;
```

As we just noted, the `spContext` variable is a smart pointer. A smart pointer is actually a C++ class that acts like a pointer to an interface, except that it handles things like reference counting automatically for you, in much the same way that Visual Basic does for object references. We'll look at smart pointers in detail later on in this chapter; for the time being, you can pretty much read a declaration like this:

```
CComPtr<IInterface> spContext;
```

As if it actually said this:

```
IInterface* spContext;
```

> At this juncture, we should point out that the Wizard-generated code isn't as good or as simple as it could be. It should at least be using the C++ `reinterpret_cast<>()` keyword rather than the old-style C cast `(void**)`. Better still, it should be using `CComQIPtr<>`, which we'll discuss in more detail later on.

This initial code *should* always succeed, but it's good coding practice to add rigorous error handling around interface negotiations. Should IIS one day decide not to support this interface, or should some strange run-time error occur in the system, the object will fail gracefully rather than crash. Even if you write code for your component that never returns anything other than `S_OK`, it's still important for a client to check for errors when any method is called, because of the possibility that some error may occur during marshaling, which will result in an error code being returned by the COM runtime. Of course, clients will generally never have such intimate knowledge of a component's inner workings; nor make such assumptions. Clients should allow for all possibilities, and never make any guesses about implementation details—they can change, and they probably will!

Once the `IScriptingContext` interface pointer has been obtained, each intrinsic object that was earlier selected in the Wizard is retrieved using interface properties and stored in a separate smart pointer variable. Each property is retrieved and stored in a similar way, so I'll just show the code that retrieves the first intrinsic object (the `Request` object) and the last intrinsic object (the `Application` object). This gives you a feel for how the cleanup code changes as more interface pointers are retrieved and must therefore be released in the case of an error:

```
// Get Request Object Pointer
hr = spContext->get_Request(&m_piRequest);
if(FAILED(hr))
{
    spContext.Release();
    return hr;
}

...

// Get Application Object Pointer
hr = spContext->get_Application(&m_piApplication);
if(FAILED(hr))
{
    m_piRequest.Release();
    m_piResponse.Release();
    m_piServer.Release();
    m_piSession.Release();
    return hr;
}
```

The `m_piRequest` and `m_piApplication` variables are defined using `CComPtr<>` in the `List.h` header file:

```
CComPtr<IRequest> m_piRequest;                   //Request Object
CComPtr<IApplicationObject> m_piApplication;     //Application Object
```

Should any of the 'property get' methods fail in `OnStartPage()`, *all* of the interface pointers that have so far been retrieved are explicitly freed by calling the `Release()` method of each `CComPtr<>`. This is done to ensure the object is not left in an intermediate state (half of the pointers are valid; half are not), and because the interface pointers that were retrieved should not live beyond the life of a page. The reason *why* the interface pointers should be released is quite simple: they have **page affinity**.

To understand what this means, consider that the `Request` object represents the data being passed to a *specific* instance of an Active Server Page, while `Response` generally represents the HTML page that is being rendered to the client. Once a page has been rendered (or if a page fails to render), the objects have no meaning, and there is no point in keeping them alive by maintaining an outstanding reference, even if our object wasn't destroyed. Of course, if our object *is* destroyed, the interfaces will automatically be released to ensure that no leaks occur.

You might wonder why we need to call `Release()` explicitly, when we just said that smart pointers will handle reference counting for you. The trouble is that the smart pointers will automatically call the `IUnknown::Release()` method *when they go out of scope*. We have a problem here in that we want to release the interface pointers, but since the smart pointer variables are members of the `CList` class, they will actually stay *in* scope. In fact, the `Release()` we are calling is a method of the `CComPtr<>` template class, not an interface method. It has been provided to solve exactly this problem.

Checking that Interface Pointers are Valid

Finally, if all of the intrinsic object interfaces are retrieved successfully, the method sets the m_bOnStartPageCalled variable to TRUE. This variable should be checked by other methods in the component *before* they attempt to use any of the intrinsic object interfaces that have been retrieved. There are two main reasons why you should perform this check:

❑ First, someone may have instantiated your component outside IIS—in a C++ or Visual Basic application or component, perhaps. If your component is dependent upon the intrinsic object interfaces provided by IIS, or has restricted functionality outside of IIS, the variable can be checked and appropriate action taken to fail or degrade method calls.

❑ Second, even if your component is created inside IIS, the user may not have created it correctly. How is this possible? Well, if an instance of a component is not instantiated using the CreateObject() method of the Server object (the IServer interface), the OnStartPage()/OnEndPage() methods will not be called, so the intrinsic object interfaces will not be initialized. Any attempt to use them would therefore result in unexpected behavior, unless m_bOnStartPageCalled is checked first.

As an alternative, you could just check that the smart pointer you want to use is not NULL.

Using the IResponse Interface

So, now that we've discussed the setup of the ASP intrinsic objects in some detail, let's add a simple Dump() method to our List component that uses the IResponse interface (held in m_piResponse) to write a simple "Hello ASP!" message back to the hosting page. We'll extend this later in the chapter to actually output the contents of our list, but for now it will act as our 'training' method.

The pi in m_piResponse stands for "Pointer to an Interface". These days, most people would use m_spResponse, where sp stands for "Smart Pointer". Our preference is for the latter, because it makes the code more explicit.

Adding the Dump() Method

Make sure that the ClassView tab is active, then right click on the IList interface and select the Add Method... menu option. Enter Dump as the method name, leave the parameter field blank, and then hit OK.

Next, expand the IList interface that is located under the CList class (this will be the class name if you've stuck with the default values) and double click on the Dump() method to display the code that's been generated. Change the method so that it looks like this:

```
STDMETHODIMP CList::Dump()
{
    if(m_bOnStartPageCalled == FALSE)
        return E_POINTER;

    m_piResponse->Write(CComVariant("Hello ASP!"));
    return S_OK;
}
```

This method is fairly simple. The first thing it does is to ensure that OnStartPage() has been called by checking the m_bOnStartPageCalled variable. As we've already mentioned, this is good coding practice if you're using IScriptingContext to access the ASP intrinsic objects. If the variable is FALSE, we return the error E_POINTER to give an indication of what has gone wrong. If the variable is TRUE, we know the intrinsic objects have been set up, so we write the "Hello ASP!" message using the Write() method of the IResponse interface that was retrieved and stored in the m_piResponse variable in the call to OnStartPage().

I've not checked the return code from the IResponse::Write() method for a couple of reasons:

❑ The chances of it ever going wrong are very small

❑ If it does go wrong, it's likely that IIS has gone wrong, in which case our object is doomed anyway.

There is no special reason why the E_POINTER return code was chosen to represent the situation where m_bOnStartPageCalled is set to FALSE, except that we know it avoids a little glitch in which IIS seems to misinterpret some return codes and display strange error messages in the browser window. One such error code is E_NOINTERFACE, which causes an Automation error to be displayed.

Compile the project, and then create the following ASP page to test it. hello.asp writes a simple message to the client browser using some static text and the text returned from the Dump() method. The important lines are highlighted:

```
<% Set oList = Server.CreateObject("BegASP.List") %>

<HTML>
    <BODY>
        The component says: <%=oList.Dump%>
    </BODY>
</HTML>
```

When an ASP page is destroyed, any objects created as part of the page are also destroyed, so we don't have to set the object pointer to Nothing explicitly unless there is a good reason for doing so. A good reason to set an object reference to Nothing sooner rather than later would be in the case of a relatively expensive resource, such as a database connection. The sooner we set the object reference to Nothing, the sooner it will release the resources it holds internally, which means another object on another page could then use those resources. This will increase overall scalability, as we discussed in Chapters 6 and 7.

View this page in your browser, and you should see the following screen:

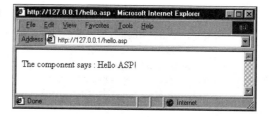

Let's Take a Closer Look

Well, that wasn't too painful, was it? All we had to do to write an ASP component using C++ was use the Wizards to generate the project and the ASP component, add a new method via a menu option, and then write four lines of code. Could it really be much simpler? Probably not, so that's my first argument for using C++ to develop ASP components: if you understand C++ and COM, writing ASP components is simple once you've become familiar with ATL and the ASP object model.

Let's revisit those four lines of code and force a situation for which the OnStartPage() method is *not* called, and prove that our error handling works. The first line of the ASP we wrote was this:

```
<% Set oList = Server.CreateObject("BegASP.List") %>
```

If we change this line to:

```
<% Set oList = CreateObject("BegASP.List") %>
```

OnStartPage() and OnEndPage() will not be called because IIS can no longer keep track of the objects being created. To confirm this does indeed cause a problem, modify the ASP page and refresh the browser, and you will be presented with this screen:

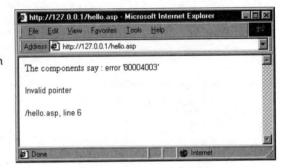

Not a very professional looking error message, but at least we've got a basic clue where the problem originates thanks to the text Invalid pointer, which corresponds to our usage of E_POINTER in the Dump() method.

Adding Verbose Error Handling to a Component

To give ourselves a far better chance of pinpointing errors as our components grow, we need to implement the ISupportErrorInfo interface and use the ATL helper function AtlSetErrorInfo() to pass back an informative message that describes where an error has occurred.

> ISupportErrorInfo and friends are the COM equivalent of C++ exceptions. You should *never* throw a C++ exception from a COM method and expect a client to catch it. This is because the client of your component could potentially be written in any programming language that abides by the COM specification. How much meaning would a C++ exception have to a Visual Basic or a Java client? None at all. COM is language-neutral, so think twice before using any language-specific constructs.

Supporting the additional interface is fairly straightforward, and it gives us a chance to look at how to implement additional interfaces in an ATL class, as well as improving the error handling for our component by using error objects. We can actually get the Wizard to add error support to our classes, but to become truly proficient you need to understand the process it goes through. Moreover, at some point, you'll probably find yourself not checking a box in the Wizard, and then several days later wishing that you had. This way, we'll kill two birds with one stone.

Supporting Error Objects

Error objects enable reasonably extensive error information to be passed from a COM object back to a client. They are created using the CreateErrorInfo() function and associated with the current **logical thread** using the COM API function SetErrorInfo(). A client can then retrieve an error object using GetErrorInfo().

> The logical thread is defined in COM as the chain of method calls between a client and a component. This chain can span across apartments and machines. If a client calls a method that gets executed on the same thread as the client, then the logical thread and the actual thread are identical. If the interface call needs to be marshaled, the method will be executed on a different thread, but since the client thread blocks until the method call returns, the illusion is created that the method is executing on the same thread. Hence the term, "logical thread".

When an error object is created using the COM API function CreateErrorInfo(), the API returns a pointer to the ICreateErrorInfo interface. This is used to add information about the error to the object. The information that can be specified includes:

- ❑ The interface that generated the error (COM errors are interface specific)
- ❑ A textual description of the source of the error (the component name, for example)
- ❑ A description of the error
- ❑ The name of a help file that contains information about the error
- ❑ A help file context identifier, which can pinpoint the error within the help file

Once the information has been specified, the error object interface can be queried for IErrorInfo, which is the interface that the call to SetErrorInfo() requires. This API associates the error object with the current logical thread, which the caller of a component can then retrieve if an error is detected.

Creating an Error Object

The following code shows how to create a simple error object and then associate it with the current logical thread (but don't add it to your component just yet):

```
CComPtr<ICreateErrorInfo> pICEI;
if(SUCCEEDED(CreateErrorInfo(&pICEI)))
{
    CComPtr<IErrorInfo> pErrorInfo;
    pICEI->SetGUID(IID_IList);

    if(lpsz != NULL)
        pICEI->SetSource(OLESTR("My List Component"));

    pICEI->SetDescription(OLESTR("Some error occurred"));
    if(SUCCEEDED(pICEI->QueryInterface(IID_IErrorInfo, (void**)&pErrorInfo)))
        ::SetErrorInfo(0, pErrorInfo);
}
```

Accessing Error Information

The client of an object can retrieve an error object using the COM API function `GetErrorInfo()`. If an error has been raised, this will return an `IErrorInfo` interface pointer that provides access to the information set using `ICreateErrorInfo`. `GetErrorInfo()` should only be called when a failed `HRESULT` is returned from a method call.

The consumer of a component *does not* query the component for the `ISupportErrorInfo` interface. That interface is actually for use by the COM runtime. When an error occurs, the COM runtime will check to see if the component supports error objects for the interface on which the method has just failed. If the interface supports error objects, COM knows that the error object for the current logical thread is valid, so it makes it available to the client via `GetErrorInfo()`. If the interface is not supported, the COM runtime will ensure that any error object is cleared. The reason why a component must support `ISupportErrorInfo` is to prevent rogue error objects created by subordinate objects (for example, components that our component might use internally) from being passed back and accessed by a client.

The following code shows how a client could retrieve the error object set by an interface method that indicates that an error has occurred:

```
hr = SomeComponent->SomeMethod();
if(FAILED(hr))
{
    CComPtr<IErrorInfo> spErrorInfo;

    hr = ::GetErrorInfo(NULL, &spErrorInfo);
    if(FAILED(hr))
    {
        printf("No error object is set \n");
        return;
    }

    CComBSTR sDescription;
    spErrorInfo->GetDescription(&sDescription);
```

The CComBSTR class is discussed later in this chapter.

In this code, we are just retrieving the description of the error by calling `spErrorInfo->GetDescription()`. As you might expect, there are methods for retrieving each piece of information set by the error object's creator:

Method	Description
GetDescription()	Returns a textual description of an error.
GetGUID()	Returns the IID of the interface that set an error.
GetHelpFile()	Returns the path of the help file that can be used to provide additional information about an error. Often, in languages like Visual Basic, you see a Help button on a dialog box that reports an error. In conjunction with the help context, this field is how it retrieves the information.
GetHelpContext()	Returns the help context ID for the error.
GetSource()	Returns the name of the component that generated the error, such as "ODBC driver-name".

So, to make our components support rich error information, we must:

- ❏ Create an error object
- ❏ Set the information in the error object
- ❏ Indicate to COM that they support errors on a per-interface basis
- ❏ Return a failed HRESULT

Adding Error Support to our Component

From the previous discussion, you'll know that in order to provide more meaningful error messages, we need *our* component to expose the ISupportErrorInfo interface. This is something new for us: we need a component that supports more than one interface (in addition to IUnknown and IDispatch). Unfortunately, we can't use ATL's Object Wizard to achieve this. Object Wizard is great at doing what it was designed to do: it writes all the boilerplate code for a *new* component that implements one new interface that you define. However, you can't use it to add new interfaces to an *existing* C++ component.

As we mentioned earlier, you can add error support using the Wizard when the component is first created, but if you don't realize that you need it at that point (or you simply forget to do it), your only recourse is to add it by hand.

Since Visual Studio 6, there has been an Implement Interface *Wizard that can add extra interfaces to an existing C++ class that represents an ATL COM component—it's available from the right-click context menu of the CList class in the ClassView. However, this Wizard is no use to us here because it can only add interfaces that have been defined in a type library, which is not the case for ISupportErrorInfo.*

Let's start editing the code that Object Wizard gave us in order to implement the ISupportErrorInfo interface. The first step is to change the class definition so that it inherits from ISupportErrorInfo:

```
class ATL_NO_VTABLE CList :
    public CComObjectRootEx<CComSingleThreadModel>,
    public CComCoClass<CList, &CLSID_List>,
    public ISupportErrorInfo,
    public IDispatchImpl<IList, &IID_IList, &LIBID_BEGASPLib>
```

This interface informs clients of our component that it (potentially) supports error objects for one or more of the other interfaces it exposes.

The COM interface ISupportErrorInfo *is defined in one of the standard header files that's included in the project already, so we don't need to add a definition of it to this class.*

The second step is to add the ISupportErrorInfo interface into the COM map:

```
BEGIN_COM_MAP(CList)
    COM_INTERFACE_ENTRY(IList)
    COM_INTERFACE_ENTRY(IDispatch)
    COM_INTERFACE_ENTRY(ISupportErrorInfo)
END_COM_MAP()
```

443

This enables clients (in this case, the COM runtime) to query for the `ISupportErrorInfo` interface successfully. ATL's implementation of `QueryInterface()` actually uses the code generated by these macros in the COM map to track down requested interface pointers. That means that if we don't put this entry into the map, then even though we've implemented the code for the interface, clients will never be able to retrieve a pointer to it—`QueryInterface()` will return a failure code whenever it is queried for.

The third step is to implement `ISupportErrorInfo`'s only method by placing this code in the `List.cpp` source file:

```
STDMETHODIMP CList::InterfaceSupportsErrorInfo(REFIID riid)
{
    static const IID* arr[] =
    {
        &IID_IList,
    };

    for(int i = 0; i < sizeof(arr) / sizeof(arr[0]); i++)
    {
        if(InlineIsEqualGUID(*arr[i], riid))
            return S_OK;
    }

    return S_FALSE;
}
```

The only method that `ISupportErrorInfo` contains is `InterfaceSupportsErrorInfo()`. As mentioned, this is used by a client to determine whether a specific interface supports error objects. The implementation of this method simply checks the interface identifier passed in against a static array. If the interface appears in the array, it supports error objects, so `S_OK` is returned. If the interface is not supported, `S_FALSE` is returned. Technically, `S_OK` and `S_FALSE` are both success codes, but `S_FALSE` is less of a success, and more of a warning.

`InlineIsEqualGUID()` is an API function supplied with COM that simply checks two GUIDs for equality, given two pointers to the GUIDs. We use this API function rather than the (apparently) more obvious

```
if((*riid) == (*arr[i]))
```

because GUIDs are actually structures rather than simple data types in C++, so the latter method might not be guaranteed to work. The `REFIID` data type passed into our method as a parameter is `#define`'d to be `IID*`—in other words, a pointer to a GUID.

Because we're only supporting error information for one interface, the code in our implementation is (arguably) unnecessarily complicated; the following code would have done the job more simply:

```
STDMETHODIMP CList::InterfaceSupportsErrorInfo(REFIID riid)
{
    if(InlineIsEqualGUID(&IID_IList, riid))
        return S_OK;
    return S_FALSE;
}
```

However, we've done it the first way so that we can illustrate how to implement this method in the general case, when there may be several interfaces for which we provide error information. This is also the way the ATL Wizard will generate support for the interface should you use it. It should be pointed out, though, that many people don't like that particular implementation because most ASP components only ever have one interface.

A Meaningful Error

Now that our component indicates to the COM runtime that it supports errors, we can make it issue a more meaningful error when `OnStartPage()` has not been called by modifying the `Dump()` method and including a call to the `Error()` method, as follows:

```
STDMETHODIMP CList::Dump()
{
    if(m_bOnStartPageCalled == FALSE)
    {
        Error("LIST.CPP - Dump() - m_bOnStartPageCalled == FALSE");
        return E_POINTER;
    }

    m_piResponse->Write(CComVariant("Hello ASP!"));
    return S_OK;
}
```

`Error()` encapsulates the code required for creating the error object for the method, setting the information, and then associating it with the current logical thread. The function is defined in `CComCoClass<>`, from which `CList` is derived. `CComCoClass<>` implements a function called `Error()` that internally calls `AtlReportError()`, which then calls `AtlSetErrorInfo()` to set the error information. In most cases, all we need to do is call `Error()`.

The `Error()` method has several overloads. Each overload accepts a different number of parameters according to the fields we want to associate with a specific error. In this code, we are calling the default overload:

```
static HRESULT WINAPI Error(LPCOLESTR lpszDesc,
                            const IID& iid = GUID_NULL, HRESULT hRes = 0)
{
    return AtlReportError(GetObjectCLSID(), lpszDesc, iid, hRes);
}
```

The end result of setting an error object for our `IList` interface is that IIS will now send a reasonable error message back to the client browser when we return a failure `HRESULT` from our `Dump()` method. When it sees that a method has returned a failure `HRESULT`, IIS will query for `ISupportErrorInfo`, check that the interface containing the method supports errors by calling `InterfaceSupportsErrorInfo()`, and then display the description field along with other pertinent information in the client browser:

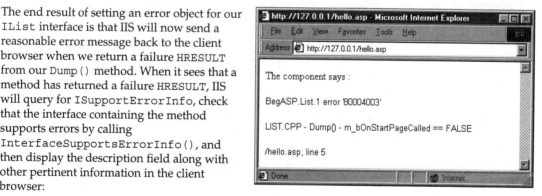

By supporting errors in this fashion, you'll find that you can save many hours of debugging should your C++ ASP components go wrong. Error handing is very important (hence the long discussion), so try and implement it correctly from day one.

445

Doing it the Easy Way

To support error objects, we purposely took
you through the steps required for
implementing an additional interface using
ATL. This is an important skill to have, but in
future we'll just use the Wizard to add error
support to our components. To do this, when
creating a new component, select the Support
ISupportErrorInfo option from the Attributes
tab:

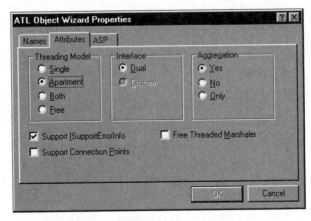

This option will only add error support for the first interface—in other words, it will ensure that the
component implements ISupportErrorInfo, and will additionally add an implementation of
ISupportErrorInfo that indicates error support for the first interface of the component you're adding.
If you decide to add additional interfaces to your component, and you want those interfaces to support
error objects, you must remember to modify ATL's implementation of the
InterfaceSupportsErrorInfo() method to include the interface identifiers in the static array.

ATL Utility Classes

We now have a simple ASP component that writes output to a client's browser via the IResponse
interface. Until now though, we've glossed over how the response interface pointer is actually held within
the class. We've indicated that it is stored as a CComPtr<>, and suggested that this is a template class that
provides smart pointer support, without saying much about how that works.

In fact, CComPtr<> is just one of several utility classes provided by ATL that you'll come across quite
frequently. In this section, we're going to look at some of the most important ones, including the string
class CComBSTR, the VARIANT utility class CComVariant, the smart pointer template CComQIPtr<>, and
of course CComPtr<> itself.

Strings, BSTR and CComBSTR

Strings are a rather delicate subject in C++. When the C language was designed, it was deemed
appropriate that a string should just be a zero-terminated array of characters, rather than being a separate
data type. At the time, this probably seemed a great idea, since it made it easy to do quite advanced string
processing by manipulating pointers and arrays of char.

An unfortunate consequence of this decision was that string manipulation tended to result in hard-to-read
code, with pointers and pointers-to-pointers all over the place. Over the last twenty years or so, the
perception of 'good' C or C++ code has shifted from "high-performance at all costs" to "easy to read and
maintain". It became apparent that something more suitable for storing strings was needed. The result was
a proliferation of wrapper classes to store strings, ranging from MFC's CString, to the Standard Template
Library's string, to ATL's CComBSTR—the one that we will be using here.

To make matters worse, there are several different ways of representing individual characters. The ASCII standard, for example, dictates that each character should be represented by a number between 0 and 255, which means that one byte is sufficient to store a character. As computing has become an international industry, however, this simple system has become inadequate, since many more bits are needed to represent all the characters in all the different languages across the world.

This has led to the development of several other standards, including the multi-byte character set (MBCS) and the UTF8 standard, both of which involve using varying numbers of bytes to represent different characters. However, the standard that COM has settled on is the Unicode standard, in which each character is represented by two bytes, allowing a potential 65,536 different characters.

Bluntly, these days, the situation for programming using strings in C++ for Windows is a mess, with a huge number of different data types that can all claim to be good ways of storing strings in different circumstances. However, if we are writing COM components, it's very easy to narrow down our choice. COM's peculiar requirements for allocating memory dictate that we should use a data type known as the BSTR. (usually pronounced "bee-struh").

BSTR stands for *basic string*, and its roots stem back to the early days of Visual Basic.

Introducing BSTR

BSTR is special because it uses the same way of storing strings that Visual Basic employs behind the scenes. If you do something like this in Visual Basic:

```
Dim strText As String
```

Then what you're *really* doing is declaring what C++ (and VB internally) knows as a BSTR. In fact, the name BSTR stands for *basic string*. Similarly, if you do something like this in Visual Basic or VBScript:

```
Dim strText
strText = "Hello"
```

Then strText will actually contain a BSTR, albeit that the BSTR itself is actually held in a placeholder that we will discuss later.

In practical terms, a BSTR is just a zero-terminated array, but it's an array of short instead of char, so that it can store Unicode characters. It is also preceded by a couple of bytes of memory that store the actual length of the string. The presence of the stored length means that the string can contain embedded zero characters, and these will not be confused with the terminating NUL.

In fact, a BSTR is just typedef'd as an unsigned short* or an LPOLESTR, but you shouldn't interchange BSTR and LPOLESTR since customary use of BSTR involves some special memory allocation and de-allocation routines. If you see BSTR in your code, you assume these routines have been followed; if you see LPOLESTR, you assume they haven't.

In order to allocate memory to store a BSTR, you should use an API function that has been specially designed for the purpose: SysAllocString(). In order to free memory that was allocated using SysAllocString(), you should use SysFreeString(). There are two reasons for this. Firstly, these functions will correctly use the preceding bytes of memory that indicate how long the string is. Secondly, and much more importantly, these functions use the **task memory allocator** that is required by COM.

The point is that when you're dealing with COM clients and components, you can easily find yourself in a situation where memory is allocated in the component and freed in the client, or vice versa. Since the client and the server might be in different processes (or even on different machines), we are clearly in a more complex situation than the C++ operators new and delete were designed to handle.

We won't go into how memory allocation works in detail, but suffice to say that Microsoft has provided two more API functions—CoTaskMemAlloc() and CoTaskMemFree()—that deal with allocating and freeing memory in such a way that everything will work cross-process according to the rules of COM. You simply use CoTaskMemAlloc() instead of new and CoTaskMemFree() instead of delete. These functions are designed for generic use for any data type, not just strings. SysAllocString() and SysFreeString() are designed specifically for BSTR, and call the other functions internally.

It might sound a bit tricky, but the code required to manipulate BSTR strings is really quite simple. This snippet, for example, shows how to initialize a BSTR that contains the text "Hello":

```
BSTR bstrText;
bstrText = ::SysAllocString(L"Hello");
```

The L in front of the string is actually standard C++ — it's a way of indicating that a string is not a standard ASCII narrow string (as indicated by the quote marks) but that it's a Unicode wide string (as required for BSTR).

While to free up the variable, you'd do this:

```
::SysFreeString(bstrText);
bstrText = NULL;
```

The last statement is not always necessary (because the allocated string might be returned via an [out] parameter, whereby the caller is responsible for freeing it) but it's useful to indicate that bstrText no longer contains anything. Also, SysFreeString() is able to cope happily with null pointers, so by setting bstrText to NULL, we ensure that no harm will be done if we inadvertently call SysFreeString() on bstrText again.

Going One Better: CComBSTR

Compared to traditional strings, the BSTR data type is a real pain for C++ programmers. We have to worry about allocating and releasing them, and if we need to manipulate them (perhaps we want to insert some characters), we have to jump through loops. Luckily, ATL provides a helper class that takes all the pain away. Enter CComBSTR.

If we want to do much manipulation with strings, we really want something more than what is basically still an array of shorts. We want to be able to add strings together in the way you do in Visual Basic. We'd like to be able to do something like this:

```
bstrNew = bstr1 + bstr2;
```

In the certain knowledge that if `bstr1` contains "`Hello `" and `bstr2` contains "`World`", the result will be "`Hello World`".

We'd also like not to have to remember to keep calling `SysAllocString()` and `SysFreeString()` — that's the sort of boilerplate code that is better off being automated and that we are prone to get wrong in at least a couple of places in a large project. And it's where ATL's `CComBSTR` class comes to our rescue.

`CComBSTR` is a wrapper class. It contains a `BSTR` as its only member variable, but it also has a number of overloaded functions and operators that make working with it easier. Declaring and initializing a value, for example, is trivial. Our original example:

```
BSTR bstrText;
bstrText = ::SysAllocString(L"Hello");
```

Now becomes:

```
CComBSTR bstrText(L"Hello");
```

Or we can even forgo the Unicode `L` prefix:

```
CComBSTR bstrText("Hello");
```

The second approach incurs a slight overhead in non-Unicode builds. This use will result in `CComBSTR` *internally using the macro* `A2WBSTR()` *to convert an ASCII string into a Unicode string. While it's not a massive overhead, do it enough times and it may become a problem.*

To free up the memory, we can simply allow `bstrText` to go out of scope—`SysFreeString()` will be called for us in the destructor. Memory allocation will also be handled automatically in situations like this:

```
bstrText = L"Hi";

// Processing
bstrText = L"Next";
```

If we were using raw `BSTR`s, we'd need to have called `SysFreeString()` explicitly, followed by `SysAllocString()` to change the contents of `bstrText`, or use the `SysReAllocString()` API that wraps these two calls.

Wherever possible, you should use `CComBSTR` to store strings in ATL components because it makes your life easier. `CComBSTR` also has two operators that enable you to pass a `CComBSTR` wherever you would typically pass a `BSTR`:

```
operator BSTR() const
{
    return m_str;
}

BSTR* operator&()
{
    return &m_str;
}
```

So we can happily write code like this:

```
CComBSTR a

SomeFunctionThatExpectsAcceptsABSTR(a);
SomeFunctionThatExpectsAcceptsAReferenceToABSTR(&a);
```

VARIANTS and CComVariant

When you write code in VBScript inside an ASP page, you don't have to specify any types for the variables you declare—it's essentially a **typeless** language, because it only supports one data type: the VARIANT. This is not a simple data type, but it's easy to use in VB and VBScript because all of the processing associated with determining the actual type being stored is hidden from us and performed by the Visual Basic runtime or script processor. In C++, however, we have to deal directly with the actual underlying details of what makes up a VARIANT.

A VARIANT is a **discriminated data structure**—a self-describing structure that contains an indicator/discriminator as part of the data content. What this means is that the structure contains a union of a large number of member variables, one for each of the data types that the VARIANT can store. Because it's a union, all these member variables occupy the same memory space, so it's not too large; a VARIANT occupies 16 bytes in total.

In addition to the union, the VARIANT contains a member called vt (the discriminator), which contains a number that indicates what data type is actually stored—and hence which of the members of the union is the one that contains valid data. vt is of type VARTYPE, which is #define'd to be a short.

To give you an idea of how this works, here's a very simplified version of the definition of the VARIANT type. It's simplified because we've removed all the lines that don't help to understand what's going on, and we've edited a few other lines. The unexpurgated definition will appear later on.

```
typedef struct tagVARIANT
{
    VARTYPE vt;         // The discriminator
    union
    {
        LONG lVal;
        BYTE bVal;
        SHORT iVal;
        FLOAT fltVal;
        DOUBLE dblVal;
        VARIANT_BOOL boolVal;
        _VARIANT_BOOL bool;
        SCODE scode;
        CY cyVal;
        DATE date;
        BSTR bstrVal;

        // Lots more data types follow
    }
} VARIANT;
```

Notice the prevalence of variable types that are just Microsoft-defined typedefs. Each of these types actually has a special identifier, such as VT_I4 for LONGs. These are detailed later on.

VARIANTs are powerful because they enable a single method parameter to represent numerous data types—strings, numbers, interface pointers, NULL values, and many others. It's even possible to store an *array* of data as another structure inside the VARIANT: the SAFEARRAY. The possible data types are known as **Automation data types**, and they're defined by the enumerator VARENUM.

A VARIANT can currently represent around 40 different data types, including NULL.

Since you cannot overload function signatures in COM like you can in C++, VARIANTs are one possible way to achieve the equivalent *basic* functionality. In fact, this is what many of the ASP interfaces do— witness the IResponse::Write() method that we used in the Dump() method of our component:

```
virtual HRESULT STDMETHODCALLTYPE Write(VARIANT varText) = 0;
```

By defining the method like this, the ASP object model allows us to write data of many different types.

VARIANT API Functions

The VARIANT structure contains only member variables—there are no member functions. This is because the VARIANT is actually a C structure rather than a C++ structure, and in common with the rest of the Windows base SDK, it needs to be able to be used by C as well as C++ programs. This makes it slightly more awkward to use, because processes such as construction and destruction don't take place automatically. Instead, Microsoft has provided some API functions that manipulate VARIANTs. (If your VARIANT contains a SAFEARRAY, there is a huge list of API functions to manipulate SAFEARRAYs.) The list here is not exhaustive; we've just described the ones that you're most likely to find useful.

Function Name	Description
VariantInit()	Initializes a VARIANT structure, setting the discriminator (the member variable vt) to VT_EMPTY.
VariantClear()	Destroys the contents of the VARIANT, along with any allocated resources.
VariantChangeType()	Does type conversions. For example, you might use this function if you want to convert a VARIANT that contains an integer to one that contains a string. The presence of this API function can be a reason for using VARIANTs to store different data types even when they're otherwise not necessary.
VariantCopy()	Copies a VARIANT. This does a "deep" copy, so the entire contents of arrays are copied, and reference counts on interface pointers are incremented.

Creating a VARIANT that Contains a String

VARIANTs are created, manipulated and destroyed using the `VariantInit()` and `VariantClear()` API functions. In order to initialize a VARIANT with a specific data type, we set the member variable vt to indicate the contained value, and then set the appropriate member to the data we want to store. The following code shows how to create a VARIANT that contains a string:

```
VARIANT varString;

VariantInit(&varString);
varString.vt = VT_BSTR;
varString.bstrVal = ::SysAllocString(L"Wrox Press");
```

This can then be used in a call to one of the ASP interfaces' methods:

```
IResponse pResponse = NULL;

...

// Initialize pResponse to point to a Response object
...

pResponse->Write(&varString);

// The resources associated with the VARIANT can now be released
VariantClear(&myString);
```

`VariantClear()` is a fairly sophisticated API function: it will check which of the Automation data types is actually stored in the VARIANT, and act accordingly to release any resources held by the VARIANT. In our example, it will call `SysFreeString()` to free the memory associated with the BSTR. If the VARIANT holds an interface pointer, `Release()` will automatically be called on it.

As a slightly more extensive example of using VARIANTs, the following code writes the message "Richard Was Born In 1972" to the client browser. It writes the messages in two parts: the first is a string (VARIANT type VT_BSTR) consisting of the first 20 characters; the second is a long integer (VARIANT type VT_I4). This code shows that the IResponse interface will perform the necessary processing to convert a VARIANT into a format suitable for the browser. In this sample, IIS isn't really doing much more than converting the number 1972 into a string, but it shows how useful VARIANTs can be when defining flexible methods:

```
VARIANT varString;

VariantInit(&varString);
varString.vt = VT_BSTR;
varString.bstrVal = ::SysAllocString(L"Richard Was Born In ");

m_piResponse->Write(varString);
VariantClear(&varString);

VariantInit(&varString);
varString.vt = VT_I4;
varString.lVal = 1972;

m_piResponse->Write(varString);
VariantClear(&varString);
```

If you take this code, paste it into the Dump() method we've written, and use the ASP page we wrote earlier (the one that *does* call Server.CreateObject()), the browser will show the following output:

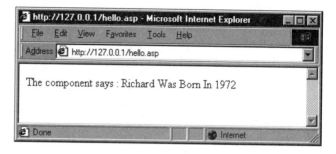

To give you an idea of the data types that can be passed using a VARIANT, here's its complete definition. Not all of these data types will be supported by IIS, so a degree of trial and error will be required depending which ones you use:

```
struct tagVARIANT {
    union {
        struct __tagVARIANT {
            VARTYPE vt;
            WORD    wReserved1;
            WORD    wReserved2;
            WORD    wReserved3;
            union {
                LONG            lVal;        /* VT_I4                   */
                BYTE            bVal;        /* VT_UI1                  */
                SHORT           iVal;        /* VT_I2                   */
                FLOAT           fltVal;      /* VT_R4                   */
                DOUBLE          dblVal;      /* VT_R8                   */
                VARIANT_BOOL    boolVal;     /* VT_BOOL                 */
                _VARIANT_BOOL   bool;        /* (obsolete)              */
                SCODE           scode;       /* VT_ERROR                */
                CY              cyVal;       /* VT_CY                   */
                DATE            date;        /* VT_DATE                 */
                BSTR            bstrVal;     /* VT_BSTR                 */
                IUnknown *      punkVal;     /* VT_UNKNOWN              */
                IDispatch *     pdispVal;    /* VT_DISPATCH             */
                SAFEARRAY *     parray;      /* VT_ARRAY                */
                BYTE *          pbVal;       /* VT_BYREF|VT_UI1         */
                SHORT *         piVal;       /* VT_BYREF|VT_I2          */
                LONG *          plVal;       /* VT_BYREF|VT_I4          */
                FLOAT *         pfltVal;     /* VT_BYREF|VT_R4          */
                DOUBLE *        pdblVal;     /* VT_BYREF|VT_R8          */
                VARIANT_BOOL    *pboolVal;   /* VT_BYREF|VT_BOOL        */
                _VARIANT_BOOL   *pbool;      /* (obsolete)              */
                SCODE *         pscode;      /* VT_BYREF|VT_ERROR       */
                CY *            pcyVal;      /* VT_BYREF|VT_CY          */
                DATE *          pdate;       /* VT_BYREF|VT_DATE        */
                BSTR *          pbstrVal;    /* VT_BYREF|VT_BSTR        */
                IUnknown **     ppunkVal;    /* VT_BYREF|VT_UNKNOWN     */
                IDispatch **    ppdispVal;   /* VT_BYREF|VT_DISPATCH    */
                SAFEARRAY **    pparray;     /* VT_BYREF|VT_ARRAY       */
                VARIANT *       pvarVal;     /* VT_BYREF|VT_VARIANT     */
                PVOID           byref;       /* Generic ByRef           */
                CHAR            cVal;        /* VT_I1                   */
                USHORT          uiVal;       /* VT_UI2                  */
                ULONG           ulVal;       /* VT_UI4                  */
                INT             intVal;      /* VT_INT                  */
```

```
          UINT          uintVal;      /* VT_UINT              */
          DECIMAL *     pdecVal;      /* VT_BYREF|VT_DECIMAL  */
          CHAR *        pcVal;        /* VT_BYREF|VT_I1       */
          USHORT *      puiVal;       /* VT_BYREF|VT_UI2      */
          ULONG *       pulVal;       /* VT_BYREF|VT_UI4      */
          INT *         pintVal;      /* VT_BYREF|VT_INT      */
          UINT *        puintVal;     /* VT_BYREF|VT_UINT     */
          struct __tagBRECORD {
              PVOID           pvRecord;
              IRecordInfo * pRecInfo;
          } __VARIANT_NAME_4;         /* VT_RECORD            */
        } __VARIANT_NAME_3;
      } __VARIANT_NAME_2;

    DECIMAL decVal;
  } __VARIANT_NAME_1;
};
```

> For an extensive description of all ATL utility classes, try reading *ATL Internals* published by Addison-Wesley. (ISBN 0-201-69589-8)

Making Life Easy: CComVariant

While VARIANTs are not difficult to create, they are somewhat tedious to program, just like BSTRs were before we introduced CComBSTR. To help us yet again, ATL provides the utility class CComVariant. This class has 16 constructors and a similar number of assignment operators, all of which make creating VARIANTs a breeze. To create a VARIANT containing a string, we can just write this:

```
CComVariant varString(L"Richard Anderson");
```

Once again, we can optionally forgo the L prefix on the string, as the CComVariant class will automatically convert the string for us. As mentioned earlier, this does introduce a slight performance overhead in non-Unicode builds.

To create a VARIANT containing a long, we would just write this:

```
CComVariant myNumber(1972L);
```

The CComVariant class derives from the VARIANT structure, so it can be used anywhere a VARIANT can be used. To demonstrate this, we can rewrite our earlier code as follows:

```
m_piResponse->Write(CComVariant(L"Richard Was Born In "));
m_piResponse->Write(CComVariant(1972L));
```

If you're using CComVariant, there's never any need to use the VariantInit() or VariantClear() functions explicitly—they are called by the constructor and destructor of CComVariant respectively. Similarly, VariantCopy() is redundant, since the =() operator is overridden to perform this functionality. Furthermore, VariantChangeType() is replaced by an easier-to-use member function, CComVariant::ChangeType().

Like CComBSTR, CComVariant can generally replace the VARIANT data type in your code and make it easier to read and less prone to bugs. However, it does have one member function that often bites the ATL newcomer because it is inconsistent with the behavior of CComBSTR. I'm talking about CComVariant::Detach().

As the name implies, this function causes the smart variable CComVariant to give up ownership of the contained variable, for example:

```
VARIANT vVar;
CComVariant vName(L"Richard")

vName.Detach(&vVar)
```

Believe it or not, this code contains a bug and is likely to crash. The problem is that the implementation of CComVariant::Detach() assumes the pointer to which the VARIANT is copied already contains a valid VARIANT. It therefore tries to free it by calling VariantClear(), but because the discriminator (vt) will be a random value, it will try to release something that hasn't really been allocated before. For the code to work reliably, we have to change it to initialize the destination VARIANT first:

```
VARIANT vVar;
CComVariant vName(L"Richard")

VariantInit(&vVar);
vName.Detach(&vVar)
```

The reason why I called this inconsistent earlier is that the equivalent CComBSTR function (CopyTo()) does not free the previous BSTR. So, to prevent bugs, always call VariantInit() before calling CComVariant::Detach() if the destination VARIANT is not already initialized. In COM interface terms, this means calling VariantInit() for any [out] parameters that are not also [in] parameters.

CComPtr<>

CComPtr<> is a smart pointer: a simple object that *acts* like a pointer to an interface, but is actually a class that contains the real pointer as a member variable. Smart pointers like CComPtr<> and CComQIPtr<> can *generally* be used interchangeably wherever a pointer to an interface is needed. The advantage of using them is that they take on the responsibility for handling reference counting. This includes:

- ❏ Calling AddRef() when an interface pointer is assigned to them
- ❏ Calling AddRef() when an interface pointer is passed via a constructor
- ❏ Calling Release() when the smart pointer is deleted or goes out of scope
- ❏ Calling Release() when one interface pointer is overwritten by another

Reference counting is very much like tracking memory: you need to make sure that every AddRef() you call is balanced at some point with a call to Release(). While this is a simple programming task, it is often complicated by functions having many possible execution paths, depending upon size and other factors such as exception handling.

> By using smart pointers we can almost guarantee that all calls to AddRef() and Release() will be balanced correctly in all circumstances.

To demonstrate using a smart pointer, we'll write another simple function to output a message via the `IResponse` interface. However, this function will accept the `IResponse` interface pointer as its only parameter. Note that what we're writing here is an ordinary C++ member function. It's not an interface method, so it can only be called internally, within the component.

```
void CList::SayHello(IResponse* pResponse)
{
    if(!pResponse)      // Check the pointer is valid
        return;

    pResponse->Write(CComVariant("Hello!"));
}
```

To invoke this function without using smart pointers, we'd need to write some code like this:

```
IResponse* pResponse = NULL;

// Initialize pResponse somehow. If it's copied from somewhere else,
//  AddRef() will need to be called on it.

SayHello(pResponse);
pResponse->Release();
```

In this code you can see quite explicitly that we've got a pointer to the `IResponse` interface, which we know matches the parameter type the function requires, so the function call should compile cleanly and work without problems.

If we rewrite the calling code using smart pointers, the code becomes slightly less intuitive. On the other hand, we no longer need to call `Release()` on the pointer, as this will be done for us in the smart pointer's destructor when it goes out of scope.

```
CComPtr<IResponse> spResponse;

// Initialize pResponse somehow. If it's copied from somewhere else,
//  AddRef() will NOT need to be called on it explicitly,
//  since the smart pointer will handle that for us.

SayHello(spResponse);
```

Note that we don't need to modify the `SayHello()` function in order to call it in this way, since the smart pointer has an operator that will make it act just as if it actually *was* defined as the data type the function requires. This magic is performed using C++ operator overloading, and in many ways it's similar to how Visual Basic works under the covers. Ultimately, of course, the two are quite different, but the result is the same: less code.

The "real" interface pointer is actually held inside the smart pointer, so in effect the following is happening without us having to do anything at all:

```
CComPtr<IResponse> spResponse;
IResponse* pRaw;

pRaw = spResponse.p;       // p is the name of the interface poiner
SayHello(pRaw);
```

For this to happen automatically in the way we saw earlier, a class has to define an operator of the type required by the function. When the compiler sees that a data type doesn't match a function parameter type, it will check to see if there is a **type cast operator** that can perform the conversion. If one exists, it will add the code to call it, and then use the result to call the real function. Provided that CComPtr<> has a type cast operator for the contained interface type, we can use it and the real interface pointer interchangeably.

For a more detailed discussion of smart pointers, check out Professional ATL COM Programming *by Dr Richard Grimes (Wrox Press, 1-861001-40-1).*

CComPtr<> Operators

Now that we've got a basic understanding of how operator overloading works, lets take a brief look at each operators that CComPtr<> overrides, and why it does it. The T represents the interface name being used with the smart pointer:

Operator	Description
operator T*() const	This is the type cast operator, and it allows the smart pointer to be passed whenever a pointer to the contained interface is required.
T& operator*() const	The deference operator returns a reference to the contained interface pointer. For example: IResponse& pResp = *m_piResponse;
T** operator&()	The address-of operator returns a pointer to the address of the contained interface pointer. This enables the smart pointer to be used when a pointer to a pointer is required—when calling IUnknown::QueryInterface(), for example.
_NoAddRefReleaseOnCComPtr<T>* operator->() const	The pointer operator returns the contained smart pointer interface. When this operator is used, a method of the contained interface is being invoked. When the normal 'dot' notation is used, the method being called is part of the smart pointer.
T* operator=(T* lp)	An assignment operator that allows a pointer to an interface to be assigned to the smart pointer. The assignment operator will always release the contained interface pointer first.
T* operator=(const CComPtr<T>& lp)	An assignment operator that enables one smart pointer to be assigned to another directly.
bool operator!() const	The logical NOT operator checks to see whether the contained interface pointer is NULL.
bool operator==(T* pT) const	Determines whether two interface pointers point to the same address. You should always use the IsEqualObject() method to determine whether two objects refer to the same COM identity, so use this method with care.

Smart Pointers and Unnecessary Reference Counts

Although smart pointers are generally very useful, you should only use a smart pointer where you need to maintain a reference count on an interface. Try not to use smart pointers when you know the additional interface count is redundant. For example, for the simple SayHello() function we described earlier on, it would be pointless to define our function as follows:

```
void CList::SayHello(CComPtr<IResponse> spResponse);
```

Each time this function is called, an unnecessary pair of calls to AddRef() and Release() will occur. While the overhead is only minimal, too many of these will result in a loss of performance.

CComQIPtr<>

CComQIPtr<> is pretty similar to CComPtr<>, except that the assignment operator has been overloaded so that you can set a CComQIPtr<> equal to a pointer of another type, and the code will implicitly call QueryInterface() for you. This is not possible with CComPtr<>.

Earlier, we mentioned that the first part of the OnStartPage() method generated by the Wizard could be simplified by using CComQIPtr<>. Rather than explicitly using QueryInterface(), we can use the assignment operator of CComQIPtr<> and then check for a NULL value, indicating that the call to QueryInterface() failed:

```
STDMETHODIMP CList::OnStartPage (IUnknown* pUnk)
{
    if(!pUnk)
        return E_POINTER;

    CComQIPtr<IScriptingContext> spContext;

    spContext = pUnk;        // QueryInterface() occurs here. This line would
                             //   cause a compilation error if spContext
                             //   had been declared as a CComPtr<>.
    if(!pUnk)
        return E_NOINTERFACE;
```

You'll surely agree that this code is much easier to read.

Adding Functionality to the List Component

So far, we've looked at how to write some basic output to the client browser by using the IResponse interface, covered in quite some detail what the ASP Object Wizard does for us, and discussed the various ATL utility classes that generally make our life easier when writing components. However, we've still got a pretty much non-functional component, so it's time to start implementing the methods we discussed at the start of this chapter, using the techniques we've examined so far.

The Standard Template Library

The list component will use the Standard Template Library (STL) to implement most of its functionality. Effectively, the component will provide a very thin COM layer around the corresponding STL class that implements a dynamic array.

In many ways, STL is like ATL. Both provide a type safe, lightweight, high performance framework for simplifying development. Where ATL is designed for the creation of COM components, STL is designed for manipulating data structures, such as lists, maps and arrays. We're not going to go into STL in detail here (it's truly a huge library); we're just going to pick out the class that is useful to us: the `vector<>` class. An STL `vector<>` is a template that allows you to create a dynamic array of objects. It's a little like the `CTypedPtrArray<>` template that MFC provides.

> *STL implementations of varying completeness have been shipped with Visual C++ since version 4.2. If you've not used it before, we suggest reading* STL Tutorial & Reference Guide *(Addison-Wesley, 0-201-63398-1).*

Supporting STL in an ATL Project

As usual, in order to create instances of classes defined in a library, we need to `#include` the appropriate header files. When using the STL, there is no need to supply an explicit path to these files, since they're in the `Include` folder of your Visual Studio installation, and therefore included in the default search path.

The STL header files are characterized by having no `.h` suffix. And the particular one that defines the `vector<>` class we're going to use is just called `vector`. So you should add the following line to the bottom of `stdafx.h`, just after the include for `atlcom.h`:

```
#include <vector>
```

When you first include an STL header file in an ATL project, you'll get a compile error warning you that C++ exception handling is used, but unwind semantics are not enabled:

warning C4530: C++ exception handler used, but unwind semantics are not enabled. Specify -GX

To redress this problem, you have to enable exception handling in your C++ project by specifying the `-GX` switch in the project options, as the warning indicates. To add this switch, just check the **Enable exception handling** option that's located on the **C/C++** tab of the **Project Settings** dialog:

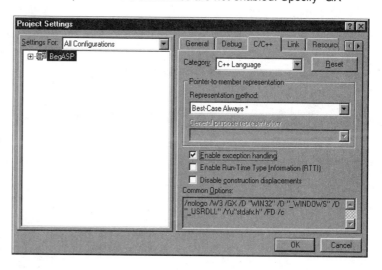

> When you enable exception handling in an ATL project, you have to remove the
> _ATL_MIN_CRT symbol from the **Preprocessor definitions** of all Release builds. This
> option appears on the **C++** tab of the **Project Settings** dialog when the **Preprocessor**
> category is selected.

Adding the Vector

We can now add the member variable m_list to our CList class definition, where it will be used to hold
the contents of our list in memory. As we want a flexible list that can hold strings, numbers and even
interface pointers, we'll use CComVariant.

Add the following line to the CList definition:

```
BOOL m_bOnStartPageCalled;          //OnStartPage successful?
std::vector<CComVariant> m_list;
```

The std:: prefix denotes that vector<> is declared within the namespace std. The template takes one
parameter that specifies the type of items that are to be contained in the list. We will use CComVariant as
the template parameter; the advantage of doing so (rather than using VARIANT) is that CComVariant will
automatically call VariantCopy() for us when we add items to the list.

Adding Items to the List

In order to add items to our list, we'll follow the
standard Visual Basic-type conventions and implement
an Add() method. Right click on the IList interface
and select the Add **Method...** menu option. Specify the
method name Add, and define the parameters like this:

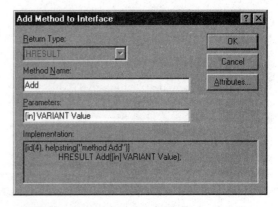

For future methods, we'll just tell you the method name and the parameters to enter.

Click **OK**, locate the definition of the Add() method, and replace the code with the following:

```
STDMETHODIMP CList::Add(VARIANT Value)
{
    m_list.push_back(Value);
    return S_OK;
}
```

The call to push_back() adds the value the caller has passed in to the end of our vector<>. Even if you
haven't encountered the STL vector<> class before, you'll find the purposes of the member functions
we'll be using are fairly obvious, and are well documented in the MSDN Library.

Retrieving Items from the List

In order to retrieve the names from our list, we'll add a method called `Item()`. This will accept a zero-based index and return the value at that position in the `vector<>`. Right click on the `IList` interface and select **Add** **M**ethod... again. This time, specify `Item` as the method name, and define the parameters as `[in] long Index, [out, retval] VARIANT* Value`. Click **OK** and then change the method to look like this:

```
STDMETHODIMP CList::Item(long Index, VARIANT *Value)
{
    // If the index exceeds the index boundaries, return an error
    if(Index < 0 || Index > m_list.size())
        return E_INVALIDARG;

    CComVariant retVal = m_list[Index];

    VariantInit(Value);
    retVal.Detach(Value);

    return S_OK;
}
```

This code is slightly more complicated than the `Add()` method. The first two lines of code ensure that the index the caller has passed in is within the addressable bounds of the `vector<>`. If the index is invalid, `E_INVALIDARG` is returned. If the index is valid, we copy the value from the list into a temporary variable called `retVal`. In doing this, `CComVariant` has made a copy of the `VARIANT` behind the scenes. The copy is then passed back to the caller by calling `Detach()`, which we examined earlier. It's important here because we're dealing with an interface method call. COM doesn't know anything about the `CComVariant` class, so interface methods must pass plain `VARIANT`s instead.

> *In COM the* callee *is responsible for allocating* `[out]` *parameters, and the* caller *is responsible for freeing them.*

Simple Test ASP Page

With the `Add()` and `Item()` methods written, we can now compile the code and test the functionality of our component as it stands.

The following changes to our `hello.asp` file will create the list object, add two strings and one number, and then display them. While simple, it demonstrates that the methods we've written work, and it shows how a `VARIANT` is a flexible yet simple way of passing and handling different data types:

```
<% set oList = Server.CreateObject("BegASP.List")
    oList.Add "Richard Anderson"
    oList.Add "rja@arpsolutions.demon.co.uk"
    oList.Add 27
%>

<HTML>
    <BODY>
        <p> name: <%=oList.Item(0) %> </p>
        <p> e-mail: <%=oList.Item(1) %> </p>
        <p> age: <%=oList.Item(2) %> </p>
    </BODY>
</HTML>
```

If you view this page in your browser, you'll see the following:

Count/Clear Methods

Two very common methods that most types of list objects support are Count() and Clear(). Thanks to STL, these methods are trivial to implement in our component. Add the Count() method to the interface, specifying the parameters string as [out, retval] long* Count.

Then, change the definition of the function to look like this:

```
STDMETHODIMP CList::Count(long *Count)
{
    if(!Count)
        return E_POINTER;

    *Count = m_list.size();
    return S_OK;
}
```

The size() method just returns the total number of items in the vector<>, so that we can return the result directly to the caller.

Next, add the Clear() method to the interface leaving the parameters string blank. Once added, change the definition of the function to look like this:

```
STDMETHODIMP CList::Clear()
{
    m_list.clear();
    return S_OK;
}
```

The Clear() method will enumerate the vector<> and release its items, freeing the memory used by any contained VARIANTs.

To test that both methods work, add the following code to the hello.asp file, just before the closing <BODY> tag:

```
        <P> count: <%=oList.count %> </P>
        <% oList.Clear %>
        <P> count after clear: <%=oList.count %> </P>
```

This additional code displays a count of the items in the list, clears it, and then displays the count again. Update your ASP page, then refresh the browser and you should see the following:

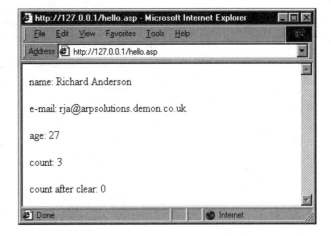

The screenshot shows that the count is 3 before the call to oList.Clear(), as expected. Once that's called, as expected, the count is shown as 0.

The Final Dump Method

The final method our component will implement is Dump(). We added the definition of this method earlier in the chapter, so just change it as follows:

```
STDMETHODIMP CList::Dump()
{
    std::vector<CComVariant>::iterator i;

    for(i = m_list.begin(); i != m_list.end(); i++)
    {
        m_piResponse->Write(CComVariant("<P>"));
        m_piResponse->Write(*i);
        m_piResponse->Write(CComVariant("</P>"));
    }
    return S_OK;
}
```

m_piResponse *will have been initialized by the call to* OnStartPage().

The final addition to hello.asp tests the Dump() method. It creates a simple list that contains the names of the authors of this book, and then calls the Dump() method after a basic title to list them:

```
<% set oList = Server.CreateObject("BegASP.List")
    oList.Add "Richard Anderson"
    oList.Add "Alex Homer"
    oList.Add "Simon Robinson"
%>

<HTML>
    <BODY>
        The authors of this book include:
        <%oList.Dump%>
    </BODY>
</HTML>
```

And here is the result:

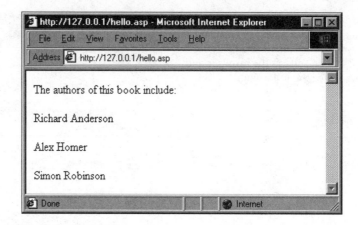

Why Use C++?

In the last part of this chapter, we're going to reprise the pros and cons of using C++ to develop ASP components. The authors of this book have combined experience of around twenty years in both C++ and Visual Basic, and in that time they've used many other languages too. These are their considered opinions.

The Good Points

Performance

C++ is quicker than Visual Basic in terms of pure code execution speed. The difference isn't massive for the code you write, but the code you call, such as the Visual Basic runtime, can be very much slower. With C++, you have total control, so you can always fine-tune code.

Size

Using ATL, you can create components that are around 30Kb or 40Kb in size, depending upon the functionality they contain. There are no additional runtime DLLs that need to be deployed or loaded when the component is used, provided that you create a "minimum dependency" project. With Visual Basic, the actual component size isn't that different, but you've got a runtime that is well over 1 megabyte in size. That isn't a huge problem for server-side ASP components, but it is still a megabyte of data that has to be loaded at least once into every process that uses your component.

Access to the Operating System

With languages like VBScript, you are restricted in the features of the operating system that you can use. Visual Basic is better, but you still have to use unfriendly declaration syntax, and any functions that require pointers become extremely complicated.

Reuse of Existing Code Base

If you've already invested in C++ development, you'll want to re-use it. By developing ASP components using C++, you can easily reuse existing C++ code.

Threading

C++ is closer to the metal, so you've got access to far more COM features. We won't discuss all of them in this book, but an important one that's discussed in the next chapter is threading models. In C++, we can create components that can efficiently be used in ASP `Session` and `Application` objects. This can also be done using Visual Basic, but it hampers scalability.

The Bad Points

It Takes Longer

C++ does take longer to learn than Visual Basic, and there is a steeper learning curve. To use it effectively, you really do have to understand C++, you really do have to understand COM, and knowledge of ATL is practically essential. To save some time, proof-of-concept work can be done by prototyping in VB or VBScript before starting your development effort proper.

It Costs More

The skill set of a C++ developer is generally more advanced than that of a typical Visual Basic programmer. This means they generally cost more to employ, and that reason alone can be enough for some companies to eschew the benefits of C++ and opt instead for Visual Basic development.

Summary

In this chapter, we've covered a lot of basic concepts that are important when writing ASP components. We started the chapter by looking at what the ATL Object Wizard does for us when we add an ASP component to a project, examining the code it created in quite some detail, and seeing how the ASP intrinsic objects are retrieved in the `OnStartPage()` method.

Next, we implemented a simple method to write information back to the client browser using the `IResponse` interface. We saw under what conditions the component would potentially fail, and discussed how to implement error objects to help us track down errors.

After that, we looked at the various utility classes that ATL provides to make developing components in C++ simpler. This included discussions of `CComBSTR`, `CComVariant`, `CComPtr<>` and `CComQIPtr<>`.

Finally, we implemented the main functionality of our component using STL, and discussed how using C++ for ASP component development can be advantageous for some types of components.

Threading, Scope and Performance

In the last chapter, we developed an environment-dependent component for ASP that was capable of holding a number of VARIANT values. We implemented the component using the STL vector<> class and the ATL CComVariant class.

Essentially, all the component did was to expose the functionality of those classes to an ASP page using COM. The list component was able to display the current list of values by accessing the ASP Response object directly and using its Write() method to create output. This is where the component's environment-dependency lies: the component must run inside of IIS for the Dump() method to work.

The ASP intrinsic objects were made accessible to the component by the implementation of the OnStartPage() method. OnStartPage() takes a single parameter: a pointer to the IScriptingContext interface. As you'll recall from the last chapter, this interface has a number of properties that expose the ASP intrinsic objects. The OnStartPage() event handler is called when a component is first created and used on a page, provided that the ASP page creates it using Server.CreateObject() function.

However, the IScriptingContext interface is considered obsolete in IIS 5, and even in IIS 4 it is considered secondary to using the **object context**, which we first demonstrated back in Chapter 3. The object context is now the preferred way of accessing the ASP intrinsic objects, and while it doesn't mean that the IScriptingContext interface is no longer supported in IIS 5, Microsoft is suggesting you only use it in legacy ASP applications. The object context, on the other hand, is part of the long-term strategy for COM+. Furthermore, the scripting context is of little use for transactional objects (where the object is created and destroyed for each method call), because after the first method call, the scripting context will not be available—MTS may well have swapped in a different component.

In this chapter, we are going to look more closely at how we can write components that take advantage of the integration between IIS and MTS, and how various factors (such as threading models and usage of the ASP intrinsic objects) can affect the overall scalability and performance of our ASP components and applications. We'll also expose some of the reasons why C++ can be better for some types of component development. Visual Basic and other languages shield us from the low-level workings of COM, making several COM threading models unavailable, but these very models are essential when writing components that are stored in the Application object.

The topics covered in this chapter will include:

- ❑ Threading, performance, and component scope
- ❑ Using the free-threaded marshaler to enable direct cross-apartment calls
- ❑ Revisiting the `List` component, making it suitable for storage in the `Application` object
- ❑ Some basic guidelines for writing good IIS applications

Abstraction and the Gory Details of C++

As C++ developers, we have far more control over how our ASP components are implemented than our colleagues who work with languages like Visual Basic. We live and work in the low-level world of Software Development Kits and Application Programming Interfaces. We are more than familiar with the feeling that we're pulling our hair out while attempting to understand why API calls aren't working, often focusing on the implementation of business logic as our secondary concern when working with a new SDK for unfamiliar APIs.

In contrast, with Visual Basic (which these days is essentially a component-based language), developers spend a greater proportion of their time implementing business logic and a lesser proportion figuring out how to call methods of an interface. The only complexity in Visual Basic is working out what references to add to our project in order to make use of other components (such as the ActiveX Data Objects) within our own component.

The fundamental differences between C++ and Visual Basic are fairly clear. First, Visual Basic is a high-level language that tries its best to shield the developer from low-level implementation details, while C++ is a low-level language that exposes all the gory details. Second, most C++ developers will probably be bald by the time they are 30.

A Brief Comparison of Visual Basic with C++

Used properly, Visual Basic and Visual C++ both have their merits. Visual Basic really doesn't have any *major* advantages over Visual C++ (that's *Visual* C++, meaning the Microsoft IDE combined with the C++ language), *if* you've got good, experienced Visual C++ developers. We're not going to start a VB vs. VC debate in this chapter; instead we're going to discuss the key differences between the two, and explain why Visual C++ is a better choice for *some* types of ASP component development. We'll also explain our rationale for saying that Visual C++ can be as quick a tool for application development as Visual Basic.

Let's start off by understanding why Visual Basic is considered to be a high-level language by looking at how it shields implementation details exposed to Visual C++ developers. As an example, we'll look at how to create an instance of a fictional COM component called `Book` using C++ and Visual Basic.

Comparing Instance Creation in Visual C++ and Visual Basic

In Chapter 10, we saw how creating instances of components in C++ required the `CoCreateInstance()` API function and the five parameters it takes. We also saw how we have to explicitly perform such tasks as calling `CoInitialize()` to instruct COM that our thread wants to use COM.

The benefit of using Visual Basic here is that code is uncomplicated. We don't have to worry about ensuring that COM is initialized; we don't need to concern ourselves with the five parameters that the C++ sample's `CoCreateInstance()` API requires, and it's the same as the way in which *all* Visual Basic objects and components are created.

This simple comparison demonstrates how Visual Basic, as a high-level language, shields the developer from low-level implementation details. This is great because it gets Visual Basic developers productive quickly, and allows them to concentrate on business logic rather than infrastructure code.

The trade-off for using Visual Basic rather than Visual C++ is quicker development for less flexibility. In this chapter, for example, we're going to look more closely at the COM threading models, and at the concept of a COM **apartment**. Visual Basic (and the `CoInitialize()` API call in C++) always gives us a **single-threaded apartment (STA)**, but in C++ it's possible to call `CoInitializeEx()` and get a **multithreaded apartment (MTA)** instead. Later in this chapter, we'll see just how significant that can be.

The Visual Basic Runtime and Abstraction of Complexity

The abstraction of `CoCreateInstance()` and various other APIs used is implemented by the Visual Basic runtime, as illustrated here:

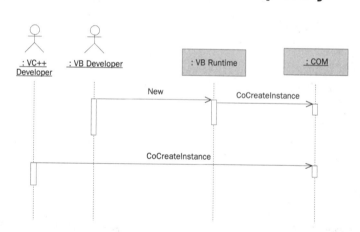

The Visual Basic runtime knows how to invoke these lower-level APIs, while the Visual Basic developer works at a higher level of abstraction using primitives such as New and `CreateObject()`. Implicitly, this means that Visual Basic needs to know about the COM APIs in order to abstract them. The Visual Basic runtime can only abstract a pre-determined number of SDKs and APIs, and we have no control over what it *does* abstract; so Visual Basic developers lose out on functionality like MTAs.

From what we've seen so far, it's reasonable to say that for STA-based applications and components, Visual Basic looks the better choice. However, it's possible that an STA-based component created using Visual C++ will execute slightly faster, and for the most part Visual C++ initializes COM the same way that Visual Basic does—it's just that we have to do more of the work ourselves. If only we could abstract the complexity out of our Visual C++ code, we'd have a strong case for using Visual C++ every time!

Abstraction of Complexity in Visual C++

The fact is that in C++, there are many SDKs and APIs that are used very frequently, and in a very similar way each time. In general, C++ developers find that they don't need all of the APIs in a given SDK, so a common practice is to develop a couple of pieces of custom code:

❑ A C++ class that makes it easier to use a set of APIs

❑ A COM component that makes it easier to use a set of APIs

This kind of abstraction hides the low-level implementation detail to the same extent as Visual Basic does. The only difference here is that *because* it's Visual C++, it gives us more control. If we want to, we can change our abstraction layer. And if we find a bug in our abstraction layer, we just fix it. If we find a bug in the Visual Basic runtime, we're stuck until Microsoft fixes it.

Abstraction through classes and components is important because it enables us (and the other developers on our team) to work at a higher level. It means that we can avoid low-level issues—what functions to call, what parameters and flags should be passed to an API, endless consultation of the help system to double-check API definitions—and focus instead on business logic and the "bigger picture".

Proficient use of abstraction in Visual C++ development can help us to produce results as quickly as we might do in Visual Basic—and in the longer term, we'll be more productive than our Visual Basic-using colleagues. This is because C++ (as a language) has more sophisticated reuse mechanisms—such as implementation inheritance, where code can be written once and then reused in several classes simply by deriving one class from another. In C++, we can simply define our class like this:

```
class MyNewClass : public MyClassWithCodeIWantToReuse;
```

In Visual Basic, one class module *can't* inherit from another class module, so we have to use alternative mechanisms like **delegation**, where one class creates another and forwards calls to its methods, like this:

```
Dim oObject As SomeClass              ' We'll delegate some work to oObject

Sub Class_Initialize                  ' Called when our object is first created
    Set oObject = New ClassCodeToReuse ' Create the object we are going to reuse
End Sub

Sub SomeFunction                      ' Use oObject's functions in this object
    oObject.SomeFunction
End Sub
```

Abstraction in Visual C++: a Competitor to Visual Basic Reuse

Let's look at how we can simplify our C++ code by using a simple form of abstraction. As an example, let's imagine we need to instantiate a number of fictional book components that all expose the interface IBook. We might want to abstract this procedure by using a helper function that encapsulates the object creation process:

```
IBook* CreateBook()
{
    IBook* pBegASP = NULL;
    CoCreateInstance(__uuidof(Book),
                     NULL, CLSCTX_ALL,
                     __uuidof(IBook),
                     reinterpret_cast<void**>(&pBegASP));

    return pBegASP;
}
```

Now, here's how we might use it:

```
int main()
{
    IBook* pBegASP = NULL;
    CoInitialize(NULL);

    pBegASP = CreateBook();

    // Do things with the object...

    pBegASP->Release();
    CoUninitialize();
    return 0;
}
```

We've created a function called CreateBook() that returns an instance of a Book. The CreateBook() function is then called in main() to create an instance of the component after COM is initialized. We still had to initialize and terminate COM, but if we need to create any other Book objects in our code, we can use the same function. In fact, creating a Book object in this way now requires the same number of lines of code as we used in the first Visual Basic code fragment in the chapter, and we no longer have to worry about the five parameters of CoCreateInstance(). All this has cost us is the initial development hit required to write the helper function. But we gain a lot of flexibility: if we decide to use a new Book component, or change the way the function works, we simply change the CreateBook() function and all of the calling code adopts our changes.

The advantage of abstraction is that it makes the main body of our code simpler to understand. By writing helper functions and classes, we also get the benefit that we isolate dependencies on SDKs and APIs in a single location. If we discover that we've made a mistake in our interpretation of the APIs (a common mistake in the C++ world, particularly with new APIs), or we have a bug related to the calls, or if we simply want to replace our old calls with newer API calls, then we can implement the necessary changes in a single location in our code. Of course, if there is a *problem* in our helper code, then that too will affect every function or class that calls it; but at least that increases our chances of finding and fixing bugs before we release the code!

Abstraction Summary

The objective of examining some of the differences between Visual Basic and Visual C++ here was to help you appreciate that the extra flexibility offered by Visual C++ doesn't necessarily compromise development time—if you abstract and simplify API calls. You can still use abstraction in Visual Basic, but the advantage of implementing Visual C++ abstraction is that we get fewer immutable "black boxes". Rather, we get complete flexibility, at the potential cost of longer development times when venturing into new SDK terrain.

In the next section, we're going to start looking at areas where C++ has advantages over Visual Basic for developing ASP components—and to understand when this extra degree of flexibility is beneficial.

Two Threading Models

As we first began to see in Chapter 2, COM provides us with a rich set of threading models that enable us to decide how much responsibility we want to take for handling access to our components. The more responsibility our components take, the more they can potentially optimize their use, and ultimately increase the performance and overall scalability of the applications using them.

In Visual Basic, threading models aren't really an issue. As of Visual Basic 6.0, we've got two choices:

❑ **Single** threading, in which all access to *all* instances of the component are serialized via a single thread.

❑ **Apartment** threading, in which all access to *one* instance of a component is serialized via a single thread, but different instances of the component can live on different threads.

The apartment threading model is fine for most types of ASP component development. However, if you want to store instances of your components within the ASP `Session` or `Application` objects, then (for performance reasons that we'll cover later in this chapter) you should really use the **free** or the **both** threading model—which means you have to use Visual C++. (Actually, you could use Visual J++ as well—but that's another book.) The free and both threading models are not available to Visual Basic, which is simply not designed for writing multithreaded applications, and does everything in its power to shield the programmer from the concept of threads.

Before we dive in and talk about the free and both threading models, and their benefits for certain types of ASP component, we'll discuss how and when we should use the threading models that *are* provided by Visual Basic. Although VB is essentially single-threaded, we'll see how the single-threaded apartment does start to introduce a few threading issues—and we'll show how Visual Basic tries to protect us from them.

The Single Threading Model

The single threading model is a *bad thing*. It stems from the early days of COM under Windows 3.1, and you really shouldn't consider using it unless the environment your using dictates it. IIS doesn't dictate it, so *steer clear*!

If you *do* use a single-threaded component in a multithreaded application like IIS, you are potentially making a large part of it (anywhere that your component is used) single-threaded. Using it means that *every single* method call to *every single* instance of the component has to be done from the *same* thread. Imagine that you've got 50 users accessing an ASP page that uses a single-threaded component, and that each page makes just one method call to the component. The 50th user has to wait for the 49th user's call to complete before its call can be processed. The 49th user will have to wait for the 48th user's call to finish. The 48th user will have to wait for the 47th user's call to finish... You get the picture. Just reading that text was painful and slow, so imagine how the 50th user will feel, waiting for the ASP page to be displayed in their browser!

The single threading model effectively tells COM that your component can't cope with threads. In fact, it tells COM that your component is seriously thread-phobic. It says that you want COM to serialize method calls to all instances of the component, so that the component can access global or local data without having to apply any synchronization.

In Chapter 2, we explained how a process could have several threads of execution that essentially run at the same time. Well, in that situation, if one thread reads a piece of data and updates, another thread could do the same thing at the same time, and one of the changes will be lost. A component that could be accessed by multiple threads needs to do some work to synchronize access to variables in order to prevent that happening. A component that declares itself to be single-threaded is basically saying that it has no such protection, so multiple threads *must* stay away!

So the bottom line is this. Don't ever use components with the single threading model attribute in ASP, and certainly don't ever buy a component that only supports single threading!

Threading Models in Visual Basic

Before version 6.0, Visual Basic either supported single threading only, or defaulted to it for new projects. In Visual Basic 6.0, apartment threading is the default. Before you finally deploy your component, always double-check your **Project Properties** dialog and select **Apartment Threading**. If your version of Visual Basic doesn't have an apartment threading option, order a new version today!

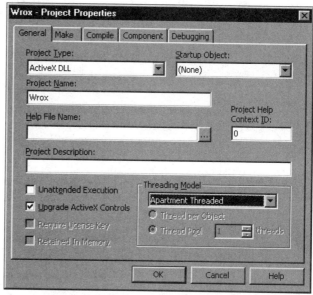

If you've built your component as an ActiveX executable, you may not have the option to select the threading model: the list box will be grayed out. However, you can tell the threading model is 'apartment' because you'll have the option to vary the thread pool, as we discussed in Chapter 2. This won't normally affect us because when writing components for use in the ASP environment, there's normally little reason to opt for out-of-process components. In our discussion of threading in this chapter, we'll concentrate on in-process components.

473

Threading Models in C++

In C++, we (as component developers) have ultimate responsibility for selecting the threading model. When you're using ATL to create an in-process component, the threading model value turns up in a **registry script (RGS)** file that's created for us by the Wizard and used to make entries for the component in the registry. The value is set according to the value selected in the **Threading Model** frame of the **Properties** dialog:

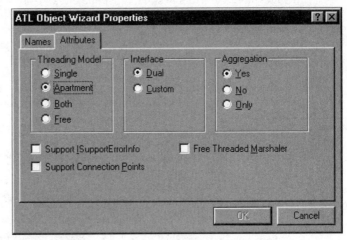

The registry script is a list of instructions that get interpreted by the **ATL Registrar** component—a COM object that is created to update the system registry when your COM server is registered. When the server is unregistered, the reverse process happens and the registry entries are removed.

Here is the script for a simple component called `AppLevelObject` that I created using the ATL Object Wizard. I've highlighted the line that contains the threading model specifier:

```
HKCR
{
    BegASP.AppLevelObject.1 = s 'AppLevelObject Class'
    {
        CLSID = s '{3B1E9957-5D7A-11D3-B95D-204C4F4F5020}'
    }
    BegASP.AppLevelObject = s 'AppLevelObject Class'
    {
        CLSID = s '{3B1E9957-5D7A-11D3-B95D-204C4F4F5020}'
        CurVer = s 'BegASP.AppLevelObject.1'
    }
    NoRemove CLSID
    {
        ForceRemove {3B1E9957-5D7A-11D3-B95D-204C4F4F5020} = s 'AppLevelObject Class'
        {
            ProgID = s 'BegASP.AppLevelObject.1'
            VersionIndependentProgID = s 'BegASP.AppLevelObject'
            ForceRemove 'Programmable'
            InprocServer32 = s '%MODULE%'
            {
                val ThreadingModel = s 'Apartment'
            }
            'TypeLib' = s '{F52A58B3-5D21-11D3-B954-204C4F4F5020}'
        }
    }
}
```

As you can probably see, an RGS file is just a generic way of adding information to the registry. HKCR is short for HKEY_CLASSES_ROOT, while each '{' marks the start of a new sub-key, and '}' marks the end. A point worth mentioning is that '%MODULE%' will be expanded when the script is executed, and replaced by the full path of the COM server containing the component. By convention, RGS files are given a name such as *ComponentName*.rgs.

If you use the *single* threading model, the first thread calling `CoInitialize()` or `OleInitialize()` (or `CoInitializeEx()` specifying an apartment type of `COINIT_APARTMENTTHREADED`) will host *all* the objects of this type that ever get created. This first thread is given special significance, and is called the **main STA**. *Every* single-threaded component will be created in the main STA, so you should consider carefully how that will affect your application. Because all these objects get instantiated in the same thread, you don't gain any of the advantages of multithreading.

That ought to be enough to convince you that the single threading model is bad; so let's look at a *much* better alternative: the apartment threading model.

The Apartment Threading Model

The **apartment threading model** is the right choice for many ASP components. And since Visual Basic supports this threading model, it's ideally suited for writing most types of ASP component that don't require outright speed of execution or operating system/SDK functions that Visual Basic cannot access. But of course, if you've got skilled Visual C++ staff, using Visual C++ can be just as productive as using Visual Basic.

So, when *should* we use Visual C++ instead of Visual Basic for writing apartment-threaded ASP components? Well, in general terms, there's not much to choose between them. However, Visual Basic does have some interesting quirks of implementation that might persuade you to prefer Visual C++. Let's recap what the apartment threading model means, and discuss how your language choice may be swayed one way or the other.

When we pick the apartment threading model, COM takes on the responsibility for ensuring that all access to a *single instance* of a component is serialized via a single thread. That same thread is used to call any of the component's methods, for the lifetime of the object. Since the calling thread is always the same, the object has **thread affinity**, and we can make various assumptions about the caller—for example, we can assume that the result of `GetThreadId()` always returns the same thread ID for the lifetime of the object. It also means that your Visual C++ components can make use of **thread local storage (TLS)**.

> *Put simply, thread local storage is a way of making a global variable that's unique for each thread. Rather than having to manage access to a global variable (as we'll discuss shortly), TLS takes care of it for you. COM and MTS make use of TLS for storing things like the object context.*

The apartment threading model is the preferred threading model for most environments, so you'll also find that it's the default threading model option in Visual C++ and Visual Basic 6.0. If we have 25 users accessing an ASP page that uses a component with this model, each call can be processed 'simultaneously' because we will have 25 active threads. In theory at least, each user will get an equal response time.

Single Threading vs. Apartment Threading

The big advantage of apartment threading over single threading is clear when we consider what happens when a multithreaded application creates an instance of a component:

❑   If the component was built using the apartment threading model, then the application creates a new thread and runs that component instance on the new thread. This allows for parallel processing.

❑   If the component was built using the single threading model, then the application creates the component instance on the application's main thread; this makes for less responsive performance because methods call to objects on the main thread must be processed in series.

> No matter how many additional CPUs we add to the machine, if the component is built using the single threading model, we can't make it run any faster.

Global Shared State

Because the apartment threading model allows simultaneous calls of methods on different component instances, there's a special consideration that we have to make: serialized access to global data.

In Visual C++, global data is available to any code running on any thread in a COM server or application. This makes it possible for two or more threads to attempt to access (or update) the same data at the same time, and this can produce unexpected results. To demonstrate the problems, we'll write a simple C++ program that counts to 30. We won't use any COM runtime calls in the code because the issue of multithreaded access is pervasive in C++, and we just want to make the basic issues clear.

A Demonstration

Being a rather sophisticated counter, our program will count to 30 using *three* threads. Each thread will invoke a function called CountToTen() that increases a global variable (called g_lCounter) by 1, ten times. The function has been designed this way in order to increase the chance that another thread will access the data at the same time, and thus break the integrity of the contained value.

The CountToTen() function that each thread will call looks like this:

```
DWORD WINAPI CountToTen(LPVOID lpParameter)
{
    long lCount = 0;                    // Local state
    for(long l = 0; l < 10; l++)
    {
        lCount = g_lCounter;            // Get the count
        Sleep(0);                       // Let another thread run
        g_lCounter = lCount + 1;        // Increase the count
    }
    return 0;
}
```

This code copies the global counter into the local variable lCount and calls the API function Sleep(). Then it increases the count, and finally it moves the incremented value back into the global counter.

The call to Sleep(0) causes the operating system to suspend the current thread and schedule (or run) another thread.

Our process has three threads, and Windows NT services threads with the same priority sequentially. We therefore know that the call to Sleep() will enable the next thread in our program to enter the function and grab the count before the original thread (which is now asleep) gets a chance to increase it. Since the second thread also calls Sleep(), the third thread will run and also grab the count before the original thread gets near it.

Can you guess the outcome and the value of the counter? Don't worry if you can't—multithreaded code is complicated, and leads to headaches if not approached with the respect it deserves. If you think you *do* know the value, have you considered the effect that multiple CPUs could have on the result? Let's look at the main body of our program and try to understand what happens:

```cpp
#include "stdafx.h"
#include "windows.h"
#include <iostream>

long g_lCounter = 0;

DWORD WINAPI CountToTen(LPVOID lpParameter);

int main()
{
    DWORD tid = 0;

    // Create the three threads
    HANDLE t1 = CreateThread(NULL, 1024, CountToTen, 0, 0, &tid);
    HANDLE t2 = CreateThread(NULL, 1024, CountToTen, 0, 0, &tid);
    HANDLE t3 = CreateThread(NULL, 1024, CountToTen, 0, 0, &tid);

    // Wait for all the threads to exit
    WaitForSingleObject(t1, INFINITE);
    WaitForSingleObject(t2, INFINITE);
    WaitForSingleObject(t3, INFINITE);

    // Display the count
    std::cout << "The count is " << g_lCounter << std::endl;

    // Close the thread handles
    CloseHandle(t1);
    CloseHandle(t2);
    CloseHandle(t3);
    return 0;
}
```

When the program is executed, it creates three threads by calling CreateThread() three times. The third parameter to CreateThread() is the function that the operating system should use as the starting execution point for the new thread. The other parameters aren't really of any interest for this example.

The return value from `CreateThread()` is a `HANDLE`; Win32 uses objects of this type to represent kernel objects like threads, processes and semaphores. The handles for each thread are saved in `t1`, `t2`, and `t3` respectively, and then used in the next three lines of code—each of which is a call to `WaitForSingleObject()`. This function puts the calling thread into a suspended state until the `HANDLE` passed in as the only parameter becomes signaled, which happens when the thread it represents terminates. This gives us an efficient way of waiting for a thread to finish once it's started. Since we don't want to display the count until all three threads have completed, we call it for each thread that is created.

Finally, we display the count, and you can see the output of this program in the screenshot below:

The value is 10 on this machine because it only has one CPU. If you have more than one CPU, the result is unpredictable. The value is 10 in this case because each thread grabs the current value before sleeping. If we've got three threads, they will all grab the value in turn, and then sleep. At any given time, all three will be holding the same value.

When each thread has grabbed the value, the first thread starts again and will increase it by 1 before placing it back into the global counter. This process is then repeated by the other two threads, which each hold the same start value in their local variable, so the value is never actually increased by more than one, no matter how many threads we create.

If you've got more than one CPU in your machine, each thread truly can run at the same time as the others, so the threads really are updating the value at exactly the same time. At most, one thread can execute on each CPU, so the only really good way of stress-testing a multithreaded application is on a machine with multiple CPUs. For our demonstration, we can't predict the value it will count up to on a machine with multiple CPUs because there is no way to predict the order in which the various threads will attempt to update the count. Running the program three or four times is quite likely to produce three or four different results.

Correcting the Code: Introducing Critical Sections

How do we modify the code so that the counting program always produces the right value (and also has predictable results for an unknown number of CPUs)? We need to modify the `CountToTen()` function to synchronize access to the global counter. There are several techniques that we can use to achieve this, but here we'll use the simplest: critical sections.

A **critical section** is an object that you can use to ensure that only one thread has access to certain pieces of code or data at any one time. What happens is that you surround any sections of code that access the data you need to protect with calls to 'enter' the critical section and to 'leave' the critical section. Once one thread has entered the critical section, no other thread can do so. If any other thread encounters a call to enter the same critical section, it will simply wait until the first thread leaves the critical section before it continues executing.

In our sample, we'll enter the critical section before manipulating the count, and leave the critical section once the global count has been updated. The modified `CountToTen()` function looks like this:

```
DWORD WINAPI CountToTen(LPVOID lpParameter)
{
    long lCount = 0;                          // Local state
    for(long l = 0; l < 10; l++)
    {
        EnterCriticalSection(&g_cs);
        lCount = g_lCounter;                  // Get the count
        Sleep(0);                             // Let another thread run
        g_lCounter = lCount + 1;              // Increase the count
        LeaveCriticalSection(&g_cs);
    }
    return 0;
}
```

We now need to declare the critical section in the global scope, and initialize it at the start of `main()` using `InitializeCriticalSection()`, *before* we create any of the threads that use it:

```
long g_lCounter = 0;
CRITICAL_SECTION g_cs;

DWORD WINAPI CountToTen(LPVOID lpParameter);

int main()
{
    DWORD tid = 0;

    // Initialize the critical section
    InitializeCriticalSection(&g_cs);

    // Create the three threads
    HANDLE t1 = CreateThread(NULL, 1024, CountToTen, 0, 0, &tid);
    HANDLE t2 = CreateThread(NULL, 1024, CountToTen, 0, 0, &tid);
    HANDLE t3 = CreateThread(NULL, 1024, CountToTen, 0, 0, &tid);

    // Wait for all the threads to exit
    WaitForSingleObject(t1, INFINITE);
    WaitForSingleObject(t2, INFINITE);
    WaitForSingleObject(t3, INFINITE);

    // Display the count
    std::cout << "The count is " << g_lCounter << std::endl;

    // Close the thread handles
    CloseHandle(t1);
    CloseHandle(t2);
    CloseHandle(t3);

    // Destroy critical section
    DeleteCriticalSection(&g_cs);
    return 0;
}
```

At the end of the program, we must also destroy the critical section using `DeleteCriticalSection()`. If you run this modified program, you will always get an output of 30.

For in-depth coverage of multi-threading and synchronization choices, the third edition of Jeffrey Richter's Advanced Windows *(ISBN 1-57231-548-2) is highly recommended.*

Component Threading Considerations

That was a rather complex program just to achieve the objective of counting to 30, but it illustrates two very important points that are relevant when writing multithreaded C++ code:

❑ If there's a possibility that your *global* state will be accessed and updated by multiple threads, then you need to perform some type of synchronization. (If the data is only going to be updated by a single thread, this protection isn't necessary.)

❑ *Local* state (such as the temporary variable in the CountToTen() function) doesn't require synchronized access, because it can only ever be accessed by one thread—the owning thread.

How does this relate to the components we write? What is considered to be global state (and what is considered to be local state) in Visual Basic and Visual C++?

Global State vs. Local State

When we create an instance of a component, the local state consists of the member variables that the component defines. In Visual C++, this means anything defined within the class statement (or any base classes of that class). In Visual Basic, on the other hand, local state consists of any variable declared outside of a subroutine or function, within a class module. Local state also includes variables that are declared within a function on the stack, as we saw in the CountToTen() function, but that local state is short lived and destroyed or freed when a function returns.

For a component that uses the apartment threading model, the following state management guidelines apply:

❑ In Visual C++, you always need to protect global state, but not local state.

❑ In Visual Basic you *never* need to protect local *or* global state!

You might be a little surprised by that last statement. We certainly were when we first discovered it.

Visual Basic and Global State

The reason why you don't have to protect global state in Visual Basic is that it doesn't actually exist in the 'global' sense. What appears to be global state is in fact **per-apartment state**. Rather than complicating the Visual Basic language with synchronization type primitives, its designers sensibly decided to give each STA its own *completely unique copy* of any global state. One copy of the global state is created and initialized for each STA in which the component is created. This initialization only occurs once per apartment, so components of the same type within the same STA share the same 'semi-global' state:

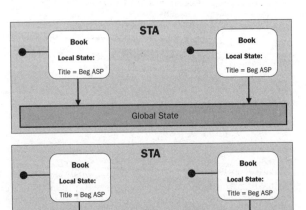

This is actually quite good news for Visual Basic programmers, because it makes their lives easier, and it also fits well with the MTS style of programming. However, if you *want* to share state between components (in order to keep a count of how many times your ASP component has encountered an error, perhaps), you have to hold this data in an external resource such as a database or (if you're using MTS) the shared property manager. You'd have to decide whether this would have an unacceptable impact on overall performance; if so, Visual C++ might be your only choice.

Visual C++ and Global State

As we've already demonstrated, C++ global state really *is* global, and this is shown here:

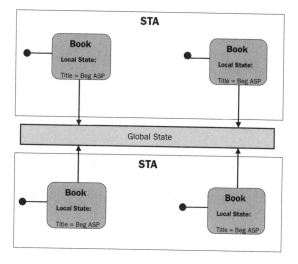

It's up to you to decide what to do with global state, and you have to enforce your own synchronization policies for individual variables.

ASP Components and the Apartment Threading Model: A Summary

Our examination of the single and apartment threading models shows that the only choice for ASP components that are written in Visual Basic is apartment threading. In fact, you should *always* avoid the single threading model unless you need it for backwards compatibility. A component developed using the single threading model will seriously compromise the scalability (and potentially the performance) of any application that uses it, because each method invoked for every component instance is serialized via a single thread—and that's a bottleneck.

If you're writing ASP components in Visual Basic that use the apartment threading model, you don't need to worry about any type of multi-threaded synchronization. You just have to remember that 'global state' is really per-apartment state: don't fall into the trap of thinking your component isn't working, when it's really just the Visual Basic runtime trying to make things easy for you.

If your component needs to share global state, then you can either share the state externally in a database or some other data source (such as the shared property manager or the Site Server Membership and Personalization Directory), or you can write the component using Visual C++. The first of these options actually fits well with the MTS programming model, so think carefully before choosing one approach over the other, even for C++ apartment-threaded components.

We'll come back to our analysis of the threading models shortly—Visual C++ still offers free threading and 'both' threading, which we've yet to examine. Before that, however, we need to take a slight detour into **component scope**.

Component Scope

The position at which you place a component instance in IIS will dictate the object's **scope**—that is, its lifetime and availability within the IIS application. Some levels of scope suit certain threading models better than others. In this section, we'll quickly revise the levels of scope used within IIS; then we can discuss how different threading models (including both threading and free threading) are best married with different scopes.

Page Scope

A component instance has **page scope** (sometimes called **page affinity**) if it is only used and referenced within an ASP page. Its lifetime is relatively short, and is related to the time that it takes to process the ASP page and generate the output to be returned to the client browser. *Any* component can be instantiated with page scope, regardless of the component's threading model.

> *Because of their dependence on the* OnStartPage() *and* OnEndPage() *functions, the components generated by the ATL Wizard for ASP components are 'expecting' to be used in this scope.*

Session Scope

A component instance has **session scope** when it is stored in the Session object. For example:

```
Set oSomeObject = Server.CreateObject("BegASP.Component")
Set Session("MySessionObject") = oSomeObject
```

This object will not be destroyed until IIS determines that the timeout value for an idle user session has been exceeded, or Session.Abandon() is called, or the component is released by either changing the reference or setting it to Nothing:

```
Set Session("MySessionObject") = Nothing
```

Again, *any* component can be instantiated with session scope, regardless of the component's threading model. However, it's generally wise to avoid creating objects with session scope, because they take up server resources and can therefore have a detrimental effect on the overall scalability of your IIS application.

Note that a session-level instance of a single-threaded or apartment-threaded component will essentially lock the user session down to a single thread: the thread used to access that component. Every request from that user must then be processed by that one thread, for the rest of the lifetime of that user session. Depending upon the number of users of your application, you could end up with large numbers of them being locked down to the same thread, even though there are lots of other free threads that could deal with the requests. The trouble is that IIS only has 25 threads to process user sessions before it does a round robin and starts reassigning. At that point you get an effect that's not dissimilar to using the single threading model—all the requests from users assigned to a single thread must be processed one at a time.

Application Scope

A component instance has **application scope** if it is stored in the `Application` object. For example:

```
Set Application("MyApplicationObject") = oSomeObject
```

This object will not be destroyed until the IIS web site or virtual directory is shut down, or (as with objects at session scope) the component instance is released by either changing the reference or setting it to `Nothing`:

```
Set Application("MyApplicationObject") = Nothing
```

No object can be given application scope using the `Set` syntax unless it aggregates the **free threaded marshaler** (FTM), which we'll discuss shortly. If you try it, the call will simply fail. Visual Basic doesn't support aggregation, which effectively means that you can't use this syntax to create application-level instances of Visual Basic components. You could use the `<OBJECT>` tag in `global.asa` to *force* a Visual Basic object into application scope, but that will still have a serious detrimental effect on the overall scalability of your IIS application, since every session that uses that component would be bottlenecked into the thread used by that component.

Two More Threading Models

There are a couple of rules of thumb that we can take away from our discussions in the previous section. Don't give application scope to *any* single- or apartment-threaded component, and only give session scope to such a component if you absolutely have to. Let's look at how the free threading and both threading models, in conjunction with Visual C++, can help overcome these restrictions.

❏   In **free threading**, access to an instance of a component can be gained from any thread. The component instance always runs in the MTA, and all access to local *and* global state has to be synchronized for updates. The component instance has no thread affinity.

❏   In **both threading**, COM effectively chooses the apartment threading or free threading model at runtime when it is creating an object, according to whether the component instance is being created in an STA or an MTA. If the caller is an STA, the component will be apartment threaded. If the caller is an MTA, the free threading model is selected. If the object is created in an STA it has thread affinity by default; otherwise it doesn't.

Apartments and Threading Models

We've still not *really* examined what an apartment is, although we've used the term on a number of occasions. A COM apartment can be thought of as the space within which a thread that uses COM is placed—a single-threaded apartment can contain only one thread. Until now, we've been talking about components that use the single and apartment threading models. Such components exist in single-threaded apartments.

> **A single-threaded apartment is associated with just one thread, which means that to this point, we've been able to treat threads and apartments as being essentially synonymous.**

A multithreaded apartment can contain any number of threads. This means that an object in a multithreaded apartment can be accessed from any of those threads. A *process* (such as IIS) can have at most one MTA, but it can have as many STAs as it needs:

❏ An STA is created whenever a thread initializes itself (by calling `CoInitializeEx()` and specifying `COINIT_APARTMENTTHREADED`, or by calling `CoInitialize()`, or by calling `OleInitialize()`). The STA is associated with that thread, and the thread is associated with only that STA. Components created in STAs are said to have **thread affinity**.

❏ An MTA can be associated with many threads. Each thread that calls `CoInitializeEx()` specifying `COINIT_MULTITHEADED` is associated with (or "enters") the MTA.

Diagrammatically, here's what a process might look like:

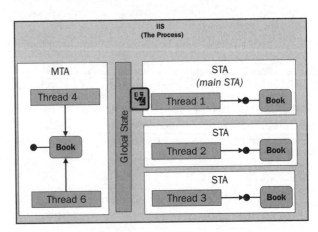

This diagram shows that only the main STA (the first one that gets created) actually has access to global state that's locked on its behalf. All other apartments have to serialize access to global state.

A thread can only be associated with one type of apartment at one time—an MTA or an STA. A thread *can* switch apartments, but it must call `CoUninitialize()` to leave one apartment before calling `CoInitialize()` to enter another one.

COM objects live within a single apartment for their entire lives. That apartment is assigned to them when they are created, and they can't change it. The methods of the object are normally only invoked by threads that belong to that apartment, but that can be changed if the **free threaded marshaler** is used—then, *any* thread can invoke the object's methods.

As we've already said, components can either be **thread-safe** or **thread-phobic**. If a component can't cope with more than one thread calling methods on the same object at the same time, but it's happy to synchronize access to global state itself, then it will be instantiated in an STA:

❑　If the caller creating the object is running in an STA, it will be created in that STA.

❑　If the caller is running in the MTA, COM will create a new STA and create the component instance there. COM will then return a **proxy object** to the MTA that will redirect calls to the STA.

> In COM, when a client and server are in different apartments, they are generally unable to communicate directly. To enable communication, the default solution is for a proxy object to be loaded into the client apartment, and a stub object into the server apartment. To the client, the proxy looks like the server. To the server, the stub looks like the client. The proxy and stub handle the process of marshaling things such as method calls from one apartment to the other.

Components that are thread-safe and happy with multiple threads calling methods of the same object (potentially simultaneously) can live in the MTA. Such components protect local and global state to synchronize updates by simultaneous method calls. This contrasts with apartment threaded components, which only synchronize their global state.

The Free Threading Model

If you want your component *always* to be instantiated in an MTA, it must be built using the **free threading model**. Why would we want to insist on instantiating the component in the MTA? Well, we would generally do that if the component creates **worker threads**.

Worker threads generally perform background tasks, and inform whichever thread created them that they have finished. If the component is instantiated in an STA, its worker threads can't communicate with it without first initializing COM. While that's not a hardship in itself, every call from the worker thread to the owner must then be marshaled, because only the thread that created an STA can legally enter it. This reduces overall performance, and may well comprise your component requirements.

If an STA instantiates a component that *insists* on running in an MTA (because its threading model is specified as 'free'), COM will simply return a proxy to the caller. This means that each method call to the MTA will be marshaled. This initially sounds surprising, because an object in the MTA expects method calls to arrive from any thread, but the calls must still be marshaled because interface pointers are **apartment sensitive**. They can only be called from the apartment within which they were created. Since the calling STA and the serving MTA are *different* apartments, the method call *must* be marshaled into the MTA.

The Both Threading Model

To gain the option of instantiating your component in *either* an MTA *or* an STA, the component can be built using the **both threading model**. This is advantageous because it means that we'll never need to marshal method calls to these instances: the component will always be created in the same apartment as the caller.

If the component is marked as using the both threading model, and the caller is STA-based, COM will make the decision to create the object in the STA, just as if it were marked as apartment threaded. There is therefore no real benefit in using this threading model for ASP components in isolation, because in practice the net result is equivalent to using an apartment-threaded component. However, that's not the end of the story, as you'll soon see.

Free Threading, Both Threading, and IIS

The objectives of the free threading and both threading models are to improve performance and throughput of a component instance that may be accessed (potentially simultaneously) by a number of different threads. However, these two threading models are generally only useful when the hosting environment or process is predominantly MTA-based. Now, IIS isn't MTA-based, so to capture the full advantage of these threading models, we need a little bit of help from the free threaded marshaler, as you'll see shortly.

The support that IIS provides for ASP is built entirely using STAs. IIS uses a pool of STAs to process page requests, and a single (distinct) STA is responsible for hosting the `Application` object. IIS uses MTS to provide this pool, as we discussed in Chapters 6 and 7.

Components with Page Scope

Components that have page scope are the situation in which it is preferable *not* to use the free or both threading models. Let's have a look why.

- ❑ If an instance of a component has page scope and is *apartment* threaded, it will be created in the same STA as the Web Application Manager object (the object responsible for processing ASP requests). In this case, method calls will be direct, and not via a proxy. In other words, method calls could not be any quicker.

- ❑ If a component instance is created at page scope and is *free* threaded, it'll be created in the MTA—so access to it will be marshaled via a proxy/stub pair. Therefore, if you're writing a component for use in IIS, then generally speaking this threading model will result in the worst overall performance.

Marshaling isn't a quick process, and the free threading model turns out to be the *slowest* choice for ASP components. Each time a method is called on an ASP page, there's a long process involved: the parameters have to be packaged up by the proxy, sent to the stub via an RPC channel, unpacked by the stub, the method invoked, any return parameters packaged up, sent back to the proxy, unpacked by the proxy, and finally returned to the WAM object. You get the picture.

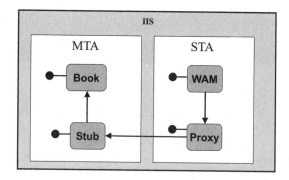

If we create a component that uses the *both* threading model at page scope, COM will create the component in the same STA as the WAM object. This is the same behavior that we'd see when creating apartment-threaded components. Unfortunately, since the both-threaded component will be protecting local state unnecessarily (using synchronization primitives like critical sections), the component will probably run more slowly than its apartment-threaded equivalent, but it's still preferable to the marshaling overhead caused by the free threading model.

> **If you know that an object is always going to be used at page scope, always use the apartment threading model for best performance.**

The Free Threaded Marshaler

You're probably starting to wonder whether the additional flexibility with threading models that C++ offers is actually of any use when writing ASP components. The problem is that IIS is an STA-based application, so it's not naturally suited to supporting components whose instances run in an MTA. In IIS, these component instances will generally be instantiated from within an STA, and therefore calls to the component instance will be cross-apartment—which means they must be marshaled. The default means of marshaling is via a proxy, and that's a relatively slow process.

However, if the free- or both-threaded component is well designed, there should be a way round this problem. Such a component is designed to run in an MTA, and should be thread-safe: it should support the synchronization required to protect it from the unmarshaled calls of other threads in the MTA. Because it's thread-safe, the component could allow *any* thread (even STA-based threads) to instantiate it without the protection of marshaling. And if we could do away with the proxy-based marshaling that comes with cross-apartment calls, then our cross-apartment calls will ultimately be more responsive.

We can bypass proxy marshaling by implementing our own **custom marshaling**. To do that, our component must implement an interface called `IMarshal` whose methods allow the *object* to dictate how it wants marshaling to occur.

Here's an overview of how custom marshaling works. When COM handles a cross-apartment call, it needs to determine how to marshal the interface pointer between apartments. To do that, it asks the object for an interface called IMarshal. *If the object supports an* IMarshal *interface, COM will use it to handle the cross-apartment call. If not, COM knows that it must use standard marshaling—usually through a proxy.*

Writing our own custom IMarshal interface is hard work, but that's where the **free threaded marshaler** (FTM) comes in. The FTM is an aggregatable COM object that provides a custom implementation of IMarshal that passes the raw interface pointer back to the caller, bypassing the proxy. When an interface pointer needs to be used outside of an apartment, COM will ask the object for IMarshal. If the component supports this interface, COM will do four things with it:

❑ Ask for the CLSID of the class that is responsible for importing the interface into the outside apartment

❑ Ask how much storage is needed to pass information about how the interface is to be imported to the outside apartment

❑ Create the storage required

❑ Ask it to put the information needed into the storage it just created

These four steps give COM all the information it needs to import the interface pointer. It whizzes the information off to the importing apartment, and then three further steps are carried out:

❑ COM creates an instance of the component that was identified by the original object's IMarshal interface in the first step above

❑ COM asks the newly-created component for the IMarshal interface

❑ COM asks IMarshal to create an interface pointer, passing the data placed into the storage by the exporting apartment

The FTM implements the IMarshal interface as described, and passes a direct pointer to the interface via storage between the two apartments, provided that they are in the same process. If the apartment importing the interface is in a different process, the FTM just implements the IMarshal methods by delegating to the COM runtime, so a proxy/stub pair is created.

By using the FTM, an interface pointer can be accessed directly from *any* apartment, and therefore by any number of threads. Any call to the interface will always be direct, provided that the apartment is within the same process. However, while this optimizes access times (because there is no proxy or stub performing marshaling), it does have an impact on how your components are implemented.

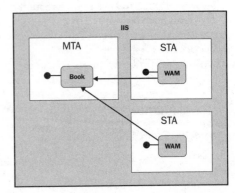

Because the FTM just provides an implementation of a COM interface (IMarshal), we can actually use it on components that use *any* threading model—single, apartment, both or free. However, it *should* only be used with both or free threading, as those specifically indicate that the component is capable of handling multithreaded access to local state, which will occur when using the FTM.

Components written using the apartment model expect calls to be serialized via one thread, so if we put an apartment-threaded object that uses the FTM in the Application *object by using the* <OBJECT> *tag (thereby giving it application scope), it would be possible for multiple ASP pages to access it at the same time. However, because the component hasn't been written to synchronize access to its local state, it will eventually break.*

Thanks to the FTM, we now have an efficient way of using the both and free threading models, removing the need for proxy/stubs. It results in an object that can be called from *any* thread—this is the whole point of using these threading models and the FTM together. It allows us to store objects in the ASP Application and Session objects without compromising the scalability of IIS. If we just stuck an STA-based object (which means any VB-developed object) into the Application or Session objects, a user session is tied down to a single thread.

The both threading model will cause the component instance to be created in the caller's apartment, resulting in direct access and therefore no proxy. When combined with the FTM, when the interface is imported into another STA, a direct pointer will still be used thanks to the IMarshal interface implemented provided by the FTM. By using the both threading model, an MTA will never be created, because ASP is STA-based.

Now that we know we can create Visual C++ ASP components with the both threading model that can be used from any apartment without *any* marshaling overhead, let's look at when and why we should use them. To do this, we have to understand a little bit about the architecture of IIS and how it processes ASP requests.

IIS Architecture

IIS is a large product with a number of features, one of which is ISAPI (Internet Server Application Programming Interface), a C API that allows a DLL to process requests for certain types of pages requested from a web server.

ASP support is implemented inside IIS as an ISAPI extension that was first introduced in version 3.0. The ASP ISAPI extension makes use of MTS to provide a scalable, component-based scripting environment for the generation of HTML pages.

MTS Integration and Page-level Objects

When the ASP handler receives a request for an ASP page, it creates a Web Application Manager (WAM) object. The WAM object is responsible for parsing the ASP page, executing any contained script (using an appropriate scripting engine), and then passing the result back into the core of IIS so it can be returned to the client.

Internally, IIS creates one or more different WAM objects depending upon the package type.

The WAM component itself is installed inside MTS. This means it's *MTS* that actually provides the STAs. MTS usually defaults to 100 threads per package, but IIS 4 reduces the threshold to 25. The number of threads is dynamic in IIS 5, so there is no fixed limit, although a maximum limit can be defined.

So, when an ASP page is requested, any script contained within the page is executed on an STA created by MTS. Any objects created within this script (using `CreateObject()` or `Server.CreateObject()`) will have page scope; these objects don't need to serialize any access to global state, because all calls will be made from a single thread. So, when you're choosing the threading model for a component that will *only* be used at page scope, the order of preference will be:

❑ Apartment threading model (for best performance)

❑ Both threading model (the component will require synchronization of local state)

❑ Free threading model (the component will require aggregation of the FTM, and its instantiation will cause creation of an MTA)

MTS and Session-level Objects

IIS and ASP ensure that, if user sessions are enabled, only one ASP request is ever active for any single user session. Multiple requests for the same user session are serialized and processed one at a time. This is why you will not find a pair of `Lock()` and `Unlock()` methods in the `Session` object: there is simply no need for them.

By default, a user session is not tied down to a specific STA, and MTS provides a pool of STAs that are used to process users' requests. To illustrate, consider a simple scenario in which we have three simultaneous active user sessions, each with one active request and two pending requests:

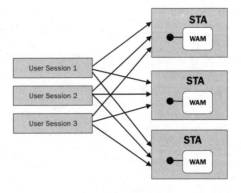

In this example, WAM objects would be created within the MTS process, on three of the least busy of the 25 STAs. We'd have at most three ASP requests being processed simultaneously, and the remaining requests queued up. A user's second request won't begin executing until their first request has completed—and MTS will assign *that* request to one of the least busy STAs. That means that it won't necessarily execute on the same STA as its predecessor.

> **In other words, user sessions just create the component instance with page scope and no STA affinity.**

A new WAM component is automatically installed into MTS by IIS every time you create a new web site or virtual directory. IIS generates a unique CLSID for the component on the fly to ensure each one can have its own unique properties, such as transaction support. These properties are dynamically configured at runtime, depending on whether the @TRANSACTION directive is used with an ASP page.

To see this integration of the two environments, we can see all of the WAM components for web sites and virtual directories that are configured to run in the same process space as IIS by looking at the **Components** folder within the **IIS In-Process Applications** package, as shown below. These are the IIS applications that run in the same address space as IIS (Inetinfo.exe), and are therefore configured as library packages.

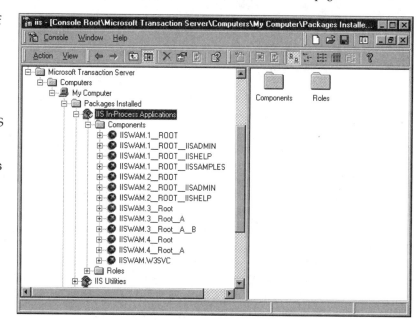

Each web site or virtual directory has one WAM component; the naming convention is IISWAM.[sequential number].[full virtual directory path].

If you configure a web site or virtual directory to run in its own process space, IIS will create a new server package inside MTS. The next screenshot shows the four packages that were installed when I created a web site called ASP with a virtual directory called A, a virtual directory called B within A, and a virtual directory called C at the same level as A. As you can see, IIS created a new package for each one, and if you look at the **Properties** tab you'll see it's configured as a server package, which shows that IIS is making use of the MTS facilities for providing process isolation. The naming convention for these server packages is IIS-{ [web site name] // [full virtual directory path].

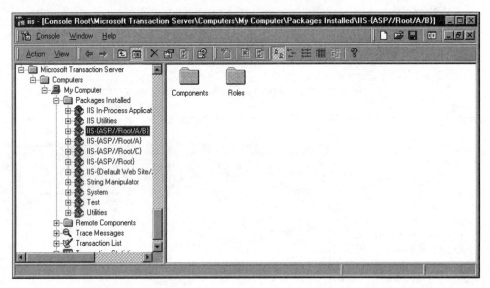

The question, therefore, is how the integration with MTS affects the way we write our IIS applications and components.

MTS is based around single-threaded apartments. Any component that wants to make use of MTS features such as role checking, activity management and automatic transaction enlistment have to be designed using the apartment threading model. MTS overrides the threading model when a component is installed, so we just have to ensure we *don't* use the FTM for components that need to be installed into MTS manually. If we do this, the context wrapper will break.

The links between MTS and IIS are pretty seamless. Apart from the Microsoft Management Console, the only other time we really see them is when we use ASP's intrinsic Server object and call the CreateObject() function. One of the benefits this has over the standard CreateObject() function is that when it's called, IIS calls the CreateInstance() method of the IObjectContext interface. (The same function also checks for the presence of OnStartPage() and OnEndPage(), and invokes them if present.) This means that if the component we are creating is transactional and the transactional attributes are compatible, it is enlisted into the caller's transaction. If we just used CreateObject(), the new component would not automatically join the transaction, and (worse still) it will be created in a different STA.

Over a large number of CreateObject() *requests, we recorded a 20-25% performance improvement when using* CreateObject() *over* Server.CreateObject(). *The reason why the latter is slower is because it performs a number of additional steps when creating a number of objects.*

When an object is created using Server.CreateObject(), the registry is accessed to check the threading model for the object being created. It uses this information to optimize the way the object is used internally. The expected behavior is that if the object's threading model is Apartment, IIS knows to lock the current user session to the ASP page's STA. IIS 5 does not perform this check, so the performance of both calls should be similar.

Indeed, in IIS 5 there is no need to use Server.CreateObject(), *because the activities it performs are now part of COM+.*

So, the moral of the story is that you should generally use Server.CreateObject() for any *transactional* objects that you create that have page scope. On the flip side, you can safely use CreateObject() for those that *aren't* transactional, provided that they don't need OnStartPage() and OnEndPage() to be invoked.

The basic integration between IIS and MTS for **IIS In-Process Applications** is shown in the figure below. The MTS executive is created inside of Inetinfo.exe, and the WAM object lives for the duration of the ASP inside an STA created by MTS. The only real difference for **IIS Out of Process** applications is that the MTS executive and the contained elements live inside Mtx.exe. A unique instance of Mtx.exe is created for each **IIS Out of Process Application**.

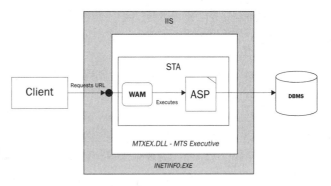

As IIS processes multiple simultaneous requests, the number of STAs used increases, as shown in the next figure. MTS automatically expands the number of available STAs, depending upon the load.

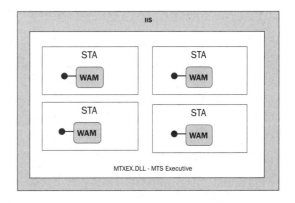

More on Component Scope

That's a brief insight into the relationship between MTS and IIS, but how does it affect our choice of threading models for the different types of components that we write? Well, for a start, storing objects in the Session object has the potential to limit the scalability of your IIS applications. If you have (say) 10,000 concurrent user sessions, and (say) 2 objects stored at the Session level, you've got 20,000 active COM objects. Assuming no cross-apartment marshaling, a small component instance might use 1Kb of memory, so around 20Mb of memory is required just for objects stored at the session level.

Each additional session requires resources for the duration of that session. Such systems are not scalable. Our servers only have a finite number of resources, so we can't take this approach for large enterprise-type IIS applications—we have to employ the MTS-style stateless programming model in order to scale. Rather than keeping lots of COM objects around, make your components stateless and rehydrate them as they become needed. Taking this approach, we could limit our web server to (say) 100 concurrent STAs, which should be able to service 10,000 user sessions quite happily. Therefore, our server no longer needs "user sessions x 2Kb", but rather "100 x 2Kb".

Once a component instance is stored at the session level, the user session will always have all requests processed by that thread. Even if the component instance is destroyed by using Set oObject = Nothing, the request is still locked down to a thread, simply because of the way IIS is written. The rationale for this behavior is fairly logical, and the overall performance loss shouldn't be that significant; it just requires consideration.

The only serious issue is that if two sessions are tied to one thread, they can only be processed sequentially. Even if no other sessions are active, the users will have to wait for each other—they can't just jump to another free thread. Given that one ASP page could take a while to process, that *could* be a serious problem.

Making the List Component Both Threaded

So far, this chapter has been rather theoretical, so let's put our newfound Visual C++ advantages into practice and make the List component from the last chapter suitable for use in both the Session and the Application object. To do this we will:

❑ Change the threading model from apartment to both

❑ Aggregate the Free Threaded Marshaler (FTM)

❑ Add synchronization code to prevent two or more threads accessing local state (the contained STL vector<> class) at the same time

When an instance of the List component is stored in the Session object, these changes will ensure that the associated user session is not locked down to a single thread. When stored in an Application object, they will ensure that multiple user sessions (and therefore multiple threads) can call the object's methods simultaneously without its state getting corrupted. IIS knows it can do this safely because it can determine that the IMarshal implementation is provided by the FTM.

To make these changes, we will *not* create a brand new component using the Wizard. Instead, I'll take you through the steps required to convert the List component we developed in the last chapter. This will give you a better insight into what ATL Wizard does when you select the various threading options.

Before we start to make the changes, though, let's see what happens if we try to put the existing List component into the Application object using the following ASP code:

```
<%
    Dim oDictionary
    Set oDictionary = Server.CreateObject("BegASP.List")
%>

<HTML>
    <HEAD>
        <TITLE>Application Level Object?</TITLE>
    </HEAD>

    <BODY>
        <%
            Set Application("Dictionary") = oDictionary
        %>
    </BODY>

</HTML>
```

This code will generate an error, as shown below. Attempting to give an object application scope fails if the object in question doesn't aggregate the free threaded marshaler. This may seem a little harsh, but given that every single ASP page or component using the object would be serialized via one thread, the performance degradation is so significant that it's not allowed using the Set syntax. We could force the issue (that is, achieve it and circumvent the default protection that IIS uses) by using the <OBJECT> tab in global.asa (IIS considers this to be an explicit declaration of our knowledge), but that doesn't get rid of the performance problem. Every call from any ASP page will be marshaled via a proxy.

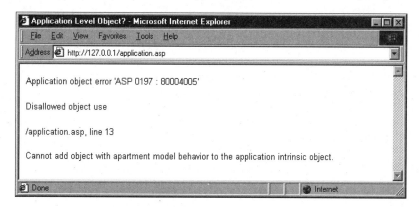

Giving *session* scope to a non-FTM object in an ASP page doesn't fail, but every future ASP request for that user session is locked down to the thread that called the Set command. As we've discussed, this isn't *as* significant, but it does still impact upon performance.

Changing the Threading Model

The first step in converting our `List` component is to change the threading model definition.

Modifying the RGS File

From the file view, double-click on `List.rgs` to bring up the registration script for the `List` component. Locate the `ThreadingModel` line, and change it from `Apartment` to `Both`:

```
HKCR
{
    BegASP.List.1 = s 'List Class'
    {
        CLSID = s '{9A5DC9C0-48E6-11D3-B926-000000000000}'
    }
    BegASP.List = s 'List Class'
    {
        CLSID = s '{9A5DC9C0-48E6-11D3-B926-000000000000}'
        CurVer = s 'BegASP.List.1'
    }
    NoRemove CLSID
    {
        ForceRemove {9A5DC9C0-48E6-11D3-B926-000000000000} = s 'List Class'
        {
            ProgID = s 'BegASP.List.1'
            VersionIndependentProgID = s 'BegASP.List'
            ForceRemove 'Programmable'
            InprocServer32 = s '%MODULE%'
            {
                val ThreadingModel = s 'Both'
            }
            'TypeLib' = s '{9A5DC9B1-48E6-11D3-B926-000000000000}'
        }
    }
}
```

Making this change causes the registry entry for the component to be updated when we next compile the project. When an instance of the component is created by COM, it now knows that it can always create the component instance in the apartment of the caller. So, if the caller is STA-based, the object will reside in that apartment and will only ever be accessed by one thread. If the caller is MTA-based, it will be created in that apartment and accessed by a number of threads, potentially simultaneously.

As the component can now be created in the MTA, we have to protect local state from multiple thread access. (If the component used global state, we would have to protect that too.)

Adding a Critical Section to Protect Local State

ATL provides us with the necessary code for creating a critical section to protect local state. If we look at the original base classes for our `List` component, we see the following:

```
class ATL_NO_VTABLE CList :
    public CComObjectRootEx<CComSingleThreadModel>,
    public CComCoClass<CList, &CLSID_List>,
    public ISupportErrorInfo,
    public IDispatchImpl<IList, &IID_IList, &LIBID_BEGASPLib>
```

The important base class with regard to threading is `CComObjectRootEx<>`. Among other useful things like reference counting, this template provides our class with two functions called `Lock()` and `Unlock()`. These functions are what we use to protect local state from being accessed by multiple components. For example:

```
STDMETHODIMP CList::SomeFunction()
{
    Lock();

    // Change some local state

    Unlock();
    return S_OK;
}
```

When our class derives from `CComObjectRootEx<CComSingleThreadModel>`, these functions are empty implementations—that is, they do absolutely nothing:

```
void Lock() {}
void Unlock() {}
```

That's fine for single- or apartment-threaded components, but it's obviously no good for this new component, so for the both (or free) threading model we need to change the parameter used in `CComObjectRootEx<>` as follows:

```
class ATL_NO_VTABLE CList :
    public CComObjectRootEx<CComMultiThreadModel>,
    public CComCoClass<CList, &CLSID_List>,
    public ISupportErrorInfo,
    public IDispatchImpl<IList, &IID_IList, &LIBID_BEGASPLib>
```

By specifying `CComMultiThreadModel` as the first parameter to `CComObjectRootEx<>`, ATL will automatically create a critical section for our COM object when it is created that is designed for protecting the local state.

The `Lock()` method will enter a critical section, blocking other threads from entering the protected section of code. The `Unlock()` function will leave the critical section and let the next thread in. Calls to `Lock()` and `Unlock()` need to be balanced; if we forget to call `Unlock()`, then the next call to `Lock()` from a different thread will block indefinitely.

Remember: critical sections are temporarily owned by the thread that calls `Lock()`. If your code forgets to call `Unlock()`, the same thread can happily call `Lock()` again without being blocked, but another thread can't.

These `Lock()` and `Unlock()` methods are implemented as follows:

```
void Lock() {m_critsec.Lock();}
void Unlock() {m_critsec.Unlock();}
```

497

m_critsec is a typedef that maps to CComAutoCriticalSection, which uses the same critical section calls we used earlier in the CountToTen example:

```
class CComAutoCriticalSection
{
public:
   void Lock() {EnterCriticalSection(&m_sec);}
   void Unlock() {LeaveCriticalSection(&m_sec);}
   CComAutoCriticalSection() {InitializeCriticalSection(&m_sec);}
   ~CComAutoCriticalSection() {DeleteCriticalSection(&m_sec);}
   CRITICAL_SECTION m_sec;
};
```

This class, which is defined in Atlbase.h, gets its name from the fact that it automatically creates the critical section in the constructor, and destroys it in the destructor. This is a general utility class that you can also use in your own code. For example, we could have used it earlier, in the CountToTen() function:

```
CComAutoCriticalSection g_cs;           // Automatically created

...

DWORD WINAPI CountToTen(LPVOID lpParameter)
{
   long lCount = 0;                     // Local state
   for(long l = 0; l < 10; l++)
   {
      g_cs.Lock();
      lCount = g_lCounter;              // Get the count
      g_lCounter = lCount + 1;          // Increase the count
      g_cs.Unlock();
   }
   return 0;
}
```

Making the Methods Thread-safe

We've now got a List component with Lock() and Unlock() functions that enable us to make the various functions in the List component thread-safe. Let's briefly run through each method and review where these functions should be called.

Add

The Add() method uses the STL vector<> class to add a new value to the end of the list. As the STL is not thread-safe, we have to make sure we synchronize access to *all* methods.

For the Add() method, the following code is all we need:

```
STDMETHODIMP CList::Add(VARIANT Value)
{
   Lock();
   m_list.push_back(Value);
   Unlock();
   return S_OK;
}
```

Clear

The Clear() method removes all entries in the list. Once again, we simply call Lock() before we use the STL method, and Unlock() afterwards:

```
STDMETHODIMP CList::Clear()
{
    Lock();
    m_list.clear();
    Unlock();
    return S_OK;
}
```

Count

The changes required to the Count() method are the same:

```
STDMETHODIMP CList::Count(long *Count)
{
    if(!Count)
        return E_POINTER;

    Lock();
    *Count = m_list.size();
    Unlock();
    return S_OK;
}
```

Dump

The Dump() method is slightly more complex than the ones we've seen so far. It makes multiple calls to the vector<> class by using an iterator. We want the Dump() method to show us a snapshot of the values at a particular point in time, so we call Lock() before the first call and Unlock() after the last call:

```
STDMETHODIMP CList::Dump()
{
    Lock();
    std::vector<CComVariant>::iterator i;

    for(i = m_list.begin(); i != m_list.end(); i++)
    {
        m_piResponse->Write(CComVariant("<p>"));
        m_piResponse->Write(*i);
        m_piResponse->Write(CComVariant("</p>"));
    }
    Unlock();
    return S_OK;
}
```

Item

Finally, the most interesting method with regard to "thread contention" is Item(). This method returns the *n*th item from the list, and it's really the only method that can result in interesting effects when being used from two threads. A thread can call it with what it *thinks* is a valid index, but by the time the code executes, the index value could be invalid. For example, consider two threads:

❑ Thread 1 calls Count() to ensure that at least one item exists in the list. There are two items, so it continues and calls Item().

❑ Thread 2 deletes the two items from the list.

❑ Thread 1 calls Item() with an index value of 1, but the call fails because the list is empty.

The problem is simply that another thread can modify the list after the call to Count (), but before the call to Item (). This makes an apparently valid index become invalid. This isn't a serious problem, but it's one of many threading problems that will leave you scratching your head thinking about alternatives, once you've spent a few hours tracking down the problem. Visual Basic programmers don't suffer from these problems, but they've not got the flexibility—each method would be called in turn, as two or more calls to the same object will not *simultaneously* occur, ever.

The most scalable solution in this case is simply for thread 1 to check the return code of the method, and perhaps make any generic error message more descriptive: "The list index is invalid; maybe the item was deleted by another thread!" We *could* implement a locking technique like the Application object does, so that a client can lock out other threads while manipulating the object, but doing so is beyond the scope of this text.

The code we've added to Item () to make it thread-safe releases the lock as soon as we've got a copy of the item from the list. We do this because at that point we've got our own copy of the item—what other threads do to the value once we've got our copy does not affect us. We can therefore release the lock early, which is very good practice as it aids throughput. The new code for Item () looks like this:

```
STDMETHODIMP CList::Item(long Index, VARIANT *Value)
{
    // If the index exceeds the index boundaries return an error
    Lock();
    if(Index < 0 || Index > m_list.size())
        return E_INVALIDARG;

    CComVariant retVal = m_list[Index];
    Unlock();

    VariantInit(Value);
    retVal.Detach(Value);

    return S_OK;
}
```

Our List component is now thread-safe, and meets all the requirements for both threading. To be a *good* both-threaded component, it must now aggregate the free threaded marshaler, to ensure that proxies are never used to access it from another apartment within the same process.

Aggregating the Free Threaded Marshaler (FTM)

As we've discussed, the free threaded marshaler is a COM object that implements the IMarshal interface. COM asks an object for this interface when a reference to it is being imported into another apartment. The default implementation of this interface that COM provides creates a proxy/stub pair to marshal calls back to the original apartment, which ensures that the method is only called via a thread that belongs to the apartment that created the object.

Our list component has no thread affinity. Because it is now also thread-safe, we don't need the protection COM adds, so we can remove the overhead of the proxy/stub. We aggregate the FTM and use its implementation of IMarshal, as shown in the figure below. Nobody knows we're using the FTM implementation of this interface; it just appears as if we are exposing and implementing it, but all method calls are redirected to the FTM object.

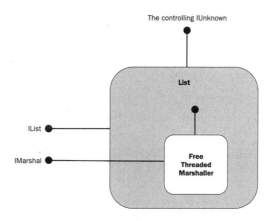

Declare the Controlling Unknown

When an object (such as the FTM) is aggregated, the object that is aggregating it is called the **controlling unknown**. It is also known as the **outer object**. Aggregated objects (you can have as many as you like) that provide the implementation of a particular interface are called **inner objects**. The outer object has to expose the interfaces of the inner object on the latter's behalf.

A client using our List component has no idea that we're using inner objects to implement its interfaces, which complies with the black-box binary reuse paradigm of COM. Furthermore, the inner component knows nothing of the outer object, except that it exists.

Another important aspect of aggregation in COM is that calls to the IUnknown methods of interfaces that are implemented by the inner object must be redirected by that object to the outer object. Because the inner object doesn't know what interfaces the outer object implements or wants to expose, it is unable (for example) to deal with calls to QueryInterface(), and so it redirects all calls to the controlling unknown.

Because an inner object needs to communicate with the outer object, ATL provides a macro called DECLARE_GET_CONTROLLING_UNKNOWN() that defines a function called GetControllingUnknown(). This function is used whenever we need a reference to the controlling unknown. For our component, we can define it thus:

```
DECLARE_REGISTRY_RESOURCEID(IDR_LIST)
DECLARE_GET_CONTROLLING_UNKNOWN()

DECLARE_PROTECT_FINAL_CONSTRUCT()
```

It might seem like overkill for our List component to do this, since it *knows* it is the outer object, but there's no reason why the List component can't actually become an inner object one day:

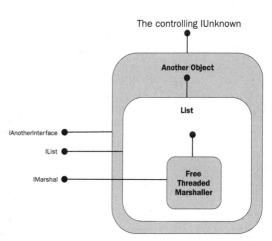

Here the "Another Object" is the outer object, and it aggregates the List component (the inner component) exposing its IList and IMarshal interfaces, while the List component aggregates the FTM exposing the IMarshal interface.

Add The Smart Pointer to Hold the FTM pointer

In order to aggregate the FTM, we must first create it. We therefore need to hold a reference to it, which for our component will be kept in m_pUnkMarshaler:

```
BOOL m_bOnStartPageCalled;                          //OnStartPage successful?
std::vector<CComVariant> m_list;
CComPtr<IUnknown> m_pUnkMarshaler;
```

Support the IMarshal Interface

Knowing that outer objects have to expose inner object interfaces explicitly, we add an entry for the IMarshal interface to the COM map, and specify the IUnknown of the FTM object:

```
BEGIN_COM_MAP(CList)
    COM_INTERFACE_ENTRY(IList)
    COM_INTERFACE_ENTRY(IDispatch)
    COM_INTERFACE_ENTRY(ISupportErrorInfo)
    COM_INTERFACE_ENTRY_AGGREGATE(IID_IMarshal, m_pUnkMarshaler.p)
END_COM_MAP()
```

Create and Destroy the FTM Object

We create the FTM object in FinalConstruct(), and release it in FinalRelease(). These methods are called when their names imply, and should be used in preference to putting code into constructors and destructors for ATL-based COM objects:

```
CList()
{
    m_bOnStartPageCalled = FALSE;
}

HRESULT FinalConstruct()
{
    return CoCreateFreeThreadedMarshaler(GetControllingUnknown(),
                                         &m_pUnkMarshaler.p);
}

void FinalRelease()
{
    m_pUnkMarshaler.Release();
}
```

The call to CoCreateFreeThreadedMarshaler() accepts the IUnknown interface of the outer object, in this case, our List component's IUnknown. However, we call GetControllingUnknown() rather than just passing its IUnknown pointer because the List component could also have been aggregated.

That's it!

We've made all the necessary code changes, so compile the project. We've now got a `List` component that can safely be used in the session or application scope without locking a user session down to a specific STA, so we'll modify the ASP code we had earlier, and try it out:

```
<%
    ' Lock other sessions out of application object
    Application.Lock

    ' If the list object isn't already created, create it.
    On Error Resume Next
    If Application("MyPageList") Is Nothing Then
        Set Application("MyPageList") = Server.CreateObject("BegASP.List")
    End If

    ' For performance reasons, take copy now
    Set oList = Application("MyPageList")
    On Error GoTo 0

    ' Let other sessions in
    Application.Unlock
%>
<HTML>
    <HEAD>
        <TITLE>Application Level Object!</TITLE>
    </HEAD>
    <BODY>
        <H1>Page View Report</H1>
        <H3>Summary</H3>

        <P>Total Page Views : <STRONG><%=oList.Count%></STRONG></P>
        <HR />
        <H3>Detail</H3>

        <%
        If oList.Count = 0 Then
            Response.Write "The list is empty."
        Else
            For i = 0 To oList.Count - 1
                Response.Write "<P>Item " & i & " is " & oList.Item(i) & "</P>"
            Next
        End If

        oList.Add "Page application2.asp view at " & Now
        %>

    </BODY>
</HTML>
```

On the first occasion we view it, the page will tell us that the list is empty because access to the page isn't logged until the *end* of the page:

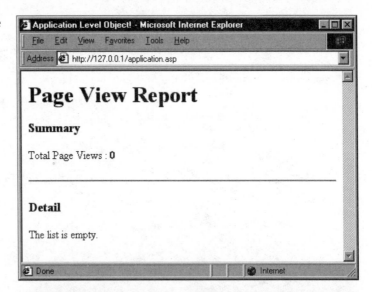

If we then refresh the page six times, we see the following output:

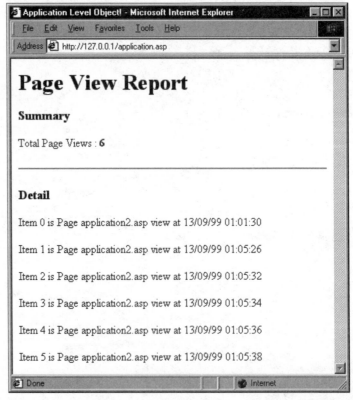

As you can see, the message added to the list at the end of each page is shown. This provides us with a neat way of logging access to our pages across multiple user sessions, which we could use in many different ways (debugging perhaps, or just logging access to a particular page).

Summary

In this chapter, we've looked at the differences between (and the advantages and disadvantages of) Visual Basic and Visual C++ for ASP component development.

We've seen that Visual Basic is a high-level language that shields us from many low-level SDK/API details and generally leads to more rapid development. Visual C++, on the other hand, exposes us to these details, making it more suitable for certain types of components.

We've seen that we have to pay special attention to component scope, and how session and application scoped objects should really be written in Visual C++ using the both threading model and the free threaded marshaler.

Finally, we've discussed the potential uses of session- and application-scoped objects.

Accessing Databases with ATL: The OLE DB Consumer Templates

In the last three chapters we've taken our first steps towards writing real world components using C++. In Chapter 10 we introduced the Active Template Library and saw how easy it is to produce simple, lightweight, C++ components. We built on that in Chapter 11 by examining some of the useful helper C++ classes that we can use to simplify handling VARIANTs and automation-compatible VB-style strings, as well as looking at how the ATL wizards can help you create a component that is aware of its ASP environment. In chapter 12 we looked more deeply at the COM threading models.

In this chapter we'll complete the range of C++ topics that we need to be aware of in order to build real components by examining how data access works in C++. This will mean our first introduction to OLE DB, through ATL's OLE DB consumer template classes. Before we do that, however, we'll start off with a discussion of the pros and cons of using ADO versus using OLE DB.

ADO and OLE DB

In Chapter 4 we described how ADO is based on OLE DB technology. To recap, OLE DB is a set of interfaces and COM components that allow you to access a data source. It is not however possible to use OLE DB directly from VB, so Microsoft added an extra layer, ActiveX Data Objects (ADO). ADO is based on dual interfaces, which means that it's easily accessible from scripting languages—indeed, it's the technology that you would normally use for data access done directly from ASP pages.

This all means that in C++ we have a choice—we can use either OLE DB or ADO to access data sources.

So which one should we use? Well there are several factors to consider, including performance, skills required and ease of coding, which we will look at in the following sections.

Performance

The main reason for using OLE DB is the same as the reason for using C++ rather than VB in the first place: Performance. When you use ADO, you have a complete extra layer to go through, as your ADO code calls up the OLE DB components. Not only that, but there's the question of data conversion. Having been designed for VB and scripting languages, ADO inevitably relies almost exclusively on variants to pass data across as parameters to its methods. This is fine for VB, which also uses variants extensively, and Scripting languages, which *must* use variants. However it's not so good for C++, since variants don't fit naturally into the C++ way of doing things. Not only are they inefficient, because you keep having to look at the vt parameter to check what data type is actually being stored, but they are quite wasteful of memory, since the full 16 bytes occupied by a VARIANT must be used even if all we are storing is a simple integer. In C++ if you want to use an integer, you will normally want a small, lightweight, integer variable. Nothing more.

However, since ADO uses variants, you'll find that if you do use ADO from C++ clients, you'll have to cope with the overhead of the ADO components converting the data they've got from the data source into variants—only so that you can manually convert the data back again after you've called the ADO methods! That kind of thing doesn't make for efficient C++ code.

Having said that it is worth pointing out that if your components are working in an ASP environment, they will need to use variants anyway in order to pass data to and from the various ASP objects— the request and response objects for example.

Skills Required

The biggest reason for using ADO if you've recently converted to C++ from VB or scripting languages is likely to be that you are already familiar with ADO. There are no new methods or components to learn about, because you've already been calling them from VB. All you need to learn is what the relevant IIDs, CLSIDs, etc. are, and where the header files are that you can find them in. You can even bypass some of that by #importing the type library into your C++ code.

Ease of Coding

This is an area that you might expect to weigh in on the side of ADO. After all, one of the reasons for Microsoft having introduced ADO was that it was easier to learn and use than OLE DB. OLE DB packed in a huge amount of functionality at a big cost in complexity. However, our belief is that that is no longer true. The reason for this is that ATL's Object Wizard is now able to generate some very convenient wrapper classes that handle the actual COM calls on the OLE DB interfaces for you. These are the ATL OLE DB consumer template classes. There is no such similar wizard for ADO.

Considering all these factors, we've adopted the viewpoint that it's so easy to use the ATL consumer template classes that there is little point covering how to use ADO in C++. In fact, you're hardly going to find any mention of COM at all in this chapter. We're going to dive straight in and show you how to use the ATL template classes, without saying anything about how the underlying OLE DB interfaces are designed. This is for the simple reason that for most normal tasks you don't need to know any of those details.

In fact, ATL's OLE DB classes take up a full third of the ATL library, which suggests, their importance. We'll only be looking at a small part of this code in this chapter though. If you do want more information, you should check up the Visual C++ Database Programming Tutorial *(1-861002-41-6) by Wendy Sarrett. This book covers how to use both ADO and OLE DB from C++, as well as the design of the OLE DB interfaces and the OLE DB object model, and, of course, includes an introductory look at some of the ATL consumer template classes.*

The Sample Dance School Database

In this chapter we're going to get down to coding quite quickly. But before we start, we'll take a quick look at the database that we are going to use for the samples in this chapter. This is a Microsoft Access database that stores details of the classes offered by a local dance school:

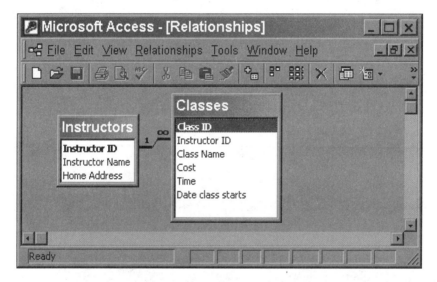

The database contains two tables. The Classes table stores the details of the weekly classes offered by the school, including such details as the cost of the class. The Instructors table contains details of the instructors who take the classes.

We'll be developing some short samples that access this database to make simple queries or simple modifications to it.

Introducing The ATL OLE DB Consumer Templates

To start off we need a project, so create an ATL in-process (DLL) server project called DanceSchool. Next, use the Object Wizard to create an ActiveX Server component, called DanceSchoolBrowser. Now we're ready to start on the OLE DB templates that this component will use.

Fire up the object wizard again, but this time select Data Access for the Category of component. This gives us two choices: Consumer and Provider. If we select Provider we'll get given the basic skeleton code to implement a new OLE DB provider. That's not what we want—we want something that can act as a client to existing providers. So we select Consumer.

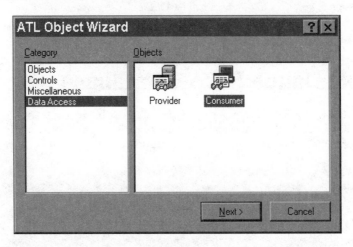

This gives us a dialog box that allows us to select the properties of the source, which basically means what provider we want to hook up to and what functionality we want to access. At present some of the options are greyed out because we haven't yet selected a data source (provider).

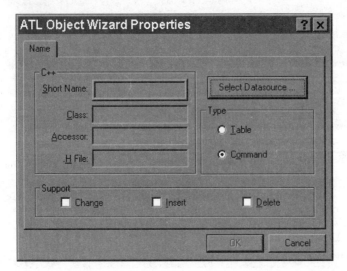

To select a provider, click on the Select Datasource button. This will bring up a list of the available providers:

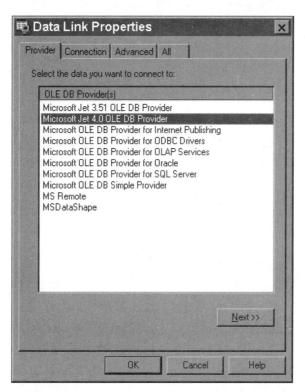

From this window you can choose the appropriate provider. The most efficient provider to use for Access databases is the Jet 4.0 one, although you could choose the ODBC driver if you wish. What happens when you click on the **Next** button is to some extent provider-specific. In the case of the Jet provider you'll need to specify the path to the .mdb file containing the database, in our case this file is Dance97.mdb (available as part of the source code downloadable from the Wrox website). With most SQL-based databases, you will then get a new dialog box asking you to select the table against which you want to make your query. For complex queries that use more than one table, you'll probably be editing the code anyway, so to be honest it doesn't matter too much what you select here. For the time being we'll go for the Classes table of the Dance School database.

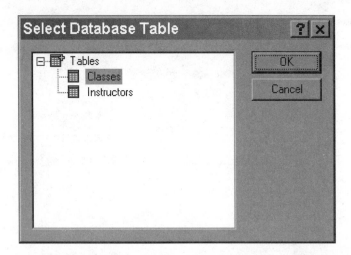

This takes us back to the Properties dialog box—but this time you can specify all the options.

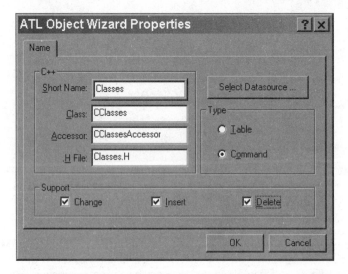

I've accepted the short name of the object—it defaults to the name of the table you've chosen, and I'm happy with that. The names of a couple of C++ classes and a header file are derived from the short name. I want to allow for the possibility that I may want to use the object to make any of the three types of modification you can make to a table—insert, delete and change records, so I've ticked all three options. If I didn't tick any of them I'd end up with a C++ class that gives me read-only functionality.

The final option is the type of object. The choice here—Table or Command—isn't particularly self-explanatory. Essentially, if you choose Table you'll get a simple to use, but very basic, C++ class that can query values in the table you've specified. If you choose Command, you get—for not much more complexity—a C++ class that you can use to make a customizable query; for SQL based databases the SQL query is there for you to edit. This is much more flexible, and I personally go for Command every time.

The Wizard Generated Code

We're done on the Wizard now, when we click on OK, our code will get generated for us. Here's what it looks like. Don't worry by the way about understanding it all now. It's presented here just to give you a feel for what the wizard has done for you. We'll explain what all this code does later on.

```
// Classes.H : Declaration of the CClasses class

#ifndef __CLASSES_H_
#define __CLASSES_H_

class CClassesAccessor
{
public:
    LONG m_ClassID;            // Primary key
    TCHAR m_ClassName[51];     // Published title of the class
    CURRENCY m_Cost;           // Price per lesson
    DATE m_Dateclassstarts;    // Date of first lesson of term
    LONG m_InstructorID;       // Foreign key to the name of the instructor in the
                               // instructor's table
    TCHAR m_Time[51];          // When in the week the class takes place
BEGIN_COLUMN_MAP(CClassesAccessor)
    COLUMN_ENTRY(1, m_ClassID)
    COLUMN_ENTRY(2, m_InstructorID)
    COLUMN_ENTRY(3, m_ClassName)
    COLUMN_ENTRY_TYPE(4, DBTYPE_CY, m_Cost)
    COLUMN_ENTRY(5, m_Time)
    COLUMN_ENTRY_TYPE(6, DBTYPE_DATE, m_Dateclassstarts)
END_COLUMN_MAP()

DEFINE_COMMAND(CClassesAccessor, _T(" \
    SELECT \
        'Class ID', \
        'Instructor ID', \
        'Class Name', \
        Cost, \
        Time, \
        'Date class starts'  \
        FROM Classes"))

    // You may wish to call this function if you are inserting a record and wish
    // to initialize all the fields, if you are not going to explicitly set all
    // of them.
    void ClearRecord()
    {
        memset(this, 0, sizeof(*this));
    }
};

class CClasses : public CCommand<CAccessor<CClassesAccessor> >
{
public:
    HRESULT Open()
    {
        HRESULT hr;

        hr = OpenDataSource();
        if (FAILED(hr))
            return hr;

        return OpenRowset();
    }
    HRESULT OpenDataSource()
    {
```

```
        HRESULT hr;
        CDataSource db;
        CDBPropSet dbinit(DBPROPSET_DBINIT);

        dbinit.AddProperty(DBPROP_AUTH_CACHE_AUTHINFO, true);
        dbinit.AddProperty(DBPROP_AUTH_ENCRYPT_PASSWORD, false);
        dbinit.AddProperty(DBPROP_AUTH_MASK_PASSWORD, false);
        dbinit.AddProperty(DBPROP_AUTH_PASSWORD, OLESTR(""));
        dbinit.AddProperty(DBPROP_AUTH_USERID, OLESTR("Admin"));
        dbinit.AddProperty(DBPROP_INIT_DATASOURCE,
                           OLESTR("E:\\VCStuff\\2882\\Chapter 13\\Dance97.mdb"));
        dbinit.AddProperty(DBPROP_INIT_MODE, (long)16);
        dbinit.AddProperty(DBPROP_INIT_PROMPT, (short)4);
        dbinit.AddProperty(DBPROP_INIT_PROVIDERSTRING, OLESTR(""));
        dbinit.AddProperty(DBPROP_INIT_LCID, (long)1033);
        hr = db.Open(_T("Microsoft.Jet.OLEDB.4.0"), &dbinit);
        if (FAILED(hr))
            return hr;

        return m_session.Open(db);
    }
    HRESULT OpenRowset()
    {
        // Set properties for open
        CDBPropSet propset(DBPROPSET_ROWSET);
        propset.AddProperty(DBPROP_IRowsetChange, true);
        propset.AddProperty(DBPROP_UPDATABILITY, DBPROPVAL_UP_CHANGE |
                            DBPROPVAL_UP_INSERT | DBPROPVAL_UP_DELETE);

        return CCommand<CAccessor<CClassesAccessor> >::Open(m_session, NULL,
                                                            &propset);
    }
    CSession m_session;
};

#endif // __CLASSES_H_
```

You'll probably have a different path to the database in your code.

Well all that work for so little code—all we've got for our efforts is one single header file called Classes.H, containing two short class template definitions. Well OK, that's not quite all. The object wizard also added a line to our precompiled header:

```
#include <atlbase.h>
//You may derive a class from CComModule and use it if you want to override
//something, but do not change the name of _Module
extern CComModule _Module;
#include <atlcom.h>
#include <atldbcli.h>
```

As you can probably guess, this line gives us all the base class definitions used by our new consumer templates. And those base classes are where most of the power of the templates lies. The stuff in Classes.H is just the small amount of code needed to customize the C++ templates for our particular database.

Let's have a look at the code in more detail. We have two C++ classes: CClasses and CClassesAccessor. We won't worry about the inheritance tree or the details of the templates these classes are based on here. What interests us is how to use them. And here is the most important point we need to notice: **the consumer template classes are *not* COM components.**

Yeah, you did hear that right. What we've got here are plain old C++ classes, nothing to do with COM at all. These classes use COM internally, to the extent that they act as clients to OLE DB providers, but those details are hidden from you. These are simply C++ classes intended to be used inside other programs. As it happens, we're going to make use of them inside our `DanceSchoolBrowser` component, but we could equally well have created these classes in an MFC project. You do need ATL support in your project for the ATL object wizard to work, but the Wizard will add that for you if you try to use if in an MFC project.

We won't be directly using the `CClassesAccessor` class here—we'll work entirely with the `CClasses` class since that allows us to do all the modifications and queries on the database that we are going to want to do. You can think of `CClasses` as the class with which we'll conduct all our operations with the database. It (mostly through its base classes) implements a lot of useful methods, but the ones you're likely to want to use are these:

- ❏ `Open()`—sets up the connection to the database

- ❏ `MoveFirst()`—grabs the information from the first row in the query, and places this information in the various member variables

- ❏ `MoveNext()`—same as `MoveFirst()`, but goes to the next row in the query (or the first row if no data has been examined yet)

- ❏ `MoveLast()`—same as `MoveFirst()`, but goes to the last row in the query

- ❏ `Close()`—closes the connection to the database

- ❏ `Insert()`—inserts a new record

- ❏ `Delete()`—deletes a record

- ❏ `SetData()`—modifies the data in the current record (the one we are examining at the moment)

Personally, I think that this set of functions could hardly be easier to use. You have one function for each of the main operations you'd normally want to carry out on the database.

One point about that though—the list of functions above mentions the **query**, but I so far haven't said anything about us setting up a query. Well the query is the command that you are going to perform against the database—and since Access understands SQL, the wizard has generated a SQL command for us. It's in the definition of the `CClassesAccessor` class, embedded in a macro:

```
DEFINE_COMMAND(CClassesAccessor, _T(" \
    SELECT \
        'Class ID', \
        'Instructor ID', \
        'Class Name', \
        Cost, \
        Time, \
        'Data class starts' \
        FROM Classes"))
```

If you check this command against the database structure, you'll find it's a command that simply returns all the fields of all the records in the `Classes` table. This is the bit that separates the Table Object Wizard choice from the Command choice. If we'd chosen Table, this command would be embedded in the class and we would not have been able to modify it. However, because we chose Command, that command is there for us to play with. For the time being, a command that retrieves all the data from the table suits us fine, so we'll leave this macro as it is.

515

We will however check out the associated member variables in the `CClassesAccessor` class:

```
class CClassesAccessor
{
public:
    LONG m_ClassID;            // Primary key
    TCHAR m_ClassName[51];     // Published title of the class
    CURRENCY m_Cost;           // Price per lesson
    DATE m_Dateclassstarts;    // Date of first lesson of term
    LONG m_InstructorID;       // Foreign key to the name of the instructor in the
                               // instructor's table
    TCHAR m_Time[51];          // When in the week the class takes place

BEGIN_COLUMN_MAP(CClassesAccessor)
    COLUMN_ENTRY(1, m_ClassID)
    COLUMN_ENTRY(2, m_InstructorID)
    COLUMN_ENTRY(3, m_ClassName)
    COLUMN_ENTRY_TYPE(4, DBTYPE_CY, m_Cost)
    COLUMN_ENTRY(5, m_Time)
    COLUMN_ENTRY_TYPE(6, DBTYPE_DATE, m_Dateclassstarts)
END_COLUMN_MAP()
```

These bits of code are important because they define:

❑ What the member variables are that are going to hold the data from the different fields

❑ How these member variables map on to the different fields in the table

Notice that the object wizard has generated us one member variable for each field, and its matched up the data types as well. In the table itself, the **Class ID** and **Instructor ID** fields are integers, so we've been given LONGs to store them in. **Class Name** and **Time** are strings with maximum length 50 in the table—so we've been given TCHAR arrays of size 51 for each (the extra character holds the trailing zero). **Cost** (defined in the table as a currency) and **Date class starts** (defined as a date) are represented by CURRENCY and DATE variables respectively.

The column map is quite intuitive to understand. The first line:

```
    COLUMN_ENTRY(1, m_ClassID)
```

simply says that the value in the first column of a record has to go in the variable m_ClassID. Checking the SQL statement the wizard generated reveals that the first column it asks for is indeed the Class ID. If we make any changes to the SQL statement, it's important to make sure we change the entries in the column map to match.

Most of the entries in the column map are simple entries that define which column we are talking about and which variable should be associated with that column. These entries are dealt with by the COLUMN_ENTRY() macro. However in some cases, additional information needs to be available concerning, for example, the precise format in which the data is mapped to the variable. In our example, you will notice that the CURRENCY and DATE variables are mapped using the COLUMN_ENTRY_TYPE() macro, which gives additional information on the data type. In general, the wizard will supply the appropriate COLUMN_ENTRY_XXX() macro for you.

Our First Code

We're now ready to actually use the consumer template class in some real code. The first thing to do is to make the classes in `Classes.H` available to the `DanceSchoolBrowser` component, which just requires a simple #include in `DanceSchoolBrowser.cpp`:

```
#include "stdafx.h"
#include "DanceSchool.h"
#include "DanceSchoolBrowser.h"
#include "Classes.H"
```

We're going to add a method to `IDanceSchoolBrowser` that displays the IDs, names and times of all the classes currently on offer. The method can be created using the usual ATL Wizard, and takes no parameters. Here's its implementation:

```
STDMETHODIMP CDanceSchoolBrowser::ListClasses()
{
    CClasses m_commandClasses;
    HRESULT hr;

    hr = m_commandClasses.Open();
    if (FAILED(hr))
        return hr;

    while ((m_commandClasses.MoveNext()) == S_OK)
    {
        m_piResponse->Write(CComVariant("\n<BR>ClassID: "));
        m_piResponse->Write(CComVariant(m_commandClasses.m_ClassID));
        m_piResponse->Write(CComVariant(", <STRONG>"));
        m_piResponse->Write(CComVariant(m_commandClasses.m_ClassName));
        m_piResponse->Write(CComVariant("</STRONG>, "));
        m_piResponse->Write(CComVariant(m_commandClasses.m_Time));
    }

    m_commandClasses.Close();
    return S_OK;
}
```

This code creates an instance of the `CClasses` class, then calls its `Open()` method to set up the connection to the database. Next, the code iterates through all the records returned from the SQL query defined in the `DEFINE_COMMAND()` macro, using the `CClasses::MoveNext()` method. This method returns `S_OK` as long as there are more rows to return. Notice how `MoveNext()` automatically places the values from the various fields into the appropriate `CClasses` member variables, as instructed by the column map macros. We don't need to take any additional action to read those values. Once the enumeration is finished, the `CClasses::Close()` method is called to terminate the connection.

We haven't bothered checking the return value of `Close()`, simply because in this case it doesn't matter to us. We're going to return from the `ListClasses()` method whether or not `Close()` succeeds (it shouldn't normally fail). However, in general, all the `CClasses` methods that we are going to be using return HRESULTs, just as if they were COM method calls (internally they will be calling OLE DB COM methods). Similarly, this code doesn't bother to check that our attempts to write output to the ASP page have succeeded. (This makes sense when you accept that if a `Write()` method failed we'd have to use the same method to write an error message to the ASP page.)

You should be able to compile this code now. Let's look at the ASP page that uses it, `DanceBrowse.asp`, which is—if that's possible—even simpler:

```
<%@LANGUAGE="VBScript"%>
<HTML>
<HEAD>
<TITLE>OLE DB Samples</TITLE>
<STYLE TYPE="text/css">
    BODY {font-family:Tahoma,Arial,sans-serif; font-size:10pt}
</STYLE>
</HEAD>
<BODY BGCOLOR=#FFFFFF>

<H1> DANCE SCHOOL </H1>

This page lists the classes offered by the dance school
<P>
<%
Set objBrowser = Server.CreateObject("DanceSchool.DanceSchoolBrowser")
objBrowser.ListClasses
%>

</BODY>
</HTML>
```

Here are the results:

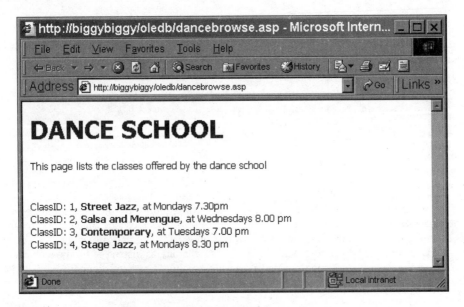

And, with this, our first database query using OLE DB is complete.

Joining Tables

That's all very well for a first query but we often want to do something more complicated than simply display one table. Most real life examples involve merging data from different tables. That's quite easy to do with the OLE DB consumer templates, but it does require some modification of the wizard-generated code. We're going to demonstrate this by adding a new method to the DanceSchoolBrowser component, called ListClassesEx(). This method lists the classes, but it also displays the name of the instructor for each class—which it needs to obtain from the Instructors table. And, just to add a bit of fun, I'm going to insist that the results are sorted in reverse order by class name. The SQL query we'll need to get that information is, using the Access dialect of SQL:

```
SELECT Classes.[Class ID], Classes.[Class Name], Classes.Time,
   Instructors.[Instructor Name] FROM Instructors INNER JOIN Classes ON
   Instructors.[Instructor ID] = Classes.[Instructor ID] ORDER BY
   Classes.[Class Name] DESC;
```

Note that this query is in slightly different format from the one in the earlier example – the names of the fields are enclosed in square brackets. That's because I generated this SQL command within Access rather than letting the ATL wizard do it for me, but the different syntax doesn't matter.

In order to accomplish this we need to create a new consumer template class. We could do it using the wizard, just as before, though it's just as easy to copy and paste the existing code into a new file called ClassesEx.H—either way we're going to have to make a couple of changes. I did it by copying and pasting, and I called my new classes CClassesEx and CClassesExAccessor. Here's the relevant portion of the code with the lines I changed highlighted:

```
class CClassesExAccessor
{
public:
    LONG m_ClassID;          // Primary key
    TCHAR m_ClassName[51];   // Published title of the class
    TCHAR m_Time[51];        // When in the week the class takes place
    TCHAR m_InstructorName[51];

BEGIN_COLUMN_MAP(CClassesExAccessor)
    COLUMN_ENTRY(1, m_ClassID)
    COLUMN_ENTRY(2, m_ClassName)
    COLUMN_ENTRY(3, m_Time)
    COLUMN_ENTRY(4, m_InstructorName)
END_COLUMN_MAP()

DEFINE_COMMAND(CClassesExAccessor, _T(" \
    SELECT \
        Classes.[Class ID], \
        Classes.[Class Name], \
        Classes.Time, \
        Instructors.[Instructor Name] \
    FROM Instructors \
    INNER JOIN Classes ON Instructors.[Instructor ID] = \
        Classes.[Instructor ID] \
    ORDER BY Classes.[Class Name] DESC;"))

    // You may wish to call this function if you are inserting a record and wish
    // to initialize all the fields, if you are not going to explicitly set all
    // of them.
    void ClearRecord()
    {
```

```
        memset(this, 0, sizeof(*this));
    }
};
```

```
class CClassesEx : public CCommand<CAccessor<CClassesExAccessor> >
{
```

Apart from the changes to the names of the classes, I've replaced the SQL statement in the
DEFINE_COMMAND() macro with the new one, completely changed the column map to match the new
SQL statement, and added a new variable to store the instructors' names. While I was at it I also took the
chance to remove the variables corresponding to columns that I wasn't using.

We just need to sort out the ListClassesEx() method on the component now. This is quite similar to
the ListClasses() method, but with the following changes: we use a CClassesEx instance rather than
a CClasses instance to generate the query, and we need to write out the extra information about the
instructor. First of all, add another #include:

```
#include "stdafx.h"
#include "DanceSchool.h"
#include "DanceSchoolBrowser.h"
#include "Classes.H"
#include "ClassesEx.H"
```

Next, add ListClassesEx() with the Wizard and implement it as follows:

```
STDMETHODIMP CDanceSchoolBrowser::ListClassesEx()
{
    CClassesEx m_commandClasses;
    HRESULT hr;

    hr = m_commandClasses.Open();
    if (FAILED(hr))
        return hr;

    while ((m_commandClasses.MoveNext()) == S_OK)
    {
        m_piResponse->Write(CComVariant("\n<BR>ClassID: "));
        m_piResponse->Write(CComVariant(m_commandClasses.m_ClassID));
        m_piResponse->Write(CComVariant(", <STRONG>"));
        m_piResponse->Write(CComVariant(m_commandClasses.m_ClassName));
        m_piResponse->Write(CComVariant("</STRONG>, "));
        m_piResponse->Write(CComVariant(m_commandClasses.m_Time));
        m_piResponse->Write(CComVariant(", taught by "));
        m_piResponse->Write(CComVariant(m_commandClasses.m_InstructorName));
    }

    m_commandClasses.Close();
    return S_OK;
}
```

We can see this new method in action using DanceBrowseEx.asp, which differs from
DanceBrowse.asp in a single line:

```
<%
Set objBrowser = Server.CreateObject("DanceSchool.DanceSchoolBrowser")
objBrowser.ListClassesEx
%>
```

The output of this ASP page is as follows:

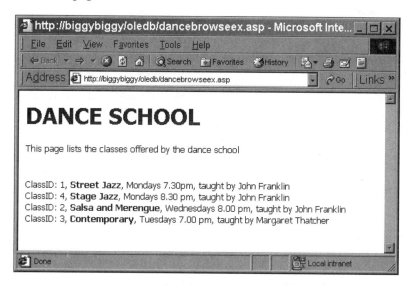

One point before I leave those particular code changes: the Wizard is clever enough to be able to generate its code from queries as well as tables. What this means is that I could have added all this new code using the Wizard if I'd first generated the appropriate query in Access. The Object Wizard would then have given me the option of using the query instead of one of the tables to generate the code. However, personally I find playing about with the code directly is much more useful in terms of helping to understand how things work—so I thought I'd do it that way.

Removing Write Functionality

I'm now going to do something else to simplify the CClassesEx class. I've decided I'm not going to want to use this particular consumer class to do any modifications with, so I'm going to remove the insert/delete/change functionality that has got copied and pasted from my old CClasses class. The relevant bit of the code here is the CClasses::OpenRowset() function, which was defined as:

```
HRESULT OpenRowset()
{
    // Set properties for open
    CDBPropSet propset(DBPROPSET_ROWSET);
    propset.AddProperty(DBPROP_IRowsetChange, true);
    propset.AddProperty(DBPROP_UPDATABILITY, DBPROPVAL_UP_CHANGE |
                        DBPROPVAL_UP_INSERT | DBPROPVAL_UP_DELETE);

    return CCommand<CAccessor<CClassesAccessor> >::Open(m_session, NULL,
                                                        &propset);
}
```

You can see from this where the change, update, and insert functionality comes from. For example, if I'd decided I didn't want delete functionality (so I want to delete the delete... Hmmm) then I'd modify that last AddProperty() call to:

```
    propset.AddProperty(DBPROP_IRowsetChange, true);
    propset.AddProperty(DBPROP_UPDATABILITY, DBPROPVAL_UP_CHANGE |
                        DBPROPVAL_UP_INSERT);
```

However, we want to do more than that—we want to remove *all* write functionality. So we'll change the `OpenRowset()` function to this:

```
HRESULT OpenRowset()
{
    return CCommand<CAccessor<CClassesExAccessor> >::Open(m_session);
}
```

By the way, don't worry about the `CDBPropSet` class, it's just an ATL class that's used to set properties on your OLE DB connection. For what we're doing we don't need to understand how it works.

Of course, using the Wizard, without requesting any write access, would have generated the same code. I thought it was more useful to do it this way—sooner or later, you're going to realise you chose the wrong options on a class you've already generated, and you want to modify them, so you may as well see now how to do that. On the same theme, it's always easier to remove functionality you don't want than to add it by hand later, so we're not doing anything out of the ordinary here.

Adding Records

Adding new records using the ATL consumer templates is easy. The hard bit is designing a user interface that lets you specify the details of the records you want to add!

We'll design another ASP page that lets you add a new instructor to the database. This is what the page will look like:

This page lists the current instructors and invites you to fill in the details of a new one. On doing so, the page adds the new instructor:

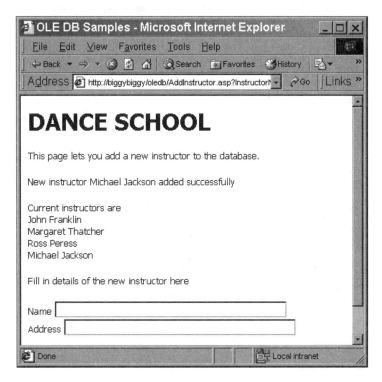

Before we detail this page, let's add the required functionality to our `DanceSchoolBrowser` component.

The first thing to do is to create a new OLE DB Consumer class with the Wizard, this time for the `Instructors` table. Leave the default name as it is for this, and request change, insert, and delete functionality for now. Next, make these simple changes to `CInstructors`:

```
class CInstructorsAccessor
{
public:
    LONG m_InstructorID;
    TCHAR m_InstructorName[51];
    TCHAR m_HomeAddress[51];
    ULONG m_InstructorIDStatus;

BEGIN_COLUMN_MAP(CInstructorsAccessor)
    COLUMN_ENTRY_STATUS(1, m_InstructorID, m_InstructorIDStatus)
    COLUMN_ENTRY(2, m_InstructorName)
    COLUMN_ENTRY(3, m_HomeAddress)
END_COLUMN_MAP()

DEFINE_COMMAND(CInstructorsAccessor, _T(" \
    SELECT \
        'Instructor ID', \
        'Instructor Name', \
        'Home Address'  \
        FROM Instructors"))
```

The new variable, and the changed entry in the column map for the Instructor ID field, relate to the fact that the Instructor ID field is set to **AutoNumber** in Access, meaning that it is generated automatically within the database. When we add the new instructor we want to avoid attempting to set this field. The `COLUMN_ENTRY_STATUS()` macro lets us specify another variable, defined as a ULONG, which can hold those sort of instructions. Setting the status variable to the value DBSTATUS_S_IGNORE will cause the consumer C++ classes not to attempt to set the corresponding field when it writes to the database.

We'll use this new consumer class by adding the following #include:

```
#include "stdafx.h"
#include "DanceSchool.h"
#include "DanceSchoolBrowser.h"
#include "Classes.H"
#include "ClassesEx.H"
#include "Instructors.H"
```

And adding a method called `AddInstructor()` with the wizard. This method has the parameters [in] BSTR bstrName, [in] BSTR bstrAddress, and its implementation is as follows:

```
STDMETHODIMP CDanceSchoolBrowser::AddInstructor(BSTR bstrName,
                                                BSTR bstrAddress)
{
    CInstructors m_commandInstructors;
    HRESULT hr;

    hr = m_commandInstructors.Open();
    if (FAILED(hr))
        return hr;

    USES_CONVERSION;
    _tcscpy(m_commandInstructors.m_InstructorName, W2T(bstrName));
    _tcscpy(m_commandInstructors.m_HomeAddress, W2T(bstrAddress));
    m_commandInstructors.m_InstructorIDStatus = DBSTATUS_S_IGNORE;
    hr=m_commandInstructors.Insert();
    m_commandInstructors.Close();

    return hr;
}
```

This method shows us that to insert a new record we simply need to set the variables in the command object to the required values of the corresponding fields, then call the `Insert()` function. Note that I've used the ATL string conversion macros (made available through the USES_CONVERSION macro) to make sure that this code will work in both UNICODE and ANSI builds.

For a full list of these macros see the topic String Conversion Macros *in the MSDN collection.*

We'll also need another, simpler, method called `ListInstructors()`. This method takes no parameters, and simply writes out a list of the instructors. Add it with the Wizard, with the following implementation:

```
STDMETHODIMP CDanceSchoolBrowser::ListInstructors()
{
    CInstructors m_commandInstructors;
    HRESULT hr;

    hr = m_commandInstructors.Open();
    if (FAILED(hr))
        return hr;
```

```
   while ((hr=m_commandInstructors.MoveNext()) == S_OK)
   {
       m_piResponse->Write(CComVariant("<BR>"));
       m_piResponse->Write(CComVariant(m_commandInstructors.m_InstructorName));
   }

   m_commandInstructors.Close();

   return hr;
}
```

This code doesn't contain anything new, so we'll move on to the ASP code that handles this,
`AddInstructor.asp`:

```
<%@LANGUAGE="VBScript"%>
<HTML>
<HEAD>
<TITLE>OLE DB Samples</TITLE>
<STYLE TYPE="text/css">
   BODY {font-family:Tahoma,Arial,sans-serif; font-size:10pt}
</STYLE>
</HEAD>
<BODY BGCOLOR=#FFFFFF>

<H1> DANCE SCHOOL </H1>

This page lets you add a new instructor to the database.

<%
on error resume next
Set objBrowser = Server.CreateObject("DanceSchool.DanceSchoolBrowser")

dim strName
strName = Request.QueryString("InstructorName")
if (not(strName = "")) then
   dim strAddress
   strAddress = Request.QueryString("InstructorAddress")
   objBrowser.AddInstructor strName, strAddress
   if (err.number = 0) then
       Response.Write "<P>New instructor " & strName & " added successfully"
   else
       Response.Write "<P>Failed to add new instructor"
   end if
end if

Response.Write "<P>Current instructors are"
objBrowser.ListInstructors
%>

<P>
Fill in details of the new instructor here
<P>
<FORM ACTION = "AddInstructor.asp" METHOD = GET>
Name <INPUT TYPE = text NAME = InstructorName ID = InstructorName MAXLENGTH=50
       SIZE=50>
<BR>Address <INPUT TYPE = TEXT NAME = InstructorAddress ID = InstructorAddress
       MAXLENGTH = 50 SIZE = 50>
<P>
<INPUT TYPE = submit>
<INPUT TYPE = reset>

</FORM>
</BODY>
</HTML>
```

This is all pretty standard stuff. We detect from the `QueryString` collection whether this page has been
called with the details of a new instructor to be added, and if so we add him or her to the database, before
displaying the form to ask for the name of the next instructor to be added.

Deleting Records

By now you'll have got a feel for how the ATL consumer template command class works, and we can move onto something a little bit trickier.

Use the wizard to add a new method, `RemoveInstructor()`, with a single parameter, `[in] long lID`. Now, we could implement this using the methods we've used so far, iterating through the records using `MoveNext()` until we find one that matches our specifications and then deleting it. However, this hardly seems efficient. What if there are 1000 instructors? OK, maybe our choice of example does mean we have to suspend logic for a while here (*1000* salsa instructors in one place?), but the point is sound. While we're accessing the records, not only could it take some time to find the right entry, but we may be locking the data while this is going on.

The easiest way to do this doesn't involve using the command classes that the object wizard has given us. Instead, we're better off creating an instance of the base `CCommand` template.

Here is the code to do this:

```
STDMETHODIMP CDanceSchoolBrowser::RemoveInstructor(long lID)
{
    CInstructors m_commandInstructors;
    HRESULT hr;

    hr = m_commandInstructors.OpenDataSource();
    if (FAILED(hr))
        return hr;

    CCommand < CAccessor<_CNoParameters> > id;
    CDBPropSet propset(DBPROPSET_ROWSET);
    propset.AddProperty(DBPROP_UPDATABILITY, DBPROPVAL_UP_DELETE);

    TCHAR szSQL[512];

    _stprintf(szSQL, _T("DELETE FROM Instructors WHERE [Instructor ID] = %d"),
            lID);

    hr = id.Open(m_commandInstructors.m_session, szSQL, &propset);
    m_commandInstructors.Close();

    return hr;
}
```

We can best understand what's going on here by comparing what we've done here with the `CInstructors` and `CInstructorsAccessor` consumer classes generated by the wizard. Those classes are respectively positioned in the class hierarchy as:

```
class CInstructors : public CCommand<CAccessor<CInstructorsAccessor> >
```

and

```
class CInstructorsAccessor
```

`CAccessor<>` is a generic template that lets you construct a class that supplies information on how to access the database. The wizard customizes this template by inserting as the parameter the accessor class that it has written. Then, the `CCommand<>` template takes this information to form a class that is able to hook up to the database an execute one SQL statement. Finally the wizard supplies our own `CCommand`-derived class, in this case `CInstructors`, again containing our own customizations.

By contrast we've declared a variable named id, of type CCommand < CAccessor<_CNoParameters> >. This is a command C++ class which has not had any customized accessor passed to it. In other words, no variables mapped on to a SQL statement that was defined in a DEFINE_COMMAND() macro.

Before we execute the SQL command, we open a connection to the data using OpenDataSource() and not Open():

```
hr = m_commandInstructors.OpenDataSource();
```

We do this because using Open() would result in a call to call OpenRowset() as well as OpenDataSource():

```
HRESULT Open()
{
    HRESULT hr;
    hr = OpenDataSource();
    if (FAILED(hr))
        return hr;

    return OpenRowset();
}
```

We don't use the default rowset created by the call as we create our own, so calling Open() would be detrimental to performance and may result in other unwanted effects.

The Open() function as we've been using it automatically executes the command we've defined. But we haven't defined one, so we can't use Open() in the way we have been. Instead, we use another overloaded form of the same function to execute our command, which accepts such details as the required SQL statement as its parameters. We've set up a string containing the SQL command to delete the appropriate item and passed it in to this version of the Open() function. Doing it this way has the advantage that we can customize the SQL command—as we've done here by inserting the appropriate instructor ID. On the other hand, the code is slightly less easy to write than it would have been using the macros and classes given to us by object wizard.

Since we are deleting instructors by their ID, we should also add a new method to list these IDs, ListInstructorsEx():

```
STDMETHODIMP CDanceSchoolBrowser::ListInstructorsEx()
{
    CInstructors m_commandInstructors;
    HRESULT hr;

    hr = m_commandInstructors.Open();
    if (FAILED(hr))
        return hr;

    while ((hr=m_commandInstructors.MoveNext()) == S_OK)
    {
        m_piResponse->Write(CComVariant("<BR><STRONG>ID:</STRONG> "));
        m_piResponse->Write(CComVariant(m_commandInstructors.m_InstructorID));
        m_piResponse->Write(CComVariant(" <STRONG>Name:</STRONG> "));
        m_piResponse->Write(CComVariant(m_commandInstructors.m_InstructorName));
    }

    m_commandInstructors.Close();

    return hr;
}
```

Again, there isn't anything new and remarkable in this code, so let's check out the ASP code, `RemoveAuthor.asp`:

```
<%@LANGUAGE="VBScript"%>
<HTML>
<HEAD>
<TITLE>OLE DB Samples</TITLE>
<STYLE TYPE="text/css">
    BODY {font-family:Tahoma,Arial,sans-serif; font-size:10pt}
</STYLE>
</HEAD>
<BODY BGCOLOR=#FFFFFF>

<H1> DANCE SCHOOL </H1>

This page lets you remove an instructor from the database.

<%
on error resume next
Set objBrowser = Server.CreateObject("DanceSchool.DanceSchoolBrowser")

dim iName
iID = Request.QueryString("InstructorID")
if (not(iID = 0)) then
    objBrowser.RemoveInstructor iID
    if (err.number = 0) then
        Response.Write "<P>Instructor removed successfully"
    else
        Response.Write "<P>Failed to remove instructor"
    end if
end if

Response.Write "<P>Current instructors are"
objBrowser.ListInstructorsEx
%>

<P>
Fill in details of the instructor here
<P>
<FORM ACTION = "RemoveInstructor.asp" METHOD = GET>
ID <INPUT TYPE = text NAME = InstructorID ID = InstructorID MALENGTH = 5
    SIZE = 5>
<P>
<INPUT TYPE = submit>
<INPUT TYPE = reset>

</FORM>
</BODY>
</HTML>
```

Modifying a Record

Modifying a record works in much the same way as adding or deleting one—except that here the relevant function in the C++ command class is `SetData()`. This is used in much the same way as `Insert()`—you set the variables in the command class to have the correct values then call `SetData()`. The only difference is that you need to have used the `MoveNext()` command to ensure you are looking at the appropriate record first, or select the appropriate record using similar techniques to those we used to delete a specific record.

We'll demonstrate the use of `SetData()` with a new `DanceSchoolBrowser` method: `UseWorkAddresses()`. The dance school has decided that the address stored for all its instructors will be the location of the dance school (despite the field still being called **Home Address**). Well, that's bureaucracy for you! So, we needs a method to rename the addresses of all the instructors. Add this method with the wizard (it doesn't take any parameters) and implement it like so:

```
STDMETHODIMP CDanceSchoolBrowser::UseWorkAddresses()
{
    CInstructors m_commandInstructors;
    HRESULT hr;

    hr = m_commandInstructors.Open();
    if (FAILED(hr))
    return hr;

    USES_CONVERSION;
    while ((m_commandInstructors.MoveNext()) == S_OK)
    {
        _tcscpy(m_commandInstructors.m_HomeAddress,
                W2T(L"The Dance School, Lancaster, UK"));
        m_commandInstructors.m_InstructorIDStatus = DBSTATUS_S_IGNORE;

        m_commandInstructors.SetData();
    }

    m_commandInstructors.Close();
    return S_OK;
}
```

This code can be called with the following trivial ASP page:

```
<%@LANGUAGE="VBScript"%>
<HTML>
<HEAD>
<TITLE>OLE DB Samples</TITLE>
<STYLE TYPE="text/css">
    BODY {font-family:Tahoma,Arial,sans-serif; font-size:10pt}
</STYLE>
</HEAD>
<BODY BGCOLOR=#FFFFFF>

<H1> DANCE SCHOOL </H1>

This page swaps instructors' addresses to work ones

<%
Set objBrowser = Server.CreateObject("DanceSchool.DanceSchoolBrowser")
objBrowser.UseWorkAddresses
%>

</BODY>
</HTML>
```

Although you'll have to open up the database manually to check that the data has changes—or modify `ListInstructors()`.

Summary

This chapter has shown the basic of using ATL's consumer template classes. We've covered how to use these classes to make simple modifications to an Access database, including:

- Linking to the database
- Reading data
- Adding records
- Deleting records
- Modifying records

We've carried this out through both simple modifications to the wizard generated code and slightly more complicated methods. At all stages we've put theory into practice by showing the ASP necessary to get everything working.

The OLE DB consumer templates go a lot deeper than we've had time to show in this one chapter. There are many more classes available besides the command class, and many more functions available in the command class. Here we've given you enough to get started with manipulating databases—and enough for us to be able to develop a fairly sophisticated cinema booking system later on in chapter 17.

MTS—Transactional Data Access and the ASP Intrinsic Objects in C++

In Chapter 7 we finished our discussion of MTS by writing a simple component based author maintenance system. The system consisted of two components:

❑ UCAuthorList—a non-transactional data centric component that provided access to a list of authors

❑ UpdateAuthor—a transactional data centric component that allowed authors details to be updated

In this chapter we are going to write a simple extension to the author maintenance system in C++, that enables us to view and delete author details. We will create two C++ components to add the extra functionality:

❑ DeleteAuthorList—a user centric component that will use the ASP intrinsic objects to display the list of authors that can be deleted

❑ DeleteAuthor—a data centric component that will enable us to delete authors

An overview of the new components is shown in the figure:

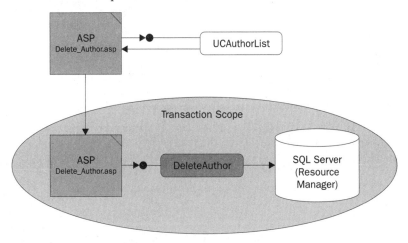

The user will view author details via the ASP page `delete_authors.asp`. This page will create the `UCAuthorList` component and invoke its `Display` method. This will render the page as shown in the figure opposite. When a **Delete** button is pressed the `delete_author.asp` ASP page will be invoked to perform the deletion.

The two new C++ components will demonstrate:

❑ Creating MTS components in C++ and using them from transactional and non-transactional ASP pages

❑ Retrieving the object context with and without the help of the ATL MTS Object Wizard

❑ How to access the ASP intrinsic objects via named properties stored in the object context, and why that is preferable to using the script context

❑ Using OLE DB to perform transactional data access across multiple tables

❑ The shortcomings of certain ATL generated wizard code

Creating the Components

The first step is to create a new ATL DLL project called BegASP using the ATL COM AppWizard, as we discussed in chapter 11. This project will host both of our components. When you create the project, leave all of the project options set to their defaults.

You may think it strange that we are leaving the **Support MTS** *box unchecked. You don't need to do this unless you are going to create interfaces that require a proxy/stub DLL. We won't be needing this in the examples given in this chapter.*

Creating the UCAuthorList Component

Once you've created the project add a new component using the ATL Object Wizard, selecting the **MS Transaction Server Component** type:

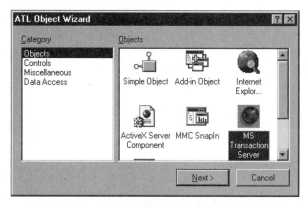

Specify the class name as UCAuthorList—UC is short for User Centric. Also, from the **MTS** tab check the Support **IObjectControl** option:

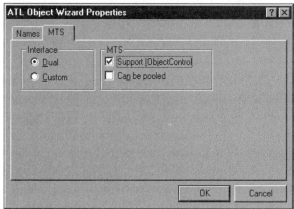

You may well notice that the Support **IErrorInfo** checkbox is missing from the MTS box, and that there is no **Attributes** tab. This is something of an oversight on the part of Microsoft, because it can and should be supported by MTS components. Fortunately, we can add this support by hand without too much effort, as you will see when we get into the code.

Unlike VB, MTS support in C++ is added to a COM server by using an include file and an import library (.lib file) rather than using a type library. This approach is taken for two reasons:

❑   It's more natural for C++ programmers to work this way

❑   C++ can access many more MTS interfaces than VB, and some of these interfaces can't be described in a compiled format using a type library

Now, let's look at the Wizard generated code. Later on we'll see how to add the required code to support MTS by hand, which is sometimes the only option when you want to retrofit existing components to use MTS, so we should have a detailed look at what's there.

mtx.h

The first thing you'll notice on top of the usual Wizard generated code is an extra #include in our class header:

```
// UCAuthorList.h : Declaration of the CUCAuthorList

#ifndef __UCAUTHORLIST_H_
#define __UCAUTHORLIST_H_

#include "resource.h"        // main symbols
#include <mtx.h>
```

This includes the required MTS support for interface and API definitions. Since we'll be hosting more than one MTS component in this project we might as well delete this line and move it to stdafx.h:

```
//You may derive a class from CComModule and use it if you want to override
//something, but do not change the name of _Module
extern CComModule _Module;
#include <atlcom.h>

#include <mtx.h>
```

By adding the mtx.h include to stdafx.h we make the definitions available to all files in the project.

IObjectControl Support

Now let's look at how the other Wizard generated code in UCAuthorList.h:

```
class ATL_NO_VTABLE CUCAuthorList :
    public CComObjectRootEx<CComSingleThreadModel>,
    public CComCoClass<CUCAuthorList, &CLSID_UCAuthorList>,
    public IObjectControl,
    public IDispatchImpl<IUCAuthorList, &IID_IUCAuthorList,
                         &LIBID_MTSWIZARDSTUFFLib>
{
public:
    CUCAuthorList()
    {
    }

DECLARE_REGISTRY_RESOURCEID(IDR_UCAUTHORLIST)

DECLARE_PROTECT_FINAL_CONSTRUCT()
```

```
DECLARE_NOT_AGGREGATABLE(CUCAuthorList)

BEGIN_COM_MAP(CUCAuthorList)
    COM_INTERFACE_ENTRY(IUCAuthorList)
    COM_INTERFACE_ENTRY(IObjectControl)
    COM_INTERFACE_ENTRY(IDispatch)
END_COM_MAP()

// IObjectControl
public:
    STDMETHOD(Activate)();
    STDMETHOD_(BOOL, CanBePooled)();
    STDMETHOD_(void, Deactivate)();

    CComPtr<IObjectContext> m_spObjectContext;

// IUCAuthorList
public:
};
```

Most of this has to do with implementing the required methods for the `IObjectControl` interface, which as we saw in Chapters 6 and 7 are:

❑ `Activate()`—called when an object is first activated.

❑ `CanBePooled()`—determines if an object can be pooled. This is not supported in MTS 2.0.

❑ `Deactivate()`—called when an object is being deactivated and destroyed. When object pooling is finally implemented in COM+ for multi-threaded components, the object will not be destroyed, just deactivated.

These methods have been declared, and the `IObjectControl` interface has been exposed. We'll see the implementations of these methods in a moment.

The Wizard has also added a member variable, `m_spObjectContext`, which is a smart pointer to contain the object context.

Note that the `DECLARE_NOT_AGGREGATABLE()` macro has been used. MTS does not support aggregation, so the Wizard adds this by default. Strictly speaking, this is optional, as `CoCreateInstance()` will return `CLASS_E_NOAGGREGATION` if you try and aggregate an MTS object. Under COM+ aggregation of this type should work, so there is no harm in no doing this.

IObjectControl Method Implementations

If you look in `UCAuthorList.cpp` you will find the following implementations:

```
HRESULT CMTSComponent::Activate()
{
    HRESULT hr = GetObjectContext(&m_spObjectContext);
    if (SUCCEEDED(hr))
        return S_OK;
    return hr;
}

BOOL CMTSComponent::CanBePooled()
{
    return FALSE;
}

void CMTSComponent::Deactivate()
{
    m_spObjectContext.Release();
}
```

This C++ code, like the Visual Basic version in Chapter 6, accesses the object context using a global function called `GetObjectContext()`. As in VB, this function accepts a pointer to the location where the returned interface should be stored. This returned interface pointer can safely be kept for the lifetime of the calling object, which is generally tied to the lifetime of a transaction.

In this code the `GetObjectContext()` function is called in `Activate()`. The returned interface pointer is managed by the smart pointer `spObjectContext`. The interface pointer is released when `Deactivate()` is called, by calling the `Release()` method of the smart pointer.

> `Activate()` and `Deactivate()` should always be used in preference to class constructors/destructors, and the ATL `FinalConstruct()`/`FinalRelease()` functions when coding for MTS.

Modifying the IDL

One change we can make is to modify the IDL for our component to specify the MTS transaction setting. To do this, we can choose from the following set of IDL attributes, defined in `mtxattr.h`:

```
TRANSACTION_REQUIRED
TRANSACTION_SUPPORTED
TRANSACTION_NOT_SUPPORTED
TRANSACTION_REQUIRES_NEW
```

This component won't support transactions, so we can use the third of these. So, `#include mtxattr.h` in the IDL file:

```
#include "mtxattr.h"
import "oaidl.idl";
import "ocidl.idl";
```

And modify the `coclass` definition of `UCAuthorList` like so:

```
[
    uuid(2DCC97E8-6925-11D3-857B-00902707906A),
    helpstring("UCAuthorList Class"),
    TRANSACTION_NOT_SUPPORTED
]
coclass UCAuthorList
{
    [default] interface IUCAuthorList;
};
```

This line associates a custom attribute with the `coclass` statement. The attribute is identified by a GUID (in this case {17093CC6-9BD2-11cf-AA4F-304BF89C0001}) using the IDL keyword `custom`. When a component is added to a package, MTS will inspect its `coclass` statement in the type library to see if one of the custom attributes it knows about is present, using `ITypeInfo2::GetCustData()`. If a recognized attribute is detected, it will automatically default the transactional support required.

VB automatically adds these customs attributes for you when you select a value in the MTSTransactionMode combo.

The ASP Intrinsic Objects and the Object Context

As we said in Chapter 3 the object context is the preferred way of accessing ASP intrinsic objects in IIS4 and IIS5 because of the integration with MTS and COM+ respectively. The scripting context object will work fine most of the time for transactional and non-transactional components inside of ASP pages, but its use should be deprecated in favor of the object context. There are some subtle problems with using the script context object for objects that are hosted in MTS, which are related to the lifetime of a transaction.

An object obtains a reference to the scripting context object by implementing the function OnStartPage(), which is called by IIS using `IDispatch::Invoke` when the object is first created. The passed in object reference to the scripting context can be stored away by the class and used later to provide access to the ASP intrinsic objects as needed. Both the OnStartPage() and OnEndPage functions are only called when an object is created using `Server.CreateObject()`, which then tracks the lifetime of the object, as well as delegating the creation to `IObjectContext::CreateInstance()`.

If an ASP page is transactional then all objects created using `Server.CreateObject()` won't actually be destroyed until the page is rendered, so there are no issues when accessing the ASP intrinsic objects. However, if a component is transactional and is used inside of a non-transactional page, IIS will still call OnStartPage()/OnEndPage() when the object is first created. Since the real object is being created and destroyed for every method call, the real object will have been destroyed by the time the OnStartPage method returns; any state and scripting context object reference will be lost.

By storing the ASP intrinsic objects inside of the object context, a component can just reach in and grab them when they are needed, and the problems described above are circumvented.

IIS exposes its ASP intrinsic objects by using the `IGetContextProperties` interface, which the object context implements to expose *named* properties. These properties are returned as VARIANTs and can be accessed as follows:

```
CComBSTR sName = "Response";
CComVariant vInterface;

// Get the IGetContextProperties interface

CComQIPtr<IGetContextProperties> spContextProperties;
spContextProperties = m_spObjectContext;

spContextProperties->GetProperty(sName, &vInterface);
```

Not surprisingly for the ASP intrinsic objects, we just use the named properties application, session, request, response and server.

My research has shown that the `IGetContextProperties` interface is not always implemented by the object context, so it appears as if it is made available by IIS using some internal MTS mechanisms that are currently undocumented. While that's not overly important, it does mean you have to ensure the interface is supported for your code to work.

To retrieve an object context that implements the `IGetContextProperties` interface reliably, an ASP component has to meet one of these conditions:

❑ Be installed in MTS and retrieve the object context only in `Activate()`. Attempting to access the object context in a class constructor or, for example, in an object's `FinalConstruct()` method results in an object context being returned that does not support the interface.

❑ Not be installed in MTS.

Accessing the Response Object

The ATL Object Wizard does not support accessing ASP intrinsic objects via the object context, so we have to roll the code by hand. This is a reflection of the fact the ASP wizard is really geared toward IIS3.

To give a complete demonstration of how to access the ASP intrinsic object using the object context, we'll access the ASP Response object via the object context. We'll add a GetResponseObject() function to UCAuthorList class in UCAuthorList.h:

```
HRESULT GetResponseObject(IResponse** ppResponse)
{
    HRESULT hr;

    // Get the IGetContextProperties interface

    CComQIPtr<IGetContextProperties> spContextProperties;
    spContextProperties = m_spObjectContext;

    if(!spContextProperties)
    {
        Error("Failed to get IGetContextProperties from the object context");
        return E_FAIL;
    }

    // Get the specific object
    CComBSTR sName = "Response";
    CComVariant vInterface;
    hr = spContextProperties->GetProperty(sName, &vInterface);
    if(FAILED(hr))
    {
        Error("Failed to retrieve the named property");
        return hr;
    }

    hr = vInterface.pdispVal->QueryInterface(__uuidof(IResponse),
                                    reinterpret_cast<void**>(ppResponse));
    if(FAILED(hr))
    {
        Error("Failed to query for the ASP interface");
        return hr;
    }

    return S_OK;
}
```

The ATL utility classes used in this code should be familiar to you by now. If not, flick back to Chapter 11 for a quick refresher.

The code asks the object context for the IGetContextProperties interface, and then uses that to retrieve a VARIANT given a named value. We know the returned VARIANT contains an automation interface (IDispatch based) that should represent the named ASP object. We use this interface pointer via the pdispVal and QI() for the IResponse interface.

pdispVal is one of the many members of a VARIANTs discriminated union, which we also discussed in Chapter 11.

The above code uses the error support provided by the `ISupportErrorInfo` interface. As already mentioned, we can't get the Object Wizard to add support for this when creating an MTS object, so let's add this support by hand.

Adding Error Support to our Component

Once again then, the first step in adding support for `ISupportErrorInfo` is to make our class inherit from it:

```
class ATL_NO_VTABLE CUCAuthorList :
    public CComObjectRootEx<CComSingleThreadModel>,
    public CComCoClass<CUCAuthorList, &CLSID_UCAuthorList>,
    public IObjectControl,
    public ISupportErrorInfo,
    public IDispatchImpl<IUCAuthorList, &IID_IUCAuthorList,
                         &LIBID_MTSWIZARDSTUFFLib>
```

Next, we add a new `COM_INTERFACE_ENTRY()` macro into the COM map so that the `ISupportErrorInfo` interface can be discovered by clients calling `QueryInterface()`:

```
BEGIN_COM_MAP(CUCAuthorList)
    COM_INTERFACE_ENTRY(IUCAuthorList)
    COM_INTERFACE_ENTRY(IObjectControl)
    COM_INTERFACE_ENTRY(IDispatch)
    COM_INTERFACE_ENTRY(ISupportErrorInfo)
END_COM_MAP()
```

Thirdly, we need to add a simple implementation of the `InterfaceSupportsErrorInfo()` method to the `UCAuthorList.cpp` source file:

```
STDMETHODIMP CUCAuthorList::InterfaceSupportsErrorInfo(REFIID riid)
{
    if(InlineIsEqualGUID(&IID_IUCAuthorList, riid))
        return S_OK;
    return S_FALSE;
}
```

And finally, you should add the associated declaration in `UCAuthorList.h`:

```
// ISupportErrorInfo
public:
    STDMETHOD(InterfaceSupportsErrorInfo)(REFIID riid);
```

Including the ASP Interface Definitions

Because we couldn't use the ATL Wizard to include the ASP support, we have to manually add the include files that define various ASP intrinsic objects and their interfaces before compiling this code. As before, open up `stdafx.h` and add this additional line:

```
extern CComModule _Module;
#include <atlcom.h>

#include <mtx.h>
#include <asptlb.h>
```

Before implementing the code to display the author details, we'll demonstrate accessing and using the intrinsic ASP objects via the object context.

We will generate a simple "Hello ASP World 2!" message by adding a function to the UCAuthorList component called Display(), invoking it using ASP.

Hello ASP World 2!

Add a new method to the UCAuthorList component (again in the header file) called Display(). As before, do this by right clicking on IUCAuthorList in the ClassView, and use the Add Method menu option. Do not specify any parameters for the method. Change the generated code as follows:

```
STDMETHODIMP CUCAuthorList::Display()
{
    HRESULT hr;
    CComPtr<IResponse> spResponse;

    hr = GetResponseObject(&spResponse);

    if(FAILED(hr))
        return hr;

    spResponse->Write( CComVariant("<HTML>Hello ASP World 2 !</HTML>"));
    return S_OK;
}
```

This code uses the GetResponseObject() function that encapsulates accessing the object context to retrieve the IResponse interface via a named property. The interface is then used to write a simple message back to the client browser, pretty much as we did in Chapter 11.

Compile the project and then add the resultant component to the Authors MTS package that we created in Chapter 7. When adding the component the ProgID should show up as BegASP.AuthorList.1. Unlike VB, VC++ uses versioning in ProgIDs, hence the ".1".

For this small demo to work the object has to be installed into MTS, simply because we are accessing the object context via the IObjectControl interface. We could move the code to get the object context into the Display() method, and it would also work. However, this should only be done for components that are not installed in MTS, but still want to use the object context approach of accessing ASP objects.

Once the component is compiled and installed into MTS, create the following ASP page, called delete_authors.asp:

```
<%
    set oUCAuthorList = Server.CreateObject("Begasp.UCAuthorList")
    oUCAuthorList.Display
%>
```

We could set the object (interface pointer) to nothing at the end of this page, but the ASP interpreter will release it when the page has been processed anyway.

You should see the result shown:

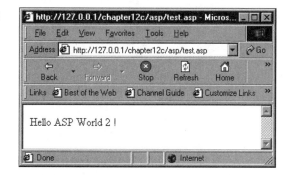

Accessing other ASP Intrinsic Objects

For each ASP object you need to access from your component you can simply write a similar function to `GetResponseObject()`, changing the named value and the requested interface. We won't actually need to use any other ASP objects for the rest of this chapter, but we'll create a `GetRequestObject()` function to complete the picture.

Make a copy of the `GetResponseObject` function and make the following changes:

- ❑ Change the function name to `GetRequestObject()`

- ❑ Change the function parameter type from `IResponse` to `IRequest` and the parameter name from `ppResponse` to `ppRequest`

- ❑ Change the named property from `Response` to `Request`

- ❑ Change the call to `QueryInterface` to use `IRequest` instead of `IResponse`

These changes are highlighted in the following implementation of `GetRequestObject`:

```
HRESULT GetRequestObject(IRequest **ppRequest)
{
    HRESULT hr;

    // Get the IGetContextProperties interface

    CComQIPtr<IGetContextProperties> spContextProperties;
    spContextProperties = m_spObjectContext;

    if(!spContextProperties)
    {
        Error("Failed to get IGetContextProperties from the object context");
        return E_FAIL;
    }

    // Get the specific object

    CComBSTR sName = "Request";
    CComVariant vInterface;
    hr = spContextProperties->GetProperty(sName,
                                          &vInterface);
    if(FAILED(hr))
    {
        Error("Failed to retrieve the named property");
        return hr;
    }
```

```
    hr = vInterface.pdispVal->QueryInterface(__uuidof(IRequest),
                                    reinterpret_cast<void**>(ppRequest));

if(FAILED(hr))
{
    Error("Failed to query for the ASP interface");
    return hr;
}

    return S_OK;
}
```

As a quick example of using `GetRequestObject()` and `GetResponseObject()` together, we'll modify the `Display` function to display any query string parameters of the `Request` object that are passed to `delete_authors.asp`. We will use the following URL in our example (which will probably need modifying to get the actual directory):

http://localhost/delete_authors.asp?Name=Richard Anderson&Born=1972&Fav Food=Pizza

This will create this output:

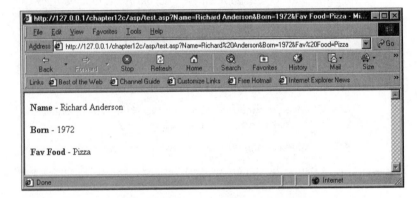

Modify the `Display()` function as follows:

```
STDMETHODIMP CUCAuthorList::Display()
{
    HRESULT hr;
    CComPtr<IResponse> spResponse;

    hr = GetResponseObject( &spResponse );
    if(FAILED(hr))
        return hr;

    CComPtr<IRequest> spRequest;

    hr = GetRequestObject( &spRequest );
    if(FAILED(hr))
        return hr;

    // Get the named/value interface

    CComPtr<IRequestDictionary> spRequestDictionary;
    hr = spRequest->get_QueryString( &spRequestDictionary );
    if(FAILED(hr))
    {
        Error("Failed to access request dictionary");
        return hr;
    }
```

```
    // Determine the number of named items

    int iCount;
    spRequestDictionary->get_Count( &iCount );

    CComVariant vName;
    CComVariant vValue;

    for( int i = 1; i <= iCount; i++ )
    {
        spRequestDictionary->get_Key( CComVariant(i), &vName );
        spRequestDictionary->get_Item( CComVariant(i), &vValue);

        spResponse->Write( CComVariant("<p><strong>") );
        spResponse->Write( vName );
        spResponse->Write( CComVariant("</strong> - ") );
        spResponse->Write( vValue );
        spResponse->Write( CComVariant("</p>") );
    }

    return S_OK;
}
```

The code used to produce this output is fairly simple, indeed, hardly any more difficult that its Visual Basic cousin. The `IRequestDictionary` interface is used to return a value or values given a name or index, and can also return the name for a named value given a valid index.

Now we've got the basic ASP & MTS building blocks let's go through the remaining steps required for extending the VB author maintenance system to have delete support.

OLE DB Consumer Classes

Our components will need access to the `authors` table in the `pubs` database, so use the ATL Object Wizard and create a new OLE DB consumer class. Specify SQL Server as the provider:

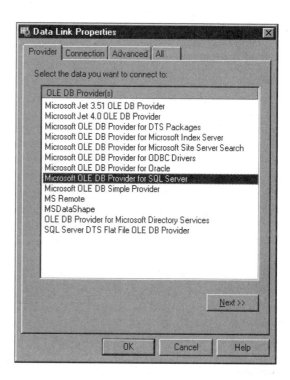

Click **OK** and select your SQL Server and specify pubs as the database:

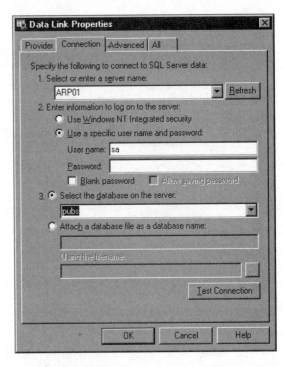

For connecting to SQL I've specified the connection to use standard security and provided a user name of SA. We'll discuss using the other option of Windows NT Integrated Security shortly.

Press **OK**, then select the authors table from the presented list. Press **OK** again and change the short name of the class to Authors, selecting the **Delete** support as shown:

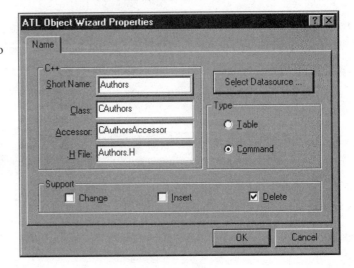

Click **OK** and the Wizard will generate two classes, as we've seen before:

- ❑ `CAuthors`—establishes the connection to the data source and opens the default rowset
- ❑ `CAuthorsAccessor`—specifies the bindings used to retrieve parameters from the table into variables

As we discussed earlier, these OLE DB consumer classes encapsulate the COM interfaces used for accessing an OLE DB provider. The only requirement for using them is that a client must have initialized the COM runtime for the calling thread.

For connecting to SQL we specified the connection to use standard security and provided a user name of `SA`. Depending upon your security requirements, you may choose integrated Windows NT security. If you do, just remember that ASP components are created under the user identify of `IWAM_MachineName` or `IUSR_MachineName`:

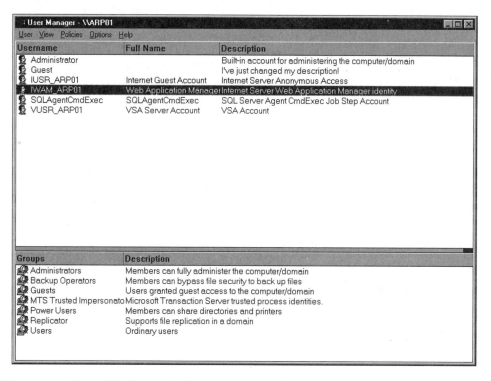

You'll have to configure SQL Server database to recognize these users, to enable access to the tables and contained data. Generally speaking this is not a wise idea because you effectively open up your SQL Server database to anonymous Internet users, which also use the `IUSR_MachineName` account. If you stick with standard security, you've got a finer grain of control of security that is controlled by your components.

As we are accessing an SQL Server database the most efficient provider to use is **OLE DB provider for SQL Server**. You can also use the **OLE DB provider for ODBC drivers** to access an SQL Server database, but this extra level of indirection adds an unnecessary overhead as shown in the figure, so it shouldn't be used in any components if at all possible.

If you do want your product to work with different OLE DB providers, modify the `OpenDataSource()` function and add generic code that reads the provider properties from a location such as the registry. The code can then set up the connection properties (such as the provider name) accordingly. Always use the most efficient mechanism, resorting to the **OLE DB provider for ODBC drivers** as a last resort!

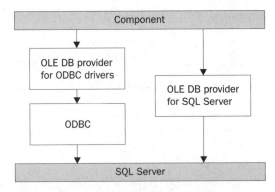

Connection to the Data Source

To see how the connection to SQL Server is established, open up the CAuthors class and you'll see the properties have been specified for this provider in the `OpenDataSource` method:

```
HRESULT OpenDataSource()
{
    HRESULT hr;
    CDataSource db;
    CDBPropSet dbinit(DBPROPSET_DBINIT);

    dbinit.AddProperty(DBPROP_UPDATABILITY, DBPROPVAL_UP_DELETE |
                       DBPROPVAL_UP_CHANGE);
    dbinit.AddProperty(DBPROP_AUTH_PERSIST_SENSITIVE_AUTHINFO, false);
    dbinit.AddProperty(DBPROP_AUTH_USERID, OLESTR("sa"));
    dbinit.AddProperty(DBPROP_INIT_CATALOG, OLESTR("pubs"));
    dbinit.AddProperty(DBPROP_INIT_DATASOURCE, OLESTR("arp01"));
    dbinit.AddProperty(DBPROP_INIT_LCID, (long)1033);
    dbinit.AddProperty(DBPROP_INIT_PROMPT, (short)4);
    hr = db.Open(_T("SQLOLEDB.1"), &dbinit);
    if(FAILED(hr))
        return hr;

    return m_session.Open(db);
}
```

Most of these properties are fairly self-explanatory. As we want to update and delete via the OLE DB provider created session (connection to the provider), we set the DBPROP_UPDATABILITY property to DBPROPVAL_UP_DELETE | DBPROPVAL_UP_CHANGE. These give the OLE DB provider hints to how we are going to use the session so it can optimize it. Similar properties are set when creating a rowset in OpenRowset(), for the same reasons, but you'll notice that OpenRowset() also adds the following property:

```
propset.AddProperty(DBPROP_IRowsetChange, true);
```

According to MSDN this property does the following: setting DBPROP_IRowsetUpdate to VARIANT_TRUE automatically sets DBPROP_IRowsetChange to VARIANT_TRUE. I think you'll agree that statement is as clear as mud! As it turns out, what the line actually means is that the rowset will be created in a mode that allows us to perform updates. The DBPROP_UPDATABILITY property doesn't allow this (on its own).

> *Strictly speaking the Wizard generated code should also be using the value* VARIANT_TRUE *rather than* true.

We don't want any GUI to be displayed if a session fails to connect, so the code also sets DBPROP_INIT_PROMPT to 4, which means don't prompt. To make this last property clearer you should change it to use the macro definition DBPROMPT_NOPROMT:

```
dbinit.AddProperty(DBPROP_INIT_PROMPT, (short)DBPROMPT_NOPROMPT);
```

There is one small problem with the Wizard generated code that the ATL Wizard provides. By default, SQL Server (and other MTS resource managers/dispensers) will *not* auto-enlist connections into any active MS-DTC transaction! Obviously that's not what we want, so we have to replace the call to db.Open() with db.OpenServiceComponents():

```
dbinit.AddProperty(DBPROP_INIT_LCID, (long)1033);
dbinit.AddProperty(DBPROP_INIT_PROMPT, (short)4);
hr = db.OpenWithServiceComponents(_T("SQLOLEDB.1"), &dbinit);
if (FAILED(hr))
    return hr;
```

OLE DB provides common services to enhance the native functionality and performance of any OLE DB provider. To use these services we have to call OpenWithServiceComponents(), which is an undocumented function that is located in CDataSource. All Wizard generated OLE DB consumers derive from CDataSource, and more documentation on this function can be located in the Visual C++ readme.

These services enable cursoring, auto transaction enlistment and session pooling. The last two features are important for transactional/scalable MTS components so you should generally use them. The session pooling provided by OLE DB is the same as the connection/resource pooling we discussed in Chapter 7.

> *Like a lot of ATL classes and functions,* OpenWithServiceComponents() *is not documented in the current release of MSDN. This is an oversight and the function is safe to use.*

Using the OLE DB Consumers Classes

For our `UCAuthorList` component to access newly created consumer classes open `UCAuthorList.cpp` and add the include for the header file `Authors.h` to it:

```
#include "stdafx.h"
#include "Begasp.h"
#include "UCAuthorList.h"
#include "Authors.h"
```

The `Display()` method called by `delete_authors.asp` will use the OLE DB consumer classes to retrieve a list of authors and generate details for each one. Each author detail line will have a **Delete** button next to it, that when pressed will invoke the transactional page `delete_author.asp`, passing in the unique ID of the author via the ID request parameter.

Change the `Display()` method to the following code:

```
STDMETHODIMP CUCAuthorList::Display()
{
    HRESULT hr;
    CComPtr<IResponse> spResponse;
    TCHAR szErrorMsg[256];

    // Get the response object

    hr = GetResponseObject( &spResponse );
    if(FAILED(hr))
        return hr;

    CComPtr<IRequest> spRequest;

    // Get the request object

    hr = GetRequestObject(&spRequest);
    if(FAILED(hr))
        return hr;

    // Access the data source / authors table
    CAuthors authors;
    hr = authors.Open();
    if(FAILED(hr))
    {
        wsprintf(szErrorMsg, _T("Open failed : %08x"), hr);
        Error(szErrorMsg);
        return hr;
    }

    // Write out the ASP header

    WritePageHeader( spResponse );

    // Write out a detail line for each author

    TCHAR szFormatLine[4096];

    while(authors.MoveNext() == S_OK)
    {
        wsprintf(szFormatLine,
            _T("<TR>")
            _T("    <TD bgcolor=\"#FFFF6C\">%s</TD>")
            _T("    <TD bgcolor=\"#FFFF6C\">%s</TD>")
```

```
                _T("    <TD bgcolor=\"#FFFF6C\">%s</TD>")
                _T("    <TD bgcolor=\"#FFFF6C\">%s</TD>")
                _T("    <TD bgcolor=\"#3AC2EF\">")
                _T("        <FORM NAME=\"A\" METHOD=\"POST\" ")
                _T("ACTION=\"delete_author.asp?au_id=%s\n\">")
                _T("            <input type=\"SUBMIT\" value=\"Delete\" name=\"B1\" />" )
                _T("        </FORM>")
                _T("    </TD>")
                _T("</TR>"),
                authors.m_auid,
                authors.m_aulname,
                authors.m_aufname,
                authors.m_phone,
                authors.m_auid );

        spResponse->Write(CComVariant(szFormatLine));
    }
    // Ensure that move next ended with S_FALSE and
    // not an error.
    if(FAILED(hr))
    {
        wsprintf(szErrorMsg, _T("Move next failed : %08x"), hr);
        Error(szErrorMsg);
        return hr;
    }
    // Close the data source

    authors.Close();

    // Write out the page footer
    WritePageFooter(spResponse);
    return S_OK;
}
```

This code opens the connection to the database, enumerates each row by calling `Authors.MoveNext()`, generating a detail line for each author, and then closes the connection. The initial page header is generated with a call to `WritePageHeader()`, and the page footer is generated with a call to `WritePageFooter()`, functions we'll see in a moment.

The ATL OLE DB consumer classes will automatically release sessions etc., so we can choose whether or not we explicitly release them by calling the `Close()` method of the various template classes. In the code above I've chosen not to.

WritePageHeader / WritePageFooter

The function for writing the page heading looks like this:

```
void CUCAuthorList::WritePageHeader(IResponse* pResponse)
{
    TCHAR szHeader[] = \
        _T("<HTML><HEAD><TITLE>Delete Authors</TITLE>")
        _T("<STYLE TYPE=\"text/css\">")
        _T(" BODY {font-family:Veranda,Tahoma,Arial,sans-serif; font-size:10pt}")
        _T("  TD {font-family:Veranda,Tahoma,Arial,sans-serif; font-size:10pt}")
        _T("</STYLE>")
        _T("</HEAD>")
        _T("<BODY BGCOLOR=WHITE>")
        _T("<H1>Delete Authors</H1>")
```

```
        _T("<HR>")
        _T("<P>Select author to delete:")
        _T("<TABLE cellspacing=\"2\" cellpadding=\"0\">")
        _T("<TR>")
        _T("   <TD bgcolor=\"#3AC2EF\"><STRONG>ID</STRONG></TD>")
        _T("   <TD bgcolor=\"#3AC2EF\"><STRONG>Last Name</STRONG></TD>")
        _T("   <TD bgcolor=\"#3AC2EF\"><STRONG>First Name</STRONG></TD>")
        _T("   <TD bgcolor=\"#3AC2EF\"><STRONG>Contact No.</STRONG></TD>")
        _T("</TR>")
        _T("<TR>")
        _T("</TR>");

    pResponse->Write(CComVariant(szHeader));
}
```

This code is fairly self descriptive and just calls IRequest::Write() to output the statically defined HTML for the header. The _T() macro just ensures the string is narrow or wide depending upon the build type—UNICODE or non-UNICODE.

The same approach is used for WritePageFooter():

```
void CUCAuthorList::WritePageFooter( IResponse* pResponse)
{
    TCHAR szFooter[] = \
        _T("</BODY>")
        _T("</HTML>");

    pResponse->Write( CComVariant( szFooter ) );
}
```

We'll also have to declare these functions in UCAuthorList.h:

```
    void CUCAuthorList::WritePageFooter( IResponse* pResponse);
    void CUCAuthorList::WritePageHeader(IResponse* pResponse);
```

Testing the UCAuthorList Component

After compiling the UCAuthorList component we can test it using the delete_authors.asp page we used earlier.

Before we do this, ensure that the default transaction attribute of the component (found in MTS explorer) is set to Does Not Support Transactions. Remember, this is important as it ensures no read-locks are created whilst the data is being read from a data source.

As a final configuration measure, ensure that the Authors package is set to be a library package, and that the web site that will serve the ASP is set to run in its own address space. This will ensure that all components for the page are created in a single instance MTX.EXE.

Viewing the ASP should display a screen that looks something like this:

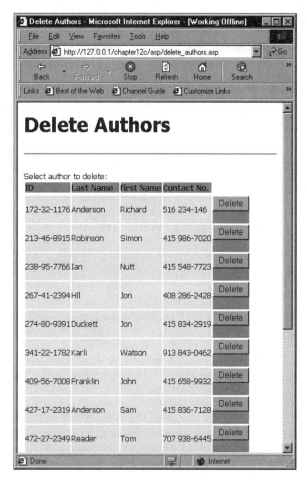

Now that the user can view the authors to be deleted, we need to write the ASP and component that enables the ACTION (for example, ACTION="delete_author.asp?au_id=238-95-7766) to be processed. Before doing that however, we'll briefly review the error handling of the UCAuthorList component.

Error Handling Is Important

The code for the Display function in the UCAuthorList component is fairly defensive with its error handling. My experience has shown that this is generally the best way to go from day one when writing ASP components, even if they are simply prototypes for proving concepts.

The reason error handling is important (other than because it's good practice) is that ASP/MTS components often run under a different user account to the interactive user, which often leads to security complications. For example, when opening a database connection to SQL Server using Windows NT integrated security you'll find that a component by default will often work outside of IIS, but will not work inside of MTS. The reason it fails inside of IIS is because SQL Server does not recognize the identity of the user requesting the connection, as the component is created under the identity of IWAM_MachineName (for applications and virtual directories running in their own process) or IUSR_MachineName.

You can, of course, just configure the database security to recognize these users, but this potentially creates a security risk for your database. It is a much better idea for COM components to access database tables using standard SQL Server security where a user ID and password are specified as properties when opening the connection.

> **For a complete discussion of MTS security see** *Professional VC++ MTS Programming* **by Dr Richard Grimes (ISBN 1-861002-39-4).**

Good Error handling does pay off

As an example of this good error-handling practice paying of I'll demonstrate the security problems that I hit when writing this chapter. When opening the database connection I didn't bother to check the HRESULT of Open() initially, so the code was like this:

```
// Access the data source / authors table
CAuthors authors;
authors.Open();
```

Because Open() had failed due to a security failure, the next call to into the class (MoveNext()) resulted in an ASSERT being thrown as shown below. Because the components were created and running as a library package at that time, and the web site containing them was configured to run in its own process space, the message box showing the error was not visible. The message box was still created and caused IIS to hang, but the message box was shown in the **WinStation** for IWAM_MachineName.

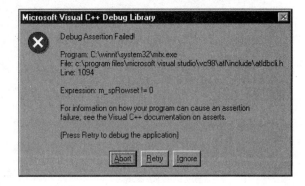

WinStations

A discussion of WinStations is beyond this chapter, but essentially they are secure containers for desktops. When you log on as an interactive user, a WinStation is created for you. All the UI elements you interact with are created in that WinStation, and no other users can access them unless they are granted permissions to access individual elements/objects.

WinStations are associated with a single user identity (principle), so when a service or MTS package runs in its own process using a different user's credentials (user name, password etc.) another WinStation is created for that user/principle. The net result of this, and my problem, was that I didn't see the ASSERT and had to keep rebooting my machine. If I'd put error handling in initially, I would have saved myself about an hour's worth of debugging time.

Debugging MTS components is discussed at the end of this chapter.

Knowing the strong feelings people have for error handling, I know that my advice may or may not be adopted. If you don't want to use error handling when writing a prototype, you should configure the user credentials of any MTS packages to be the interactive user.

Tip—Seeing those ASSERTS!

When developing new components you'll often find that ASSERTs may occur because a method parameter is invalid or an object's state is not right for a particular called method. By default you won't see any ASSERTs of ASP components that are running inside of IIS. IIS runs without using the security credentials of the interactive users, so any message boxes raised will appear in a different WinStation—an invisible one!

To get around this during the earlier development cycle, do the following:

❑ Change your web site or virtual directory to run in its own process, as we described in Chapter 6

❑ Select the associated MTS package that IIS creates to achieve process isolation and bring up its properties using the context menu

❑ Select the identity tab and change the account to be the interactive user:

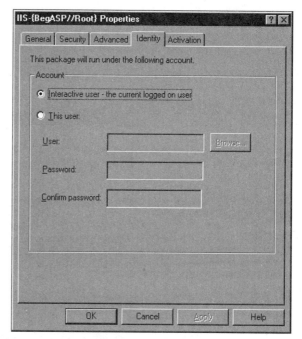

When you press **OK** you'll get a warning, which basically says you shouldn't change the properties unless you know what you are doing. You do, so you can ignore this message, but remember to change them back when you have finished your developments and enter the production testing stage.

Creating the DeleteAuthor Component

Now that we've created the component to display the deletion UI, we need to write the component for actually deleting an author.

The `pubs` database that ships with SQL Server has a number of tables with foreign keys that prevent one row from being deleted whilst another row is referencing it, which is quite a common feature of databases. This is true for the `pubs` database, so to delete an author we have to delete a row from *two* tables:

❑ `titleauthor`—links authors to books

❑ `authors`—details relating to an individual author

The relationship between these tables is shown in the figure below:

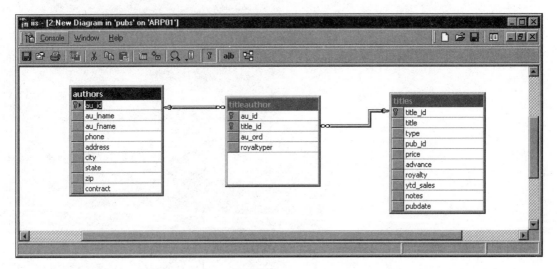

The database can have many authors and many titles. Each author can be associated with many titles, and each title can have more than one author.

Having to delete rows from two tables is a good test for our transaction. In the `DeleteAuthor` component we won't delete a row from the `titles` table if there are no associated authors, we'll simply remove any rows from the `titleauthor` table that reference the author being deleted (there could be one or more). We have to do this first as this table has a foreign key to the `authors` table. If we try and delete the author without first deleting the associated rows in the `titleauthor` table the operation will fail. Once all rows from the `titleauthor` table are removed we'll remove the row from the `authors` table.

In a real life system you might want to warn the user that deleting an author may result in one or more books not being associated with any author, or maybe provide a maintenance screen that shows authorless books.

Creating the DeleteAuthor Component

The `DeleteAuthor` component is a data centric component that is environment neutral—it accesses data and doesn't use the ASP object model. I've taken this approach simply to demonstrate the alternatives. I've not used the ASP intrinsic objects simply because I didn't want to overly complicate the sample code.

Because this is a data centric class we could have given the class a prefix of DC (Data Centric) to make its role more explicit.

This time round we'll create a simple object and add the MTS support by hand. As already mentioned, it is useful to know how to do this, as it's sometimes the only option you have with existing components. So, add the `DeleteAuthor` component with the Object Wizard, making sure you check the ISupportErrorInfo box and the No box in the Aggregation frame for the reasons we discussed earlier. Both of these values are located on the Attributes tab.

Adding MTS Support

We don't need to include `mtx.h`, as we placed this in `stdafx.h`. The changes we need to make are:

❑ Derive our class from `IObjectControl`

❑ Add `IObjectControl` to the COM map

❑ Implement the methods of `IObjectControl`

❑ Add a smart pointer to hold the object context interface

❑ Modify the IDL to specify that a transaction is required

The changes to `DeleteAuthor.h` are as follows:

```
class ATL_NO_VTABLE CDeleteAuthor :
    public CComObjectRootEx<CComSingleThreadModel>,
    public CComCoClass<CDeleteAuthor, &CLSID_DeleteAuthor>,
    public IObjectControl,
    public ISupportErrorInfo,
    public IDispatchImpl<IDeleteAuthor, &IID_IDeleteAuthor,
                         &LIBID_MTSWIZARDSTUFFLib>
{
public:
    CDeleteAuthor()
    {
    }

DECLARE_REGISTRY_RESOURCEID(IDR_DELETEAUTHOR)
DECLARE_NOT_AGGREGATABLE(CDeleteAuthor)

DECLARE_PROTECT_FINAL_CONSTRUCT()

BEGIN_COM_MAP(CDeleteAuthor)
    COM_INTERFACE_ENTRY(IDeleteAuthor)
    COM_INTERFACE_ENTRY(IObjectControl)
    COM_INTERFACE_ENTRY(IDispatch)
    COM_INTERFACE_ENTRY(ISupportErrorInfo)
END_COM_MAP()
```

557

```
// IObjectControl
public:
    STDMETHOD(Activate)();
    STDMETHOD_(BOOL, CanBePooled)();
    STDMETHOD_(void, Deactivate)();

    CComPtr<IObjectContext> m_spObjectContext;

// ISupportsErrorInfo
    STDMETHOD(InterfaceSupportsErrorInfo)(REFIID riid);

// IDeleteAuthor
public:
};
```

We can implement these methods in `DeleteAuthor.cpp` in the standard way:

```
HRESULT CDeleteAuthor::Activate()
{
    HRESULT hr = GetObjectContext(&m_spObjectContext);
    if (SUCCEEDED(hr))
        return S_OK;
    return hr;
}

BOOL CDeleteAuthor::CanBePooled()
{
    return FALSE;
}

void CDeleteAuthor::Deactivate()
{
    m_spObjectContext.Release();
}
```

And modify the IDL using the `TRANSACTION_REQUIRED` attribute:

```
[
    uuid(2DCC97EA-6925-11D3-857B-00902707906A),
    helpstring("DeleteAuthor Class"),
    TRANSACTION_REQUIRED
]
coclass DeleteAuthor
{
    [default] interface IDeleteAuthor;
};
```

Adding the Delete Method

Once the component is created add an include for `Authors.H`:

```
// DeleteAuthor.cpp : Implementation of CDeleteAuthor
#include "stdafx.h"
#include "BegASP.h"
#include "DeleteAuthor.h"
#include "Authors.H"
```

Next, add a `Delete()` method to the
`IDeleteAuthor` interface that takes one BSTR
value called au_id:

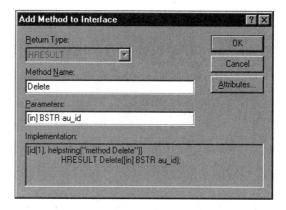

*In C++ and other langauges it is common to give variables/properties a prefix to indicate their type,
such as s for string. However, my experience shows that this simply confuses people that are script
oriented, so whether you use such 'Hungarian notation' is entirely up to you. For this example I
haven't.*

The main body of the `Delete()` method should be implemented as follows:

```
STDMETHODIMP CDeleteAuthor::Delete(BSTR au_id)
{

    USES_CONVERSION;
    HRESULT hr;

    // ensure the object context is available

    if (!m_spObjectContext)
    {
        Error("Please ensure you've installed the object into MTS");
        return E_FAIL;
    }

    // Open the datasource

    CAuthors authors;
    hr = authors.OpenDataSource();
    if (FAILED(hr))
    {
        Error("Failed to open database connection for deletion");
        return hr;
    }

    // The command/accessor defined to have no parameters

    CCommand < CAccessor<_CNoParameters> > id;
    CDBPropSet propset(DBPROPSET_ROWSET);
    propset.AddProperty(DBPROP_UPDATABILITY, DBPROPVAL_UP_DELETE);

    TCHAR szSQL[512];

    // Delete any title the author has written.

    wsprintf(szSQL,
            _T("DELETE FROM dbo.titleauthor WHERE au_id = '%s'"),
            W2T(au_id));
```

```
hr = id.Open( authors.m_session,szSQL, &propset );
if (FAILED(hr) )
{
    Error("Failed to delete titleauthor ");
    return hr;
}

// Delete the author

wsprintf(szSQL,
         _T("DELETE FROM dbo.authors WHERE au_id = '%s'"),
         W2T(au_id));

hr = id.Open(authors.m_session,szSQL, &propset);
if (FAILED(hr))
{
    Error("Failed to delete author");
    return hr;
}

authors.Close();

m_spObjectContext->SetComplete();
return S_OK;
}
```

Just like the `Display()` method in the `UCAuthorList` component I've got lots of error handling, which as I've said is always a good idea. We already discussed this, so we'll just focus on the interesting new bits of this code. Note that I'm not calling `IObjectControl::SetAbort()` when an error occurs. The reason for this is that MTS will automatically abort a transaction if a COM exception is raised using `SetErrorInfo`—remember this is what `Error()` calls under the covers.

In this code, as we had to do once in the last chapter, we don't use the default rowset. Instead, we create our own, so calling `Open()` would be detrimental to performance and we use `OpenDataSource()` instead.

After the call to `OpenDataSource()`, we create our rowset using a special no parameters accessor:

```
CCommand < CAccessor<_CNoParameters> > id;

CDBPropSet propset(DBPROPSET_ROWSET);
propset.AddProperty(DBPROP_UPDATABILITY, DBPROPVAL_UP_DELETE);

CHAR szSQL[512];

wsprintf(szSQL,
         _T("DELETE FROM dbo.titleauthor WHERE au_id = '%s'"),
         W2T(au_id));

hr = id.Open(authors.m_session,szSQL, &propset);
```

`CAccessor<_CNoParameters>` is used when an SQL statement does not pass in parameters or expect any to come out. This is fine for our `DELETE` statements, because like the update statement in Chapter 6, we build the complete SQL command ourselves, before executing it by calling `Open()`.

Rather than building a SQL command like this code does, you could use a simple accessor that contains a single member variable for identifying the author to be deleted. Whether or not you prefer this approach is up to you. I would recommend you use accessors if your parameters will contain reserved characters such as the single quotes, which would cause the technique I'm using to fail *unless* you double them up. For more details on using in parameter accessors, see *ATL COM Programmer's Reference* by Dr Richard Grimes (ISBN 1-861002-49-1).

Finally, if all goes well the code closes the data connection and says it's happy with the transactional state by calling SetComplete():

```
authors.Close();

m_spObjectContext->SetComplete();
```

That's all the code required for the DeleteAuthor component, so compile it, and install it into the Authors MTS package, which should now contain 4 components:

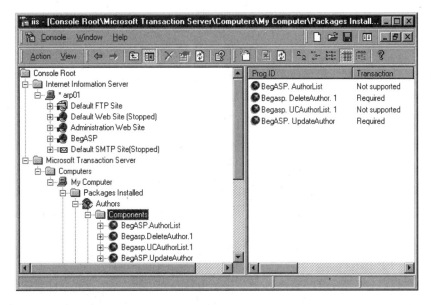

Note that the DeleteAuthor component transactional setting should be set to Required. This will have been done automatically by the IDL change made earlier.

Doing a Delete

Because the DeleteAuthor component is data centric and environment neutral it doesn't access the ASP object model. Consequently, the delete_author.asp ASP page for the UI is slightly larger because it contains all the HTML for the page. The basic structure for the ASP is the same as the update_author.asp page we saw in chapter 7, so I've highlighted the main differences and won't discuss it any further:

```
<%@TRANSACTION=REQUIRED%>

<HTML>
<HEAD>
<TITLE>Delete Author</TITLE>
<STYLE TYPE="text/css">
    BODY {font-family:Veranda,Tahoma,Arial,sans-serif; font-size:10pt}
    TD {font-family:Veranda,Tahoma,Arial,sans-serif; font-size:10pt}
</STYLE>
<BODY BGCOLOR=WHITE>

<H1>Delete Author</H1>
<HR>
```

```
<P>Time Before Query Start : <%=now%></P>
<%
   set oDeleteAuthor = Server.CreateObject("Begasp.DeleteAuthor")
   oDeleteAuthor.Delete Request.QueryString("au_id")
   set oDeleteAuthor = Nothing
%>
<P>Time After Query Start : <%=now%></P>

</FORM>
</BODY>
</HTML>

<%

' Called if the transaction succeeds

Sub OnTransactionCommit()
   Response.Write "<hr />"
   Response.Write "<p><strong>Transaction Committed - Author Deleted</strong></p>"
   Response.Write "<p><a href='delete_authors.asp'>Back to author list</a></p>"
End Sub

' Called if the transaction fails

Sub OnTransactionAbort()
   Response.Write "<hr />"
   Response.Write "<p><strong>Transaction Aborted - Deletion Failed</strong></p>"
   Response.Write "<p><a href='delete_authors.asp'>Back to author list</a></p>"
End Sub

%>
```

Now we've got the deletion component installed into MTS, and the ASP page has been created, we can happily delete authors by pressing the **Delete** button from the delete_authors.asp page. When you do press the **Delete** button you'll see the delete confirmation screen appear shortly afterwards:

If you delete an author, use the back to author list hyperlink to review to the complete author list. You should see the author you selected has disappeared!

Sometime you have to refresh the author list because SQL Server doesn't immediately make the changes available.

To prove that the MTS transaction really works across an ASP and two database tables you can change the `DeleteAuthor` method to call `SetAbort()` rather than `SetComplete()`. By doing this, no matter what you do the author information will never be deleted, and the delete author ASP will tell you the transaction has failed. If you make the changes and the authors are still deleted, you've made one of two mistakes:

❑ Not called `OpenWithServiceComponent()` in the components `OpenDataSource()` method. This will result in the deletions occurring outside of the transaction.

❑ Forgotten to refresh the MTS catalog when you recompiled the component.

I can't help you with the first problem, but I can alleviate the second problem by automating the catalog refresh.

Tip—Automatically Refreshing the MTS Catalog

As we discussed in the early MTS chapters the MTS catalog is not integrated within the COM registry. This means you have to refresh MTS each time you recompile an MTS hosted component so MTS can manipulate the registry entries from the component, redirecting its creation via `MTX.EXE` or `MTXEX.DLL` depending upon the package type.

Because re-registering your components is easy to forget you should automate the process using a post build command—`MTXREREG.EXE`.

To automate the process, bring up the project settings and add the following command in the Post-build step tab:

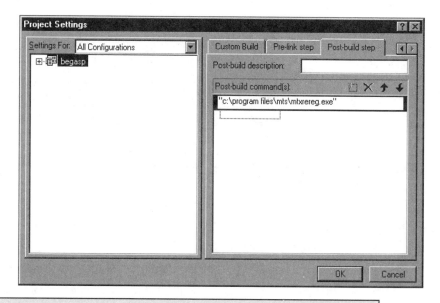

Note that I have specified double quotes around the command, which *are* needed.

Once you've added this command, you should notice an extra step appearing in the output window when you next compile:

```
Output                                                                    ×
----------------------Configuration: begasp - Win32 Debug----------------
Compiling...
UCAuthorList.cpp
Linking...
LINK : warning LNK4076: invalid incremental status file "Debug/begasp.ilk";
    Creating library Debug/begasp.lib and object Debug/begasp.exp
Performing registration
RegSvr32: DllRegisterServer in .\Debug\begasp.dll succeeded.
Creating browse info file...
Mtxrereg: Refreshing all locally registered Mtx components...
         Done: All Mtx components were refreshed.

◄ ► \ Build ⟨ Debug ⟩ Find in Files 1 ⟩ Find in Files 2 ⟩ Results ⟩ SQL Debugging ⟨    ◄┃ ►
```

MTXSTOP

Whilst on the subject of MTS utility programs, if you want to shut down all MTS packages in an automated fashion you can use the MTXSTOP command. This can be run from a command line as shown in the figure below, but unfortunately it is an asynchronous command, so the shutdown of all packages could complete some time after the program finishes execution. This makes it a but unreliable if you use it as pre-link option inside of Visual C++, to enable you to always compile a DLL that would otherwise be in use by an MTS package/process.

This MTXSTOP command is great on a development machine, but remember to use it carefully on any production machines.

```
Command Prompt                                                    _ □ ×

C:\>mtxstop
Mtxstop: Stopping all application server processes...

C:\>_
```

Debugging ASP Components

No matter how good you think your code is, there will always be a time when something very strange happens and you'll need to debug it whilst running under IIS4 and MTS. As we've discussed, often you'll find a component works fine outside of an ASP and IIS, but use it inside and strange things start happening, like security checks!

Debugging MTS hosted components isn't that difficult to do once you've got the right steps, but getting those steps right in the first place can be a real struggle. The main challenge is making sure the VC debugger is correctly set up so that it attaches to the executable and loads the component.

Debugging with Visual Studio is made a lot simpler when you can specify an executable to launch that you know will load your component. We know that IIS uses MTS to perform its process isolation, so all we have to do is make Visual Studio launch that surrogate process/package (MTX.EXE).

Step 1—Use an Isolation Process

The first step is to configure the web site or virtual directory to run in its own process space. Bring up the properties for the entry in the MMC, select the **Home Directory** tab and check the **Run in separate memory space (isolated process)** option:

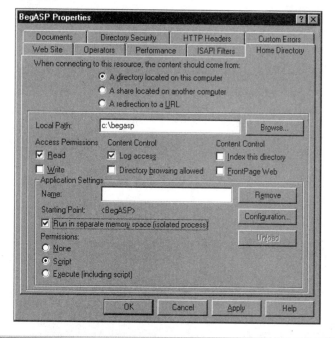

When this option is selected a new MTS package will be created. For this web site (called **BegASP**) we see the `IIS-{BegASP//Root}` package is created:

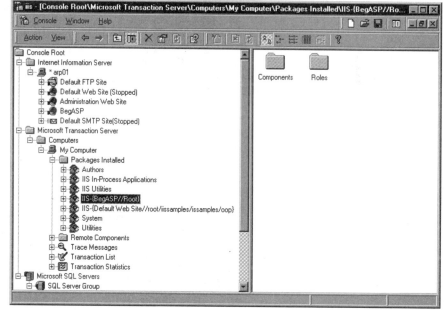

By selecting this option IIS will create an instance of `MTX.EXE` to provide the process isolation for the site, and all components created using `Server.CreateObject` will be created inside of this process space, provided they are defined to run in their own server package. That would of course launch another instance of `MTX.EXE`.

Step 2—Change the IIS/MTS Package Security Credentials

When IIS automatically creates an MTS package to provide process isolation it uses the identity `IWAM_MachineName`, as shown in the following screen:

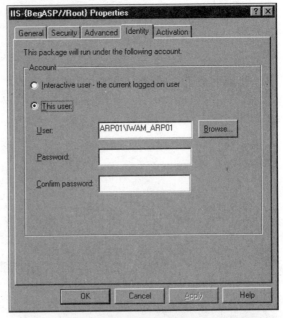

My machine is called `ARP01`, so the identity is `IWAM_ARP01`. The `ARP01\` prefix is simply the Windows NT domain name.

For the Visual Studio debugger to work, we have to change this identity to be the interactive user. Debugging across WinStations doesn't work, as we've already noted. If you forget to change this then the debugger will exit prematurely and you won't be told why. As a general rule check for this in the event log. For this problem you'd see the following entry:

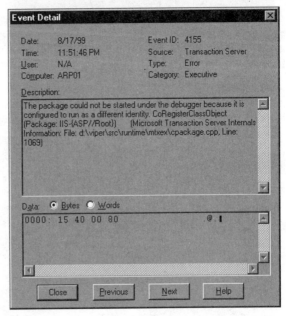

Change the account to be the Interactive User, press OK and ignore the following message box you'll be prompted with:

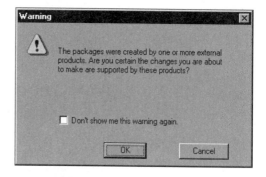

This message is warning you that the package is automatically managed by another application, in this case IIS. You can safely ignore this warning when changing the user identity, so check the Don't show me this warning again option.

You should never add your own components to an IIS managed package. The configuration will be lost if your change the web site configuration in IIS.

Step 3—Only for MTS Hosted Components

If the component you wish to debug is hosted in MTS make sure the Package activation type is set to Library Package:

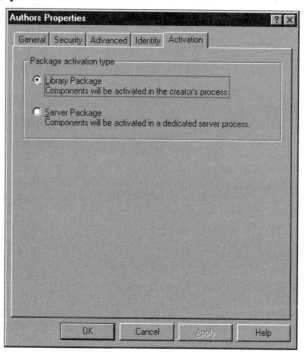

If you don't do this and leave the option set to Server Package two copies of MTX.EXE will be launched:

❑ One for IIS and any non-hosted MTS component

❑ One for hosting the MTS based components

You could launch two copies of Visual Studio using the techniques we'll discuss, but for now make sure the option is set to library.

Step 4—Make Sure the Web Site Isn't Running

Right click on the web site or virtual directory and from the home directory tab press the Unload button if it is enabled:

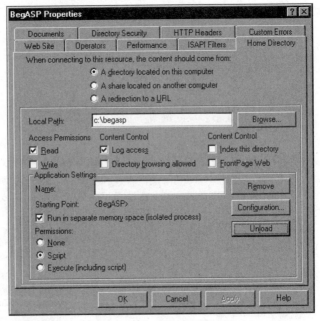

Pressing the Unload button will cleanly shutdown any running instances of MTX.EXE. If this is left running and you try debugging it you'll just get an error in the event log and then debugger will stop. If you forcibly shutdown the MTS package by using the package shutdown option from the MTS explorer, you'll invalidate the proxy/interface IIS has to the package. This results in IIS making an internal note of the error. Once a certain number of these errors have occurred, IIS will not service any more URL requests, and will display the unhelpful message "Error 500 - Internal Server Error". Translated, this error means reboot!

Step 5—Setting the Debugger Option

Now that we've set the groundwork outside of Visual Studio, we can load the project containing the component to be debugged.

Bring up the project settings and select the Debug tab. Change the executable for debug session to be:

```
C:\WINNT\SYSTEM32\MTX.EXE
```

Change this path depending upon the location of your Windows system directory location.

To get MTX.EXE to load a specific package we use the /P command in conjunction with the package's unique GUID. To determine the GUID assigned to a package bring up the properties of the package:

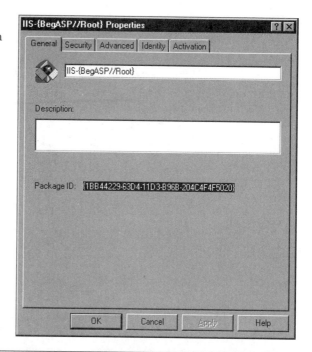

Select the GUID and then paste it into the program argument fields, prefixing it with "/P:", as shown here:

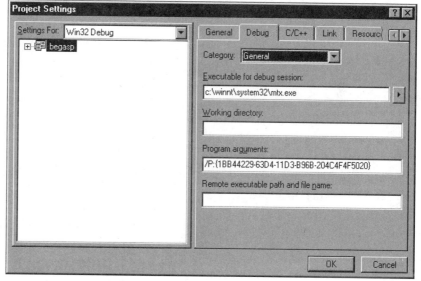

Running the Debugger

That's it, you're ready to go. Provided you've followed these steps carefully and not skipped any, you can set break points in your components' code and the debugger will break as expected:

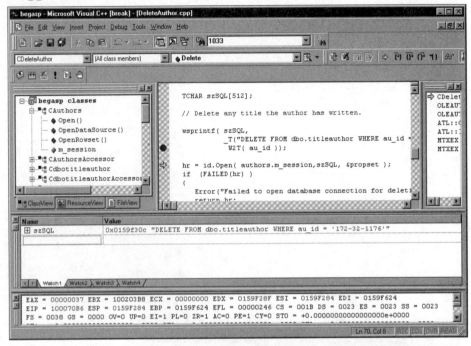

If you find your breakpoints aren't working, or you start the debugger and it just returns within a few seconds, double/triple check each step I've described, and check the event log for helpful messages from the MTS executive. If you change the web site or virtual directory settings in IIS your manual changes to the MTS package configuration may get overridden, so remember to pay special attention to the identity tab if your debugging stops working.

As a final note, remember that a transaction has a default timeout of 60 seconds. If your debugging is likely to take longer than this time, you can increase the duration for all packages by bringing up the properties for My Computer in the MTS explorer:

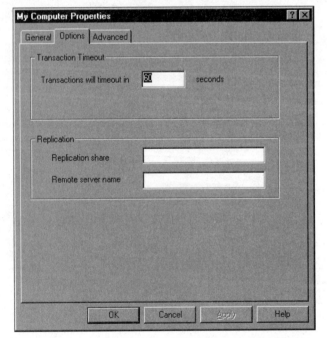

You'll probably want to reset this to 60 seconds when you've finished debugging.

Debugging VB code

As well as being able to debug C++ components the Visual Studio IDE can also debug VB components in an identical fashion. To enable this you have to create the PDB files for your VB components, by checking the **Create Symbolic Debug Info** option located on the project settings:

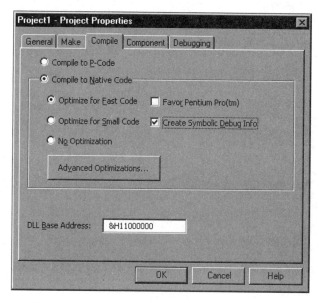

You can load VB code and set break points just like you can with VC++ code.

Summary

The main focus of this chapter has been using C++ to create MTS hosted components that are transactional.

We started by looking at how to access the ASP objects using named properties exposed by the object context using the IGetContextProperties, and said that this should be used in preference to the scripting context.

We then used the ASP Request and Response objects to perform a simply dump of input parameters.

Next, we implemented the UCAuthorList and DeleteAuthor components. These both used OLE DB, and we saw how the default Wizard generated code has to be changed for transactions to work.

Finally, we took a brief look at how we can debug C++ components that are used by IIS. We'll refer back to this knowledge in Chapter 17 when we create a cinema booking system.

Document Management
Case Study—Part 1

One of the most exciting new language technologies to hit the Web development arena is **Extensible Markup Language** (or **XML**). XML has been closely followed by a number of associated developments such as the **Extensible Stylesheet Language** (**XSL**). Together, they are providing us with a whole new set of emerging possibilities for handling information on a multi-platform network like the Internet.

We don't intend to spend a lot of time in this case study describing the basics of XML or the current language standards and related proposals. Instead, we'll have a look at one approach to using components when working with text-based information such as XML and HTML.

The case study is split over two chapters, and will demonstrate how we can use XML as a core part of an application. As a result you should get some ideas as to how you might use similar techniques in your own working environment. We'll look at how we can automate the storage and retrieval of information that is held in text files on disk, and at the same time provide index and search information to allow users to look up information in a number of ways. By the end of the next chapter we will have an application that indexes and searches text files, which we will call the **Text File Indexed Storage System**. To implement this system, we'll be using a two custom components: one that will provide read/write access to the content of text-based HTML and XML files; the other for interacting with a database, both exposing its contents and receiving updates in XML. We'll also be using a component that is part of the standard Internet Explorer 5 installation, although there is also a standalone version available that is free to download, and we will use it on the server instead of the client.

In this first chapter of two, we'll start with a look at some of the basic issues that are involved with text-based information storage, and the problems that are immediately obvious. After that, we'll cover the design of our application, and the design and creation of the two main custom components. In the next chapter, we'll look at how we can use these components as part of our application.

So, the plan for this chapter is to look at:

- ❏ How and why we might use text-based information storage and how to manage it
- ❏ How we might use components to automate tasks in managing text-based information
- ❏ How we can build task-specific components to help with XML-based tasks
- ❏ How we design the complete application, and plan the components we'll need
- ❏ How we build the components, and test them in simple VB applications

So, to start off, let's think about why we might want to use text-based storage techniques anyway.

Why Use Text-based Information Storage?

The first question to ask is, "Why should we consider using text-based storage anyway?" After all, the industry has spent many years perfecting the relational database, and modern database systems are highly efficient at storing all kinds of information. Why bother with old-fashioned methods that imply the need for serial access and slow disk-based contiguous file reads, when data can be fetched and cached automatically by SQL Server, Oracle, Informix or DB2?

One answer is that we probably *already* keep most of our real 'business information' in text-based files, or files that can easily be converted into plain text. At present, these are likely to be HTML pages and special formats like Microsoft Word and other word-processor formats. We may have PowerPoint and Excel files as well. However, in the future (so we keep hearing) we'll all be using XML to store our information instead. Almost all of the modern business and office applications can save their data in HTML format now, and certainly most will have both HTML and XML 'Save As' options soon.

In other words, it's likely that most of our business **information** (such as quotations, letters and product documentation)—as opposed to traditional business **data** such as the sales figures and customer lists stored in a relational database system—can be (or is already) stored as a text file of some type. So we need to find some techniques that can help us keep track of this information, in particular we need to automate and manage some kind of indexing and search facility that allows us to find and retrieve information from these text-based files.

Did Somebody Mention XML?

If you were concentrating during the last few paragraphs, you'll have noticed that we sneaked a reference to XML in there. It's a fair bet that almost everybody connected with the IT industry, in any way at all, has heard of XML. But do you know much about it? Do you know what it is and, more importantly, what it can do?

Extensible Markup Language is an initiative that finally reached a standard at the World Wide Web Consortium (W3C) in February 1998. While XML is strongly related to our old favorite HTML, and looks very similar in terms of the syntax and format, it is actually quite different. XML is defined a lot more strictly than HTML in terms of syntax, and yet it has no intrinsic 'meaning' in the way that HTML does.

The 'Meaning' of HTML and XML

When we talk about HTML as having a 'meaning', we are referring to the way that certain elements (which are predefined in HTML) can be used to achieve a certain fixed effect. For example, a <TABLE> element in HTML always means a section of rows and columns in the page. By enclosing a series of <TR>, <TH> and <TD> elements within the <TABLE> element, we can construct a table. OK, so it won't look exactly the same in every browser, but the overall effect is likely to be very similar.

In XML, there is no pre-defined meaning for any element other than certain **processing instructions** (which we meet in a moment). We can make up our own tags to mean what we want them to mean. So, we can quite legally create an XML construct using a <TABLE> element, which will have a completely different meaning:

```
<?xml version="1.0" ?>
<TABLE>
  <SHAPE>Oval</SHAPE>
  <NUMBER_OF_LEGS>4</NUMBER_OF_LEGS>
  <FINISH>African Walnut</FINISH>
</TABLE>
```

The first line here is called a processing instruction; this is a special one saying that the document is an XML document. Of course, the big question is, "What happens when I load this page into a browser?" The answer depends on one thing—does the browser know what to do with a <TABLE> element? If it is a special browser that has been custom built to display furniture details then it might automatically give us a picture of an appropriate dining table—it may even be decorated with a few silver candlesticks, crystal glasses and surrounded by contented diners! However, if it's just Internet Explorer or Netscape Navigator, then the chances are we'll get something less useful—because these browsers are only designed to style and format known tags in HTML. Here is what we would see if we loaded this simple XML document into Internet Explorer 5:

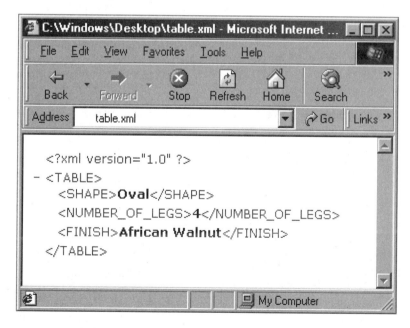

Now, if there was a standard way of defining furniture, the furniture manufacturers and retailers may decide to get together and create a language for marking up furniture descriptions using XML. They would have created an **application** of XML (i.e. an application of the language) that is specific to their own requirements, and standardized across their industry. And once that's been done, software companies can easily build programs that work with this new furniture description language, perhaps a *Chaise-Long Explorer* or a *Coffee-table Navigator*.

The reason why this is so important is because HTML has become a language for how to display data on the Web, while XML is just a method of marking up data, so that the data is self-describing. An XML document contains no rules for how the document should be displayed, these are kept in a separate style sheet. And because the XML file is self-describing data, it can be used for several different purposes—not just for display in a web browser.

XML as a Display Mechanism

Hopefully, the preceding section has made you think about the core reason why XML is basically different to HTML—the fact that it has no intrinsic meaning until someone (or some group of people) applies specific meanings to suit their own circumstances. This freedom provides us with all kinds of ways to use XML, boosted by the fact that it is independent of all the platforms and implementations that can make HTML so difficult to work with.

> When it comes to displaying your XML in a browser, you can either use Cascading Style Sheets (the same ones that are used in HTML), or XSL—Extensible Stylesheet Language.

XML is also the solution to more fundamental problems than just displaying data on a web page, such as:

❑ How do we move information around complex networks like the Internet?

❑ How do we store data in multi-platform environments and on different operating systems?

After all, if we can get the storage and transport of the information right, we can display it afterwards in any way we like. We can build platform-specific display tools that all understand the same dialect of XML and display it in the correct format. And in fact, everyone can display it differently if that's appropriate, as long as they can understand what it actually **means**.

Using XML for Storage and Data Transport

So, I can use XML to produce a list of things, for example I can create tags to store information about each of the music CDs in my collection:

```
<CD_LIBRARY>
  <COMPACT_DISK>
    <TITLE> Songs About XML </TITLE>
    <ARTIST>The Wrox Choir</ARTIST>
    <TRACKLIST>
      <TRACK>
        <NUMBER>1</NUMBER>
        <SONG_TITLE>It's So Elementary</SONG_TITLE>
      </TRACK>
```

```
        <TRACK>
          <NUMBER>2</NUMBER>
          <SONG_TITLE>Let's Play Tag</SONG_TITLE>
        </TRACK>
        ...
        ... other tracks here
        ...
        <TRACK>
          <NUMBER>14</NUMBER>
          <SONG_TITLE>What Is The Meaning</SONG_TITLE>
        </TRACK>
      </TRACKLIST>
    </COMPACT_DISK>
    ...
    ... other disks here
    ...
</CD_LIBRARY>
```

Here it is easy to see what each element means, and I can make sense of the information. So, when my friends want to borrow a CD, they can check to see if I own a copy of it. All they need is my XML CD list—as long as they know what each element means and how the elements are structured. In fact, we can each provide a list of our own CDs, so that we can swap and share them around more easily.

> Note that in XML all tags must either have a corresponding closing tag
> `<COMPACT_DISK>` `</COMPACT_DISK>`, or must have a closing slash at the end of the
> tag `<COMPACT_DISK/>`.

So, XML provides us with a format for information to be stored in. Furthermore, it is pure text so we can easily send it across a network in this simple format, and we can be sure that all systems will be able to read it irrespective of the platform, operating system, network transport protocol or other software that they use. All we need to do is provide each user of the information with the meaning of each element, and they will be able to use it.

Learning About XML

This has been a simplistic and rudimentary look at XML, it is only aimed at ensuring that you understand the main principles and objectives of using it to store information. In this case study, we're using it purely in that form, together with some task-specific display formatting that you'll meet in the next chapter.

But, as you can probably guess, there is a lot more to XML that you should consider learning about. XML is set to become a key part of many future developments in computing, including data transport, presentation, storage, and other situations. It's likely that we'll see most new applications (including databases, office applications, and other tools) moving towards using and supporting it. Already it's a big part of Oracle 8i, Microsoft Office 2000 and Internet Explorer 5.

Wrox has produced several books aimed at different aspects of XML, including:
IE5 XML Programmer's Reference (ISBN 1-861001-57-6)
Professional XML (ISBN 1-861003-11-0)
XML Design and Implementation (ISBN 1-861002-28-9)
Designing Distributed Applications with XML and ASP (ISBN 1-861002-27-0)

Storing and Retrieving XML

XML is a resolutely text-based format for holding information, which makes it difficult to know the best way to physically store it on our servers. We could use the text-type fields of a database system, which would give easy access to each block of text. We could also add fields (that indicate the attributes of the information, such as a title, a description, or a set of keywords) to each record. We could even provide separate indexes for the information, in another table or file of some type.

However, this destroys the one aspect of the information that we've already found to be key—the fact that it is pure text means that it is easily transportable between disparate systems and platforms. Once we convert it into fields in a database, can we be sure that it is going to be as freely accessible and available? What if we have to change some of the information to fit into relational database structures, or break it into sections to meet database-specific limitations? How do we get it back into text format again, and can we do it without changing anything within it?

One solution would be to leave it stored as text files on disk, we could easily copy it from one place to another over a network. And if we ensure that we only use the standard 7-bit ASCII character set, we can send it across the Internet as it stands, with no need for translation into an intermediate format. In other words, there's no chance of it being changed accidentally as it crosses the boundaries between our disparate platforms and operating systems.

Working With Text Files

Once we move to a pure text-based information storage paradigm, we have to do some serious rethinking about how we are going to actually work with the information. The simple relational database access techniques that we are so used to using will no longer work, and we have to look at alternatives. As you have probably already guessed, we're going to provide these alternatives as server-based components.

Text files are very easy to access, but suffer from a couple of major problems:

❑ They often have little or no concrete structure, when compared to the rigid structure that is forced upon us by a database system.

❑ We can usually only access them in serial form, i.e. we start at the beginning and read data until we find what we want. So, how can we tackle these problems?

Structuring Text File Information

If our text information is in a format that *does* provide structure (or even better, a format that demands structure) then we solve the first problem immediately. Unfortunately, HTML is not ideal for forcing structure upon the user. In theory, the heading elements <H1> to <H6> indicate a natural hierarchy within an HTML document, but we all know that this tends to fall by the wayside. The current use of many different formatting techniques generally destroys the intrinsic structure of an HTML page, where an <H1> header is supposed to be the primary header, and so on.

XML is a more obvious candidate, as it forces a more strict use of structure (called **well-formedness**). Also, the fact that each element means exactly what the group of users wants it to mean permits structure to be defined very closely. As an example, if we were displaying our CD collection with HTML, we might use something like:

```
<DIV><FONT FACE="Fantasy" SIZE="16">My CD Library</FONT></DIV>
<DIV><FONT FACE="Arial" SIZE="12">
Title: <B>Songs About XML</B> by <B>The Wrox Choir</B><P>
<OL>
<LI> It's So Elementary </LI>
<LI>Let's Play Tag</LI>
...
... other tracks here
...
<LI>What Is The Meaning</LI>
</OL></DIV>
<HR>
...
... other disks here
...
<A HREF="mailto:me@myaddress.com">Contact me</A>
```

If you compare this with the XML version we looked at earlier, you can see that XML can provide a huge advantage as far as structuring the information is concerned.

Using Serial File Access

What about our second problem with text files—the limitations of serial file access? It's a problem that we can't solve easily. It is especially apparent if the files are large, and we need information that is stored near the end of the file.

We can help by keeping the size of our data files down to the minimum, and by using several smaller files instead of one large file. So long as we can properly index the contents (a task we're going to accomplish in this case study), several small files will be more efficient anyway. Also modern disk caching technologies, and super-fast disks with read-ahead buffers make text-file access faster than it has ever been. In any case, the Web depends on servers reading text files (i.e. HTML pages) from disk or disk cache all the time—so why are we worrying?

In fact, the problems we've just been discussing are part of the driving force behind an ongoing development in XML, such as XLink, XPointer and XML Fragment Interchange. For some time the W3C have seen that making a text-based information system more efficient requires a new way of accessing text files. It needs to be done without having to read the whole file from disk, and without sending it all across a network for users to search out the information they want in the file. So, what are these advancements?

Text File Access Techniques and Components

Although we will not be using the techniques mentioned in the following section during this case study, they are good background to see what we will be doing. One proposal for a way of accessing text files efficiently, aimed particularly at XML files, is called **X-Pointer**. It is a specification, still in development, for specifying parts of an XML-format document that are to be the targets for links, in much the same way that we currently use the <A> element to identify a target anchor within an HTML page. For example, in a traditional HTML page, the following link:

```
...
<A HREF="chapter03.html#chap03">Jump to Chapter 3</A>
...
```

would jump to the following anchor point in a page named chapter03.html:

```
...
<A NAME="chap03"><H1>Chapter 3</H1></A>
...
```

Extracting Sections of a Text File

X-Pointer (together with the associated new linking language, called **XLink**—XML Linking Language) provides several ways that the page author can specify the location(s) in the target document that a link points to—and it does this in a much more generic and flexible way than HTML. It might be by physical position, by element name, or by logical document section. And, even better, it will enable just one block of text content to be sent over the network to the requestor—rather than the whole page, as is the case with the HTML technique. Our first component will implement a similar technique to access our text files.

Transferring Text Data

We'll also be using a second custom component to help us work with text when it is structured data held in a relational database rather than unstructured information in a text-based file. If we have such data that *is* stored in a normal relational database, we often have to transfer it across a network for display or when it needs updating. In a disparate platform and operating system environment, the obvious format for transferring this data is as plain text. Or, even better, how about XML?

Sending data from one place to another as XML is easy enough. After all it is only text, so any client or server should be able to handle it correctly. If we wrap our information up using XML elements, we can send it from one place to another as though it were a recordset:

```
<RECORDSET>
  <RECORD>
    <CUST_ID>MART03</CUST_ID>
    <CUST_NAME>Martins Stores</CUST_NAME>
    <CUST_ADDR>1429 East Central Street</CUST_ADDR>
    <CUST_TOWN>Chicago</CUST_TOWN>
    <CUST_STATE>IL</CUST_STATE>
  </RECORD>
  <RECORD>
    <CUST_ID>HANK17</CUST_ID>
    <CUST_NAME>Hank Smith Industries</CUST_NAME>
    <CUST_ADDR>Uptown Forge</CUST_ADDR>
    <CUST_TOWN>Los Angeles</CUST_TOWN>
    <CUST_STATE>CA</CUST_STATE>
  </RECORD>
...
... other records here
...
</RECORDSET>
```

Creating this text format from a database using ASP is easy enough, though a component that executes compiled code would be more efficient. When we come to update the original data, however, things are a little more complicated. We can send back a similarly structured XML file containing the updates required, but then we have to parse the file on the server and apply the changes to the original records. This requires some intensive processing, so it is an ideal task for a component.

The Text File Indexed Storage System Case Study

Having seen a number of situations where we are already using text based storage, and also having identified new areas where we will be using text based storage, we will need a way of managing this information so that we know what is in each file. To help us keep track of the information stored in these text files, the next two chapters will provide an application for cataloging the contents of them. This may involve indexing more than one part of the file, so that we can provide details of different areas within a file, such as what is contained in the sub headings. In the case study we will come across three components: two of which we shall build, and one that is free for download.

At the end of the exercise we will be able to generate indexes for the HTML and XML files we have on our server, which provide hyperlinks directly to each section of the content. As the following screen shot of an index shows, we are gathering three things: a heading, some keywords and a sample of the content (of course, your final index will probably be a lot longer).

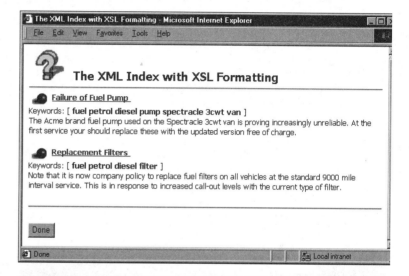

In addition we will also be able to search the text files:

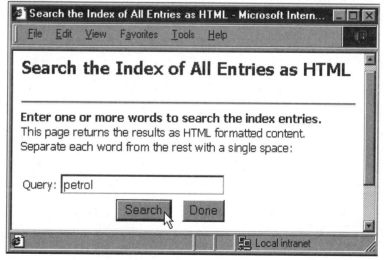

Application Requirements

In order to achieve the aims of the case study, we need to be able to do two things:

❑   Specify the parts of the text documents that we want to index, the header, keywords and sample content, and then copy them into a database

❑   Insert text as pointers into the part of the original file that is indexed so that we can go directly to the relevant section

So, let's see how we achieve these two tasks.

Collecting Index Information

All of the index entries will be stored in a database. So, we will obviously need a way to specify which parts of the text files to index, so that we can copy that information into the database. In order to determine this we must ask what we want to store and index. For a start, we will be indexing a heading for the section, any keywords (where possible) within a specified pair of tags, and an extract of the content. To do this we will allow the user to provide six items of information:

❑   The path of the file to index

❑   The name of the file to index

❑   The heading element, to index as the topic heading

❑   The keywords element

❑   Start of content element

❑   End of content Element

Users can provide this information using this screen:

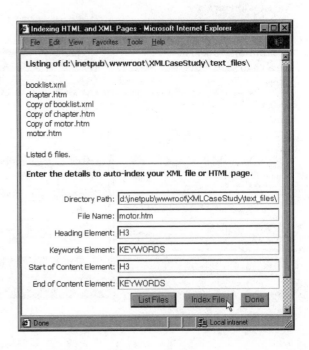

So, in this example the text between the <H3> headings will be treated as the heading to display in the index, the text between the <KEYWORDS> tags will be stored as the keywords related to the item, and the sample of content will be the text kept between the closing <H3> and opening <KEYWORDS> tags. We will also be storing the name and path of the file, along with the entry we will be adding into the HTML or XML file so that we can directly access the appropriate section (which is very similar to the HTML <A> anchor element).

Inserting Specific Index Points

At the same time that we copy content that we want to index into the database, we'll also write a marker into the actual text file we are indexing to identify the point that each topic appears. This is what allows users to go directly to the appropriate part of the file from each link. We will be inserting an anchor element something like:

```
<A NAME="unique_anchor_name">The original topic heading here</A>
```

Of course, we will have to store this in the database with the text we have copied from the HTML and XML files, otherwise we would not know where to point the index entries to. Using a combination of the file path and the index point, users will be able to go directly to the right topic without scrolling.

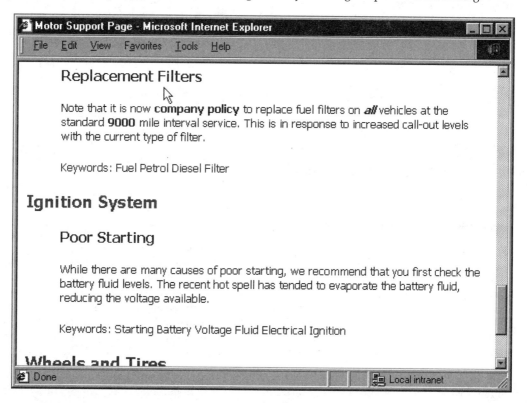

We will be writing our first component to handle the retrieval of this information from the text files and to insert anchor elements.

Using the Database Index Information

It is from the index data stored in a relational database that the index page and the search results will be generated. So, we need a way to retrieve the data from the database and update/enter it. And that is where our second component comes in; we will be building a component for our data access.

Searching the Indexed Data

As mentioned earlier, users will also be able to search the contents of the database of index entries. In order to achieve this we will remove the tags from the database content, allowing a full text search that will provide results that are uninhibited by existing formatting.

How It all Fits Together

The following diagram shows how the whole process fits together. The text files are processed to copy the index entries into the database. The database entries are then used to generate index list pages, and for searching (the search pages use the same process to format the search results as the index listing pages). All of the results pages are directly linked to the text files in the appropriate place.

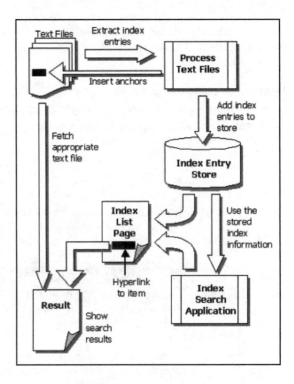

Will It Work With XML As Well?

Before we go off and start building stuff, let's just consider one problem area. Will the whole application work just the same with XML as it would with HTML? The answer is no. There are two areas where we need to adapt our design for use with XML.

First, when we use an `<A NAME="...">` anchor element in HTML it acts as a simple anchor for a hyperlink to directly access that section of the file. In XML, however, there are no tags set aside for things such as anchor elements. In other words, we can't just scroll to that point in the page using an `<A HREF="#...">` hyperlink. As we saw, XML tags mean whatever you want them to. In order for it to become an anchor element, we would have to supply a role for the element using an XPointer. However it is not yet a standard (you have to remember that XML is still young and that it will take some time for XML's related standards to fully mature). We'll come back to addressing this problem at the end of the next chapter. For now, we'll just insert the anchor elements as we do for HTML.

Second, we need to think about how we are going to structure and display our index data. We could use either XML or HTML. Again, XML has no built in concept of hyperlinks, so producing links would probably be more difficult than using HTML. However, by using a separate XML-based language called **Extensible Stylesheet Language** (**XSL**), we can format the XML page in Internet Explorer 5 to include working hyperlinks.

In our example, we'll actually build parallel index and search pages—one set using HTML and one set using XML—so that you can see the different techniques. There are also several opportunities here to introduce more custom components, and we'll discuss these as we go along.

Other Application Requirements

To show you some other aspects of working with XML and components, we'll also incorporate a couple of other peripheral activities into the overall application. We'll provide a mechanism for editing the contents of the index entry table in the database, using XML as the data transfer protocol. This means that the client doing the actual editing could be on a different platform or operating system—one that doesn't support any of the proprietary data access technologies we are used to.

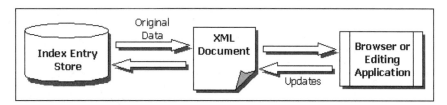

In the next part of this chapter we'll briefly look at another part of the application, and see how we can create the text files in the first place. Once we go down the route of text-based document and information management, we will probably want to integrate data from other sources into the system. One aspect of this is to convert data that is currently stored in a relational database into text-based form, and then process it through our document management system.

Dynamically Created Text Files

Converting relational database information into text file data could be a problem if the data also needs to stay in the database for other reasons, for example if it is used by several other applications. If we are not careful, we'll end up with data in the database and the text files getting out of sync unless we regularly keep updating the text files. Solutions include using either a component or raw ASP code to rewrite the text file on a regular basis:

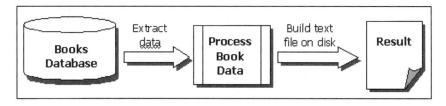

In ASP, we would create a new text file on disk (replacing any existing one with the same name) iterate through the data in the database, take the values from each field in each record and wrap them in XML. So let's see how this is done.

To show you how this works we have a list of book details in an Access database and we want to be able to create an XML version of these book details. So, we will use ASP to wrap the data from the database in XML tags and then write them into a text file on disk.

We first set the variables we'll need, create the new text file, and write into it the opening lines of our XML document (the setup instructions for the database we use are included with the sample files):

```
...
<%
'fill in with your connection string details
strConnect = "DRIVER={SQL Server};SERVER=___;DATABASE=___;UID=___;PW=___"

'fill in with your file path details
strFileName = "D:\InetPub\WWWRoot\XMLCaseStudy\xml_booklist.xml"

'create new file, overwriting any existing one
Set objFSO = CreateObject("Scripting.FileSystemObject")
Set objFile = objFSO.CreateTextFile(strFileName, True)

'write XML page headings to file
QUOT = Chr(34) 'double-quote character
strDate = Year(Now) & "-" & Right("00" & Month(Now), 2) & "-" _
        & Right("00" & Day(Now), 2)
objFile.WriteLine "<?xml version=" & QUOT & "1.0" & QUOT & " ?>"
objFile.WriteLine "<!-- Created " & QUOT & strDate & QUOT & " -->"
objFile.WriteLine "<BOOKLIST>" & CRLF
...
```

Then we create an ADO recordset containing the book details, and iterate through each record fetching the field values and creating the strings that we want for our XML file:

```
...
'select all the book details from database
Set oConn = Server.CreateObject("ADODB.Connection")
oConn.Open strConnect
strSQL="SELECT * FROM BookList ORDER BY kBookCode"
Set oRs = oConn.Execute(strSQL)
Do While Not oRs.EOF
  strBookCode = oRs("kBookCode")
  strISBN = "1-86100" & Left(strBookCode, 1) & "-" & Mid(strBookCode, 2, 2) _
          & "-" & Right(strBookCode, 1)
  datRelease = CDate(oRs("dReleaseDate"))
  strRelDate = Year(datRelease) & "-" & Right("00" & Month(datRelease), 2) _
          & "-" & Right("00" & Day(datRelease), 2)
  strKeywords = oRs("tKeywords")
  ...
```

Now we can write out to our text file the current XML record describing the book record in our database, then loop round to do the next record:

```
...
'write the details out to the file
objFile.WriteLine "<BOOKINFO>"
objFile.WriteLine "  <ISBN>" & strISBN & "</ISBN>"
objFile.WriteLine "  <BOOK_TITLE>" & oRs("tTitle") & "</BOOK_TITLE>"
objFile.WriteLine "  <RELEASE_DATE>" & strRelDate & "</RELEASE_DATE>"
objFile.WriteLine "  <DESCRIPTION>" & oRs("tDescription") & "</DESCRIPTION>"
objFile.WriteLine "  <KEYWORDS>" & oRs("tKeywords") & "</KEYWORDS>"
objFile.WriteLine "  <COVER_IMAGE_URL>http://webdev.wrox.co.uk/webdev/wd_images/" _
        & strBookCode & ".gif</COVER_IMAGE_URL>"
objFile.WriteLine "  <MORE_INFO_URL>http://www.wrox.co.uk/Store/Details.asp?Code=" _
        & strBookCode & "</MORE_INFO_URL>"
objFile.WriteLine "</BOOKINFO>" & CRLF
```

```
   oRs.MoveNext
   Response.Write "Done " & strISBN & "<BR>"
Loop
objFile.WriteLine "</BOOKLIST>"
oRs.Close
objFile.Close
%>
...
```

When we're all finished, we add the final closing XML document element, and close the text file. You'll find this sample page, named `make_booklist_xml.asp`, with the other sample files for this case study. The result is an XML file that looks like the next screenshot:

We can process this file on a regular basis, and keep it in our text file store, so that our users can search for information about the current books and always get the latest information.

The simple ASP code that we used above in the page `make_booklist_xml.asp` is ideally suited for conversion to an ActiveX DLL component that is specific just to this task—but that's a job for you to do when you've got some spare time on your hands.

The Components We'll Need

To get the initial parts of our Text File Indexed Storage System application working, we'll be using two custom components. The first provides a way to access our text-based documents to capture whatever sections of the information we need (in our example the heading, keywords and content), and at the same time insert anchor pointers into the file we are reading.

The second component will expose the database content as XML and accept XML to update database entries. The creation of the XML document uses a similar technique to that shown in the previous section, with XML as the transport protocol.

In the remainder of this chapter, we'll design, build and test these two components. These will form the backbone of the final application, which we'll be describing in more detail in the next chapter. The production of the index/content pages, the search pages, and the way we locate the original document again are topics that we'll be looking at there, once we have built the components that these pages rely upon. We will also show you how to set up the sample files at the start of the next chapter so that you can see how it all fits together while reading about the different pages that make up the application.

Designing and Building the Components

By now, you will have seen many components being built and so we won't be describing the process in detail. What we will look at is the way we implement the requirements of the application in the component, and the way that the code works to achieve the desired result. Much of the code is string handling (as you'd expect when handling text files), and is commented throughout so you should have no problem understanding it and adapting the components to your own requirements. The source code and compiled components can be downloaded with the rest of the samples for this book from http://webdev.wrox.co.uk/books/2882/.

Both of the components are cut-down versions of commercial components, which you can try by downloading the free evaluation versions from the Wrox Web Developer site. You can also read about them and download them from the Stonebroom Software site at http://www.stonebroom.com/.

The Text File Access Component (WX2882TX.dll)

This component is the simpler of the two, and is based on some reasonably simple string handling techniques. It's written using Visual Basic, and uses no other sub-components. It has a single class file named **XMLTX**. We've also provided a test application written in VB (Form1.frm), which is compiled into an application named Project1.exe.

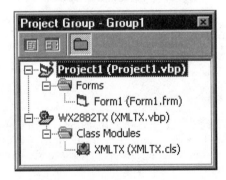

Designing the Interface

The first step is to think about what we want to achieve, and from that define the component's interface, which gets information into and out of the component. Firstly, the component will need to provide access to an HTML or XML text file, and collect the content from specific parts of that file. As we saw earlier, we need to collect the header, the keywords (if there are any), and an extract. The most obvious part is the content of a specific element, such as:

```
<H1>We will return this content</H1>
```

This will allow us to extract the heading for a topic, based on the element that the page author uses for each topic. Then, if the author has included a particular element that contains the topic keywords, we can use the same technique to return the keywords:

```
<KEYWORDS>We will return this content</KEYWORDS>
```

This won't work with the traditional `<META>` element that is placed in the `<HEAD>` section of an HTML document and used for document keywords in HTML because these don't have a closing tag—i.e. they don't conform to the correct syntax for XML. We'll have to depend on page authors to include them for us, or add them ourselves before we process the documents.

The other thing we want to find is an 'extract' or 'description' of the topic. If the author provides this in a separate element, we can use the same technique as with the heading and keywords. However, in most cases there will be no specific element holding a description, so we'll do something different. We'll return the content that is located between two different elements. For example, suppose the document contains this:

```
<H1>The first topic heading</H1>
<KEYWORDS>Keywords for the first topic</KEYWORDS>
This is the text of the first topic, and the part that we'll
extract to form the description of the topic.
<H1>The next topic heading</H1>
<KEYWORDS>Keywords for the next topic</KEYWORDS>
```

What we'll do is provide the opportunity to extract the text that lies between the end of the closing `</KEYWORDS>` element and the beginning of the next `<H1>` element. In other words, we'll allow the user to specify the 'start' and 'end' elements, and we'll extract all the content that lies in between these two elements.

The final piece of information we need is the instance number of the element that we're searching for. A document is likely to contain many instances of each heading and keywords element, so we'll allow the user to specify which instance they want. Notice that, for this to work, there must be the same number of keyword elements as there are heading elements, otherwise a read of, say, the fifth instance of a heading element and the fifth instance of a keywords element will return content that applies to two different topics.

All of this functionality will be exposed by one public method called `ReadContent()`.

Note that the components we are building here are designed to be generic, so that they can be used in different situations. While our component can accept an instance number, the application we are building will not give the user this option—it is just used internally.

589

XML documents should follow a strict structure; for example our CD list has the same elements for each CD instance, in the same order. In fact, XML often forces this to be the case when a structural definition (called a document type definition) is provided as part of the XML document. However, discussion of this whole topic is well beyond the space allowance we have in this book. You will find more information in the other XML-focused titles listed earlier.

While we are collecting the information from the text files to write into a database for the index, we will also need to write the anchor points into the files so that the users of the system can follow a link directly to the part of the file they are interested in. So, we will provide a second public method `WriteContent()` in our text file access component, which adds an anchor point into the source document.

The final public method, `FileListing()`, will list all of the files in a given folder. This is very useful so that we can see the names of the files available for index while running the application, and make sure that we have the correct file name and path for the file we want to index.

So, here are the three public methods:

Method	Description
ReadContent(DocumentName, StartElementName, StartInstance, EndElementName, MatchesFound)	Extracts the required text based on the parameters provided
WriteContent(NewContent, DocumentName, StartElementName, StartInstance, MatchesFound)	Adds the anchor pointer into the source document
FileListing(FileListRoot, FileSpecification, ListSeparator, MatchesFound)	Lists the files within a folder

The ReadContent() Method

This method will extract the required text based on the parameters provided:

```
Public Function ReadContent(ByVal DocumentName As String, _
                            ByVal StartElementName As String, _
                            Optional ByVal StartInstance As Integer = 1, _
                            Optional ByVal EndElementName As String = "", _
                            Optional MatchesFound As Variant = 0) _
                            As String
```

Here, we have parameters for the full path and name of the document to be processed, `DocumentName`, and the name of the element we want the content from, `StartElementName`. We also provide a parameter for the instance of this element in the document, `StartInstance`, and the name of the element to end at when we are extracting content from between two elements (rather than the content of a single element), `EndElementName`. All these are input parameters, and then there is a single optional in/out parameter that will—once the method returns—contain the number of times the component found matching element names. If the method succeeded and found our element(s) we'll use this parameter to return the number of matches found, otherwise we will return 0 if an element was not found, and –1 if there was an error (such as the document not being available).

The content of the element (if it was found) will be returned as the value of the method. In the simplest form, we can use the component's `ReadContent()` method in an ASP using VBScript like this, just providing the documents path and the element whose content we want to retrieve:

```
<%
Set objXMLTX = Server.CreateObject("Prog_ID")
strDocument = "c:\mydocs\thisone.htm"
strElement = "H1"
Response.Write objXMLTX.ReadContent(strDocument, strElement)
%>
```

If there is an error or no match, our component will return an error message. And if all goes well, the code shown here will return the content of the first `<H1>...</H1>` element in the document, because the default value for the element instance number is 1. Alternatively, we could return the content between the end of the third `<H3>` element and the start of the next `<CENTER>` element, and monitor the number of matches by specifying the following parameters in our ASP code:

```
<%
Set objXMLTX = Server.CreateObject("Prog_ID")
strDocument = "c:\mydocs\thisone.htm"
strStartElement = "H3"
strEndElement = "CENTER"
intInstance = 3
Dim intMatchesFound  'to hold count of matches
strContent = objXMLTX.ReadContent(strDocument, strStartElement, _
                    intInstance, strEndElement, intMatchesFound)
If intMatchesFound > 0 Then
   Response.Write "Content of element(s) is: " & strContent
ElseIf intMatchesFound = 0 Then
   Response.Write "No matching element(s) found."
Else
   Response.Write "Error accessing document: " & strDocument
End If
%>
```

And, of course, these examples will work equally well with an XML document, which is likely to have a more strictly controlled structure anyway.

The WriteContent() Method

Retrieving content is only part of the task. We also need to be able to insert new content into our text documents to create the target anchor elements. However, in this case, we don't need to worry about content between different elements, only updating the content of a single element by adding the anchor tag inside it. So, our second method looks like this:

```
Public Function WriteContent(ByVal NewContent As String, _
                    ByVal DocumentName As String, _
                    ByVal StartElementName As String, _
                    Optional ByVal StartInstance As Integer = 1, _
                    Optional MatchesFound As Variant = 0) _
                    As String
```

The `DocumentName`, `StartElementName`, `StartInstance` and `MatchesFound` parameters are the same as in the `ReadContent()` method. We don't need an `EndElementName` parameter this time as we are inserting the text into the start element, but we do need a parameter, `NewContent`, to contain the new content that we'll insert into the element, replacing the existing content. We'll also use the value of the function to return the original content of the element, or an error message if it wasn't found or an error occurred:

```
<%
Set objXMLTX = Server.CreateObject("Prog_ID")
strDocument = "c:\mydocs\thisone.htm"
strStartElement = "H1"
intInstance = 3
Dim intMatchesFound    'to hold count of matches
strNewContent = "This is the replacement text"
strOldContent = objXMLTX.WriteContent(strNewContent, strDocument, _
                         strStartElement, intInstance, intMatchesFound)
If intMatchesFound > 0 Then
    Response.Write "Previous Content was: " & strOldContent
ElseIf intMatchesFound = 0 Then
    Response.Write "No matching element found."
Else
    Response.Write "Error accessing document: " & strContent
End If
%>
```

The FileListing() Method

Because we're accessing text document files, one thing that will be useful is a way of listing the files in a folder on disk, so as to help establish the full and correct filename of the document required. We have included a simple file listing method in the component, which can return the full file listing of a directory as a string. It allows the user to select files based on a DOS file specification pattern (such as `"*.xml"`), and also permits the use of custom list separator characters:

```
Public Function FileListing(ByVal FileListRoot As String, _
             Optional ByVal FileSpecification As String = "*.*", _
             Optional ByVal ListSeparator As String = "<BR>" & vbCrLf, _
             Optional MatchesFound As Variant = 0) As String
```

The following ASP VBScript code could, for example, be used to build an HTML `<SELECT>` list showing just the XML files in a specific folder on the server:

```
<%
Set objXMLTX = Server.CreateObject("class_string")
Dim intMatchesFound    'to hold count of matches
strFolder = "c:\mydocs\"
strFileSpec = "*.xml"
strListSeparator = "<OPTION>"
strFileList = objXMLTX.FileListing(strFolder, strFileSpec, _
                         strListSeparator, intMatchesFound)
%>

<SELECT>
<% = strFileList %>
</SELECT>
...
```

Having seen the interface that we have to provide for our component, we'll move on to look at how the methods in this interface are implemented in code.

Implementing the Component

We won't be listing each method in its entirety, mainly because we don't expect you to type them in yourself. All the source code is provided with the samples for this book, which you can download from http://webdev.wrox.co.uk/books/2882/.

In addition to the public functions we have just seen, which implement the interface, we also have a number of private methods, which we shall meet after going through ReadContent() and WriteContent().

The ReadContent() Method

The ReadContent() method starts with assignment of the parameter values to local internal variables, so that they can be used more efficiently and to prevent any errors in our code attempting to update the original parameter values. Then we execute two Private functions that we define elsewhere within our component: ValidateInputs() and SearchFile().

The first of these, ValidateInputs(), checks that the parameters all contain legal values, and then it opens the source document text file. The file number is returned from this function in the intFileInput parameter (this number comes from using the VB FreeFile() function in the private OpenDocumentFile() function). The second private function, SearchFile(), does the work of retrieving the content that we want. If either of these functions fails, we return -1 as the value of the MatchesFound parameter, and an error message as the value of the ReadContent() method itself:

```
. . .
m_DocName = Trim(DocumentName)         'local member variables
m_StartElemName = LCase(Trim(StartElementName))
m_ElemStart = StartInstance
m_EndElemName = LCase(Trim(EndElementName))
m_Matches = 0
. . .
strError = ValidateInputs(m_DocName, m_StartElemName, m_ElemStart, _
                  m_EndElemName, intFileInput)
If Len(strError) Then
    MatchesFound = -1
    ReadContent = "ERROR: " & strError
    Exit Function
End If

strError = SearchFile(strContent, m_DocName, m_StartElemName, _
        m_ElemStart, m_EndElemName, intFileInput, False, "", m_Matches)
If Len(strError) Then
    MatchesFound = -1
    ReadContent = "ERROR: " & strError
Else
    MatchesFound = m_Matches
    ReadContent = strContent
End If
. . .
```

Before we look at the custom functions that do the real work, we should take a look at the main body of the WriteContent() method.

The WriteContent() Method

You can see that `WriteContent()` only varies from `ReadContent()` in a few places. Basically, it has to do much the same as the `ReadContent()` method, but on top of finding the appropriate sections of the file it also has to insert the new content. So, it makes sense to share the internal functions and use parameters to control the different parts of the processes:

```
...
m_NewContent = NewContent          'local member variables
m_DocName = Trim(DocumentName)
m_StartElemName = LCase(Trim(StartElementName))
m_ElemStart = StartInstance
m_Matches = 0
...
strError = ValidateInputs(m_DocName, m_StartElemName, m_ElemStart, _
                          "", intFileInput)
If Len(strError) Then
    MatchesFound = -1
    WriteContent = "ERROR: " & strError
    Exit Function
End If

strError = SearchFile(strContent, m_DocName, m_StartElemName, _
            m_ElemStart, "", intFileInput, True, m_NewContent, m_Matches)
If Len(strError) Then
    MatchesFound = -1
    WriteContent = "ERROR: " & strError
Else
    MatchesFound = m_Matches
    WriteContent = strContent
End If
...
```

In this case, you can see that we don't have to specify an end element name of the `ValidateInputs()` function because the `WriteContent()` method doesn't accept this parameter. And for this reason, the `SearchFile()` function also omits the end element parameter. Here `SearchFile()` also has `True` for the seventh parameter, which specifies that it should replace the existing content with the string provided in the next (eighth) parameter. When the `ReadContent()` method calls this private function, it uses `False` for the seventh parameter to indicate that it is only reading content, and provides an empty string for the new content parameter.

The Private Functions

Here are the private functions that are used within our component:

Method	Description
`ValidateInputs(strDocName, strStartName, intInstance, strEndName, intFNum)`	Checks that the values provided in the parameters fall within acceptable boundaries.
`SearchFile(strExistingContent, strDocName, strStartElemName, intElemStart, strEndElemName, intInFile, blnPutContent, strNewContent, intFound)`	Does the real work of the component by scanning the document for matching entries and replacing them where appropriate.
`OpenDocumentFile(strDocName, blnToWrite)`	Opens a document file for reading or writing.

Method	Description
ReadDocumentFile(intFileNum)	Reads in a block of text from the file for processing within the component.
GetFilePath(strFullName, strNameOnly, strFileExtension)	Splits the complete path and filename of the input document into separate path, filename and file extension parts
TryKillFile(strFName)	Attempts to delete an existing file.
DoFileRename(strFrom, strTo)	Renames an existing file.
GetNextElementMatch(strElemName, strProcess, intStartPos, strEndPtn)	Moves the internal pointer to the next matching element instance.

As we've seen in the previous sections, the two main internal functions are `ValidateInputs()` and `SearchFile()`. The `ValidateInputs()` function is simple enough—the main body of it looks like this:

```
Private Function ValidateInputs(strDocName As String, _
                                strStartName As String, _
                                intInstance As Integer, _
                                strEndName As String, _
                                intFNum As Integer) _
                                As String
  ...
  If Len(strDocName) = 0 Then Error 60000
  If Len(strStartName) = 0 Then Error 60001
  If intInstance = 0 Then Error 60003
  intFNum = OpenDocumentFile(strDocName, False)
  If intFNum = 0 Then Error 60007
  ValidateInputs = ""
  ...
```

Both the `ReadContent()` and `WriteContent` methods call `ValidateInputs()` to ensure that each parameter contains a legal value.

`ValidateInputs()` then calls another private function named `OpenDocumentFile()`, which is used to open the source document text file. It returns a DOS-type file number that we'll use to access the file in the rest of the public method. If the file can't be opened, the file number will be zero and we return an error message string from our `ValidateInputs()` function, which will halt the current `ReadContent()` or `WriteContent()` method execution.

All the functions contain error-handling code (not show above) which creates custom error messages to be passed back to the caller. By raising numbered internal error events with the `Error` statement, we can catch them in our error-handler and decide from the error number what message to return.

Opening the document file is easy enough. However, we will also use this function to open our output file if we are writing new content, so we need to check the value of the `blnToWrite` parameter first. This Boolean parameter indicates whether or not the function is being called by the `ReadContent()` or `WriteContent()` method, and hence whether it will open the file for reading or writing:

```
Private Function OpenDocumentFile(strDocName As String, _
                                  blnToWrite As Boolean) _
                                  As Integer

    On Error GoTo FODF_ERR
    Dim intFileNum As Integer

    intFileNum = FreeFile()
    If blnToWrite Then
        Open strDocName For Output As #intFileNum
    Else
        Open strDocName For Input As #intFileNum
    End If
    OpenDocumentFile = intFileNum
    Exit Function

FODF_ERR:
    OpenDocumentFile = 0
    Exit Function
End Function
```

Writing Updated Text Files

Before we look at how we might find the target elements in our text file, let's briefly consider how we are going to update the text file if we are writing new content. We can't just 'poke' new values into the file, like we do when we update a database using a SQL INSERT statement. We have to read the existing file from the disk and write a copy back to disk that is identical except for the insertions or changes we make, which depend on the values specified by the user.

This means that we must open a temporary output file as well as the input file, and copy the content of the input file to it as we search for our target element. It also means that, after we find the target element(s), we have to insert any new content and then continue to copy from the old file to the new one until all the existing content has been copied across.

If we have specified that we want to write new content to the text file, we use the private function called `SearchFile()` to handle the copying and replacing of files. This same function also scans the document and replaces content. At the start of the function, we create a temporary filename, and then use the `OpenDocumentFile()` method again, this time to create a new temporary output file which we can write to using this temporary name:

```
...
If blnPutContent Then
    Randomize
    strTempName = Format(Now, "mmddhhnnss") & CStr(Int(Rnd * 10000))
    strFPath = GetFilePath(strDocName, strFName, strFExt)
    strOutFileName = strFPath & "~" & strTempName & ".tmp"
    intOutFile = OpenDocumentFile(strOutFileName, True)
    If intOutFile = 0 Then Error 60002
End If
...
```

The `GetFilePath()` function is a simple routine that splits the complete path and filename of the input document into separate path, filename and file extension parts so that we can write our new file into the same folder. The `OpenDocumentFile()` function is the one that we saw at the end of the previous section. The first parameter is the temporary filename and the second parameter, `blnToWrite`, is set to `True` to indicate that we want to open the file for writing rather than reading.

Once the `SearchFile()` function has finished copying the updated content to this temporary file, it closes it. Then it goes through a series of steps that delete any existing backups of the original input file, rename the original input file to a backup file extension, and then rename the new file to the original input filename:

```
...
Close intInFile
If blnPutContent Then
    Close intOutFile
    strBackFileName = strFPath & strFName & ".bak"
    If Not TryKillFile(strBackFileName) Then Error 60010
    If Not DoFileRename(strDocName, strBackFileName) Then Error 60011
    If Not DoFileRename(strOutFileName, strDocName) Then Error 60012
    strTempName = Format(Now - 2, "mmdd") 'clear old temp files
    strTempName = strFPath & "~" & strTempName & "*.tmp"
    blnDummy = TryKillFile(strTempName)
End If
...
```

This code makes use of two more simple custom functions, `TryKillFile()` and `DoFileRename()`, shown next. `TryKillFile()` attempts to delete an existing file given the file name:

```
Private Function TryKillFile(strFName As String) As Boolean
    On Error GoTo FTKLF_ERR
    TryKillFile = False
    If Len(Dir(strFName)) Then Kill strFName
    TryKillFile = True
FTKLF_ERR:
End Function
```

While the `DoFileRename()` function renames the new temporary file to the original file name:

```
Private Function DoFileRename(strFrom As String, strTo As String) As Boolean
    On Error GoTo FDOFRN_ERR
    DoFileRename = False
    Name strFrom As strTo
    DoFileRename = True
FDOFRN_ERR:
End Function
```

Searching for Matching Elements

Finding the target element in our source text file is really just a matter of reading text from the input file into a string and then using the Visual Basic `InStr` function to locate the element opening tag. From there, we can use the `InStr` function again (starting from the end of the opening tag) to find the closing element tag and then extract and return the content between these tags.

Alternatively, if we are looking for a section of content **between** two different elements (or two different instances of elements with the same name), we just have to use `InStr` again to find the start tag of the next element. Then we can return the content between the closing tag of the first element and the opening tag of the second one.

Of course, in reality, things are never that simple. We are going to read the text from the file in distinct 'blocks' of around 8KB (an arbitrary number that seems to give a good balance between performance and memory usage). So, we have to consider what happens when the end tag isn't in the same string (block of text) as we read from the text file (i.e. it is further on in the file). In this case we'll have to save the content after the opening tag while we read the next block of text from disk. We also need to think about how XML elements that have the closing '/>' characters on a separate line will behave if we only read up to the end of the line before, for example:

```
<MYELEMENT TYPE="SPECIAL"
           VALUE="UNKNOWN"
           BINARY_KEY="34567DE98CA4A67842DCC8243BF456732"
           OWNER="Index_service_marker"
/>
```

What our custom `SearchFile()` function does is shown in the following outline. You can see how we get round some of the problems, and how we handle the situation where we are updating the file rather than just reading it. You will find the complete function and the other supporting functions in the source code that we supply.

The first part of the code opens a temporary file, using the code we saw earlier, reads a block from the file, and searches for the opening tag of the required element. When it finds the tag, it calls our `GetNextThisElementMatch()` function:

```
...
If blnPutContent Then
    'open temporary file to write to
End If
...
strStartPtn = "<" & strStartElemName  'calculate start element pattern match
strLine = ReadDocumentFile(intInFile) 'read block of text from file

Do While Len(strLine) > 0
    ...
    intStartPos = InStr(strLine, strStartPtn) 'look for opening element tag
    If intStartPos Then                       'at least one match in line

        'use another custom function to find matching end element tag pattern
        blnFoundTarget = GetNextThisElementMatch(strStartElemName, strEndPtn)
        ...
```

The `GetNextThisElementMatch()` function is described later on. For the meantime, just accept that when it returns, the second parameter will contain the matching end tag for the start element name that we provide in the first parameter. It also returns `True` if it found the end tag, in other words this is a legal instance of the element we're looking for. This means that our code can check that we want this element. Although it is only used internally in our application (not implemented in the user interface for our component) the user could provide a `StartInstance` value, stored here in `intEStart`, which is decremented each time a matching element is found. When it reaches zero, we've reached the first instance of the element that we want to extract or update:

```
    ...
    If blnFoundTarget Then

        'decrement the 'instance' counter
        If intEStart > 0 Then intEStart = intEStart - 1

        'if it is zero, this is the element instance we want
        If intEStart = 0 Then
            ...
```

So, now we can save the current content up to the start of the element if we are going to replace it (i.e. when we are writing out the updated file to disk), and then get the position of the 'end tag' string that was returned by the GetNextThisElementMatch() function. Of course, if the end tag isn't in the same block of text that we are currently processing, we have to keep reading blocks from the original file until we find it. And, in this case, if we are updating the file by inserting new content, we have to write each block of text back out to the disk as well:

```
...
If blnPutContent Then
    'save line content up to start tag
    'for output when writing to file
    ...
End If

'look for the matching element end pattern in the text
intEndPos = InStr(intStartPos + 1, strLine, strEndPtn)
Do While (intEndPos = 0) And (Len(strLine) > 0)
    'if the end element tag isn't in this block of text, then
    'save it and read the next block until we do find it
    strFoundText = strFoundText & Mid(strLine, intStartPos)
    intStartPos = 1
    strLine = ReadDocumentFile(intInFile)
    intEndPos = InStr(strLine, strEndPtn)
Loop
...
```

At this point, we either found the end tag or we reached the end of the file. If we did find the end tag, we can insert the replacement text if required, and collect the existing content of the element. One complexity occurs when we are looking for text between two elements, rather than within a single element. In this case the code has to first find the end of the current element's end tag, then find the start of the next element's start tag, and then extract the content. If we are inserting new content, we add this to the output string that will be written to the disk:

```
...
If intEndPos > 0 Then        'end element tag found
    If blnPutContent Then
    '... insert replacement content

    'set found text to contents of this element
    strFoundText = strFoundText _
                & Mid(strLine, intStartPos, intEndPos - intStartPos)

    If Len(strEndElemName) Then
        'span to next element of type End Element Name
        intStartPos = intEndPos + Len(strEndPtn)
        'find start of 'end span' element
        strFoundText = ""
        strEndPtn = "<" & strEndElemName
        'search for start of this element and then extract the
        'text between end of first element and start of this one
        ...
    End If

    'save the content for output to the updated file it required
    If blnPutContent Then strPrintLine = strPrintLine & strWriteContent
    intStartPos = intEndPos  'ready to look for next element instance

Else    'end element tag not found, so exit with error
    Error 60003
End If
...
```

Now we can increment the count of matching elements, and move the start position marker to just after the end position of the last element we found. In addition, we can write out the currently saved content to disk if we are updating the file. We also need to do this if there is no match in the current block of text:

```
            . . .
            intFound = intFound + 1

        End If     'look for next instance of matching element

      End If     'end of found target element

      intEndPos = intStartPos + 1
      intStartPos = InStr(intEndPos + 1, strProcess, strStartPtn)

      If blnPutContent Then
          Print #intOutFile, strPrintLine; 'write the remaining line to file
      End If

    Else  'no match in line

        'if we are updating the file we have to write line to output
        If blnPutContent Then Print #intOutFile, strLine;

    End If
    . . .
```

Having completed all the tasks required on the current block of text in the file, we could read the next block and look for matches within it. Once we've found all matching instances, we can copy the remainder of the file to the new disk file, and set the return value from our function.

```
    . . .
    strLine = ReadDocumentFile(intInFile)   'read the next block of text

Loop 'for each block of text

'copy rest of existing file to new file if replacing content
Do While (blnPutContent) And (Len(strLine))
    Print #intOutFile, strLine;
    strLine = ReadDocumentFile(intInFile)
Loop
. . .
If blnPutContent Then
    'close and rename temporary file
    . . .
End If
. . .
strExistingContent = strThisContent   'return the found content
. . .
```

The GetNextThisElementMatch() function that we saw in the code above is used to decide what the end tag of an element will look like, based on the start tag that was located by the InStr function. It has to cope with XML elements that may have no closing tag, for example <MYELEMENT NAME="THISONE" />. It also sets the intStartPos parameter to the position in the string of the end of the element, so that the main routine can carry on and look for the closing tag without getting confused by any attributes within the element opening tag. Here is the code for GetNextThisElementMatch():

```
...
intElemLen = Len(strElemName)
strTemp = Mid(strProcess, intStartPos + intElemLen + 1, 1)
If (InStr("/> ", strTemp) > 0) Then
   intEndPos = InStr(intStartPos, strProcess, ">")
   If intEndPos = 0 Then
      GetNextThisElementMatch = False   'no end tag exists
      Exit Function
   End If
   strTemp = Trim(Mid(strProcess, intStartPos + 1, intEndPos - intStartPos))
   If Right(strTemp, 2) = "/>" Then
      strEndPtn = "<" & strTemp        'this is a single tag element, so we
      intStartPos = intStartPos - 1 'set the start point at this element
   Else
      strEndPtn = "</" & strElemName & ">" 'end pattern is a normal closing tag
      intStartPos = intEndPos + 1
   End If
   GetNextThisElementMatch = True
Else
   GetNextThisElementMatch = False
End If
...
```

Of course, this will all fall apart if the element is one of those HTML elements that doesn't have a closing tag, and doesn't include a slash in their single tag either, for example <HR>. This means that our component can't be used to find this type of element in an HTML page.

The FileListing() Method

The final method that our component provides is the FileListing method. This uses some basic Visual Basic techniques to return a list of filenames from the current directory using the Dir function. If preferred, you could implement this using the FileSystemObject instead:

```
...
m_FileSpec = FileSpecification    'local member variables
m_ListSeparator = ListSeparator
m_FileListRoot = FileListRoot
...
MatchesFound = -1
intCount = 0
If Len(m_FileListRoot) = 0 Then Exit Function
If Right(m_FileListRoot, 1) <> "\" Then m_FileListRoot = m_FileListRoot & "\"
strFoundFile = Dir(m_FileListRoot & m_FileSpec, vbArchive + vbNormal + vbReadOnly)
Do While Len(strFoundFile)
   If Left(strFoundFile, 1) <> "." Then
      strFileList = strFileList & m_ListSeparator & strFoundFile
      intCount = intCount + 1
   End If
   strFoundFile = Dir
Loop
MatchesFound = intCount
FileListing = strFileList
...
```

And that's all there is to the component; it is ready to be compiled and used as part of our applications. The next step is to see if it works.

Testing the Component with Visual Basic

We've provided a simple VB test application and its source files with the component so that you can try it out, and check your own modifications to it.

> *Remember that you have to register the* wx2882tx.dll *component before using this sample application. VB will do this for you on the machine where you compile the component.*

The test application contains a series of text boxes where you can enter values for the various parameters, and three buttons—one for each method:

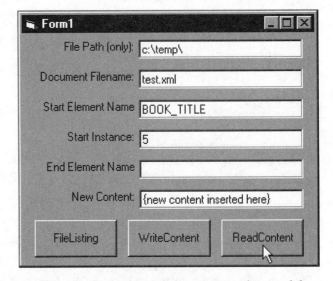

The **ReadContent** button uses the first five text box values to build up the parameter values, and then calls the `ReadContent()` method. The code that runs when the button is clicked looks like this:

```
...
Dim objTX As New WX2882TX.XMLTX    'create the component instance
...
DocumentName = Text1.Text & Text2.Text
StartElementName = Text3.Text
StartInstance = Text4.Text
EndElementName = Text5.Text
strResult = objTX.ReadContent(DocumentName, StartElementName, _
                      StartInstance, EndElementName, intMatches)
MsgBox "Result is: " & vbCrLf & strResult & vbCrLf & vbCrLf _
              & "Number of matches = " & intMatches
...
```

The results are displayed in a normal message box:

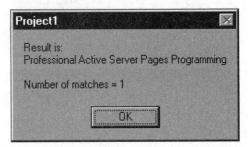

The WriteContent button executes similar code, but this time it uses the New Content text box value and not the End Element Name value. It calls the `WriteContent()` method of our component to update the target XML file, leaving the original as a backup copy. This is what the code for the WriteContent button looks like:

```
...
Dim objTX As New WX2882TX.XMLTX   'create the component instance
...
DocumentName = Text1.Text & Text2.Text
StartElementName = Text3.Text
StartInstance = Text4.Text
NewContent = Text6.Text
strResult = objTX.WriteContent(NewContent, DocumentName, _
                StartElementName, StartInstance, intMatches)
MsgBox "Old content was: " & vbCrLf & strResult & vbCrLf & vbCrLf _
                & "Number of matches = " & intMatches
...
```

And here's the result. You can see the backup file `test.bak` (the original `test.xml` file after being renamed) and the replacement text that has been written into the newly created `test.xml` file:

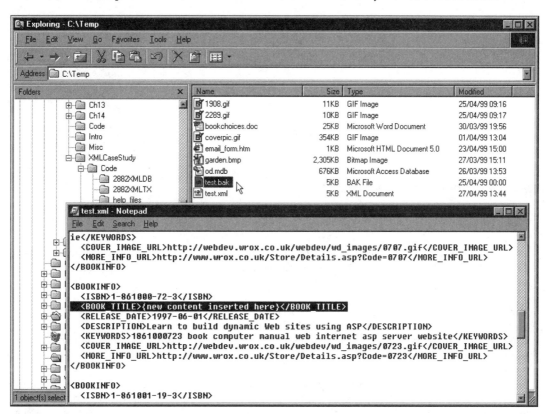

Finally, this is the code that is executed when the **FileListing** button is clicked:

```
...
Dim objTX As New WX2882TX.XMLTX   'create the component instance
...
FileListRoot = Text1.Text
FileSpecification = "*.*"
ListSeparator = vbCrLf
strResult = objTX.FileListing(FileListRoot, FileSpecification, _
            ListSeparator, intMatches)
MsgBox "Result is: " & vbCrLf & strResult & vbCrLf _
                    & "Number of matches = " & intMatches
...
```

The result is a simple listing of the files in the current folder:

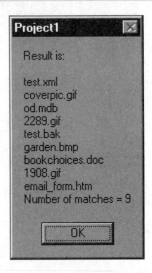

Other Document Parsing Techniques

If you have already been experimenting with XML in IE5 or other applications, you will probably be wondering why we haven't used the Document Object Model (DOM) to get at the contents of a document. The DOM can expose an entire valid and well-formed XML document as a tree structure, and IE5 contains one of the many parser applications that can achieve this. In fact, the tree structure is defined by the W3C, in an attempt to persuade all manufacturers to produce compatible parsers and applications.

More than that, the standard set out by the W3C also defines the methods that should be available to access and manipulate the contents of the DOM tree. So, we could load an XML document into our parser application, and use these standard methods to retrieve and modify the content of any of the elements.

But, there is one big problem. We've already decided that we want to support HTML text files as far as possible, and it's highly unlikely that any of these will be structured in such a way that they are well-formed enough to be successfully loaded by an XML parser. In particular, single tag elements such as `<HR>` and `<BR>` are illegal, and so are any instances of elements that omit optional end tags, such as `<LI>` or `<P>`.

However, we will be looking at a specific instance later in the next chapter where we are always going to be parsing valid XML files. There, we'll see how we can use an XML parsing component to access document content.

Having seen the Text File Access component we now need to look at how the Database Access Component works, because the two work together in the application to achieve the results that we need. While the File Access Component allows us to manipulate the text files, selecting and replacing their content, we still need a way of getting the extracted information to and from the database. So, the final section of this chapter will look at how we interact with the database.

The Database Access Component (WX2882DB)

Our second custom component is the more complex one of the pair, as it uses ActiveX Data Objects (ADO) to access a data store, as well as depending on the same kind of string handling techniques we used in the previous component. Again, it's written using Visual Basic, and contains a single class named XMLDB. We've also provided a test application written in VB (Form1.frm), which is compiled into an application named Project1.exe.

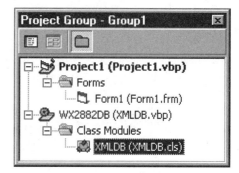

The database access component has two tasks to achieve. First, it must be able to create an XML document that represents a recordset already stored in the database, using the values stored in a database table. Second, it must be able to add new records to and update existing values in the database, based on the contents of another XML document that represents a recordset containing the changes required.

We've seen earlier in this chapter how we can represent data as a recordset (in the section on dynamically creating text files, before we got stuck into the case study), so the first task should be easy enough. However, the second one prompts some extra considerations. Still, let's get the interface details sorted out first.

Designing the Interface

We know that we'll need two separate methods in our component, one to create the outgoing XML document, and one to accept and process incoming XML to add to the database or update existing content. Here are the two public functions, which we expose as the interface:

Method	Description
GetXML(ConnectionString, QueryString, KeyFieldName)	Returns a string that is the matching records from the database formatted as XML.
PutXML(ConnectionString, XMLString)	Uses information in the XML document to update the original records in the database.

Again, we will look at the values we want to get into and out of our component, and then move on from the interface to the implementation and the `Private` functions that do the work behind the scenes.

The GetXML() Method

The `GetXML()` method should be the easiest to implement, even though it requires three parameters:

```
Public Function GetXML(ByVal ConnectionString As String, _
                       ByVal QueryString As String, _
                       ByVal KeyFieldName As String) _
                    As String
```

Obviously, we need to be able to connect to the database, and a single connection string is the easiest way to specify this. We also need a query that will specify the data to read from the database and include in the XML recordset. We'll return the XML recordset document as the value of the function. That still leaves us with one extra parameter—the `KeyFieldName`.

To see why we need the name of the key field, think about how we're going to update the original data when we edit it. We need a way to link each record that we get sent back from our client with the original record that it was created from. We are going to let people update the database entries using the following screen:

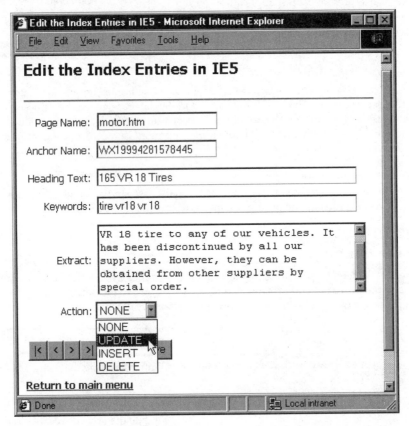

This takes the XML recordset, displays the data in a form and allows the user to change the values before sending them back to the database for updating. To make sure that we update the correct record, we need to be able to tell which record in the database they intended to edit.

To do this, we'll use the value in the primary key field of each record to identify it. In other words, if a record has a primary key field named CUST_ID with a value of BOND007, we'll include the clause CUST_ID='BOND007' in our XML record. You'll probably recognize this as part of a SQL WHERE clause—and it should give you a hint as to how we're going to update the original data.

The PutXML() Method

The PutXML() method will accept and process an XML document created by the user, or more likely an XML document that was created by the component and then edited by the user. This document can contain just details of the additions and changes that are required to our database records, rather than all the data from all the records that we originally sent to the client. This makes it a reasonably efficient way to transmit data across the network.

So, the only two parameters we need are the same database connection string as was used when creating the original XML recordset document before editing it, and the new XML document that contains the changes, delivered as a string:

```
Public Function PutXML(ByVal ConnectionString As String, _
                       ByVal XMLString As String) As Long
```

We'll return the number of records that were successfully modified as the value of the function. If there is an error, however, we'll return a specific error code number instead. To help the user decide what went wrong, we'll also add a Public enumeration to our component that contains these error numbers:

```
Public Enum PUTXMLERROR
    PX_NO_TABLE_NAME = -100
    PX_NO_UPDATE_ACTION = -101
    PX_NO_RECORD_MATCH = -102
    PX_RECORD_MATCH_ERROR = -103
    PX_TOO_MANY_FIELDS = -104
    PX_ELEMENT_NAME_MISSING = -105
    PX_DATATYPE_ATTR_MISSING = -106
    PX_SQL_EXEC_ERROR = -107
End Enum
```

Implementing the Component

As with our previous text file access component, we'll move on to look at how the methods of our interface are implemented in code. And, again, we won't be listing each function in its entirety: all the source code is provided with the samples for this book, which you can download from http://webdev.wrox.co.uk/books/2882/.

The private functions we will be implementing are:

Method	Description
`GetFieldType(intFieldType)`	Returns the field type, such as `"TEXT"`, `"NUMERIC"`, etc.
`FormatFieldValue(varValue, strDataType, strFormat)`	Converts value between the correct formats required for XML or a database table.
`GetTableName(strXML)`	Returns the name of the database table from the XML document.
`MoveNextRecord(strXML)`	Moves the pointer to the next record in the XML document.
`GetElementName(strXML, blnPeekOnly)`	Returns the name of an element from the XML document.
`GetDataType(strXML)`	Returns the data type of an element from the XML document.
`GetElementValue(strXML)`	Returns the value of an element from the XML document.

The GetXML() Method

Building up an XML document from a database is easy. We just have to iterate through each record in the appropriate table or query result recordset, and then for every record we find we iterate through the fields. For each field, we wrap the value in XML tags that contain the field name, and we wrap each complete record in another XML element to indicate the boundaries of each record. Finally, we add a single opening and closing tag to the whole XML document, probably using the table name:

```
<MY_DATA_TABLE>
  <RECORD>
    <FIELD1>value of field 1 in record 1</FIELD1>
    <FIELD2>value of field 2 in record 1</FIELD2>
    ... more fields
  </RECORD>
  <RECORD>
    <FIELD1>value of field 1 in record 2</FIELD1>
    <FIELD2>value of field 2 in record 2</FIELD2>
    ... more fields
  </RECORD>
  ... more records
</MY_DATA_TABLE>
```

However, to be able to update the original data, we need more than this. We already discovered that we need some kind of 'record match' clause, such as `KEY_FIELD='key_value'`. We also need to indicate the data types in the XML, so that we can create a correctly formatted SQL statement later on to update the original values (as you'll see when we look at the `PutXML()` method implementation). Finally, we need some way of indicating the action we want to take with the record, so we'll need an `UpdateAction` field in each record as well.

After some experimentation, it turns out that we need to produce an XML document that looks something like the following example, which uses data from the sample `BookList` database that you'll meet again later on. The 'A2X' part of some of the XML elements indicates that these are a custom fields, added to make updating of the original data easier (it comes from the name of the commercial component, ASP2XML):

```xml
<?xml version="1.0"?>
<BookList>
  <A2X_Record>
    <A2X_RecordNumber>00001</A2X_RecordNumber>
    <A2X_UpdateAction>NONE</A2X_UpdateAction>
    <A2X_RecordMatch>kBookCode='0448'</A2X_RecordMatch>
    <kBookCode A2X_DataType="TEXT">0448</kBookCode>
    <dReleaseDate A2X_DataType="DATE">1996-12-01 00:00:00</dReleaseDate>
    <tTitle A2X_DataType="TEXT">Instant JScript Programming</tTitle>
  </A2X_Record>
  <A2X_Record>
    <A2X_RecordNumber>00002</A2X_RecordNumber>
    <A2X_UpdateAction>NONE</A2X_UpdateAction>
    <A2X_RecordMatch>kBookCode='0707'</A2X_RecordMatch>
    <kBookCode A2X_DataType="TEXT">0707</kBookCode>
    <dReleaseDate A2X_DataType="DATE">1998-04-15 00:00:00</dReleaseDate>
    <tTitle A2X_DataType="TEXT">Professional IE4 Programming</tTitle>
  </A2X_Record>
  ... more records here
</BookList>
```

This XML document contains the values of the fields in the database, plus some extra specialist elements that help us to manage updates to the data when we return it to the server. The A2X_UpdateAction element tells the component whether this record is to be updated or left as it is, saving processing if the client sends back all the records instead of just the changed ones. It can be set to UPDATE, DELETE or INSERT to tell the component what to do with the record.

The A2X_RecordMatch element provides a link to the original record in the database in case the client decides to change the value of the record key field. Finally, the A2X_RecordNumber element is included so that during debugging the client can see which record was being processed if an error occurs. It does not reflect any record number in the database, only in our XML document.

The function code to create this format is easy enough to follow. The only complex part is discovering the data type of the original field, and formatting the data in the appropriate way for XML, based on the data type. The first part of the GetXML() function creates a connection to the data source, and opens it:

```
...
Dim oConn As Object        'using Object is slower than early binding using
Dim oRs As Object          'the New keyword and a specific object variable
Dim objField As Object     'type, but prevents ADO version dependency
...
Dim QUOT As String
QUOT = Chr(34)             'double-quote character
m_ConnectString = Trim(ConnectionString)    'local member variables
m_QueryString = Trim(QueryString)
m_KeyFieldName = Trim(KeyFieldName)
...
'get the table name from the query string
intCharPos = InStr(UCase(m_QueryString), "FROM ")
If intCharPos Then
   m_TableName = Trim(Mid(m_QueryString, intCharPos + 5))
   intCharPos = InStr(m_TableName, " ")
   If intCharPos Then m_TableName = Left(m_TableName, intCharPos - 1)
Else
```

```
    GetXML = "ASP2XML Error: Table Name must be included in SQL Query "
    Exit Function
End If

'open connection to data source
Set oConn = CreateObject("ADODB.Connection")
oConn.Open m_ConnectString
Set oRs = oConn.Execute(m_QueryString) 'execute the user's query
If Err.Number > 0 Then
    GetXML = "ASP2XML Error: Failed to access database: " & Err.Description
    Exit Function
End If
If oRs.EOF Then
    GetXML = "ASP2XML Error: No records matched your query"
    Exit Function
End If
...
```

Now we can iterate through the records to create our XML output string. Notice that we start with the special XML processing instruction line: `<?xml version="1.0"?>`. This is required for most clients that understand XML to accept it as a valid XML file. The record numbers are created by our function, for use mainly in indicating errors later on and to help the user keep track of which records were updated:

```
...
'create XML string header
strXML = "<?xml version=" & QUOT & "1.0" & QUOT & "?>" & vbCrLf

'add table name as root element
strXML = strXML & "<" & m_TableName & ">" & vbCrLf & vbCrLf
lngRecNum = 0

Do While Not oRs.EOF

    'add our specific identifier elements to the XML
    lngRecNum = lngRecNum + 1
    strRecNum = Right("00000" & CStr(lngRecNum), 5)
    strXML = strXML & " <A2X_Record>" & vbCrLf _
            & " <A2X_RecordNumber>" & strRecNum & "</A2X_RecordNumber>" _
            & vbCrLf & " <A2X_UpdateAction>NONE</A2X_UpdateAction>" & vbCrLf
    ...
```

The next step is to create the element that will hold the 'match details'. Recall that this is what we'll use to associate the 'record' in the XML document that is returned to our component to the original record in the database when we come to update the values in this record. We use our own private functions `GetFieldType()` and `FormatFieldValue()` to discover the type of data for the field, and format the value it contains as legal XML:

```
    ...
    'add match details for WHERE update clause elements to the XML
    strDataType = GetFieldType(oRs(m_KeyFieldName).Type)
    strKeyMatch = strFieldName & "=" _
            & FormatFieldValue((oRs(strFieldName).Value), strDataType, "SQL")
    strXML = strXML & " <A2X_RecordMatch>" & strKeyMatch _
            & "</A2X_RecordMatch>" & vbCrLf
    ...
```

This will produce the `<A2X_RecordMatch>` element for this record in our XML document, for example:

```
<A2X_RecordMatch>kBookCode='0448'</A2X_RecordMatch>
```

We can now loop through all the fields in this record and extract the values, format them as required for the XML, and add them as elements to the XML document:

```
    ...
    'now get values from each field in the query result set
    For Each objField In oRs.Fields
        'add elements for each field and its value to the XML
        strDataType = GetFieldType(objField.Type)
        strFieldName = objField.Name
        strFieldValue = FormatFieldValue((objField.Value), strDataType, "XML")
        strXML = strXML & "  <" & strFieldName & " A2X_DataType=" _
                & QUOT & strDataType & QUOT & ">" _
                & strFieldValue & "</" & strFieldName & ">" & vbCrLf
    Next

    strXML = strXML & "  </A2X_Record>" & vbCrLf & vbCrLf
    oRs.MoveNext    'move to next record

Loop
...
'add closing table name root element tag
getXML = strXML & "</" & m_TableName & ">" & vbCrLf
...
```

As we mentioned, GetXML() uses two custom Private functions that we have created elsewhere within our component, GetFieldType() and FormatFieldValue().

The GetFieldType() function is used so that we can determine what data type to use as an attribute of the tags containing the database content. This function is just a Case statement that uses the integer field type returned by ADO as the Type property of each field. The named constants we use in the Case statement are defined in the global declaration section of our component:

```
Private Function GetFieldType(ByVal intFieldType As Integer) As String
    Select Case intFieldType
        Case adBoolean
            GetFieldType = "BOOLEAN"

        Case adDate, adDBDate, adDBTime, adDBTimeStamp, adFileTime, adDBFileTime
            GetFieldType = "DATE"

        Case adEmpty, adBSTR, adVariant, adChar, adWChar, _
            adVarChar, adVarWChar, adLongVarWChar
            GetFieldType = "TEXT"

        Case adLongVarChar   'text block data
            GetFieldType = "#-Memo Data-#"

        Case adIDispatch, adError, adIUnknown, adUserDefined, _
            adGUID, adChapter, adPropVariant
            GetFieldType = "#-Undefined-#"

        Case adBinary, adVarBinary, adLongVarBinary
            GetFieldType = "#-Binary Data-#"

        Case Else 'numeric -in SQL
            GetFieldType = "NUMERIC"

    End Select
End Function
```

Notice that we are really only interested in four formats, "BOOLEAN", "DATE", "TEXT" and "NUMERIC". We're only doing this so that we can include the data in our XML documents or SQL statements in the correct format, and these are the only four basic types of data that are treated differently from each other as far as the text format goes. You'll see what we mean in the listing of the FormatFieldValue() function next.

Our custom FormatFieldValue() function is used in both the GetXML() and PutXML() methods. It is used to format the field value correctly for either an XML document (as text) or the correct string format for a SQL statement as required by the database. For example, SQL server returns Boolean values as -1 (True) or 0 (False), while a user of the XML document will probably prefer to see the words TRUE or FALSE.

To indicate the conversion type to be applied to the value, the FormatFieldValue() function accepts a parameter named strFormat. If strFormat is "XML", as in the GetXML() function, we're formatting the data from a database table so that it is suitable for use in an XML document. If the value of the strFormat() parameter is "SQL" then we're formatting data taken from an XML document so as to make it suitable for inserting into a database table with a SQL statement:

```
Private Function FormatFieldValue(ByVal varValue As Variant, _
                                  ByVal strDataType As String, _
                                  ByVal strFormat As String) _
                                  As String
   FormatFieldValue = ""
   If IsNull(varValue) Or IsEmpty(varValue) Then Exit Function

   Select Case strDataType
      Case "BOOLEAN"
         Select Case strFormat
            Case "XML"
               If varValue Then
                  strResult = "TRUE"
               Else
                  strResult = "FALSE"
               End If
            Case "SQL"
               If UCase(varValue) = "TRUE" Then
                  strResult = "-1"
               Else
                  strResult = "0"
               End If
         End Select

      Case "DATE"
         Select Case strFormat
            Case "XML"
               strResult = Year(varValue) & "-" _
                           & Right("0" & Month(varValue), 2) & "-" _
                           & Right("0" & Day(varValue), 2) & " " _
                           & Right("0" & Hour(varValue), 2) & ":" _
                           & Right("0" & Minute(varValue), 2) & ":" _
                           & Right("0" & Second(varValue), 2)
            Case "SQL"
               If varValue = "" Then
                  strResult = "NULL"
               Else
                  strResult = "'" & Year(varValue) & "-" _
                              & Right("0" & Month(varValue), 2) & "-" _
                              & Right("0" & Day(varValue), 2) & " " _
                              & Right("0" & Hour(varValue), 2) & ":" _
                              & Right("0" & Minute(varValue), 2) & ":" _
                              & Right("0" & Second(varValue), 2) & "'"
```

```
                    End If
            End Select

        Case "TEXT"
            Select Case strFormat
                Case "XML"
                    strResult = varValue
                Case "SQL"
                    strResult = Replace(varValue, "'", "''")
                    strResult = "'" & strResult & "'"
            End Select

        Case "NUMERIC"
            Select Case strFormat
                Case "XML"
                    strResult = CStr(varValue)
                Case "SQL"
                    If varValue = "" Then
                        strResult = "NULL"
                    Else
                        strResult = CStr(varValue)
                    End If
            End Select

        Case Else
            'we can't handle this type (i.e. image or memo types) so
            'we just use the text data type description as the value
            strResult = strDataType

    End Select

    FormatFieldValue = strResult
    ...
End Function
```

So, we can now use the `GetXML()` method to create the XML document that defines our recordset, and send it to the client for editing or display.

The PutXML() Method

When the client has finished editing our XML document, we can use it to update the source data. This is a more complex process, which we'll show you in outline next. To see all the code in full detail, you can examine the source that is supplied with the samples for this book:

```
...
'we use an array to hold the field values for each record as we
'build the appropriate SQL query string to update the source data
Dim arrFields(255, 1) As String        '0 = field name, 1 = new value
...
m_ConnectString = ConnectionString      'local member variables
m_XMLString = XMLString
...
'extract table name from XML string
strTableName = GetTableName(m_XMLString)
If Len(strTableName) = 0 Then      '... Error

'open connection to data source
Set oConn = CreateObject("ADODB.Connection")
oConn.Open m_ConnectString
...
```

Having opened the connection to our database, we position an 'internal pointer' variable at the first record in the XML document ready to start processing the records it contains. We keep a count of updated records in the variable lngNumUpdated:

```
...
'chop XML string at start of next (first) record using a custom function
'this function returns the current record number
lngRecNumber = MoveNextRecord(m_XMLString)
lngNumUpdated = 0

Do While lngRecNumber > 0
...
```

To process each record, we use the GetElementName() and GetElementValue() functions we've defined elsewhere in the component. This first thing to check is whether this record needs to be updated, or whether the user simply left it in (with no intention of updating it) when the document is returned. If it is an update to the data, we get the match value. It must be present for a DELETE or UPDATE action to succeed, otherwise we don't know which record to delete or update:

```
...
'get next element name using another custom function
'this should be the update action required
If GetElementName(m_XMLString) <> "A2X_UpdateAction" Then '... Error
strUpdateAction = UCase(GetElementValue(m_XMLString))
If (strUpdateAction = "UPDATE") _
Or (strUpdateAction = "INSERT") _
Or (strUpdateAction = "DELETE") Then

    'get next element name - should be record key match string
    If GetElementName(m_XMLString) <> "A2X_RecordMatch" Then '... Error
    strRecordMatch = GetElementValue(m_XMLString)
    If (strUpdateAction = "UPDATE") Or (strUpdateAction = "DELETE") Then
        If Len(strRecordMatch) = 0 Then  '... Error
    End If
...
```

For an UPDATE or an INSERT action, we need to collect all the values for the record that we are inserting or updating. We do this by deciding where the record ends (with the closing </A2X_Record> tag), and looping through each element up to that point collecting the filed names and values. These values are placed in the array we declared earlier, remembering to format the field appropriately for use in a SQL statement:

```
...
If (strUpdateAction = "UPDATE") Or (strUpdateAction = "INSERT") Then
    'figure out what the end of record/document tags are
    intNumFields = 0
    strRecordCloseTag = "</A2X_Record>"
    strTableCloseTag = "</" & strTableName & ">"

    'loop through the elements (fields) in this record
    Do While (Left(m_XMLString, Len(strRecordCloseTag)) _
            <> strRecordCloseTag) _
    And (Left(m_XMLString, Len(strTableCloseTag)) <> strTableCloseTag)
        intNumFields = intNumFields + 1
        If intNumFields > 255 Then   '... Error

        'get next element name for data source record field name
        strFieldName = GetElementName(m_XMLString)
        If Len(strFieldName) = 0 Then  '... Error
        arrFields(intNumFields, 0) = strFieldName  'store in array
```

```
                    'get field data type string from A2X_DataType attribute
                    strDataType = GetDataType(m_XMLString)
                    If Len(strDataType) = 0 Then       '... Error

                    'get field value and format according to data type
                    strFieldValue = GetElementValue(m_XMLString)
                    strFieldValue = FormatFieldValue(strFieldValue, strDataType, "SQL")
                    arrFields(intNumFields, 1) = strFieldValue   'store in array

            Loop    'to get value for next field

        End If
        ...
```

Now that we've got all the values for this record, we can build a suitable SQL statement and fire it off to our database to update the record. There is a different process for each type of update, i.e. INSERT, DELETE or UPDATE:

```
            ...
            'got all field values so build SQL query string to update record
            Select Case strUpdateAction
                Case "UPDATE"
                    If intNumFields > 0 Then
                        strSQL = "UPDATE " & strTableName & " SET "
                        For intThisField = 1 To intNumFields
                            strSQL = strSQL & arrFields(intThisField, 0) & "=" _
                                & arrFields(intThisField, 1) & ", "
                        Next
                        strSQL = Left(strSQL, Len(strSQL) - 2)
                        strSQL = strSQL & " WHERE " & strRecordMatch
                    End If

                Case "INSERT"
                    If intNumFields > 0 Then
                        strSQL = "INSERT INTO " & strTableName & "("
                        For intThisField = 1 To intNumFields
                            strSQL = strSQL & arrFields(intThisField, 0) & ", "
                        Next
                        strSQL = Left(strSQL, Len(strSQL) - 2) & ") VALUES ("
                        For intThisField = 1 To intNumFields
                            strSQL = strSQL & arrFields(intThisField, 1) & ", "
                        Next
                        strSQL = Left(strSQL, Len(strSQL) - 2) & ")"
                    End If

                Case "DELETE"
                    strSQL = "DELETE FROM " & strTableName & " WHERE " & strRecordMatch

            End Select

            'execute the SQL query string to update the data source
            oConn.Execute strSQL
            If Err.Number > 0 Then    '... Error
            lngNumUpdated = lngNumUpdated + 1

        End If
```

Finally, we finish off by moving to the next record, and when all have been processed we can return the number that we updated:

```
lngRecNumber = MoveNextRecord(m_XMLString) 'move to start of next record

    Loop    'do again for next record
    ...
    putXML = lngNumUpdated
    ...
End Function
```

As you can see from the code, there are several other private functions included in this component, which are used to parse the XML string:

Private Function	Description
GetTableName()	Parses the XML string for the name of the database table, which should be the root element name.
MoveNextRecord()	Finds the starting point of the next record in the XML, and returns the rest of the XML string and the record number.
GetElementName()	Parses the XML string to find the next element name, and returns the rest of the XML string and the element name.
GetDataType()	Parses the XML after the GetElementName function has removed the element name, finds the data type for the current element, and returns the rest of the XML string and the data type.
GetElementValue()	Parses the XML after the GetDataType function has removed the data type, finds the value for the current element, and returns the rest of the XML string and the element value.

You can examine these custom functions in the source code that is included with the samples for this book.

Testing the Component with Visual Basic

Again, we've provided a simple VB test application that uses our component. It provides text boxes for the parameters that the component expects, and buttons to run the two methods GetXML and PutXML. To use it, you must have a database table available, to which you have read and write access permission.

> Remember that you have to register the wx2882db.dll component before using this sample application. VB will do this for you on the machine where you compile the component.

We've provided a simple Access database named XMLCaseStudy.mdb containing the tables you'll see in this and the next chapter. We've also included SQL scripts with the downloadable samples, which you can use to create the databases on your own SQL Server or similar database server. You then need to build the connection string either using:

```
DRIVER={driver_name};SERVER=server_name;DATABASE=db_name;UID=user;PW=password
```

Or by creating a System DSN on the server that points to the relevant database, and specify that in the connection string as:

```
SERVER=server_name;DSN=your_system_dsn
```

Setup notes have been included with the download files to help you get the application working on your server.

The GetXML() Method in Action

This screenshot shows the test application with our connection string entered in the top text box. We're using the `BookList` table that we created from the sample SQL script, and have selected a single record based on the primary key field named `kBookCode`:

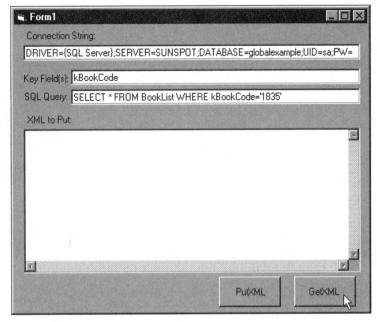

When we click the **GetXML** button, the following code extract is executed:

```
Dim objClass As New WX2882DB.XMLDB
...
strConnect = Text1.Text
strKeyFields = Text2.Text
strQuery = Text3.Text
strResult = objClass.GetXML(strConnect, strQuery, strKeyFields)
MsgBox strResult
...
```

The result is an XML document that defines the recordset containing this single record:

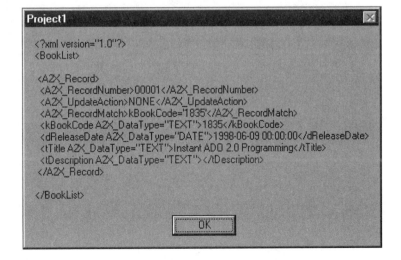

The PutXML() Method in Action

To update the original data, we have to edit the XML document created by the GetXML() method, or provide an appropriate XML document with the correct structure. In the next screenshot, we've entered the document into the lower multi-line text box of the sample application (in fact, in the sample application that we provide, this is already in place). We've also manually changed the <A2X_UpdateAction> element value to UPDATE, and edited the values of the date and description field elements:

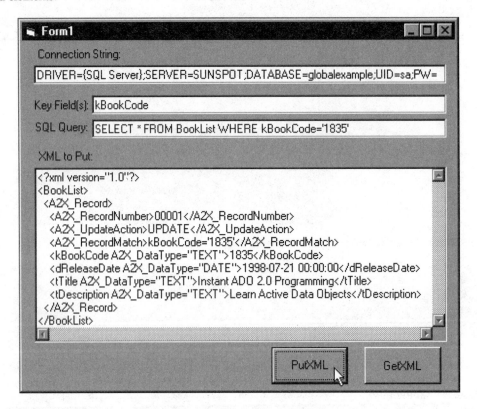

Clicking the PutXML button executes the following code extract:

```
...
Dim objClass As New WX2882DB.XMLDB
...
strConnect = Text1.Text
strXML = Text4.Text
intResult = objClass.PutXML(strConnect, strXML)
MsgBox intResult & " record(s) modified."
...
```

This applies the updates to the database, and displays the number of records that were modified. If there is an error, you'll get a numeric error value returned instead, which equates to one of the errors defined within the component's PUTXMLERROR enumeration (which we examined when designing our component):

Providing the update succeeded, we can view the results by clicking the GetXML button again. You can see the changed release date and the new description:

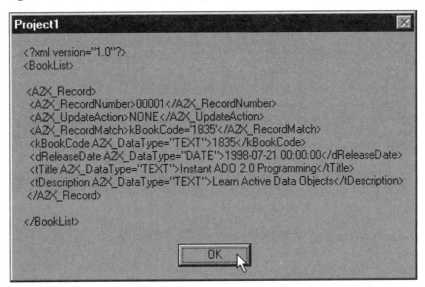

The component can also carry out insertions of new records and deletion of existing ones, as you'll no doubt have noticed from looking at the PutXML method implementation earlier on. We've included some HTML pages with the sample code that discuss ways of using an XML document to modify a database. You'll find these files in the help_files subfolder of the main XMLCaseStudy folder.

XML Case Study Part 1 - Summary

In this chapter, we've explored some of the reasons why text-based information storage might be useful. We've also explored some of the issues that we have to overcome before we can put our Text File Indexed Storage System application into practice. In particular, the fact that text files provide only serial access, and that they often lack internal structure, are the two main issues—but we believe that our custom components can help to provide work-arounds for these problems.

So, we laid out our plans for a text-based information storage and retrieval application that can use existing HTML and XML documents as the source data, index it to provide easy access and searching features, and present the results to the user on demand. To make it work, we discovered that we will require at least two custom components, and we showed you how we designed and built these specifically for the task in hand.

We also saw the components in action in test environments, using simple VB applications. By taking advantage of the Project Group feature of VB4 and above, we can use these test applications to fine-tune and debug our components as we build them. This is far quicker than installing them on a Web server and trying them out with an ASP page each time. It also allows us to single-step though the component code and track down those recalcitrant bugs in a flash.

In the next chapter, we'll continue this case study by looking at how we are going to use these two shiny new components, and also explore where other componentization opportunities exist. We had to concentrate on building our two components in this chapter so that we could show their implementation and functionality in the next chapter, as both components interact with each other. Now we shall move on to cover how we can create and use the text-file indexes to display information on demand, how we can format it, and how we might solve the problems of keeping the index information up to date. We'll start with setting up the Text File Indexed Storage System application so that you can see how the parts integrate as you read.

Document Management Case Study—Part 2

This chapter forms the second and final part of our Text File Indexed Storage System case study. In the previous chapter, we looked at why we might consider such an approach to information management, and the issues that are involved in implementing it. We produced a broad design for our application, and created two custom components that will carry out the most intensive parts of the process. Having built the components in the last chapter we will be spending more time in this chapter focusing on how we use the components from within a full application.

In this chapter, we'll look at how we implement the complete Text File Indexed Storage System application. We'll be using our two custom components within ASP pages, and at the same time we'll look for opportunities to improve the application by converting other parts of the various operations into custom components that enforce our business rules.

We've provided all the code for this application with the samples for this book, and we'll describe the setup issues shortly, before we get too involved. You should have no problems getting the whole thing working on your own Web server using the components and other files that we have supplied.

We've divided the application into five sections, and we'll cover each part separately:

- ❑ Processing both HTML and XML documents, which represent source text files
- ❑ Editing and maintaining the index store data in our database table
- ❑ Creating the static HTML and XML index pages and formatting the information
- ❑ Implementing a dynamic search feature in both HTML and XML
- ❑ Retrieving and displaying the original HTML document or XML-based information

We'll start with a brief resume of the application design, so that you can see how all these parts fit together, and take a look at how to install the samples.

The Overall Application Design

In the previous chapter, we produced a top-level design for our Text File Indexed Storage System. We process the source text files, and store details of each one in an index store database. From this, we can build both static index pages that display all the index entries, and also create dynamic search pages where users can search the index entries in the database and display lists of those that match.

Both the static index lists and the dynamic search result pages will contain hyperlinks, so that the target document can be retrieved and displayed on demand. If it's an HTML page, we'll even scroll down the page in the browser window to show the relevant topic.

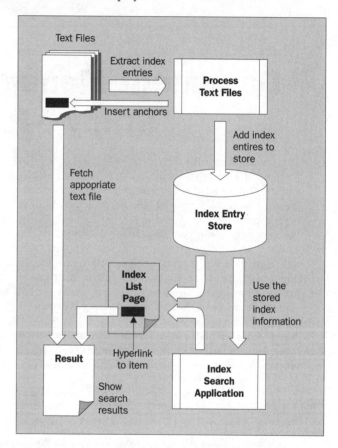

Setting up the Sample Files

The only setup issues that you need to be aware of are installing and registering the components, creating the database tables and the connection strings, copying the HTML and ASP pages to your Web server, and changing some of the path names. You can download all the sample files for the complete application from our Web site at http://webdev.wrox.co.uk/books/2882/. We have included extra setup instructions in the download if you require them.

Installing and Registering the Components

Our application uses the two custom components that we created in the previous chapter, the ActiveX DLLs `wx2882db.dll` and `wx2882tx.dll`. These are provided ready-compiled with the samples, or you can compile them yourself from the supplied source code. Copy the DLLs to the folder on your Web server where you keep your custom components. Then either open a DOS **Command** window, change to the folder containing your components and register them by typing:

```
regsvr32 wx2882db.dll
regsvr32 wx2882tx.dll
```

Or go to **Run** from the **Start** menu and type the following, making sure you use the pathname for your component:

```
regsvr32 c:\Winnt\System32\inetsrv\components\wx2882db.dll
regsvr32 c:\Winnt\System32\inetsrv\components\wx2882tx.dll
```

We'll also be using one other component in this application, which is provided as part of Internet Explorer 5. The file you want is `msxml.dll`, and, if you have IE5 installed on your server, it will probably be in your **Winnt\System32** (NT) or **Windows\System** (Win 9x) folder.

If you don't have IE5 installed on your Web server, you can download a standalone version of the component from the Microsoft site at **http://msdn.Microsoft.com/xml/** in the Developer Downloads section. This still requires IE4.01 with SP1 or later on the Web server.

Creating the Database Tables

As we saw when developing our database access component in the last chapter, our application requires a database called `XMLCaseStudy.mdb`. This needs to include a table named `PageIndex` to be available for storing the index entries. We've provided a sample Microsoft Access database with the downloads, it is called `XMLCaseStudy.mdb`. Alternatively, you can create it in a server database system such as SQL Server using the script `build_pageindex.sql` that we've also supplied:

```
CREATE TABLE dbo.PageIndex (
    kItemCode int IDENTITY (1, 1) NOT NULL ,
    tPageName varchar (255) NULL ,
    tHeading varchar (255) NULL ,
    tAnchorName varchar (255) NULL ,
    tKeywords varchar (255) NULL ,
    tExtract varchar (255) NULL ,
    CONSTRAINT PK_PageIndex_1__12 PRIMARY KEY  NONCLUSTERED
    (
        kItemCode
    )
)
```

The Database Connection String

As we saw in the data access component, we are using a parameter to hold a connection string to the database. In our example you can use a connection string such as:

```
DRIVER={SQL Server};SERVER=your_server;DATABASE=your_db;UID=user;PW=password
```

Alternatively, you can create a **System DSN** for it using the **ODBC32** applet in **Control Panel**. You can then use a connection string such as:

```
SERVER=your_server_name;DSN=your_dsn_name
```

The next screenshot shows the PageIndex table in design view in Microsoft Access.

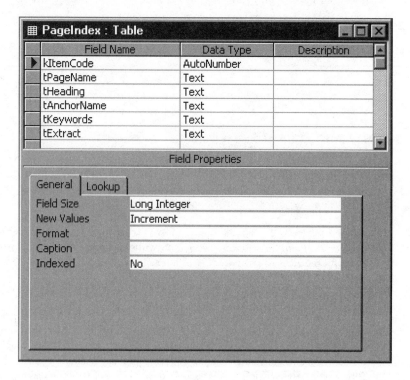

The BookList Table

If you are not using the sample Microsoft Access database that already contains the BookList table, and you didn't create or use the BookList table in the previous chapter to test the second component that we built, the second SQL script that we supply, build_booklist.sql, creates the table and populates it with a list of books:

```
CREATE TABLE dbo.BookList (
    kBookCode varchar (4) NOT NULL ,
    dReleaseDate datetime NULL ,
    tTitle varchar (255) NULL ,
    tDescription varchar (255) NULL ,
    tKeywords varchar (255) NULL
)
```

Installing the HTML and ASP Pages

The only other task is to copy all the HTML and ASP pages to your Web server, maintaining the same directory structure as is stored in the samples Zip file. If you place them in a directory named XMLCaseStudy directly under the WWWRoot folder of your default Web site, it will save you having to edit some of the pages to change the absolute paths to the text files. However, you will still have to go through the files and alter the database connection string. There is a read me file named File_Changes_Required.txt in the setting_up folder of the samples that tells you the ones you need to change.

Also remember that, if you are using Internet Information Server 3.0, you will also have to create an **alias** for this folder and give it Execute and well as Read permission.

The Application Main Menu

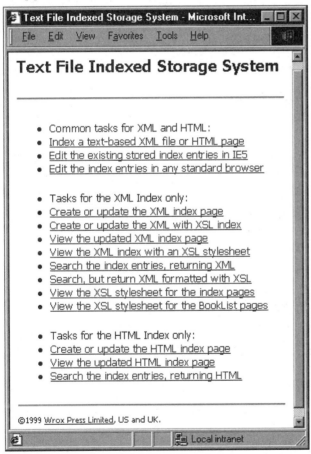

As there are many files in the Text File Indexed Storage System application, we've provided a default page that provides a link to each one so that you can run them easily without having to keep typing the URLs into your browser. Simply open the URL http://your_server_name/ XMLCaseStudy/ and you should see this page.

You can download all the sample files for the complete application from our Web site at http://webdev.wrox.co.uk/books/2882/.

So, let's get on and look at the pages that make up the application and make use of the components we developed in the last chapter.

627

Processing the Source Text Files

The first step in our application is processing the source text files to create the index store. As we saw in the last chapter, we'll extract a topic title or heading, a set of keywords where available, and a short extract of the content. At the same time we'll insert into the text file an HTML-style anchor element to identify each topic heading, so that when we reload the file in the future we can scroll directly to this topic. As you'll have guessed, both of these tasks will make use our text file access component.

Indexing HTML and XML Pages

The page that does all the work of indexing the text files is autoindex_pages.asp. This uses the now common ASP technique of housing both an input <FORM> to collect the values for a process, and the ASP code that carries out that process, in the same ASP page. In other words, the contents of the form are posted back to the same page that created the form in the first place.

The HTML FORM Section

The <FORM> section of our page contains six text boxes and three buttons. The HTML code looks like this:

```
. . .
<!************ display controls to enter parameters ***************>
<FORM ACTION="<% = Request.ServerVariables("SCRIPT_NAME")%>" METHOD="POST">
<TABLE>
 <TR><TD ALIGN="RIGHT">Directory Path:</TD>
     <TD ALIGN="LEFT"><INPUT TYPE="TEXT" NAME="txtPathName" SIZE="35"
                             VALUE="<% = strPathName %>"></TD></TR>
 <TR><TD ALIGN="RIGHT">File Name:</TD>
     <TD ALIGN="LEFT"><INPUT TYPE="TEXT" NAME="txtFileName" SIZE="35"
                             VALUE="<% = strFileName %>"></TD></TR>
 <TR><TD ALIGN="RIGHT">Heading Element:</TD>
     <TD ALIGN="LEFT"><INPUT TYPE="TEXT" NAME="txtHeadingElement" SIZE="35"
                             VALUE="<% = strHeadingElement %>"></TD></TR>
 <TR><TD ALIGN="RIGHT">Keywords Element:</TD>
     <TD ALIGN="LEFT"><INPUT TYPE="TEXT" NAME="txtKeywordsElement" SIZE="35"
                             VALUE="<% = strKeywordsElement %>"></TD></TR>
 <TR><TD ALIGN="RIGHT">Start of Content Element:</TD>
     <TD ALIGN="LEFT"><INPUT TYPE="TEXT" NAME="txtContentStart" SIZE="35"
                             VALUE="<% = strContentStart %>"></TD></TR>
 <TR><TD ALIGN="RIGHT">End of Content Element:</TD>
     <TD ALIGN="LEFT"><INPUT TYPE="TEXT" NAME="txtContentEnd" SIZE="35"
                             VALUE="<% = strContentEnd %>"></TD></TR>
 <TR><TD ALIGN="RIGHT" COLSPAN="2">
     <INPUT TYPE="SUBMIT" VALUE="List Files" NAME="cmdList">  
     <INPUT TYPE="SUBMIT" VALUE="Index File" NAME="cmdIndex">  
     <INPUT TYPE="SUBMIT" VALUE="Done" NAME="cmdDone"></TD></TR>
</TABLE>
</FORM>
. . .
```

The result is a page where the user can enter the values we'll need to process the text file. The two 'action' buttons allow them to produce a listing of files in a directory or start the indexing process. Note that the file path and name are entered into two separate text boxes in this page:

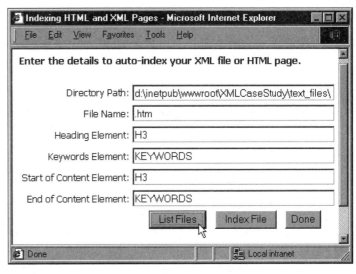

Here, our text file access component can be called upon to provide a file listing as well as accessing the contents of text files. We'll look at the file listing capability first.

The ASP code that does all the work is all kept in the first part of the `autoindex_pages.asp` page (the form section we've just seen comes at the end of the page, so the user can enter a new set of values for the next process). After setting the connection string of our database, along with a few default values for the controls, we check to see if there was any value provided in the `txtPathName` control. If there was, it indicates that the user submitted the form by clicking one of the SUBMIT buttons, if not it will have just been loaded ready for a path to be specified:

```
...
<%
'fill in with your connection string details
strConnect = "DRIVER={SQL Server};SERVER=___;DATABASE=___;UID=___;PW=___"

'set default values for controls
strPathName = "c:\inetpub\wwwroot\XMLCaseStudy\text_files\"
strFileName = "motor.htm"
strHeadingElement = "H3"
strKeywordsElement = "KEYWORDS"
strContentStart = "H3"
strContentEnd = "KEYWORDS"
QUOT = Chr(34)     'double quote character

'see if there was a path name parameter
If Len(Request.Form("txtPathName")) Then

  'collect all the input parameter values
  strPathName = Request.Form("txtPathName")
  If Right(strPathName, 1) <> "\" Then strPathName = strPathName & "\"
  strFileName = Request.Form("txtFileName")
  strFullPath = strPathName & strFileName
  strHeadingElement = Request.Form("txtHeadingElement")
  strKeywordsElement = Request.Form("txtKeywordsElement")
  strContentStart = Request.Form("txtContentStart")
  strContentEnd = Request.Form("txtContentEnd")

  'create the component instance
  Set objTX = Server.CreateObject("WX2882TX.XMLTX")
  Dim intMatches  'to hold resulting number of matches found
  intMatches = 0
  ...
```

In the code above, if we do get some values from the user, we collect them in local variables and build up the full path and name of the file they specified. Then we create the component instance together with a variable to hold the number of matches found. We'll come back to this after looking at listing the contents of the directory.

Listing the Directory Contents

To list the directory contents, we just have to call the `FileListing()` method of our text file access component, and supply the path of the directory, the file pattern to match (.htm or .xml), the separator character (in this case `<BR>`), and our `intMatches` variable:

```
...
  If Len(Request.Form("cmdList")) Then
    'build a list of all the files in this folder
    strResult = objTX.FileListing(strPathName, "*.*", "<BR>", intMatches)
    If intMatches >= 0 Then
      Response.Write "<B>Listing of " & strPathName & "</B><P>"
      Response.Write strResult & "<P>Listed " & intMatches & " files.<HR>"
    Else
      Response.Write "<B>Error listing files</B>.<HR>"
    End If
  Else
    'build the index and update the page/file
    ...
```

On return, `intMatches` will contain the number of files found, or -1 if there was an error. Here's the result for our `XMLCaseStudy\ text_files\` folder. You can see the three sample text files we provide, plus copies of each one so that you can experiment and repeat the process by deleting the file you index and copying the 'spare' one:

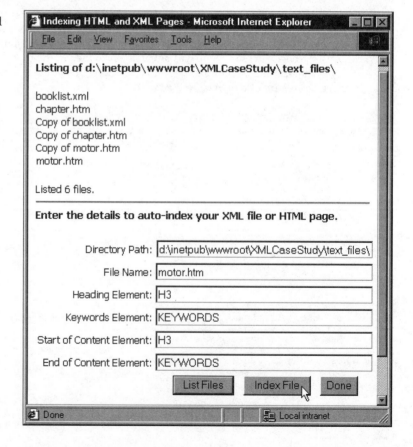

Having listed the files in an appropriate directory, the **File Name:** option allows the user to enter the name of the file to index. We will look at indexing three different examples of pages: a structured HTML page, an unstructured HTML page, and an XML document.

Indexing a Structured HTML Page

If the user clicked the **Index File** button, we now need to start off the indexing process. The default values in the page are correct for `motor.htm` (the first of our files), a structured HTML document that describes motor vehicle support issues. The next screenshot shows what the `motor.htm` page looks like:

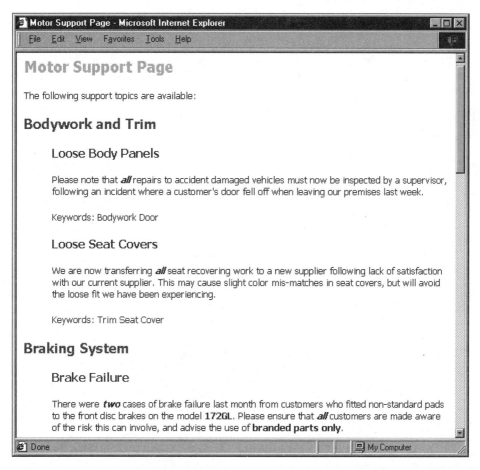

The code in this page follows a regular repeating pattern, making it ideal for indexing with our automated system. For each topic, there is an `<H3>` heading, a few sentences of text in a `<P>` element, along with keywords between two `<KEYWORDS>` tags:

```
...
<H3>Loose Seat Covers</H3>
<P>We are now transferring <B><I>all</I></B> seat recovering work to a new supplier
following lack of satisfaction with our current supplier .... etc.</P>
Keywords: <KEYWORDS>Trim Seat Cover</KEYWORDS>
...
```

Iterating Through the Headings

To index this file, we start by creating and opening a connection to our index store database, and then we enter a loop that will be executed for each topic-heading element in the document. By using a variable named `intStartInstance` in our ASP page to keep track of the topic-heading number, we can access this same topic several times. We do this once to get the content of the heading element, once to get the contents of the keywords element, and once to get the 'abstract' (the content between the start and end content elements specified in the form page). Then, once we've finished processing our matching `<H3>` element, the `intStartInstance` variable can be incremented, allowing us to go to the next instance of the element that we want to index.

Here our ASP page first calls the `ReadContent()` method of our custom component to get the content of the `<H3>` heading element (which we collected along with the other parameters from the text boxes on the form). When we are reading text from between an opening and closing tag using `ReadContent()` we omit the optional 'end element' parameter which is only used if we want to get the content from between two different elements (such as for the sample content).

```
...
  Else
    'build the index and update the page/file
    Response.Write "Processing file: <B>" & strFullPath & "</B> ...<BR>"
    'create and open a connection to the index table
    Set objCon = Server.CreateObject("ADODB.Connection")
    objCon.Open strConnect
    intStartInstance = 1   'start at first heading instance
    intCount = 0           'number of entries added
    Do
      'read content of this heading element instance
      strHeadingContent = objTX.ReadContent(strFullPath, strHeadingElement, _
                          intStartInstance, , intMatches)
      If intMatches > 0 Then   'got a heading instance so ...
        'read content of keywords element for this heading
        strKeywords = objTX.ReadContent(strFullPath, strKeywordsElement, _
                      intStartInstance, , intMatches)
        If intMatches > 0 Then
          strKeywords = CleanString(LCase(strKeywords))
        Else
          strKeywords = ""   'no keywords
        End If
        'get first 255 chars of content between start and end elements
        strResult = objTX.ReadContent(strFullPath, strContentStart, _
                    intStartInstance, strContentEnd, intMatches)
        If intMatches > 0 Then   'got some text so index this element instance
          strExtract = Left(CleanString(strResult), 254)
          ...
```

If we do get any matches to this heading, we call the component's `ReadContent()` method again to get the contents of the 'keywords' element. And if we find any content here, we call a custom function to 'clean' the string of any unwanted characters (as we will see in a moment, this cleaning involves removing markup characters).

The final part of the code shown above also uses `ReadContent()` with the start and end element names provided by the user, so as to collect the content of the document between these two elements. In our case, this is the content between the `<H3>` and the `<KEYWORDS>` elements. After 'cleaning' the string, we take the first 254 characters of this as the extract. This ensures that it will fit in a normal 255-character database `varchar` (or similar) type of field.

The CleanString() Function

We intend to display the headings, keywords and extracts from our index store in both HTML and XML format later on, and so we have to consider what they will actually contain. It's likely that there will be HTML elements and other formatting content if we have drawn them from an HTML page, or XML elements and processing instructions if we have drawn them from an XML text file.

To be able to display them safely in either an HTML or XML page, without causing errors to appear in the structure of that page (for example, if we have an opening `<B>` tag but no matching closing `</B>` tag in the extract), we should remove any contentious content.

This is what our `CleanString()` function does. It removes all HTML/XML elements, double-quotes, carriage returns, ampersands '&' (which define entities in XML and special characters in HTML) and all stray opening and closing '<' and '>' tag characters:

```
Function CleanString(strInput)
  strOutput = Replace(strInput, Chr(34), "")   'remove double quotes
  strOutput = Replace(strOutput, Chr(13), "")  'remove carriage returns
  strOutput = Replace(strOutput, Chr(10), "")  'remove line feeds
  strOutput = Replace(strOutput, "&", "")      'remove ampersands

  'remove all XML or HTML elements by searching for '<' and '>'
  'characters and using only the text that is outside them. This
  'will include the content of the elements (the stuff between the
  'tags) as well as the text between the elements themselves.
  intOpenElem = InStr(strOutput, "<")
  Do While intOpenElem > 0
    If intOpenElem > 1 Then
      strLeft = Left(strOutput, intOpenElem - 1)
    Else
      strLeft = ""
    End If
    intCloseElem = Instr(strOutput, ">")
    If (intCloseElem < Len(strOutput)) And (intCloseElem > intOpenElem) Then
      strRight = Mid(strOutput, intCloseElem + 1)
    Else
      strRight = ""
    End If
    strOutput = strLeft & strRight
    intOpenElem = InStr(strOutput, "<")
  Loop
  CleanString = Trim(Replace(strOutput, ">", ""))
End Function
```

Adding the Anchor Element

Now that we've extracted the values we want for the heading, the keywords and an 'abstract', the next task is to add an anchor element to the original text-based file page, to indicate the point where the topic starts. We create a unique anchor name (in strict HTML it must start with an alphabetic character), and from that we build the complete `<A NAME="..." >Heading Text</A>` element, which sits inside the heading element. For example:

```
<H3><A NAME="WX1999428103222417">Instant VBScript Programmer's Reference</A></H3>
```

We get the heading text from the `strHeadingContent` variable, and we'll insert it into the document using our component's `WriteContent()` method:

```
...
Randomize
intRand = CInt(Rnd * 1000) - 1    'create unique anchor name
strAnchor = "WX" & CStr(Year(Now)) & CStr(Month(Now)) & CStr(Day(Now)) _
        & CStr(Hour(Now)) & CStr(Minute(Now)) & CStr(Second(Now)) _
        & CStr(intRand)
strNewContent = "<A NAME=" & QUOT & strAnchor & QUOT & ">" _
            & strHeadingContent & "</A>"
'update the content of the element with new anchor
strResult = objTX.WriteContent(strNewContent, strFullPath, _
        strHeadingElement, intStartInstance, intMatches)
...
```

Providing all goes well (i.e. the return value of `intMatches` is greater that zero), we'll build a suitable SQL statement containing the heading, keywords and abstract, and fire it off at our index store database. Notice that we have to 'double' all the apostrophes (i.e. convert ' to '') to match SQL syntax requirements, and also 'clean' the heading string in `strHeadingContent` to ensure it's stored in the database as plain text without any HTML or XML content:

```
If intMatches > 0 Then    'successfully inserted anchor so ...
    'add index to database, first create SQL string
    strExtract = Replace(strExtract, "'", "''")    'format apostrophes
    strKeywords = Replace(strKeywords, "'", "''")
    strHeadingContent = CleanString(strHeadingContent)
    strHeadingContent = Replace(strHeadingContent, "'", "''")
    strSQL = "INSERT INTO PageIndex (tPageName, tHeading, " _
        & "tAnchorname, tKeywords, tExtract) " _
        & "VALUES ('" & strFileName & "', '" & strHeadingContent _
        & "', '" & strAnchor & "', '" & strKeywords _
        & "', '" & strExtract & "')"
    objCon.Execute strSQL
    Response.Write "Heading '" & strHeadingContent & "' indexed as <B>" _
            & strAnchor & "</B>.<BR>"
    intCount = intCount + 1
Else  'could not add index anchor entry to text file
    Response.Write "<B>" & strResult & "</B><BR>"
End If
Else  'no content found to link to heading
    If intCount = 0 Then
        Response.Write "<B>Cannot find content element &lt;" _
                & strContentElement & "&gt;</B><BR>"
    End If
End If
Else  'no match found for heading
    If intCount = 0 Then
        Response.Write "<B>Cannot find heading element &lt;" _
                & strHeadingElement & "&gt;</B><BR>"
    End If
End If
intStartInstance = intStartInstance + 1  'go to next heading
Loop While intMatches > 0

objCon.Close
Set objCon = Nothing
Response.Write "Added <B>" & CStr(intCount) & "</B> index entries.<HR>"
End If  'end of processing page
End If
%>
...
```

The remainder of this code section displays status messages and handles situations where we don't find any matching elements. Then it increments the `intStartInstance` variable ready to access the next topic, and goes round the loop again. Only when there are no further matches to the topic-heading element for this instance, i.e. we've indexed all of them, does the loop exit. The screenshot opposite shows the result after indexing the Motor Support page:

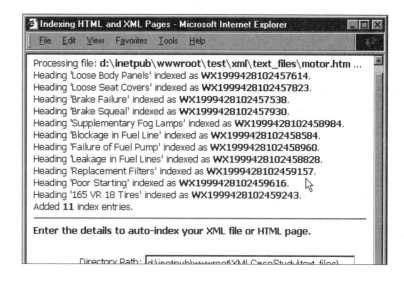

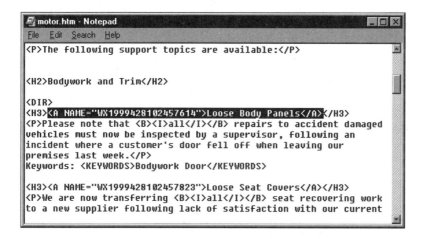

If we now view the source of the Motor Support page residing on our server, we can see the anchors that our page has inserted as it indexed the document.

Indexing a Non-Structured HTML Page

The page we've just indexed is probably not very representative of the kinds of HTML pages that you have on your server. Let's face it—most HTML pages are made up of a mixture of all kinds of elements, often with little or no overall structure to the elements themselves. For example, we used Microsoft Word to convert a sample chapter from one of the Wrox books to HTML for use on our Web site:

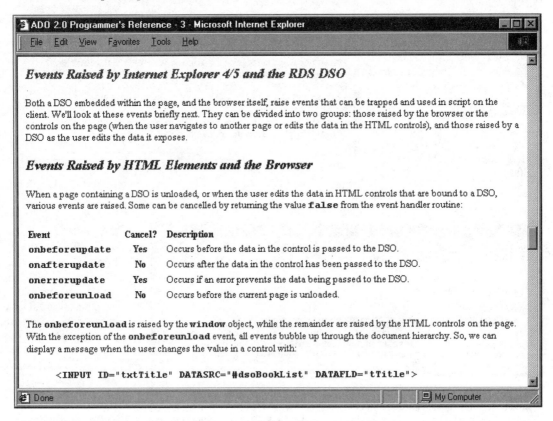

This page (`chapter.htm`) looks fine, but if you view the HTML source you'll find that it's a rare mixture of all kinds of formatting elements, as well as the actual text content. There is no obvious topic-heading element, because the whole formatting exercise has involved the use of <P> elements combined with appropriate <FONT> elements. Before we could even think about indexing it, we had to go through it manually adding a specific element—we chose <H3>—around each topic heading (although we actually used a text editor with a 'search and replace' feature to speed up the process).

There is no obvious element containing keywords, so we'll leave this value empty when we index the file. And as there is no obvious element that marks the start or end of any description or extract, we'll just use the entire text content between the consecutive <H3> headings and retain the first 254 characters, so it will do fine as an extract of the topic contents. The whole indexing process will use our CleanString() function to remove all the non-text content. The next screenshot shows the values we used, and the result of the indexing process:

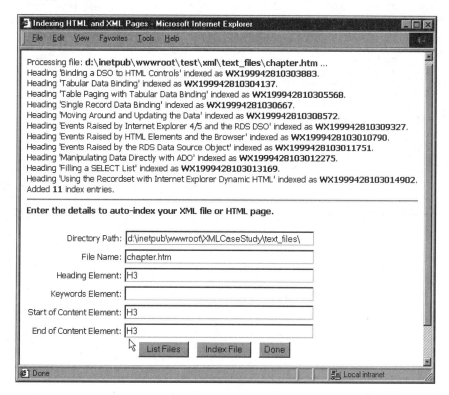

If we now view the HTML source of the chapter, we can see the new anchors. You can also see what we mean about the file being a rare mixture of formatting elements and text!

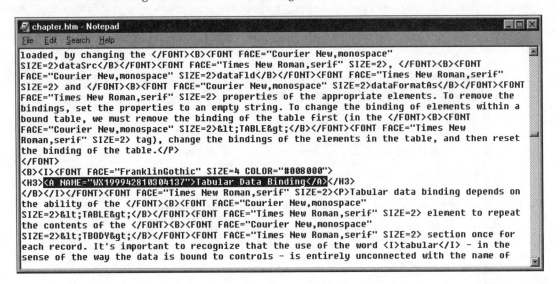

Indexing the BookList XML Page

OK, so you're wondering where all the XML in this case study has gone. The next file we'll index is an XML document, which contains a list of books and their descriptions. The following screenshot shows the file displayed in Internet Explorer 5. You can see that this time we should have an easy indexing task because the document contains an obvious heading element <BOOK_TITLE>, a <KEYWORDS> element, and a description held in a <DESCRIPTION> element:

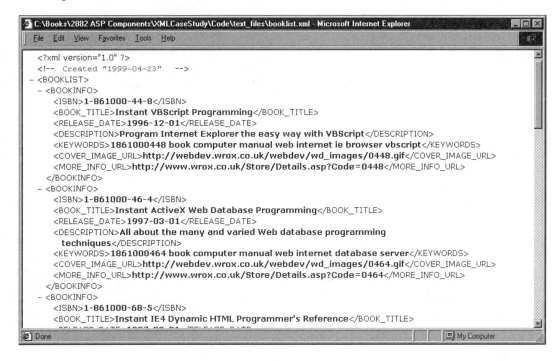

One difference here is that our indexing page expects a start and end element to be specified for the 'extract' or 'description', and it uses the content between these two elements. So, we have to enter the two surrounding element names, `</RELEASE_DATE>` and `<KEYWORDS>` to get back the content of the description element (remember that the process removes all the XML element tags automatically). The next screenshot shows the results and the values we used:

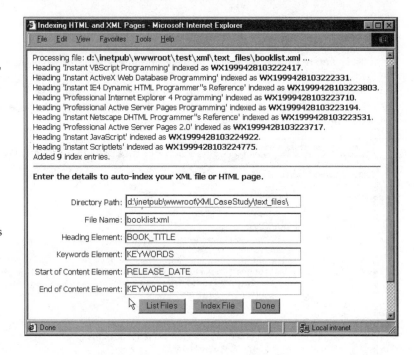

And, again, we can look at the source of the XML page and see the anchor elements that we've inserted:

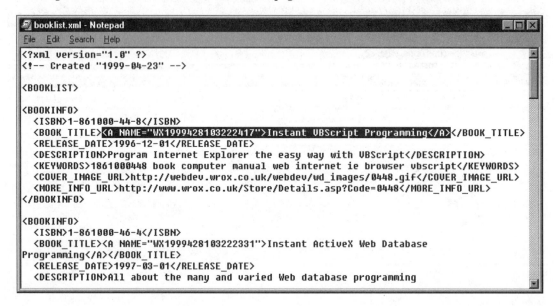

Viewing the Results in our Index Store

Having worked through three text documents, let's have a look at what we have collected in the way of index information in our example. We've used SQL Server to store the index entries (you might be using the supplied Access database instead), and to view them we've linked our `PageIndex` table to a client-side copy of Microsoft Access (using the **Get External Data | Link Tables** option). You can see the result in the next screenshot:

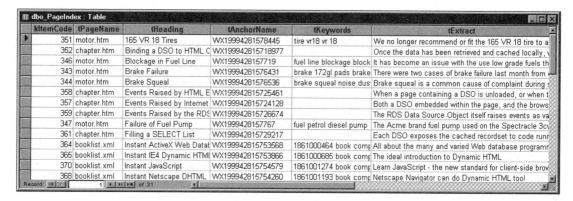

It all seems to have worked fine. We have the page name and anchor name, some keywords where they were available, and the text extract from each topic. The next step is to look at how we can edit this information should we need to add or update it manually for any reason.

Editing and Updating the Index Entry Store

Our index store now contains pure text entries, with all the HTML/XML-specific content such as elements and special characters removed. As this is an automated process, using our text file access component, there may be times when we want to edit the content of the index store. If we want to edit this data on a remote client machine, we first need to decide how we will transfer the data across the network. We could use server-side ASP to create a list of all the index entries (probably as a table), and then create a specific page for each record that they want to edit using HTML controls on a `<FORM>`. When users submit the form, we could use the contents to update the original record in the database. However, this technique is not bandwidth friendly if there are a lot of changes to make. Instead we will look at a solution that uses XML.

Using XML as a Data Transfer Protocol

In the previous chapter, we looked at how we can use XML to transfer data across a network, by wrapping up the individual data values in XML element tags and sending it across the network as pure text, as shown in the next diagram:

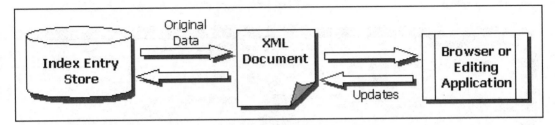

We then went on to build a custom component that can create this XML from a data source and, better still, manage updates that are returned to the server as XML as well. We'll put this component to use in our application to allow us to edit the PageIndex data on our server. In fact, we'll show you two ways that it can be used, depending on the way that you intend to edit the data and the client application you use.

This process will involve creating an XML document on the server containing the details you want to edit and sending it to the client. The client will then have to display it in a way that will allow users to edit the relevant data. We will be providing two implementations of this, the first for users running Internet Explorer 4 or 5, the second for earlier browsers. The client then has to create an XML document to return to the database containing the required updates.

Luckily we built the database access component in the last chapter to handle the conversion of the database content into XML and to receive XML to update the database, and we shall be using it here.

Creating the XML Document

The first step is to be able to create the outgoing XML document that contains all the index entry data that we want to edit. This is done with get_xml.asp, and uses our database access component's GetXML() method to build the XML document:

```
<%
'fill in with your connection string details
strConnect = "DRIVER={SQL Server};SERVER=___;DATABASE=___;UID=___;PW=___"

strQuery = "SELECT * FROM PageIndex ORDER BY tHeading"
strKeyField = "kItemCode"

Set objDB = Server.CreateObject("WX2882DB.XMLDB")
strResult = objDB.GetXML(strConnect, strQuery, strKeyField)
Response.ContentType = "text/xml"   'tell the client it's an XML file
Response.Write strResult
%>
```

We're sending all the index entries to the client in this example, though on a large system you would probably add a form that allowed the user to select a set of entries to edit. Instead of using a SQL query such as:

```
SELECT * FROM PageIndex ORDER BY tHeading
```

as we're doing here, you could add a WHERE clause based on the user's enquiry to limit the output to a specific set of records. The result, either way, is an XML file that looks something like this next section of code:

```
<?xml version="1.0"?>
<PageIndex>

 <A2X_Record>
  <A2X_RecordNumber>00001</A2X_RecordNumber>
  <A2X_UpdateAction>NONE</A2X_UpdateAction>
  <A2X_RecordMatch>kItemCode=351</A2X_RecordMatch>
  <kItemCode A2X_DataType="NUMERIC">351</kItemCode>
  <tPageName A2X_DataType="TEXT">motor.htm</tPageName>
  <tHeading A2X_DataType="TEXT">165 VR 18 Tires</tHeading>
  <tAnchorName A2X_DataType="TEXT">WX19994281578445</tAnchorName>
  <tKeywords A2X_DataType="TEXT">tire vr18 vr 18</tKeywords>
  <tExtract A2X_DataType="TEXT">We no longer recommend ... etc.</tExtract>
 </A2X_Record>

 <A2X_Record>
  ...
  ... etc.
  ...
 </A2X_Record>

</PageIndex>
```

Now that we have the XML to send to the client, we will start to look at the two different ways we can edit the content of the Index Store database. First we will create a version for IE4 and 5 users, then we will come back and revisit the problem so that users with earlier browsers can still edit the content of the Index Store.

XML Data Binding in Internet Explorer

One of the clever tricks that Internet Explorer has been able to do since version 4.0 is to manage **client-side data binding**. This allows us to associate objects or controls on a page with a data source. What this means is that we can send data to the client across the network and cache it there. The client can display the cached data, allow the user to sort, filter and modify it, and then package up the changes and send them back to the server to update the data source.

By using client-side data binding we are able to provide a simple page for users to edit the contents of the index entry store. We can cache data from the index entry store on the client and allow the client to edit entries easily and efficiently, before returning them to the database to update the content.

All this can happen automatically when you use a SQL data source and Microsoft's own **Remote Data Service** technology. Unfortunately, however, when we come to use XML as the data transport mechanism, much of the automation disappears. Still, we can add the features we want ourselves to produce a very intuitive and efficient client-side application using an **XML Data Island**.

To find out more about Remote Data Services, check out Professional ADO RDS Programming with ASP (ISBN 1-861001-64-9) from Wrox Press.

Creating a Data Island

Data islands were introduced with Internet Explorer 5. They allow us to include or reference an XML document within an HTML page, and script against it. We create an XML Data Island in a page using the new <XML> element (which is an HTML element, not an XML element). The XML can then either be added inline, in the HTML file between the <XML> tags, or in an external file using a reference to its location. The <XML> tag takes an ID attribute, which allows us to specify a name that we can use to reference the data island, and the SRC attribute to specify a source for the XML data (in this case our get_xml.asp page).

This is an extract from our sample page edit_ie5_index.htm:

```
...
<!-- create the XML data island -->
<XML ID="dsoData" SRC="get_xml.asp"></XML>
...
```

So, now we can bind HTML controls to the XML that is returned by get_xml.asp referring to it as dsoData.

> Note that because this is an HTML element and **not** an XML element, it must have a separate closing tag—you can't use <XML ID="dsoData" SRC="get_xml.asp" />.

An XML Data Island exposes the XML Data Source Object (DSO). In IE4 the DSO is a Java applet, and the <XML> element is not supported. Instead, we can use the **Microsoft Java Parser for XML**, which is packaged with the latest Java Virtual Machine and available from http://www.microsoft.com/java/. The equivalent code that we use to instantiate it is:

```
<APPLET CODE="com.ms.xml.dso.XMLDSO.class"
  ID="dsoData" WIDTH=400 HEIGHT=50 MAYSCRIPT=true>
  <PARAM NAME="URL" VALUE="get_xml.asp">
</APPLET>
```

In Internet Explorer 5 the DSO is a COM object. The DSO exposes XML encoded text not only as data rowsets, but also as XML DOM parse trees. When a data island is loaded with a page, Internet Explorer transparently loads the data into a parse tree and offers several COM interfaces for our use. The standard DSO interfaces allow XML elements to participate in data binding as if data were coming from a database. The DSO parses the XML content and keeps bound elements synchronized with the parse tree, exposing each top-level child as a 'row' of data.

The Databound HTML Controls

With our data island in place holding the XML, we can add HTML controls to our page and bind them to our data island. The only difficulty is that, because we have included the A2X_DataType attribute in each data element, we have to use a separate table for each element (an explanation follows the code).

The table is bound to the XML data in the data island using the DATASRC attribute. This takes the value of the ID attribute used in the <XML> element preceded by a #. The DATAFLD attribute specifies the element from the XML file to be displayed as a 'field' in the XML recordset. In this case we are using tPageName, which is the name of the page that has been indexed. Then we bind the control that lets us move between records to the $TEXT property of the field to get the actual value—in this case the page name. The $TEXT value represents the element content.

```
...
<TABLE>
 <TR>
  <TD ALIGN="RIGHT">Page Name:</TD>
  <TD>
   <TABLE DATASRC="#dsoData" DATAFLD="tPageName"><TR><TD>
    <INPUT TYPE="TEXT" DATASRC="#dsoData" DATAFLD="$TEXT" NAME="tPageName">
   </TD></TR></TABLE>
  </TD>
 </TR>
...
```

The Reason for Nesting Tables

Because IE has to support the XML data format created by newer versions of ADO, it doesn't always behave quite as you would expect. ADO can produce an XML document from a database automatically. However, the structure of the resulting document is quite different from that we normally expect to see in our XML documents. Instead of placing the values from the database fields into the elements as content, like we have done in our component (i.e. surrounding them with XML element tags that are the field name), ADO currently places the values of all the fields as attributes within the XML elements.

This means that the XML DSO treats attributes as though they were values (i.e. content) of elements, in the respect that each attribute within an XML element is treated as a separate XML element that follows the one containing these attributes. So, our XML field elements, which contain an attribute named A2X_DataType, are treated as being two separate elements. Therefore the value (i.e. the content) of our element is treated as the child of an element named A2X_DataType.

To get at the value of this child, we have to bind a <TABLE> to the main 'field' element in our XML, and then use "$TEXT" as the name of the field to bind a control within that table to. $TEXT is providing the value of the top-level element's content, and its use exposes the child whose content we want to expose. In effect, we are binding to the child of the child of the field element, which is the value we want.

Our example page also contains controls that are bound to the remaining data fields of the XML 'recordset', plus a <SELECT> list bound to the A2X_UpdateAction field. Note that this particular field doesn't have an A2X_DataType attribute, so we can bind to it directly:

```
...
<TABLE DATASRC="#dsoData" DATAFLD="tAnchorName"><TR><TD>
 <INPUT TYPE="TEXT" DATASRC="#dsoData" DATAFLD="$TEXT" SIZE="20">
</TD></TR></TABLE>
...
<TABLE DATASRC="#dsoData" DATAFLD="tHeading"><TR><TD>
 <INPUT TYPE="TEXT" DATASRC="#dsoData" DATAFLD="$TEXT" SIZE="45"
       VALUE="Data loading, please wait ...">
</TD></TR></TABLE>
...
<TABLE DATASRC="#dsoData" DATAFLD="tKeywords"><TR><TD>
 <INPUT TYPE="TEXT" DATASRC="#dsoData" DATAFLD="$TEXT" SIZE="45">
</TD></TR></TABLE>
...
<TABLE DATASRC="#dsoData" DATAFLD="tExtract"><TR><TD>
 <TEXTAREA DATASRC="#dsoData" DATAFLD="$TEXT" ROWS="5" COLS="40"></TEXTAREA>
</TD></TR></TABLE>
...
<SELECT NAME="selUpdate" DATASRC="#dsoData" DATAFLD="A2X_UpdateAction" SIZE=1>
 <OPTION VALUE="NONE">NONE
 <OPTION VALUE="UPDATE">UPDATE
 <OPTION VALUE="INSERT">INSERT
 <OPTION VALUE="DELETE">DELETE
</SELECT>
...
```

645

This is what it looks like when we open the page, and after the XML document has been loaded. You can see that we've edited the description in the **Extract:** control, and we're changing the **Action:** to UPDATE:

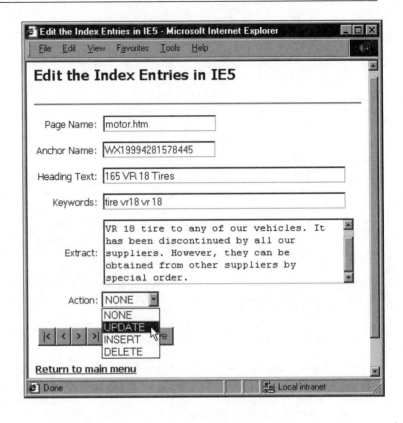

The Button-Bar Controls

At the bottom of the page are the controls that we use to move around the recordset and add new records. There is also a **Save** button that transmits all the changes we've made to the XML data back to the server. The next section of code shows the HTML that creates the buttons:

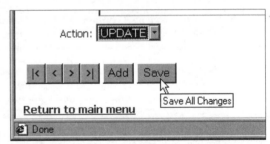

```
...
<button onclick="dsoData.recordset.MoveFirst()" title="First Record"
    id="cmdFirst"> |&lt; </button>
<button onclick="if (! dsoData.recordset.BOF) dsoData.recordset.MovePrevious()"
    title="Previous Record"> &lt; </button>
<button onclick="if (! dsoData.recordset.EOF) dsoData.recordset.MoveNext()"
    title="Next Record"> &gt; </button>
<button onclick="dsoData.recordset.MoveLast()" title="Last Record">
     &gt;| </button> 
<button onclick="fnAddRecord();" title="Add New Record">Add</button> 
<button onclick="fnSaveChanges();">Save</button>     
</TD></TR></TABLE>

<FORM NAME="frmUpdate" ACTION="update_index.asp" METHOD="POST">
  <INPUT TYPE="HIDDEN" NAME="txtXML">
</FORM>
...
```

The buttons call various methods that are exposed by the DSO's interface, which our <XML> element (or Java applet if you are using IE4) created in the page. The data island exposes the XML data as an ADO-style recordset object, which (just as in a normal ADO recordset) has a range of Movexxxx methods as well as the BOF (beginning of file) and EOF (end of file) properties we use in the code above. The Add and Save buttons call custom JavaScript functions elsewhere in the page, which we'll look at next. There is also, after the buttons, a HIDDEN control on a FORM, into which we'll place the XML document that we will use to submit the changes back to our server.

The Custom Page Functions

The two JavaScript functions in the page are used to add a new record to the locally cached recordset, and to send the changes back to the server. Adding a new record, when we are updating the content, is simple enough:

```
function fnAddRecord() {
  dsoData.recordset.addNew();              // add a new record
  document.all('selUpdate').value='INSERT'; // set UpdateAction value to INSERT
  document.all('tPageName').focus();        // put cursor in the Page Name box
}
```

To save the changes back to the server requires a bit more work. The first step is to make sure that all the edits in the current record are saved into the locally cached recordset, by changing which record is the 'current' one. We do this here by scrolling to the last and then back to the first record. Then we create a reference to the recordset and create the first part of the XML document that we'll be returning to our custom component on the server:

```
function fnSaveChanges() {
  dsoData.recordset.MoveLast();
  dsoData.recordset.MoveFirst();
  var intChanges = 0;    // number of changed records
  var objRS = dsoData.recordset;
  // create string to hold XML updates document
  var strUpdates = '<?xml version="1.0"?>\n' + '<PageIndex>\n';
  ...
```

Creating the XML Document to Return

Now we can loop through the cached recordset and collect the values of any records that have been changed—in other words those that have a value other that 'NONE' for the A2X_UpdateAction field. This reduces network traffic and server load from our component. For each one, we add a record to the XML document containing all the A2X fields and the data fields from the cached recordset. Note that, for the fields that have the A2X_DataType attribute, we have to extract the value from the $TEXT property of the field value, as we did when binding them to our HTML controls:

```
...
while (! objRS.EOF) {
  if (objRS('A2X_UpdateAction') != 'NONE') {
    strUpdates += ' <A2X_Record>\n'
            + ' <A2X_RecordNumber>' + objRS('A2X_RecordNumber')
            + '</A2X_RecordNumber>\n'
            + ' <A2X_UpdateAction>' + objRS('A2X_UpdateAction')
            + '</A2X_UpdateAction>\n'
            + ' <A2X_RecordMatch>' + objRS('A2X_RecordMatch')
            + '</A2X_RecordMatch>\n'
            + ' <tPageName A2X_DataType="TEXT">'
            + objRS.fields('tPageName').value.fields('$TEXT')
            + '</tPageName>\n'
            + ' <tHeading A2X_DataType="TEXT">'
```

```
                          + objRS.fields('tHeading').value.fields('$TEXT')
                          + '</tHeading>\n'
                          + '    <tAnchorName A2X_DataType="TEXT">'
                          + objRS.fields('tAnchorName').value.fields('$TEXT')
                          + '</tAnchorName>\n'
                          + '    <tKeywords A2X_DataType="TEXT">'
                          + objRS.fields('tKeywords').value.fields('$TEXT')
                          + '</tKeywords>\n'
                          + '    <tExtract A2X_DataType="TEXT">'
                          + objRS.fields('tExtract').value.fields('$TEXT')
                          + '</tExtract>\n'
                          + '  </A2X_Record>\n';
      intChanges++;
    }
    objRS.MoveNext();
  }
  dsoData.recordset.MoveFirst();
  strUpdates += '</PageIndex>\n';
  //put updates string into hidden control on form
  document.all('txtXML').value = strUpdates;
  // submit form to server where another ASP page will update data source
  document.all('frmUpdate').submit();
}
```

Once we've looped through all the records, the code (above) adds the closing XML document element tag. Then it places the complete document string into the hidden HTML control on the page, and submits the form containing it to our server.

Updating the Source Data on the Server

On the server, the request is collected by a page named `update_index.asp`. It simply takes the XML string and (after displaying some status messages) passes it to our custom component's `PutXML()` method. The return value is either the number of records updated, or a negative error number value:

```
...
<%
'fill in with your connection string details
strConnect = "DRIVER={SQL Server};SERVER=___;DATABASE=___;UID=___;PW=___"

strXML = Request.Form("txtXML")
If Len(strXML) > 0 Then    'we have some values to update
  ...
  Response.Write "<PRE>" & Server.HTMLEncode(strXML) & "</PRE>"
  ...
  'create the component instance
  Set objDB = Server.CreateObject("WX2882DB.XMLDB")
  strResult = ""           'to hold the error/result value
  intNumUpdated = objDB.PutXML(strConnect, strXML)

  If intNumUpdated > 0 Then
    Response.Write "<P>Updated " & intNumUpdated & " record(s)</P>"
  ElseIf intNumUpdated = 0 Then
    Response.Write "<P>No matching records to update</P>"
  Else
    Response.Write "<P>Error " & intNumUpdated & ". Failed to update data</P>"
  End If
End If
%>
...
```

Here's the result. You can see from the XML document displayed that we have sent back just one edited record, and that the data source has been successfully updated:

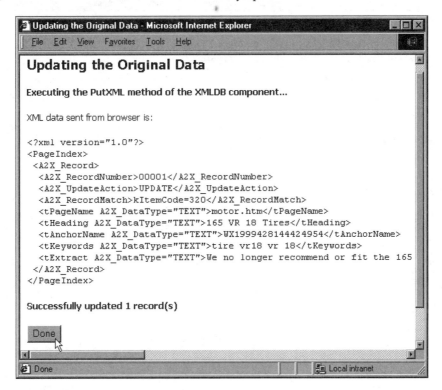

Editing the XML Document in Other Browsers

What happens if we don't have IE4 or IE5 available to edit our XML document through data binding? Well, we can always fall back on old-fashioned technology. Our sample page edit_all_index.asp uses a simple <TEXTAREA> control to display the XML document we create, allowing the user to edit it to their heart's content. Once they're happy with the changes, they can delete any records that haven't changed and submit the XML document back to our custom component, just like we did in the IE5 version:

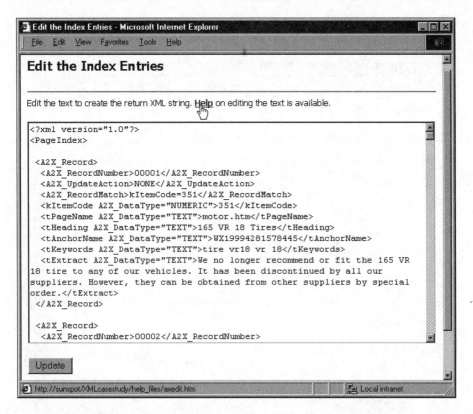

We've also included a link to some Help files at the top of the page, which show users how to edit the XML document so they can make changes to the database. And, of course, they can create their own documents if they wish, as long as they follow the correct structure and format.

To create this page, we simply use our custom component's GetXML() method to create the XML string:

```
...
'fill in with your connection string details
strConnect = "DRIVER={SQL Server};SERVER=___;DATABASE=___;UID=___;PW=___"

strQuery = "SELECT * FROM PageIndex ORDER BY tHeading"
strKeyField = "kItemCode"
Set objDB = Server.CreateObject("WX2882DB.XMLDB")
strXML = objDB.GetXML(strConnect, strQuery, strKeyField)
...
```

And then we insert it into the <TEXTAREA> control using <% = strXML %>. Note that the control has the same name as our HIDDEN control in the IE5 version of the page (txtXML), and is on a form that is submitted to the same ASP page (update_index.asp) to update the data source. This allows the same ASP page to be used with both this and the IE5 versions of the client-side 'updates' page:

```
...
<FORM ACTION="update_index.asp" METHOD="POST">
  <TEXTAREA ROWS="20" COLS="75" NAME="txtXML"><% = strXML %></TEXTAREA><P>
  <INPUT TYPE="SUBMIT" NAME="cmdUpdate" Value="Update">
</FORM>
...
```

You could, of course, create all kinds of different user-interfaces to edit the data, either using a text area like this example or in some automated fashion using different types of controls. You could even create an application that automatically generated the XML documents to add new records, without fetching a document first. They could all use the same update_index.asp page, and so offer a whole range of possibilities.

Creating and Updating the Index Lists

Now that we've processed our text files, created and stored our index entries, and edited them to correct any errors or inconsistencies, we're ready to use the data to retrieve the information on demand. The way we've chosen to do this in our example gives users two separate options—either they can read through an index list (rather like a contents list), which shows all the entries, or they can search for specific entries that match one or more words that they provide.

Returning XML and HTML Index Lists

In order to demonstrate how we can use the index data in different ways, we've provided both an XML and an HTML version of the index page and the search page. And for the XML versions we allow our users to display either plain XML data (as a document), or a copy of the data that is formatted using **Extensible Stylesheet Language** (XSL). The next diagram shows an outline of this part of the process in more detail:

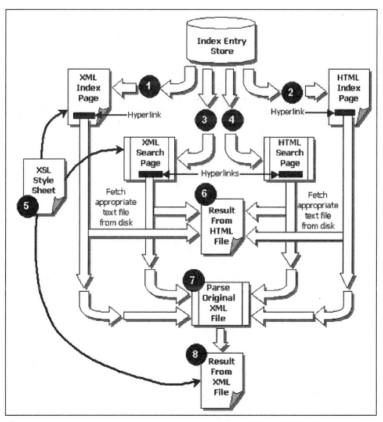

The files that carry out each step of the process are described in the table below:

File name(s)	Description
make_xml_index.asp	Uses the data in the index store to create and write to disk an XML document named xml_index.xml, which contains all the index entries in alphabetical order by topic heading. Can also create a copy of the file named xsl_index.xml, which uses an XSL stylesheet to display the contents.
make_html_index.asp	Uses the data in the index store to create and write to disk an HTML formatted document named html_index.html, which contains all the index entries in alphabetical order by topic heading.
xml_search.asp	Allows the user to enter search words and returns a list of all the matching topics in the index store, displayed as an XML document. Can also create the list in a form that uses an XSL stylesheet to display the entries.
html_search.asp	Allows the user to enter search words and returns a list of all the matching topics in the index store, displayed as an HTML page.
basic.xsl and booklist.xsl	XSL stylesheets that are designed to format the index entry lists (basic.xsl) and the lists of books (booklist.xsl).
{ the HTML result }	The original source HTML text file containing the topic information, from which the index entries were taken, scrolled in the browser window to display the appropriate topic.
show_xml.asp	Used to extract an individual topic from an XML document on demand, and display it formatted by an appropriate XSL stylesheet.
{ the XML result }	An XML document containing the appropriate topic, drawn from the original source XML text file containing the topic information, and from which the index entries were taken in the first place.

Creating the Index List Pages

In the previous chapter, we saw how we can use ASP to create a text file on disk, drawing the information from a database and wrapping it in the appropriate XML or HTML elements. Both our HTML and XML index pages are created this way, using the index entries stored in our PageIndex database table. The only real differences between the two processes are the ways that we organize and lay out the index entry information in the text file.

The HTML Index List

The ASP page `make_html_index.asp` is used to create the HTML index page. The first section is where we set up the values for things like the connection string to the database and the path to the text file that we'll be creating. We also need the path to the folder where our original text files reside, because we'll be including hyperlinks to them in the page:

```
...
<%
'fill in with your connection string details
strConnect = "DRIVER={SQL Server};SERVER=___;DATABASE=___;UID=___;PW=___"

'fill in with your file path details
strFileName = "D:\InetPub\WWWRoot\XMLCaseStudy\html_index.htm"

'change this to point to your text file store directory if different:
strTextPath = "/XMLCaseStudy/text_files/"
...
```

Now we can create the text file on disk, replacing any file with the same name, and write into it the HTML for the start of our index page:

```
...
'create new file, overwriting any existing one
Set objFSO = CreateObject("Scripting.FileSystemObject")
Set objFile = objFSO.CreateTextFile(strFileName, True)

'write new HTML page headings to the file
QUOT = Chr(34) 'double quote character
objFile.WriteLine "<html><head><title>Index of Pages</title>"
objFile.WriteLine "<style type=" & QUOT & "text/css" & QUOT & ">"
objFile.WriteLine "BODY {font-family:Tahoma,Arial,sans-serif; font-size:10pt}"
objFile.WriteLine "H3 {font-family:Tahoma,Arial,sans-serif; " _
                & "font-size:14pt; font-weight:bold}"
objFile.WriteLine "</style></head><body>"
strDate = Year(Now) & "-" & Right("00" & Month(Now), 2) & "-" _
        & Right("00" & Day(Now), 2)
objFile.WriteLine "<h3>Index of Pages</h3>Created: " & strDate & "<HR>"
...
```

Creating the Index Entries in the Page

The next step is to iterate through the records in the index store table, and assemble the information from them into the correct format for our page. We want to use the topic heading as a hyperlink that will open the original page at the appropriate point, using the anchor name that is also stored in our `PageIndex` table:

```
...
'select all index entries from index store database
Set oConn = Server.CreateObject("ADODB.Connection")
oConn.Open strConnect
strSQL="SELECT * FROM PageIndex ORDER BY tHeading"   'or use a WHERE clause
Set oRs = oConn.Execute(strSQL)                      'to split the index list
Do While Not oRs.EOF                                 'over several pages ...

  'get values from database
  strPageName = oRs("tPageName")
  strHeading = oRs("tHeading")
  strAnchor = oRs("tAnchorName")
  strKeywords = oRs("tKeywords")
  strExtract = oRs("tExtract")
  If LCase(Right(strPageName, 4)) = ".xml" Then
```

```
      'this is an XML file, so needs a different URL
      strPageName = "show_xml.asp?page=" & strPageName & "|" & strAnchor
   Else
      strPageName = strTextPath & strPageName & "#" & strAnchor
   End If

   'write the details out to the file
   objFile.WriteLine "<B><A HREF=" & QUOT & strPageName & QUOT & ">" _
                  & strHeading & "</A></B><BR>"
   If Len(Trim(strKeywords)) Then
      objFile.WriteLine "Keywords: [ <B>" & strKeywords & "</B> ]<BR>"
   End If
   objFile.WriteLine strExtract & "<P>"

   oRs.MoveNext
Loop
...
```

Notice the section that creates the HREF for our hyperlink. If the page we're linking to is a normal HTML page we just need to use the path to our 'text file store' folder, the page name, and the anchor name, so we get a hyperlink such as:

```
<A HREF="/XMLCaseStudy/text_files/motor.htm#WX199942183511023">Topic Heading</A>
```

Displaying XML Topic Information—The Problem

If the original file is an XML file, this kind of anchor isn't going to be any use. The browser won't recognize an <A> element in an XML page as being an anchor link. Rather than discuss how we're going to solve this problem now, we'll content ourselves with inserting the URL of another page named show_xml.asp that will retrieve an XML file. We'll look at this page in detail later in the chapter.

We also need to send the filename of the XML target document and the anchor name to the show_xml.asp page, so that we can open the appropriate file at the correct place. Therefore, we add them to the query string. However we can't use a # character here because it causes the string to be truncated when we read it using ASP. So, we'll delimit the two values with a vertical bar (or pipestem) character (|) instead. The result of all this activity is a hyperlink for XML source files that looks something like:

```
<A HREF="show_xml.asp?page=booklist.xml|WX199942183511023">Topic Heading</A>
```

Finishing Off Our Text File for the HTML Index Page

To finish off our HTML index page, once we've iterated through all the records, we add some HTML to the end of our page to create the button that returns the user to the default page:

```
'write out HTML for the SUBMIT button to return to the default page
objFile.WriteLine "<hr><form action=" & QUOT & "default.htm" & QUOT & ">"
objFile.WriteLine "<input type=" & QUOT & "submit" & QUOT & " value=" _
                  & QUOT & "Done" & QUOT & ">"
objFile.WriteLine "</form>"
objFile.WriteLine "</body></html>"
oRs.Close
objFile.Close
%>
...
```

The following screenshot shows the page as it looks in the browser, with each topic heading being a hyperlink to the original document. At the bottom of the page, you can see the button to open the default menu page, and in the status bar you can see the address that the selected hyperlink points to:

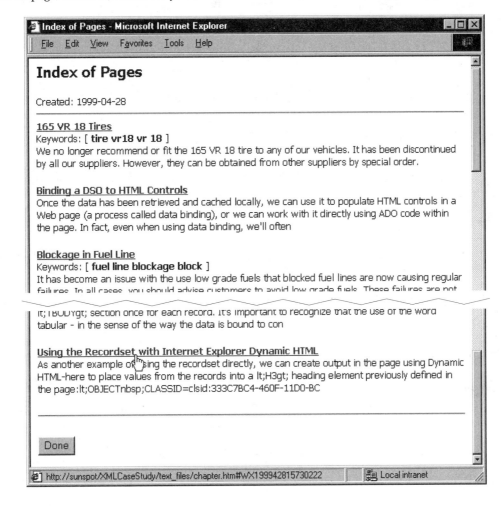

Note that the task this ASP code accomplishes would be an ideal candidate for a custom business component, built as an ActiveX DLL and installed on the server like the other two custom components that we've used.

The XML Index List

As you can probably imagine, the task of creating the XML format index page is very similar to that of creating the HTML formatted version. In fact, we will actually use this ASP page to create two different XML-formatted index lists.

❑   One will be purely XML data, reflecting the index entries in our index store database.

❑   The other will contain the same data, but we'll arrange for it to be linked to an XSL stylesheet that will display the contents in a much more attractive and intuitive way, including functional links.

To use the same ASP page to create two separate files requires a parameter to be supplied that indicates which one we are creating each time the page is opened. In our make_xml_index.asp page, we first look for a parameter named xsl in the query string. This will only appear if the page was opened using something like make_xml_index.asp?xsl=yes. If it does appear, we set a flag to indicate that in this instance we're building the XSL formatted version of the document, and then select the appropriate filename:

```
...
<%
If Len(Request.QueryString("xsl")) Then blnIncludeXSL = True 'use stylesheet
...
'fill in with your own file path details
If blnIncludeXSL Then
  strFileName = "D:\InetPub\WWWRoot\XMLCaseStudy\xsl_index.xml"
Else
  strFileName = "D:\InetPub\WWWRoot\XMLCaseStudy\xml_index.xml"
End If
...
```

Linking to an XSL Stylesheet

If we are building the XSL-formatted version, we have to include a link to the stylesheet at the beginning of the page. For our basic.xsl stylesheet, this requires something along the lines of:

```
<?xml-stylesheet type="text/xsl" href="basic.xsl" ?>
```

So, this is the code in our make_xml_index.asp ASP page that creates the headings for the XML document:

```
...
'write XML page headings to file
objFile.WriteLine "<?xml version=" & QUOT & "1.0" & QUOT & " ?>"
If blnIncludeXSL Then      'include XSL stylesheet
  objFile.WriteLine "<?xml-stylesheet type=" & QUOT & "text/xsl" & QUOT _
                    & " href=" & QUOT & "basic.xsl" & QUOT & "?>"
End If
objFile.WriteLine "<!-- Created " & QUOT & strDate & QUOT & " -->"
...
```

Creating the Index Entries in XML

Now we carry on in the same way as we did when creating the HTML index page. We loop through all the records in the `PageIndex` table of our index entry store, fetching the values of each field into variables and then building up the structure of the index page from these. We also have to do some similar—but slightly different—manipulation of the page name and anchor name (from which we'll later create the proper `HREF` value), depending on whether the index entry refers to an XML or an HTML page:

```
...
Do While Not oRs.EOF
   ...
   ... get values from recordset
   ...
   If LCase(Right(strPageName, 4)) = ".xml" Then
      'this is an XML file, so needs a different URL and anchor
      strPageName = "show_xml.asp?page=" & strPageName
      strAnchor = "|" & strAnchor
   Else
      strPageName = strTextPath & strPageName
      strAnchor = "#" & strAnchor
   End If

   'write the details out to the file
   objFile.WriteLine "  <INDEXITEM>"
   objFile.WriteLine "    <PAGE_NAME>" & strPageName & "</PAGE_NAME>"
   objFile.WriteLine "    <HEADING_TEXT>" & strHeading & "</HEADING_TEXT>"
   objFile.WriteLine "    <ANCHOR_NAME>" & strAnchor & "</ANCHOR_NAME>"
   objFile.WriteLine "    <KEYWORDS>" & strKeywords & "</KEYWORDS>"
   objFile.WriteLine "    <EXTRACT>" & strExtract & "</EXTRACT>"
   objFile.WriteLine "  </INDEXITEM>"

   oRs.MoveNext
Loop
...
```

The end of the code section above shows how we create a relatively simple format for our XML document, mirroring the original index entries in our database quite closely. The exception is the manipulation of the page name and the anchor name, as you can see in the next screenshot:

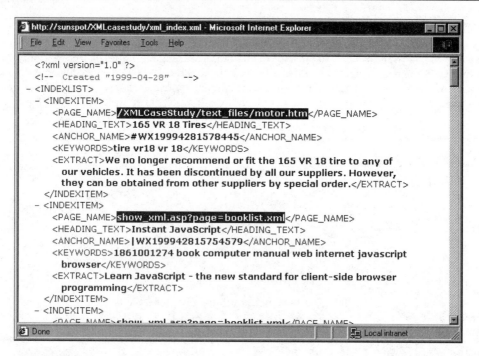

Obviously, this page could be useful in lots of ways. It provides a complete index to the stored text information, by topic, and includes all the data required to retrieve and display it. It would form an ideal basis for a search engine, and as it is pure XML, it can easily be transmitted over a network or sent to other people as a disk file.

The Basic XSL Index Stylesheet

Here we've met the first of our XML-oriented problems. The XML file is fine for storing the information, and using it as the basis for a custom application. For example, we could use this document to populate an IE5 XML data island, and work with the contents through data binding or script as though they were records in a normal ADO recordset.

However, as far as display in the browser is concerned, the plain XML file on its own isn't exactly attractive or easy to read, and there are no hyperlinks to other documents. To get round this, let's see what we can do with the version of the XML document in which we included a link to an XSL stylesheet. This document includes the line:

```
<?xml-stylesheet type="text/xsl" href="basic.xsl" ?>
```

This tells the browser to fetch the XSL stylesheet from the location specified in the `href` attribute, and use it to format the XML document that contains this instruction.

XSL Stylesheets in General

We don't have room in this chapter to discuss even the basics of XSL in any detail, as it is quite a complex technology when you take into account all the options it provides. However, to give you a feel for what it can do, and how it can solve some of the problems that we've already identified when working with XML, we'll step through a simple IE5 stylesheet taken from the examples for this chapter and then see the results.

Formatting the Root Element

The stylesheet we use to format the XML index page is named `basic.xsl`. It consists of a series of **templates** that are identified by the `<xsl:template>` element. Each one tells the browser how to format or process the content of any elements that match that template's `match` attribute. The first template includes the attribute `match="/"`, which means that it will only match the root element of our XML document. As you can see, it is mainly creating HTML code:

```
<xsl:stylesheet xmlns:xsl="http://www.w3.org/TR/WD-xsl">

<!-- template for the single root element -->
<xsl:template match="/">
  <HTML>
  <HEAD>
  <TITLE>The XML Index with XSL Formatting</TITLE>
  <STYLE TYPE="text/css">
    BODY        {font-family:Tahoma,Arial,sans-serif;
                 font-size:10pt; font-weight:normal}
    .heading    {font-family:Tahoma,Arial,sans-serif;
                 font-size:14pt; font-weight:bold}
    .itemhead {font-family:Tahoma,Arial,sans-serif;
                 font-size:10pt; font-weight:bold}
  </STYLE>
  </HEAD>
  <BODY>
  <DIV CLASS="heading">
    <IMG SRC="question.gif" ALIGN="BOTTOM" HSPACE="10" />
    The XML Index with XSL Formatting
  </DIV>
  <HR></HR> <!-- make it legal by adding dummy end tag -->
  <!-- iterate through all the INDEXITEM elements -->
  <xsl:for-each select="//INDEXITEM" order-by="+HEADING_TEXT">
    <xsl:apply-templates select="HEADING_TEXT" />
    <xsl:apply-templates select="KEYWORDS" />
    <xsl:apply-templates select="EXTRACT" />
  <P /> <!-- make it legal by adding dummy end slash -->
  </xsl:for-each>
  <HR /> <!-- make it legal by adding dummy end slash -->
  <!-- HTML button to return to main menu page -->
  <FORM ACTION="default.htm">
    <INPUT TYPE="submit" VALUE="Done" />
  </FORM>
  </BODY>
  </HTML>
</xsl:template>
...
```

It creates the outline of the page that you'll see when this template formats the XML document. However, notice the section that contains other `xsl` elements. This consists of an `<xsl:for-each>` element, which will select all the XML `<INDEXITEM>` elements and sort them by ascending order on the value of their `<HEADING_TEXT>` element.

Applying Other Templates

Within the `<xsl:for-each>` element are three `<xsl:apply-templates>` elements, each of which selects a particular XML element that is contained within the `<INDEXITEM>` element. As the XSL engine in the browser parses each one of the `<xsl:apply-templates>` elements, it will look for another template that matches the selected XML element. So all we have to do is provide templates for each of these XML elements.

It's also usual to include a template that uses a wildcard character, which will match (and display) the content of any element for which we omit a specific template, but it depends on the outcome we're looking to achieve. If we do include a wildcard template, it must come before the more specific ones:

```
...
<!-- elements that don't match any other template -->
<xsl:template match="*">
  <xsl:value-of /><BR />
</xsl:template>
...
```

In this template, we simply use the `<xsl:value-of>` element to output the value of the XML element, followed by an HTML `<BR>` element. This template is actually used to output our XML `<EXTRACT>` element content, as we haven't provided any other that will match this element in our stylesheet.

> *Notice that our stylesheet has to conform to XML syntax rules, so we include a closing slash character in the `<BR />` element. The browser doesn't mind about this, and still recognizes it as a normal `<BR>` element. The alternative is to add a dummy closing element instead, for example `<BR></BR>`.*

Creating HTML Anchors in an XML Document

The remainder of our XSL stylesheet contains the templates to format the contents of the XML `<HEADING_TEXT>` and `<KEYWORDS>` elements. For the `<HEADING_TEXT>` elements, we use HTML code to insert the image of a ball at the left, and then add an opening `<A>` element that will be formatted by the CSS styles defined at the top of the page (created by the root element template).

```
...
<!-- create HTML link element from heading -->
<xsl:template match="HEADING_TEXT">
  <IMG SRC="ball_red.gif" ALIGN="MIDDLE" HSPACE="5"/>
  <A CLASS="itemhead">
    <xsl:attribute name="HREF">
    <xsl:value-of select="..//PAGE_NAME" /><xsl:value-of select="..//ANCHOR_NAME" />
    </xsl:attribute>
    <xsl:value-of />
  </A><BR />
</xsl:template>
```

We want this `<A>` element to display a hyperlink to the original source text file, using the values from the XML `<PAGE_NAME>` and `<ANCHOR_NAME>` elements in the source document. We can create the HREF attribute for the `<A>` element using an `<xsl:attribute>` element, with the name being the name of the attribute we want, and the content between the opening and closing `<xsl:attribute>` tags being the value of that attribute. By using the `<xsl:value-of>` element with different select attribute values, we can insert the values of the XML elements. So, the template above will actually create equivalent HTML code that looks something like this:

```
<IMG SRC="ball_red.gif" ALIGN="MIDDLE" HSPACE="5"/>
<A CLASS="itemhead"
  HREF="/XMLCaseStudy/text_files/motor.htm#WX199942183511023">
  Blockage in Fuel Line
</A><BR />
```

Adding the Document Keywords

The final template in our XSL stylesheet matches the XML `<KEYWORDS>` elements in the document. We use an `<xsl:if>` element to check the value of the element content. If it is not equal to an empty string (`*` means the current element), the template outputs the text `"Keywords: [<B>"` followed by the contents of the `<KEYWORDS>` element from the XML document and ending with `"]</B><BR />"`:

```
<!-- only show keywords if they are available -->
<xsl:template match="KEYWORDS">
  <xsl:if match="* [. $ne$ '']" >
    Keywords: [ <B><xsl:value-of /></B> ]<BR />
  </xsl:if>
</xsl:template>
```

And here's the result. It looks very similar to the HTML index page we created earlier, but has the added images to brighten it up. The hyperlinks look and work exactly the same, because what we've effectively done is simply **transformed** the XML into HTML for display in the browser:

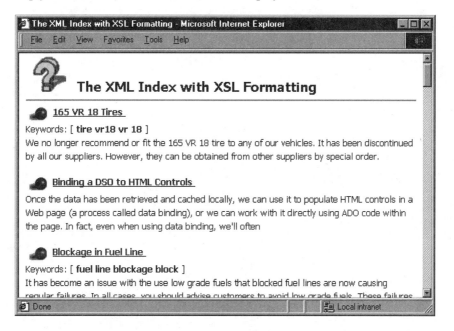

So, What Does XML and XSL Offer over HTML and CSS?

The great thing is that, by using XSL in this way, we haven't had to change the original XML document at all, other than to insert the link to the XSL stylesheet. In fact, if you view the source of the page from the browser's View menu, what you see is the original XML document. You don't see the HTML that we've transformed it into.

This means that applications can download and use the XML document *without* applying the stylesheet, or even provide a *different* stylesheet and use it to format the same document in a different way. On top of that the structured nature of the information means that it can be used in other applications that read and parse it automatically, perhaps as part of a bigger overall indexing project. Our output index file becomes the source input for the next stage of the process.

661

Also, as we saw earlier in this chapter, we might even be tempted to use data binding to display (and even edit) the final XML document if that was appropriate in our application. And, of course, we could build custom search pages that use the XML index page as their input.

Implementing the Search Feature

If we want to search for information, rather than read through a list as provided by our index pages, we can use the XML index page as an input to some kind of custom search engine, component or ASP page—as we intimated at the end of the previous section. However, we can also use ASP to search the index entries in the database table directly, and display any that match our search criteria.

We'll very briefly look at how the ASP search feature is implemented in our sample pages. The techniques for displaying the index entries that match our search criteria are identical to those we used to create the index pages. In effect, all we are doing is creating dynamic index pages that contain a selection of the index entries, rather than static ones that contain all the entries. Therefore, we won't be reprinting and describing *all* of the code again.

The HTML Output Search Page

To create the input form of our HTML search page, `html_search.asp`, we use some simple HTML:

```
...
<FORM ACTION="<% = Request.ServerVariables("SCRIPT_NAME")%>" METHOD="POST">
<TABLE>
 <TR>
  <TD ALIGN="RIGHT">Query:</TD>
  <TD ALIGN="LEFT"><INPUT TYPE="TEXT" NAME="txtQuery" SIZE="25"
                    VALUE="<% = Server.HTMLEncode(strQuery) %>"></TD>
 </TR>
 <TR><TD ALIGN="RIGHT" COLSPAN="2">
     <INPUT TYPE="SUBMIT" VALUE="Search" NAME="cmdSearch">  
     <INPUT TYPE="SUBMIT" VALUE="Done" NAME="cmdDone"></TD>
 </TR>
</TABLE>
</FORM>
...
```

This gives us the simple form we need to enter simple criteria and submit the page back to itself for processing by ASP code elsewhere in the same page. Note that we have to use the `Server.HTMLEncode` function to prevent characters that are not legal HTML from corrupting the value of the text box.

If the **Done** button is clicked, we simply redirect the user to the default menu page. However, if the **Search** button is clicked, and we have a value that was sent from the **Query** text box, we can search for matching entries:

```
<%
...
If Len(Request.Form("cmdDone")) Then Response.Redirect "default.htm"
...
strQuery = Trim(Request.Form("txtQuery"))
If Len(Trim(strQuery)) > 0 Then
  'build a suitable SQL statement to search for matching entries
  ...
```

To find matching index entries we use a SQL statement, and execute it against the index entries data store. We build the SQL statement by converting the string of search words into an array with the VBScript `Split` function (which converts a space-delimited string into an array automatically), and then iterating through the array adding each word to the WHERE clause:

```
  ...
  arrQuery = Split(strQuery)
  strWhere = " WHERE "
  For intLoop = 0 to UBound(arrQuery)
    strWhere = strWhere & "tHeading LIKE '%" & arrQuery(intLoop) _
           & "%' OR tKeywords LIKE '%" & arrQuery(intLoop) & "%' OR "
  Next
  strWhere = Left(strWhere, Len(strWhere) - 4)  'strip off last OR part
  ...
```

This will create a WHERE clause that looks something like:

```
WHERE tHeading LIKE '%word1%' OR tKeywords LIKE '%word1%'
OR tHeading LIKE '%word2%' OR tKeywords LIKE '%word2%'
OR tHeading LIKE '%word3%' OR tKeywords LIKE '%word3%'
```

Once we've got the WHERE clause, we can add it to the rest of the SQL statement and execute it against our `PageIndex` table. If we do get any matches, we can then iterate through the records and display them in exactly the same way as we did in the `make_html_index.asp` page. The only difference is that now we will be writing them direct to the browser through the ASP `Response` object, rather than to a disk-based text file.

```
  ...
  'now select the matching index entries
  QUOT = Chr(34)
  Set oConn = Server.CreateObject("ADODB.Connection")
  oConn.Open strConnect
  strSQL="SELECT * FROM PageIndex " & strWhere & " ORDER BY tHeading"
  Set oRs = oConn.Execute(strSQL)

  If oRs.EOF Then  'no matching index entries found
    Response.Write "No index entries matched your query:" & strQuery
  Else
    Response.Write "These index entries matched your query:" & strQuery
    'then display a list of matching entries
    ...
```

Here's what the HTML search page looks like after a successful search. The input controls are added after the search results so that the user can refine their search if required:

The XML Output Search Page

The second search page that we've provided, `xml_search.asp`, returns the matching index entries it finds as XML rather than HTML. The code it uses to do this is exactly the same as we've seen in our previous examples. It uses the same technique to parse the criteria string and build the SQL statement as the HTML search page. Then when it comes to listing the matching entries, it uses the same technique as the XML index page, except that they are written direct to the browser through the ASP `Response` object, and not to a disk-based text file.

Passing on the XSL Parameter

Where the page is unusual is that it has to serve a dual purpose of creating the results as either plain XML, or for formatting with an XSL stylesheet. As well as adding the appropriate `<xsl-stylesheet>` element to the XML if an XSL stylesheet is to be used, we also have to ensure that the parameter is passed on when the user clicks the Search button. As with the ASP page that created the XML index, we specify that XSL formatted output is required by adding the parameter `xsl=yes` to the query string when we open the page.

> *There is no option built into the test application to say that you want the XSL formatted version. To see this just add `xsl=yes` to the end of the URL.*

When the user clicks the **Search** button, the page is reloaded and the ASP code in the page is executed to build a list of matching pages. Therefore, we need to check if the parameter is present, and if so, add it to the query string of the `ACTION` attribute of the form in the page:

```
...
<%
strFormURL = Request.ServerVariables("SCRIPT_NAME")
If Len(Request.QueryString("xsl")) Then strFormURL = strFormURL & "?xsl=yes"
%>
<FORM ACTION="<% = strFormURL %>" METHOD="POST">
...
```

Choosing XML or HTML

The other point is that, unlike the HTML search page, we can't output some XML to indicate the matching index entries, then add some HTML to create the text box, **Search** and **Done** buttons. We have to do one or the other—XML or HTML. So, if the search is successful, the `xml-search.asp` page just returns the list of matching topics as XML. If it fails, we display the HTML controls for specifying the criteria and doing the search. And of course, if there are no criteria (because the page is being loaded for the first time and not through the **Search** button), we'll display the HTML part.

This means that the overall design of the page has to be different from the HTML version. The first step is to check to see if we got a string for the criteria. If the `xsl` parameter appears in the query string, we use ASP to generate the XML list of index entries, adding the link to the XSL stylesheet. After generating the XML document, the `Response.End` statement prevents any further output being sent from the page. If we didn't get any criteria in the request, we just skip the rest of the ASP script section, and instead output the HTML part for the user to enter the criteria and start the search process:

```
<%
...
strQuery = Trim(Request.Form("txtQuery"))
If Len(Trim(strQuery)) > 0 Then
   ...
   ... ASP code to create the XML document with matching index entries
   ...
   Response.End   'stop processing after sending XML file
End If
%>
<HTML>
...
... HTML to create the text box and buttons to start a search
...
</HTML>
```

Here's the result if we do get a match, showing the two entries that match the same criteria, 'petrol', that we used in the HTML search page:

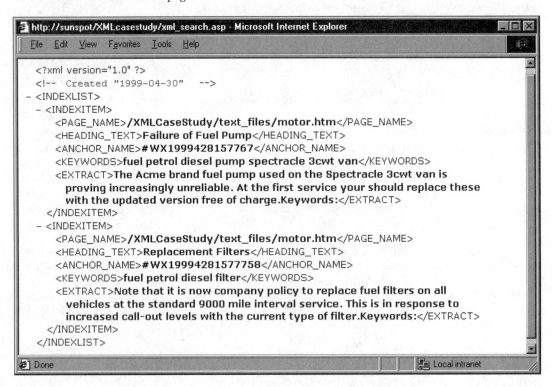

```
<?xml version="1.0" ?>
<!-- Created "1999-04-30"   -->
- <INDEXLIST>
  - <INDEXITEM>
      <PAGE_NAME>/XMLCaseStudy/text_files/motor.htm</PAGE_NAME>
      <HEADING_TEXT>Failure of Fuel Pump</HEADING_TEXT>
      <ANCHOR_NAME>#WX1999428157767</ANCHOR_NAME>
      <KEYWORDS>fuel petrol diesel pump spectracle 3cwt van</KEYWORDS>
      <EXTRACT>The Acme brand fuel pump used on the Spectracle 3cwt van is
        proving increasingly unreliable. At the first service your should replace these
        with the updated version free of charge.Keywords:</EXTRACT>
    </INDEXITEM>
  - <INDEXITEM>
      <PAGE_NAME>/XMLCaseStudy/text_files/motor.htm</PAGE_NAME>
      <HEADING_TEXT>Replacement Filters</HEADING_TEXT>
      <ANCHOR_NAME>#WX19994281577758</ANCHOR_NAME>
      <KEYWORDS>fuel petrol diesel filter</KEYWORDS>
      <EXTRACT>Note that it is now company policy to replace fuel filters on all
        vehicles at the standard 9000 mile interval service. This is in response to
        increased call-out levels with the current type of filter.Keywords:</EXTRACT>
    </INDEXITEM>
  </INDEXLIST>
```

If we elect to return the search results as XSL-formatted XML, we get the following page instead. This is, of course, the same XSL stylesheet as we use to format the XML index list document:

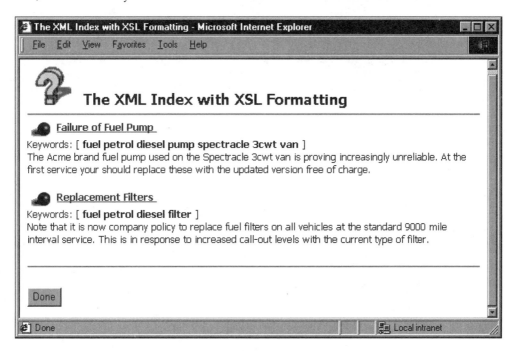

Retrieving and Displaying the Original Document

So, we can now create the index lists and view them to find a topic, or we can search for specific topics that contain certain keywords. There's just one thing left to look at, and it actually opens a whole new can of worms as far as XML is concerned. But let's work up to that in an orderly manner.

Displaying HTML Topics

We've already seen that we can open the original topic from our HTML or XSL-formatted index list pages or search pages with no problem. They contain hyperlinks of the form:

```
<A HREF="/XMLCaseStudy/text_files/motor.htm#WX199942183511023">Topic Heading</A>
```

These are standard HTML hyperlinks that will load the original page and scroll to the anchor defined in the HREF attribute:

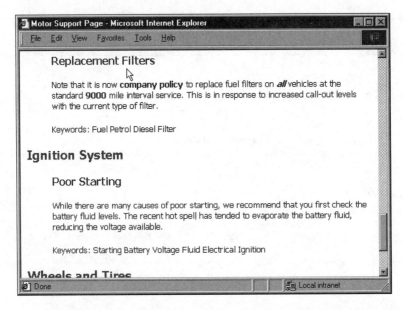

However, this is wasteful on bandwidth, and not particularly user friendly—especially if you have large documents. The whole page is sent over the network to the client, and the scrolling process can't take place until the document is loaded so there is often a delay.

The answer to this is to use small documents where possible. In fact, you might even consider building your application in such a way that it breaks each topic out into a separate document as it processes the source text files. That way, you would only have to send the appropriate topic file on demand.

However, if the source files contain related topics, which the user might like to read through, maintaining them as a complete single page might be better—it all depends on your own network bandwidth, information structure, and user requirements.

But all this still doesn't solve the main problem that we identified earlier. What happens when the target topic is in an XML document rather than an HTML page?

Displaying XML Topic Information—The Solution

We've discovered earlier in this chapter that, if the original file is an XML file, the normal <A> element isn't going to work like an anchor in HTML. The browser just won't recognize it in an XML page as meaning anything at all. Our solution was to send the page name and anchor to another page, in an attempt to put off addressing the problem until we actually had to.

We also discovered that we couldn't use a hash '#' character in a query string, because it causes the string to be truncated when we read it using ASP. Instead, we delimit the two values with the vertical bar ('pipe') character (|) instead. So, we end up with a hyperlink to our XML source topic files that looks something like this:

```
<A HREF="show_xml.asp?page=booklist.xml|WX199942183511023">Topic Heading</A>
```

All that remains, then, is to provide the `show_xml.asp` page that will display the appropriate part of the XML topic file.

What We Need To Do

To extract a subsection from an XML file earlier in this chapter we used the custom component that we built in the previous chapter. However, that can only extract the content of an element, or the content between two elements. In the current situation, we need to extract a whole section of XML from the source file. We need the entire content of the element for the selected topic.

In the case of our `booklist.xml` document, you can see from the next screenshot that the anchor we inserted surrounds only the heading text (in this case the book title). What we want to extract for display, however, is the entire `<BOOKINFO>` element and all its content. We also need to wrap it in a `<BOOKLIST>` element, and add the XML version header instruction as well. Only then will it be compatible with the original XML file, i.e. be a true extract that we can format with the same XSL stylesheet:

```
<?xml version="1.0" ?>
<!-- Created "1999-04-23" -->

<BOOKLIST>

<BOOKINFO>
  <ISBN>1-861000-44-8</ISBN>
  <BOOK_TITLE><A NAME="WX1999428103222417">Instant VBScript Programming</A></BOOK_TITLE>
  <RELEASE_DATE>1996-12-01</RELEASE_DATE>
  <DESCRIPTION>Program Internet Explorer the easy way with VBScript</DESCRIPTION>
  <KEYWORDS>1861000448 book computer manual web internet ie browser vbscript</KEYWORDS>
  <COVER_IMAGE_URL>http://webdev.wrox.co.uk/webdev/wd_images/0448.gif</COVER_IMAGE_URL>
  <MORE_INFO_URL>http://www.wrox.co.uk/Store/Details.asp?Code=0448</MORE_INFO_URL>
</BOOKINFO>

<BOOKINFO>
  <ISBN>1-861000-46-4</ISBN>
  <BOOK_TITLE><A NAME="WX1999428103222331">Instant ActiveX Web Database
Programming</A></BOOK_TITLE>
  <RELEASE_DATE>1997-03-01</RELEASE_DATE>
  <DESCRIPTION>All about the many and varied Web database programming
```

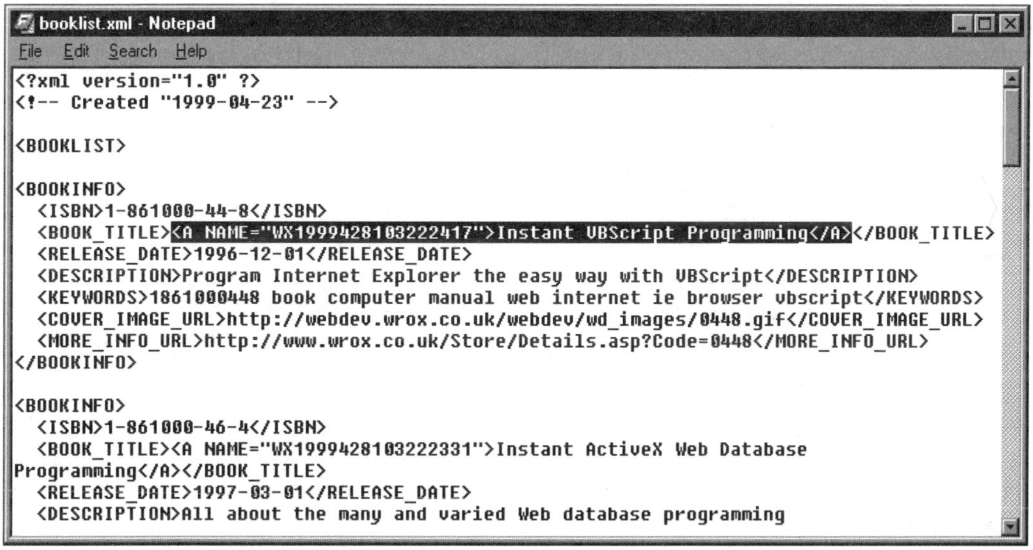

To be able to select the appropriate book, and extract the entire `<BOOKINFO>` element, we're going to need another technique, as our custom component is not going to be able to handle this task without a huge amount of extra work. Instead, we'll use another component, which Microsoft supplies as part of their Internet Explorer 5 browser. If you followed the setup instructions at the start of this chapter, you should already have this installed on your server and be ready to go.

The component we use, `msxml.dll`, is the XML parser that is part of IE5. However, it's also a fully COM-compliant DLL, just like those we've been building ourselves, and so we can instantiate it and use it in our own applications. We'll be using it to access the XML topic pages and extract the relevant entries from them for display when the user selects an XML page in the index list or search page.

The show_xml.asp File

The `show_xml.asp` page starts with code to set the path to the source text files folder, followed by code to extract the page name and anchor name from the query string:

```
...
<%
'change this to point to your text file store directory if different:
strXMLPath = "d:\inetpub\wwwroot\XMLCaseStudy\text_files\"

'get values from request
strPageName = Request.QueryString("page")
strAnchorName = Mid(strPageName, InStr(strPageName, "|") + 1)
strPageName = Left(strPageName, InStr(strPageName, "|") - 1)
...
```

Instantiating the XML Parser

Now we can get on and instantiate the XML parser component, and load up the original source XML file. After it's loaded, we check the error code to see if all went well. If this worked, we can start creating the XML document to return to the user. Notice that we specify the content type of the response, so the browser will know that it's XML (although it will recognize the opening `<?xml ...?>` element so this isn't absolutely necessary, but it's better to play safe):

```
...
'create an instance of the MS XML Parser on the server
Set objXML = Server.CreateObject("microsoft.XMLDOM")

'load the original XML document that we want to display
objXML.load(strXMLPath & strPageName)

'see if it loaded OK, i.e. is a well-formed XML file
If objXML.parseError.errorCode = 0 Then

  'completed loading OK so create pure XML to return
  Response.ContentType = "text/xml"
  ...
```

Creating the XML Headers

In our application, we have only one sample XML file, the book list file, and in the `show_xml.asp` page we will take special action for this file so that we can format the results using an XSL stylesheet. For other XML files, where we don't know the structure, we'll omit the stylesheet link and use a different root element, `<SELECTION_RESULT>`, instead. So, the next section of our code sets the required root element name and creates the XML document header elements:

```
...
strRootElement = "SELECTION_RESULT"
QUOT = Chr(34)
CRLF = Chr(13) & Chr(10)
strDate = Year(Now) & "-" & Right("00" & Month(Now), 2) _
        & "-" & Right("00" & Day(Now), 2)

'create the XML document headers
Response.Write "<?xml version=" & QUOT & "1.0" & QUOT & " ?>"
```

```
Response.Write "<!-- Created " & strDate & " -->" & CRLF

'add style sheet for special case of the BookList document
If strPageName = "booklist.xml" Then
  Response.Write "<?xml-stylesheet type=" & QUOT & "text/xsl" & QUOT _
                 & " href=" & QUOT & "booklist.xsl" & QUOT & "?>"
  strRootElement = "BOOKLIST"
End If
...
```

Parsing the XML Document

Now the real work starts. We have to find the correct <A> element, then go back up the XML 'element tree' (in much the same way as the left-hand pane of Windows explorer exposes your file structure) until we reach the element (or **node**) that defines the original topic section. In the case of the book list file, this will be the <BOOKINFO> element.

Working with the XML parser means that you have to know about the XML **Document Object Model (DOM)**. We can't expect to cover all the theory here, but basically what is happening is that we are creating a **pattern**, rather like we used in our XSL stylesheet earlier, that will select a single node in the document. In this case, it's the <A> element with the value of our anchor name for its NAME attribute. Then the code uses the selectSingleNode() method of the parser object to create a reference to that 'anchor' element.

Having done that, it gets a reference to the parent node's parent node, which should in most cases be the topic-containing element such as <BOOKINFO>. Then it can output the opening root element tag, the entire XML content of the topic node including its opening and closing element tags (all obtained from its xml property), and finish off with the closing root element tag:

```
...
'find the <A> tag with the required NAME attribute
strXSLPattern = "//A[@NAME='" & strAnchorname & "']"
Set objAnchorNode = objXML.selectSingleNode(strXSLPattern)

'then get the parent's parent's node, i.e. the enclosing element
Set objOwnerNode = objAnchorNode.parentNode.parentNode

'create the opening XML 'root' element
Response.Write "<" & strRootElement & ">" & CRLF

'output the XML content of the found item node
Response.Write objOwnerNode.xml

'create the closing XML 'root' element
Response.Write "</" & strRootElement & ">" & CRLF

Else
...
```

Providing Error Information

If the parser cannot load and parse the document for any reason, it sets the errorCode property of the parser's parserError object to a non-zero value. Our page will have detected this and, instead of trying to extract XML from the document, will instead run the following section of code.

This sets the return content type to `"text/html"` and sends back an error message. The `parserError` object provides a whole range of properties that identify the error in more detail:

```
...
Else
  'error loading document so create HTML error page
  Response.ContentType = "text/html"
%>
  <HTML>
  <HEAD>
  <TITLE>Error Extracting XML Sub-Tree</TITLE>
  </HEAD>
  <BODY>
  <H3>Error Extracting XML Sub-Tree</H3>
<% 'create the error message
  strError = "<B>Invalid XML file !</B><BR>" _
             & "File URL: " & objXML.parseError.url & "<BR>" _
             & "Line No.: " & objXML.parseError.line & "<BR>" _
             & "Character: " & objXML.parseError.linepos & "<BR>" _
             & "File Position: " & objXML.parseError.filepos & "<BR>" _
             & "Source Text: " & objXML.parseError.srcText & "<BR>" _
             & "Error Code: " & objXML.parseError.errorCode & "<BR>" _
             & "Description: " & objXML.parseError.reason
  Response.Write strError
  Response.Write "</BODY></HTML>"
End If
%>
```

Displaying the Result

The result, if the parser succeeds in extracting it, is a pure XML document. If the source file was our `booklist.xml` text file, the resulting XML will look something like this:

```
<?xml version="1.0" ?>
<?xml-stylesheet type="text/xsl" href="booklist.xsl" ?>
<!-- Created "1999-04-23" -->
<BOOKLIST>
 <BOOKINFO>
  <ISBN>1-861000-46-4</ISBN>
  <BOOK_TITLE>Instant ActiveX Web Database Programming</BOOK_TITLE>
  <RELEASE_DATE>1997-03-01</RELEASE_DATE>
  <DESCRIPTION>All about the many and varied Web ...etc.</DESCRIPTION>
  <KEYWORDS>1861000464 book computer manual web internet server</KEYWORDS>
  <COVER_IMAGE_URL>http://webdev.wrox.co.uk/wd_images/0464.gif</COVER_IMAGE_URL>
  <MORE_INFO_URL>http://www.wrox.co.uk/Details.asp?Code=0464</MORE_INFO_URL>
 </BOOKINFO>
</BOOKLIST>
```

When we display this XML in the browser, the XSL style sheet (a second one called `booklist.xsl`) that is attached to it means that we get a nicely formatted page containing the book cover image, details and description. The cover image and the title are both hyperlinks, which will take you to the page on our Web site that describes the book in more detail:

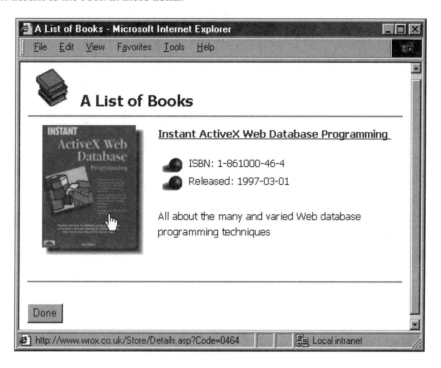

The BookList XSL Stylesheet

The page you saw in the previous screenshot was formatted by an XSL stylesheet named `booklist.xsl`, which we've included with the samples for this book. It uses basically the same techniques as we described for the `basic.xsl` stylesheet earlier in this chapter, but is in fact much simpler. There are no conditional elements such as `<xsl:if>`, and so the main focus is on the way each element is transformed into HTML to get the layout and effects you see. You can load the stylesheet into your browser to view the source. Alternatively if you want to experiment with it you can open it in NotePad or your favorite text editor.

> For more information about using XML and XSL in Internet Explorer 5, we recommend the Wrox Press book XML IE5 Programmer's Reference, ISBN 1-861001-57-6.

Part 2 Summary

The XML Case Study and the associated application and components have taken two whole chapters to describe, and by now you can see that they cover a wide range of topics—many of which may be new to you if you haven't started working with XML yet. However, hopefully these chapters have convinced you that XML is a powerful new technique, which you can't afford to ignore as it provides many opportunities for building better Web-based applications.

We've used two custom components and one standard Microsoft-supplied component in our application, though there is plenty of room to convert other parts of the process to components if required, depending on how you structure your own application and what data formats you settle on. Building code with ASP, and then converting the code to an ActiveX DLL component, provides even faster development and prototyping than working directly in a compiled language, and for VBScript/Visual Basic the conversion from VBScript is really simple—most ASP code works in VB directly as it is.

Our case study application demonstrates different ways of achieving the same (or similar) results, and this is intentional because it both increases the chances of it being applicable to your situation, as well as spreading across several related topics to give you a broader view of the possibilities. However, putting it all together, we've looked at:

- Processing different types of source text files, i.e. HTML pages and XML documents
- Editing and maintaining the index store data in our database table
- Creating the static HTML and XML index pages and formatting the information
- Implementing a dynamic search feature in both HTML and XML
- Retrieving and displaying the original HTML document or XML-based information

Amongst these topics should be something that has whetted you appetite, and persuaded you to get involved in XML, XSL, and text-based information storage and management.

The Rocks Cinema Application

In this chapter, we're going to use our knowledge of C++ to develop a full-blown application that uses ASP. We'll start by introducing the case study which is the focus of this chapter. This is an application allowing customers to book seats at a cinema, and managers to update the cinema schedule. We'll spend quite some time designing this application—it's always better to do this and save headaches later.

Then we'll dive into the C++ code required to get everything to work. This will use a lot of the techniques seen earlier in the book—particularly the OLE DB database access. We'll interrupt this coding frequently to test out what we've done so far using simple console applications.

When our components are functional we'll move on to build the ASP pages required for the project to work, which turns out to be quite simple in comparison with the work done to build the components. But then again, as this book has stressed time and again, the components are reusable.

Introducing the Cinema Application

Our application is a cinema booking system. It is designed to handle all aspects of booking tickets in a cinema—and since this is an up-to-date, fully technology aware cinema, it naturally allows its customers to book tickets over the web.

So let's look at the people who are going to want to use the system. The 'actors', as we tend to call them when formally developing use-case scenarios. We have:

❑ **Managers**—the people who configure the system, choose what films are going to get shown when, and check they are actually making some money.

❑ **Sales Team**—staff able to make bookings and answer queries on behalf of customers who drop in or phone up.

❑ **Customers**—will view show times and book tickets over the Internet.

More precisely, what each actor needs to do is this:

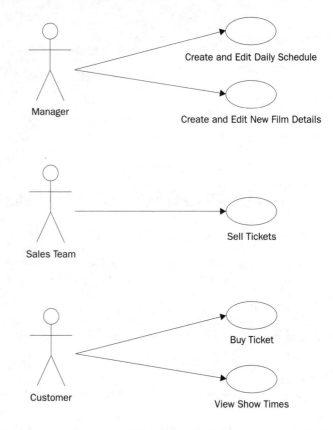

Application Architecture

Now we've seen what the application needs to be able to do, let's see how it's designed.

We can start off with a big simplification. The sales team and the customers are doing exactly the same thing—they both need to view performance times and make bookings. The real difference would be that whereas customers booking over the web must supply a credit card number, the sales team might be accepting payment in cash. However we're going to simplify things by assuming that the cinema is so amazingly advanced that it no longer accepts cash payments, and all bookings must be made by credit card. This allows us to use the same ASP page for customers and the sales team.

With this simplification, the cinema booking application will require the following:

❑ A database containing details of films, times, and tickets availability.

❑ An ASP page that allows customers to view details of films, and book tickets by supplying a credit card number. This same page can be used by the sales team in the cinema, to book tickets and answer queries on behalf of customers.

❑ An ASP page that allows the cinema management to modify the films and showings in the database—that is, add new films and showings, and remove out-of-date ones. This page must be password protected.

❑ A COM component (the `FilmBooker` component) written in C++, which interfaces with the ASP page that makes the bookings.

❑ A COM component (the `CinemaManager` component) written in C++, which interfaces with the ASP page to modify the films and showings.

❑ A COM component (the `DatabaseAccessor` component) written in C++, which modifies the database.

You can see how this fits together in this diagram:

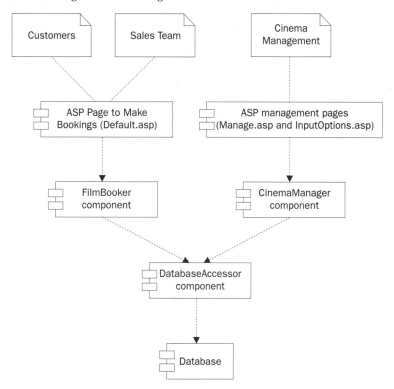

Notice how the functionality of interfacing with the database has been separated from interfacing with the ASP pages—these tasks are handled by different components. We discussed this in Chapter 5.

Since this isn't a database book, we won't go into the details of database design. However, you can download the Access database from the Wrox Press site, along with all the source code for the cinema booking application.

Any readers of criminal disposition will be disappointed to hear that we won't be presenting any 'real' source code to authenticate the credit card numbers either. Instead we'll just take a simple algorithm, whereby a credit card number is considered correct if it doesn't start with a '2' or '3'.

The User Interface

Before we perform a more in-depth analysis of these components, let's take a time out and skip forward to the end result. Taking a look at the full solution, while not being something that is possible in the normal design process, will help to give you a better understanding of what's going on in the rest of the chapter.

This section is divided into two parts. We'll start by looking at what users first see when they log on, and how they go about booking tickets, then examine the administration side, seeing how adding and removing films etc. is achieved.

Booking Tickets

This may be done by end users over the Internet or by the sales staff. The relevant ASP page is called `Default.htm`, to emphasize that this is quite close to being the default page that Rocks Cinemas might want end users to see when they visit their web site. This is what it looks like when you first connect to it:

So we have a list of the films currently on offer, with a brief description of each one. If we scroll down we get to the list of showing times:

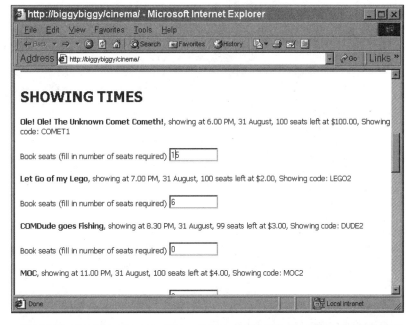

The showing times part of the page is embedded in an HTML form, so that you can fill in the numbers of seats you want to book for each film. Finally, at the bottom of the page is the bit where you have to fill in your own details allowing the booking to be made, along with the usual small print.

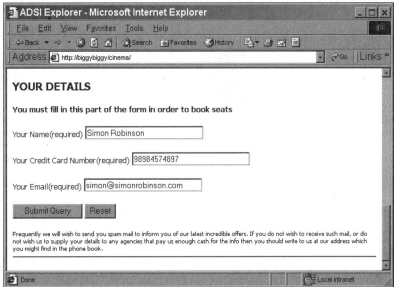

So booking could hardly be simpler: you fill in your name, credit card number, and e-mail address, as well as the numbers of tickets you want. From the previous screenshots, you can see that I've asked for 15 tickets to see Ole! Ole!, and 6 tickets to see Let Go of my Lego (obviously I've got a lot of friends!). If I submit the form with these details on it, I get to see this:

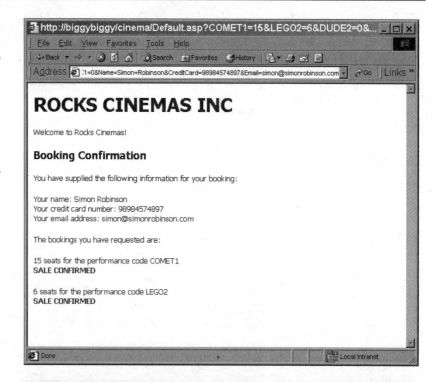

The bookings have been made for me—as I confirm by going back to the previous page and refreshing it to check the numbers of seats now available:

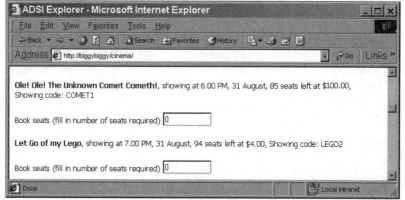

I guess if this was a real cinema, you'd probably want an extra screen in there, giving you the chance to see what bookings you'd made and how much it was going to cost you, with a Confirm button that you had to press before the sale actually went through. But even though this is supposedly a real-world sample, it's still a sample for a book, so I reckon I'm allowed to simplify it a bit. In real life you probably wouldn't want your credit card number going unencrypted tagged on to the end of a URL via the HTTP Get protocol, as is done in this sample, but I wanted to do it that way so I could prove that the GetRequestVariables() function I'll develop in this chapter works for the QueryString collection. Oh, and before you rush off and buy things using my credit card number, I should point out that I just used a random series of digits!

Administration

There are four things the managers would want to do with the database:

❑ Add new films

❑ Remove old films that are no longer being shown

❑ Add new showings

❑ Cancel showings

In fact, our sample implements all of these except adding new showings, for which we just have a couple of empty stub functions. The code for adding a showing would be quite complex as there are a lot of variables involved (date, showing code, film ID, price, etc.) but it wouldn't illustrate any new principles, so we've left it 'as an exercise'. If you want to play with the sample a lot, you can always directly add some showings to the underlying Access or SQL Server databases.

Since there are four possible actions, the relevant ASP page, `Manage.asp`, simply presents the four options.

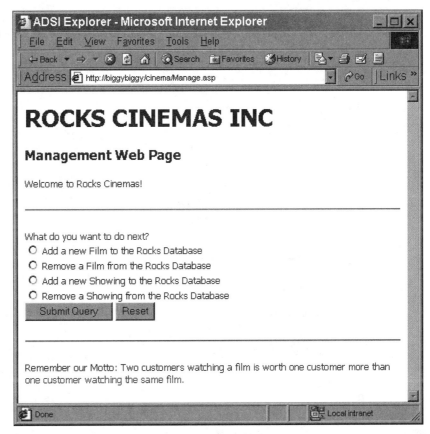

You simply click on the radio button you want, and submit. This takes you to a different ASP page, `InputOptions.asp`, which deals with presenting you with an appropriate form to specify all the information about your action (name of the new film, or which film you want to remove, etc.). For example, if I select Add a New Film, I get this:

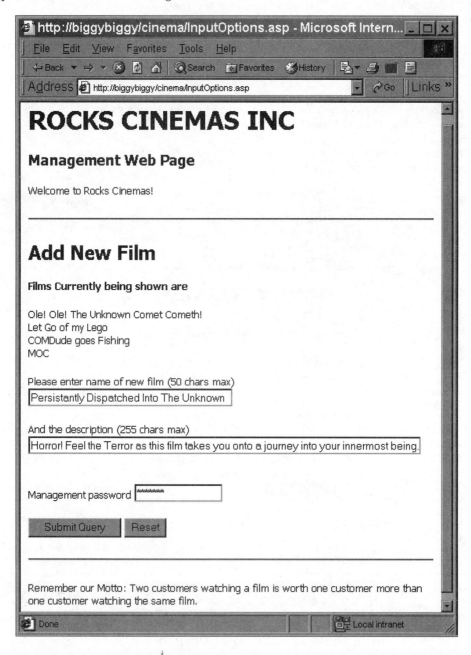

I've typed in the details of the new film and the password, and when I hit Submit Query, the film will get added to the database, and I'll get taken back to the Manage.asp page (which is the page responsible for making the modifications). Note also that it is at this point that security enters the frame; this page won't let me make any modifications to the database unless I supply the management password. (For this sample, the password has been hard coded into one of the components—it's comdude.)

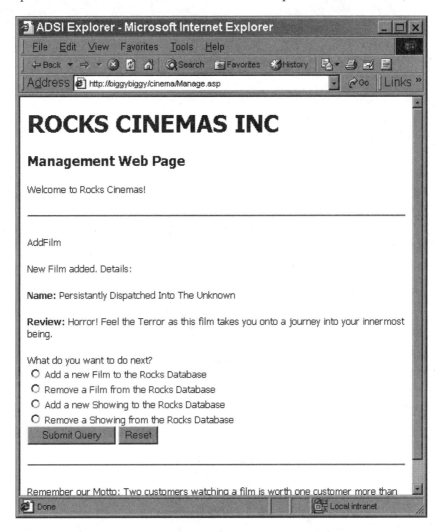

Although the film is now recorded in the database, you would still need to add some showings before customers could book tickets to see it.

As another example, if you opt to remove a showing `InputOptions.asp` will present you with this page:

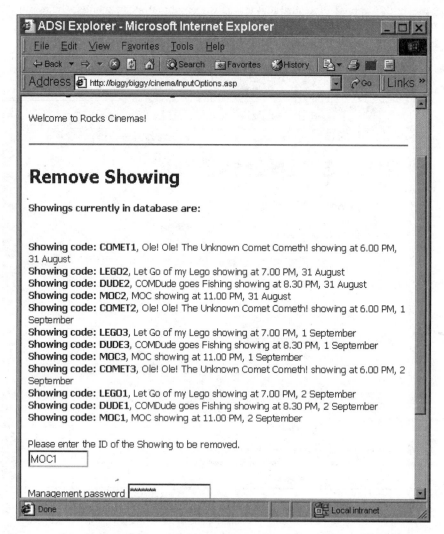

Hopefully you've got the idea, without our having to show you screenshots of every other possible action! Next we'll take a look at the database design, and go into more detail about the components we'll be using.

The Database

The database needs to contain details of films and tickets sold. We're also storing customer details—just in case the cinema wants to use them to send out mailshots to its customers.

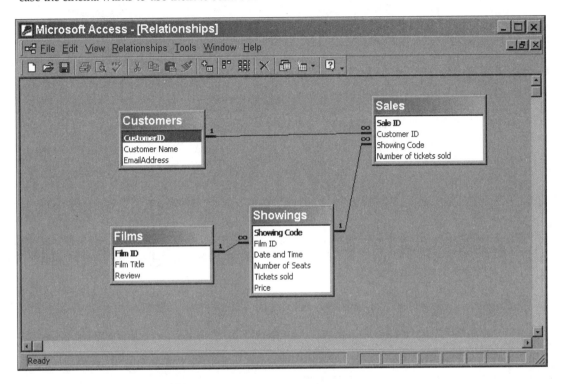

Here we have the following tables:

- ❑ **Films**—this stores the title and a quick review of each film to help customers choose what they want to watch.

- ❑ **Showings**—this stores details of what films are being showed when, and how many tickets can be booked.

- ❑ **Sales**—this simply stores details of each sale of tickets.

- ❑ **Customers**—like all true ethical companies, this cinema likes to keep tabs on who its customers are, in order to be able to con them into buying, sorry, tempt its customers with lots of special deals. This table allows them to do just that.

To see how we go about getting this data through to users, let's examine the components we're going to need.

Component Specification

The best way to design our components is to look at the specific functionality they should provide. This will lead logically into a set of methods they should expose, and with knowledge of both the structure of the database and the capabilities of ASP we'll be able to fully map out the code we need to write.

Let's look at each component in turn.

The FilmBooker Component

This component needs to provide the following services:

- Output a list of film showings
- Book tickets for film showings

Data exchange with the ASP pages that use this component can be achieved using the Request and Response objects, so both of these services can be carried out using simple methods requiring no parameters:

- ListFilms()—retrieves performance information from the DatabaseAccessor component and displays the full list of film showings, including the input controls necessary for the user to perform bookings.
- ConfirmBooking()—extracts booking requests from the data entered by the user, validates this, and (if necessary) updates the database through the DatabaseAccessor component.

The IDL is therefore:

```
interface IFilmBooker : IDispatch
{
    //Standard Server Side Component Methods
    HRESULT OnStartPage([in] IUnknown* piUnk);
    HRESULT OnEndPage();
    [id(1), helpstring("method ListFilms")] HRESULT ListFilms();
    [id(2), helpstring("method ConfirmBooking")] HRESULT ConfirmBooking();
};
```

The CinemaManager Component

This is the component used by the administration pages. As already specified, the functions this should perform are:

- Add and remove films
- Add and remove showings

In order to facilitate this, we'll include four methods to display forms for each of these processes as well as four methods to actually carry out these processes. Each method will first need to read data via the `DatabaseAccessor` component. The full set of methods exposed is thus:

❑   `DisplayAddFilmForm()`, `AddFilm()`—for adding films.

❑   `DisplayRemoveFilmForm()`, `RemoveFilm()`—for removing films.

❑   `DisplayAddShowingForm()`, `AddShowing()`—for adding showings.

❑   `DisplayRemoveShowingForm()`, `RemoveShowing()`—for removing showings.

Note that none of these methods need parameters, for the same reason as in the `FilmBooker` component. The IDL for these methods looks like this:

```
interface ICinemaManager : IDispatch
{
    //Standard Server Side Component Methods
    HRESULT OnStartPage([in] IUnknown* piUnk);
    HRESULT OnEndPage();
    [id(1), helpstring("method AddFilm")]
        HRESULT AddFilm();
    [id(2), helpstring("method RemoveFilm")]
        HRESULT RemoveFilm();
    [id(3), helpstring("method AddShowing")]
        HRESULT AddShowing();
    [id(4), helpstring("method RemoveShowing")]
        HRESULT RemoveShowing();
    [id(5), helpstring("method DisplayAddFilmForm")]
        HRESULT DisplayAddFilmForm();
    [id(6), helpstring("method DisplayAddFilmForm")]
        HRESULT DisplayRemoveFilmForm();
    [id(7), helpstring("method DisplayAddFilmForm")]
        HRESULT DisplayAddShowingForm();
    [id(8), helpstring("method DisplayAddFilmForm")]
        HRESULT DisplayRemoveShowingForm();
};
```

The DatabaseAccessor Component

The set of methods exposed by this component are perhaps the easiest to (qualitatively) describe; we've already seen what the other two components need, and these processes must propagate through to the data via this component. However in this case we do also need to decide on the parameters, since we have got to pass data between the database accessor and the other components.

With that in mind, let's dive in and say what we'll need this component to do. It should be able to:

❑   Provide a list of films being shown

❑   Provide a list of film showings

❑   Record customer info (if the customer is a first-time booker), and retrieve IDs of existing customers

❑   Make bookings

❑   Add and remove films and showings

These capabilities lead us to the following set of methods; the associated functionality will help us to decide what parameters they should take:

- ❑ GetFilmInfo()—returns a list of films in array form along with the total count of films.

- ❑ GetShowingsInfo()—returns a list of showings, also with a count.

- ❑ GetCustomerID()—accepts a name and e-mail address, returns the customer ID (which may be new if the customer is new).

- ❑ MakeSale()—makes a booking based on customer ID, showing ID and number of seats required.

- ❑ AddFilm()—adds a film to the database. The film title and review are required, the film ID is returned.

- ❑ AddShowing()—adds a film showing to the database. This requires a film ID, the date and time of the showing, the number of seats available, and the cost of a ticket. The showing ID should be returned.

- ❑ RemoveShowing()—Removes a showing from the database, using the showing ID.

- ❑ RemoveFilm()—Removes a film by its ID.

As far as parameters are concerned, we'll use BSTRs for all the strings, including the showing ID (which, as we saw earlier, will be something like COMET1), longs for the other IDs, and ints for the counts of films and showings. However we'll also combine the strings. A lot of these functions need to return lots of strings, and determine how many strings they'll be returning as well. That means arrays of [out] parameters containing strings where the size of the arrays are determined by the method call. That's not the easiest of things to do in IDL, so we'll simplify this by concatenating all the strings into a single string, separated by @ signs. The resultant IDL code for these methods is therefore:

```
interface IDatabaseAccessor : IUnknown
{
    [helpstring("method GetFilmInfo")]
        HRESULT GetFilmInfo([out] int* piNFilms,
            [out] BSTR* pbstrFilmInfo);
    [helpstring("method GetShowingsInfo")]
        HRESULT GetShowingsInfo([out] int* piNShowings,
            [out] BSTR* pbstrShowingsInfo);
    [helpstring("method UpdateCustomers")]
        HRESULT GetCustomerID([in] BSTR bstrCustomerName,
            [in] BSTR bstrCustomerEmail,
            [out] long* plCustomerID);
    [helpstring("method MakeSale")]
        HRESULT MakeSale([in] long lCustomerID,
            [in] BSTR bstrShowing,
            [in] int iNSeats);
    [helpstring("method AddFilm")]
        HRESULT AddFilm([in] BSTR bstrName,
            [in] BSTR bstrReview,
            [out] long* plID);
    [helpstring("method AddShowing")]
        HRESULT AddShowing([in] long lFilmID,
            [in] DATE dtDate,
            [in] long lSeats,
            [in] CURRENCY cyCost,
            [out] BSTR* pbstrID);
    [helpstring("method RemoveShowing")]
        HRESULT RemoveShowing([in] BSTR bstrShowingCode);
    [helpstring("method RemoveFilm")]
        HRESULT RemoveFilm([in] long lFilmID);
};
```

Note that this is a custom interface; we don't need a dual as this component will not be accessed by script.

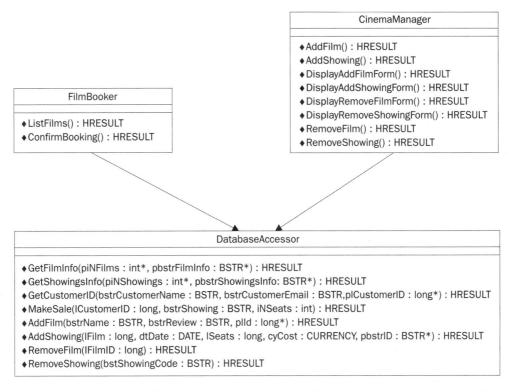

Now we know what the overall structure of our application will look like, we can start to assemble our code.

The Code

In this section we'll look at each component in turn, starting with the DatabaseAccessor component, and work our way up to the ASP pages.

The DatabaseAccessor Component

This component will be held in an ATL DLL project called CinemaDatabase. Create this project, add a simple (non aggregatable, custom interface) object called DatabaseAccessor, and add the methods detailed earlier.

Before we add the implementations of our methods, we need to set up our OLE DB consumer classes.

OLE DB Consumer Classes

We'll need to add four consumer classes to our project, one for each of the tables in the database. The access permissions required for these classes are as follows:

Table to access	Change	Insert	Delete
Customers	✗	✓	✗
Films	✗	✓	✓
Sales	✗	✓	✗
Showings	✓	✓	✓

To use the Access database you should use the **Microsoft Jet 4.0 OLE DB Provider**. Later on, when we use SQL Server, you'll need to use the **Microsoft OLE DB Provider for SQL Server**. Either way, four header files will be generated; include each of them in `DatabaseAccessor.cpp`:

```
#include "stdafx.h"
#include "CinemaDatabase.h"
#include "DatabaseAccessor.h"
#include "Utilities.h"
#include "Films.h"
#include "Showings.h"
#include "Customers.h"
#include "Sales.h"
```

We'll now examine the functions that use these accessor classes, starting with the simpler ones that just read data from the database.

Returning a List of Films

First up, let's look at how we return a list of films, using the `GetFilmInfo()` method that we defined earlier. This is how it is implemented:

```
STDMETHODIMP CDatabaseAccessor::GetFilmInfo(int *piNFilms, BSTR *pbstrFilmInfo)
{
    HRESULT hr;
    CFilms commandFilms;

    CComBSTR bstrResult;

    hr = commandFilms.Open();
    if (FAILED(hr))
        return hr;

    int iNFilms = 0;
    while ((hr=commandFilms.MoveNext()) == S_OK)
    {
        ++iNFilms;
        bstrResult += commandFilms.m_FilmTitle;
        bstrResult += "@";
        bstrResult += commandFilms.m_Review;
        bstrResult += "@";
        bstrResult += IntToBstr(commandFilms.m_FilmID);
        bstrResult += "@";
    }
```

```
commandFilms.Close();
    *pbstrFilmInfo = bstrResult;
    *piNFilms = iNFilms;

    return S_OK;
}
```

This should be mostly self-explanatory. Most of the code is devoted to constructing the string that contains the information about the films. Note how we've kept this simple, passing an array (the size of which would have to be determined at runtime) could be tricky, so as we mentioned earlier this method packs all the data into a single BSTR, separating fields by "@"s. So, you'd best make sure you don't book a film called "The @ of Doom".

Note the use of CFilms, one of the OLE DB consumer template command classes that we just created. The CFilms class is there to return information from the Films table. We'll modify this generated code slightly, shown below as the highlighted lines:

```
class CFilmsAccessor
{
public:
    LONG m_FilmID; // The primary key used to identify the film in other tables
    TCHAR m_FilmTitle[51]; // The title of the film
    TCHAR m_Review[256];   // Optional text describing the film
    ULONG m_FilmIDStatus;

BEGIN_COLUMN_MAP(CFilmsAccessor)
    COLUMN_ENTRY_STATUS(1, m_FilmID, m_FilmIDStatus)
    COLUMN_ENTRY(2, m_FilmTitle)
    COLUMN_ENTRY(3, m_Review)
END_COLUMN_MAP()

DEFINE_COMMAND(CFilmsAccessor, _T(" \
    SELECT \
      [Films].[Film ID], \
      [Films].[Film Title], \
      [Films].[Review] \
    FROM Films ")) \
```

A status variable for the FilmID has been introduced, because this is a primary key field that is automatically generated by the database—so we need the option to avoid setting it later on when we come to add new films from the management ASP page.

A Quick Test

It is often a good idea to check that everything is working properly at this stage of development. To accomplish this, compile the code we have so far, and create a new Win32 Console Application in a subdirectory of CinemaDatabase, called ConsoleTest. Add a C++ file called ConsoleTest.cpp, containing the following code:

```
#include <windows.h>
#include <tchar.h>
#include "..\CinemaDatabase.h"

int main()
{
    CoInitialize(NULL);
```

```
        IDatabaseAccessor* pDBA = NULL;
        CoCreateInstance(__uuidof(DatabaseAccessor),
                         NULL,
                         CLSCTX_INPROC_SERVER,
                         __uuidof(IDatabaseAccessor),
                         reinterpret_cast<void**>(&pDBA));

        BSTR bstrFilms;
        int intFilms;

        pDBA->GetFilmInfo(&intFilms, &bstrFilms);
        pDBA->Release();

        MessageBoxW(NULL, bstrFilms, L"Films", MB_OK);

        CoUninitialize();
        return 0;
}
```

This code simply creates an instance of our `DatabaseAccessor` object using standard VC COM code, retrieves a list of films showing, and outputs this to a message box. If all goes well you should see the full list of films (including embedded @s):

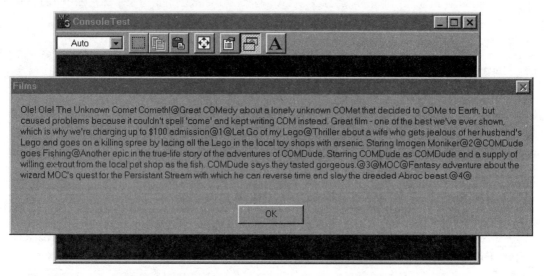

Returning a List of Showings

The `GetShowingsInfo()` function works in pretty much the same way as the `GetFilmInfo()` method.

```
STDMETHODIMP CDatabaseAccessor::GetShowingsInfo(int* piNShowings,
                                                BSTR* pbstrShowingsInfo)
{
    HRESULT hr;
    CShowings commandShowings;

    CComBSTR bstrResult;
    CComVariant buffer;
    SYSTEMTIME systDateAndTime;
    TCHAR tchrDate[12];
    TCHAR tchrTime[8];
```

```
        hr = commandShowings.Open();
        if (FAILED(hr))
        return hr;

        int iNShowings = 0;
        while ((hr=commandShowings.MoveNext()) == S_OK)
        {
            ++iNShowings;
            bstrResult += commandShowings.m_FilmTitle;
            bstrResult += "@";
            bstrResult += commandShowings.m_ShowingCode;
            bstrResult += "@";
            VariantTimeToSystemTime(commandShowings.m_DateandTime, &systDateAndTime);
            GetTimeFormat(NULL, NULL, &systDateAndTime, _T("h':'mm tt"), tchrTime,
                        8);
            GetDateFormat(NULL, NULL, &systDateAndTime, _T("MMM dd yyyy"), tchrDate,
                        12);
            bstrResult.Append(tchrTime);
            bstrResult += ", ";
            bstrResult.Append(tchrDate);
            bstrResult += "@";
            buffer = commandShowings.m_NumberofSeats;
            buffer.ChangeType(VT_BSTR);
            bstrResult.AppendBSTR(buffer.bstrVal);
            bstrResult += "@";
            buffer = commandShowings.m_Ticketssold;
            buffer.ChangeType(VT_BSTR);
            bstrResult.AppendBSTR(buffer.bstrVal);
            bstrResult += "@$";
            buffer = commandShowings.m_Price;
            buffer.ChangeType(VT_BSTR);
            bstrResult.AppendBSTR(buffer.bstrVal);
            bstrResult += "@";
        }

        commandShowings.Close();
        *pbstrShowingsInfo = bstrResult;
        *piNShowings = iNShowings;

        return S_OK;
    }
```

This code uses a handy method of CComVariant to convert various types of data into BSTRs: CComVariant::ChangeType(). We also use a couple of system APIs to convert the DATE variable into a more readable format.

The main difference here is that we use a different consumer template class, CShowings. CShowings is slightly more complicated than CFilms, since it needs to return information from two different tables (to get the film title relating to the film ID), so it requires a few more modifications to the wizard-generated code.

```
class CShowingsAccessor
{
public:
    DATE m_DateandTime;        // Date and time of this performance
    LONG m_FilmID;             // Foreign key that identifies the film showing
    LONG m_NumberofSeats;      // Number of tickets that may be sold
    CURRENCY m_Price;          // The price of each ticket for this performance
    TCHAR m_ShowingCode[11];   // Primary key that identifies this performance
    LONG m_Ticketssold;        // The number of tickets already sold. Number of
                               // seats minus Tickets sold gives number of
                               // tickets left to sell.
    TCHAR m_FilmTitle[51];
    ULONG m_ShowingCodeStatus;
```

```
BEGIN_COLUMN_MAP(CShowingsAccessor)
    COLUMN_ENTRY(1, m_FilmTitle)
    COLUMN_ENTRY_STATUS(2, m_ShowingCode, m_ShowingCodeStatus)
    COLUMN_ENTRY_TYPE(3, DBTYPE_DATE, m_DateandTime)
    COLUMN_ENTRY(4, m_NumberofSeats)
    COLUMN_ENTRY(5, m_Ticketssold)
    COLUMN_ENTRY(6, m_FilmID)
    COLUMN_ENTRY_TYPE(7, DBTYPE_CY, m_Price)
END_COLUMN_MAP()

DEFINE_COMMAND(CShowingsAccessor, _T(" \
    SELECT \
    [Films].[Film Title], [Showings].[Showing Code], \
    [Showings].[Date and Time], [Showings].[Number of Seats], \
    [Showings].[Tickets sold], \
    [Showings].[Film ID], \
    [Showings].[Price] \
    FROM Showings \
    INNER JOIN Films ON [Films].[Film ID] =[Showings].[Film ID] \
    ORDER BY [Date and Time];"))
```

A Quick Test

You can test this method in a very similar way to the last one – just replace the call to GetFilmInfo() with GetShowingsInfo():

```cpp
#include <windows.h>
#include <tchar.h>
#include "..\CinemaDatabase.h"

int main()
{
    CoInitialize(NULL);

    IDatabaseAccessor* pDBA = NULL;
    CoCreateInstance(__uuidof(DatabaseAccessor),
                    NULL,
                    CLSCTX_INPROC_SERVER,
                    __uuidof(IDatabaseAccessor),
                    reinterpret_cast<void**>(&pDBA));

    BSTR bstrShowings;
    int intShowings;

    pDBA->GetShowingsInfo(&intShowings, &bstrShowings);
    pDBA->Release();

    MessageBoxW(NULL, bstrShowings, L"Showings", MB_OK);

    CoUninitialize();
    return 0;
}
```

Getting the Customer ID

The GetCustomerID() method is the first one in the project that adds new records. This method looks to see if customers with supplied names are already in the database, and adds them if they're not there. This function also uses the ATL conversion macros to convert between the UNICODE strings required in BSTR and the ANSI strings that will be retrieved from the database if the project settings do not specify a UNICODE build.

```
STDMETHODIMP CDatabaseAccessor::GetCustomerID(BSTR bstrCustomerName,
                                              BSTR bstrCustomerEmail,
                                              long *plCustomerID)
{
    CCustomers commandCustomers;
    HRESULT hr;

    USES_CONVERSION;

    // attempt to locate this customer
    hr = commandCustomers.Open();
    if (FAILED(hr))
        return hr;

    while((hr = commandCustomers.MoveNext()) == S_OK)
    {
        if (CComBSTR(bstrCustomerName) == commandCustomers.m_CustomerName)
        {
            // found the customer!
            *plCustomerID = commandCustomers.m_CustomerID;
            commandCustomers.Close();
            return S_OK;
        }
    }
    // not found customer -> add customer
    _tcscpy(commandCustomers.m_CustomerName, W2T(bstrCustomerName));
    _tcscpy(commandCustomers.m_EmailAddress, W2T(bstrCustomerEmail));
    commandCustomers.m_CustomerIDStatus = DBSTATUS_S_IGNORE;
    hr = commandCustomers.Insert();
    if (FAILED(hr))
    {
        commandCustomers.Close();
        return hr;
    }
    hr = commandCustomers.GetData();

    *plCustomerID = commandCustomers.m_CustomerID;

    commandCustomers.Close();
    return hr;
}
```

As before, we are using an additional status variable, so the following changes need to be made to CCustomers:

```
class CCustomersAccessor
{
public:
    TCHAR m_CustomerName[31];
    LONG m_CustomerID;
    TCHAR m_EmailAddress[51];
    ULONG m_CustomerIDStatus;

BEGIN_COLUMN_MAP(CCustomersAccessor)
    COLUMN_ENTRY_STATUS(1, m_CustomerID, m_CustomerIDStatus)
    COLUMN_ENTRY(2, m_CustomerName)
    COLUMN_ENTRY(3, m_EmailAddress)
END_COLUMN_MAP()

DEFINE_COMMAND(CCustomersAccessor, _T(" \
    SELECT \
        CustomerID, \
        `Customer Name`, \
        EmailAddress \
        FROM Customers"))
```

697

A Quick Test

To test this method we need to make slightly more changes to our console application:

```
#include <windows.h>
#include <tchar.h>
#include "..\CinemaDatabase.h"

int main()
{
    CoInitialize(NULL);

    IDatabaseAccessor* pDBA = NULL;
    CoCreateInstance(__uuidof(DatabaseAccessor),
                    NULL,
                    CLSCTX_INPROC_SERVER,
                    __uuidof(IDatabaseAccessor),
                    reinterpret_cast<void**>(&pDBA));

    wchar_t buffer[20];
    BSTR bstrName = SysAllocString(L"Roger Moore");
    BSTR bstrEmail = SysAllocString(L"rogerm@eyebrows.org");
    long lngID;

    pDBA->GetCustomerID(bstrName, bstrEmail, &lngID);
    _ltow(lngID, buffer, 10);
    MessageBoxW(NULL, buffer, L"Roger Moore Added, ID=", MB_OK);

    pDBA->GetCustomerID(bstrName, bstrEmail, &lngID);
    _ltow(lngID, buffer, 10);
    MessageBoxW(NULL, buffer, L"Roger Moore Retrieved, ID=", MB_OK);

    SysReAllocString(&bstrName, L"Sean Connery");
    SysReAllocString(&bstrEmail, L"seanc@thankyoumishmoneypenny.com");

    pDBA->GetCustomerID(bstrName, bstrEmail, &lngID);
    _ltow(lngID, buffer, 10);
    MessageBoxW(NULL, buffer, L"Sean Connery Added, ID=", MB_OK);

    pDBA->Release();
    CoUninitialize();
    return 0;
}
```

This code demonstrates how GetCustomerID() updates the database behind the scenes. We look up the ID for Roger Moore, and because it's the first time he's booked tickets to Rocks Cinemas, GetCustomerID() adds him to the database. We then display the ID that's been assigned to him. Next, we try looking up Roger's ID again: if all goes well we should get the same ID back as before. As a final test we try looking up another new customer, Sean Connery. This time we should receive an ID one greater than Roger's, obviously proof that Sean was a greater James Bond.

Making a Sale

The MakeSale() method is slightly complicated by the fact that not only does an entry need to be made in the sales table, but the number of seats remaining in the showings table needs to be adjusted.

First of all we search for the showing we need to book seats for, returning `E_FAIL` if we either can't find it, or discover that there aren't enough seats left:

```
STDMETHODIMP CDatabaseAccessor::MakeSale(long lCustomerID, BSTR bstrShowing,
                                         int iNSeats)
{
    USES_CONVERSION;

    // check if there are enough seats for this showing
    CShowings commandShowings;
    HRESULT hr;
    hr = commandShowings.Open();
    if (FAILED(hr))
        return hr;

    // locate this showing
    bool bFound = false;
    while ((hr = commandShowings.MoveNext()) == S_OK)
    {
        if (CComBSTR(bstrShowing) == commandShowings.m_ShowingCode)
        {
            // found showing! - check there's enough seats...
            bFound = true;
            int iSeatsRemaining = commandShowings.m_NumberofSeats -
                commandShowings.m_Ticketssold;
            if (iSeatsRemaining < iNSeats)
                return E_FAIL;
            break;
        }
    }
    if (!bFound)
        return E_FAIL;
```

After deciding that the sale is possible, we record it in the `Sales` database:

```
    // record the sale
    CSales commandSales;
    hr = commandSales.Open();
    if (FAILED(hr))
        return hr;

    commandSales.m_CustomerID = lCustomerID;
    _tcscpy(commandSales.m_ShowingCode, W2T(bstrShowing));
    commandSales.m_Numberofticketssold = iNSeats;
    commandSales.m_SaleIDStatus = DBSTATUS_S_IGNORE;
    hr = commandSales.Insert();
    commandSales.Close();
    if (FAILED(hr))
    {
        commandShowings.Close();
        return hr;
    }
```

Finally, we update the number of seats remaining in the `Showings` database:

```
    // adjust the remaining number of seats in the showing
    commandShowings.m_Ticketssold += iNSeats;
    commandShowings.m_ShowingCodeStatus = DBSTATUS_S_IGNORE;
    hr = commandShowings.SetData();
    commandShowings.Close();

    return hr;
}
```

We also have to make a (by now) familiar change to `CSales`:

```
class CSalesAccessor
{
public:
LONG m_CustomerID; // Foreign key that identifies customer
LONG m_Numberofticketssold; // Number of tickets this customer has bought
LONG m_SaleID; // Primary key - this is only here to stop Access complaining
TCHAR m_ShowingCode[11]; // Foreign key that identifies the performance these
                         // tickets were sold for
ULONG m_SaleIDStatus;

BEGIN_COLUMN_MAP(CSalesAccessor)
    COLUMN_ENTRY_STATUS(1, m_SaleID, m_SaleIDStatus)
    COLUMN_ENTRY(2, m_CustomerID)
    COLUMN_ENTRY(3, m_ShowingCode)
    COLUMN_ENTRY(4, m_Numberofticketssold)
END_COLUMN_MAP()

DEFINE_COMMAND(CSalesAccessor, _T(" \
    SELECT \
        `Sale ID`, \
        `Customer ID`, \
        `Showing Code`, \
        `Number of tickets sold`  \
        FROM Sales"))
```

A Quick Test

Let's test this by getting Roger Moore to book tickets until there aren't any left:

```
#include <windows.h>
#include <tchar.h>
#include "..\CinemaDatabase.h"

int main()
{
    CoInitialize(NULL);

    IDatabaseAccessor* pDBA = NULL;
    CoCreateInstance(__uuidof(DatabaseAccessor),
                     NULL,
                     CLSCTX_INPROC_SERVER,
                     __uuidof(IDatabaseAccessor),
                     reinterpret_cast<void**>(&pDBA));

    wchar_t buffer[20];
    BSTR bstrName = SysAllocString(L"Roger Moore");
    BSTR bstrEmail = SysAllocString(L"rogerm@eyebrows.org");
    long lngID;

    pDBA->GetCustomerID(bstrName, bstrEmail, &lngID);

    BSTR bstrShowing = SysAllocString(L"COMET1");
    HRESULT hr = pDBA->MakeSale(lngID, bstrShowing, 30);
    if (SUCCEEDED(hr))
        MessageBoxW(NULL, L"Lucky Roger Moore bought some tickets!",
                    L"Success", MB_OK);
    else
        MessageBoxW(NULL, L"Poor Roger Moore can't buy any tickets.",
                    L"Failure", MB_OK);

    pDBA->Release();
    CoUninitialize();
    return 0;
}
```

If you run this a few times, Roger will soon exhaust the ticket supply.

Well, we've now implemented enough of the methods for the `FilmBooker` component to function, so let's leave the `DatabaseAccessor` component for now and move on, taking one more step towards the ASP solution we're aiming for.

The FilmBooker Component

The `FilmBooker` component is, thankfully, a lot simpler than the `DatabaseAccessor` component! This component will be part of a project called `CinemaBookings`, another ATL DLL. Create this project and add a non-aggregatable **ActiveX Server Component**, called `FilmBooker`. Add the two methods `ConfirmBooking()` and `ListFilms()` to `IFilmBooker`—we'll implement them in a bit. First, though, we'll add a few helper functions:

Helper Functions

Add the following declarations to `FilmBooker.h`:

```
IResponse* GetResponse() const;
IRequest* GetRequest() const;
HRESULT GetBookingDetails(CComBSTR &bstrName, CComBSTR &bstrEmail,
                          CComBSTR &bstrCreditCard, int &iNBookings,
                          CComBSTR **parrbstrShowings, int **parriNSeats);
HRESULT GetRequestVariables(CComPtr<IRequestDictionary> spDictionary,
                            int &iNValues, CComBSTR **parrbstrNames,
                            CComBSTR **parrbstrValues);
HRESULT BreakUpBstr(CComBSTR &bstrInput, LPWSTR *ppszResults, int iNVals);
```

The implementation of the first two of these is trivial—we'll just use them to gain access to the respective ASP objects. Add these to `FilmBooker.cpp`:

```
IResponse* CFilmBooker::GetResponse() const
{
    return m_piResponse;
}

IRequest* CFilmBooker::GetRequest() const
{
    return m_piRequest;
}
```

Here `m_piRequest` and `m_piResponse` are the variables supplied by the object wizard. We won't add any other member variables, either to this component or to any of the others that we develop, since we need the project to be compatible with MTS—so we don't want it to have any identifiable state.

We'll see the code for `GetBookingDetails()`, `GetRequestVariables()` and `BreakUpBstr()` later. These are all utility functions used by our component: we'll detail them at the appropriate times.

You'll also need to include the files necessary to access the `DatabaseAccessor` component:

```
#include "stdafx.h"
#include "CinemaBookings.h"
#include "FilmBooker.h"
#include "Utilities.h"
#include "../CinemaDatabase/CinemaDatabase.h"
#include "../CinemaDatabase/CinemaDatabase_i.c"
```

The ListFilms() Method

This method starts off by getting an instance of the `DatabaseAccessor` component to handle the interaction with the database. We then call the `GetFilmInfo()` method of this object, which returns all the names, IDs, and reviews of each film along with the number of films, in the form of a single (and large) `BSTR` and a count, as we saw earlier. We'll use a global function, `BreakUpBstr()` (shown later), to unpack all the information.

```
STDMETHODIMP CFilmBooker::ListFilms()
{
    HRESULT hr;

    // get details of each film: Title and review
    CComPtr<IDatabaseAccessor> spDatabase;
    hr = CoCreateInstance(CLSID_DatabaseAccessor, NULL, CLSCTX_INPROC_SERVER,
                          IID_IDatabaseAccessor, (void**)&spDatabase);
    if (FAILED(hr))
        return hr;

    CComBSTR bstrResult;
    int iNFilms;
    hr = spDatabase->GetFilmInfo(&iNFilms, &bstrResult);
    if (FAILED(hr))
    {
        GetResponse()->Write(CComVariant(
            "We are currently unable to connect to the cinema database."
            "\nWe apologise for the inconvenience and suggest you try again "
            "later."));
        return hr;
    }

    LPWSTR *ppszTokens = new LPWSTR[iNFilms*3+1];
    hr = BreakUpBstr(bstrResult, ppszTokens, iNFilms*3);
    if (FAILED(hr))
        return hr;
```

You might notice after the first few `if (FAILED(hr))` tests we don't bother printing out much in the way of explanatory error messages. This is only a sample, and most of the possible errors we are detecting here are the sorts of things that should never happen anyway...

After the call to `BreakUpBstr()`, the array `ppszTokens` is an array of strings, each string being one of the bits of data for a film. The order goes: name of 1st film, review of 1st film, ID of 1st film, name of 2nd film, etc. We then display the information for each film:

```
    // write out details of films
    GetResponse()->Write(CComVariant("\n<hr><h2>FILMS SHOWING</h2>"));
    GetResponse()->Write(CComVariant("\nWe are currently showing "));
    GetResponse()->Write(CComVariant(iNFilms));
    GetResponse()->Write(CComVariant(" films:<p>"));

    for (int i=0 ; i<iNFilms*3 ; i+=3)
    {
        GetResponse()->Write(CComVariant("<strong>"));
        GetResponse()->Write(CComVariant(ppszTokens[i]));
        GetResponse()->Write(CComVariant("</strong><br>"));
        GetResponse()->Write(CComVariant(ppszTokens[i+1]));
        GetResponse()->Write(CComVariant("<p>"));
    }
```

Then we do pretty much the same thing all over again with the showings. This time we use the `DatabaseAccessor` method, `GetShowingsInfo()`. Again we get the information back in one long `BSTR` and use our function, `BreakUpBstr()`, to sort out the data. This time, the `ppszTokens` array will contain six pieces of text for each showing, in the order: film title of 1st showing, showing code, date and time, number of seats, tickets sold, price, film title of 2nd showing, etc.

```
// get details of each showing
bstrResult = "";
int iNShowings;
hr = spDatabase->GetShowingsInfo(&iNShowings, &bstrResult);
if (FAILED(hr))
{
    GetResponse()->Write(CComVariant(
        "We are currently unable to connect to the cinema showings database."
        "\nWe apologise for the inconvenience and suggest you try again "
        "later."));
    return hr;
}

delete [] ppszTokens[0];
delete [] ppszTokens;
int iNShowingsStrings = iNShowings*6;
ppszTokens = new LPWSTR[iNShowingsStrings+1];
hr = BreakUpBstr(bstrResult, ppszTokens, iNShowingsStrings);
if (FAILED(hr))
{
    GetResponse()->Write(CComVariant(
        "Conversion failed."));
    return hr;
}
```

Next we display the details of the showings:

```
GetResponse()->Write(CComVariant("\n<hr><h2>SHOWING TIMES</h2>"));

// start up form
GetResponse()->Write(CComVariant("\n<form action = \"Default.asp\""
    "Method = Get>"));

for (i=0 ; i<iNShowingsStrings ; i+=6)
{
    GetResponse()->Write(CComVariant("<strong>"));
    GetResponse()->Write(CComVariant(ppszTokens[i]));
    GetResponse()->Write(CComVariant("</strong>, showing at "));
    GetResponse()->Write(CComVariant(ppszTokens[i+2]));
    GetResponse()->Write(CComVariant(", "));
    int iNSeatsLeft = _wtoi(ppszTokens[i+3])-_wtoi(ppszTokens[i+4]);
    GetResponse()->Write(CComVariant(iNSeatsLeft));
    GetResponse()->Write(CComVariant(" seats left at $"));
    GetResponse()->Write(CComVariant(ppszTokens[i+5]));
    GetResponse()->Write(CComVariant(", Showing code: "));
    GetResponse()->Write(CComVariant(ppszTokens[i+1]));
    GetResponse()->Write(CComVariant("\n<p>"));

    GetResponse()->Write(CComVariant("\n Book seats (fill in number of "
        "seats required) "));
    GetResponse()->Write(CComVariant("<input type = text value = 0 size=10 "
        "name = \""));
    GetResponse()->Write(CComVariant(ppszTokens[i+1]));
    GetResponse()->Write(CComVariant("\" id = \""));
    GetResponse()->Write(CComVariant(ppszTokens[i+1]));
    GetResponse()->Write(CComVariant("\"> <p>"));
}
```

And lastly, we output the part of the form that allows the user to fill in their own details, and the small print.

```
if (iNShowings == 0)
{
    GetResponse()->Write(CComVariant("<p>There are currently no films you "
        "can book for<p>"));
    return E_FAIL;
}
else
{
    GetResponse()->Write(CComVariant("\n<hr>"));
    GetResponse()->Write(CComVariant("<h3> YOUR DETAILS</h3>"));
    GetResponse()->Write(CComVariant("<strong>You must fill in this part of "
        "the form in order to book seats</strong>"));

    GetResponse()->Write(CComVariant("\n<p>Your Name (required) "
        "\n<input type = \"text\" name = \"Name\" id = Name "
        "value = \"\" size = 30>"));
    GetResponse()->Write(CComVariant("\n<p>Your Credit Card Number "
        "(required) \n<input type = text name = CreditCard "
        "id = CreditCard value = \"\" size = 30>"));
    GetResponse()->Write(CComVariant("\n<p>Your Email (required) "
        "\n<input type = text name = Email id = Email value = \"\" "
        "size = 30>"));

    GetResponse()->Write(CComVariant("\n<p><input type = submit>"));
    GetResponse()->Write(CComVariant("\n<input type = reset>"));
    GetResponse()->Write(CComVariant("\n</form>\n"));

    GetResponse()->Write(CComVariant("\n<p><small>Frequently we will wish "
        "to send you spam mail to inform you of our latest incredible "
        "offers. If you do not wish to receive such mail, or do not wish "
        "us to supply your details to any agencies that pay us enough cash "
        "for the info then you should write to us at our address which you "
        "might find in the phone book.</small>"));

    GetResponse()->Write(CComVariant("<hr>"));
}
delete [] ppszTokens[0];
delete [] ppszTokens;

return S_OK;
}
```

The ConfirmBooking() Method

The first task of this method is to get at the information in the `QueryString()` collection. This is handled by one of the member functions we declared earlier, `GetBookingDetails()`, which returns the name, e-mail address, and credit card details entered. It also places a list of the bookings in the arrays `arrbstrShowings` and `arriNSeats`. `arrbstrShowings` contains the showing codes of the showings for which seats have been booked, while `arriNSeats` contains the corresponding numbers of seats booked.

```
STDMETHODIMP CFilmBooker::ConfirmBooking()
{
    HRESULT hr;

    GetResponse()->Write(CComVariant("<h3> Booking Confirmation</h3>"));

    CComBSTR bstrName, bstrEmail, bstrCreditCard;
    int iNBookings;
    CComBSTR *arrbstrShowings;
    int *arriNSeats;
    hr = GetBookingDetails(bstrName, bstrEmail, bstrCreditCard, iNBookings,
                    &arrbstrShowings, &arriNSeats);
```

We check that all the information is there then perform our extra-simple credit card validation routine.

```
if (FAILED(hr) || bstrName == "" || bstrEmail == "" || bstrCreditCard == "")
{
    GetResponse()->Write(CComVariant("Sorry, but you haven\'t filled in all "
        "the required information. Please use the Back button on your "
        "browser to return to the cinema bookings form and fill in all "
        "required fields."));
    return E_FAIL;
}

// test for validity of credit card - this would normally be a much
// tougher test!
if (bstrCreditCard[0] == '2' || bstrCreditCard[0] == '3')
{
    GetResponse()->Write(CComVariant("Sorry, your credit card number has "
        "been rejected. If you have mistyped it then please use the Back "
        "button on your browser to return to the cinema bookings form and "
        "correct the information."));
    return E_FAIL;
}
```

At this point we need to talk to the database, so we need an `IDatabaseAccessor` pointer. When we've got this, we first want to get the customer ID corresponding to the customer name that was entered; if the customer does not have an ID in the database, we'll quietly create one behind the scenes. Even if we didn't want to store the customer information, it's really needed as a foreign key in the sales table of the database. That's all handled in the `IDatabaseAccessor::GetCustomerID()` method, as we saw earlier.

```
// bind to database component
CComPtr<IDatabaseAccessor> spDatabase;
hr = CoCreateInstance(CLSID_DatabaseAccessor, NULL, CLSCTX_INPROC_SERVER,
                      IID_IDatabaseAccessor, (void**)&spDatabase);
if (FAILED(hr))
    return hr;

// attempt to get a customer ID - adding this customer to the database if
// appropriate
long lCustomerID;
hr = spDatabase->GetCustomerID(bstrName, bstrEmail, &lCustomerID);
if (FAILED(hr))
{
    GetResponse()->Write(CComVariant(
        "We are currently unable to connect to the customer database."
        "\nWe apologise for the inconvenience and suggest you try again "
        "later."));
    return hr;
}
```

Then there's a fair bit more of displaying information, and embedded in that a call to `IDatabaseAccessor::MakeSale()`, which will make an entry for the sale in the database. This call is embedded in a loop that iterates through all the bookings the customer has asked for.

```
        GetResponse()->Write(CComVariant("\n<p>You have supplied the following "
            "information for your booking:"));
        GetResponse()->Write(CComVariant("\n<p>Your name:  "));
        GetResponse()->Write(CComVariant(bstrName));
        GetResponse()->Write(CComVariant("\n<br>Your credit card number:  "));
        GetResponse()->Write(CComVariant(bstrCreditCard));
        GetResponse()->Write(CComVariant("\n<br>Your e-mail address:  "));
        GetResponse()->Write(CComVariant(bstrEmail));

        GetResponse()->Write(CComVariant("\n<p>The bookings you have requested "
            "are:<br>"));
        for (int i=0 ; i< iNBookings ; i++)
        {
            GetResponse()->Write(CComVariant("\n<p>"));
            GetResponse()->Write(CComVariant(arriNSeats[i]));
            GetResponse()->Write(CComVariant(" seats for the performance code "));
            GetResponse()->Write(CComVariant(arrbstrShowings[i]));

            // attempt to make the sale
            hr = spDatabase->MakeSale(lCustomerID, arrbstrShowings[i],
                                arriNSeats[i]);
            if (SUCCEEDED(hr))
                GetResponse()->Write(CComVariant("<br><strong>SALE "
                    "CONFIRMED</strong>"));
            else
                GetResponse()->Write(CComVariant("<br><strong>Sale "
                    "Rejected</strong><br>This may be because you have attempted to "
                    "book more seats than are available, or for some other reason."));
        }

    return S_OK;
}
```

The next thing to do is to take a closer look at the `GetBookingDetails()` and `GetRequestVariables()` helper functions, which, as already mentioned, handle extracting data from the `QueryString` collection. First off though, we need to examine this collection in more detail, by looking at the `Request` object.

The Request Object

The question of how to get at the data in the various collections encapsulated in the request object is something that you will need to be familiar with when writing components that interact with ASP pages. This is also one area where it has to be admitted that you really see the benefits of VB hiding what is really going on. In VB and VBScript, you can write code like this:

```
if (Request.QueryString("Action")="Add") then
```

You've no chance of getting away with anything like that in C++— beneath the `QueryString` collection lies a whole chain of COM interfaces that VB is able to navigate silently and automatically in order to retrieve the string you're looking for. You have to explicitly walk through these interfaces in any C++ code you write. It's the same story for the `Form()` collection, or any of the other collections in the `Request` object.

As a taster, the diagram shows roughly how you have to navigate through the various components. Taking the `QueryString` collection as an example, you can see from the figure the chain of components that leads you to the strings in the collection:

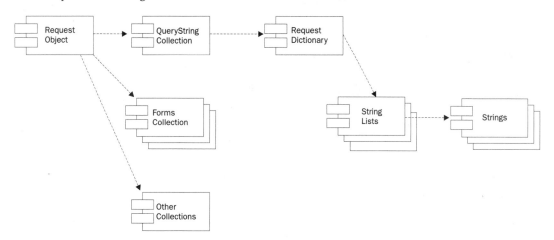

In more detail: the `Request` object exposes an interface, `IRequest`, and the `QueryString` collection is in fact implemented as an automation property on this interface. This means that in C++ you would actually call the method, `get_QueryString()`. The value you get for this property is an interface pointer to the `IRequestDictionary` interface. `IRequestDictionary` is a general-purpose interface designed to allow enumeration of the data in one of the `Request` object's collections. You'll recover this same interface from any of the `QueryString`, `Form`, `ServerVariables`, `Cookies` and `ClientCerticicate` collections.

If you have much C++ programming experience prior to this book, you may be wondering 'why `IRequestDictionary`? Why not simply use something like `IEnumVARIANT` to enumerate the properties?' Well, the reason is that each property in these `Request` object collections has a name as well as a value. Standard COM enumerators are designed to deal with collections of values only. Something more sophisticated is needed here, hence the new interface.

`IRequestDictionary` contains methods that allow you to enumerate through the *names* of the values. It also has a method, `get_Item()`, to which you pass the name of a value as a parameter and from which you get back a `VARIANT` that contains the value.

So far, so good—now's where it gets more complicated. You might expect that this `VARIANT` would contain a `BSTR` with the value in. But that's not possible because there may be more than one value with a given name. So, at the very least you would need a `SAFEARRAY`. However, Microsoft have chosen not to do it this way. Instead this `VARIANT` contains an `IDispatch` pointer. You need to `QueryInterface()` this pointer for the interface `IStringList`.

`IStringList` is designed to allow you to enumerate a list of strings, so it almost looks like we're there. But we have one more hurdle to cross. `IStringList` won't let you get at the strings directly. Instead, it exposes a `get__NewEnum` property that gives you an enumerator. This enumerator exposes `IEnumVariant`, which (finally) does give you a set of `VARIANT`s, each one of which contains a `BSTR`.

By the time you've got here, it does look like pretty serious overkill for wrapping the string up in one component after another, but all we can say is that's the way it's been done, so we have to live with it.

To make it clearer how to code round this, we first present some sample code that enumerates through the collections, then we'll go over the interfaces involved in a bit more detail.

The GetRequestVariables() Function

This is the function we'll develop to allow access to the strings in a collection. Although it's presented here as a utility function for our FilmBooker component, it's designed to work with both the QueryString and Form collections. It starts off by assuming the calling function has already retrieved the IRequestDictionary pointer, and returns (via its other parameters) an integer, iNValues, that says how many different named values are in the collection, and two arrays of BSTRs. The memory for these arrays is allocated within GetRequestVariables() and should be freed in the calling function. One of these arrays contains the names of the values, and the other contains the values themselves. There is one simplification, though. We assume that there is only one value for each name. In fact, for each name, we only look for one value, then once we've found it we move on to the next name.

The code starts off by checking how many values are in the dictionary by checking out the IRequestDictionary::get_Count() method:

```
HRESULT CFilmBooker::GetRequestVariables(
    CComPtr<IRequestDictionary> spDictionary, int &iNValues,
    CComBSTR **parrbstrNames, CComBSTR **parrbstrValues)
{
    HRESULT hr;

    // find out how big the collection is
    hr = spDictionary->get_Count(&iNValues);
    if (FAILED(hr))
        return hr;
```

Next we extract the enumerator that will allow us to enumerate through the names in the dictionary. You can start to get a feel for why it's called a dictionary here—it contains lots of names each of which has one or more values, just as a real dictionary has lots of words (names) each of which has one or more definitions (values).

```
    // get the enumerator
    CComQIPtr<IEnumVARIANT, &IID_IEnumVARIANT> spEnumerator;
    IUnknown *spEnum;
    hr = spDictionary->get__NewEnum(&spEnum);
    spEnumerator = spEnum;
    if (spEnumerator == NULL)
        return E_FAIL;
```

Now we enumerate through the names and for each one we use the IRequestDictionary::get_Item() method to get a variant that (after a few more steps) will give us the corresponding values. Well, actually we do a bit of simplifying here. We already know how many names there are so instead of doing the enumeration in a while loop, we'll just ask for them all in one go. That'll give us an array of VARIANTs that we can step through—each VARIANT in the array contains one name, which we'll place in our parrbstrNames array that will get returned to our calling function.

```
    // enumerate through the names
    ULONG cFetched;
    CComVariant *arrvarNames = new CComVariant[iNValues];
    hr = spEnumerator->Next(iNValues, arrvarNames, &cFetched);
    if (FAILED(hr) || cFetched != unsigned(iNValues))
        return E_FAIL;

    *parrbstrNames = new CComBSTR[iNValues];
    for (int i=0; i<iNValues ; i++)
    {
        if (arrvarNames[i].vt != VT_BSTR)
            return E_FAIL;
        (*parrbstrNames)[i] = arrvarNames[i].bstrVal;
    }
```

We've now completed the first half of our task—we've got the names of the values. Now we just need the values themselves. For this we use the `get_Item()` method of the request dictionary. For each name, the result gets placed in the VARIANT, `varTemp`, and we extract the string list from it.

```
    // got all the names: Now need the values
    *parrbstrValues = new CComBSTR[iNValues];
    CComVariant varTemp;
    for (i=0 ; i<iNValues ; i++)
    {
        hr = spDictionary->get_Item(arrvarNames[i], &varTemp);
        if (varTemp.vt != VT_DISPATCH)
            return E_FAIL;
        CComQIPtr<IStringList> spStringList;
        spStringList = varTemp.pdispVal;
        if (spStringList == NULL)
            return E_FAIL;
```

Almost there now. From the string list, we get the enumerator that exposes IEnumVARIANT. We're only interested in the first value for each name, so we just call `IEnumVARIANT::Next()` once (we know there must be at least one value there or the name wouldn't have shown up inside the request dictionary).

```
        ULONG cFetched;
        CComVariant varInnerTemp;
        hr = spStringList->get__NewEnum(&spEnum);
        spEnumerator = spEnum;
        // no while loop as we only want the first value.
        hr=spEnumerator->Next(1, &varInnerTemp, &cFetched);
        if (hr != S_OK || cFetched != 1 || varInnerTemp.vt != VT_BSTR)
            return E_FAIL;
        (*parrbstrValues)[i] = varInnerTemp.bstrVal;
    }

    return S_OK;
}
```

So that's how we can extract the members of the collection. In your component code, assuming you've created a standard ActiveX Server component, the `m_piRequest` variable points to the request object. You would call this function using something like this in order to enumerate over the `QueryString` collection:

```
    CComPtr <IRequestDictionary> spDictionary;
    int iNValues;
    CComBSTR *arrbstrNames, *arrbstrValues;

    hr = m_piRequest->get_QueryString(&spDictionary);
    hr = GetRequestVariables(spDictionary, iNValues, &arrbstrNames,
                             &arrbstrValues);
```

If you wanted to extract data from the forms collection, it'd be more like:

```
CComPtr <IRequestDictionary> spDictionary;
int iNValues;
CComBSTR *arrbstrNames, *arrbstrValues;

hr = m_piRequest->get_Form(&spDictionary);
hr = GetRequestVariables(spDictionary, iNValues, &arrbstrNames,
                                       &arrbstrValues);
```

Get the idea?

Before we leave this topic, we'll take a quick pass over the new interfaces we've mentioned here.

IRequest

This is the first interface you'll encounter on the request object. It has the following methods:

Method	Description
get_Form()	Gets an IRequestDictionary* pointer to the Forms collection
get_QueryString()	Gets an IRequestDictionary* pointer to the QueryString collection
get_Cookies()	Gets an IRequestDictionary* pointer to the Cookies collection
get_ServerVariables()	Gets an IRequestDictionary* pointer to the ServerVariables collection
get_ClientCertificate()	Gets an IRequestDictionary* pointer to the ClientCertificate collection
get_Item()	Retrieves the value of the named item, which could be in any of the above collections
get_TotalBytes()	Gets the total size in bytes of the request object
BinaryRead()	Copies the request object to a SAFEARRAY where its contents can be read directly in binary form

IRequestDictionary

This is the interface that allows you to enumerate over any one of the request object collections.

Method	Description
get__NewEnum()	Gets an IEnumVARIANT* pointer that allows you to enumerate the names in the collection
get_Item()	Gets a VARIANT that allows access to the values corresponding to a given name in the collection
get_Count()	Gets the number of names in the collection
get_Key()	Gets a unique identification for a given item

IStringList

This interface allows enumeration of a list of strings

Method	Description
get_Count()	Gets how many items are in the list
get__NewEnum()	Gets an IEnumVARIANT* pointer that allows you to enumerate through the strings in the list
get_Item()	Retrieves a named item from the list

The GetBookingDetails() Function

At the heart of this function is a call to the GetRequestVariables() function that we developed above. Its implementation is as follows:

```
HRESULT CFilmBooker::GetBookingDetails(CComBSTR &bstrName,
                                       CComBSTR &bstrEmail,
                                       CComBSTR &bstrCreditCard,
                                       int &iNBookings,
                                       CComBSTR **parrbstrShowings,
                                       int **parriNSeats)
{
    HRESULT hr;

    // get all the request variables out of the collection
    CComPtr <IRequestDictionary> spDictionary;
    hr = GetRequest()->get_QueryString(&spDictionary);
    int iNValues;
    CComBSTR *arrbstrNames, *arrbstrValues;

    hr = GetRequestVariables(spDictionary, iNValues, &arrbstrNames,
                             &arrbstrValues);

    if (FAILED(hr))
        return hr;
```

The rest of this function is to do with interpreting the arrays. We need to identify the name, credit card number, and e-mail address from the arrays returned from GetRequestVariables(). The loop that does this also counts how many bookings have actually been made. This is not particularly related to the number of elements of the QueryString() collection, since most of these elements will be zeros from where the customer has not made bookings (but the form on the Default.asp page returns the information for all showings anyway)—so we need to pick out the elements with non-zero values.

```
    // count how many showings bookings have been made for - this is how
    // big the arrays parrbstrShowings and parriNSeats must be made
    iNBookings = 0;
    int *arriBookingMade = new int[iNValues];
    for (int i=0 ; i<iNValues ; i++)
    {
        arriBookingMade[i] = 0;
        if (arrbstrNames[i] == "Name")
            bstrName = arrbstrValues[i];
        else if (arrbstrNames[i] == "CreditCard")
            bstrCreditCard = arrbstrValues[i];
        else if (arrbstrNames[i] == "Email")
            bstrEmail = arrbstrValues[i];
```

```
        else
        {
            arriBookingMade[i] = _wtoi(arrbstrValues[i]);
            if (arriBookingMade[i])
            ++iNBookings;
        }
    }
```

The information from that pass through the elements of the collection tells us how many bookings were made—and hence how much memory to allocate for the arrays that will hold the booking information. All that remains is to allocate the memory and copy the information into the arrays.

```
    // copy the valid bookings into the parrbstrShowings and parriNSeats
    // parameters
    *parrbstrShowings = new CComBSTR[iNBookings];
    *parriNSeats = new int[iNBookings];
    int j=0;
    for (i=0 ; i<iNValues ; i++)
    {
        if (arriBookingMade[i])
        {
            (*parriNSeats)[j] = arriBookingMade[i];
            (*parrbstrShowings)[j] = arrbstrNames[i];
            ++j;
        }
    }

    return S_OK;
}
```

The BreakUpBstr () Function

Finally, let's take a look at BreakUpBstr(), which is used to retrieve information from @ separated strings. This function is implemented like this:

```
HRESULT BreakUpBstr(CComBSTR &bstrInput, LPWSTR *ppszResults, int iNVals)
{
    if (iNVals == 0)
        return S_OK;
    LPWSTR pszInput = new wchar_t[bstrInput.Length()+1];
    wcscpy(pszInput, bstrInput.m_str);
    int i=0, j=1;
    ppszResults[0] = pszInput;
    for(i=0 ; pszInput[i] != L'\0' && j<=iNVals && i<5000; ++i)
    {
        if (pszInput[i] == L'@')
        {
            pszInput[i] = '\0';
            ppszResults[j++] = pszInput+i+1;
        }
    }
    if (j != iNVals+1)
        return E_FAIL;
    return S_OK;
}
```

This function basically tours round the string, looking for @ characters, and assumes each one marks a new string. It includes a check that the number of strings so retrieved is the same as the number the calling function said it was expecting (via the iNVals parameter).

And with that we are done with the FilmBooker component!

Booking Tickets—ASP Page

There seems little point in testing this component with a console application as we did for the `DatabaseAccessor` component. In fact, this would be difficult anyway; we need access to the ASP objects. Instead, lets dive in and write our `default.asp` page:

```
<%@LANGUAGE="VBScript"%>
<HTML>
<HEAD>
<TITLE>ADSI Explorer</TITLE>
<STYLE TYPE="text/css">
    BODY {font-family:Tahoma,Arial,sans-serif; font-size:10pt}
</STYLE>
</HEAD>
<BODY BGCOLOR=#FFFFFF>

<h1> ROCKS CINEMAS INC </h1>

Welcome to Rocks Cinemas!
<%

on error resume next

Set objFilmViewer = Server.CreateObject("CinemaBookings.FilmBooker")

if (Request.QueryString("Name") = "") then
    objFilmViewer.ListFilms
else
    objFilmViewer.ConfirmBooking
end if

%>

</BODY>
</HTML>
```

This is possibly the simplest bit of the project. The user interface is handled entirely by the `FilmBooker` component. The `Default.asp` page detects whether it is supposed to be confirming a booking by whether a customer name has been filled in on the form and sent to it via the HTTP `Get` protocol.

The Management Files

We've now presented code that illustrates all the basic principles, so from this point on we'll increasingly not show the C++ code in detail, but refer you to the source code on the Wrox Press website. The code for the `CinemaManager` component is a case in point—since this code doesn't demonstrate any new concepts. We'll also skip the `DatabaseAccess` methods that this component uses.

We'll quickly go over the ASP pages themselves, though, since they are slightly more complicated due to the number of possible actions managers might want to do.

Management ASP Pages

As we mentioned, there are two pages here: `Manage.asp` and `InputOptions.asp`. `Manage.asp` is the page you will head for first, since it gives you the radio buttons from which you can select which action you want to take. Submitting this will take you to the `InputOptions.asp` page, which is responsible for displaying the detailed form that asks you questions like the name of the film you want to add (if you're adding a film) or which film you want to delete (if you're removing one). `InputOptions.asp` won't work unless it is called with the information from the form in `Manage.asp` supplied using the HTTP `Post` protocol. Once you've filled in the form, you get taken back to `Manage.asp`. `Manage.asp` not only gives you the choice of what you want to do next, but also detects if it has been called in response to a previous request, and takes the appropriate action—adding a film or whatever.

Here's `Manage.asp`:

```
<%@LANGUAGE="VBScript"%>
<HTML>
<HEAD>
<TITLE>ADSI Explorer</TITLE>
<STYLE TYPE="text/css">
    BODY {font-family:Tahoma,Arial,sans-serif; font-size:10pt}
</STYLE>
</HEAD>
<BODY BGCOLOR=#FFFFFF>

<h1> ROCKS CINEMAS INC </h1>

<h3> Management Web Page </h3>
Welcome to Rocks Cinemas!
<p>

<hr>
<form action = "InputOptions.asp" method = post id=form1 name=form1>

<%
on error resume next

' display any specific stuff outstanding from options being processed
Dim strPassword
strPassword = Request.Form("password")

dim objManager
set objManager = Server.CreateObject("CinemaManagement.CinemaManager")
Response.Write Request.Form("CurrentAction")
if (Request.Form("CurrentAction") = "AddFilm") then
    objManager.AddFilm
elseif (Request.Form("CurrentAction") = "RemoveFilm") then
    objManager.RemoveFilm
elseif (Request.Form("CurrentAction") = "AddShowing") then
    objManager.AddShowing
elseif (Request.Form("CurrentAction") = "RemoveShowing") then
    objManager.RemoveShowing
end if
' now display form to ask what user wants to do next
%>

<input type = hidden name = password id = password
value = "<% = strPassword %>" size = 15>
<p>
What do you want to do next?
<br> <input type = radio name = AddFilm id = AddFilm>
    Add a new Film to the Rocks Database
<br> <input type = radio name = RemoveFilm id = RemoveFilm>
    Remove a Film from the Rocks Database
```

```
<br> <input type = radio name = AddShowing id = AddShowing>
   Add a new Showing to the Rocks Database
<br> <input type = radio name = RemoveShowing id = RemoveShowing>
   Remove a Showing from the Rocks Database
<br> <input type = submit> <input type = reset>
</form>
<hr>
<p>
Remember our Motto: Two customers watching a film is worth one customer more
than one customer watching the same film.

</BODY>
</HTML>
```

As you can see it basically contains the code to display the form. Notice the hidden control to contain the password. This is present in order to remember the user's password between successive calls to the InputOptions.asp page, in which the password is actually entered.

The InputOptions page is quite similar:

```
<%@LANGUAGE="VBScript"%>
<HTML>
<HEAD>
<TITLE>ADSI Explorer</TITLE>
<STYLE TYPE="text/css">
   BODY {font-family:Tahoma,Arial,sans-serif; font-size:10pt}
</STYLE>
</HEAD>
<BODY BGCOLOR=#FFFFFF>

<h1> ROCKS CINEMAS INC </h1>

<h3> Management Web Page </h3>
Welcome to Rocks Cinemas!
<p>

<hr>
<form action = "Manage.asp" method = post id=form1 name=form1>

<%
on error resume next

Dim strPassword
strPassword = Request.Form("password")

dim objManager
set objManager = Server.CreateObject("CinemaManagement.CinemaManager")
if (Request.Form("AddFilm") = "on") then
   objManager.DisplayAddFilmForm
   Response.Write "<br> <input type = hidden "_
      & "name = CurrentAction id = CurrentAction value = AddFilm>"
elseif (Request.Form("RemoveFilm") = "on") then
   objManager.DisplayRemoveFilmForm
   Response.Write "<br> <input type = hidden "_
      & "name = CurrentAction id = CurrentAction value = RemoveFilm>"
elseif (Request.Form("AddShowing") = "on") then
   objManager.DisplayAddShowingForm
   Response.Write "<br> <input type = hidden "_
      & "name = CurrentAction id = CurrentAction value = AddShowing>"
elseif (Request.Form("RemoveShowing") = "on") then
   objManager.DisplayRemoveShowingForm
   Response.Write "<br> <input type = hidden "_
      & "name = CurrentAction id = CurrentAction value = RemoveShowing>"
end if
%>
```

```
<p>Management password <input type = password name = password id = password
value = "<% = strPassword %>" size = 15>
<p> <input type = submit> <input type = reset>
</form>
<hr>
<p>
Remember our Motto: Two customers watching a film is worth one customer more
than one customer watching the same film.
</BODY>
</HTML>
```

This ASP page hands almost all responsibility for displaying the page over to the `CinemaManager` component—the only stuff handled by the VBScript in the ASP page is the small amount that's common to all the actions the user might want to do—basically entering the password. There's also another hidden control, the `CurrentAction` control, which is used to communicate back to the `Manage.asp` page what action needs to be taken when the submit button is pressed.

Example Summary

Well if there's one lesson from this sample it's clearly that even fairly simple real-world examples can quickly generate a lot of code! The Rocks Cinemas database has consumed an entire chapter, without our even beginning to consider questions of real security—like having different management accounts—or of other functionality like generating statistics on sales, or allowing bookings to be cancelled—the kind of stuff that would be considered essential in a real cinema. On the other hand, look how far we have come—we do have the basis of a workable cinema bookings application. Not only that, but although there's a large quantity of code, most of it is relatively straightforward. A lot of the functions we've just presented were taken up largely by all the `Write()` statements needed to write text to the web page. All the hard stuff was still handled automatically for us by the various ATL wizards.

The Rocks Cinema project demonstrates many of the principles of writing good, maintainable, code. It exhibits a clear separation between the user interface (the web page), the backend database, and the two middle-tier components—servicing respectively the ASP page and the database. A more complex application, written along the same general principles, should be quite scalable.

If you've been paying close attention you'll have noticed that some of the database access we've presented here isn't exactly optimal. If you refer back to the discussion in Chapter 13, you'll see that using `MoveNext()` repeatedly to find a record has its faults. It is far better to use a customised SQL statement to extract the data you require. If you were to upsize this case study to SQL server this would become far more of an issue—with potentially many more users on line you really wouldn't want to lock the database for any longer than strictly necessary.

On this note, we could use the techniques developed in Chapter 14 to migrate to a combination of SQL Server and MTS. This would require converting the database into a SQL Server one, changing the OLE DB consumers, and adding MTS transaction support to the `DatabaseAccessor` class. The end result, a combination of the techniques from throughout this book, would be on a par with many of the commercial solutions available today.

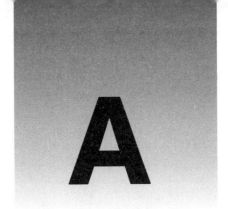

Active Server Pages Object Model

This appendix offers a handy reference to the Active Server Pages **object model**, and in each case provides the properties, methods and events for the object, along with their collections.

The Request Object

Together, the `Request` object and the `Response` object form the 'conversational mechanism' of ASP. The `Request` object is responsible for controlling how the user sends information to the server. Using the `Request` object, the server can obtain information about what the user wants – either explicitly (e.g. through programmed ASP code) or implicitly (e.g. through the HTTP headers).

Collections	Description
ClientCertificate	Client certificate values sent from the browser. Read Only
Cookies	Values of cookies sent from the browser. Read Only
Form	Values of form elements sent from the browser. Read Only
QueryString	Values of variables in the HTTP query string. Read Only
ServerVariables	Values of the HTTP and environment variables. Read Only

Property	Description
TotalBytes	Specifies the number of bytes the client is sending in the body of the request. Read Only

Method	Description
BinaryRead	Used to retrieve data sent to the server as part of the POST request

The Response Object

The Response object is responsible for sending the server's output to the client. In this sense, the Response object is the counterpart to the Request object: the Request object gathers information from both the client and the server, and the Response object sends, or resends, the information to the client by writing to the HTTP data stream.

Collection	Description
Cookies	Values of all the cookies to send to the browser.

Properties	Description
Buffer	Determines whether the page is to be buffered until complete
CacheControl	Determines whether proxy servers are allowed to cache the output generated by ASP
Charset	Appends the name of the character set to the content-type header
ContentType	HTTP content type (e.g. "Text/HTML") for the response
Expires	Number of minutes between caching and expiry, for a page cached on the browser
ExpiresAbsolute	Explicit date and/or time of expiry for a page cached on a browser
IsClientConnected	Indicates whether the client has disconnected from the server
PICS	Adds the value of a PICS label to the pics-label field of the response header
Status	Value of the HTTP status line returned by the server

Methods	Description
AddHeader	Adds or changes a value in the HTML header
AppendToLog	Adds text to the web server log entry for this request
BinaryWrite	Sends text to the browser without character-set conversion
Clear	Erases any buffered HTML output
End	Stops processing the page and returns the current result
Flush	Sends buffered output immediately
Redirect	Instructs the browser to connect to a different URL
Write	Writes variable values, strings etc. to the current page as a string

The `Response` interface elements can be divided into groups, like this:

Response Items	Description
`Write, BinaryWrite`	Inserts information into a page
`Cookies`	Sends cookies to the browser
`Redirect`	Redirects the browser
`Buffer, Flush, Clear, End`	Buffers the page as it is created
`Expires, ExpiresAbsolute, ContentType, AddHeader, Status, CacheContol, PICS, Charset`	Sets the properties of a page
`IsClientConnected`	Checks the client connection

The Application Object

Each application is represented by an instance of the `Application` object. This object stores variables and objects for application-scope usage. It also holds information about any currently-active sessions.

Collections	Description
`Contents`	Contains all of the items added to the application through script commands
`StaticObjects`	Contains all of the objects added to the application with the `<OBJECT>` tag

Methods	Description
`Lock`	Prevents other clients from modifying application properties
`Unlock`	Allows other clients to modify application properties

Events	Description
`OnStart`	Occurs when a page in the application is first referenced
`OnEnd`	Occurs when the application ends, i.e. when the web server is stopped

The Session Object

The Session object is used to keep track of an individual browser as it navigates through your web site.

Collections	Description
Contents	Contains all of the items added to the session through script commands
StaticObjects	Contains all of the objects added to the session with the <OBJECT> tag

Method	Description
Abandon	Destroys a Session object and releases its resources

Properties	Description
CodePage	Sets the codepage that will be used for symbol mapping
LCID	Sets the locale identifier
SessionID	Returns the session identification for this user
Timeout	Sets the timeout period for the session state for this application, in minutes

Events	Description
OnStart	Occurs when the server creates a new session
OnEnd	Occurs when a session is abandoned or times out

The Server Object

The main use of the Server object is to create components.

Property	Description
ScriptTimeout	Length of time a script can run before an error occurs

Methods	Description
CreateObject	Creates an instance of an object or server component
HTMLEncode	Applies HTML encoding to the specified string
MapPath	Converts a virtual path into a physical path
URLEncode	Applies URL encoding including escape chars to a string

The ObjectContext Object

When we use MTS (Microsoft Transaction Server) to manage a transaction, we have the functionality within our script to commit (or to abort) the transaction. This functionality is provided by the `ObjectContext` object.

Methods	Description
SetComplete	Declares that the script knows no reason for the transaction not to complete. If all participating components call `SetComplete` then the transaction will complete. `SetComplete` overrides any previous `SetAbort` method that has been called in the script
SetAbort	Aborts a transaction initiated by an ASP

Events	Description
OnTransactionCommit	Occurs after a transacted script's transaction commits
OnTransactionAbort	Occurs if the transaction is aborted

ADO Object Summary

Microsoft ActiveX Data Objects 2.1 Library Reference

Properties or methods new to version 2.1 are shown *italicized*.

All properties are read/write unless otherwise stated.

Objects

Name	Description
Command	A Command object is a definition of a specific command that you intend to execute against a data source.
Connection	A Connection object represents an open connection to a data store.
Error	An Error object contains the details about data access errors pertaining to a single operation involving the provider.
Errors	The Errors collection contains all of the Error objects created in response to a single failure involving the provider.
Field	A Field object represents a column of data within a common data type.
Fields	A Fields collection contains all of the Field objects of a Recordset object.
Parameter	A Parameter object represents a parameter or argument associated with a Command object based on a parameterized query or stored procedure.
Parameters	A Parameters collection contains all the Parameter objects of a Command object.

Table Continued on Following Page

Name	Description
Properties	A Properties collection contains all the Property objects for a specific instance of an object.
Property	A Property object represents a dynamic characteristic of an ADO object that is defined by the provider.
Recordset	A Recordset object represents the entire set of records from a base table or the results of an executed command. At any time, the Recordset object only refers to a single record within the set as the current record.

Command Object

Methods

Name	Returns	Description
Cancel		Cancels execution of a pending Execute or Open call.
CreateParameter	Parameter	Creates a new Parameter object.
Execute	Recordset	Executes the query, SQL statement, or stored procedure specified in the CommandText property.

Properties

Name	Returns	Description
ActiveConnection	Variant	Indicates to which Connection object the command currently belongs.
CommandText	String	Contains the text of a command to be issued against a data provider.
CommandTimeout	Long	Indicates how long to wait, in seconds, while executing a command before terminating the command and generating an error. Default is 30.
CommandType	CommandTypeEnum	Indicates the type of Command object.
Name	String	Indicates the name of the Command object.

Name	Returns	Description
Parameters	Parameters	Contains all of the `Parameter` objects for a `Command` object.
Prepared	Boolean	Indicates whether or not to save a compiled version of a command before execution.
Properties	Properties	Contains all of the `Property` objects for a `Command` object.
State	Long	Describes whether the `Command` object is open or closed. Read only.

Connection Object

Methods

Name	Returns	Description
BeginTrans	Integer	Begins a new transaction.
Cancel		Cancels the execution of a pending, asynchronous `Execute` or `Open` operation.
Close		Closes an open connection and any dependant objects.
CommitTrans		Saves any changes and ends the current transaction.
Execute	Recordset	Executes the query, SQL statement, stored procedure, or provider specific text.
Open		Opens a connection to a data source, so that commands can be executed against it.
OpenSchema	Recordset	Obtains database schema information from the provider.
RollbackTrans		Cancels any changes made during the current transaction and ends the transaction.

Properties

Name	Returns	Description
Attributes	Long	Indicates one or more characteristics of a Connection object. Default is 0.
CommandTimeout	Long	Indicates how long, in seconds, to wait while executing a command before terminating the command and generating an error. The default is 30.
ConnectionString	String	Contains the information used to establish a connection to a data source.
ConnectionTimeout	Long	Indicates how long, in seconds, to wait while establishing a connection before terminating the attempt and generating an error. Default is 15.
CursorLocation	CursorLocationEnum	Sets or returns the location of the cursor engine.
DefaultDatabase	String	Indicates the default database for a Connection object.
Errors	Errors	Contains all of the Error objects created in response to a single failure involving the provider.
IsolationLevel	IsolationLevelEnum	Indicates the level of transaction isolation for a Connection object. Write only.
Mode	ConnectModeEnum	Indicates the available permissions for modifying data in a Connection.
Properties	Properties	Contains all of the Property objects for a Connection object.
Provider	String	Indicates the name of the provider for a Connection object.
State	Long	Describes whether the Connection object is open or closed. Read only.
Version	String	Indicates the ADO version number. Read only.

Events

Name	Description
BeginTransComplete	Fired after a BeginTrans operation finishes executing.
CommitTransComplete	Fired after a CommitTrans operation finishes executing.
ConnectComplete	Fired after a connection starts.
Disconnect	Fired after a connection ends.
ExecuteComplete	Fired after a command has finished executing.
InfoMessage	Fired whenever a ConnectionEvent operation completes successfully and additional information is returned by the provider.
RollbackTransComplete	Fired after a RollbackTrans operation finishes executing.
WillConnect	Fired before a connection starts.
WillExecute	Fired before a pending command executes on the connection.

Error Object

Properties

Name	Returns	Description
Description	String	A description string associated with the error. Read only.
HelpContext	Integer	Indicates the ContextID in the help file for the associated error. Read only.
HelpFile	String	Indicates the name of the help file. Read only.
NativeError	Long	Indicates the provider-specific error code for the associated error. Read only.
Number	Long	Indicates the number that uniquely identifies an Error object. Read only.
Source	String	Indicates the name of the object or application that originally generated the error. Read only.
SQLState	String	Indicates the SQL state for a given Error object. It is a five-character string that follows the ANSI SQL standard. Read only.

Errors Collection

Methods

Name	Returns	Description
Clear		Removes all of the Error objects from the Errors collection.
Refresh		Updates the Error objects with information from the provider.

Properties

Name	Returns	Description
Count	Long	Indicates the number of Error objects in the Errors collection. Read only.
Item	Error	Allows indexing into the Errors collection to reference a specific Error object. Read only.

Field Object

Methods

Name	Returns	Description
AppendChunk		Appends data to a large or binary Field object.
GetChunk	Variant	Returns all or a portion of the contents of a large or binary Field object.

Properties

Name	Returns	Description
ActualSize	Long	Indicates the actual length of a field's value. Read only.
Attributes	Long	Indicates one or more characteristics of a Field object.
DataFormat	Variant	Identifies the format that the data should be displayed in.
DefinedSize	Long	Indicates the defined size of the Field object. Write only.

Name	Returns	Description
Name	String	Indicates the name of the Field object.
NumericScale	Byte	Indicates the scale of numeric values for the Field object. Write only.
OriginalValue	Variant	Indicates the value of a Field object that existed in the record before any changes were made. Read only.
Precision	Byte	Indicates the degree of precision for numeric values in the Field object. Read only.
Properties	Properties	Contains all of the Property objects for a Field object.
Type	DataTypeEnum	Indicates the data type of the Field object.
UnderlyingValue	Variant	Indicates a Field object's current value in the database. Read only.
Value	Variant	Indicates the value assigned to the Field object.

Fields Collection

Methods

Name	Returns	Description
Append		Appends a Field object to the Fields collection.
Delete		Deletes a Field object from the Fields collection.
Refresh		Updates the Field objects in the Fields collection.

Properties

Name	Returns	Description
Count	Long	Indicates the number of Field objects in the Fields collection. Read only.
Item	Field	Allows indexing into the Fields collection to reference a specific Field object. Read only.

Parameter Object

Methods

Name	Returns	Description
AppendChunk		Appends data to a large or binary Parameter object.

Properties

Name	Returns	Description
Attributes	Long	Indicates one or more characteristics of a Parameter object.
Direction	ParameterDirectionEnum	Indicates whether the Parameter object represents an input parameter, an output parameter, or both, or if the parameter is a return value from a stored procedure.
Name	String	Indicates the name of the Parameter object.
NumericScale	Byte	Indicates the scale of numeric values for the Parameter object.
Precision	Byte	Indicates the degree of precision for numeric values in the Parameter object.
Properties	Properties	Contains all of the Property objects for a Parameter object.
Size	Long	Indicates the maximum size, in bytes or characters, of a Parameter object.
Type	DataTypeEnum	Indicates the data type of the Parameter object.
Value	Variant	Indicates the value assigned to the Parameter object.

Parameters Collection

Methods

Name	Returns	Description
Append		Appends a `Parameter` object to the `Parameters` collection.
Delete		Deletes a `Parameter` object from the `Parameters` collection.
Refresh		Updates the `Parameter` objects in the `Parameters` collection.

Properties

Name	Returns	Description
Count	Long	Indicates the number of `Parameter` objects in the `Parameters` collection. Read only.
Item	Parameter	Allows indexing into the `Parameters` collection to reference a specific `Parameter` object. Read only.

Properties

Methods

Name	Returns	Description
Refresh		Updates the `Property` objects in the `Properties` collection with the details from the provider.

Properties

Name	Returns	Description
Count	Long	Indicates the number of `Property` objects in the `Properties` collection. Read only.
Item	Property	Allows indexing into the `Properties` collection to reference a specific `Property` object. Read only.

Property Object

Properties

Name	Returns	Description
Attributes	Long	Indicates one or more characteristics of a `Property` object.
Name	String	Indicates the name of the `Property` object. Read only.
Type	DataTypeEnum	Indicates the data type of the `Property` object.
Value	Variant	Indicates the value assigned to the `Property` object.

Recordset Object

Methods

Name	Returns	Description
AddNew		Creates a new record for an updateable `Recordset` object.
Cancel		Cancels execution of a pending asynchronous `Open` operation.
CancelBatch		Cancels a pending batch update.
CancelUpdate		Cancels any changes made to the current record, or to a new record prior to calling the `Update` method.
Clone	Recordset	Creates a duplicate `Recordset` object from an existing `Recordset` object.
Close		Closes the `Recordset` object and any dependent objects.
CompareBookmarks	CompareEnum	Compares two bookmarks and returns an indication of the relative values.
Delete		Deletes the current record or group of records.

Name	Returns	Description
Find		Searches the Recordset for a record that matches the specified criteria.
GetRows	Variant	Retrieves multiple records of a Recordset object into an array.
GetString	String	Returns a Recordset as a string.
Move		Moves the position of the current record in a Recordset.
MoveFirst		Moves the position of the current record to the first record in the Recordset.
MoveLast		Moves the position of the current record to the last record in the Recordset.
MoveNext		Moves the position of the current record to the next record in the Recordset.
MovePrevious		Moves the position of the current record to the previous record in the Recordset.
NextRecordset	Recordset	Clears the current Recordset object and returns the next Recordset by advancing through a series of commands.
Open		Opens a Recordset.
Requery		Updates the data in a Recordset object by re-executing the query on which the object is based.
Resync		Refreshes the data in the current Recordset object from the underlying database.
Save		Saves the Recordset to a file.
Seek		Searches the recordset index to locate a value
Supports	Boolean	Determines whether a specified Recordset object supports particular functionality.
Update		Saves any changes made to the current Recordset object.
UpdateBatch		Writes all pending batch updates to disk.

Properties

Name	Returns	Description
AbsolutePage	PositionEnum	Specifies in which page the current record resides.
AbsolutePosition	PositionEnum	Specifies the ordinal position of a Recordset object's current record.
ActiveCommand	Object	Indicates the Command object that created the associated Recordset object. Read only.
ActiveConnection	Variant	Indicates to which Connection object the specified Recordset object currently belongs.
BOF	Boolean	Indicates whether the current record is before the first record in a Recordset object. Read only.
Bookmark	Variant	Returns a bookmark that uniquely identifies the current record in a Recordset object, or sets the current record to the record identified by a valid bookmark.
CacheSize	Long	Indicates the number of records from a Recordset object that are cached locally in memory.
CursorLocation	CursorLocationEnum	Sets or returns the location of the cursor engine.
CursorType	CursorTypeEnum	Indicates the type of cursor used in a Recordset object.
DataMember	String	Specifies the name of the data member to retrieve from the object referenced by the DataSource property. Write only.
DataSource	Object	Specifies an object containing data to be represented as a Recordset object. Write only.
EditMode	EditModeEnum	Indicates the editing status of the current record. Read only.
EOF	Boolean	Indicates whether the current record is after the last record in a Recordset object. Read only.

Name	Returns	Description
Fields	Fields	Contains all of the `Field` objects for the current `Recordset` object.
Filter	Variant	Indicates a filter for data in the `Recordset`.
Index	String	Identifies the name of the index currently being used.
LockType	LockTypeEnum	Indicates the type of locks placed on records during editing.
MarshalOptions	MarshalOptionsEnum	Indicates which records are to be marshaled back to the server.
MaxRecords	Long	Indicates the maximum number of records to return to a `Recordset` object from a query. Default is zero (no limit).
PageCount	Long	Indicates how many pages of data the `Recordset` object contains. Read only.
PageSize	Long	Indicates how many records constitute one page in the `Recordset`.
Properties	Properties	Contains all of the `Property` objects for the current `Recordset` object.
RecordCount	Long	Indicates the current number of records in the `Recordset` object. Read only.
Sort	String	Specifies one or more field names the `Recordset` is sorted on, and the direction of the sort.
Source	String	Indicates the source for the data in a `Recordset` object.
State	Long	Indicates whether the recordset is open, closed, or whether it is executing an asynchronous operation. Read only.
Status	Integer	Indicates the status of the current record with respect to match updates or other bulk operations. Read only.
StayInSync	Boolean	Indicates, in a hierarchical `Recordset` object, whether the parent row should change when the set of underlying child records changes. Read only.

Events

Name	Description
EndOfRecordset	Fired when there is an attempt to move to a row past the end of the Recordset.
FetchComplete	Fired after all the records in an asynchronous operation have been retrieved into the Recordset.
FetchProgress	Fired periodically during a length asynchronous operation, to report how many rows have currently been retrieved.
FieldChangeComplete	Fired after the value of one or more Field objects have been changed.
MoveComplete	Fired after the current position in the Recordset changes.
RecordChangeComplete	Fired after one or more records change.
RecordsetChangeComplete	Fired after the Recordset has changed.
WillChangeField	Fired before a pending operation changes the value of one or more Field objects.
WillChangeRecord	Fired before one or more rows in the Recordset change.
WillChangeRecordset	Fired before a pending operation changes the Recordset.
WillMove	Fired before a pending operation changes the current position in the Recordset.

Method Calls Quick Reference

Command

Command.Cancel

Parameter = Command.CreateParameter(*Name As String, Type As DataTypeEnum,_
     Direction As ParameterDirectionEnum, Size As Integer, [Value As Variant]*)

Recordset = Command.Execute(*RecordsAffected As Variant, Parameters As Variant, _
     Options As Integer*)

Connection

Integer = Connection.BeginTrans

Connection.Cancel

Connection.Close

Connection.CommitTrans

Recordset = Connection.Execute(*CommandText As String, RecordsAffected As Variant, _
     Options As Integer*)

Connection.Open(*ConnectionString As String, UserID As String, Password As String, _
     Options As Integer*)

Recordset = Connection.OpenSchema(*Schema As SchemaEnum, [Restrictions As Variant], _
     [SchemaID As Variant]*)

Connection.RollbackTrans

Errors

Errors.Clear

Errors.Refresh

Field

Field.AppendChunk(*Data As Variant*)

Variant = Field.GetChunk(*Length As Integer*)

Fields

Fields.Append(*Name As String, Type As DataTypeEnum, DefinedSize As Integer, _
     Attrib As FieldAttributeEnum*)

Fields.Delete(*Index As Variant*)

Fields.Refresh

Parameter

Parameter.AppendChunk(*Val As Variant*)

Parameters

Parameters.Append(*Object As Object*)
Parameters.Delete(*Index As Variant*)
Parameters.Refresh

Properties

Properties.Refresh

Recordset

Recordset.AddNew([*FieldList As Variant*], [*Values As Variant*])
Recordset.Cancel
Recordset.CancelBatch(*AffectRecords As AffectEnum*)
Recordset.CancelUpdate
Recordset = *Recordset*.Clone(*LockType As LockTypeEnum*)
Recordset.Close
CompareEnum = *Recordset*.CompareBookmarks(*Bookmark1 As Variant, Bookmark2 As Variant*)
Recordset.Delete(*AffectRecords As AffectEnum*)
Recordset.Find(*Criteria As String, SkipRecords As Integer, _*
    SearchDirection As SearchDirectionEnum, [Start As Variant])
Variant = *Recordset*.GetRows(*Rows As Integer, [Start As Variant], [Fields As Variant]*)
String = *Recordset*.GetString(*StringFormat As StringFormatEnum, _*
    NumRows As Integer, ColumnDelimeter As String, RowDelimeter As String, _
    NullExpr As String)
Recordset.Move(*NumRecords As Integer, [Start As Variant]*)
Recordset.MoveFirst
Recordset.MoveLast
Recordset.MoveNext
Recordset.MovePrevious
Recordset = *Recordset*.NextRecordset([*RecordsAffected As Variant*])
Recordset.Open(*Source As Variant, ActiveConnection As Variant, _*
    CursorType As CursorTypeEnum, LockType As LockTypeEnum, _
    Options As Integer)
Recordset.Requery(*Options As Integer*)
Recordset.Resync(*AffectRecords As AffectEnum, ResyncValues As ResyncEnum*)
Recordset.Save(*FileName As String, PersistFormat As PersistFormatEnum*)
Recordset.Seek(*KeyValues As Variant, SeekOption As SeekEnum*)
Boolean = *Recordset*.Supports(*CursorOptions As CursorOptionEnum*)
Recordset.Update([*Fields As Variant*], [*Values As Variant*])
Recordset.UpdateBatch(*AffectRecords As AffectEnum*)

Microsoft Transaction Server Type Library Reference

This appendix should provide a list of the objects, methods, and properties which can be used within your programs to allow you to make use of the Microsoft Transaction Server.

Global Methods

Name	Description
GetObjectContext	Obtains a reference to the IObjectContext that's associated with the current MTS Object
SafeRef	Used by an object to obtain a reference to itself that's safe to pass outside its context

Objects

Name	Description
ObjectContext	Provides access to the current objects context
SecurityProperty	Used to determine the current object's caller or creator
ObjectControl	Used to define context specific initialization and cleanup procedures and to specify whether or not the objects can be recycled

ObjectContext

Methods

Name	Returns	Description
CreateInstance	Variant	Creates an object using current object's context.
DisableCommit		Indicates that the object is not yet finished its work and any attempt to commit the transaction will force an abort.
EnableCommit		Indicates that the object is not yet finished its work but would allow the transaction to commit.
IsCallerInRole	Boolean	Returns TRUE if the caller's Userid is included in the identified role.
IsInTransaction	Boolean	Returns TRUE if this object context has an active transaction.
IsSecurityEnabled	Boolean	Returns TRUE if security is enabled.
SetAbort		Indicates that the object has completed its work and the transaction must be aborted.
SetComplete		Indicates that the object has completed its work and a transaction can be committed.

Properties

Name	Returns	Description	Type
Count	Integer	Get number of named properties.	Read only
Item	Variant	Get a named property	Read only
Security	SecurityProperty	Returns the security object	Read only

SecurityProperty

Methods

Name	Returns	Description
GetDirectCallerName	String	Returns the Name of the direct caller
GetDirectCreatorName	String	Returns the Name of the direct creator
GetOriginalCallerName	String	Returns the Name of the original caller
GetOriginalCreatorName	String	Returns the Name of the original creator

Constants

Error_Constants

Name	Value	Description
mtsErrCtxAborted	-2147164158	The transaction was aborted
mtsErrCtxAborting	-2147164157	The transaction is aborting
mtsErrCtxActivityTimeout	-2147164154	The activity timed out
mtsErrCtxNoContext	-2147164156	There is no object context
mtsErrCtxNoSecurity	-2147164147	There is no security context
mtsErrCtxNotRegistered	-2147164155	The context is not registered
mtsErrCtxOldReference	-2147164153	The context has an old reference
mtsErrCtxRoleNotFound	-2147164148	The role was not found
mtsErrCtxTMNotAvailable	-2147164145	The Transaction Monitor is not available
mtsErrCtxWrongThread	-2147164146	Execution on wrong thread

XactAttributeEnum

Name	Value	Description
adXactAbortRetaining	262144	Performs retaining aborts, so calling Rollback automatically starts a new transaction
adXactCommitRetaining	131072	Performs retaining commits, thus calling CommitTrans automatically starts a new transaction. Provider dependant.

Microsoft Message Queue Object Library Reference

This appendix lists the objects, properties, and methods available to the programmer to be able to implement the Microsoft Message Queue from within Web applications.

Objects

Name	Description
MSMQApplication	Obtains the machine identifier
MSMQCoordinatedTransaction Dispenser	Use to obtain an MSMQ DTC Transaction Object (MSMQTransaction)
MSMQEvent	Allows implementation of a single event handler to support multiple queues
MSMQMessage	A message to be queued
MSMQQuery	Allow the querying of existing public queues
MSMQQueue	An MSMQ Queue
MSMQQueueInfo	Provides Queue Management
MSMQQueueInfos	Allows selection of public queues
MSMQTransaction	An MSMQ Transaction Object
MSMQTransactionDispenser	Used to create new MSMQ Internal Transaction Objects

MSMQApplication

Methods

Name	Returns	Description
MachineIdOfMachineName	String	Global function used to map a machine pathname to a unique identifier. For example, this identifier can be used to construct a format name for a computer so that its journal queue can be opened.

MSMQCoordinatedTransactionDispenser

Methods

Name	Returns	Description
BeginTransaction	IMSMQTransaction	Method used to obtain a new transaction from a transaction dispenser.

MSMQEvent

Methods

Name	Returns	Description
Arrived		User-defined method invoked when a message arrives at a queue.
ArrivedError		User-defined method invoked when an error is returned while reading messages asynchronously.

MSMQMessage

Methods

Name	Returns	Description
AttachCurrentSecurityContext		Method used to associate the current security context with a message.
Send		Method used to send a message to the destination queue. Can optionally be part of a transaction.

Properties

Name	Returns	Description	Type
Ack	Integer	Property indicating what kind of acknowledgement message is returned. Possible values defined by MQMSGACKNOWLEDGEMENT enumeration.	Read/Write
AdminQueueInfo	IMSMQQueueInfo	Property indicating the administration queue for the message.	Read/Write
AppSpecific	Integer	Property containing application-specific information.	Read/Write
ArrivedTime	Variant	Property indicating when the message arrived at its destination queue. Type is Variant Date.	Read only
AuthLevel	Integer	Property indicating the authorization level of a message. Possible values defined by MQMSGAUTHLEVEL enumeration.	Read/Write

Table Continued on Following Page

Name	Returns	Description	Type
Body	Variant	Property containing the message body. It is a Variant type and can contain any intrinsic type and persistent object.	Read/Write
BodyLength	Integer	Property indicating the length (in bytes) of the message body.	Read only
Class	Integer	Property indicating the class of message. Possible values defined by MQMSGCLASS enumeration.	Read only
CorrelationId	Variant	Property indicating the correlation identifier (array of bytes) of the message.	Read/Write
Delivery	Integer	Property indicating the delivery mode of a message. Possible values defined by MQMSGDELIVERY enumeration.	Read/Write
DestinationQueueInfo	IMSMQQueueInfo	Property indicating the destination queue of the message. Typically used when reading response messages, or messages in machine journals or dead-letter queues.	Read only
EncryptAlgorithm	Integer	Property indicating which encryption algorithm to use when encrypting the message body of a private message.	Read/Write
HashAlgorithm	Integer	Property indicating which hash algorithm to use when authenticating the message.	Read/Write
Id	Variant	Property containing the MSMQ-generated identifier (array of bytes) of the message.	Read only
IsAuthenticated	Boolean	Property indicating whether a message was or was not authenticated.	Read only
Journal	Integer	Property indicating journaling option for message. Possible values defined by MQMSGJOURNAL enumeration.	Read/Write
Label	String	Property indicating the label of the message.	Read/Write
MaxTimeToReachQueue	Integer	Property indicating the amount of time MSMQ has to deliver the message to its destination queue.	Read/Write

Name	Returns	Description	Type
MaxTimeToReceive	Integer	Property indicating the amount of time the receiving application has to retrieve the message from its destination queue.	Read/Write
Priority	Integer	Property indicating the priority level of a message. Range must be between MQ_MIN_PRIORITY and MQ_MAX_PRIORITY.	Read/Write
PrivLevel	Integer	Property indicating the privacy level of a message. Possible values defined by MQMSGPRIVLEVEL enumeration.	Read/Write
ResponseQueueInfo	IMSMQQueueInfo	Property indicating the response queue for the message.	Read/Write
SenderCertificate	Variant	Property containing the security certificate of a message. Type is an array of bytes.	Read/Write
SenderId	Variant	Property containing the sender identifier of the message. Type is an array of bytes.	Read only
SenderIdType	Integer	Property indicating what type of identifier is attached to the message. Possible values are defined by MSMQSENDERIDTYPE enumeration.	Read/Write
SentTime	Variant	Property indicating when the message was sent. Type is Variant Date.	Read only
SourceMachineGuid	String	Property identifying the computer where the message originated.	Read only
Trace	Integer	Property indicating tracing option for message. Possible values defined by MQMSGTRACE enumeration.	Read/Write

MSMQQuery

Methods

Name	Returns	Description
LookupQueue	IMSMQQueueInfos	Produces a collection of public queues that match a specified selection criteria. Queries the MSMQ information store.

MSMQQueue

Methods

Name	Returns	Description
Close		Method to close an open instance of a queue.
EnableNotification		Method to enable asynchronous notification of arriving messages. It can use the queue's implicit cursor. The user-defined MSMQEvent_Arrived event handler is invoked when a message arrives at the location specified by the optional Cursor parameter (default is first message in the queue), or a timeout occurs. The user-defined MSMQEvent_ArrivedError is invoked if the asynchronous message retrieval results in an error.
Peek	IMSMQ Message	Method to synchronously peek at the first message in the queue, regardless of the implicit cursor position. Optional parameters include ReceiveTimeout (default set to INFINITE), WantDestinationQueue (default set to False), and WantBody (default set to True).
PeekCurrent	IMSMQ Message	Method to synchronously peek at the current message in queue (message pointed at by the implicit cursor). The implicit cursor is not advanced. Optional parameters include ReceiveTimeout (default set to INFINITE) and Transaction (default set to MTS Transaction).
PeekNext	IMSMQ Message	Method to synchronously peek at the next message in the queue. When called, the implicit cursor is first advanced and then the message is returned. Optional parameters include ReceiveTimeout (default set to INFINITE) and Transaction (default set to MTS Transaction).
Receive	IMSMQ Message	Method to synchronously retrieve a message from a queue. It always removes the first message in queue regardless of the position of the implicit cursor. Optional parameters include ReceiveTimeout (default set to INFINITE), Transaction (default set to MTS Transaction), WantDestinationQueue (default set to False), and WantBody (default set to True).

Name	Returns	Description
ReceiveCurrent	IMSMQ Message	Method to synchronously remove the current message from the queue. Retrieves the message at the position pointed to by the implicit cursor. Optional parameters include ReceiveTimeout (default set to INFINITE) and Transaction (default set to MTS Transaction).
Reset		Method that resets the queue's implicit cursor to the beginning of the queue.

Properties

Name	Returns	Description	Type
Access	Integer	Property indicating the access mode of a queue. Possible values defined by MQACCESS enumeration.	Read only
Handle	Integer	Property indicating the internal MSMQ handle of an open queue instance. Useful for directly calling MSMQ APIs.	Read only
IsOpen	Boolean	Property indicating whether or not the queue object refers to an open instance of a queue.	Read only
QueueInfo	IMSMQQueueInfo	Property referring to an MSMQQueueInfo instance describing the queue.	Read only
ShareMode	Integer	Property indicating the share mode of a queue. Possible values defined by MQSHARE enumeration.	Read only

MSMQQueueInfo

Methods

Name	Returns	Description
Create		Method that creates a new queue. The PathName property is required to create a queue. The FormatName property is updated when the queue is created. Optional parameters include IsWorldReadable (default set to False) and IsTransactional (default set to False).
Delete		Method used to delete queue. The PathName property must be specified to delete a queue.
Open	IMSMQQueue	Method used to open a queue. The PathName property must be specified to open a queue. Parameters include Access (send, peek, or receive) and ShareMode (exclusive or all).
Refresh		Method used to refresh the properties of a public queue from the MSMQ information store.
Update		Method used to update the MSMQ information store with the public queue's current properties.

Properties

Name	Returns	Description	Type
Authenticate	Integer	Property that specifies whether or not the queue only accepts authenticated messages. If the authentication level of the message does not match the authentication level of the queue, the message is rejected by the queue. Possible values are defined by the MQAUTHENTICATE enumeration.	Read/Write
BasePriority	Integer	Property that specifies the base priority for all messages sent to a public queue. The queue's base priority has no effect on the order of the messages in the queue, or how messages are read from the queue.	Read/Write
CreateTime	Variant	Property that indicates the time and date when the queue was created. Type is Variant Date.	Read only

Name	Returns	Description	Type
FormatName	String	Property that identifies the queue. The format name of a queue is generated by MSMQ when the queue is created, or generated later by the application.	Read/Write
IsTransactional	Boolean	Property indicating whether the queue is transactional or non-transactional. If the queue is transactional, all messages sent to the queue must be part of a transaction.	Read only
IsWorldReadable	Boolean	Property that indicates who can read messages in the queue. If False, then the queue has the default MSMQ security: all users can send messages to the queue but only the owner of the queue can read messages from it. Otherwise all users can read its messages.	Read only
Journal	Integer	Property that specifies if the messages retrieved from the queue are copied to the queue's journal queue. Possible values are defined by the MQJOURNAL enumeration.	Read/Write
JournalQuota	Integer	Property that specifies the maximum size (in kilobytes) of the journal queue.	Read/Write
Label	String	Property indicating the label of the queue.	Read/Write
ModifyTime	Variant	Property that indicates the time and date when the queue's properties were last modified. Type is Variant Date.	Read only
PathName	String	Property indicating pathname (physical location) of the queue.	Read/Write
PrivLevel	Integer	Property that specifies the privacy level that is required by the queue. The privacy level determines how the queue handles private (encrypted) messages. Possible values are defined by the MQPRIVLEVEL enumeration.	Read/Write
QueueGuid	String	Property indicating the identifier of the public queue.	Read only
Quota	Integer	Property that specifies the maximum size (in kilobytes) of the queue.	Read/Write
ServiceTypeGuid	String	Property identifying the type of service provided by the queue.	Read/Write

MSMQQueueInfos

Methods

Name	Returns	Description
Next	IMSMQQueueInfo	Method used to reset the implicit cursor to the start of a collection of queues produced by MSMQQuery.LookupQueue.
Reset		Method used to reset the implicit cursor to the start of a collection of queues produced by MSMQQuery.LookupQueue.

MSMQTransaction

Methods

Name	Returns	Description
Abort		Method used to abort an MSMQ transaction.
Commit		Method used to commit an MSMQ transaction.

Properties

Name	Returns	Description	Type
Transaction	Integer	Property that indicates the underlying "magic cookie" used by a transaction dispenser.	Read only

MSMQTransactionDispenser

Methods

Name	Returns	Description
BeginTransaction	IMSMQTransaction	Method used to obtain a new transaction from a transaction dispenser.

Constants

MQACCESS

Name	Value	Description
MQ_PEEK_ACCESS	32	Messages can only be looked at, and can not be removed from the queue
MQ_RECEIVE_ACCESS	1	Messages can be retrieved from the queue or peeked at.
MQ_SEND_ACCESS	2	Messages can only be sent to the queue

MQAUTHENTICATE

Name	Value	Description
MQ_AUTHENTICATE	1	The queue only accepts authenticated messages
MQ_AUTHENTICATE_NONE	0	The default. The queue accepts authenticated and non-authenticated messages

MQCALG

Name	Value	Description
MQMSG_CALG_DES	26113	Hashing algorithm used when authenticating messages
MQMSG_CALG_DSS_SIGN	8704	Hashing algorithm used when authenticating messages
MQMSG_CALG_MAC	32773	Hashing algorithm used when authenticating messages

Table Continued on Following Page

Name	Value	Description
MQMSG_CALG_MD2	32769	Hashing algorithm used when authenticating messages
MQMSG_CALG_MD4	32770	Hashing algorithm used when authenticating messages
MQMSG_CALG_MD5	32771	The Default. Hashing algorithm used when authenticating messages
MQMSG_CALG_RC2	26114	Hashing algorithm used when authenticating messages
MQMSG_CALG_RC4	26625	Hashing algorithm used when authenticating messages
MQMSG_CALG_RSA_KEYX	41984	Hashing algorithm used when authenticating messages
MQMSG_CALG_RSA_SIGN	9216	Hashing algorithm used when authenticating messages
MQMSG_CALG_SEAL	26626	Hashing algorithm used when authenticating messages
MQMSG_CALG_SHA	32772	Hashing algorithm used when authenticating messages

MQDEFAULT

Name	Value	Description
DEFAULT_M_ACKNOWLEDGE	0	Default value for the Acknowledgement property of a Message
DEFAULT_M_APPSPECIFIC	0	Default value for the AppSpecific property of a Message
DEFAULT_M_AUTH_LEVEL	0	Default value for the AuthLevel property of a Message
DEFAULT_M_DELIVERY	0	Default value for the Delivery property of a Message
DEFAULT_M_JOURNAL	0	Default value for the journal property of a Message
DEFAULT_M_PRIORITY	3	Default value for the Priority property of a Message

Name	Value	Description
DEFAULT_M_PRIV_LEVEL	0	Default value for the PrivLevel property of a Message
DEFAULT_M_SENDERID_TYPE	1	Default value for the SenderId property of a Message
DEFAULT_Q_AUTHENTICATE	0	Default value for the Authenticate property of a Queue
DEFAULT_Q_BASEPRIORITY	0	Default value for the BasePriority property of a Queue
DEFAULT_Q_JOURNAL	0	Default value for the Journal property of a Queue
DEFAULT_Q_JOURNAL_QUOTA	-1	Default value for the JournalQuota property of a Queue
DEFAULT_Q_PRIV_LEVEL	1	Default value for the PrivLevel property of a Queue
DEFAULT_Q_QUOTA	-1	Default value for the Quota property of a Queue
DEFAULT_Q_TRANSACTION	0	Default value for the Transaction property of a Queue

MQERROR

Name	Value	Description
MQ_ERROR	-1072824319	Generic error code.
MQ_ERROR_ACCESS_DENIED	-1072824283	Access to the specified queue or computer is denied.
MQ_ERROR_BAD_SECURITY_CONTEXT	-1072824267	Security context specified by PROPID_M_SECURITY_CONTEXT is corrupted.
MQ_ERROR_BUFFER_OVERFLOW	-1072824294	Supplied message body buffer is too small. A partial copy of the message body is copied to the buffer, but the message is not removed from the queue.
MQ_ERROR_CANNOT_IMPERSONATE_CLIENT	-1072824284	MSMQ information store server cannot impersonate the client application. Security credentials could not be verified.

Table Continued on Following Page

Name	Value	Description
MQ_ERROR_COMPUTER_ DOES_NOT_SUPPORT_ ENCRYPTION	-1072824269	Encryption failed. Computer (source or destination) does not support encryption operations.
MQ_ERROR_CORRUPTED_ INTERNAL_ CERTIFICATE	-1072824275	MSMQ-supplied internal certificate is corrupted.
MQ_ERROR_CORRUPTED_ PERSONAL_CERT_STORE	-1072824271	Microsoft® Internet Explorer personal certificate store is corrupted.
MQ_ERROR_CORRUPTED_ SECURITY_DATA	-1072824272	Cryptographic function (CryptoAPI) has failed.
MQ_ERROR_COULD_NOT_ GET_ACCOUNT_INFO	-1072824265	MSMQ could not get account information for the user.
MQ_ERROR_COULD_NOT_ GET_USER_SID	-1072824266	MSMQ could not get the specified sender identifier.
MQ_ERROR_DELETE_CN_ IN_USE	-1072824248	Specified connected network (CN) cannot be deleted because it is defined in at least one computer. Remove the CN from all CN lists and try again.
MQ_ERROR_DS_ERROR	-1072824253	Internal error with MQIS.
MQ_ERROR_DS_IS_FULL	-1072824254	MSMQ information store is full.
MQ_ERROR_DTC_ CONNECT	-1072824244	MSMQ cannot connect to the Microsoft® Distributed Transaction Coordinator (MS DTC).
MQ_ERROR_ FORMATNAME_BUFFER_ TOO_SMALL	-1072824289	Specified format name buffer is too small to contain the queue's format name.
MQ_ERROR_ILLEGAL_ CONTEXT	-1072824229	The lpwcsContext parameter of MQLocateBegin is not NULL.
MQ_ERROR_ILLEGAL_ CURSOR_ACTION	-1072824292	An attempt was made to peek at the next message in the queue when cursor was at the end of the queue.
MQ_ERROR_ILLEGAL_ FORMATNAME	-1072824290	Format name specified is not valid.
MQ_ERROR_ILLEGAL_ MQCOLUMNS	-1072824264	Indicates that pColumns is NULL.
MQ_ERROR_ILLEGAL_ MQQMPROPS	-1072824255	No properties are specified by the MQQMPROPS structure, or it is set to NULL.

Name	Value	Description
MQ_ERROR_ILLEGAL_ MQQUEUEPROPS	-1072824259	No properties are specified by the MQQUEUEPROPS structure, or it is set to NULL.
MQ_ERROR_ILLEGAL_ OPERATION	-1072824220	The operation is not supported on this specific platform.
MQ_ERROR_ILLEGAL_ PROPERTY_SIZE	-1072824261	The specified buffer for the message identifier or correlation identifier is not the correct size.
MQ_ERROR_ILLEGAL_ PROPERTY_VALUE	-1072824296	Property value specified in the PROPVARIANT array is illegal.
MQ_ERROR_ILLEGAL_ PROPERTY_VT	-1072824295	VARTYPE specified in the VT field of the PROPVARIANT array is not valid.
MQ_ERROR_ILLEGAL_ PROPID	-1072824263	Property identifier in the property identifier array is not valid.
MQ_ERROR_ILLEGAL_ QUEUE_PATHNAME	-1072824300	MSMQ pathname specified for the queue is not valid.
MQ_ERROR_ILLEGAL_ RELATION	-1072824262	Relationship parameter is not valid.
MQ_ERROR_ILLEGAL_ RESTRICTION_PROPID	-1072824260	Property identifier specified in MQRESTRICTION is invalid.
MQ_ERROR_ILLEGAL_ SECURITY_DESCRIPTOR	-1072824287	Specified security descriptor is not valid.
MQ_ERROR_ILLEGAL_SORT	-1072824304	Illegal sort specified.
MQ_ERROR_ILLEGAL_ SORT_PROPID	-1072824228	Property identifier specified in MQSORTSET is not valid.
MQ_ERROR_ILLEGAL_USER	-1072824303	User is not legal.
MQ_ERROR_ INSUFFICIENT_ PROPERTIES	-1072824257	Not all properties required for the operation were specified.
MQ_ERROR_ INSUFFICIENT_ RESOURCES	-1072824281	Insufficient resources to complete operation (for example, not enough memory). Operation failed.
MQ_ERROR_INTERNAL_ USER_CERT_EXIST	-1072824274	Internal user certificate exists
MQ_ERROR_INVALID_ CERTIFICATE	-1072824276	Security certificate specified by PROPID_M_SENDER_CERT is invalid, or the certificate is not correctly placed in the Microsoft® Internet Explorer personal certificate store.

Table Continued on Following Page

Name	Value	Description
MQ_ERROR_INVALID_HANDLE	-1072824313	Specified queue handle is not valid.
MQ_ERROR_INVALID_OWNER	-1072824252	Object owner is not valid. Owner was not found when trying to create object.
MQ_ERROR_INVALID_PARAMETER	-1072824314	One of the IN parameters supplied by the operation is not valid.
MQ_ERROR_IO_TIMEOUT	-1072824293	MQReceiveMessage I/O timeout has expired.
MQ_ERROR_LABEL_BUFFER_TOO_SMALL	-1072824226	Message label buffer is too small for received label.
MQ_ERROR_LABEL_TOO_LONG	-1072824227	Message label is too long. It should be equal to or less than
MQ_ERROR_MACHINE_EXISTS	-1072824256	Machine with the specified name already exists.
MQ_ERROR_MACHINE_NOT_FOUND	-1072824307	Specified machine could not be found in MQIS.
MQ_ERROR_MESSAGE_ALREADY_RECEIVED	-1072824291	Message pointed at by the cursor has already been removed from the queue.
MQ_ERROR_MESSAGE_STORAGE_FAILED	-1072824278	Recoverable message could not be stored on the local computer.
MQ_ERROR_MISSING_CONNECTOR_TYPE	-1072824235	Specified a property typically generated by MSMQ but did not specify PROPID_M_CONNECTOR_TYPE
MQ_ERROR_MQIS_READONLY_MODE	-1072824224	MQIS database is in read-only mode.
MQ_ERROR_MQIS_SERVER_EMPTY	-1072824225	The list of MSMQ information store servers (in registry) is empty.
MQ_ERROR_NO_DS	-1072824301	No connection with the Site Controller server. Cannot access the MQIS.
MQ_ERROR_NO_INTERNAL_USER_CERT	-1072824273	No internal certificate available for this user.
MQ_ERROR_NO_RESPONSE_FROM_OBJECT_SERVER	-1072824247	No response from MQIS server. Operation status is unknown.
MQ_ERROR_OBJECT_SERVER_NOT_AVAILABLE	-1072824246	Object's MSMQ information store server is not available. Operation failed.

Name	Value	Description
MQ_ERROR_OPERATION_CANCELLED	-1072824312	Operation was cancelled before it could be started.
MQ_ERROR_PRIVILEGE_NOT_HELD	-1072824282	Application does not have the required privileges to perform the operation.
MQ_ERROR_PROPERTY	-1072824318	One or more of the specified properties caused an error.
MQ_ERROR_PROPERTY_NOTALLOWED	-1072824258	Specified property is not valid for the operation (for example, specifying PROPID_Q_INSTANCE when setting queue properties).
MQ_ERROR_PROV_NAME_BUFFER_TOO_SMALL	-1072824221	The provider name buffer for cryptographic service provider is too small.
MQ_ERROR_QUEUE_DELETED	-1072824230	Queue was deleted before the message could be read. The specified queue handle is no longer valid and the queue must be closed.
MQ_ERROR_QUEUE_EXISTS	-1072824315	Queue (public or private) with the identical MSMQ pathname is registered. Public queues are registered in MQIS. Private queues are registered in the local computer.
MQ_ERROR_QUEUE_NOT_AVAILABLE	-1072824245	Error while reading from queue residing on a remote computer.
MQ_ERROR_QUEUE_NOT_FOUND	-1072824317	Public queue is not registered in MQIS. This error does not apply to private queues.
MQ_ERROR_RESULT_BUFFER_TOO_SMALL	-1072824250	Supplied result buffer is too small. MQLocateNext could not return at least one complete query result.
MQ_ERROR_SECURITY_DESCRIPTOR_TOO_SMALL	-1072824285	Supplied security buffer is too small.
MQ_ERROR_SENDER_CERT_BUFFER_TOO_SMALL	-1072824277	Supplied sender certificate buffer is too small.
MQ_ERROR_SENDERID_BUFFER_TOO_SMALL	-1072824286	Supplied sender identification buffer is too small to hold sender identification.
MQ_ERROR_SERVICE_NOT_AVAILABLE	-1072824309	Application was unable to connect to the Queue Manager.

Table Continued on Following Page

Name	Value	Description
MQ_ERROR_SHARING_ VIOLATION	-1072824311	Sharing violation when opening queue. The application is trying to open an already opened queue that has exclusive read rights.
MQ_ERROR_SIGNATURE_ BUFFER_TOO_SMALL	-1072824222	The signature buffer is too small.
MQ_ERROR_STALE_ HANDLE	-1072824234	Specified handle was obtained in a previous session of the Queue Manager service.
MQ_ERROR_SYMM_KEY_ BUFFER_TOO_SMALL	-1072824223	The symmetric key buffer is too small.
MQ_ERROR_ TRANSACTION_ENLIST	-1072824232	Cannot enlist transaction.
MQ_ERROR_ TRANSACTION_IMPORT	-1072824242	MSMQ could not import the specified transaction.
MQ_ERROR_ TRANSACTION_ SEQUENCE	-1072824239	Transaction operation sequence is incorrect.
MQ_ERROR_ TRANSACTION_USAGE	-1072824240	Either the queue or the message is not transactional. Transaction messages can only be sent to a transaction queue, and transaction queues can only receive transaction messages.
MQ_ERROR_ UNSUPPORTED_ ACCESS_MODE	-1072824251	Specified access mode is not supported. Supported access modes include MQ_PEEK_MESSAGE, MQ_SEND_MESSAGE, and MQ_RECEIVE_MESSAGE.
MQ_ERROR_ UNSUPPORTED_DBMS	-1072824302	Current version of Database Management System is not supported
MQ_ERROR_ UNSUPPORTED_ FORMATNAME_ OPERATION	-1072824288	Requested operation is not supported for the specified format name (for example, trying to open a queue to receive messages using a direct format name).
MQ_ERROR_USER_ BUFFER_TOO_SMALL	-1072824280	Supplied buffer for user is too small to hold the returned information.
MQ_ERROR_WRITE_NOT_ ALLOWED	-1072824219	Write operations to MQIS are not allowed while an MSMQ information store server is being installed.

MQJOURNAL

Name	Value	Description
MQ_JOURNAL	1	When a message is removed from the queue it is stored in the queue journal
MQ_JOURNAL_NONE	0	The default. Messages are not stored in a journal queue when they are removed from the queue

MQMAX

Name	Value	Description
MQ_MAX_Q_LABEL_LEN	124	The maximum length of the queue label
MQ_MAX_Q_NAME_LEN	124	The maximum length of the queue name

MQMSGACKNOWLEDGEMENT

Name	Value	Description
MQMSG_ACKNOWLEDGMENT_FULL_REACH_QUEUE	5	Posts positive and negative acknowledgements depending upon whether or not the message reached the queue. This can happen when the 'time-to-reach-queue timer expires, or when a message cannot be authenticated
MQMSG_ACKNOWLEDGMENT_FULL_RECEIVE	14	Post a positive or negative acknowledgement depending on whether or not the message is retrieved from the queue before its time-to-be-received timer expires.
MQMSG_ACKNOWLEDGMENT_NACK_REACH_QUEUE	4	Posts a negative acknowledgement when the message cannot reach the queue. This can happen when the time-to-reach-queue timer expires, or a message can not be authenticated
MQMSG_ACKNOWLEDGMENT_NACK_RECEIVE	12	Posts a negative acknowledgement when an error occurs and the message cannot be retrieved from the queue before its time-to-be-received timer expires.
MQMSG_ACKNOWLEDGMENT_NEG_ARRIVAL	4	Indicates a negative message arrival
MQMSG_ACKNOWLEDGMENT_NEG_RECEIVE	8	Indicates a negative message receive

Table Continued on Following Page

765

Name	Value	Description
MQMSG_ACKNOWLEDGMENT_ NONE	0	The default. No acknowledgement messages are posted.
MQMSG_ACKNOWLEDGMENT_ POS_ARRIVAL	1	Indicates a positive message arrival
MQMSG_ACKNOWLEDGMENT_ POS_RECEIVE	2	Indicates a positive message receive

MQMSGAUTHLEVEL

Name	Value	Description
MQMSG_AUTH_LEVEL_ ALWAYS	1	The message must be authenticated when it arrives at the destination queue
MQMSG_AUTH_LEVEL_ NONE	0	The default. The message does not have to be authenticated when it arrives at the destination queue

MQMSGCLASS

Name	Value	Description
MQMSG_CLASS_ACK_ REACH_QUEUE	2	The original message reached its destination queue
MQMSG_CLASS_ACK_ RECEIVE	16384	The original message was retrieved by the receiving application
MQMSG_CLASS_NACK_ ACCESS_DENIED	32772	The sending application does not have access rights to the destination queue
MQMSG_CLASS_NACK_ BAD_DST_Q	32768	The destination queue is not available to the sending application
MQMSG_CLASS_NACK_ BAD_ENCRYPTION	32775	The destination Queue Manager could not decrypt a private (encrypted) message
MQMSG_CLASS_NACK_ BAD_SIGNATURE	32774	MSMQ could not authenticate the original message. The original message's digital signature is not valid.
MQMSG_CLASS_NACK_ COULD_NOT_ENCRYPT	32776	The source Queue Manager could not encrypt a private message
MQMSG_CLASS_NACK_ HOP_COUNT_EXCEEDED	32773	The original message's hop count is exceeded

Name	Value	Description
MQMSG_CLASS_NACK_NOT_TRANSACTIONAL_MSG	32778	A non-transaction message was sent to a transactional queue
MQMSG_CLASS_NACK_NOT_TRANSACTIONAL_Q	32777	A transaction message was sent to a non-transactional queue
MQMSG_CLASS_NACK_PURGED	32769	The message was purged before reaching the destination queue
MQMSG_CLASS_NACK_Q_DELETED	49152	The queue was deleted before the message could be read from the queue
MQMSG_CLASS_NACK_Q_EXCEED_QUOTA	32771	The original message's destination queue is full
MQMSG_CLASS_NACK_Q_PURGED	49153	The queue was purged and the message no longer exists
MQMSG_CLASS_NACK_REACH_QUEUE_TIMEOUT	32770	Either the time-to-reach-queue or time-to-be-received timer expired before the original message could reach the destination queue
MQMSG_CLASS_NACK_RECEIVE_TIMEOUT	49154	The original message was not removed from the queue before its time-to-be-received timer expired
MQMSG_CLASS_NORMAL	0	Indicates a normal MSMQ message
MQMSG_CLASS_REPORT	1	Indicates a report message

MQMSGCURSOR

Name	Value	Description
MQMSG_CURRENT	1	Notification starts when a message is at the current cursor location
MQMSG_FIRST	0	The default. Notification starts when a message is in the queue
MQMSG_NEXT	2	The cursor is moved, then notification starts when a message is at the new cursor location

MQMSGDELIVERY

Name	Value	Description
MQMSG_DELIVERY_EXPRESS	0	The default. The message stays in memory until it can be delivered
MQMSG_DELIVERY_RECOVERABLE	1	In every hop along its route, the message is forwarded to the next hop or stored locally in a backup file until delivered, thus guaranteeing delivery even in the case of a machine crash

MQMSGIDSIZE

Name	Value	Description
MQMSG_ CORRELATIONID_ SIZE	20	Size of CorrelationID byte array
MQMSG_MSGID_SIZE	20	Size of MessageID byte array

MQMSGJOURNAL

Name	Value	Description
MQMSG_DEADLETTER	1	If the message time-to-be-received or time-to-reach-queue setting expires, keep the message in the dead letter queue on the machine where time expired
MQMSG_JOURNAL	2	If the message is transmitted (from the originating machine to the next hop), keep it in the machine journal on the originating machine
MQMSG_JOURNAL_NONE	0	The default. The message is not kept in the originating machine's journal

MQMSGMAX

Name	Value	Description
MQ_MAX_MSG_LABEL_ LEN	249	Maximum length of the message Label property

MQMSGPRIVLEVEL

Name	Value	Description
MQMSG_PRIV_LEVEL_ BODY	1	The message is a private (encrypted) message
MQMSG_PRIV_LEVEL_ NONE	0	The default. The message is a non-private (clear) message

MQMSGSENDERIDTYPE

Name	Value	Description
MQMSG_SENDERID_ TYPE_NONE	0	SenderID is not attached to the message
MQMSG_SENDERID_ TYPE_SID	1	The default. The SenderID property contains a SID for the user sending the message

MQMSGTRACE

Name	Value	Description
MQMSG_SEND_ROUTE_TO_REPORT_QUEUE	1	Each hop made by the original message generates a report that is recorded in a report message, which is sent to the report queue specified by the source Queue Manager
MQMSG_TRACE_NONE	0	The default. No tracing for this message

MQPRIORITY

Name	Value	Description
MQ_MAX_PRIORITY	7	Maximum queue priority
MQ_MIN_PRIORITY	0	Minimum queue priority

MQPRIVLEVEL

Name	Value	Description
MQ_PRIV_LEVEL_BODY	2	The queue accepts only private (encrypted) messages
MQ_PRIV_LEVEL_NONE	0	The queue accepts only non-private (clear) messages
MQ_PRIV_LEVEL_OPTIONAL	1	The default. The queue does not force privacy, and accepts both clear and encrypted messages

MQSHARE

Name	Value	Description
MQ_DENY_NONE	0	The queue is available to everyone for sending, peeking, or retrieving messages.
MQ_DENY_RECEIVE_SHARE	1	Messages can only be retrieved by this process.

MQTRANSACTION

Name	Value	Description
MQ_MTS_TRANSACTION	1	Specifies that the call is part of the current MTS transaction
MQ_NO_TRANSACTION	0	Specifies the call is not part of a transaction
MQ_SINGLE_MESSAGE	3	Sends a single message as a transaction
MQ_XA_TRANSACTION	2	Specifies that the call is part of an externally coordinated, XA compliant, transaction

MQTRANSACTIONAL

Name	Value	Description
MQ_TRANSACTIONAL	1	All messages sent to the queue must be done through an MSMQ transaction
MQ_TRANSACTIONAL_ NONE	0	Default. No transaction operations can be performed on the queue

MQWARNING

Name	Value	Description
MQ_INFORMATION_ DUPLICATE_PROPERTY	1074659333	Property already specified with same value. When duplicate settings are found, the first entry is used and subsequent settings are ignored.
MQ_INFORMATION_ FORMATNAME_BUFFER_ TOO_SMALL	1074659337	Supplied format name buffer is too small. Queue was still created.
MQ_INFORMATION_ ILLEGAL_PROPERTY	1074659330	Specified identifier in property identifier array aPropID is not valid.
MQ_INFORMATION_ OPERATION_PENDING	1074659334	Asynchronous operation is pending.
MQ_INFORMATION_ PROPERTY	1074659329	One or more of the specified properties resulted in a warning. Operation completed anyway.
MQ_INFORMATION_ PROPERTY_IGNORED	1074659331	Specified property is not valid for this operation (for example, PROPID_M_SENDERID is not valid; it is set by MSMQ when sending messages).
MQ_INFORMATION_ UNSUPPORTED_ PROPERTY	1074659332	Specified property is not supported by this operation. This property is ignored.

RELOPS

Name	Value	Description
REL_EQ	1	The default. Queue searching operator. Find only items that are Equal to the search string
REL_GE	6	Queue searching operator. Find only items that are Greater Than or Equal to the search string
REL_GT	4	Queue searching operator. Find only items that are Greater Than to the search string
REL_LE	5	Queue searching operator. Find only items that are Less Than or Equal to the search string
REL_LT	3	Queue searching operator. Find only items that are Less Than to the search string
REL_NEQ	2	Queue searching operator. Find only items that are Not Equal to the search string
REL_NOP	0	Queue searching operator.

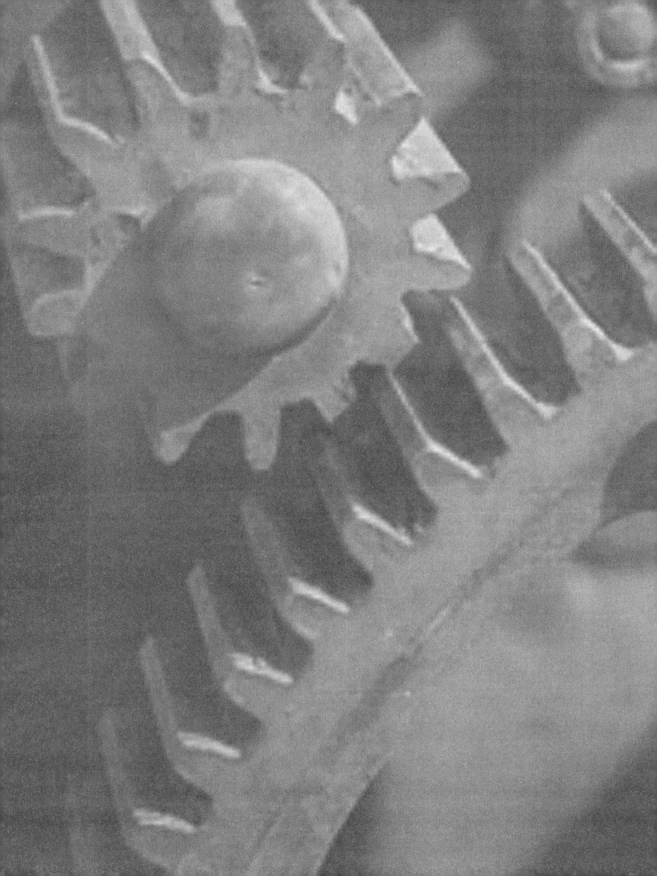

COM & The System Registry

It should be clear by now that the System Registry plays a very important part in the proper functioning of COM. Furthermore, since the system and application configurations, the user preferences and the security database (under NT) are all stored in the registry, the registry is vital to the health and well being of the system as a whole.

In this appendix, we'll introduce the registry editor, and we'll cover how to use it in order to examine and modify many of the vital entries related to COM object operations.

The registry editor may be used to:

- ❏ View registry entries
- ❏ Add, delete and modify registry entries
- ❏ Backup the registry

We can use this tool, as a viewer, to take a look at how the COM runtime buries away the essential information.

The registry editor is not the best tool for simply viewing COM entries and so we'll also look at another tool provided by Microsoft, that you will have seen throughout the book: OLEView.

OLEView may be used to:

- ❏ Browse, in a structured way, all of the Component Object Model (COM) classes installed on your machine.
- ❏ See the registry entries for each class in an easy-to-read format.
- ❏ Configure any COM class on your system. This includes Distributed COM activation and security settings.
- ❏ Configure system-wide COM settings, including enabling or disabling DCOM.
- ❏ Test any COM class, simply by double-clicking its name. The list of interfaces that class supports will be displayed. Double-clicking an interface entry allows you to invoke a viewer that will "exercise" that interface.
- ❏ Activate COM classes locally or remotely. This is great for testing DCOM setups.
- ❏ View type library contents. Use this to figure out what methods, properties, and events an ActiveX Control supports!

The Registry

The registry is little more than a database. It stores data in a hierarchically structured tree. Each node in the tree is called a **key**. Each key can contain both **subkeys** and data entries called **values**.

The Registry Editor

Find the registry editor on your system and run it. In Windows 9x, it's called `Regedit.exe`. When it loads you will see an Explorer style interface. There are six subtrees that are displayed in the left pane, each of which has associated keys and information:

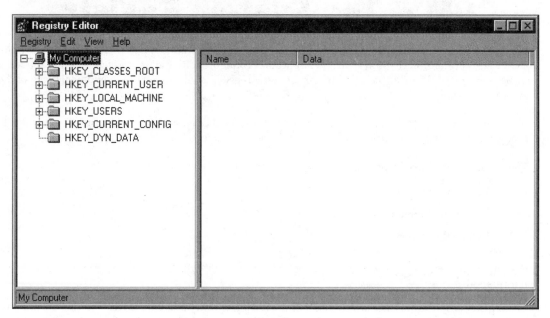

In Windows NT 4.0, it is called `Regedt32.exe`. On running it, you'll find that only five subtrees are displayed and this time, each subtree has its own window:

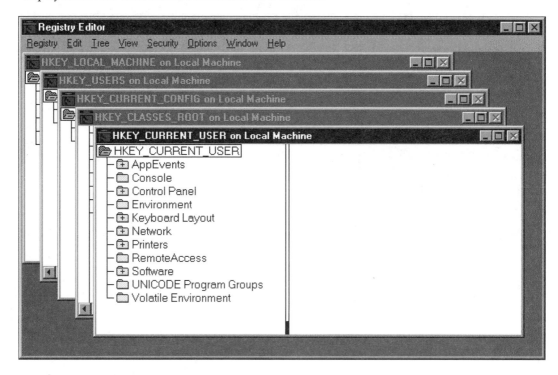

Windows NT does also have `Regedit.exe`. *Each program just allows you to do slightly different things and the differences are not relevant to our discussion here.*

Backing up the Registry

Before you go playing about with the registry it's always a good idea to create a backup copy, just in case anything goes wrong.

This is easily done by using the Export Registry File... entry on the File menu. This allows you to save a copy of the registry:

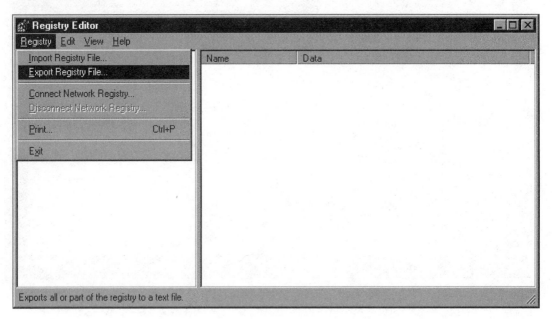

Enter COM, Stage Right

The subtree that we, and COM, are interested in is the HKEY_CLASSES_ROOT subtree. When we expand this subtree, we'll typically find a very large list of keys. One interesting key is the CLSID key. Try expanding this one:

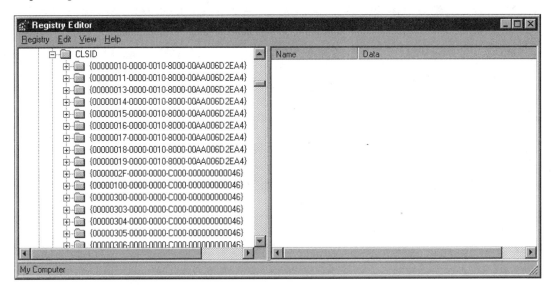

You'll be greeted with a large list of CLSIDs, remember them? These, as we know, are actually 'names' or 'keys' for classes of COM objects. If you expand any one of them, you'll see that they have additional subkeys (attributes) which describe the class further. The attributes you see listed here are dependent upon the type of component.

DLLs

DLLs have a key called `InprocServer32`. This key indicates to the COM runtime that the CLSID represents an in-process server or DLL. The named values under this subkey typically include a `(Default)` and a `ThreadingModel`:

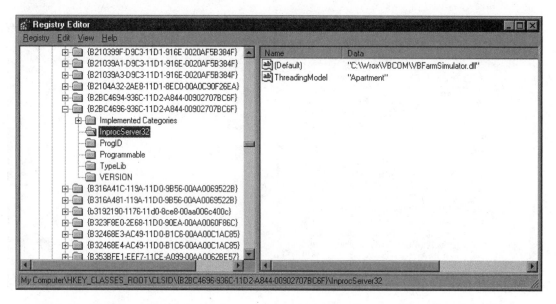

The COM runtime looks into the `(Default)` value to find out where the DLL is located. The `ThreadingModel` value gives COM an indication, unsurprisingly, of what sort of threading model the server will support.

EXEs

For COM objects that are local server based, you'll find a `LocalServer32` key that will provide the COM runtime with a path to find the server EXE:

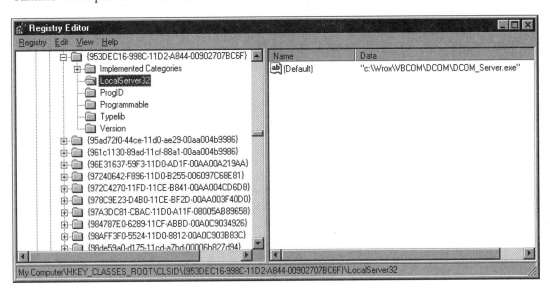

You'll also see a lot of other keys, which are covered in the table below.

Controls

Controls also have an `InprocServer32` key, because they are also in-process servers, which provides COM with the location of the OCX file. However, they also have a `Control` key that marks the server as an ActiveX control:

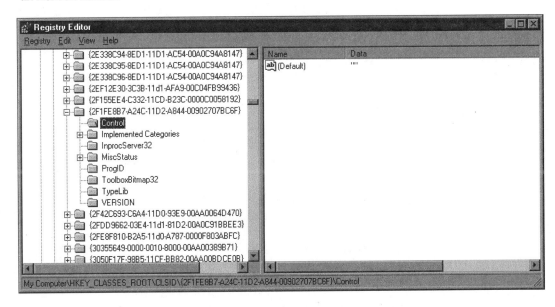

The COM Attributes in Full

The following table summarizes some of the many keys that you'll find under
`\HKEY_CLASSES_ROOT\CLSID\{-----}`

Key Name	Applies To	Comment
InprocServer	16/32-bit servers	Path to 16/32-bit DLL on same machine. Implements an in-process server.
InprocServer32	32-bit servers	Path to 32-bit DLL on same machine. Implements an in-process server.
InprocHandler32	32-bit servers	An object handler is nothing more than a piece of code that implements the interfaces expected by a container when an object is in its loaded state (i.e. it isn't running yet). In other words, it's a glue object that provides the interfaces but doesn't necessarily provide the full functionality.
LocalServer32	32-bit servers	Path to 32-bit EXE on same machine. Implements a local server running in a separate process.
Insertable	32-bit servers	Indicates that the 32-bit server can be used by existing 16-bit applications.
ProgId		A programmatic identifier. The default value of the key is a human readable string uniquely (but not universally) identifying a class that can appear in an Insert Object dialog box.
Verb	OLE objects	Verbs are specific actions the object can execute that are meaningful to the end user. A container (client app) looks at this key in the registry to find out what verbs the object supports, in order to present them to the user, typically in a pop-up menu.
Control		If the key is present, the object is a control.
Typelib		Type library ID for the object.
MainUserType		The constant name referring to the currently installed version of the server.
AuxUserType		Auxiliary names, for example, a short name for the class, a real-world name for the application when necessary to present to the user, etc.
DefaultIcon		Contains icon information for iconic representations of the object. It includes the full path to module (DLL or EXE) where the icon resides and the index of the icon within the executable.

This list is certainly not exhaustive, and any particular pair of COM objects can establish their own private use of keys associated with the CLSID. What we attempt to cover here are the most common ones that we may encounter in our ActiveX programming activities. This explains how COM can know so much about a class given a CLSID. The `ProgId` entry above, for example, is an interesting entry - it gives a human readable string for locating a CLSID. If you go up a level to HKEY_CLASSES_ROOT you can scroll through this subtree and find a string relating to your class. Under this key you will find a `Clsid` subkey which you can copy to the clipboard and search the registry for.

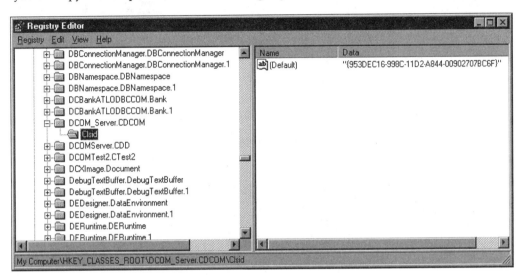

This makes it unnecessary to use and remember CLSIDs in most programming activities.

Type Libraries

One final key that I want to look at is `TypeLib`. It is also found under HKEY_CLASSES_ROOT and if you expand this node then you will again find a large list of GUIDs:

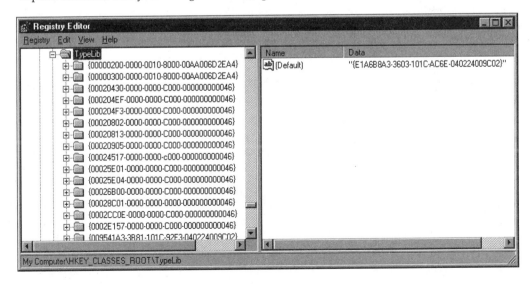

This is what Visual Basic uses to provide the list of components in the **References** dialog:

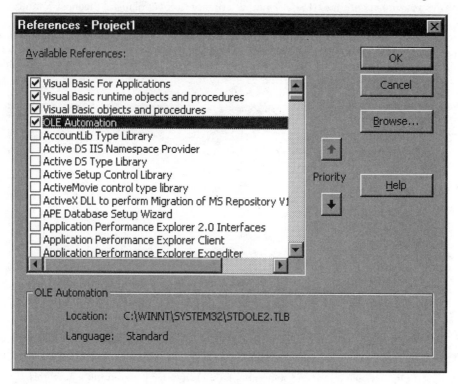

Object Browsing Made Easier: OLEView

After working with the registry editor for a while during COM programming and debugging, you'll wish you had a more intelligent tool available. The problem with the registry editor is that it isn't specific to COM, and relies on you as the intelligent filter to get to the information you need.

Microsoft has released an excellent tool that practically makes the registry editor obsolete as a viewer. The tool is called the Object Viewer, in the form of `Oleview.exe`. This tool combs the entire registry, looking up all the OLE objects and controls, stores and sorts all the relevant object information entries, and then presents the compiled information in an easy-to-use format that can be browsed.

> *`Oleview.exe` is now a standard item including with distributions of Visual Studio 6. However, you can still download the latest version of it Microsoft's website.*

Sounds too good to be true? You can try Object Viewer for yourself. Once started, Object Viewer displays all its collected information on two panes:

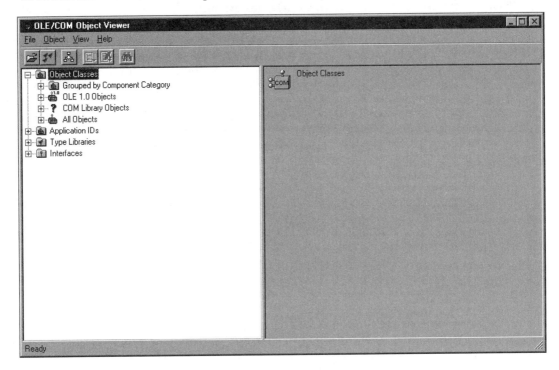

The left pane is a tree view displaying all the various COM objects, AppIDs, Type Libraries and Interfaces that are installed on the system. The right pane displays information about the registry settings, and additional settings, associated with the item selected in the right pane:

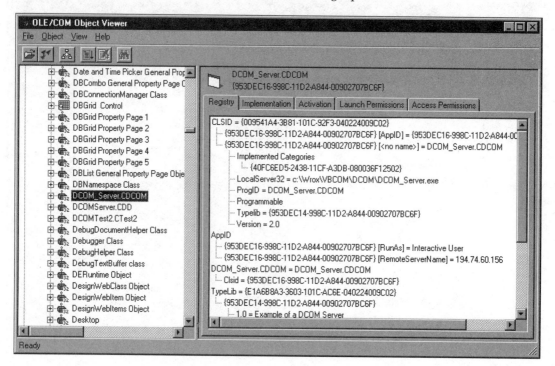

The left pane also provides a certain degree of component grouping allowing you to more easily locate types of components. However, for your ActiveX DLLs and EXEs you are more likely to use the All Objects node:

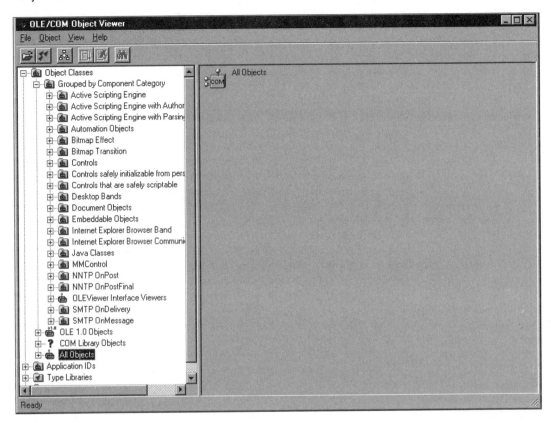

Instantiating Objects using OLEView

One of the most useful functions provided by OLEView is its ability to instantiate and instance of any COM object. This provides a quick and easy method of checking that your component can be instantiated properly and is especially useful for testing remote DCOM components.

Creating an instance is very easy to do. Simply select the object you wish to create an instance of in the left pane and then either double-click the entry or expand the node. If you do this you will find a list of all the interfaces the object supports:

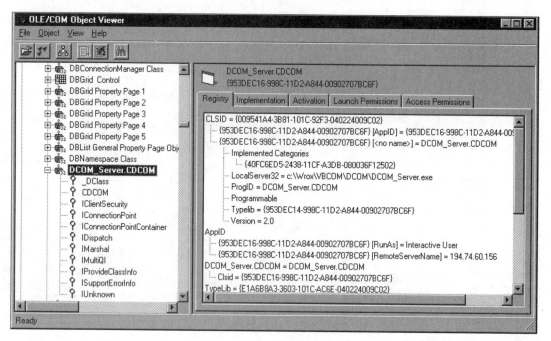

To release the instance right-click on the object entry and select <u>R</u>elease Instance. The node should then retract. Simply contracting the node with the - box will not release the object instance.

If you want to test a DCOM component by instantiating the object on another machine then you need to right-click on the object and select Create Instance <u>O</u>n... This will bring up a dialog asking for the name or IP address of the machine on which you want to create an instance:

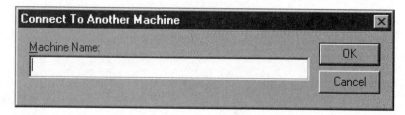

Viewing Type Libraries

Another useful feature of OLEView is that it allows you to view the type library for any given component. There are several ways that you can do this:

- ❏ Expand the Type Libraries node in the left pane and scroll through all type libraries registered on the system

- ❏ Find the COM object for the type library you are interested in and from the pop-up menu you get by right-clicking, select View Type Information...

- ❏ Hit the View TypeLib button on the tool bar or select View TypeLib... from the File menu. Either of this will bring up the Open dialog and allow you to browse your hard disk for the type library file.

Any of these methods will open a new window, the ITypeLib Viewer, which allows you to browse the interfaces and coclasses your object supports:

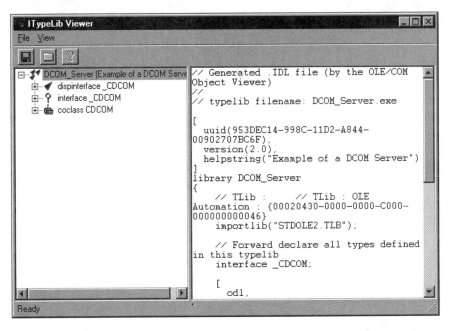

Unfortunately, OLEView is just that, a viewer. If you want to adjust and tweak object registry setting directly, you'll still need to use the registry editor. Therefore, you will frequently find instances of Visual Studio, Object Viewer, and the registry editor all opened on the typical COM developer's desktop (and the manager asks why COM developers need at least 64MB of memory, and a 21-inch monitor!).

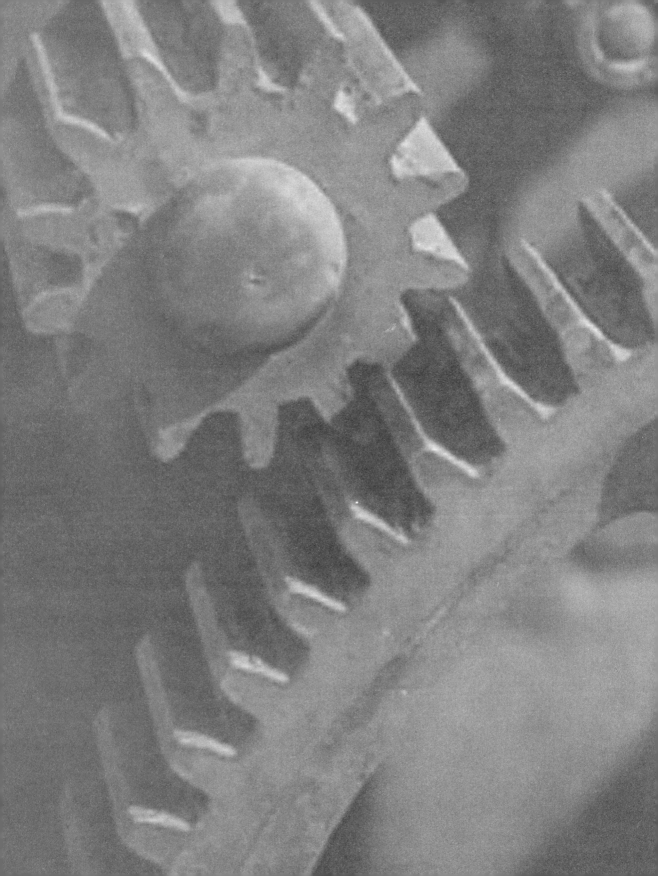

Support and Errata

One of the most irritating things about any programming book is when you find that bit of code you've just spent an hour typing simply doesn't work. You check it a hundred times to see if you've set it up correctly and then you notice the spelling mistake in the variable name on the book page. Of course, you can blame the authors for not taking enough care and testing the code, the editors for not doing their job properly, or the proofreaders for not being eagle-eyed enough, but this doesn't get around the fact that mistakes do happen.

We try hard to ensure no mistakes sneak out into the real world, but we can't promise that this book is 100% error free. What we can do is offer the next best thing by providing you with immediate support and feedback from experts who have worked on the book and try to ensure that future editions eliminate these gremlins. The following section will take you step by step through the process of posting errata to our web site to get that help. The sections that follow, therefore, are:

- ❑ Wrox Developers Membership
- ❑ Finding a list of existing errata on the web site
- ❑ Adding your own errata to the existing list
- ❑ What happens to your errata once you've posted it (why doesn't it appear immediately)?

There is also a section covering how to e-mail a question for technical support. This comprises:

- ❑ What your e-mail should include
- ❑ What happens to your e-mail once it has been received by us

So that you only need view information relevant to yourself, we ask that you register as a Wrox Developer Member. This is a quick and easy process, that will save you time in the long-run. If you are already a member, just update membership to include this book.

Wrox Developer's Membership

To get your FREE Wrox Developer's Membership click on **Membership** in the top navigation bar of our home site – http://www.wrox.com This is shown in the following screenshot:

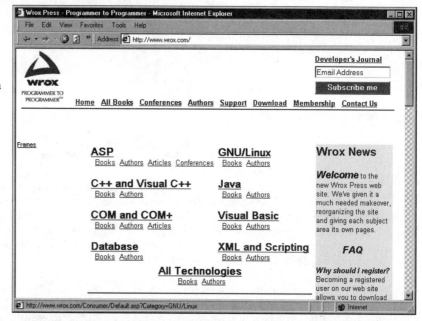

Then, on the next screen (not shown), click on **New User**. This will display a form. Fill in the details on the form and submit the details using the **Register** button at the bottom. Before you can say 'The best read books come in Wrox Red' you will get the following screen:

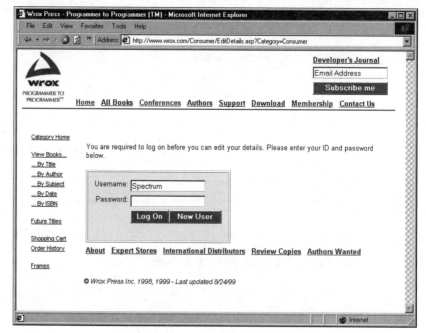

Type in your password once again and click **Log On**. The following page allows you to change your details if you need to, but now you're logged on, you have access to all the source code downloads and errata for the entire Wrox range of books.

Finding an Errata on the Web Site

Before you send in a query, you might be able to save time by finding the answer to your problem on our web site – `http:\\www.wrox.com`.

Each book we publish has its own page and its own errata sheet. You can get to any book's page by clicking on **Support** from the top navigation bar.

Halfway down the main support page is a drop down box called **Title Support**. Simply scroll down the list until you see **Beginning ASP Components**. Select it and then hit **Errata**.

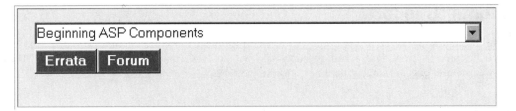

This will take you to the errata page for the book. Select the criteria by which you want to view the errata, and click the **Apply criteria** button. This will provide you with links to specific errata. For an initial search, you are advised to view the errata by page numbers. If you have looked for an error previously, then you may wish to limit your search using dates. We update these pages daily to ensure that you have the latest information on bugs and errors.

Add an Errata : E-mail Support

If you wish to point out an errata to put up on the website or directly query a problem in the book page with an expert who knows the book in detail then e-mail support@wrox.com, with the title of the book and the last four numbers of the ISBN in the subject field of the e-mail. A typical email should include the following things:

❑ The **name, last four digits of the ISBN** and **page number** of the problem in the Subject field.

❑ Your **name, contact info** and the **problem** in the body of the message.

We won't send you junk mail. We need the details to save your time and ours. If we need to replace a disk or CD we'll be able to get it to you straight away. When you send an e-mail it will go through the following chain of support:

Customer Support

Your message is delivered to one of our customer support staff who are the first people to read it. They have files on most frequently asked questions and will answer anything general immediately. They answer general questions about the book and the web site.

Editorial

Deeper queries are forwarded to the technical editor responsible for that book. They have experience with the programming language or particular product and are able to answer detailed technical questions on the subject. Once an issue has been resolved, the editor can post the errata to the web site.

The Authors

Finally, in the unlikely event that the editor can't answer your problem, s/he will forward the request to the author. We try to protect the author from any distractions from writing. However, we are quite happy to forward specific requests to them. All Wrox authors help with the support on their books. They'll mail the customer and the editor with their response, and again all readers should benefit.

What We Can't Answer

Obviously with an ever growing range of books and an ever-changing technology base, there is an increasing volume of data requiring support. While we endeavor to answer all questions about the book, we can't answer bugs in your own programs that you've adapted from our code. But do tell us if you're especially pleased with the routine you developed with our help.

How to Tell Us Exactly What You Think

We understand that errors can destroy the enjoyment of a book and can cause many wasted and frustrated hours, so we seek to minimize the distress that they can cause.

You might just wish to tell us how much you liked or loathed the book in question. Or you might have ideas about how this whole process could be improved. In which case you should e-mail `feedback@wrox.com`. You'll always find a sympathetic ear, no matter what the problem is. Above all you should remember that we do care about what you have to say and we will do our utmost to act upon it.

Index

Symbols